500+
All-American
Family Adventures

500+
All-American
Family Adventures

Debbie K. Hardin

The Countryman Press
Woodstock, Vermont

Interior photographs by the author unless otherwise specified
Book design and composition by Faith Hague

Published by The Countryman Press, P.O. Box 748, Woodstock, VT 05091

Distributed by W. W. Norton & Company, Inc., 500 Fifth Avenue, New York, NY 10110

Printed in the United States of America

10 9 8 7 6 5 4 3 2 1

500+ All-American Family Adventures
978-0-88150-989-2

Frontispiece photo: An interesting angle on the Supreme Court Building © Debbie K. Hardin

Front cover photographs: (Left to right from top left) Library of Congress, © Debbie K. Hardin; Courtesy Emilee Legg; Cataldo Mission, Photo Peg Owens, courtesy Idaho Tourism; Iditarod Trail Sled Dog Headquarters, Courtesy of the Library of Congress; Glacier Bay NP and Preserve, © Debbie K. Hardin; Noah Webster House, Courtesy Library of Congress; Alcatraz, Courtesy Juliane Preimesberger; Totems at Pu'uhonua o Honaunau, Courtesy National Park Service; Katmai NP and Preserve, Courtesy National Park Service; California Palace of Fine Arts, © Debbie K. Hardin; Chinatown, San Francisco, Courtesy John Preimesberger; Rose Parade roses, © Debbie K. Hardin; Kings Canyon NP and Sequoia NP, © Debbie K. Hardin; Fort Pulaski National Monument, Courtesy National Park Service; Mesa Verde, Courtesy National Park Service; Rocky Mountains NP, Courtesy National Park Service; Redwoods NP, © Debbie K. Hardin; Yosemite Valley, © Debbie K. Hardin; Yucca Cove, Canyon de Chelly, Courtesy National Park Service; Kennedy Space Center, Courtesy NASA; Acadia NP, Courtesy National Park Service; Andersonville NHP, Courtesy National Park Service; Haleakala NP, Courtesy National Park Service; Dry Tortugas NP, Courtesy National Park Service; Lincoln Boyhood home, Courtesy National Park Service; Desota NWR, Courtesy U.S. Fish and Wildlife Service; Kennedy Presidential Library and Museum, © Debbie K. Hardin; Antietam National Battlefield, Courtesy National Park Service; Tuzigoot National Monument, Courtesy National Park Service; Fort Smith, Courtesy National Park Service; Harvard University, © Debbie K. Hardin; Babe Ruth Museum, Courtesy Library of Congress; Gateway Arch, Courtesy National Park Service; Boston Massacre site, Courtesy Jon Preimesberger; Sojourner Truth Memorial, Courtesy Library of Congress; Wilson's Creek National Battlefield, Courtesy National Park Service; Chrysler Museum, Courtesy Library of Congress; New Bedford Whaling Museum, Photo John Robson, Courtesy National Park Service; Benjamin Harrison Home, Courtesy National Park Service; Hovenweep National Monument, Courtesy National Park Service; Mission Basilica San Diego de Alcala, © Debbie K. Hardin; Carlsbad Caverns, Courtesy National Park Service; Sutter's Mill, © Debbie K. Hardin; Statue of Liberty, Courtesy National Park Service; Biscayne NP, Courtesy National Park Service; New Salem Historic Site, Courtesy Library of Congress; Bryce NP, © Debbie K. Hardin; USS Constellation, Courtesy Library of Congress; Glacier Valley, Montana © Debbie K. Hardin

To my favorite travel companions: Juliane and Jon

contents

INTRODUCTION

Introduce your kids to America through travel: There's no better way to learn about this beautiful, vast country. See firsthand America's natural wonders by hiking through the hoodoos of Bryce Canyon in Utah or riding the waves at Waikiki Beach in Hawaii. Experience the spirit of the nation and the lasting influence of inspiring people who have made America great by reading the Constitution of the United States in the National Archives in Washington, DC, or walking in the footsteps of explorers Lewis and Clark along the Columbia River in Oregon. Learn about the literary and artistic culture of America by visiting Ernest Hemingway's house in Key West, Florida, or touring Norman Rockwell's studio in Stockbridge, Massachusetts. Exposing children to all the country has to offer, and introducing them to the talented, bighearted people who populate it, is one of the best ways to raise kids who understand and appreciate their American heritage. As American writer Henry Miller put it, "One's destination is never a place, but a new way of looking at things." Open their eyes to the wonder of this country, and in so doing raise your children to be well-educated Americans and good citizens of the world.

Let's be honest: Family travel also needs to be *fun*! A vacation or even a day trip is a chance to get away from the everyday routine, and for siblings to make lifelong memories that will transport them out of their ordinary rivalries and help them bond as friends. Family adventures also offer parents the chance to enjoy their children (and each other!) away from the confines of work schedules, car pools, ballet practice, soccer games, and homework. These respites from the everyday are often the stuff of indelible memories.

So how do we as parents sneak a little education into weekend trips and vacations alike? If kids know a trip is "educational," they may not be open to the possibilities. The key is to make the education that is inherent in all travel as much fun as those activities we do for pure entertainment. It's a lot like sneaking vegetables into pizza or adding oatmeal to cookies: If you plan the educational sites in your vacations well, your children will barely notice they're there. That's where this book comes in: In the pages that follow I'll be your personal tour guide through this astounding country, sharing advice to help you introduce your children to the treasures the United States has to offer with a fun, kid-friendly, engaging approach that will enable you make the most of every family trip. Along the way I'll offer guidance on staying within your budget and insider tips that will help you maximize your experience. I'll also offer hints throughout for extending the educational opportunities by finding even more adventures to enjoy.

How This Book Is Organized

This book offers travel suggestions and a synopsis of 500+ of the most engaging, educational destinations in the United States. I chose each of the sites because of its significance to the American experience, with options that highlight American history, arts and culture, industry, and natural wonders. I've also included sites that illuminate important Americans, and I've mixed in opportunities to learn about the multicultural richness of the nation. Don't think of this book as a pedagogical bucket list: Think of it instead as an inspirational road map that will motivate you to discover opportunities to augment your children's education through meaningful, interesting travel.

I've grouped the 500+ proposed adventures by state (with an additional section on Washington, DC, at the end of the book), and I've organized the entries in each state in alphabetical order. This presentation will help you find a nearby adventure that's right for your family, no matter where in the country you live or how far afield you're able to travel. In large states like California and history-rich states like Virginia and Massachusetts, I've included more options than for smaller, less populated states; but you'll find something to explore in every locale. A detailed table of contents and a voluminous index will help you find whatever you're looking for, wherever you're looking for it. In addition, I've included a chart (see appendix A at the back of the book) that will help you match your children's interests with travel adventures around the country. You'll also find stunning color photographs of attractions and a handy information box at the top of each entry that provides contact information, pricing, tips on the best times of year to visit, and suggested age ranges.

So what makes for an all-American travel adventure with children? The strength of America lies in its inexhaustible opportunities, and this holds true for vacation adventure options. Each state, even each city, offers hundreds of worthy options vying for your time and money. To help you find the best options for your family, in this book I've concentrated on those sites and attractions that offer real insight into the American experience *and* that offer maximum impact, through either an entertaining and educational experience or a profound and thoughtful one. Every attraction highlighted in this book was chosen because it allows children to actively interact with their surroundings, and each helps illuminate the legacy of the United States by introducing a meaningful American icon, whether the adventure focuses on soaking in the majesty of the American landscape in sites like the Rocky Mountains in Colorado or the rugged seascapes of coastal Maine; stepping into history at a Civil War battle reenactment in Arkansas or trekking through the rugged early settlements of the colonists in Virginia; exploring ancient archaeological wonders in Arizona or picking through fossils in Wyoming; or experiencing popular American culture by touring Elvis's Graceland in Tennessee or comparing handprints with the stars of the silver screen at Grauman's Chinese Theatre in California. I've included plenty of active adventures that are quintessentially American, too, like sledding the Iditarod Trail in Alaska and spelunking through the otherworldly stalagmites and stalactites

of Carlsbad Caverns in New Mexico. And for true sports lovers, I've offered vacation suggestions that include pilgrimages to famous ballparks, hands-on excursions like whitewater rafting and surfing, and opportunities to watch professional athletes like rodeo riders and race car drivers in action.

The people of the United States have been this country's greatest strength since the early days of the Republic, so I've included dozens of attractions that honor the memories of great Americans as well, like the iconic architect Frank Lloyd Wright's studio in Illi-

> ## The people of the United States have been this country's greatest strength since the early days of the Republic.

nois and the real Little House on the Prairie at the Ingalls' Homestead in South Dakota. Because the rich culture of the immigrants who established America and who have toiled through the years to make it great is the foundation of our society, I've included sites that celebrate America's diversity at destinations like the Polynesian Cultural Center in Hawaii, the Acadian Village in Louisiana, and the Basque Museum in Idaho.

A caveat on coverage: America is vast, and it's impossible in a single book to chronicle *each* important and worthy site. I've included all the definitive American destinations (Gettysburg, the White House, the Liberty Bell, and so on) and also chosen other iconic and important sites to allow for the full spectrum of American attractions scattered as evenly as possible across the country. Are there other adventures worthy of exploring in the United States? You bet. Have I left out somebody's favorite historical attraction or natural wonder? Undoubtedly. Will you be able to teach your children about the experience of being American by visiting the attractions I *have* included? Absolutely.

HOW TO USE THIS BOOK

This book has been designed to be part history book, part travel guide, and part wish list. Read it from cover to cover to get a comprehensive, contextual understanding of the important events and influential people that have had lasting influence on the United States, or approach the book like a reference work. Look for adventures that will suit your family's interests—or find educational sites that will open up new horizons for children and parents alike.

Suggested Age Ranges

I've included a minimum age range for all entries in the book, and you'll notice that most of them start at 5 or 7 years old. But take these recommendations with a grain of salt: If you have a particularly mature child—or a particularly immature one—adjust the ranges up or down accordingly. And if you have several children who fall into distinctively different age categories, use your own instincts about what is likely to engage your family. Some older children might be bored by attractions designed for younger kids—and some younger children might not understand sites aimed at older kids—but that doesn't mean that children outside of the recommended age ranges will not get something educational or fun (or better yet, both!) from the adventure at hand.

None of the sites is explicitly recommended for kids younger than 3. But don't leave babies and toddlers at home! Although such young kids will probably not remember excursions made before they are 3 or 4, they are at an age when any sort of unusual environment is likely to stimulate their senses and excite their brains. Babies of 6 months will benefit from a trip to the museum (or a trip to the grocery store!) if only because the sights, sounds, and shapes will be new and will help them understand and learn to navigate the world around them. Toddlers will enjoy and learn from exposure to novel situations as well: A trip to the beach or the zoo will widen their frame of reference, give them a sense of a world larger than their home or preschool, and offer them the chance to try out new skills like walking, talking, and waiting patiently for their turns. In addition, travel is like any other skill: The more you practice, the better you become. Traveling with babies and very young children will teach them to be better travelers at older ages, when they will truly be primed to learn about the history, culture, and natural wonders of America that are explored in this book.

Price Ranges

Throughout I've offered price ranges for attractions, based on a single entry for one day. Most national parks discussed sell weeklong passes for a vehicle transporting an entire family; prices range from $10 to $25 for these passes—but note that the prices indicated in the At a Glance information boxes at the top of each entry reflect the average day price per person. Please be aware in general that prices can (and do!) change dramatically from year to year, so if budgeting is important to you, be sure to check websites in advance for the most up-to-date rates. Note that most sites in this book charge considerably less for children than adults. Many sites also offer discounts for seniors, active military personnel, and AAA members—and it's always a good idea to look for website specials. Prepurchasing tickets to attractions online almost always saves time, and often saves money as well.

Happy Travels

I am a writer, editor, and mother—and travel has been the best teacher in my life. I was born and raised in Southern California; I spent childhood vacations and long weekends camping in local deserts, playing in the surf at nearby beaches, and observing from the backseat on innumerable cross-country trips to visit grandparents. As a young adult I moved to the nation's capital, where I had the honor of serving in the White House as a writer and editor for President Bill Clinton. My daughter was born in Washington, DC, where she visited national monuments and world-class art museums, went to plays and ballets at the incomparable Kennedy Center, and hunted Easter eggs on the White House lawn—all before she entered preschool. More than a decade ago we moved back to my hometown of San Diego, which has become our family's home base, and we've exhaustively explored the region, including the spectacular national parks of the West and vast expanses of all manner of wilderness, from Death Valley to the Sierra Nevadas, from Glacier Bay to the Grand Canyon. From her first family vacation on the Outer Banks in North Carolina when she was only a few months old, to our recent college tours on the East Coast, my husband and I have tried to introduce our daughter to everything this country has to offer. Now I'm inviting you and your family to come along for the ride: Buckle your seat belts and be prepared to learn about this country in a way you may never have imagined. Happy travels!

—Debbie K. Hardin

Acknowledgments

Thank you to the many public relations specialists who helped me throughout the process of research for this book, especially Cliff Allen, Wendalyn Baker, Marge Bateman, Kirstin Beal, Staci Best, William F. Bomar, Andrea Carneiro, Camila Clark, Peggy Collins, Jennifer Forte Cuomo, Lena Dakessian, Dawn Dawson-House, Danielle DiBenedetto, Andrea Ferreira, Kate Fox, Joe Giessler, Ally Goddard, Kim Hatcher, Lori Hogan, Ruth Hammon, Jennifer Ireland, William R. Iseminger, Lorie Juliano, Eric Kerr, Heather Kincade, Amy Larson, Pat Laurel, Stefanie S. LeBrun, Helen Lin, Ann Lindblad, Jaime Majewski, Leigh Massey, Joseph A. Milano, Kristin R. Mooney, Chris Moran, Leah Mulkey, Shalyn Murphy, Susan I. Newton, Meaghan Owen, Peg Owens, Ginny Poehling, Elizabeth Purcell, Scooter Pursley, Jeleesa Randolph, Becky Rex, David Ritchie, Nancy Sartain, Janet L. Serra, Donnie Sexton, Steve Shaluta, Stacy Ann Shreffler, Christina Simmons, Gina Speckman, Susan Steckman, Kelly Strenge, Jennifer Stringfellow, Kristi Turek, Emily J. Waldren, Laurel Williams, and Leslie Wright.

Writing is a long and lonely process, and so I am indebted to the guidance provided by my publisher, Kermit Hummel, who helped me clarify my vision for this project. I also appreciate the help and encouragement provided by the managing editor at Countryman Press, Lisa Sacks; the capable and good-humored copy editor, Laura Jorstad; the production editor, Doug Yeager; production manager Fred Lee; text designer Faith Hague; and cover designer Vicky Shea.

Finally, a special thanks also to my friends and family who shared travel tips and photographs: Charles Arensman, Susie Bright, Linda Frandsen, S. P. Gonzalez, Emilee Legg, Jo Legg, Kevin Legg, Ann Passantino, David Preimesberger, Mel Preimesberger, James H. Pugh, Cindy Simpson, Brinda Taylor, and Rosi Weiss. Finally, special thanks to my husband and daughter, Jon and Juliane Preimesberger, for sharing many memorable travel adventures with me over the years.

ALABAMA

1 Ivy Green

CONTACT 256-383-4066, www.helenkellerbirthplace.org; 300 N. Commons St. W., Tuscumbia

PRICING	$–$$
BEST TIME TO VISIT	June through mid-July
AGE RANGE	3 and older

Helen Keller's Birthplace   Courtesy Alabama Tourism Department

Helen Keller was a well-known American activist and spokesperson for the disabled community and an inspiration for those with physical and mental challenges. Keller was born a healthy baby in 1880, but at 19 months she suffered an illness that left her deaf and blind. She spent the next several years in relative isolation because she was unable to communicate. On a recommendation from inventor Alexander Graham Bell, her parents hired Anne Sullivan, a private teacher, to work with Helen. Sullivan is remembered as the "miracle worker" who spent countless hours teaching Helen to communicate with her hands using a form of sign language. The seminal moment in Helen's life came when she understood her first word. Sullivan spelled out w-a-t-e-r as she held young Helen's hand under a stream from the family well. Helen went on to learn Braille, and she was the first deaf and blind person to earn a bachelor's degree. In her adult life, Helen was a political activist, author, and speaker. She was a fierce champion of women's rights, as well as a proponent for education for disabled individuals. Through her prolific writing and teaching, she encouraged Americans to treat disabled individuals with dignity and respect, and in so doing became a role model for millions of Americans.

At Keller's birthplace, known as Ivy Green, guests can tour the pretty white clapboard house where Keller lived with her family as well as the small cabin

Sullivan used as her sleeping quarters and schoolroom. The house is furnished in period detail, and the grounds are extensive. Kids can walk through the inviting lawn and garden and touch the pump where Helen learned her first word. On site is an exhibit of Keller's extensive Braille library as well as her Braille typewriter.

2 Moundville Archaeological Park

CONTACT 205-371-8732, http://moundville.ua.edu; 13075 Moundville Archaeological Park, Moundville

PRICING	$$
BEST TIME TO VISIT	Year-round
AGE RANGE	7 and older

Moundville was a ceremonial and political capital of the ancient Mississippian culture and one of the most important sites from the Middle Mississippian era in the United States. This U.S. historic site includes 32 of the characteristic platform mounds for which the ancient Mississippian people are known; archaeologists estimate that the site was occupied from approximately AD 1000 to 1450. At the height of its influence, the settlement was home to 1,000 people who lived within a 300-acre, three-walled community bordered by the Black Warrior River.

The Mississippian people were an agrarian culture that originated in the Mississippi River Valley

> From June through mid-July, William Gibson's play about Keller and Sullivan—*The Miracle Worker*—is performed live on the grounds. Children will enjoy the moving drama, which is particularly poignant in this setting.

Orange Beach   Courtesy of Gulf Shores and Orange Beach Tourism

PRICE KEY
$ free–$5
$$ $6–10
$$$ $11–20
$$$$ $21+

Moundville Archaeological Park

Courtesy Bill Bonner, Moundville Archaeological Park

give you the sense that you are walking through a Mississippian village. On display are exquisite pottery, handwoven clothing, jewelry, tools, and ceremonial feather decorations. Look for the famous Duck Bowl, one of the best-known and most beautiful artifacts from the Mississippian culture.

There are several tours available at the park, including the kid-friendly Southeastern Indian Games program that teaches participants how the sports of lacrosse and stickball originated and offers them a chance to play both, as well as a form of Native American football; and the Dream Catchers and Talking Feathers program, in which participants learn to weave sinew, beads, and feathers into an authentic Native craft.

and lived from about 800 to 1500 throughout what is now the southeastern United States. This Native group was believed to be especially skilled at agriculture, cultivating maize and then trading surpluses of the crop for items like mica, copper, and shells, which researchers believe they imported to create the fine pottery and embossed copper artwork that has been found at the site.

Visitors to the archaeological park will first be struck by the impressive, large mounds, believed to be built for ceremonial and burial purposes. There is a half-mile wooden boardwalk on the property that allows visitors to walk or bike through the region to get close to the mounds and to appreciate the natural beauty of the region. The highlight is a trip to the on-site museum to view the 200 spectacular artifacts found during excavations. Step inside and you are surrounded by murals and life-sized dioramas that

> Visit the park during the first full week of October (Wednesday through Saturday) to catch the Moundville Native American Festival, which features performers, artisans, and educators who celebrate the Native American heritage of the region. Look for demonstrations of basket making, listen to storytellers share ancient legends, and watch as toolmakers craft arrowheads and spears by hand. The festival includes an extensive children's area where kids can dress up like southeastern Native Americans, make shell necklaces, and play ancient games.

3 Selma to Montgomery Historic Trail

CONTACT www.nps.gov/semo; located on U.S. 80, extending 54 miles from Selma to Montgomery, Alabama

PRICING	Fees vary by venue
BEST TIME TO VISIT	Year-round
AGE RANGE	10 and older

In 1965, Martin Luther King Jr. and the Southern Christian Leadership Conference focused their efforts to extend civil rights on the voting rights campaign in Selma, where they sought to register all black citizens of age. To bring visibility to the cause, activists attempted a highly publicized symbolic march from Selma to Montgomery, Alabama's state capital. As the media recorded the events for the world to see, the marchers were met with brutal resistance by local and state authorities. In what was the first of three attempts, known later as "Bloody Sunday," hundreds of marchers set off on March 7 from the Brown Chapel AME Church, only to be met soon afterward on the Edmund Pettus Bridge in Selma by local law enforcement agents wielding billy clubs and tear gas. It took two more attempts, and the federal protection of thousands of National Guard troops, for the marchers to finally succeed. Those participating walked for three straight days and nights from Selma to Mont-

The Voting Rights Act outlawed discriminatory voting practices throughout the country.

gomery, and in so doing they brought awareness of the discrimination black Americans in the South faced. The march and its aftermath were responsible in large measure for the passage of the Voting Rights Act that President Lyndon Johnson signed into law later the same year. The Voting Rights Act outlawed discriminatory voting practices throughout the country, giving a voice and a vote to previously disenfranchised black citizens.

Today visitors can retrace the steps of the activists who risked their lives to protect democracy and stand up for civil rights by following the march route—now a historic trail. Begin at Brown Chapel AME Church, where Reverend King and others organized the marchers. Then follow trail markers to U.S. 80, which leads to the Alabama state capitol in Montgomery. Along the way, check out the many illuminating stops in both Selma and Montgomery:

- **Civil Rights Monument** (400 Washington Ave., Montgomery): This memorial to the 40 people who died for the struggle for civil rights from 1954 (the year of the momentous *Brown v. Board of Education* case) to 1968 (when Reverend King was assassinated) is a moving tribute, designed by Maya Lin, the artist responsible for the Vietnam Memorial in Washington, DC.

Edmund Pettus Bridge, Selma   Courtesy Alabama Tourism Department

- **The Lowndes County Interpretive Center** (7001 U.S. 80 W., White Hall): This interpretive center is midway between Selma and Montgomery and offers a 30-minute video overview and interactive exhibits that tell the story of the historic march.
- **Martin Luther King Jr. Street Historic Walking Tour** (Selma): Take a self-guided tour along Martin Luther King Jr. Street in Selma, which includes 20 memorials that highlight the historic march and the voting rights movement. Along the route is Brown Chapel AME Church (410 Martin Luther King St., Selma). This church was pivotal in organizing the Selma-to-Montgomery marches. Now a national historical monument, Brown Chapel is open for tours (with reservations in advance).
- **National Voting Rights Museum and Institute** (334-418-0800, http://nvrmi.com; 6 U.S. 80 E., Selma). This privately owned museum and education complex is a memorial to the many activists who took part in the march.
- **Rosa Parks Museum** (252 Montgomery St., Montgomery): Located on the campus of Troy University, the Rosa Parks Museum is an interactive experience that is dedicated to the woman who spearheaded another important civil rights event: the Montgomery bus boycotts. Be sure to visit the "time machine" in the children's wing of this museum.

4 Tuskegee Airmen National Historic Site

CONTACT 334-727-6390, www.nps.gov/tuai; Moton Field, 1616 Chappie James Ave., Tuskegee

PRICING	$
BEST TIME TO VISIT	Year-round
AGE RANGE	7 and older

The Tuskegee Institute, a traditionally African American college in Alabama, was the site of a "military experiment" during World War II. As hard as it is to imagine today, at the time commanders in the air force were not convinced African Americans were capable of being trained as military pilots, navigators,

Road Trip Survival Kit

Family road trips are an American rite of passage, but they can be tedious and fractious (especially for parents). Ward off crankiness by loading your automobile with items that will anticipate emergencies, suppress boredom, keep children engaged, and make the long hours on the road pass a little quicker.

- **Essentials preparation:** Always keep your car stocked with a first-aid kit, a roadside emergency kit, and car-cleanup supplies (glass cleaner, a roll of paper towels, and some wet wipes). It's also a good idea to keep the car packed with a flashlight and fresh batteries—and an even better idea to have a flashlight available for each child on board.

- **Healthy snacks:** Stay away from sugary treats that can spike hyperactivity (which can lead to exhaustion later on) and instead pack protein-rich, low-carb nibbles like nuts and jerky. If you're traveling with multiple children, portion out the snacks in advance in disposable Baggies or reusable containers that are clearly labeled with the owner's name. Bring along a small cooler for bottled water.

- **Portable exercise equipment:** Bring a jump rope, small ball, or Frisbee that kids can play with for brief (intense) bursts of activity during refueling stops. Challenge them to see how much they can accomplish in a short period of time—you'll be amazed at how well even five minutes of exercise works to combat the fidgets.

- **Nap accessories:** Make sure all passengers have a small pillow (neck rolls work particularly well in the car) and a comfy blanket. Nothing makes a long road trip pass faster for passengers than sleeping through most of it.

- **Toilet:** For very young children just out of diapers, consider bringing along a kid-sized portable potty. Although you'll still have to pull off the road to access the tot-sized john, for children who haven't yet trained their bladders, having an always-accessible restroom option is invaluable.

- **Music:** Let every family member bring along a few favorite CDs, and take turns acting as DJ. (Don't rely on the car radio for entertainment; even satellite radio reception isn't reliable in some heavily forested areas.)

A break from the car

Courtesy Emilee Legg

- **Books on CD:** Pick an audio book that the whole family can enjoy—an Agatha Christie mystery, for example, or a Harry Potter tome.

- **Car games:** In addition to electronic Game Boy gadgets, pack some low-tech games that kids and parents can play together, like Mad Libs or a travel version of Boggle; in addition, have in your back pocket a couple of impromptu games, like 20 Questions and License Plate Bingo.

- **Portable audio and visual equipment:** Don't be a hero. If your kids like to watch videos, let them bring along portable DVD players, laptops, or iPads. Likewise, if your teenager just can't live without her tunes, let her enjoy her iPod or Pandora—but consider limiting the time these solitary devices are in use, to promote familial sociability. And agree in advance that all electronics will be left in the trunk once you arrive at your destination.

- **Flexibility:** If the kids can't stand the car one more moment, be flexible enough to pull off the road to spend 15 minutes at a park or playground. Even some rest stops along highways make for a pretty place to let little ones breathe some fresh air.

Airplane from the Tuskegee Airmen era

From The George F. Landegger Collection of Alabama Photos in Carol M. Highsmith's America, courtesy of the Library of Congress

5 U.S. Space and Rocket Center

CONTACT 256-837-3400, www.spacecamp.com; 1 Tranquility Base, Huntsville

PRICING	$$$
BEST TIME TO VISIT	Year-round
AGE RANGE	5 and older

mechanics, bombardiers, and support staff, and this experiment was meant to challenge this notion. Training began in 1941 (and was completed in 1946), and the successful graduates of the program became the Tuskegee Airmen. Before the Tuskegee Airmen, no African American had ever served as a U.S. military pilot; in 1941, a squadron of Tuskegee Airmen became the first black Americans ever to be deployed to active duty. Although they were segregated—as was the rest of the American military at the time—and although they were subject to racial discrimination, often intended to discredit their considerable accomplishments, the Tuskegee Airmen served the country with distinction and honor and contributed importantly to the Allied success in the war. More than 16,000 men and women—predominantly African Americans—took part in the training, in the process shattering discriminatory practices that had been in place in the U.S. military for decades and paving the way for greater opportunities for minorities within military and federal service.

The Tuskegee Airmen National Historic Site at Moton Field, where the airmen received their flight instruction, memorializes their accomplishments. Visit the Hangar #1 Museum, which offers two segments to explore. Start at the orientation room to view a short video that offers historical context on the site and on the pilots' training. Then head to the museum to view exhibits honoring the soldiers, including a fascinating oral history project in which the airmen tell their stories in their own words, two World War II–era training planes, a parachute-folding table, and other exhibits that tell the story of the Tuskegee heroes.

In the early days of space exploration, the United States and the former Soviet Union pushed the limits of science and technology in an effort to win the Cold War "space race," marked by the 1957 launch of the first satellite, the Soviet Sputnik, and the 1969 landing of U.S. *Apollo 11* on the moon. In the past several decades, the U.S. space program, headed up by the National Aeronautics and Space Administration (NASA), has focused its efforts on the space shuttle program and its involvement in the International Space Station, and NASA continues to challenge the boundaries of the human imagination.

The U.S. Space and Rocket Center in Huntsville offers the world's largest museum dedicated to space exploration. See the *Apollo 16* capsule, the original Mercury and Gemini capsule trainers, and a full-sized replica of the *Apollo 11 Saturn V*. In addition to myriad fascinating exhibits, the center offers an incomparable chance to experience what it must be like to blast off in space. There are dozens of thrilling simulators

U.S. Space and Rocket Center   Courtesy Alabama Tourism Department

and interactive exhibits to explore. In the G Force Accelerator, for example, you will experience 3 g's as you spin (and spin and spin!) in a capsule, eventually lifting you off your seat. And in the Space Shot, you'll feel 4 g's as you blast upward 150 feet in less than three seconds, culminating in two to three seconds of weightlessness during a free fall.

Young astronauts 8 and under (accompanied by an adult) will not want to miss the Kids Cosmos Energy Depletion Zone, where they can crawl around in a re-creation of the space station. For older space

Many of the simulator rides at the U.S. Space and Rocket Center have height restrictions that range from 4 to 5 feet. Be sure to check ahead to make sure your little aviator isn't *too* little to enjoy the attractions.

cadets, check out the Apollo Cockpit Trainer, a simulator that puts you on a mission to the moon. (Note: This simulator is similar to what Apollo astronauts trained on before actual missions.) For a slightly tamer experience, try the Discovery Theater, which offers visitors a chance to understand the scientific principles behind space exploration. There are also IMAX and 3-D films on site daily.

If you have longer to explore, check out the *awesome* space and aviation camps the center offers. Space camp programs are offered to families with children as young as 7 years old; there are also longer camps for teenagers, who train in simulators and take part in math and science classroom instruction. The Aviation Challenge is available for children, adults, and families; weekend programs include simulated jet fighter pilot training, survival training, and leadership programs.

Alaskan floatplane © Debbie K. Hardin

ALASKA

6 Alaska Native Heritage Center

Alaska Native Heritage Center

CONTACT	907-330-8000, www.alaskanative.net; 8800 Heritage Center Dr., Anchorage
PRICING	$$$$
BEST TIME TO VISIT	Year-round, but outside exhibits will be more accessible in summertime
AGE RANGE	5 and older

Although Alaska was one of the last territories in the United States to achieve statehood (in 1959), the enormous region has been populated since about 12,000 BC by descendants of peoples from Asia who crossed over what was then the Bering land bridge. The vast expanse of Alaska—with incredible climatic and geographic challenges for settlers—was sparsely populated for millennia. In the 18th century, Russian explorers, trappers, and missionaries established settlements, but it was not until the Yukon Gold Rush in the 1890s that U.S. citizens made their way to the area in search of mining claims.

As a result of this long and rich history, the cultural legacy of Alaska is tremendous, and there is no better place to learn about the customs and traditions of the Native peoples, past and present, than at the fascinating Alaska Native Heritage Center, which is just outside downtown Anchorage. This well-designed and thoughtful complex features cultural exhibits on Alaska's 11 major cultural groups and offers numerous interactive experiences to captivate the imagination of children. Start exploring the center with the introductory film *Stories Shared, Stories Given*, shown regularly in the museum theater, which offers amazing scenes of Alaska's majestic scenery as well as a riveting history of the people who have called the state home. Then head to the Gathering Place to enjoy Native storytelling, music, and dance demonstrations.

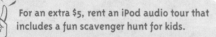

For an extra $5, rent an iPod audio tour that includes a fun scavenger hunt for kids.

Do not miss the Kodiak dancers, who put on a colorful and uplifting show. The Hall of Cultures features the artwork of Alaskan Natives, such as Athabascan dolls trimmed in beaver fur and intricate beading, Yu'pik baskets finely crafted of grass, and hand-carved canoes by the Tlingit people.

The center also offers the opportunity to see Native artisans demonstrate their crafts, which on any given day might include fine beadwork on clothing, delicate basket weaving, and large-scale wood carving. There are plenty of opportunities for kids to try their hand at crafts as well.

Perhaps the most intriguing exhibits can be found outside the museum: Sited alongside a picturesque lake on the property are six re-created authentic Native dwellings furnished with original artifacts that will give children of sense of how Native people of the past lived and give them insight into the traditions that modern-day ancestors carry on today. Be sure to check out the massive whale bones at the Inupiaq site.

7 Denali National Park and Preserve

CONTACT www.nps.gov/dena; AK 3/George Parks Hwy., Denali

PRICING	$$
BEST TIME TO VISIT	Summer
AGE RANGE	7 and older

Denali is the Native Alaskan term for "the great one," and it's the original name of Mount McKinley, the tallest mountain in North America. An American explorer who came along in the 20th century renamed the mountain after President William McKinley—a rather odd move given McKinley had no connection to the mountain or to Alaska. The region was designated a national park in 1917, in part to protect the native Dall sheep. Today the park comprises the expansive, perpetually snowcapped Alaska Range (of which Mount McKinley is a part); the landscape also includes bogs, spongy patches of tundra, hardwood forests, and vast tracts of open space.

Visiting Denali is unlike visiting most other national parks in the United States: The majority of the park is inaccessible to visitors, which means you can expect solitude and a true wilderness experience. Although there are 6 million acres, Denali National Park has only one road, the Denali Park Road, and it is has extremely limited access: The road is just over 90 miles long, and only the first 15 miles are paved and available to the public. The paved portion is open from late May through early September, and it runs from the park entrance to the Savage River. Travel beyond the first 15 miles of the road is limited to foot travel or bus tours, which cost from $25 to $110 per person

Denali is one of the few national parks that allows off-trail hiking, and thus your routes are limited only by your imagination, your stamina, and your sense of navigation. Be careful about choosing your pathway—and remembering it. But finding your way without a trail, although daunting at first, is easier than is sounds, because with a few exceptions the tundra allows for visibility for miles, making it easy to orient yourself to the park road. If you're interested in this kind of hiking adventure, try taking a shuttle bus a few miles into the park, ask to be let off, and then hike back toward the park entrance.

Denali is famously home to grizzly bears, and it is a rare visitor who doesn't spot at least one (usually from the window of a tour bus). The park is also home to black bears, Dall sheep, moose, caribou, gray wolves, beavers, pikas, snowshoe hares, foxes, and numerous birds. Because of the remote nature of the park, wildlife viewing is easy, either from the trails or from the aforementioned tour buses. Bring along binoculars so that children can help spot the wildlife.

Mount McKinley in Denali National Park and Preserve   Courtesy Jon Preimesberger

8 Glacier Bay National Park and Preserve

CONTACT 907-697-2230, www.nps.gov/glba/index.htm; Glacier Bay National Park, P.O. Box 140, Gustavus

PRICING	Park entrance: $; boat trips require separate fees
BEST TIME TO VISIT	Summer
AGE RANGE	7 and older

As the name implies, Glacier Bay National Park is one of the best places in the world to view glaciers—the park offers 16 spectacular specimens, representing at least four glacial periods. Glaciers are massive rivers of ice made from compacted snow that over thou-

PRICE KEY
$ free–$5
$$ $6–10
$$$ $11–20
$$$$ $21+

Alaskan glacier

© Debbie K. Hardin

grate to and from Mexico. Orcas, or killer whales, can be seen throughout the bay year-round. To spot any type of whale, look about a mile offshore for water spouts 8 to 15 feet tall, the by-product of whales breathing through their blowholes. Generally the whales blow four or five spouts, then sound (dive down) for about five minutes. You're apt to see the head or the tail surfacing shortly after a spout, and if you're really lucky you'll see a whale breach. In good visibility and calm waters, it isn't unusual to see evidence of several whales in your vicinity in Glacier Bay at the same time, and the experience is unforgettable.

Ways to See Glacier Bay

It takes some advance planning to navigate Glacier Bay, and there are a couple of options:

- **By boat:** Because the park is largely a water preserve, the best way to see Glacier is by boat. This can range from full-scale, weeklong luxury cruises carrying 2,000 guests; to daylong vessel tours that carry several hundred guests through the bay and alongside glaciers, with onboard naturalists; to charter boats that can design an itinerary just for your family; to private vessels (including canoes and kayaks)—although note that permits are required if you plan to use your own boat.

- **By foot:** Backpacking through the expanse of wilderness is not for the faint of heart (or the inexperienced camper or hiker). The park is without trails, the geography is challenging, and the weather conditions are often severe. But for those looking for a true wilderness experience, Alaska in general, and Glacier Bay in particular, offer rewards like no other place in America.

- **With the guidance of park rangers:** Rangers lead guests on day hikes through rain forests and along beaches, and provide evening programs that can include stargazing, hikes by moonlight, and campfire talks. Drop by the Glacier Bay National Park Visitor Center, located upstairs in the Glacier Bay Lodge, to sign up.

sands of years has compressed and moves under the force of its own weight. The glaciers in the park date to the last "little ice age," which took place 4,000 years ago. Today these glaciers flow from the land to the water 3 to 6 feet every day, so the scenery is ever-changing. In addition to the movement (which really isn't discernible without the aid of a stop-action camera), it is all but certain that if you pause long enough before a glacier, you will see it "calve"—in other words, watch a chunk of ice break off from the glacier and fall into the water. You'll get the biggest bang for your buck if you head to the West Arm of the bay. It is here you will see perhaps the most spectacular of the park's glaciers: Johns Hopkins Glacier, an ever-evolving and enormous hunk of prehistoric ice.

The park also has magnificent examples of ocean coastline, fjords, rivers, lakes, and majestic snowy mountain ranges that can be explored. The diverse ecosystem is home to fascinating wildlife like brown and black bears, sea otters, mink, moose, beavers, mountain goats, and porpoises, but probably the most popular wildlife sighting in Glacier are the whales. Humpback whales migrate to Glacier Bay in the summer to feed in the nutrient-rich glacial waters; massive humpbacks are commonly viewed in the lower portion of Glacier Bay, particularly Whidbey Passage and the vicinity of South Marble Island. If you're game to visit the bay in a kayak, look for humpbacks surrounding the Beardslee Islands and the Hugh Miller Inlet. Gray whales are generally found along the outer coast in spring and fall, when they mi-

9 Iditarod Trail Sled Dog Headquarters

CONTACT 907-376-5155, ext. 108, www.iditarod.com; Mile 2.2 Knik Goose Bay Rd., Wasilla

PRICING	$
BEST TIME TO VISIT	Summer
AGE RANGE	3 and older

Called the "Last Great Race on Earth," the Iditarod is a fiercely competitive, uniquely American extreme dogsled race run through 1,500 miles of treacherous terrain, generally in below-zero temperatures, in whiteout conditions, and in the limited daylight available in this part of the world. The route runs from Anchorage to Nome, and it is completed over the course of 10 to 17 days in early spring. Each musher, as the humans who compete are called, commands 12 to 16 sled dogs along the snowy Iditarod Trail, now designated a National Historic Trail. This impressive competition of humans against the forces of nature is a much-beloved tradition in Alaska, and is a favorite spectator sport for many fans around the world.

The Iditarod Trail Sled Dog Race Headquarters is a tiny memorial to this epic competition. On site is a small museum that showcases Iditarod memorabilia, trophies, videos, and photographs. If you and your family are traveling through the area, do not miss the chance to meet the dogs of the Iditarod at this site. In summer, visitors can climb aboard a sled and take an exhilarating ride along the actual Iditarod Trail.

Iditarod Trail shelter, Glovin   Courtesy of the Library of Congress

Bears feeding on salmon   Courtesy National Park Service

10 Katmai National Park and Preserve

CONTACT 907-246-3305, www.nps.gov/katm; P.O. Box 7, King Salmon

PRICING	$
BEST TIME TO VISIT	July and September
AGE RANGE	5 and older

The remote region of Katmai fell under federal protection in 1918, when it was designated a national monument to protect the 40-square-mile Valley of Ten Thousand Smokes, an enormous ash flow deposited by the Novarupta Volcano. Decades later, in 1980, Katmai was officially proclaimed a national park, and although the volcanoes are still a draw for many, this bit of wilderness is most famous for the incredible opportunities it offers for viewing bears. Tens of thousands of visitors flock to Katmai each year to watch brown bears feed on sockeye salmon as they swim upriver to spawn. A recent government survey estimates that the park is home to more than 2,000 bears, one of the greatest concentrations of these animals in the country.

Katmai National Park and Preserve does not have road access, so visitors must instead catch flights or arrange for boat trips into the park. Although the experience can be pricey, a ride via floatplane over the pristine wilderness and rugged coastline can be as memorable as visiting the park. There are a number of commercial flights available from Anchorage to King Salmon, the entry point to Katmai. It's also possible to charter flights and boat trips into the park from Homer and Kodiak.

Once you arrive, head to Brooks Camp, where in July and September the area is literally crawling with bears: You can see them along the trails, walking alongside the river, and most spectacularly feeding in the waterfalls. There are three viewing platforms located in Brooks Camp, situated along the side of the Brooks River. The greatest bear activity near these platforms comes during the salmon migration, from late June through July. Arrive at the Falls Platform early in the day: It provides the most spectacular views, and there is a maximum capacity of 40, which is managed by an on-site waiting list. Guests are allowed to remain on this platform for an hour.

There are few bears in the Brooks region in early June, so if you arrive at this time, check out the coastline of Halo Bay and Swikshak Lagoon to see bears feeding on sedge and grasses. In August, look for bears on the coastline at Geographic Harbor and inland at Moraine Creek.

11 Klondike Gold Rush Park

CONTACT 907-983-2921, www.nps.gov/klgo; headquarters at 2nd and Broadway, Skagway

PRICING	$
BEST TIME TO VISIT	Summer
AGE RANGE	5 and older

In 1896, gold was discovered in a small creek in the Yukon Territory, bordering Alaska in northwest Canada—and this discovery set off a clamor among prospectors, more than 40,000 of whom passed through Skagway and nearby Dyea en route to their future fortunes (so they hoped—very few prospectors actually found significant amounts of gold). The gold rush lasted approximately two years, and in its wake the Alaskan frontier towns experienced possibly the

Skagway, Alaska, the heart of the Klondike Gold Rush Park   © Debbie K. Hardin

most colorful, lawless period in the state's history.

The little town of Skagway was right in the middle of the prospecting action. It was founded by William Moore, a former steamboat captain who eventually watched tens of thousands of prospectors trek through his homestead on the way to the Canadian gold. It took average gold seekers three months to outfit themselves for prospecting and make it through the rugged terrain. But the Klondike Gold Rush ended almost as suddenly as it had begun, and burgs like Dyea were transformed into ghost towns, while Skagway diminished greatly in size and importance.

The Klondike Gold Rush National Historical Park commemorates the gold rush era in a 13,000-acre park that includes the six-block historical district of Skagway where prospectors came to outfit themselves for their adventure, the now-desolate Dyea, and the rugged Chilkoot and White Pass Trails that they used to reach the Yukon. Start your visit at the park visitor center, housed in the 1901 White Pass and Yukon Route Railroad Depot, and be sure to see *Days of Adventure, Dreams of Gold*, a 30-minute introduction to the history of the region. This is also the starting point of several walking tours through Skagway. The National Park Service has restored 15 of the many historic public buildings, saloons, and shops in downtown Skagway, including the 1910 Mascot Saloon Museum (3rd and Broadway) and the Moore House and Cabin (at 5th and Spring St.)—don't miss the chance to glimpse an early homestead. Visit nearby Dyea to catch the 33-mile Chilkoot Trail, one of two main routes to the Klondike. The trail actually predates the

There are two segments of this historic park: one in Skagway, and a second in Seattle, Washington, where most miners began their journey.

gold rush; it was first created by the Native Tlingit people as a trade route to Canada. A hike along this extremely challenging trail allows you to imagine what it must have been like for the prospectors (although it's not recommended for young children or inexperienced hikers of any age). The trail begins at the Taiya River Bridge near Dyea and ends at Lake Bennett. Expect it to take three to five days to make the trek.

12 Sitka National Historical Park

CONTACT 907-747-0110, www.nps.gov/sitk; 103 Monastery St., Sitka

PRICING	$
BEST TIME TO VISIT	Summer
AGE RANGE	7 and older

The first European settlers to brave the extreme wilderness of Alaska were Russian colonists, who were attracted to the area's vast natural resources as early as the 18th century. By the mid-1700s, the first Russian fur-trading posts and the communities that supported them were settled throughout the Aleutian Islands and along the coast. In addition to the trappers and traders came Russian missionaries, who established the Russian Orthodox Church in these regions. As was the case with Natives on the mainland of the United States, the Native Alaskans were exposed to numerous new diseases brought by the colonists, and many of the Alaskans died as a result.

In 1795, Alexandr Baranov, a successful fur trader and businessman, claimed Sitka Sound as Russian territory, and soon brought in hunting parties in search of sea otter skins. Shortly afterward, Sitka (then known as Novo-Arkhangelsk) became the primary settlement of Russians in Alaska. The Natives in the region at first tried to live peacefully alongside the colonists, but when the colonists proved less cooperative they tried to rebuff the settlers by force. In the early 19th century, Native clans destroyed a Russian trading post in retaliation for the encroachment on their hunting grounds. The Russian response took the form of the Battle of Sitka, in 1804, what was to be the last major armed conflict between colonists and Alaska Natives. The Russian-American Company, headed by Baranov, and the Imperial Russian Navy bombarded the Tlingit nation's clan of Sheet'ká Kwáan, quickly defeating the outgunned Natives and driving them permanently from their ancestral lands.

After the Alaska Purchase, in which the Alaska territory was bought by the United States from Russia in 1867, Sitka city became the first capital. The Sitka National Monument commemorates the Battle of Sitka and also preserves Northwest Coast totem pole

Sitka National Historical Park   Courtesy National Park Service

artworks, which adorn the park's 2 miles of scenic pathways. Visitors today can see the Tlingit fort from the Battle of Sitka and the battlefield. Also here is the Russian Bishop's House, one of the last remaining buildings from the Russian colonial era. Before exploring the battlefield and remaining buildings on site, start your visit in the park auditorium with the 12-minute video *The Voices of Sitka*, which tells the stories of historic people of the region as well as modern-day Sitkans. Also within the visitor center is the Southeast Alaska Indian Cultural Center, where you can observe Native artists creating traditional arts and crafts.

13 Totem Bight State Historical Park

CONTACT 907-247-8574, http://dnr.alaska.gov/parks/units/totembgh.htm; Ketchikan Ranger Station, 9883 N. Tongass Hwy., Ketchikan

PRICING	$
BEST TIME TO VISIT	Summer
AGE RANGE	5 and older

The Native peoples of the Pacific Northwest—particularly those living in the area that is now called the Inside Passage of Alaska—are famed totem pole carvers. Traditional totem poles are a visual way to tell a story—a kind of signpost to mark a clan's territory, recount a familiar legend, memorialize a historic event, or serve as a funerary sculpture—and the artisans use animals, human figures, and mythical creatures as a vehicle for their narrative. The totems were historically carved out of cedar logs by hand, and then painted using natural pigments in bright tones of red, green, and black. Up until the early 20th century, most Alaskan villages and many clans lived with a wide variety of totem poles to express their history and communicate their cultural ideals with visitors.

But by the early 1900s in southeast Alaska, many clans left their villages and moved to the burgeoning cities to find work, leaving the totem poles behind to rot or become overgrown by the forest. Recognizing the cultural importance of totem poles, in 1938 the USDA Forest Service instituted a program to preserve and reconstruct the beautiful but fragile pieces of artwork. Using Civilian Conservation Corps funds, they hired Native artisans to either repair abandoned totem poles or replicate them. The project continued until the funds ran out in World War II, at which point a collection of totem poles and a re-created community house (called a clan house) were gathered. When Alaska became a state in 1959, the site was designated a state historical park. Several years later it was added to the National Register of Historic Places.

Totem Bight State Historical Park, as it is now called, offers one of the world's largest collections of hand-carved totem poles, all of which are replicas carved by Native artists copying decaying originals found in the area. From the parking lot, walk along a level, well-maintained pathway through a lush hemlock-and-cedar forest to view the impressive collection. Notice that the totem poles face the sea, an homage to the original placement of totem poles meant to show outsiders approaching from the ocean the history and wealth of the village. Children will particularly enjoy walking through the clan house.

Artifact from Totem Bight State Historical Park

Courtesy Totem Bight State Historical Park

The tiny oval hole at the front of the house was purposely made small, to force a visitor to enter head-first—in the most vulnerable position, should the visit be unwelcome!

14 White Pass and Yukon Railway

CONTACT 800-343-7373, www.wpyr.com; 231 2nd Ave., Skagway

PRICING	$$$$
BEST TIME TO VISIT	Summer
AGE RANGE	5 and older

Aboard the White Pass and Yukon Railway © Debbie K. Hardin

The White Pass and Yukon Railway was built in 1898, during the Klondike Gold Rush, and it represents an engineering marvel: The 110-mile route was blasted through the rugged mountainside in just over two years. It took thousands of individuals and hundreds of tons of explosives to tame the challenging geography. The railway climbs upward 3,000 feet, heading through tunnels, bridges, and perilous-looking trestles, and in its day transported materials and personnel making their living off the natural resources in the area—first gold and then other precious minerals. Operations along the line were suspended in 1982, when the route was no longer needed for mining, but the railway was reopened several years later as a tourist attraction. Guests today can ride vintage passenger coaches along the route, from Skagway, Alaska, to Carcross, Yukon, Canada. No passports are required; you will not get out of the train once you cross the border. The train rolls up the route one way and back the other (the benches are cleverly designed to reverse, so no one has to endure the trip backward). The 20-mile trek takes about three hours, and passes through awe-inspiring views of waterfalls, mountains, and glaciers. The excursions are narrated and offer an interesting glimpse into the gold rush days.

Arizona

15 Canyon de Chelly National Monument

CONTACT 928-674-5500, www.nps.gov/cach; 3 miles off U.S. 191, Chinle

PRICING	$
BEST TIME TO VISIT	Fall through spring (summer can be prohibitively hot)
AGE RANGE	7 and older

There is something magical about the American Southwest, as witnessed by the large number of national parks and federally protected lands that preserve both the anthropological importance of an area inhabited thousands of years ago and the unusual natural beauty of the region. Canyon de Chelly in the northeastern part of the state is one such special place.

Canyon de Chelly offers a glimpse at the legacy of the Native Pueblo people, also called Anasazi, and includes their captivating cliff dwellings, artifacts, and petroglyphs. It is also a serene and beautiful place, perfect for contemplation and quiet drives. The colorful cliffs, the three canyons that fall within the park, and the impossibly blue sky highlight the astonishing desert scenery. The National Park Service administers and manages the park resources in concert with the Navajo Nation, which owns the land. Access to the canyon floors is thus restricted, and you can venture into the canyon only with an authorized Navajo guide or on a group tour with a park ranger. The exception is the White House Ruin Trail, a 600-foot switchback descent that leads to the White House Ruin, the most accessible and best-preserved ancient dwelling in the park. Allow two hours for a round-trip hike; although the path is relatively short, it is rigorous and can be extremely hot in the late spring and summer.

If the steep trail is too much for your family, the

> From March through November, the Navajo Nation within Canyon de Chelly observes Mountain Daylight Saving Time. However, the surrounding areas of Arizona observe Mountain Standard Time all year long.

Yucca Cove, Canyon de Chelly Courtesy National Park Service

next best way to explore the park on your own is via the North and South Rim Drives, which begin at the visitor center and run along the canyon edge to several overlooks with lovely views. If you have time for only one drive—each will take a few hours—take the South Rim Drive, which offers more chances to pull off the road and observe the canyon. Look for the park's most distinctive geological feature along this route: Spider Rock, a sandstone spire that rises 800 feet from the canyon floor (at the junction of Canyon de Chelly and Monument Canyon), which can be seen from this roadway.

If you have a full day or more to visit, prearrange for a guided tour into the canyon; the rangers at the visitors center can offer information on the best options for your family. Getting into the canyons will give you the best views of the archaeological sites and will give you an up-close view of the sheer cliffs.

16 Casa Grande Ruins National Monument

CONTACT 520-723-3172, www.nps.gov/cagr/contacts.htm; 1100 W. Ruins Dr., Coolidge

PRICING	$
BEST TIME TO VISIT	Fall through spring (summer can be prohibitively hot)
AGE RANGE	10 and older

As long ago as the early 13th century, the Ancient Sonoran Desert People developed wide-scale irriga-

Sedona red rocks Courtesy Greater Phoenix Convention and Visitors Bureau

Casa Grande Ruins National Monument

17 Grand Canyon National Park

CONTACT 928-638-7888, www.nps.gov/grca/index.htm; Grand Canyon National Park

PRICING	$
BEST TIME TO VISIT	Spring and fall (summertime is prohibitively hot, and trails can be icy in winter)
AGE RANGE	7 and older

tion farming and a sophisticated trading system in the heart of the desert that allowed them to settle and live for hundreds of years in what is now the American Southwest. The Casa Grande Ruins National Monument northeast of Coolidge preserves one of these Native farming communities and a group of original structures, including the impressive Casa Grande, which translates to the "great house." The community was abandoned in about 1450, and because the Sonoran people who built it left no written records, archaeologists can only guess at the purpose of the mysterious primary structure. Some believe the four-story, 11-room Casa Grande was a temple; others argue that it was more likely a watchtower. Still others believe it could simply have been a particularly large home. Casa Grande, and the other surrounding structures, were made of caliche, a mixture of the indigenous clay, sand, and calcium carbonate that is rock-hard when dry.

Start your trip with a stop at the visitor center (where you'll need to pay the entrance fee) and watch the 15-minute orientation video. You'll also find a small museum, bookstore, and facilities on site. Because of the desolate nature of the area, be sure to bring along supplies—plenty of water, especially in warmer months, and snacks. A shaded picnic area near the visitor center overlooks an ancient sports field that children will enjoy.

The Grand Canyon is one of the most famous sites in the United States, and is considered one of the natural wonders of the world. This awe-inspiring area offers sublime vistas across the mile-deep chasm, ample opportunities for outdoor adventures, and plenty of chances for kids to learn about geology and the vast history of the earth on display in the layers of this canyon. The bulk of the must-see sites are on the popular South Rim. Here the views are so expansive and the colors of the stone and bright blue sky so vivid that it's easy to spend hours simply staring into the canyon—and there are seemingly limitless vantage points from which to do just that.

Active families will want to descend into the canyon and take advantage of dozens of one-of-a-kind adventures. Perhaps the best-known option for tour-

Overlooking the South Rim of the Grand Canyon

Encourage children 10 years old and younger to read *Brighty: Of the Grand Canyon*, by Marguerite Henry, before traveling to the Grand Canyon. This children's novel tells the story of a beloved burro who lives in the canyon and witnesses historic events that are important to the park's history. This makes for a nice introduction to the park—but be prepared for your kids to *beg* for a mule ride!

Heard Museum   Photo by Craig Smith, courtesy the Heard Museum

ing the canyon is via mule train—a chance to saddle up and experience the canyon like a real cowpoke. These tours are wildly popular and, for South Rim departures, are usually booked up to 13 months in advance. Guests can opt for a day trip or an overnighter (which includes a stay at the fabulous Phantom Ranch, a secluded bunkhouse at the base of the canyon). Mule train participants must be able to turn over control to their mules as they traverse the steep cliffs of the Grand Canyon—but the good news is that the safety record of these animal tours is impeccable. Note that riders must be at least 7 years old for one-hour trips, 10 years old for half-day trips, and 12 years old for daylong trips. In addition, guests must weigh less than 200 pounds when fully outfitted (yes, they will make you climb on a scale to prove you're eligible), be at least 4 feet 7 inches tall, and speak English well enough to follow simple commands. Pregnant women are not allowed, and if you are at all frightened of heights, forget about it: The mules walk the outside of extremely narrow trails that look over dizzying drops.

18 Heard Museum

CONTACT 602-252-9757, www.heard.org; 2301 N. Central Ave., Phoenix

PRICING	$–$$
BEST TIME TO VISIT	Year-round
AGE RANGE	5 and older

Showcasing the heritage and living culture of Native Americans from the Southwest, the Heard Museum is one of the largest collections of Native arts and crafts in the country and includes artifacts, clothing, weapons, jewelry, beads, and contemporary art. The museum was founded in 1929 by Dwight B. and Maie Bartlett Heard to house their personal collection of artworks, many of which were archaeological artifacts from the La Ciudad Indian ruin.

There are more than 40,000 objects on display at the Heard, exhibited across 10 galleries. One of the favorite permanent exhibits is the Barry Goldwater collection of 437 historic Hopi kachina (often called "dolls," but historically these were not intended to be toys). Also on exhibit is a collection of artifacts that tell the story of the 19th-century boarding school experiences of Native Americans. It is little known that during this period Native children were taken from their homes and families (often by force) and educated in a way that was meant to erase their cultural identification. The collection includes old uniforms, oral interviews, heartbreaking photographs, and memorabilia that provide insight into this misguided attempt to "civilize" Native Americans.

Guided tours of the museum are available, and there are hands-on activities and crafts for children year-round. The museum is the site of several well-attended festivals, too. If you're in town in November, don't miss the annual Spanish Market, with strolling mariachis and artisan demonstrations. The first weekend in March the museum hosts the Indian Fair and Market, which includes live entertainment and the opportunity to buy Native arts and crafts from hundreds of artists.

19 Meteor Crater

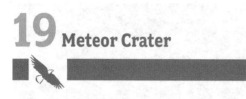

CONTACT 928-289-5898, www.meteorcrater.com; exit 233 off I-40, near Winslow

PRICING	$–$$
BEST TIME TO VISIT	Year-round
AGE RANGE	7 and older

More than 50,000 years ago, an asteroid traveling approximately 26,000 miles per hour struck the earth at this desolate spot in northern Arizona, outside of Winslow. The result was a meteor crater that is close to a mile across, 2.4 miles in circumference, and more than 500 feet deep. This is the biggest, most visible crater in the United States, and it is pretty impressive! The attraction is privately owned, and entrance includes exhibits and an educational center that is entertaining, especially for young children. Start your visit at the meteor welcome center to see *Collisions and Impacts*, a 10-minute film that explains the science and history behind the crater. The center is also home to a 1,400-pound meteor fragment, exhibits on astronaut training, and an actual Apollo space test capsule—it's interesting stuff. Guests can step outside to view the depths of the crater from several outlook points. You can also take guided tours around the rim of the meteor—but reserve any hiking for fall through early spring; summer heat in this part of Arizona is generally oppressive.

Meteor Crater Courtesy Northern Arizona USA

20 Montezuma Castle National Monument

CONTACT 928-567-3322, www.nps.gov/moca; exit 289 off I-17, Camp Verde

PRICING	$
BEST TIME TO VISIT	Fall through spring
AGE RANGE	10 and older

Tucked into a white limestone mountain, 70 feet off the ground, Montezuma Castle is an impressive 20-room cliff dwelling built over multiple levels that has existed on this spot in central Arizona for at least 1,000 years. It is one of the best-preserved cliff dwellings in the United States, built and inhabited by what are now known as the Sinagua people—so named by Spanish explorers, who dubbed them the people "without water," because most of their ruins are in dry, desert locales. The Sinagua left no written records, so we don't know what they called themselves. In fact, we know little about these ancient people, aside from the fact that they lived in this place for 400 years and then disappeared suddenly, about 600 years ago. Archaeologists and anthropologists believe they farmed the surrounding lands between the 12th and 14th centuries. When Europeans rediscovered the cliff dwelling in the 1860s, they mis-

Montezuma Castle National Monument

Courtesy National Park Service

named it for the Aztec emperor Montezuma II because they mistakenly believed that the emperor had been involved in its construction. In fact, the whole moniker is misleading: The dwelling is less a "castle" than a multifamily townhouse.

Up until 1951 visitors to the ruins were able to climb a series of ladders and walk through Montezuma Castle. At that time, however, concerns for the safety of visitors and the integrity of the structure led to the removal of the ladders. Today guests can hike a third-of-a-mile loop to see the structure from below—still a remarkable sight. The Montezuma Castle Visitor Center is also worth a visit; it houses Sinagua artifacts, such as the tools they used to construct the dwelling, bone needles and gemstone ornaments, and stones used for grinding corn.

21 Petrified Forest National Park

Petrified log　　　　　　　　　　　© Debbie K. Hardin

CONTACT 928-524-6228, www.nps.gov/pefo; northern Arizona between I-40 and U.S. 180

PRICING	$
BEST TIME TO VISIT	Fall through spring
AGE RANGE	3 and older

Fossils provide us with a glimpse into the distant past, and the Petrified Forest in northern Arizona offers the world's largest collection of fossilized wood. The area was once home to a forest of conifers, which over millennia were buried in ash and silt. After tens of thousands of years, the wood tissue was gradually replaced with quartz—which is surprisingly colorful and unusually beautiful. These striking fossils are set amid a stark landscape that might as well be on the Moon given the scarcity of vegetation, the otherworldly colors of the hills, and the unusual mineral formations.

The park offers two distinct areas. Less visited, but equally spectacular, is the northernmost portion that includes the multihued badlands known as the Painted Desert. The vast, deserted wilderness really does look like it has been washed with watercolors of yellow, blue, orange, and red. Head to Pintado Point, a high spot on the rim of the desert, for the best views.

The southernmost section of the park is the real attraction for kids: This is where you'll find the greatest concentration of petrified wood. Look for massive logs and small bark-like chunks. The fossils date to the late Triassic period, more than 200 million years ago—even before the Jurassic period when dinosaurs were prominent.

The park is also home to an impressive collection of petroglyphs, but these can be hard to find on your own. Sign up for a guided ranger tour through the backcountry for the chance to see some of these ancient rock paintings. If you have the time, you'll also want to check out the Cultural Demonstrator Program within the park, which provides the opportunity for Native Americans from the region to share their history and traditional crafts with visitors.

22 Pueblo Grande Museum and Archeological Park

CONTACT 602-495-0900, http://phoenix.gov/recreation/arts/museums/pueblo/index.html; 4619 E. Washington St., Phoenix

PRICING	$–$$
BEST TIME TO VISIT	Year-round
AGE RANGE	7 and older

Pueblo Grande is an expansive archaeological museum and site of a Native Hohokam village that is be-

Pit House, at Pueblo Grande Museum and Archaeological Park   Courtesy Greater Phoenix Visitors Bureau

lieved to be more than 1,500 years old. *Hohokamis* is a Pima word used to identify Native peoples who lived in the Sonoran Desert, surrounding the Gila River and lower Salt River, from the 7th through 14th centuries. Hohokam are believed to have been farmers who cultivated maize, beans, squash, agave, tobacco, and cotton, and who harvested myriad wild plants as well. They used a sophisticated system of canals to irrigate their crops—an innovation that allowed them to survive for centuries in the harsh, arid desert environment of the Southwest. They were also skilled potters and jewelry artisans. Hohokam people are likely ancestors of the Tohono O'odham and Akimel O'odham peoples from southern Arizona.

> *Hohokamis is a Pima word used to identify Native peoples who lived in the Sonoran Desert.*

Visitors to the archaeological park can hike the outdoor trail that allows easy viewing of a platform mound and ball court ruin, replicated houses, and native plants. The on-site museum features three galleries, including a children's hands-on gallery and a theater. Collections are dedicated to preserving objects and documents from the Pueblo Grande site and include excavated archaeological artifacts taken from the Phoenix metropolitan area. The museum also collects historic and contemporary Native American art objects; especially well represented are artifacts from

cultures that developed along the Salt River Valley, such as the Akimel O'odham (Pima) and Piipash (Maricopa).

23 San Xavier del Bac

CONTACT 520-294-2624, www.sanxaviermission.org; 1950 W. San Xavier Rd., Tucson

PRICING	$
BEST TIME TO VISIT	Year-round
AGE RANGE	10 and older

Spanish Jesuits in the late 17th century founded missions throughout the Sonoran Desert for the purpose of religious conversion of Native peoples, including the Tohono O'odham and the Pima who lived (and continue to live) near Tucson; the missions were also a convenient way for Spain to get a toehold on territory in America. San Xavier del Bac is a stunning example of mission architecture and is simply spectacular, inside and out. The church is located a few miles southwest of Tucson on what is now the Tohono O'odham San Xavier Reservation. The original building of San Xavier was destroyed in 1770. The church as it stands now was redesigned and completed in 1797 using Native labor. Once Mexico gained its independence from Spain in 1821, the region became part of Mexico, and the last Spanish missionary left soon after. In 1848 the region became a territory of the United States, and in 1913 Franciscan friars returned to the mission, where they continue to work and live today.

The church is still an active parish (and thus it's better to avoid visiting on Sunday mornings). Most other days, guests can take 45-minute guided tours to learn more about the ornate interior. There is also a museum on site offering a 20-minute orientation

> If you can visit in the spring, come for the San Xavier Festival, held the Friday night after Easter, which offers a lovely torchlit parade of Tohono O'odham and Yaqui tribe members.

San Xavier del Bac

Photo by James Randklev @ Metropolitan Tucson Convention and Visitors Bureau

video. The lavish, European-style church is incongruous in its dusty setting—it almost seems like a mirage. In fact, some people have called the church the "white dove of the desert."

24 Tombstone

CONTACT Tombstone Chamber of Commerce, 888-457-3929, www.tombstonechamber.com

PRICING	Prices vary by attraction
BEST TIME TO VISIT	Year-round
AGE RANGE	12 and older

When most Americans think of the "Wild West," they think of frontier towns like Tombstone. In its heyday, this was a hardscrabble, lawless place, full of miners and cowboys out to strike it rich. The boomtown offered no end of possibilities for those looking for trouble, in saloons, brothels, and gambling halls. Tombstone is most famously associated with the 30-second gunfight at the O.K. Corral (which in fact took place on Fremont Street, *near* the corral) in the late 19th century, in which the McLaury and Clanton clans had a bloody run-in with the lawmen of the area: Wyatt Earp and his brothers, along with Doc Holliday.

The town grew quickly, seemingly out of nothing, after prospector Ed Schieffelin discovered silver in 1877 and miners flocked to the area to stake their claims. Legend has it that before Schieffelin struck it rich, he was warned away from the area by soldiers from nearby Fort Huachuca, who were on constant guard against marauding Apaches; the soldiers joked that the only stone Schieffelin would find in the wilderness would be his own tombstone. When Schieffelin *did* discover silver, he had the last laugh: He named his first mine The Tombstone, and soon after the growing town acquired the same name. At its peak, the population was estimated to reach 20,000—and it was at the time one of the fastest-growing cities in the West.

Today Tombstone is a National Historic Site, and although you can still hear the occasional gunshot ring out, rest assured the sounds are coming from one of the numerous reenactments around the city. Children will enjoy being surrounded by living (entertaining) history, and aside from the somewhat sordid past, the area is now mostly kid-friendly. Walk along the town's wooden boardwalks, visit historic sites, attend an Old West show, and wet your whistle with a sarsaparilla in one of a number of re-created (and PG-rated) saloons. Be sure to visit the Good Enough Mine (520-255-5552; PO Box 219), which once belonged to the man who discovered the silver lode that started the rush to Tombstone. Guests don hard hats and reflective safety gear and descend into the mine for a 45-minute tour through the dark and damp tunnels. It's a fascinating look into the past, but avoid this if you are claustrophobic or if your kids are frightened of the dark. Children must be accompanied by an adult, and no one shorter than 48 inches may tour the mine.

You won't want to miss the O.K. Corral (520-457-3456, www.ok-corral.com; 326 E. Allen St.). The site of the famous shootout is now a museum, with kitschy life-sized animatronics that dramatize the gunfight. Every afternoon at 2, see a live reenactment on the site as well. Nearby is the Tombstone Western Heritage Museum (520-457-3800, www.thetombstone-museum.com; 6th and Fremont St.), which offers a glimpse at many of Wyatt Earp's personal effects, as well as a large collection of antique guns, photos, and documents.

25 Tuzigoot National Monument

Tuzigoot National Monument   Courtesy National Park Service

CONTACT 928-634-5564, www.nps.gov/tuzi; Tuzigoot
National Monument, Camp Verde

PRICING	$
BEST TIME TO VISIT	Fall through spring
AGE RANGE	7 and older

Tuzigoot is the largest and best-preserved of the many Sinagua pueblo ruins in the Verde Valley; the site comprises a complex village built by the ancient people, who were farmers and traders. The 110-room pueblo was built in about AD 1200 and was inhabited for approximately 400 years. Tuzigoot (an Apache word for "crooked water," referring to the unusual shape of nearby Pecks Lake) has two easy trails you can use to explore the area. The Ruins Loop is a third of a mile that winds in and around the pueblo and affords nice views of the Verde River. The Tavasci Marsh Overlook Trail is a half-mile out-and-back pathway that winds through native vegetation. Stop by the visitors center to see Sinagua artifacts found on the site, such as tools, eating vessels, and jewelry. Note that the parking lot leading to the site is locked at 5 PM.

Discount passes are available if you purchase tickets for both Tuzigoot and Montezuma Castle (see above).

Arkansas

26 Buffalo National River

CONTACT 870-439-2502, www.nps.gov/buff; 402 N. Walnut, Harrison

PRICING	$
BEST TIME TO VISIT	Year-round
AGE RANGE	7 and older

Rafting the Buffalo National River Courtesy Arkansas Tourism Office

The lovely Buffalo National River is one of the few waterways in the United States that hasn't been dammed, thanks to a 1972 act of Congress that protected the area from industrial uses by designating it a national river. It flows freely through towering limestone bluffs for nearly 150 miles, from the Boston Mountains in the Ozarks, through the scenic Springfield and Salem Plateaus, finally meeting up with the White River in the northeast. Along its length you can find lazy stretches of gently flowing water and quiet pools and wilder lengths rushing along rapids.

Most visitors come to float the river, whether by inner tube, canoe, kayak, or inflatable raft, and the expansive waterway is suited to most abilities. For those looking for a peaceful, relaxing outing, head to the lower river to find gentle currents and slow-moving water; for those looking for a more adrenaline-fueled adventure, check out the whitewater in the upper portion of the river: Here you'll find natural springs, caves, and sinkholes where the river is surrounded by 500-foot bluffs and dramatic rock formations. Look for the Hemmed-in-Hollow waterfall about half a mile from the upper river, a 200-foot beauty that is one of the largest in middle America. Whatever float trip you envision, you can bring your own craft or rent boats from dozens of park concessioners, who will make arrangements to pick you up at the end of your river run. The National Park Service maintains a website with updated water levels and temperatures (http://ar.water.usgs.gov/buffaloriver/), so that you can plan the river adventure that is right for your family.

There are a number of developed campgrounds along the river; visitors are also allowed to camp throughout much of the region along the river on sand- and gravel bars, so long as you stay 100 feet from the water and keep off private property.

27 Clinton Presidential Library and Museum

CONTACT 501-374-4242, www.clintonlibrary.gov; 1200 President Clinton Ave., Little Rock

PRICING	$–$$
BEST TIME TO VISIT	Year-round
AGE RANGE	7 and older

The Clinton Presidential Library and Museum in Little Rock is a recent addition to a collection of presidential libraries across the country, and the exhibits and holdings provide an unparalleled look into the presidency of Bill Clinton (b. 1946), the 42nd president of

Clinton Presidential Library and Museum

Courtesy Clinton Presidential Library and Museum

28 Crater of Diamonds State Park

CONTACT 870-285-3113, www.craterofdiamondsstate park.com; 209 State Park Dr., Murfreesboro

PRICING	$–$$
BEST TIME TO VISIT	Year-round
AGE RANGE	5 and older

the United States, and the life of Americans in the 1990s. The stunning glass-and-steel building cantilevers over the Arkansas River, a clever analogy to Clinton's campaign promise to build a "bridge to the 21st century." There are three floors of exhibit space, housed on extensive grounds, and there are countless opportunities for children to interact with exhibits and get a firsthand look into the American presidency.

Start off a museum tour with a 12-minute orientation film narrated by President Clinton himself, which tells the story of his life and presidency. Move on to permanent exhibits, including a collection of gifts presented to the president and Mrs. Clinton by other heads of state: Kids will want to see the 5-foot Swiss-chalet-style cat house designed for First Cat Socks and presented to the Clintons by Sitterdorf, Switzerland. Other fun exhibits include the limousine and Secret Service exhibit, where guests can view one of the 1993 Cadillac Fleetwood Broughams that was used during Clinton's presidency; and *Holidays in the White House*, which includes a collection of the much-coveted wooden Easter eggs used in the annual White House Easter Egg Roll on the Monday after Easter. The highlight of any visit is the chance to tour the precisely re-created Oval Office, which features reproductions of the furniture, artwork, and collections at the time Clinton was president. Encourage children to ask docents about the HMS *Resolute* Desk, the original version of which was a gift to Rutherford B. Hayes by Queen Victoria. It was constructed from timbers of a British Arctic exploration ship, and the original has been used as the official presidential desk by most of the U.S. presidents since that time, including John F. Kennedy, Jimmy Carter, Ronald Reagan, Bill Clinton, and Barack Obama.

For kids (and their parents) who like to hunt for buried treasure and don't mind getting their hands dirty, this is a one-of-a-kind adventure: Crater of Diamonds is the only diamond-producing site in the world that is open to the public and one of the few sites within the United States where the precious stones have been found. The valuable gems were first discovered in Murfreesboro in 1906, by a farmer who owned the land at the time. Since then, more than 75,000 diamonds have been unearthed, including a 40-carat stone (the largest ever mined in the United States).

Start at the visitor center to get tips on finding diamonds and to see them in their natural state, so you know what you're looking for. Park staff at the center will help you identify your finds at the end of the day. Note that diamonds at this site come in all colors, but you're most likely to find white, brown, and yellow diamonds. You may also find other gems, such as agate, amethyst, garnet, and quartz. While you're at the visitor center, check out the Strawn-

Hunting for treasure at Crater of Diamonds State Park

Courtesy Arkansas Tourism Office

PRICE KEY
$ free–$5
$$ $6–10
$$$ $11–20
$$$$ $21+

You can buy or rent tools at Crater of Diamonds, or bring your own. You'll need a bucket and a trowel or small shovel. You may also want a screen through which to sift the soil, knee pads, and a camp stool. Be sure to bring a hat and wear sunscreen; there is very little cover here, and the 37 acres of plowed field—the eroded surface of an ancient volcanic pipe—is very dusty, so on particularly dry days you might appreciate a kerchief to tie around your nose and mouth.

Wagner Diamond, a 1-carat gem that has the highest quality rating that a diamond is given: It is nearly flawless.

29 Fort Smith National Historic Site

CONTACT Fort Smith Convention and Visitors Bureau, 479-783-8888, www.fortsmith.org; 2 N. B St., Fort Smith

PRICING	$
BEST TIME TO VISIT	Year-round
AGE RANGE	10 and older

Fort Smith epitomizes the history of the American frontier during the 19th century—the good, the bad, and the ugly. Fort Smith was both a bastion of law and order during a time when bandits and outlaws ruled the open Plains and a symbol for one of the most shameful national tragedies in the country: It was here that Native Americans being forcefully relocated from the East to "Indian Territory" (modern-day Oklahoma) ended their "Trail of Tears."

Fort Smith sits on the border of Arkansas and Oklahoma, in the Ozark Mountains, and today encompasses two fort sites, along with barracks and an original courthouse. The first fort was built in 1817, at Belle Point along the Arkansas River, and the soldiers stationed here were tasked with keeping the peace between the warring Osage and Cherokee peoples. The second Fort Smith was garrisoned from 1838 to 1871. Although the fort was never actually used for defense purposes, it was a training location and a supply depot for the U.S. Army. During the American Civil War it was manned by both the Confederate army, which occupied the fort until 1863, and Union troops, who maintained command from 1863 until the war was over. During this period the town attracted people fleeing from the bloody war, runaway slaves, and more than its fair share of criminals hoping that the vast expanse of wilderness would give them free rein. Saloons, gambling halls, and brothels flourished. Federal troops left the post of Fort Smith in 1871 and were replaced by U.S. deputy marshals, who patrolled the increasingly lawless area, an enormous expanse of geography that included all of the Indian Territory. The film *True Grit* made the Fort Smith U.S. deputy marshals (like the fictional Rooster Cogburn) famous, and it reminded the modern audience of the notorious "hanging judge" of the district, Isaac Parker, who sent 79 people to the gallows during his 21-year bench.

While the frontier developed and grew, in the 1830s the U.S. government mandated that Native Americans living in the Southeast be forcibly marched across the country, to Indian Territory—lands reserved by the U.S. government for the Cherokee, Chickasaw, Choctaw, Creek, and Seminole peoples. Tens of thousands of men, women, and children from the so-called Five Civilized Tribes were driven at bayonet point from their homes in Alabama, Mississippi, and other southern states all the way to western Arkansas and eventually into what is today Oklahoma—making Fort Smith their last stop. This tragic event is referred to as the Trail of Tears; more than 10,000 Native Americans died from exposure, diseases, starvation, or violence during their removal. Many died soon after arriving.

Fort Smith   Courtesy National Park Service

30 Historic Washington State Park

CONTACT 870-983-2684, www.historicwashingtonstate
park.com; off U.S. 30, Washington

PRICING	$–$$
BEST TIME TO VISIT	Year-round
AGE RANGE	7 and older

Historic Washington State Park is a 19th-century museum village preserving the legacy of this pioneer town that was once a stop along the Southwest Trail from St. Louis, Missouri, to Fulton (about 12 miles from Washington). Today the site protects more than 30 carefully restored or re-created structures, including classic examples of Southern Greek Revival and Federal architecture, Gothic Revival, and more humble hand-hewn timber framing. Guests can walk the plank-board sidewalks along streets that have never been paved in the town's history, tour the public buildings and homes, witness historic reenactments, and ride in an authentic surrey.

Different historic buildings are open on different days. Start with a visit to the 1874 Hempstead County Courthouse, which serves as a visitor center and box office. Check out the Print Museum to learn about the history of the only Arkansas newspaper to print throughout the Civil War and to learn about printing equipment from the 19th century; the Blacksmith Shop, with two working forges and interpreters to explain the craft; the Trimble House, a single-family home with period furnishings; the Clardy/Goodlet

> There are seasonal historical and educational programs in the park, which include demonstrations in Dutch oven cooking, classes on traditional dances like the Virginia Reel and the Pattie-Cake Polka, and an introduction to blacksmithing. Popular festivals include Civil War weekend reenactments throughout the year; the Five Trails Rendezvous in February that commemorates the five Native American trails in the area; and a Victorian Era Christmas Ball in December.

*Reenactors at work, Historic Washington
State Park* Courtesy Arkansas Tourism Office

Kitchen, a detached structure that is often the site of pioneer cooking demonstrations; the Royston Log House, which offers an exhibit on the tools, materials, and techniques of building a log home on the frontier; the Simon Sanders House and Urban Farmstead, which offers a fascinating program called *Her Work Is Never Done* chronicling the life of a household slave during the antebellum period; and the Candle Shop, where kids can see demonstrations of candle making and then dip their own souvenirs.

31 Little Rock Central High

CONTACT www.nps.gov/chsc; 2120 Daisy Bates Dr.,
Little Rock

PRICING	$
BEST TIME TO VISIT	Year-round
AGE RANGE	10 and older

In 1954 the U.S. Supreme Court issued its groundbreaking decision in *Brown v. Board of Education*, which was to have repercussions throughout the country. In this case the court held that segregated schools are unconstitutional, and as a result schools around the nation were compelled to integrate. But the transition was not a smooth one in many areas of the country, and especially not in Little Rock. The Lit-

Little Rock Central High   Courtesy National Park Service

tle Rock School Board initially complied with the high court's ruling, in 1957 allowing what came to be called the Little Rock Nine—nine African American students—to enroll in Little Rock Central High, a previously all-white school. However, when the term began and the Little Rock Nine were set to attend their first classes, Arkansas governor Orval Faubus sided with segregationists and prevented them from entering the school, ordering the state's National Guard to physically block them from the facility. The students missed what was to have been their first day of school, and on leaving the premises were followed by an attending mob, viciously harassed, and threatened with lynching. For two weeks the African American students were advised to stay home for their own safety.

President Dwight D. Eisenhower eventually sent federal troops to escort the students into the school and to enforce the desegregation that was ordered by the Supreme Court. The military presence remained in place at the school for the rest of the school year, with each student being escorted to classes. Under federal protection, the Little Rock Nine finished out the school year. However, the following year, Faubus closed all the high schools; white students attended private schools, but the African American students were

forced to attend schools in other states or to enroll in correspondence courses. The school board reopened the schools in the fall of 1959, and although there was continued violence, two of the original nine students returned, this time protected by local police; they went on to graduate from Little Rock Central High.

The drama played out on national television, eliciting outrage from many incredulous viewers. The events surrounding the Little Rock Nine are considered a turning point in the civil rights movement. Designated a National Historic Monument, Little Rock High School, now called Central High School National Historic Site, stands as a memorial commemorating the often-violent struggle over school desegregation. Across the intersection from the facility (which is still a working school), the National Historic Site Visitor Center displays interactive exhibits on the 1957 events.

32 Louisiana Purchase State Park

CONTACT 870-572-2352, www.arkansasstateparks.com/louisianapurchase; AR 362, Brinkley

PRICING	$
BEST TIME TO VISIT	Year-round
AGE RANGE	7 and older

The Louisiana Purchase of 1803 was the largest land acquisition in the history of the United States, nearly

> Check out the oral history listening stations, where you can learn about the events at Little Rock High firsthand from the participants. On Monday, Wednesday, and Friday during the school year, rangers offer 30-minute guided tours of the high school; these must be arranged (501-374-1957) at least two weeks in advance.

Louisiana Purchase State Park   Courtesy Arkansas Tourism office

There are no facilities whatsoever at the Louisiana State Park. Plan accordingly.

doubling the size of the country at that time. President Thomas Jefferson presided over the transaction, purchasing close to 900,000 square miles of unmapped wilderness from France for the bargain price of $15 million. The territory included all or parts of what now make up 15 U.S. states (including all of Arkansas, Iowa, Kansas, Missouri, Nebraska, and Oklahoma; plus chunks of Colorado, Louisiana, Minnesota, Montana, New Mexico, North Dakota, South Dakota, Texas, and Wyoming) and two Canadian provinces (Alberta and Saskatchewan)—and today makes up close to 25 percent of the land in the United States.

The state park encompasses the site from which all surveys of the vast property acquired in the Louisiana Purchase originated. Visitors to the area today can stroll along a boardwalk that winds through a (very) swampy area to see the monument marking the starting point of the 1815 surveys President James Madison commissioned 12 years after the initial purchase. Along the way are interpretive panels that tell the story of the Louisiana Purchase, the survey, and the inhabitants of the park. The rare headwater swamp conserves an unusual habitat for many bird species, including the belted kingfisher, the pileated woodpecker, and the barred owl, which makes this park a nice stop for birders as well as history buffs.

33 Ozark Folk Center State Park

CONTACT 800-264-3655, www.ozarkfolkcenter.com; 1032 Park Ave., Mountain View

PRICING	$$$
BEST TIME TO VISIT	Year-round
AGE RANGE	5 and older

The Ozarks is a mountainous region in the central United States that stretches across five states: Arkansas, Illinois, Kansas, Missouri, and Oklahoma. It has a strong cultural legacy of artisan crafts and "old-

Broom making, Ozark Folk Center State Park
Courtesy Arkansas Tourism Office

time" music. The Ozark Folk Center is dedicated to sharing the heritage of the Ozark Mountain people in a fun, entertaining way that is extremely kid-friendly and very much hands-on. The lively center offers workshops in American folk music, herb gardening, and pioneer crafts. The village has a rotating cadre of more than 20 artisans on site to demonstrate skills such as basket weaving, broom making, pottery throwing, quilting, soap making, coopering, doll making, and musical instrument construction.

Children have plenty of opportunities to get active while visiting the park. The Folk Kids' Club is open to every child on entry. Kids pick up a scavenger hunt packet that will help them explore the offerings at the park, and in the process have the opportunity to take a turn at weaving, modeling a coonskin hat, and playing a hand-wrought musical instrument. The Kids' Young Pioneers program is for children 7 to 14 and allows participants to work with artisans to learn a craft or skill and complete a project in dozens of activities common to the Ozark mountain people, including square dancing, corn shucking, yarn spinning, and apple-head doll making.

In addition to myriad opportunities to participate in arts and crafts, the Folk Center is a fabulous place to experience live music. Traditional Ozark folk music is presented regularly in the park in the craft grounds during the day and in the Ozark Folk Center's 1,000-seat Music Theater in the evenings. Guests will be treated to traditional fiddle and banjo folk songs and dance music from the region, as well as tunes played with dulcimers, autoharps, and mandolins.

34 Parkin Archeological State Park

CONTACT 870-755-2500, www.arkansasstateparks.com/parkinarcheological; at the junction of U.S. 64 and AR 184 N., Parkin

PRICING	$
BEST TIME TO VISIT	Year-round
AGE RANGE	7 and older

The Parkin Archeological Park in northeastern Arkansas preserves the site of a Native American village that existed on the site during the Mississippian period, from about AD 1000 to 1550. Artifacts found at the site indicate that Hernando de Soto's expedition visited the village in 1541. De Soto is the Spanish explorer credited as the first European to cross the Mississippi River while looking for gold and for a shortcut to China. The village was originally 17 acres boxed in by the St. Francis River on one side and a hand-dug

Headpots are believed to be either portraits of deceased ancestors or trophies.

water moat on the other three sides. Visitors today can see a large earthen platform mound built by the Natives that is believed to be the foundation of the village chief's home.

Excavations are ongoing. The visitor center includes a laboratory where guests can observe scientists cleaning, sorting, and cataloging artifacts. The on-site museum includes intact items that have been uncovered over the years, including unique "headpots," a Native art form that is found only in this region. The small headpots, a little smaller than an actual head, are made from clay and were originally painted with vibrant colors. They are believed to be either portraits of deceased ancestors or trophies, made by tribal artisans in the form of the visage of a warrior's victims.

35 Prairie Grove Battlefield State Park Civil War Reenactment

CONTACT 479-846-2900, www.arkansasstateparks.com/prairiegrovebattlefield; 506 E. Douglas St., Prairie Grove

PRICING	$
BEST TIME TO VISIT	Year-round (and every other December to view the reenactment)
AGE RANGE	10 and older

This 838-acre park preserves the site of the Battle at Prairie Grove, one of the most important battles of the Civil War in northwest Arkansas. On December 7, 1862, the Confederate Army of the Trans-Mississippi battled the Union Army of the Frontier. In one day of bloody fighting, there were nearly 3,000 casualties. This horrific engagement was the last major battle in the area.

To commemorate the historic event, and to honor the thousands who were killed, every even-numbered year the park hosts Arkansas's largest battle reenactment—and one of the most extensive, most colorful reenactments in the country. Guests can take tours through re-created army camps, watch demonstrations of battlefield cooking, witness military drills, and chat with docents who will interpret the events that took place during the battle. In the afternoon each day during the reenactment, you can watch attacks and

Prairie Grove Battlefield State Park Courtesy Arkansas Tourism Office

counterattacks by Union and Confederate infantry and cavalry, all staged on the actual battlefield.

If you visit anytime other than the biannual reenactment, you can walk along the 1-mile Battlefield Trail to see where the heaviest fighting took place, or take the 5-mile driving tour. On site is a historic Ozark village. The visitor center offers interpretive exhibits to help children understand the circumstances of the battle and the historical significance of the Civil War.

36 Toltec Mounds Archeological State Park

Toltec Mounds   Courtesy Arkansas Tourism Office

CONTACT 501-961-9442, www.arkansasstateparks.com/ toltecmounds; 490 Toltec Mounds Rd., Scott

PRICING	$
BEST TIME TO VISIT	Year-round
AGE RANGE	7 and older

The 100-acre Toltec Mounds near Little Rock is one of the largest archaeological sites in the Lower Mississippi River Valley. Preserved here are three monumental mounds dating to an ancient civilization. The historic earthworks are the remains of the governmental and ceremonial center that was inhabited from AD 650 to 1050 by the Plum Bayou Culture. The Plum Bayou were agriculturists who farmed domesticated plants like barley and maygrass; they were also hunters, living off the deer, turkey, and rabbits native to the area. The mounds were constructed gradually over a 300-year period, and at one time 18 mounds were arranged around two rectangular open spaces that were used as ceremonial religious sites. Of the remaining mounds, one is nearly 50 feet high and another nearly 40. Archaeologists believe that some of the mounds were used as platforms for viewing the ceremonies, and others were the foundations for dwellings used by religious leaders. One construction has been identified as a burial mound.

It isn't known why the site was abandoned or where the Plum Bayou people may have gone from here. Later Native Americans in the region occasionally used the site for their own ceremonies and rituals, including burials. It is considered a sacred place by the Native Americans still living in the region. Note: The use of the word *Toltec* is misleading. In the 1800s, locals believed that the Native Americans of the region were not culturally advanced enough to undertake such an ambitious construction project and instead attributed the mounds to the Toltecs and Aztecs in Mexico, whom they mistakenly believed lived in the area at one time. Experts later proved that the mounds were actually built by the ancestors of local Native tribes.

california

37 Alcatraz

CONTACT 415-981-7625, www.nps.gov/alca; San Francisco Bay, accessed via ferries that leave from Fisherman's Wharf

PRICING	Prices vary by ferry and tour
BEST TIME TO VISIT	Year-round
AGE RANGE	10 and older

Alcatraz from the San Francisco Bay Courtesy Juliane Preimesberger

Thanks in part to Hollywood folklore, which glorified the site in dozens of movies and television shows, Alcatraz is known as a historical penitentiary for criminals so dangerous and so crafty that they had to be secured in an island prison. Alcatraz Island is isolated in the middle of San Francisco Bay—tantalizingly close to the city—and "The Rock," as the maximum-security prison was sometimes called, was home to some of the most notorious people in the country. From 1934 to 1963, the detention facility famously housed the likes of gangster Al Capone, murderer "Machine Gun" Kelly, and "Birdman" Robert Franklin Stroud (known for his love of birds, although contrary to popular belief he didn't keep pets in Alcatraz). During its nearly 30 years as a federal penitentiary, Alcatraz claimed that no prisoner *successfully* escaped. (Several dozen men made attempts but were either retrieved, killed by guards, or imagined to have drowned when they tried to swim the cold and rough waters of the San Francisco Bay.)

Before its storied role as the most dreaded penitentiary in the country, the facility also served as a military outpost: From 1850 to 1934 troops were stationed on the island to protect the San Francisco Bay Area. Even in its military capacity, however, the advantages of the island as a remote prison were evident: Alcatraz began housing military prisoners here during the Civil War as early as 1861. In 1907, Alcatraz was designated an official U.S. military prison, and a

few years later construction began on a concrete cell block meant to be impenetrable. The prison was also the holding place for conscientious objectors during World War I.

Today guests can take boat trips to the island and then tour the facility with the help of national park rangers or via self-guided audio tours, enjoy the outdoor gardens, and take in premier views of the Golden Gate Bridge and the city—imagining all the while how prisoners must have felt seeing the city as so close, yet so far.

38 Cabrillo National Monument

CONTACT 619-557-5450, www.nps.gov/cabr; 1800 Cabrillo Memorial Dr., San Diego

PRICING	$
BEST TIME TO VISIT	Year-round
AGE RANGE	7 and older

On September 28, 1542, Portuguese explorer Juan Rodriquez Cabrillo, sailing on behalf of Spain, became the first European of record to set foot on the West Coast of the United States. He sailed his flagship, the *San Salvador*, from Mexico into the San Diego Bay, just off the peninsula of Point Loma, one of the southernmost points in California, in search of a trade route between Mexico and the Spice Islands in Asia. Cabrillo never found the shortcut to the riches for which he was looking, but he did claim the newfound area for Spain. Cabrillo named the spot San Miguel and then

Be sure to purchase tickets in advance; because of limited space and popularity of the site, Alcatraz often sells out weeks in advance.

California Palace of Fine Arts, San Francisco   © Debbie K. Hardin

PRICE KEY
$ free–$5
$$ $6–10
$$$ $11–20
$$$$ $21+

> Also within the park is the picturesque Old Point Loma Lighthouse, which dates to 1855. Visitors can peek into the re-created living space of the light keeper and his family. From December through March, this is one of the best vantage points (on dry land) to watch the annual gray whale migration to Mexico.

quickly moved on in search of another discovery. Cabrillo died during the expedition, not too long after stopping in San Diego. Spanish missionaries renamed the region San Diego more than 100 years later.

The Cabrillo National Monument memorializes Cabrillo's landing with a statue of the conquistador looking out over the San Diego Bay. The on-site visitor center presents an informative film, *In Search of Cabrillo*, and offers exhibits that include artifacts representing Cabrillo's life, along with a scale model of Cabrillo's flagship. Throughout the summer, there are ranger-led programs that offer more insight into Cabrillo's voyage.

Cabrillo National Monument © Debbie K. Hardin

39 Chinatown San Francisco

CONTACT www.sanfranciscochinatown.com; starting at Grant Ave. and Bust St., San Francisco

PRICING	$
BEST TIME TO VISIT	Year-round
AGE RANGE	All ages

San Francisco's Chinatown is the largest and oldest Chinese community outside of Asia. The "city within a city" covers 24 square blocks, and is one of the most densely populated areas in the United States. The area was founded in the mid-19th century and served as home to Chinese immigrants beginning in the 1850s; the immigrants congregated in this spot largely because in other areas they were forbidden to live and set up businesses. Many of the early residents of Chinatown worked for the Transcontinental Railroad; when gold was discovered nearby in Sutter's Mill, Chinese immigrants flooded the area for employment in the mines or as independents in search of instant wealth.

Today there are several hundred restaurants, grocery stores, import shops, stores that sell spices and herbal remedies, and boutiques that specialize only in teas. It is possible to stroll the streets and hear very little English. The most recognizable landmark of the characteristic neighborhood is the ornate, dragon-festooned Gateway to Chinatown, located on the corner of Grant Avenue and Bush Street. Look for the ornate Bank of Canton, formerly the Chinese Telephone Exchange; the building dates to 1891 and served as the first public telephone pay station. The original station was destroyed in the 1906 earthquake in San Francisco but was quickly rebuilt and today very

> Visit Chinatown in August through early October to check out the Night Market Fair. Held in Portsmouth Square in the heart of Chinatown, this market offers food, entertainment, and late-night shopping—much as you might encounter on an evening foray in Hong Kong.

Wares for sale in Chinatown, San Francisco

Courtesy Jon Preimesberger

much resembles an ancient temple. Another worthy architectural find is now the Bank of America, which boasts 60 dragon medallions on the exterior, along with gold dragons on its front doors and columns. Chinatown is a great place to sample authentic foods. Kids will particularly enjoy Dim Sum, a lunchtime favorite in which carts full of dumplings, soup, and small side dishes are brought directly to your table: Pick whatever looks good to you, and servers will keep a running tab. Another surefire hit with children is the Golden Gate Fortune Cookie Factory (415-781-3956; 56 Ross Alley), where you can see fortune cookies made and sample freshly baked specimens.

40 Death Valley National Park

CONTACT www.nps.gov/deva; off CA 190, southeastern California

PRICING	$
BEST TIME TO VISIT	Late fall through early spring; summer is prohibitively hot
AGE RANGE	7 and older

Death Valley: The name doesn't conjure a family-friendly vacation, and for good reason. In the late spring and throughout the summertime, the temperatures can top out at an oppressive 120 degrees. The

> Hiking in the harsh environment of Death Valley requires extreme caution and common sense. Each person should drink a gallon of water per day—more if it is especially hot. Wear a hat, sunscreen, and thick-soled shoes, and watch where you step (to avoid unfriendly animals and plants). Take care to stay on established trails, to avoid getting lost. And don't hike in the summer months. It's scorching.

valley picked up its forbidding name in the mid-19th century, when a group of gold prospectors got lost here and assumed it would be the place where they died. On being rescued and leaving the area, they reportedly called back, "Good-bye, Death Valley." But despite the ominous moniker, Death Valley National Park is a natural wonder not to be missed: Here you'll find seasonal snowcapped peaks, unusual expanses of salt flats, colorful badlands, undulating sand dunes, and the lowest and driest spots in the country. More than 1,000 plant species thrive in the park, including dozens that are found nowhere else in the world. There are also hundreds of species of animals that make their home in this seemingly desolate place, including gophers, desert mice, kangaroo rats, squirrels, jackrabbits, foxes, bobcats, coyotes, mountain lions, and the elusive bighorn sheep.

The park is part of the larger Mojave Desert, and comprises 3.4 million acres, making it the largest national park in the Lower 48. The valley is 130 miles long and as much as 13 miles wide, and there are a surprising number of unique, beautiful places to explore—none more intriguing than The Racetrack, a

Death Valley National Park

Courtesy National Park Service

crazy site that is sure to excite the imagination of children. The area is a dry lake bed infamous for its mysterious "moving rocks." Although no one is on record as having actually seen the rocks move, there are tracks across the powdery surface of the lake bed that suggest that they must. Some of the largest rocks have tracks up to 1,500 feet in length. Scientists believe that a combination of light rain on the surface of the lake bed (which becomes quite slick when wet) and extremely high winds explains the locomotion.

41 Disneyland

CONTACT 714-781-4400, http://disneyland.disney.go.com; 1313 Harbor Blvd., Anaheim

PRICING	$$$$
BEST TIME TO VISIT	Year-round
AGE RANGE	All ages

Walt Disney sprinkled the real estate in Anaheim, California, with pixie dust back in 1955 when he opened the doors to what has become one of the most famous, most beloved family travel destinations in the world. The delightful Disneyland Resort pioneered the modern theme park, and although the franchise has spread around the globe, all things Disney remain quintessentially American. Touting itself as the "happiest place on earth," Disneyland really does offer something to enchant every visitor, from tykes in strollers to thrill-seeking teenagers to nostalgic grandparents. The theme park is ideal for families looking for a wholesome experience: The streets are perpetually clean; the "cast members" (as employees are called) are ever-cheerful; and the visual appeal of the imaginative gardens and storybook architecture is compelling even if you don't step foot on a ride.

The 85-acre park is divided into various themed "lands" that offer attractions built on a central theme, beginning with Main Street, a re-creation of an idyllic midwestern town. Pass through Main Street to Sleeping Beauty's Castle, modeled on real castles in southern Germany, that serves as the iconic centerpiece of the park. Each of the eight lands radiates out from

California Adventure is a Golden State—themed amusement park adjacent to Disneyland, opened in 2001 to expand the offerings at The Disneyland Resort. Like Disneyland, the park is subdivided into themed areas that feature elaborately designed rides and attractions. Guests will find a beach-themed region that offers old-fashioned boardwalk rides and games; a Hollywood main street that provides a peek into the movie industry; and a gold-country region that is anchored by Grizzly Mountain. California Adventure has many of the most impressive and thrilling attractions at any of the Disney parks and also offers a nightly water, music, and lights spectacular (World of Color) that is well worth battling the crowds to experience.

this central castle. The elaborately designed areas include the rough-and-tumble Adventureland; the glittery, frothy Fantasyland (a toddler favorite); the Old West Frontierland; the cartoon-inspired Mickey's Toontown (the most likely place to spot Mickey and his gal pal, Minnie); and the futuristic Tomorrowland. Families can immerse themselves in the many rides, shows, and attractions that capitalize on Disney films. Live entertainment is available throughout the park all day long, including daily parades and fireworks extravaganzas on the weekends and throughout the summer, and live musical groups.

42 El Presidio de Santa Barbara State Historic Park

CONTACT 805-965-0093, www.sbthp.org; 123 E. Canon Perdido St., Santa Barbara

PRICING	$
BEST TIME TO VISIT	Year-round
AGE RANGE	7 and older

The original Santa Barbara presidio was founded in 1782 as a military fort built by soldiers accompanying the Spanish missionaries, who were establishing churches along the coast of what was then known as Alta California. The remains are among the oldest structures on the West Coast of the United States. The presidio served to protect the Catholic padres at the nearby Santa Barbara Mission from Native uprisings, and also did duty as military headquarters and government center for a large expanse of wilderness that fell north of Los Angeles and south of San Luis Obispo.

Today El Presidio de Santa Barbara Historic Park in downtown Santa Barbara comprises most of the original presidio site. Only two sections of the original presidio quadrangle still stand: El Cuartel, onetime home to a soldier assigned to the fortress and the oldest adobe building in Santa Barbara; and remnants of Cañedo Adobe, an authentic whitewashed mud-and-straw dwelling. Also on site is a reconstruction of the Spanish fort, including a small chapel, living quarters for the presidio commander and his soldiers, and a bell tower. Visitors to the park can also see the Rochín adobe, built in 1856 by José María Rochín, who was married to Lorenza Ordaz de Rochín, a descendant of Francisco Ortega, the first commander of the presidio. Docent-led tours are available daily.

Olvera Street in Old Los Angeles

Courtesy Los Angeles Tourism and Convention Board

43 El Pueblo de Los Angeles Historic Park

CONTACT Visitor center, 213-628-1274, www.ci.la.ca.us/elp; in the Avila Adobe, E10 Olvera St., Los Angeles

PRICING	$
BEST TIME TO VISIT	Year-round
AGE RANGE	7 and older

El Pueblo de Los Angeles State Historic Park is near the site of the first settlement in what is now Los Angeles (the original pueblo was washed away in a flood in 1815, and the site was soon relocated farther from the Los Angeles River). It preserves some of the West Coast's oldest structures. The original settlement was the second town born from Spanish colonization during the missionary period and the home to 44 pioneers who migrated to the region from Mexico in 1781. Since its humble founding, the area thrived first under Spanish rule until 1821, then under Mexican authority,

and from 1847 onward under U.S. rule; it has grown to be one of the world's largest cities. Today this thriving historic district, at the heart of downtown LA, is a great place to celebrate cultural diversity.

El Pueblo serves as a living museum that reflects the city's multicultural heritage. The historic district comprises 27 historic buildings, 11 of which are open to the public as businesses or museums. Start your visit on historic, festive Olvera Street (213-628-1274, www.olvera-street.com), an open-air marketplace overflowing with Mexican restaurants, shops, and often populated with strolling musicians. Then check out some of the most important historical buildings, including the Avila Adobe—onetime home to Francisco Avila, a successful cattle rancher, and the city's oldest surviving residence, dating to 1818; the Nuestra Señora La Reina de Los Angeles Church, which dates to 1822; and the Pico House, originally a luxury hotel built in 1870 by Pío Pico, the last Mexican governor of Alta California. Children will enjoy visiting the Plaza Firehouse Museum, the Chinese American Museum, and the Italian American Museum as well. Free guided tours of El Pueblo are available Tuesday through Saturday. (Call ahead for reservations: 213-628-1274.)

44 Getty Villa Malibu

CONTACT 310-440-7300, www.getty.edu; 17985 Pacific Coast Hwy., Malibu

PRICING	$; parking (which must be pre-arranged) $$$
BEST TIME TO VISIT	Year-round
AGE RANGE	7 and older

J. Paul Getty (1892–1976) was an American industrialist and oil baron who at one time was considered the richest person in the United States. Throughout his life, Getty collected invaluable art and antiquities from around the world, which upon his death he endowed to the J. Paul Getty Institute, now overseen by several museums and research institutions that maintain his collections.

The Getty Villa, perched atop a hill in lovely Malibu with stunning views of the Pacific Ocean, was the onetime home of the mogul, and is modeled after a Roman country house near Pompeii. In keeping with its classical design, the museum highlights ancient Greek, Etruscan, and Roman artwork. Featured are an array of immaculately preserved Greek urns and glassware, sculptures, and mosaics. Look for the most famous piece in the collection, *The Victorious Youth*, salvaged from the Adriatic Sea off Italy and now re-

Getty Villa Malibu   © Debbie K. Hardin

Check out the nearby Getty Center (310-440-7300, www.getty.edu; 1200 Getty Center Dr., Los Angeles), a miraculous arts center compound sprawling over 750 acres amid the foothills of the Santa Monica Mountains, which was built in the late 20th century to house J. Paul Getty's modern art collection, including Van Gogh's famously expensive *Irises*. Kids will want to stop by the Family Room, which offers children ages 5—13 hands-on opportunities to create their own artwork.

siding in gallery 201—but be quick about it: Italy wants this particular piece back, claiming rightful ownership even though the piece is of Greek origin. Although the number and quality of antiquities at the villa is astounding, the structure itself is perhaps the most appealing aspect of this museum, especially the stunning Outer Peristyle, which features a long narrow pool surrounded by statues and encircled by a formal garden. Children will enjoy the Family Forum, on the ground floor, which encourages hands-on participation with activities like sketching on a replica of an ancient urn.

45 Golden Gate Bridge

CONTACT www.goldengatebridge.org; San Francisco Bay, San Francisco

PRICING	$
BEST TIME TO VISIT	Year-round
AGE RANGE	All ages

The Golden Gate Bridge connects the city of San Francisco with Marin County, and it is an internationally recognized architectural landmark. The iconic structure is synonymous with the Golden State, and remains a masterpiece of engineering. When it was completed in 1937, it was the world's tallest, longest suspension bridge. It took a little more than four years to build, and was hailed as having one of the best safety records of any such structure: A net sus-

Golden Gate Bridge   © Debbie K. Hardin

Grauman's Chinese Theatre   Courtesy Jon Preimesberger

pended beneath the floor of the bridge rescued nearly 20 workers from what otherwise would have been a fatal fall. Note that the bridge isn't really golden: It's actually a shade of rusty red, and maintenance workers must continuously touch up the paint. It's great fun to cross, either by car or via the pedestrian walkway on the eastern side. The bridge is 1.7 miles one way—and if you're walking, be aware that it can get very windy. On clear days, the San Francisco cityline is stunning from this vantage point.

46 Grauman's Chinese Theatre

CONTACT 323-461-3331, www.chinesetheatres.com; 6925 Hollywood Blvd., Hollywood

PRICING	$
BEST TIME TO VISIT	Year-round
AGE RANGE	5 and older

Grauman's Chinese Theatre opened its doors in 1927 with the premier of *The King of Kings*, a Cecil B. DeMille extravaganza, and has since become an icon of Hollywood and the movie industry. It remains a working theater, but it is renowned for the famous hand- and footprints immortalized in an expanse of concrete that fronts the elaborate facade of the building.

Legend has it that a starlet of the day inspired the tradition of leaving prints when she accidentally stepped into a patch of wet concrete shortly after the theater was opened. Since then, celebrities have been leaving their hand- and footprints in the concrete in front of this theater, and doting fans have flocked to see them for decades. Luminaries like Cary Grant, George Clooney, and the young cast of *Harry Potter* have left their marks over the years.

While you're in Hollywood, check out the Hollywood Walk of Fame (www. hollywoodchamber.net), on Hollywood Boulevard, between La Brea Avenue and Gower Street and on Vine Street between Yucca Street and Sunset Boulevard, where the sidewalks are emblazoned with stars commemorating old Hollywood, like Bob Hope and Bing Crosby, as well as more recent superstars that kids are likely to recognize, such as Adam Sandler, Christina Aguilera, Matt Damon, and Johnny Depp.

47 Hearst San Simeon State Historical Monument

CONTACT 800-444-4445; www.hearstcastle.com; 750 Hearst Castle Rd., San Simeon

PRICING	$$$–$$$$
BEST TIME TO VISIT	Year-round
AGE RANGE	7 and older

Best known as Hearst Castle, this lavish estate is a monument to the American dream. It was begun in 1865, when successful miner George Hearst purchased 40,000 acres of land along the central coast of California as a weekend getaway for his family and friends. Eventually his son, the famous newspaper magnate William Randolph Hearst, inherited the property—which by then had grown to 250,000 acres. In 1919, W. R. is said to have communicated to renowned American architect Julia Morgan that he "would like to build a little something." Hearst named the ever-evolving property "La Cuesta Encantada"—The Enchanted Hill. More than 25 years later, Morgan and Hearst had developed a magnificent, rambling mansion that comprises 65 rooms and 127 acres of pools, gardens, and terraces, filled to the brim with artwork and priceless antiquities. In its heyday, Hollywood luminaries, royalty, and presidents enjoyed Hearst's legendary hospitality in this spectacular site. The castle and grounds were opened to the public in 1958 as a state historical monument.

Hearst San Simeon State Historical Monument

There are several tours available that take visitors through the mansion, gardens, and ancillary structures. Tour 1 is recommended for first-time visitors and includes a film beforehand that gives an introduction to Hearst and his opulent way of life; the movie, along with the docent spiel on the history of the man and his times, is quite interesting, and children are sure to learn as much about the golden age of the 1920s as they do about the art and architecture on display in the mansion.

48 John Muir National Historic Site

CONTACT 925-228-8860, www.nps.gov/jomu; 4202 Alhambra Ave., Martinez

PRICING	$
BEST TIME TO VISIT	Year-round
AGE RANGE	7 and older

John Muir (1838–1914) is synonymous with the wilderness preservation movement and the influential Sierra Club that he founded; he's known to many as the "Father of the National Parks" in the United States. Muir was born in Scotland and spent his life as a naturalist, preservationist, inventor, and passionate wilderness writer (best known for his book *The Yosemite*). He moved to the West Coast of the United States as a young man and immediately headed to Yosemite Valley, where he was to spend many years living and exploring, and for a season working as a shepherd. Muir was a keen student of geology, and he was the first to realize that the Yosemite Valley had been sculpted by glaciers (contrasted with the conventional wisdom of the time, which held that the sheer cliffs and dramatic rock formations were a product of a cataclysmic earthquake). Muir was a persuasive and influential lobbyist, and he convinced President Teddy Roosevelt to protect the Grand Canyon, Mount Ranier, Sequoia, and Yosemite as national parks. He was an outspoken advocate of forests and open spaces throughout his life, and as a result has numerous tributes bearing his name throughout the state of California, including dozens of schools,

John Muir National Historic Site

Photo by Thaddeus Shay, courtesy National Park Service

trails, and parks. Although in his youth Muir preferred to roam the countryside with little more than a loaf of bread and bedroll, later in life he settled down with his wife, Louisa Strengtzel, near her family on a 2,600-acre fruit orchard in Martinez (although he often returned to Yosemite for long stretches).

The John Muir National Historic Site preserves the 17-room Victorian mansion Muir shared with his wife and two daughters for the latter several decades of his life, along with 9 acres of the original fruit orchards. (If you visit during harvest season, you can have a taste of the Muir orchard fruit. As it ripens, it is picked by park staff and distributed in boxes around the park, for guests to sample at no charge.) Start at the visitor center with a short orientation film on Muir's life (shown on demand throughout the day). The lovely mansion, furnished with period pieces, is open for self-guided tours. Also on site is an 1849 adobe, open to the public.

Check out the Tunnel Log in Sequoia National Park. This fallen giant sequoia has been carved out so that cars can drive through it—a kitschy experience that harks back to the gimmicks of the early days in the national parks. Come early in the morning to avoid traffic (and afford yourself the luxury of stepping out and photographing your vehicle heading through the tree).

Kings Canyon and Sequoia National Parks are often missed by visitors not because they lack natural beauty—both have this in abundance—but because of their proximity to the much more popular Yosemite, which is nearby. But don't overlook them. Both have acres of giant sequoia forests, raging whitewater rivers, deeply carved canyons, hundreds of miles of hiking trails, and the breathtaking granite formations that the High Sierra is known for, generally without the crowds that often plague Yosemite. Sequoia National Park was established in 1890, thanks to the efforts of environmentalist John Muir and the Sierra Club, in large part to protect some of the world's largest living things: Giant sequoias (*Sequoiadendron giganteum*) are the biggest trees (by mass—California redwoods are taller) in the world, and among the oldest living things. They are indigenous only to the southern Sierra Nevada range of California. The spectacular trees are almost mind boggling in scale: They can grow to 250 to 300 feet tall, more than 100 feet wide in diameter, and can live as long as 2,500 to 3,000 years. Their almost-furry, cinnamon-colored bark can grow to more than 2 feet thick, and this is the true secret to their survival: Because of their ex-

49 Kings Canyon and Sequoia National Parks

CONTACT Kings Canyon Visitor Center, 559-565-4307; on CA 180, 3 miles northeast of the Kings Canyon Park entrance Giant Forest Museum Center, 559-565-4480; on CA 198, in the Giant Forest

PRICING	$
BEST TIME TO VISIT	Year-round
AGE RANGE	3 and older

Sequoia Tunnel Log

© Debbie K. Hardin

Smarter than the Average Bear

Kings Canyon, Sequoia, and Yosemite parks are all smack in the middle of bear country, and it is imperative that visitors "bear-proof" their cars before entering the area, to avoid dangerous encounters with the animals or damage to unattended vehicles. On average one car *a day* is damaged by bears in these parks. Never store food or beverages in your automobile, even if it is "hidden"; bears have an unbelievably strong sense of smell, and some say they can even detect food in unopened cans. Also remove all cosmetics that have scents, including lip gloss, makeup, sunscreen, moisturizing lotions, wet wipes, and bug

Foraging bear

Courtesy National Park Service

spray. Purchase a bear-proof container to store such items while hiking, or make use of bear-proof food-storage lockers that are available in camping and picnic areas throughout the parks. You might think your doughnuts are safe locked inside your car if you park it in the middle of a busy parking area in the middle of a tourist zone: Think again. Smarter-than-average park bears have learned that this is *exactly* where to find treats, and can often be seen sniffing through such crowded lots in search of a snack.

ceptionally thick insulation, giant sequoias are not as susceptible to fires as most other trees.

Sequoia lies to the south, and Kings Canyon is divided into two distinct sections, north and east of Sequoia National Park, with Sequoia National Forest separating the two. Both Sequoia National Park and Kings Canyon National Park have extensive backcountry areas, enough to provide weeks' worth of solitary hiking and camping to those looking for real outdoor adventure. In Kings Canyon, don't miss the General Grant Tree within the Grant Grove. The General Grant is more than 267 feet tall and nearly 108 feet around. And in Sequoia, check out the equally impressive General Sherman Tree, which is considered the largest living tree in the world because of its mass. It weighs about 2.7 million pounds—and is thought to be more than 2,000 years old.

> *The General Grant is more than 267 feet tall and nearly 108 feet around.*

50 La Brea Tar Pits

CONTACT www.tarpits.org; Hancock Park, Wilshire Blvd., Los Angeles

PRICING	$
BEST TIME TO VISIT	Year-round
AGE RANGE	7 and older

For millennia, tar has been bubbling up in the springs in La Brea, now situated in downtown Los Angeles. In prehistoric times, animals like woolly mammoths and saber-toothed tigers sometimes wandered too close to the tar and got stuck in the muck. Today archaeologists painstakingly pick through the black goo, and over the years have amassed a huge collection of prehistoric skeletons, many of which are displayed at the on-site Page Museum. Visitors today can stroll around the park to see the tar pits, which include life-sized models of prehistoric animals. The fabulous Page

La Brea Tar Pits
© Debbie K. Hardin

Museum displays fossils from the ice age, representing 650 species, including dire wolves, ground sloths, and short-faced bears. For kids who are interested in science, check out the Fishbowl Lab, where you can watch paleontologists working in a glass-walled laboratory preserving fossils.

51 Manzanar

CONTACT 760-878-2194, www.nps.gov/manz; off U.S. 395, 9 miles north of Lone Pine

PRICING	$
BEST TIME TO VISIT	Year-round
AGE RANGE	10 and older

On December 7, 1941, as World War II raged on in Europe, the Imperial Japanese Navy attacked the Pacific Fleet stationed at Pearl Harbor, in Honolulu, Hawaii, killing more than 2,400 people and wounding 1,200 more. The surprise air attack also destroyed 188 planes and eight battleships. The events of the "day of infamy" were shocking to Americans, and the fear and panic this act of war incited at times reached hysterical levels. Cultural misunderstandings and outright racism gripped the nation, and hatred was misdirected at Japanese Americans living on the West Coast. Some believed individuals of Japanese descent—even if they had been living in the United States for several generations—were possible spies or, worse, terrorists who would mastermind another attack on U.S. soil.

Note that Manzanar is far removed from cities and towns: Arrive with a full tank of gas, and plenty of water and food.

In an act that seems almost incomprehensible today, in 1942 President Franklin Roosevelt passed Executive Order 9066, which called for mandatory removal of Japanese Americans living in western coastal regions of the country and for their forced incarceration in military-style internment camps. More than 120,000 individuals of Japanese descent (nearly a third of whom were children) were rounded up, forced to leave their homes and abandon most of their possessions, and taken to isolated camps in the desert. Families were made to live in barracks and eat in communal dining halls; they were often separated from extended family members. The conditions were harsh, thanks to poor housing, extreme weather, and the limitations on the internees' liberties. Most internees lived and worked in these camps for three years; many were forced to take an oath of loyalty while interned, or were punished for refusing to do so. In early 1945, the internees were finally allowed to return home. They were given only train fare, a very small amount of spending money, and meals en route. Most internees returned home to find that their property and businesses were gone—and some had to be evicted from the camps when they wouldn't leave because they knew they no longer had a home to return to. Years later, in 1988, President Ronald Reagan signed the Civil Liberties Act that provided $20,000 in restitution to the survivors of these internment camps, and in

Historic photo of Manzanar internment camp
Photo by Ansel Adams. From the Library of Congress Collection

1989 President George H. W. Bush offered a formal apology to all those who lived through the relocations.

In total there were 10 internment camps, called "relocation centers" at the time. Manzanar in the Owens Valley was the first to open, and is the best preserved today. A visit to the remote site is a sobering experience. Guests can take a self-guided driving tour that passes by a baseball field, the camp cemetery, a Japanese garden built by internees, re-created barracks, and a restored mess hall. Be sure to stop in to the interpretive center, which displays photos, artifacts, and documents from the time; the center also shows an excellent 20-minute film, *Remembering Manzanar*, that will provide interesting background. To get a fuller understanding of this site, arrange for a ranger-led tour. There are several tour options, which include basic introductions to everyday life at Manzanar; garden tours; and bus tours. Reservations for all tours should be made at least a month in advance.

52 Mission Basilica San Diego de Alcala

CONTACT 619-281-8449, www.missionsandiego.com; 10818 San Diego Mission Rd., San Diego

PRICING	$
BEST TIME TO VISIT	Year-round
AGE RANGE	7 and older

Father Junipero Serra, along with explorer Gaspar de Portolá, arrived in San Diego in 1769 to establish Mission San Diego de Alcalá, the first of 21 Spanish missions in California. The missions were placed a day's walk from one another, and stretch from San Diego to Sonoma on a 650-mile route that is known as El Camino Real, or The Royal Highway (named after the Spanish royalty who funded the missions). The San Diego mission was originally located on Presidio Hill, but the fathers moved it 6 miles inland in 1774 for better farmland and a more reliable source of water. The mission today has been rebuilt many times after it was destroyed by fires, and the current mission is a remodel designed to look like the church in 1813. Self-guided tours take visitors through Father

Mission Basilica San Diego de Alcala   © Debbie K. Hardin

Many of the California missions have been relocated over the years, and most have been rebuilt because of fire or construction deficiencies, but each is a remarkable example of early architecture, and each is surprisingly unique and well worth a visit, not just because of their historical importance but also because they are truly beautiful structures, cared for lovingly through earthquakes, Native uprisings, and shifting political fortunes. From south to north, the missions are: San Diego de Alcalá, San Diego (1st mission); San Luis Rey de Francia, Oceanside (18th mission); San Juan Capistrano (7th mission); San Gabriel Arcangel, San Gabriel Valley (4th mission); San Fernando Rey de Espana, San Fernando Valley (17th mission); San Buenaventura, Ventura (9th mission); Santa Barbara (10th mission); Santa Ines, Solvang (19th mission); La Purisima Conception, Lompoc (11th mission); San Luis Obispo de Tolosa, San Luis Obispo (5th mission); San Miguel Arcangel, San Miguel (16th mission); San Antonia de Padua, Jolon (3rd mission); Nuestra Senora de la Soledad, Soledad (13th mission); San Carlos Borromeo de Carmelo, Carmel (2nd mission); San Juan Bautista (15th mission); Santa Cruz (12th mission); Santa Clara de Asis, Santa Clara (8th mission); San Jose, Fremont (14th mission); San Francisco de Asis, Mission Dolores, San Francisco (6th mission); San Rafael Arcangel, San Rafael (20th mission); and San Francisco Solano, Sonoma (21st mission).

Serra's apartment, a small chapel, and a lovely garden that offers pretty views of the 50-foot bell tower. Also on site is the Padre Luis Jayme Mission Museum (Jayme was Serra's successor). Archaeological excavation is ongoing, and with advance arrangements, older children can pitch in and help dig for the day.

53 National Steinbeck Center

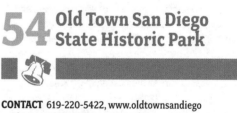

CONTACT 831-775-4726, www.steinbeck.org; 1 Main St., Salinas

PRICING	$$–$$$
BEST TIME TO VISIT	Year-round
AGE RANGE	10 and older

Pulitzer Prize–winning author John Steinbeck (1902–68) is considered one of the great American writers of the 20th century. He is probably best remembered for his novel *The Grapes of Wrath*, a social commentary set during the Great Depression that follows a family of migrant workers driven from their home in Oklahoma to seek their fortunes in California. Other works include *Of Mice and Men*, *East of Eden*, *In Dubious Battle*, and *Cannery Row*, many of which are deeply political and offer insight into the American psyche at the time. Steinbeck was awarded the Nobel Prize for literature in 1962.

The National Steinbeck Center in the author's hometown of Salinas houses the largest collection of Steinbeck papers in the country, and offers numerous rotating exhibits that explore the political and philosophical underpinnings of Steinbeck's writing. The Rabobank Agricultural Hall within the museum is dedicated to the life of migrant agricultural workers in the United States, reflecting Steinbeck's great interest in the topic. The interactive exhibit allows guests to explore the history of the Salinas Valley agricultural industry as well as the many cultural influences that migrant workers have had on the region.

The center is the site of educational programs that memorialize the life and work of Steinbeck through multimedia art presentations, lectures, films, panel discussions, art receptions, and commu-

Steinbeck bust in Monterey
Photograph in the Carol M. Highsmith Archive, Library of Congress, Prints and Photographs Division

nity events like the yearly Steinbeck Festival and the annual Day of the Dead celebration. Art classes are held weekly at the center, where children and parents can paint, sculpt, and learn the art of the short story.

54 Old Town San Diego State Historic Park

CONTACT 619-220-5422, www.oldtownsandiego guide.com; 4002 Wallace St., San Diego

PRICING	$
BEST TIME TO VISIT	Year-round
AGE RANGE	5 and older

Old Town San Diego was the site of the first European settlement on the West Coast of what is now the United States. The pueblo grew hand in hand with the adjacent San Diego Presidio, a military outpost that was originally charged with protecting the Spanish missionaries who built the San Diego Mission. Soon after the mission and presidio were established, the mission was moved upriver, but the presidio remained (preserved now as Presidio Park), and this

Old Town San Diego State Historic Park   © Debbie K. Hardin

55 Queen Mary

CONTACT	877-342-0738, www.queenmary.com; 1126 Queen's Hwy., Long Beach
PRICING	$$$$
BEST TIME TO VISIT	Year-round
AGE RANGE	7 and older

Moored since 1967 in Long Beach, about 30 miles south of downtown Los Angeles, the once-fabulous *Queen Mary* cruise ship was originally built by Cunard in the mid-1930s as part of its luxury transatlantic ocean liner fleet. After she had served only a few years as the favored transportation for the elite, World War II put an end to pleasure travel between the United States and Europe, and the ship was commandeered by the U.S. government and used as a military transport from 1940–46. During this period the ship carried more than 750,000 army and navy personnel to and from the war—ferrying as many as 16,000 troops at any given time, often cramming soldiers into four-decker bunk beds. In 1947 the *Queen Mary* resumed passenger service, sailing for 20 more years before being retired.

The ship now serves as a museum and a hotel. Start your exploration by walking through a self-guided gallery that tells the story of the great ship;

small settlement continued to thrive in its shadows.

Today the restored and reconstructed buildings at this site in Old Town San Diego make up a western version of Colonial Williamsburg. With docents and shopkeepers in period costumes, historic reenactments and period demonstrations, and nearly 40 themed buildings—some museums and some shops—that highlight the early pueblo era of 1821–72, Old Town gives visitors a chance to step into history. Museum exhibits highlight the commercial and personal lives of the missionaries, Spanish colonists, wealthy Mexican families, and the native Kumeyaay Indians who lived in early San Diego. Visitors can tour the Blackhawk Livery Stables and view historic carriages; wander through the original newspaper office of the *San Diego Union*; visit the old courthouse museum; and stroll through the Robinson Rose Building, the onetime house and law offices of prominent attorney James W. Robinson, which currently serves as the park's visitor center. La Casa de Estudillo, built for a former commander of the presidio, has been preserved with period furniture and decorations. The adjacent entertainment zone known as Fiesta de Reyes (2754 Calhoun St.) is chock-full of historically themed restaurants and shops.

Queen Mary   © Debbie K. Hardin

look for the faithful miniature, which is a perennial kid magnet. Also fun to explore is the ship's bridge, which is filled with traditional nautical equipment, and the upper deck, which offers stunning views of the Long Beach harbor. Guests can also take audio tours to further explore. For those interested in such things, the ever-popular paranormal tours (some with added special effects designed to scare the wits out of participants) will guide you through to discover the ship's purported ghosts. (Note: The "haunted" tours are intense; save these for kids 13 years and older.) Families will not want to miss the World War II Tour to learn about the *Grey Ghost* (as the ship was nicknamed during wartime, because she was painted gray) and her efforts to help the Allied forces.

56 Redwood National Park

Redwood National Park © Debbie K. Hardin

CONTACT 707-464-6101, www.nps.gov/redw/index.htm; 1111 2nd Street, Crescent City

PRICING	$
BEST TIME TO VISIT	Year-round
AGE RANGE	3 and older

Stand in awe alongside the tallest living things in the world at Redwood National Park, an unusually beautiful ecosystem that includes spectacular coastal scenery, expansive prairies, oak woodlands, prime wildlife spotting, and the aforementioned really big trees. The coastal redwoods for which this region is famous can top out at more than 300 feet, and some are older than 2,000 years. The magnificent trees grow naturally only in the few hundred miles of coastline along the Pacific Ocean, running from Northern California to the Oregon border. The park preserves all that remains of what was once a 2-million-acre forest of the evergreen giants.

In addition to the federally managed preserve, the park also comprises three state parks, the totality of which is split into two distinct regions: the southern section, near Trinidad, that includes the Prairie Creek Redwood State Park; and the northern section, near Crescent City, close to the Oregon border, which includes the Jedediah Smith Redwoods State Park and the Del Norte Coast Redwoods State Park. There are hundreds of amazing tree specimens in the park, but don't miss the obviously named (and easily accessible) Big Tree, which is estimated to be 1,500 years old and reaches more than 300 feet into the sky. You'll find the Big Tree along the Foothill Trail, in Prairie Creek Redwood State Park. If you were to hug this tree, you would need to join forces with many friends to encircle its more than 60-foot circumference. And don't miss Fern Canyon (at U.S. 101 and Davison Rd.), a quarter-mile canyon that rims the outline of a shallow river at the north end of Gold Bluffs Beach; the canyon walls are steep verticals overgrown with massive emerald-green ferns, dripping with precipitation and cascading in every direction. The trail is easy and the scenery is breathtaking, but depending on the time of year, you'll have to hike through sections of shallow river to get the best views. Dinosaur aficionados and movie buffs will recognize the scenery from movies *Jurassic Park II* and *Star Wars*, some scenes of which were filmed here.

57 Ronald W. Reagan Presidential Library and Museum

CONTACT 805-577-4000, www.reaganlibrary.com; 40 Presidential Dr., Simi Valley

PRICING	$$–$$$
BEST TIME TO VISIT	Year-round
AGE RANGE	7 and older

Ronald Reagan (1911–2004) was the 40th president of the United States, serving two consecutive terms from 1981–1989. He was the 33rd governor of California as well, and before that a stage and film actor. The Republican president—a particular favorite with many conservatives—was most famously credited with contributing to the end of the Cold War between the United States and the then Soviet Union, and was in the White House when the Berlin Wall came down.

At the Ronald Reagan Presidential Library in Simi Valley, north of Malibu, visitors can step aboard the actual Boeing 707 that was used as *Air Force One* during the tenure of seven presidents; view a U.S. Marine Helicopter Squadron One aircraft up close; and witness a U.S. Army MP patrol a re-creation of Checkpoint Charlie, the former border crossing of the Berlin Wall. Guests can also walk through an amazingly accurate re-creation of the Oval Office during the Reagan administration, complete with a jar of jelly beans (the president's favorite sweet treat) on the desk and Reagan's collection of Remington bronze

Ronald W. Reagan Presidential Library and Museum
Courtesy of the Ronald W. Reagan Presidential Library and Museum

saddles on the bookshelves. The grounds of the library are open to explore, and those wishing to can pay their respects at President Reagan's grave site. The library is also a repository for more than 60 million pages' worth of documents, more than 1.5 million photographs, tens of thousands of audio- and videotapes, and more than 40,000 artifacts, some of which are on rotating display in the museum.

58 Rose Parade

CONTACT 626-449-ROSE, www.tournamentofroses.com; parade route runs along Colorado Blvd., Pasadena

PRICING	$
BEST TIME TO VISIT	January 1 (or January 2, if New Year's Day falls on a Sunday)
AGE RANGE	All ages

The Tournament of Roses, better known as the Rose Parade in Pasadena, is a New Year's celebratory parade that coincides with the college football game known as the Rose Bowl. The beloved parade is known for extravagant floats that are covered exclusively in flowers and plant materials; the entertainment also includes marching bands and equestrian groups. The event is televised around the world and attracts tens of millions of viewers. If you're interested in seeing this quintessential American parade in person, reserve bleacher seating well in advance (think 12 months beforehand), or—if you're game for adventure—camp out the night before along the parade route on Colorado Boulevard. (Local law enforcement will allow folks to overnight it in sleeping bags, but no tents are permitted.)

If you can't make the parade, check out the Tournament of Roses House and Wrigley Gardens (626-449-4100; 391 S. Orange Grove Blvd., Pasadena), which is open for afternoon tours, February through August. Part of what's known as Millionaire's Row, this gorgeous white Italian Renaissance-style mansion and onetime home to William Wrigley Jr. (chewing gum magnate) is now the headquarters for the Pasadena Tournament of Roses Association, the group

Roses waiting to be added to Tournament of Roses Parade floats   © Debbie K. Hardin

Meercats at the San Diego Zoo   Courtesy San Diego Zoo

that sponsors the Rose Parade. The beautiful interior boasts inlaid marble floors and ornate plaster ceilings. On display are the tiaras worn by former Rose Parade queens and their royal court princesses, along with other parade memorabilia. The 4.5-acre garden in the back is abloom with a magnificent display of more than 1,500 varieties of roses and camellias.

59 San Diego Zoo

CONTACT 619-234-3153, www.sandiegozoo.org; 2920 Zoo Dr., San Diego

PRICING	$$$$
BEST TIME TO VISIT	Year-round
AGE RANGE	All ages

The famous San Diego Zoo put the city on the tourist map, and remains one of the finest zoological parks in the world. The more-than-100-acre site is home to 3,500 rare and endangered animals, including one of the very few exhibits of panda bears outside of China and a gorilla enclosure that is considered by conservationists one of the most forward-thinking in the

During the entire month of October, the zoo is free to children, which is a nice benefit if you're traveling with little ones, but note that the congestion increases as a result.

world. The extensive botanical gardens contain more than 700,000 exotic plants, many of these endangered species as well. The zoo was one of the first in the world to create animal habitats that do not resemble traditional animal enclosures. Animals that would normally cohabitate in the wild are housed together in "biomes" that simulate their natural habitat, in the least restrictive environment possible to ensure the safety of the animals and visitors.

60 Sutter's Mill

CONTACT Coloma Valley Chamber of Commerce, www.coloma.com, off CA 49 and Lotus Rd., Coloma

PRICING	$
BEST TIME TO VISIT	Year-round
AGE RANGE	5 and older

The 1849 California gold rush attracted thousands of miners to central and northeastern California, all looking to make their fortune from the precious metal. It's estimated that during the height of the era, there were more than 300,000 49ers (as the miners were called) and individuals making their livelihoods off the miners living and working in the area.

The gold frenzy began in early 1848, when James Marshall found a chunk of the precious metal at Sutter's Mill in Coloma. Prospectors—men, women, and sometimes children—from around the world moved to

Panning for gold

© Debbie K. Hardin

the area over the next two years, first staking out portions of rivers to pan for gold, and later using more sophisticated methods of excavation, such as hydraulics and hard-rock blast-mining techniques. A handful of these folks met with spectacular success, bringing immense wealth to the region and its citizens as businesses like sundry stores, mining equipment suppliers, and saloons sprang up to support the burgeoning mining industry. But as quickly as the miners flocked to California, they abandoned most of the boomtowns once the gold deposits were played out.

The gold rush had enormous lasting effects, including a population explosion in nearby San Francisco—one of the few boomtowns that didn't bust; incorporation of California into the United States (at the time of the gold rush, the land was in Mexican territory, although it was under military occupation after the Mexican-American War); expansion of the railways; degradation of the environment because of careless mining practices and pollution; and widespread disease among Native Americans in the region, who had no immunity to many of the diseases the 49ers brought with them.

Sutter's Mill today is ensconced in the Marshall

You can purchase pans at the visitor center and try your own luck in the American River, near the first gold discovery site. Throughout the year there are Living History Days in which costumed docents interpret the events of the gold rush.

Gold Discovery Park, the highlight of which is a replica of the original sawmill where Marshall found the first nugget of gold that started the mad dash for wealth. There's also an on-site museum that offers an interesting film that provides a historical overview, a working blacksmith shop, and a monument to Marshall.

61 Yosemite National Park

CONTACT 209-372-0200, www.nps.gov/yose; P.O. Box 577; Yosemite National Park

PRICING	$
BEST TIME TO VISIT	Year-round (but note that Tuolumne Meadows and the road to Glacier Point are closed from late fall through early spring)
AGE RANGE	3 and older

Yosemite National Park, located in the Sierra Nevadas, about three hours east of San Francisco, California, is one of the most beautiful natural wonders of the world, thanks to stunning glacier-carved valleys, sculptural granite cliffs, dramatic waterfalls, and groves of ancient sequoias. The 1,200-square-mile park has been protected by the U.S. federal government since 1890, when the region became one of the nation's first national parks, and it remains a shining example of both the natural beauty of the United States and the resolve of Americans to protect our treasures.

Compact Yosemite Valley boasts the must-see icons of the park, and for this reason is heavily trafficked, especially in summertime. The one-way loop road around the valley is often jammed with cars, especially during "rush hour," at sunset when day-trippers leave. (Avoid adding to the stream of cars while in the valley by using the Yosemite Hybrid Shuttle. It is free, it makes frequent stops, and the routes are easy to understand.) Don't miss these highlights:

• **El Capitan** is an imposing granite cliff overlooking the valley, and is wildly popular with rock climbers. Because of its smooth, flat face, expect stunning displays of reflected color at sunset and sunrise.

- Rising 4,800 feet, the graceful granite rock formation that is **Half Dome**—so striking because a glacier rubbed off the lower portion of the otherwise round feature—can be seen throughout the valley. Hardcore hikers trek to the top with the aid of rope lines, which are left in place year-round.
- **Mariposa Grove** in the southernmost portion of the park is an enchanting forest of enormous sequoia trees. Come to this less visited spot to see black bears, which scrabble over the trails at dawn and dusk.
- **Wawona** is 4 miles north of Mariposa Grove, anchored by the historic Wawona Hotel. Adjacent is the Pioneer History Center, where you'll find a collection of restored historical buildings and information signs posted to allow for self-guided tours. Kids will not want to miss a hair-raising 10-minute wagon ride from the Wells Fargo Building on weekends.
- At 2,425 feet, **Yosemite Falls** is the highest waterfall in North America. It is fed almost entirely by snowmelt, so its character changes significantly with the seasons. In spring it roars through the valley, creating pools and streams in its wake; in late fall, it dries up entirely. A hike to the base of the falls is an easy half-mile trek from the main road and is manageable even for parents pushing strollers.

Beyond the valley, about 30 miles south, Glacier Point is accessible via a winding road. Expect the drive to take close to an hour, even with good road conditions. High elevations make for spectacular panoramic views of the valley and a near-eye-level vista of Half Dome. From December through early April, the same road in is plowed up to Badger Pass, a popular ski resort. And Tuolumne Meadows is a wildflower-strewn subalpine area north of the valley, with jaw-dropping views of the surrounding granite cliffs, small lakes and ponds, and miles of easy, flat hiking trails that are ideal for young children. Again because of high elevation and heavy snowfall, CA 120 (also called Tioga Road) to Tuolumne Meadows is open only from late May through early November. When visiting in-season, don't miss the 39-mile stretch along Tioga Road, from Crane Flat to Tuolumne—one of the most scenic drives in California.

Although it is hard to have a true wilderness experience in crowded Yosemite—especially in the summer, and especially in the Yosemite Valley area—this

Yosemite Valley, with Bridal Veil Falls in the background
© Debbie K. Hardin

overabundance of civilization has its upside: The park has innumerable activities for families throughout the year:

- **Art classes:** The Yosemite Art and Education Center offers free drawing and painting classes spring through fall, for adults and children. (Some classes are designed so that parents and kids can create together.) You can also buy supplies here.
- **Biking:** There are more than 12 miles of paved bike paths through Yosemite Valley, and these are ideal for bypassing the clotted roadway. Off-road biking is not permitted in the park. Pathways are level and easily navigable for young children.
- **Fishing:** Lakes are open to fishing year-round, and rivers and streams from late April through mid-November. Individuals 16 and older must have a valid California fishing license. If you forget your rod and reel or any other angling supplies, you can find what you need at the Yosemite Village Sport Shop.
- **Galleries:** The Ansel Adams Gallery displays original signed works by the noted Yosemite photographer. You'll also find artwork by other contemporary photographers and a good collection of handmade jewelry and kids' books.
- **Rafting:** A favorite pastime in the summer is a river raft down the Merced River, which cuts through the heart of Yosemite Valley. The gentle current makes for an easy ride, and relaxed paddling will open up some of the most breathtaking vistas in the park. The river is open to rafting from Stoneman Bridge, near Curry Village, to Sentinel Beach, a few miles

Four More to Explore Along the Northern California Coast

Choosing 500+ family-friendly adventures across the expanse of the United States means making some tough choices about coverage, and nowhere was this more difficult than the Northern California coast. The rugged shoreline is magnificent, and dozens of beach cities offer small-town charm, a family-friendly atmosphere, and plenty of opportunities to learn about nature with your children. Here are four favorites in brief:

- **Carmel-by-the-Sea:** Carmel is a quaint, upscale village that is fun to explore on foot—although weekends can be crowded. To miss the hordes and keep your children's attention, avoid the shops and boutiques and head instead to the Carmel River State Beach (www.parks.ca.gov/?page_id=567), which boasts 100 acres along the sparkling Carmel Bay—although note that the waters are extremely rough and aren't recommended for swimming. And just to the south is Point Lobos State Natural Reserve (www.parks.ca.gov/?page_id=571), with walking trails leading through a forest of Monterey cypress. Kids will enjoy the Sea Lion Point Trail here, which offers good peeks at the resident sea lions.

- **Point Reyes National Seashore:** The dramatic cliffs, pretty dunes, and long expanses of shoreline make this one of the favorite beach destinations in Northern California. For a quick lesson in geology, head to the Bear Valley Visitor Center to pick up the Earthquake Trail, a short pathway to see the effects of the calamitous earthquake that nearly destroyed nearby San Francisco in 1906.

- **Santa Cruz:** This vaguely retro enclave is a surfer's mecca, and children and teenagers will appreciate the lively boardwalk amusement park. Curious kids will also enjoy the touristy Mystery Spot (www.mysteryspot.com), a place that seems to defy the laws of gravity (see balls roll up!). Another favorite here is the Santa Cruz Surfing Museum (www.santacruzsurfingmuseum.org), housed in an old lighthouse, which chronicles more than 100 years of wave riding.

- **Trinidad:** At the southernmost point of the Redwood National Park, Trinidad is a quiet, welcoming town that offers hiking, beachcombing, and exploring. Patrick's Point State Park is a great place to ride bikes and watch for migrating gray whales in season. Pint-sized treasure hunters will not want to miss Agate Beach, a protected cove covered with pebbles—many of them semiprecious agates, which are fun to collect.

Enjoying the coastline

Courtesy James H. Pugh

downstream. From late May through the end of July, rent rafts for four to six people at the Curry Village Recreation Center (209-372-4386) for approximately $20 per person. Note that children of any age must weigh at least 50 pounds to qualify for the raft rental; the Yosemite concessionaire is *unbending* about this rule. You can also bring your own inflatable rafts; the rental office has an air hose available to the public. If you float your own boat downstream, you can still catch a ride back on the Curry Village bus at the end.

- **Ranger programs:** There is a ranger-led hike or program for every age, ability level, and interest in Yosemite; examples include campfire talks, photo-safari hikes, and nighttime stargazing programs. Check schedules in the visitors center for times and meeting places. Don't miss the Junior Ranger program for children 5–12. Purchase an inexpensive activity booklet, available at most ranger stations; children complete a certain number of paper-and-pencil activities, participate in a ranger-led program, and fill a trash bag full of litter. After tackling the assigned tasks, children return to a ranger station to receive their official Junior Ranger badge.

- **Theater:** Live theater programs are available summer evenings and are staged in a comfortable indoor venue near the visitor center. In past seasons, a talented actor has staged a series of moving one-man shows about environmentalist John Muir. The content of these dramas are appropriate for children of all ages, but best suited for kids 8 and older.

- **Winter sports:** Although many roads and trails are closed during the snowy season, Yosemite offers numerous possibilities for winter sports, including cross-country skiing and snowshoeing on the park trails; downhill skiing and snowboarding at the Badger Pass Ski Area; and ice skating at one of the world's most romantic outdoor rinks in Curry Village.

COLORaDO

62 Cave of the Winds

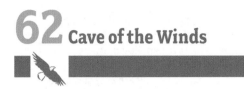

CONTACT 719-685-5444, www.caveofthewinds.com;
U.S. 24 W., Manitou Springs

PRICING	$$$–$$$$
BEST TIME TO VISIT	Summertime
AGE RANGE	7 and older

The Cave of the Winds, just west of Colorado Springs, was discovered in 1880 by two boys on a church outing, and it is believed to be more than 500 million years old. It was named for an Apache legend that maintains the Great Spirit of the Wind resides within the caves of this area. The surrounding Pike's Peak region is dramatically picturesque, and the cave itself is beautiful, with surprisingly colorful stalactites, stalagmites, and "cave flowers" (particularly attractive crystal formations).

Spelunkers can choose one of two cave tours: The Discovery Tour takes you along a mile-long trail that meanders past underground geological formations with fanciful names like Fat Man's Misery and the Giant's Bleeding Heart. The tour takes about 45 minutes. Beware: At one point the lights are shut off, allowing guests to experience the cave in total blackout darkness, which can be a little intense for young children. The Lantern Tour is slightly more physical, and guests must wriggle through several low passageways and tight tunnels. The pathway is lighted only by the lanterns carried by those on the tour. This more rigorous, authentic trek into the cave requires attention to footing because of the uneven pathway and low overheads. It takes about an hour and a half, and isn't recommended for children younger than 7. Whatever tour you choose, be sure to bring a jacket, because the interior is chilly even in the summer.

63 Colorado Trail

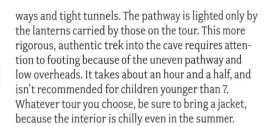

CONTACT www.coloradotrail.org; running from Denver to Durango

PRICING	$
BEST TIME TO VISIT	Summer
AGE RANGE	10 years and older

The 485-mile Colorado Trail runs from just outside of Denver, in Waterton Canyon State Park, to Durango, and offers myriad outdoorsy opportunities for athletic families along a route that cuts through some of the most beautiful scenery in America. The established and well-marked trail is open to hikers, bikers, and horseback riders. Mountain bikers are allowed in some nonwilderness portions. The trail passes through seven national forests and eight mountain ranges, climbing to more than 13,000 feet at the highest point and dipping to 5,500 feet at its lowest. It

Cave of the Winds
Photo by Matt Inden, Weaver Multimedia Group, courtesy of Colorado Tourism Office

On the Colorado Trail
Courtesy Rosi Weiss

Rainbow Lake, Telluride   Photo Denise Chamber, Weaver Multimedia Group, courtesy of Colorado Tourism Office

PRICE KEY
$ free–$5
$$ $6–10
$$$ $11–20
$$$$ $21+

takes about five to six weeks to through-hike the entirety of the trail, but families can make a day of it by choosing one of the 28 segments, which range from 10 to 32 miles. Be sure to download trail maps before you set off, and check weather conditions in advance. Come prepared with sufficient food and water; wear sunscreen; and carry first-aid supplies. Portions of this trail are quite remote, and it's possible to travel for hours without seeing other people—which is a joy if you're looking for a true wilderness adventure, but the desolation can be dangerous if you aren't prepared properly.

64 Comanche National Grassland

CONTACT USDA Forest Service, 719-384-2181, www.visit lajunta.net/comanche.html; 1420 E. 3rd St., La Junta

PRICING	$
BEST TIME TO VISIT	Spring and fall
AGE RANGE	5 and older if biking or horseback riding; hiking should be reserved for kids 10 and older

Dinosaur aficionados will not want to miss the Comanche National Grasslands. The more than 400,000 acres of wild and desolate grasslands offer enough solitude to let your imagination run wild and dream about what it would have been like 150 million years ago, when dinosaurs roamed this part of the world—but what's even better, you can actually get a glimpse of dino life here. The ancient animals trekked through the mud along the shores of a now-extinct lake at the site, and miraculously, distinct dinosaur footprints that were left behind remain today. And there are a *lot* of prints. The park rangers have cataloged more than 1,300 visible tracks—making this the largest collection of dinosaur tracks in the world. There's really nothing like standing in the footprint of a brontosaurus to get kids thinking about the history of life on earth.

It takes some perseverance to reach the dinosaur tracks: The prints are far from the roads that cross through the grasslands. You'll need to hike, bike, or ride a horse about 5 miles (along a flat trail) through the Picketwire Canyon to reach them. Pick up maps to the site at the Comanche National Grassland visitor center in La Junta to minimize the route (if you start in the wrong spot, the hike could be closer to 10 miles). Be sure to bring along plenty of water and food: This is quite a remote spot, and there is no drinking water available in the canyon. Dress appropriately for the season, and check the weather in advance: The area is prone to flash floods.

The grasslands are also an excellent place to spot living animals. There are more than 300 species of mammals, birds, insects, and reptiles that make their home in the grasslands here, including familiar species like the pronghorn, swift fox, and golden eagle. After being inspired by the Jurassic tracks, kids will be especially fascinated by the unusual and often brightly colored collared lizards, which are reminiscent of dinosaurs: These modern-day reptiles can grow up to a foot long and run on their hind legs.

65 Dinosaur National Monument

CONTACT 435-781-7700, www.nps.gov/dino; 4545 U.S. 40, Dinosaur

PRICING	$
BEST TIME TO VISIT	Spring and fall
AGE RANGE	5 and older

This fascinating and beautiful park straddles Colorado and Utah and preserves an impressive number of relics from the Jurassic period. Paleontologist Earl Douglass came to the region in the early 20th century looking for mammal fossils for the Carnegie Museum in Pittsburgh, Pennsylvania. What he found instead was an enormous collection of dinosaur bones. Since the discovery in 1909, the Carnegie Quarry—as it is now called—has produced some of the finest dinosaur fossils ever unearthed, many of which are displayed in museums throughout the world. But many fossils remain, and this is arguably one of the best sites in the country to see dinosaur bones outside a museum.

Douglass Quarry Fossils, Dinosaur National Monument
Courtesy National Park Service

Scientists believe that dinosaurs were originally drawn to the area for water, which at one time was abundant. However, a drought some 150 million years ago caused the fresh water supply to dry up, and the dinosaurs died. After decades, the skeletons were buried under sand and silt, and after thousands of years they eventually fossilized in place. Millions of years of geology buried the bones under layers of rock, but shifting tectonic plates pushed these layers back to the surface, partially exposing them for Douglass's eventual discovery.

The biggest draw at this national monument is the newly reopened, remodeled Quarry Exhibit Hall (which falls over the Utah border, just north of Jensen). The impressive structure is built into a cliff and hovers over a mountainside that is embedded with more than 1,500 dinosaur bones, which have been partially excavated so that visitors can readily see the amazing variety and number of fossils. The concentration of skeletons is believed to be particu-

larly dense here because the so-called Bone Wall on display is thought to have been the site of one of the last watering holes before the region went dry.

If you and your family want to hit the paths to look for dinosaurs, check out the Fossil Discovery Trail, which is studded with interpretive signs along the way to point out fossils. Expect to see dinosaur bones alongside smaller fossils like fish and small mammals embedded in the layers of rock visible along this route.

The park is undeniably popular because of the rich fossil deposits, but there are other attractions to recommend it, including beautiful river-carved canyons, colorful mesas, and abundant wildlife. The park is also home to pictographs (rock paintings) and petroglyphs (pictures carved into the rock), left behind by the Fremont People, who lived here more than 1,000 years ago. These are on display at a number of sites near the park visitor center.

66 Durango & Silverton Narrow Gauge Railroad

CONTACT 970-247-2733, www.durangotrain.com; 479 Main St., Durango

PRICING	Prices vary according to duration of trip and class of travel
BEST TIME TO VISIT	Year-round; winter packages are magical
AGE RANGE	All ages

This beautifully restored coal-fired steam-engine train runs from a historic 1882 depot in charming Durango, through the San Juan National Forest to Silverton, a well-preserved mining town designated a National Historic Landmark. The route winds 200 feet above the Animas River and offers breathtaking views of the Animas Gorge and the impressive peaks. Train lovers will not want to miss the chance to check out this vintage locomotive, which offers several classes of service, including open-air gondolas and antique coach cars. (Beware: First class is reserved for passengers 16 and older.)

There are a number of package tours available

In addition to the wonderful Junior Ranger program at Dinosaur National Monument (similar to Junior Ranger programs offered at most national parks throughout the country), this park also offers a fun (and free) Junior Paleontologist program. Kids can pick up an age-appropriate booklet at a visitor center, complete a number of paper-and-pencil activities about fossils, participate in a ranger program, and be sworn in as a junior protector of Dinosaur National Monument, complete with official-looking badge.

Durango & Silverton Narrow Gauge Railroad
Photo by Matt Inden, Weaver Multimedia Group, courtesy of Colorado Tourism Office

from the Durango & Silverton group, including rail trips that are combined with horseback riding through stunning mountains; four-wheeling through the beautiful Colorado backcountry; and rafting on the Animas River.

Perhaps the most magical rail adventure offered by this group is the Polar Express trip, which runs from mid-November through the end of December. Fans of the beloved children's book *Polar Express* will notice that many details from the story are incorporated into the train ride. Children are encouraged to arrive in their PJs; every passenger enjoys hot chocolate and a cookie; the onboard crew leads everyone in carols; and the ride culminates in a visit from Santa himself, who gives each child aboard a small gift that is sure to be meaningful for those kids (and their parents) who love the storybook.

67 Florissant Fossil Beds National Monument

CONTACT 719-748-3253, www.nps.gov/flfo; Florissant

PRICING	$
BEST TIME TO VISIT	Spring and fall
AGE RANGE	7 and older

Imagine prehistoric Colorado during the Oligocene epoch, during which flowering plants, insects, birds, and mammals flourished. Some 35 million years ago, the dinosaurs had long ago gone extinct, but it would

be thousands of years before humans evolved. Amid this lush and fertile landscape, a series of sudden volcanic eruptions transformed the region, engulfing every living thing with volcanic mud, ash, and pumice. After millennia the organisms fossilized in layers of shale. What's left today is one of the most diverse fossil deposits in the country, including petrified redwood stumps up to 14 feet in diameter, along with detailed fossils of smaller plants and animals, like ferns, butterflies, caterpillars, mollusks, and early ancestors of horses and pigs. Paleontologists have collected more than 60,000 specimens in the area that is now federally protected as the Florissant Fossil Beds National Monument.

Visit the park today to see meadowlands, forests, and abundant seasonal wildflowers (from which the region got its name). Start at the visitor center, which offers an interesting 15-minute orientation film, along with geological exhibits and fossil displays. Outside the visitor center, check out petrified redwood stumps. You can also catch two easy interpretive trails from here: Look for more fossilized stumps along the Ponderosa Loop and the Petrified Forest Trail.

The park features an active archaeology program, which includes excavation demonstrations, ranger-led walks, and—in the summertime—daily paleontology demonstrations at the Fossil Excavation Site. Kids can get hands-on experience at the on-site field lab here by examining fossils under microscopes and using excavation tools to clean specimens. The Junior Ranger program offers the opportunity for kids to dig for fossils. Note: The park is accessible only during daytime hours.

Junior Ranger program at the Florissant Fossil Beds National Monument
Courtesy National Park Service

68 Hovenweep National Monument

CONTACT 970-562-4282, www.nps.gov/hove; McElmo Canyon Rd., Cortez

PRICING	$
BEST TIME TO VISIT	Fall through spring
AGE RANGE	7 and older

More than 10,000 years ago, Paleoindians moved through the region in a seasonal migration to hunt and gather food. But it wasn't until approximately 1,000 years ago that Native peoples settled in the region permanently, practicing rudimentary agriculture and continuing to hunt the bounty of animals. Anthropologists believe that by 1200 more than 2,500 individuals lived at the site now known as Hovenweep.

Ancestral Puebloan people built small villages, or pueblos, throughout the region. The stacked-stone structures at Hovenweep National Monument (which stretches across Colorado and Utah) that remain today as ruins were constructed sometime between 1200 and 1300, and demonstrate sophisticated craftsmanship and great beauty. Hovenweep includes a variety of structures, in various sizes and shapes, including circular and rectangular towers and kivas (ceremonial structures that are generally rounded). Some structures were clearly meant to be dwellings, but researchers are less sure of the purposes of the towers, which tend to be narrow and several stories

Hovenweep National Monument   Courtesy National Park Service

tall. Possibly because of a drought or possibly because of territorial wars among Native peoples, the Ancestral Puebloans disappeared from the area by about the 14th century.

Visitors to the park today can enjoy the solitude and beauty of the surrounding high desert while they explore the many architectural remains. The park includes six pueblos (some of which fall within Utah). Start exploring at the Square Tower Group trail, a 2-mile loop that begins at the park's visitor center and passes by the greatest concentration of structures, including the impressive Square Tower, a three-story structure that is believed to be a ceremonial site. Other ruins include the Cutthroat Castle Group, a large outcropping of structures with several kivas; the Holly Group, which includes the picturesque Tilted Tower; and the Cajon Group, a small village that includes pictographs.

69 Mesa Verde National Park

CONTACT 970-529-4465, www.nps.gov/meve; off U.S. 160 W., Mesa Verde

PRICING	$
BEST TIME TO VISIT	Spring and fall
AGE RANGE	7 and older

As far back as AD 600, Ancestral Puebloans farmed throughout what is now southwestern Colorado. Beginning around 750, these Native peoples began to build clusters of dwellings in small villages (pueblos) at the tops of mesas. Perhaps for added protection, by 1200 they moved into the crevices and overhangings of canyons—which both protected the inhabitants of the ancient pueblos from severe weather (and perhaps neighboring tribes) and protected the structures of the pueblos themselves, which were made of sandstone, wood beams, and mortar. By the 1300s, the Ancestral Puebloans had abandoned these pueblos and fled the region. No one knows why.

In the late 19th century, two ranchers chasing stray cattle through the area discovered a great cache of these amazing dwellings. The site was dubbed

Mesa Verde (Spanish for "green table"). Today the park preserves more than 4,500 archaeological sites, 600 of which are the spectacularly beautiful and well-preserved cliff dwellings. Start your visit at the Far View Visitor Center to pick up maps. Note that only two cliff dwellings are open for self-guided tours, so while you're there, be sure to purchase tickets to view others you might be interested in seeing. Next head to the Chapin Mesa Archeological Museum where you can view a film on Ancestral Puebloan culture and explore artifacts and Native crafts, including exquisite pottery, on display. (Note: The visitor center closes from mid-October through mid-April, at which time tour tickets must be purchased at the Chapin museum.) Catch the Spruce Tree House Trailhead from the museum. The quarter-mile trail will take you to the cliff dwelling known as Spruce Tree House (one of

Cliff dwellings at Mesa Verde   Courtesy National Park Service

If you're so inclined, you can climb down a ladder into one of the kivas.

the dwellings that is open for self-guided tours); although the structures throughout the park are painstakingly maintained by park service archaeologists, this structure is 90 percent original stonework and it's a great place to observe the considerable craftsmanship that went into designing and building these dwellings. The structure is 200 feet wide, with eight kivas (ceremonial rooms located belowground); if you're so inclined, you can climb down a ladder into one of the kivas. This is likely the easiest dwelling to tour, thanks to a paved trail and no steps or ladders—but the walk to reach Spruce Tree House is steep nevertheless and includes many switchbacks.

These cliff dwellings are at 7,000 feet elevation, and tours include a lot of climbing. The trails are steep, and you must often climb up and down ladders and/or stairs. Make sure to wear hiking boots or other sturdy footwear; avoid the worst of the heat in the summertime; and be realistic about the physical stamina and abilities of everyone in your family before setting out on this particular adventure.

There are several other cliff dwellings in the park that can be visited, but only via guided tours that require separate ticket purchase. During busy summer months, you may be limited in the number of dwellings your can tour. If you have the time, check out these stunning archaeological sites:

- **Balcony House:** This dwelling has 40 rooms, and is one of the best-preserved sites in the park. Watch children carefully on this tour: The dwelling is entered via a 32-foot ladder, and it is necessary to pass through some narrow tunnels as well. (Skip this if you have claustrophobia or a fear of heights.)

- **Cliff Palace:** A 150-room dwelling that was once home to 100 individuals, this is one of the largest dwellings in the park. Archaeologists believe it could have had religious or ceremonial importance. This is one of the most popular sites in the park, and often the most crowded. Consider taking the first or last tours of the day, to avoid the worst of the congestion.

- **Long House:** This is the second largest dwelling in the park, and is particularly lovely—although the tour is quite strenuous and includes a white-knuckle wooden ladder. This dwelling is only accessible from Memorial Day to Labor Day.

Note that during summer months, when the road is open, the Wetherill Mesa Drive offers spectacular overlooks across the cliff dwellings, if you find you just aren't up for the strenuous climbing to tour the dwellings.

70 Pike's Peak

CONTACT City of Colorado Springs, 719-385-7325, www.springsgov.com; located 10 miles west of Colorado Springs

PRICING	$–$$$
BEST TIME TO VISIT	Year-round
AGE RANGE	7 and older

Known as the most visited mountain in the United States, Pikes Peak is 14,000 feet in elevation. The granite mountain was carved into its characteristic craggy shape by glaciers that passed through the region in the last ice age, nearly 11,000 years ago. The beautiful rosy hue of the granite is thanks to large concentrations of potassium feldspar: At sunrise and sunset, when the light catches it at its best, the granite seems to glitter. The iconic mountain became part of America thanks to the Louisiana Purchase in 1803. Since that time it has become emblematic for Americans. In the mid-19th century, gold prospectors coming to Colorado declared it would be "Pike's Peak or Bust." Not long after, the peak served as the inspiration for Katharine Lee Bates to write "America the Beautiful," which was originally penned as a poem.

Although it isn't the highest mountain in Colorado (or even close to it), Pike's Peak *is* the farthest east in the Rocky Mountain chain and one of the easiest to access. Visitors can hike, drive, or take the rails to the summit:

- **Pikes Peak Highway:** Undoubtedly the most popular way to reach the top of Pike's Peak, this 19-mile-long roadway offers nothing less than stunning views—which on clear days can extend across the state line. The drive is slow and winding, with numerous white-knuckle switchbacks. There are plenty of opportunities to pull off and enjoy the lookouts. At the top is a large plaque commemorating the writing of "America the Beautiful." The road in theory is open year-round, but it's subject to closure in poor weather conditions—which are frequent in winter.
- **Barr Trail:** This 13-mile one-way trail to the summit is the most popular for hikers. The elevation gain on the way up is nearly 8,000 feet, and because it requires about 10 hours to walk, this adventure is appropriate only for very experienced hikers in optimal shape. Pick up the trailhead in Manitou Springs, off Ruxton Avenue. Halfway up is Barr Camp, where backpackers can rest for the night. There is no potable water here, but overnight visitors can prearrange to dine at the site.
- **Pikes Peak Cog Railway:** Operating since 1891, this cog railway (which uses a gear wheel that meshes into a specially designed track, giving it the needed traction to get up the peak) takes you 8.9 miles up the mountain, for a round trip lasting about three hours. Once at the top, visitors may get off the train for half an hour to look around and take photos. The depot is located in Manitou Springs, on Ruxton Avenue. The train runs year-round.

However you make your way to the summit, conditions there are likely to be extreme: Because of the high elevation, the air is thin—with only about 60 percent of the oxygen available in the atmosphere at sea level. Many people are prone to altitude sickness, which usually presents itself as dizziness and/or a headache that can quickly deteriorate to nausea and fainting. The temperatures are chilly—often 30 degrees cooler than at the base of the mountain—and snow is possible any time of the year. In addition, high winds and thunderstorms are common in the spring and summer. The summit is so high that you'll often be higher than the clouds—which makes for a surreal sense of being above it all, but in these conditions the visibility is limited. In short, get to the top—or as near to it as you can—but don't plan to stay *too* long.

Pike's Peak   Courtesy National Park Service

71 Rocky Mountain National Park

CONTACT 970-586-1206, www.nps.gov/romo; 1000 U.S. 36, Estes

PRICING	$
BEST TIME TO VISIT	Spring through early fall
AGE RANGE	5 and older

The history of the Rocky Mountains goes back to 80 million years ago, when geological forces upthrust the formidable ridges. Through several ice ages, the latest one as recent as 11,000 years ago, glaciers have slowly sculpted scenic valleys through these peaks, and erosion from rain and snowfall has further weathered them, creating a scenic region that today presents visitors with postcard-perfect scenes of snowcapped mountains, alpen forests, flower-strewn meadows, crystal lakes, and ethereal waterfalls. More than a century after the U.S. government acquired the portion of land that is now Rocky Mountain National Park as part of the Louisiana Purchase, in 1915 the Congress set aside this portion of the Rocky Mountains so that the beauty of the area could be preserved and enjoyed for generations to come.

Within the 416 square miles of the park boundaries, there are more than 60 mountains that stretch higher than 12,000 feet—with the highest, Longs Peak, rising to 14,259 feet—and it is these dramatic mountains that are the greatest draw for visitors. The

Elk herd, Rocky Mountain National Park

Courtesy National Park Service

Continental Divide splits the park into east and west sides, each of which has a distinct personality. (The Continental Divide—also known as the Great Divide—is the point in the United States at which waterways drain either east, to the Atlantic Ocean, or west, to the Pacific Ocean.)

Start your visit with a stop at the Beaver Meadows Visitor Center to enjoy a 20-minute orientation film on the park called *Spirit of the Mountains*. This is a good place to pick up trail maps and any last-minute supplies as well. There are a number of ways to explore the park, making it accessible for just about anyone, regardless of age or athletic ability.

Scenic Roadways

One of the most popular—and physically easiest—ways to get some of the most startling views is via two popular scenic roadways in the park that will allow you to drive along rivers, through subalpine forests, and to mountain summits. There are opportunities along the way to pull off at lookout points to take photos or catch short trails.

- **Old Fall River Road:** Motoring along this one-way gravel road is an adventure. The speed limit is 15 mph, along steep uphill grades and around sharp switchbacks, and there are no guardrails. The 11-mile road runs from Horseshoe Park (near the Fall River Entrance to the park) to Fall River Pass, nearly 12,000 feet above sea level.
- **Trail Ridge Road:** The more heavily trafficked Trail Ridge Road is easily the most popular scenic drive in the park. It runs from Estes Park in the east to Grand Lake in the west, along 48 miles of paved roadway, and offers visitors a chance to view forests, tundra, seasonal alpine wildflowers, and abundant wildlife.

Hiking

Hiking through Rocky Mountain National Park is more challenging than in regions at lower elevations. Unless everyone in your family is in top physical condition and used to extensive hiking, take it easy in this park and concentrate on shorter day hikes that do not have tremendous changes in elevation. The trails that follow are appropriate for most children 7 and older and can be accomplished in a few hours.

There is no lodging within the Rocky Mountain National Park. To minimize the amount of driving and to fully immerse yourself in a true wilderness experience, consider bunking at one of the five family campgrounds. The settings are majestic and the costs extremely affordable (expect about $20 a night), but be prepared to rough it: The campsites offer no water, electric, or sewer hookups. Aspenglen, Glacier Basin, and Moraine Park campgrounds take reservations, and it is recommended you make summer plans several months in advance.

- **Alberta Falls:** Pick up the trailhead for this easy half-mile hike at Glacier Gorge Junction and follow it for views of a spectacular waterfall. This is one of the best scenic payoffs for an easy hike that the park has to offer.
- **Bear Lake Loop:** This heavily trafficked, very easy half-mile loop follows the rim of the namesake lake; there are interpretive signs along the way to orient children to the flora and fauna of the region.
- **Cub Lake:** For a slightly more difficult trek, try the Cub Lake Trail, a 2.3-mile hike to a pretty mountain pond.
- **Deer Mountain:** Starting at Deer Ridge Junction, this 3-mile hike is moderately strenuous, thanks to an elevation gain of 1,000 feet (culminating in a total elevation of 10,000 feet), but it is nevertheless one of the easier summit hikes in the park.
- **Upper Beaver Meadows:** An easy 1.5-mile trek with minimal elevation change, this scenic hike winds through a meadow that is particularly lovely when the wildflowers are peaking; look for elk along Beaver Creek.

Horseback Riding

If you have experienced equestrians in your family or if you've never spent a day in the saddle, riding in Rocky Mountain National Park is a quintessentially American experience that will please just about everyone: The crisp mountain air, jaw-dropping scenery, and great variety of terrain are enough to bring out anyone's inner cowboy.

There are two stables located within the park—Glacier Creek Stables and Moraine Park Stables—and many others operated by concessionaires outside the park boundaries. The park offers more than 250 miles of trails open to horses. Favorite horse trails include Big Meadows, with trailheads at Green Mountain and Tonahutu; Lawn and Ypsilon Lakes, accessed at Lawn Lake; Lost Lake, accessed at Dunraven Glade; and Thunder and Finch Lakes, accessed at Wild Basin and Finch Lake.

Wildlife Viewing

Regardless of how you choose to explore, don't miss the opportunity to view wildlife, which can be seen throughout the park, via the roadways, the trails, and even sometimes near heavily populated visitor centers. Look for bighorn sheep, black bears, coyotes, marmots, moose, mule deer, and tiny pika. The park is home to several species of endangered or protected birds, including the bald eagle, the least tern, the Mexican spotted owl, the whooping crane, and the yellow-billed cuckoo. The rock stars of the park, however, are the impressive North American elk, also known as wapiti. In autumn, expect to see elk in the Kawuneeche Valley, Horseshoe Park, Moraine Park, and Upper Beaver Meadows. The animals are best spotted early in the morning or just as dusk falls, and you are most apt to notice them along the edges of clearings.

Elk mating season starts in August and runs through October, and is marked by the distinctive mating bugle that adult males engage in to ward off rivals. These calls are quite loud and a little unsettling, starting out as deep bellows and often rising to high-pitched squeals. Calves can be seen in May and June.

72 Ski Colorado

CONTACT	See contact information associated with each resort below
PRICING	Fees vary
BEST TIME TO VISIT	Late November through April
AGE RANGE	5 and older

When many of us think of Colorado, we think about winter sports in a pristine, fairy-tale setting: The

Snowboarding in Colorado
Photo by Matt Inden, Weaver Multimedia Group, courtesy of Colorado Tourism Office

bright blue skies, snow-clad alps, and a citizenry that is passionate about outdoor life have contributed to Colorado's bounty of some of the best snow skiing and snowboarding in the world. And thanks to an elevation of 14,000 feet or more and countless impressive peaks, the Colorado ski season tends to start earlier and end later than many ski resorts in other parts of the country—some resorts in the state open in mid-October and close in late May.

Here are a handful of favorite ski destinations, located in some of the most picturesque regions of Colorado:

- **Arapahoe Basin** (888-ARAPAHOE, www.arapahoe basin.com): Known for having *the* longest ski season in North America, the resort recently added a quad chairlift, which they estimate has cut in half the time to get from the base to the middle of the mountain. The resort offers a range of programs and lessons for children, starting as young as 3 years old. Look for the quirky Arapahoe Basin "Beach," site of barbecues, live music, and parties.
- **Breckenridge Ski Resort** (970-452-5000, www.breckenridge.com): This resort offers a variety of terrain that appeals to athletes at every level, from long groomed trails to steep chutes, to lots of family-friendly bunny slopes. If you like extreme boarding, check out the Rocky Mountain Park and Pipe Camp, for skiers and snowboarders at least at an intermediate level; there are two age divisions, for children 7–13 and for those 14 and older.

- **Copper Mountain** (800-404-3858, www.copper colorado.com): This beautiful resort offers year-round ski and snowboard camps that will appeal to teenagers into extreme sports. Copper Mountain also offers sledding and tubing runs.
- **Durango Mountain Resort** (800-982-6102, www.durangomountainresort.com): This is an ideal ski resort for families with young kids, thanks to plenty of accessible slopes and a child-friendly atmosphere. The Burton Learn-to-Ride Kids Center offers snowboarding instructions for children, along with kid-sized snowboards for rent.
- **Snowmass** (800-525-6200, www.aspensnowmass.com): Located in Aspen, which is synonymous with the rich and famous, the real star of this enormous ski resort is "Snowmassive," a 4,400-foot slope that is the highest vertical rise in the country, allowing for a 5.3-mile run. Look for the Treehouse Kids' Center, the focal point of kids' ski instruction in Aspen, which also includes a family-inclusive climbing gym, a teen center, and regular kid-friendly programming.
- **Steamboat** (800-922-2722, www.steamboat.com): Known as Ski Town USA, Steamboat knows a good thing when it finds it: This resort has trademarked the light, dry snow here—dubbed Champagne Powder. Steamboat boasts kids-only terrain and lifts. And after hitting the slopes during the day, children will enjoy the chance to ride horse-drawn sleighs through snow-dusted pine trees.
- **Telluride** (866-287-5015, http://tellurideskiresort.com): This pretty Victorian town is the backdrop for some of the most expert ski runs in the nation. Telluride EcoAdventures offers kids' programs that include education and outdoor fun, and can include activities like ice sculpting and snow cave building.
- **Vail** (970-476-5601, www.vail.com): Vail boasts 193 trails, 5,289 skiable acres, and seven back bowls, making it one of the largest ski regions in the country. The area also offers snowshoeing, cross-country skiing, ski biking, tubing, and kid-sized snowmobiles. The upscale surroundings are a favorite with deep-pocket singles and families, with plenty of luxury shopping, dining, and pricey accommodations as well.

73 U.S. Mint

CONTACT 303-572-9500, www.usmint.gov;
320 W. Colfax Ave., Denver

PRICING	$
BEST TIME TO VISIT	Year-round
AGE RANGE	5 and older

In 1792, shortly after the U.S. Constitution was ratified, Congress passed the Coinage Act establishing the precedent for building mints to manufacture and distribute money. There are six mint facilities throughout the country, but only two are accessible to the public: The original mint in Philadelphia and the mint in Denver, which was constructed in 1863, shortly after gold was discovered in Colorado.

The U.S. Mint in Denver produces coins only. Public tours of this facility allow visitors to learn about the stages of the minting process, including the design of original coins through the actual creation of the coins (called "striking"). Visitors cannot stroll the production floor, for obvious reasons, but can observe coin striking from windows that look down on the process. The 30-minute tour is informative, interesting, and serious—the tour guides and guards that accompany the public tours do not tolerate jokes about security.

Arrange for a tour several weeks in advance by making online reservations. The tours are free and are conducted Monday through Friday from 8 AM until 2 PM, excluding all federal holidays. Be sure to arrive 15 minutes before the tour starts: Late arrivals *will* miss out. There is a standby line for those who miss their scheduled tours or for those who forget to make reservations—but don't count on getting in this way. Because this is a high-security federal institution, expect screening for every member of the family, no matter how young. Leave behind strollers; purses, diaper bags, and totes of all kinds (although wallets are allowed); food, drink, and tobacco products; and of course all weapons. There are no storage lockers on site. You can carry cell phones and cameras, but you won't be allowed to use them inside the facility, so might as well leave these behind as well. You may also carry an umbrella.

connecticut

74 Amistad Memorial

CONTACT	165 Church St., New Haven
PRICING	$
BEST TIME TO VISIT	Year-round
AGE RANGE	10 and older

Slavery existed long before the first Europeans arrived in America: The shameful practice of forced, unpaid labor helped build Roman aqueducts and other monuments in the ancient world and was tolerated in many cultures across the globe. But it is one of the saddest truths in American history that early colonists brought slavery to the New World, and the U.S. Founders legalized the practice for centuries. Indeed, slaves were responsible for much of the back-breaking work involved in building the early colonies and then sustaining large farms and plantations that propelled the growth of the fledgling nation. Slaves are even credited with helping to build the White House and the U.S. Capitol Building.

The U.S. Constitution, drafted in 1787, prevented Congress from changing the existing laws in America regarding importation of slaves until 1808. As soon as it was constitutionally possible, on January 1, 1808, Congress made illegal additional importation of slaves—although the institution of slavery remained legal and, because of the many descendants of slaves already in the country, remained well entrenched, especially in the U.S. South. Most northeastern states nevertheless chose on their own to abolish slavery. By 1804, slavery was nearly abolished in U.S. states north of the infamous Mason-Dixon line (running north of Maryland and including Delaware). It was

> It was not until the 1865 passage of the 13th Amendment to the U.S. Constitution that slavery was abolished in the United States.

New Haven Lighthouse ©enfi/iStockphoto.com

not until the 1865 passage of the 13th Amendment to the U.S. Constitution that slavery was abolished completely in the United States, after the bloody American Civil War.

In the midst of the struggle for abolition—and after the congressional ban in the United States that declared importation of slaves to this country as an act of piracy—a Spanish shipped dubbed *La Amistad* was en route to Cuba carrying human cargo, including 52 adults and four children, who had been abducted in Africa and were being brought to the island for slave labor. On July 2, 1839, one of the captives—Sengbe Pieh (who was later known as Joseph Cinqué)—led his fellows in an onboard revolt. The 50-some individuals broke free from their shackles in the cargo hold in which they were being imprisoned, stormed the decks, and overpowered their captors. The Africans demanded they be returned home, and ostensibly the overpowered ship's crew agreed. However, the navigator on board lied to them about the course they were sailing, and instead of heading back to Africa steered the ship north, eventually passing by Long Island, New York, where the ship was spotted by a U.S. Revenue Cutter Service ship patrolling the area. The U.S. Navy officials took the ship's occupants captive, and the Africans aboard were transported to New Haven, Connecticut, to have their fate determined in a U.S. court.

The trial of these displaced Africans received an enormous amount of attention. Because importing slaves to the Americas was by this point illegal, the court had to consider the capture of the Africans and their illegal transportation in determining whether the human cargo should be considered salvage and thus the property of the officers who took custody of

Amistad Memorial   Courtesy Michael Marsland, Yale University

the ship outside of New York or of the property of the wealthy Cubans who had paid for their capture and passage, or if they should be treated as free individuals. The point was argued through a series of trials, and the bitterly contested case was eventually appealed to the U.S. Supreme Court. The Court ruled in 1841 that because the Africans had been illegally captured and transported, they were to be considered free. In 1842, those captives of *La Amistad* who were still alive were returned to their home, in what is now Sierra Leone in Africa.

To commemorate this important event in the abolitionist cause, the 14-foot Amistad Memorial was erected on the spot where the captive Africans were imprisoned during the trials. The bronze sculpture designed by artist Ed Hamilton depicts three scenes from the *Amistad* drama: Pieh in Africa before he was kidnapped, the courtroom during the trial, and Pieh ready to board the ship taking him back home to Africa. The memorial was dedicated in 1992, and is well worth visiting to remember the struggles of enslaved people and other abolitionists in the 19th century.

75 Eli Whitney Museum and Workshop

CONTACT 203-777-1833, www.eliwhitney.org;
915 Whitney Ave., Hamden

PRICING	Cost of workshops varies
BEST TIME TO VISIT	Year-round
AGE RANGE	3 and older

Eli Whitney (1765–1825) was an American inventor most famous for creating the cotton gin, a machine that automated the process of separating usable cotton fiber from the rest of the cotton plant—an invention that would quickly revolutionize cotton production and ultimately change the course of the history of slavery in America. Cotton was especially well suited to growing in the South, and Whitney's invention made farming cotton a much more profitable endeavor; as a result, large cotton plantations in the South grew wealthy—but not without the consider-

> Whenever possible, make reservations for building workshops in advance—but if you aren't able to plan ahead, visit on Saturday, when some workshops are offered on a walk-in basis.

able labor investment needed, which was usually supplied by slaves.

The incredible Eli Whitney Museum and Workshop memorializes the work of this influential American by sparking the creativity and problem-solving abilities in children as young as toddlers in a way that allows them to use their senses and naturally quizzical natures to learn and discover an empowering environment. Using self-guided methods of discovery, children work through a series of "essential experiments" to allow them to uncover truths about the natural world, the properties of energy, and their own inherent ability to teach themselves.

The museum on site includes permanent exhibits such as the water lab, in which children can uncover the mechanics of hydroelectric power, and a model of Whitney's 1825 factory. There is also a historic site based on a manufacturing village that Whitney designed, including a forge, an armory, a factory model, and a covered bridge. Traveling exhibits have included disparate collections such as model trains, bottle caps, and playing cards. The true magic of this place is in the workshops presented for children as young as 3. Longer workshops (which must be reserved in advance) have included building elaborate wooden toys; transforming household items like rubber bands and springs into inventions inspired by da Vinci and Archimedes; and constructing Praxinscopes, century-old animation devices. In addition, the museum offers shorter walk-in workshops on weekends that guide children through building things like mobiles, toy paddleboats, rubber-band cars, pinball machines, magnetic pendulums, model sailboats, electromagnets, and simple musical instruments like xylophones and violins. The museum provides all the raw materials and tools needed, and each workshop is guided by patient, knowledgeable folks in a safe environment. Children (and adults) who like to make things will find this place irresistible.

76 Mark Twain House

CONTACT 860-247-0998, www.marktwainhouse.org;
351 Farmington Ave., Hartford

PRICING	$$–$$$
BEST TIME TO VISIT	Year-round
AGE RANGE	7 and older

Born Samuel Langhorne Clemens (1835–1910), the prolific American writer and humorist who published under the name Mark Twain is responsible for some of the most enduring characters and best-read novels in American literature, including the beloved *Adventures of Tom Sawyer* and *Adventures of Huckleberry Finn*. This museum preserves the home Clemens shared with his wife, Olivia; the couple commissioned the construction of the beautiful home in 1873 and lived there until 1891. Clemens wrote many times how superior he believed the house to be over any other he lived in before or since. The on-site museum offers a number of enlightening exhibits on the man and his work. Start out your visit viewing the excellent Ken Burns mini documentary on the iconic author, and then check out the more than 16,000 artifacts on permanent display, including Clemens's last pair of eyeglasses, a love letter written by Clemens to his wife, and a great many family photographs.

Mark Twain House   Courtesy Connecticut Commission on Culture and Tourism

77 Mashantucket Pequot Museum and Research Center

CONTACT 800-411-9671, www.pequotmuseum.org;
110 Pequot Trail, Mashantucket

PRICING	$$–$$$
BEST TIME TO VISIT	Year-round
AGE RANGE	5 and older

The Pequot people are a group of Native Americans from the region that is now Connecticut. In the early 17th century, when there were more than 2,000 Pequots living in the Thames Valley, they survived as hunters and fishermen, and also cultivated grain. When the British first arrived, the colonists and the Pequots enjoyed a mutually beneficial relationship, living near each other without incident and trading peacefully. However, as with so many interactions between Natives and the newly arrived Europeans who sought to claim the New World as their own, the colonists' expanding encroachment on land and hunting grounds proved troublesome to the Pequots, and in the summer of 1636 coexistence seemed to become intolerable for both parties. Puritan clergymen regarded the Pequots as "infidels," and as a result of the increasing intolerance and because of escalating violence perpetrated by the Pequots, the local colonists became determined to drive them from the region. At this point, Captain John Mason, along with Native warriors from other tribes, attacked the Pequot settlement at Mystic, setting the village on fire and slaughtering residents. After this bloody encounter, the Pequots were decimated, and many survivors left the area altogether. Others were later killed or captured by other Native tribes, and some were even sold into slavery in the colonies. In 1655, the Pequot tribe was placed under the control of the colonial government in Connecticut and the remaining members settled along the Mystic River. Today it is believed that there are 3,000 Pequot descendants.

To remember the legacy of the Pequots, and to celebrate the traditions that the living Pequots carry

Mashantucket Pequot Museum and Research Center
Courtesy Mashantucket Pequot Museum and Research Center

78 Mystic Seaport

CONTACT	www.mysticseaport.org; Greenmanville Ave., Mystic
PRICING	$$$–$$$$ (special events and tours require separate fee)
BEST TIME TO VISIT	Spring and summer
AGE RANGE	5 and older

on today, as well as explore Native American culture in all its forms, in the late 20th century the massive Mashantucket Pequot Museum and Research Center was opened to the public. The sleek, modern museum is one of the largest such facilities in the United States, and it offers engaging and stimulating exhibits that allow guests to learn about Native life and America before the Industrial Age. Guests walk through life-sized dioramas that illustrate more than 18,000 years of Native history, including a re-created Native home, and view full-sized replicas of 17th-century canoes. Visitors can also stroll outside to see Native agricultural techniques. Children will especially enjoy the re-created 1550-era Pequot Village on display. Kids can crawl into a furnished wigwam to see Native women preparing a meal and children playing. There are a number of other interactive experiences at the museum, including video programs that allow children to experience a caribou hunt, life during the last ice age, and daily existence at the fort at Mashantucket. The museum also hosts Native craft demonstrations, live musical and dance performances, storytelling, educational seminars, and annual festivals. Touring exhibits include artwork by contemporary Native artists, dance exhibitions, and documentaries. There are also two extensive libraries on site, one just for children.

Before Mystic was famous for pizza (and the Julia Roberts movie set here), this quaint New England seaside community was known for the beloved maritime museum called the Mystic Seaport. Today this impressive and extensive 17-acre complex comprises a collection of galleries housing nautical artwork and artifacts, a preservation shipyard, a jaw-dropping collection of historic sailing vessels, a charming 19th-century coastal village, and plenty of themed shopping and dining—enough to keep a family entertained for days.

Children will want to head to the water first off to climb aboard the historic tall ships; onboard reenactors dressed in period costumes will tell them stories of seafaring, and perhaps offer to let them take the helm or hoist a sail. Don't miss the chance to promenade on the *Charles W. Morgan*, a one-of-a-kind 1841 wooden whale ship. Or board the *Sabino*, a 100-year-old coal-fired steamboat that offers cruises in the scenic harbor. Next head over to the Preservation Ship-

Mystic Seaport   Courtesy Mystic County

yard, where you can watch craftsmen preserve and restore antique vessels using 19th-century tools and techniques.

The re-created 19th-century village offers myriad opportunities to explore restored original structures (many of them moved from their original sites around New England) and watch maritime artisans like wood-carvers, coopers, and ship smiths ply their trades. Throughout the village there are costumed reenactors ready to tell you and your family about the seafaring life. The highlight within the village for most kids will be the Boardman School, a traditional one-room schoolhouse where pupils learned approved subjects like spelling, geography, reading, writing, and Latin. The headmaster of the school is generally on site to explain the rules of grammar school, chide visitors for their "uneducated" use of slang, and lead willing participants through an energetic alphabet drill.

There are several other opportunities for children to learn and have fun, including the Treworgy Planetarium, where older children can discover how early navigators found their way by watching the stars; the Discovery Barn (for kids 8 and older), where they can learn how to tie knots and interpret semaphores; the Playground, filled with a wooden lobster boat, a sailing ship, and a fishing dragger, all kid-sized for children to climb through and play on; and the Children's Museum (for kids 7 and younger), where tykes can dress up like sailors, cook in a pretend galley, and swab the decks. There's also fun period shopping and dining, carriage rides, and live period entertainment.

79 Noah Webster House

Noah Webster   Courtesy Library of Congress

CONTACT 860-521-5362, www.noahwebsterhouse.org; 227 S. Main St., West Hartford

PRICING	$–$$
BEST TIME TO VISIT	Year-round
AGE RANGE	7 and older

Noah Webster was born in West Hartford in 1758 and lived during the formative years of the American colonial period and the Revolution. In addition to being a pioneer in the field of education, he was also an outspoken abolitionist, successful textbook author and editor, and early advocate for copyright protection laws. As part of his work to improve public education in the fledgling country, Webster is widely credited with regularizing American spelling and grammatical instruction; he found it unpatriotic that American children would be educated with British instructional materials, so he decided to write his own textbook, *A Grammatical Institute of the English Language*, to teach schoolchildren to read, spell, and pronounce words in a uniquely American way. This so-called blue-backed speller, nicknamed for its colorful cover, came to be the most successful American book at the time, selling 100 million copies. It was used in classrooms for more than 100 years. Most famously, Webster is also remembered as the father of the American dictionary (*A Compendious Dictionary of the English Language*, first published in the early 19th century).

This small museum preserves Webster's birthplace and offers a glimpse into his early colonial life. Begin a tour of the facility at the visitor center with an orientation film that will provide an overview of Webster's contributions to the nation, and then explore the period-decorated home with the help of costumed docents. Be sure to check out the Discovery Learning Space, which offers a number of hands-on opportunities for kids to explore Webster's childhood years, including a colonial kitchen where children can dress up in period costumes.

80 Wadsworth Atheneum

CONTACT 860-278-2670, www.thewadsworth.org;
600 Main St., Hartford

PRICING	$–$$
BEST TIME TO VISIT	Year-round
AGE RANGE	7 and older

The Wadsworth Atheneum is the oldest public art museum in the United States, comprising close to 50,000 pieces, touring exhibits, and a lovely sculpture garden. The museum was founded in 1842 by early art patron Daniel Wadsworth, who actively collected Roman and Greek antiquities; surrealist paintings; and—most notably—a huge collection of Hudson River School paintings. Hudson River School artists created quintessentially American, romantic landscapes that celebrated the natural beauty of the Hudson River Valley and surrounding regions. Also included in the museum's collection are African American arts and crafts, American and European impressionist works, and theatrical costumes. The five interconnected structures that make up the facility are remarkable in their own right, and include the iconic Gothic Revival Wadsworth Building (dating to 1844), a Tudor Revival (dating to 1910), and a modernist building (built in 1969).

Wadsworth Atheneum   Courtesy Allen Phillips, Wadsworth Atheneum

81 Windham Textile and History Museum

CONTACT 860-456-2178, www.millmuseum.org;
411 Main St., Willimantic

PRICING	$–$$
BEST TIME TO VISIT	Year-round
AGE RANGE	7 and older

For more than 150 years, until the late 20th century, the textile industry was an economic and social force throughout New England, and Willimantic was a major player in the region's industrial prowess. The Windham Textile and History Museum preserves the history of this important American industry and chronicles its effects on the culture, economy, and lives of the people who worked in the mills.

The museum is housed in the former headquarters of the American Thread Company's Willimantic Mills. At the height of its success, in the early 20th century, the Willimantic Mills was the largest thread mill in North America, the largest factory in Connecticut, and employer to more than 3,500 people. Although work in the mills was hard—even into the later years when much of the labor was automated—the Willimantic Mills instituted a number of firsts to make the process a little easier: This was the first factory to install electric lights and the first to allow coffee breaks. Through the years the mill workers manufactured threads used on major-league baseballs, U.S. Army uniforms, and spacesuits used by NASA.

The museum offers a glimpse into the harsh working conditions of the 19th century and displays technological advancements in the industry through the years. When visiting the museum, be sure to see the *Thread Mill Square* exhibit, which includes a replication of a typical home of a working family at the end of the 19th century. Look for early examples of commercial products like washing detergent and packaged foods. Then move on to the *Workers' House* display, which re-creates a communal kitchen and displays a typical bedroom (complete with chamber pot). Finally, don't miss the museum's collection of more than 75 antique sewing machines—many of them surprisingly beautiful.

Beyond College Visits

Colleges and universities across the country present a unique opportunity for parents to expose their children to the idea of higher learning at a very young age. High schoolers will want to sign up for official campus tours intended for prospective students. Such tours are generally led by current students, and they offer a glimpse into the history, architecture, and campus life of each prospective school. Harvard University in Boston, for example, offers small tours through Harvard Yard, past historic dorm rooms, and to the university library, the largest collection of books in this country aside from the Library of Congress.

Most campuses of any size offer exciting sporting events to witness, old trees to climb, and large expanses of open area where kids can run off excess energy. Here are a handful of other suggestions for making universities across the country into educational, fun day trips:

- **Basilica of the Sacred Heart** (http://basilica.nd.edu/museums-and-tours): This ornate church in Indiana, near South Bend, is one of the loveliest outside of Europe, with an intricate interior and impressive architecture, and it is the centerpiece of the University of Notre Dame, one of the most beloved Catholic universities in the country. The stained glass in this stunning chapel is especially dazzling on a sunny day.

- **Hoover Tower Observation Platform** (www.stanford.edu/dept/visitorinfo): On the lovely Palo Alto, California, campus of Stanford University, this 285-foot tower offers views that extend across the beautiful

mission-style campus to nearby San Francisco (on a clear day). Kids will enjoy seeing the enormous 48 bells housed in the tower—although the platform is closed during the periodic carillon concerts, which often feature songs not normally thought of as organ tunes (like scores from Led Zeppelin and the Beatles).

- **Michigan State University Museum** (http://museum.msu.edu): In East Lansing, this expansive museum has exhibits on the natural world, including a nice collection of dinosaur artifacts; an anthropology collection featuring the world's largest set of artifacts from the Great Lakes area; and cultural and folk art, including textile and quilt collections, Indian dance regalia, and a U.S. presidential campaign button collection.

- **Phoebe A. Hearst Anthropology Museum** (http://hearstmuseum.berkeley.edu/index.php): Check out the oldest and largest anthropological collection in the western United States at this free museum in the heart of the University of California—Berkeley campus, near Oakland. Look for conservators at work, and be sure to ask questions; staff are happy to explain their craft.

- **Sarah P. Duke Gardens** (www.hr.duke.edu/duke gardens): Sprawling across 55 acres across from the Duke University medical school in Durham, North Carolina, this lovely oasis full of flower gardens and ponds is great for young children who want to burn off a little energy exploring a pristine setting.

- **Yale Peabody Museum** (http://peabody.yale.edu): This kid-friendly museum offers exhibits on the natural world, focusing on geology, biology, paleontology, and anthropology. The museum is located on the beautiful, gothic Yale campus in New Haven, Connecticut.

Stanford University campus in California   © Debbie K. Hardin

DELAWARE

82 Fort Delaware State Park

Fort Delaware · Courtesy Delaware Tourism

CONTACT 302-834-7941, www.destateparks.com/park/fort-delaware; Pea Patch Island

PRICING	$$–$$$
BEST TIME TO VISIT	Late spring through summer (closed September through early spring)
AGE RANGE	All ages

Fort Delaware is an immaculately preserved Union fortress, dating to 1859 and originally built to protect the ports of Wilmington and Philadelphia. It was also a onetime holding facility for Confederate prisoners during the American Civil War, and people who are in the know about such things consider it to be haunted by the souls of the prisoners who died here. The picturesque granite-and-brick fortress is located on Pea Patch Island and accessible only via a half-mile ferry ride from Delaware City. (No private boats are allowed to dock on the island.) Once you land, you'll be taken by jitney from the dock to the fort, where costumed interpreters act the part of 1864 soldiers. Among the reenactors you are likely to encounter while taking a self-guided tour are the Fort Delaware laundress, who will invite you to roll up your sleeves and help her tackle ring around the collar with only a scrub board and a piece of lye soap; the ordnance sergeant, who will show you around the ammunition stored at the fort; the blacksmith and his apprentice, who may enlist you to hammer out a replacement part for one of the fort's cannons; and the hospital surgeon, who will share 17th-century operating tools and tell a few grisly tales about common medical procedures of the day. You'll have the opportunity to watch the infantry drill, hear prisoners describe their elaborate escape attempts, and pick up a few gourmet tips from the cooks at Fort Delaware.

The park is open for tours from the spring through the summer. In September and October, regular tours are discontinued, but you can arrange for a variety of candlelit ghost tours that explore the paranormal particularities of the fort. These package tours are restricted to adults and children 12 and older, and can include dinner at a nearby restaurant in Delaware City, a hands-on experience using electronic magnetic field detectors and temperature sensors, and more than a few hair-raising ghost stories. Whenever you visit, be sure to reserve tickets in advance (877-98-PARKS).

83 Hagley Museum and Library

ONTACT www.hagley.org; 200 Hagley Rd., Wilmington

PRICING	$$–$$$
BEST TIME TO VISIT	Year-round
AGE RANGE	7 and older

Eleuthère Irénée du Pont (1771–1834), a French immigrant who came to the United States in 1799, founded the well-known E. I. du Pont de Nemours, a modern-day chemical company originally begun in 1802 as a gunpowder mill. Throughout the more than 200 years of its history, the company has been responsible for developing such recognizable materials as nylon, Kevlar, Teflon, and neoprene. As a result of this enormous success in American industry, the du Pont descendants were some of the richest and most influential American citizens in the 19th and 20th centuries.

The Hagley Museum is the site of the gunpowder works and the original du Pont home, and it's a wonderful place to learn about early American life and industry. The museum is spread across more than 200 acres along the Brandywine River, and in addition to the gunpowder works and the home the property in-

Cape Henlopen Courtesy Delaware Tourism

Hagley Museum and Library   Courtesy Delaware Tourism

cludes a restored mill, a barn (look for the 1911 electric car housed here), a restored office building, and a workers' community.

Start your visit with a tour of the Georgian-style home, called Eleutherian Mills, which is filled to the brim with antique furnishings and the memorabilia of the five generations of du Ponts who passed through here. Then head to the Hagley Powder Yard, which includes a picturesque waterwheel that was the source of the energy used to run the machines, a working machine shop full of period equipment, storehouses, and enormous stone mills.

The museum has a number of wonderful programs for kids, where children make their own paper decorations and enjoy treats and story time; a Valentine's Day event where kids and parents can craft their own greeting cards and then write verses on them with a quill pen; and a spectacular fireworks show held over two nights in June.

84 John Dickinson Plantation

CONTACT 302-739-3277, http://history.delaware.gov/museums/jdp/visitors.shtml; 340 Kitts Hummock Rd., Dover

PRICING	$
BEST TIME TO VISIT	Year-round (open Wednesday–Saturday)
AGE RANGE	7 and older

Few Americans of any era can boast credentials like those belonging to John Dickinson (1732–1808): This Founder served as a militia officer in the American Revolution; was a Continental Congressman from both Delaware and Pennsylvania; acted as a delegate to the 1787 Constitutional Convention; was one of the wealthiest people in the British colonies; and authored the influential *Letters from a Farmer in Pennsylvania* (a collection of essays against the Townshend Acts), which earned him the nickname "Penman of the Revolution." The John Dickinson Plantation preserves his childhood home, built in 1740, and comprises a beautiful brick mansion, reconstructed outbuildings, a log dwelling, and acres of farmland.

Visitors can tour the home, called Poplar Hall, and see the elegant yet simple period furnishings. Costumed reenactors throughout the plantation lead tours that allow guests to experience what life must have been like for the many people who called the plantation home in the late 1700s—the privileged Dickinson family, poor white tenants, slaves, and free black residents. Children will especially enjoy demonstrations that they may be called on to participate in, like grinding spices for a cook preparing a holiday feast for the wealthy plantation owners, stoking the fires for a blacksmith fashioning farming implements, or dipping candles to light the mansion.

John Dickinson Plantation   Courtesy Delaware Tourism

85 Nemours Mansion and Gardens

CONTACT 302-651-6912, www.nemoursmansion.org; DE 141 and Alapocas Rd., Wilmington

PRICING	$$$
BEST TIME TO VISIT	May through December (closed the rest of the year)
AGE RANGE	7 and older

Alfred I. du Pont (1864–1935), the great-grandson of the founder of the E. I. du Pont Gunpowder works (which was eventually to transform into one of the largest and most successful chemical companies in the world), was an industrialist and philanthropist, renowned for being a man of the people despite his fabulous wealth and power. Over the course of his career he developed more than 200 patents, and as a result of his forward thinking is credited with bringing the du Pont company into the 20th century.

Alfred built the magnificent 300-acre estate he called Nemours for his second wife, Alicia. The five-story, 77-room, 47,000-square-foot palace was meant to be a "modern Versailles" and a love letter to Alicia—who eventually left him, regardless. Guests today can tour the stunning structure, which is grandly decorated with enormous chandeliers, museum-quality oil paintings, gilded furniture, and Persian rugs: This lovely mansion is the very picture of opulence. The grounds are no less impressive. A section called the Long Walk features a 1-acre pool with jets that shoot water 12 feet into the air; the Sunken Gardens are built from Italian

Nemours Mansion and Gardens   Courtesy Delaware Tourism

travertine, accented with statuary carved in Carrara marble—all adornments to a spectacular family pool; and the Four Borders comprises 8,500 square feet of annuals and perennials, cleverly encapsulated within mixed herbaceous borders. When visiting, do not miss seeing the stunning *Achievement*, a 23-karat-gold-leafed sculpture that overlooks a maze garden.

86 Rehoboth Beach

CONTACT www.rehoboth.com; off DE 1, Rehoboth Beach

PRICING	Varies by attraction
BEST TIME TO VISIT	Late spring through fall
AGE RANGE	All ages

Rehoboth Beach is the kind of all-American, family-friendly beach that parents dream about: The ocean is sparkling and the sand is soft; the mile-long boardwalk offers strolling and biking opportunities along the coast; and there are plenty of wholesome activities to keep kids and their adults entertained, even on rainy days.

Perhaps the best part of the resort is that it feels vintage, thanks to Victorian architecture and the old-timey wooden boardwalk. But this historic feel isn't re-created: A good percentage of the businesses, be they hotels, restaurants, or amusement sites, have been on this boardwalk for decades. The oceanside Funland Amusement Park (http://funlandrehoboth.orbs.com) has been family owned for more than 50 years, and the colorful (and noisy!) attraction is a perennial kid pleaser, offering an extensive arcade with pinball and video games; more than a dozen midway games; an electronic shooting gallery; and rides like boats, a carousel, a tot slide, bumper cars, and the ever-popular Haunted Mansion. Many of the rides are appropriate for toddlers, but there are a

Bikes are allowed on the Rehoboth boardwalk only from 5 to 10 am during the peak tourist season, running from May 15 through September 15.

Early morning on Rehoboth Beach   Courtesy Jon Preimesberger

Winterthur Museum   Photo Jeannette Lindvig, courtesy Winterthur Museum

handful of thrillers that will please tweens and teens, too. The park is open Mother's Day through Labor Day, and the attractions are pay-as-you-go—so you can stop in for an hour or make a day of it when the beach weather isn't prime.

Another longtime boardwalk resident, Dolles Saltwater Taffy opened its doors in 1926, and the distinctive white-and-blue building and the bright red sign are icons at the beach. In addition to purchasing peanut brittle, caramel corn, and some of the best saltwater taffy on the eastern seaboard, you can have fun watching the on-site old-fashioned taffy machine at work, pulling the original confection recipe.

The aquatic wildlife just offshore has also been a longtime attraction: It's nearly impossible to visit the area and *not* see dolphins. In late spring through summertime, look for the playful animals just off the coastline; they generally travel in groups of a dozen or more. It's also possible you'll spot a humpback whale; the Delaware Bay is rich in marine life, so whales can be seen throughout the year feeding (more so from March through December).

87 Winterthur Museum

CONTACT www.winterthur.org; 5105 Kennett Pike, Winterthur

PRICING	$–$$$
BEST TIME TO VISIT	Spring and summer (for the gardens)
AGE RANGE	7 and older

Another fabulous mansion once belonging to the influential du Pont family, Winterthur (pronounced *winter tour*) also offers one of the most important collections of American decorative arts in the world. The museum was created by Henry Francis du Pont (1880–1969), an avid collector and gardener, who opened his childhood home and the surrounding 1,000 acres of grounds for visitors to enjoy.

The glorious 175-room mansion is filled to the brim with more than 90,000 decorative objects made or used in America between 1640 and 1860. The collection includes glass, furniture, paintings, textiles, ceramics, and fine metalwork. The equally impressive on-site library comprises more than 100,000 books, including some 20,000 rare imprints, focusing on decorative American objects and life in America from the 17th through the early 20th centuries.

The crowning jewels of the property are the astonishing grounds. The mansion is surrounded by naturalistic woodlands and meadows, plus an additional 60 acres of highly manicured gardens. The stunning gardens are shockingly colorful and offer something of interest nearly year-round. Look for a profusion of fragrant lilacs in the Sundial Garden in late April; an explosion of pink, red, magenta, purple, and white from azaleas and dogwoods in the Azalea Woods in early to mid-May; delicate primroses and hearty orange daylilies in the woodlands in July; crepe myrtles and begonias surrounding the Reflecting Pool in September; and glorious autumnal colors throughout the property in late October.

Destin Beach   Courtesy Emerald Coast Convention and Visitors Bureau

FLORIDA

88 Biscayne National Park

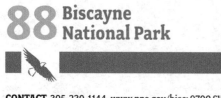

CONTACT 305-230-1144, www.nps.gov/bisc; 9700 SW 328 St., Homestead

PRICING	$
BEST TIME TO VISIT	Year-round
AGE RANGE	10 and older

Biscayne Bay, within the Biscayne National Park, offers arguably the best snorkeling in the continental United States and some of the most beautiful tropical water in the world. In the backyard of Miami, this spectacular and varied park preserves astonishing coral reefs, clear blue waters, and a collection of beautiful coral islands, known as keys. There are more than 500 species of fish in the park, along with dozens of species of coral, manatees, birds, and butterflies, making this one of the best places in America to spot wildlife.

More than 95 percent of the park is underwater. To see much of the park, then, you'll need a boat. There are no bridges or ferries to the keys, and there's only 1 mile of road traversing the entire park. If you don't have a boat of your own, or don't have enough boating experience to rent one, you can arrange a charter via a private concessioner (call 305-230-1100 for reservations). The concessioner can also provide snorkeling equipment and lessons. (For those who are unafraid of the water, snorkeling is really quite easy and something children 10 and older can pick up

Underwater world at Biscayne National Park
Courtesy National Park Service

almost immediately.) Other fun family outings in the park include glass-bottomed boat trips, canoe and kayak tours, and park ranger talks.

89 Castillo de San Marcos National Monument

CONTACT 904-829-6506, www.nps.gov/casa; 1 S. Castillo Dr., St. Augustine

PRICING	$–$$
BEST TIME TO VISIT	Year-round (weekdays are significantly less crowded)
AGE RANGE	7 and older

The Castillo de San Marcos is the oldest masonry fort in the United States and the only extant 17th-century fort in North America. The exceptionally beautiful star-shaped structure was constructed from a stone called coquina, a kind of limestone made up of fossilized shells—a material that proved to be ideal for deflecting attacks through time. Over 200 years, the fort flew six flags and served a surprising variety of roles.

The seaside settlement of what is now St. Augustine was founded by Spanish admiral Pedro Menéndez de Avilés in 1565 at the site of what was a Native American village. Before the Castillo de San Marcos (and its nine wooden sister forts) existed, St. Augustine was attacked in 1596 by Sir Francis Drake, an English navigator and explorer. Drake's fleet of 20 ships and 2,000 men burned down the town. A generation later, Robert Searles, an English pirate, launched an assault on the Spanish settlers; and it wasn't long before English colonization also threatened the settlement. What was then called the Presidio of San Augustin was important in Spanish trade (defending the primary trade route to Europe), and in response to the repeated onslaughts Queen Mariana of Spain ordered the construction of a stone fortification that would thwart all would-be conquerors. Construction of the fort lasted more than 20 years, and was completed in 1695; for generations the massive fort served its purpose for Spain. No invaders ever took the fort by force.

In 1763, however, through the Treaty of Paris that

Castillo de San Marcos   Courtesy National Park Service

90 Dry Tortugas National Park

CONTACT	www.nps.gov/drto; off Key West
PRICING	Park admission: $; Ferry ride: $$$$
BEST TIME TO VISIT	Mid-October through mid-January to see Bush Key; mid-October through mid-March to see Middle and East Keys; year-round for Loggerhead Key, Garden Key, and Fort Jefferson
AGE RANGE	7 and older

ended the Seven Years War, Britain gained possession of what is now the state of Florida, including St. Augustine. Not long after, with the start of the American Revolution, St. Augustine served as a British loyalist bastion. At this time the fort was improved, and for a period served as a military prison. In a treaty settlement after the Revolution, Spain once again regained control of St. Augustine and the fort, and held control of it from 1784 to 1821.

In mid-1821, Spain ceded control of Florida to the United States. On their assumption of power, the Americans immediately changed the name of the *castillo* to Fort Marion. The fort was modified during the American territorial period, and it was used first as a jail for rebellious local Seminole Natives, and later for Native Americans captured from the West as American pioneers pushed ever farther into Native lands. In 1845 Florida became a Union state—only to join the Confederacy in 1860 during the American Civil War. Union forces occupied Fort Marion in 1862, after the USS *Wabash*, a Union gunboat, claimed St. Augustine. During the Spanish American War in 1898, the fort was again used primarily as a prison, holding nearly 200 U.S. Army deserters. At the start of the 20th century, the fort was decommissioned.

Today the cannon-ball-scarred structure bears witness to its remarkable 300-plus-year history. The fort's original name has been restored, and now the monument comprises 20 acres, including a reconstructed section of the original city wall and the St. Augustine city gate. History comes alive at the *castillo* through historical reenactments, ranger talks, museum exhibits, and myriad seasonal events. Don't miss the regular (noisy!) weapons demonstrations at the *castillo*, when park employees fire off the cannons and demonstrate other weaponry of the day.

A visit to the Dry Tortugas is like a visit to an unspoiled Caribbean island: This national park about 70 miles west of Key West comprises 100 miles of mostly water, and includes seven small coral islands. The tiny islands are set amid crystal-clear aquamarine waters, and the area is renowned for its colorful coral reefs (there are 30 species of coral within the preserve) and diverse sea life. Added to the natural beauty are shipwrecks and legends of sunken treasure, which makes this a favorite diving and snorkeling destination. The park got its name from famed explorer Juan Ponce de León, who passed through the islands in 1513. Ponce de León was taken by the number of turtles on the island at the time (*tortugas* means "turtles" in Spanish). The islands are referred to as "dry" because there is no surface fresh water.

At the heart of the park, on Garden Key, is Fort Jefferson, the largest masonry fort in the Western Hemisphere. The fort was intended to protect the United States's gateway to the Gulf of Mexico. Plans for the site were under way for years, but its remote location caused delays in construction, and it wasn't begun until 1846—although it remains unfinished because engineers feared that additional bricks would

Fort Jefferson, and Garden Key on which it is located, offers no services. Bring all food, drinks, and all other supplies you will need. Plan to pack out your trash as well.

PRICE KEY	
$	free–$5
$$	$6–10
$$$	$11–20
$$$$	$21+

Fort Jefferson, Dry Tortugas National Park

Courtesy National Park Service

place undue stress on the structure and cistern system. The distinctive structure boasts 2,000 arches and decorative brickwork throughout. The fort was a military outpost, and also served for a few years as a remote federal prison, at one time housing Samuel Mudd, the doctor who treated John Wilkes Booth after he assassinated President Abraham Lincoln. Guided tours are offered at the fort daily.

To get to this remote park, you'll need to arrange passage on a ferry, charter boat, or seaplane. It takes about 45 minutes to fly or 2.5 hours to arrive by boat—and passage is pricey. If the cost and travel time dissuade you from making this merely a day trip, consider camping overnight. A 13-site *primitive* campground is available on Garden Key, a short walk from the public dock. Sites can accommodate up to six people and three tents, and are available on a first-come, first-served basis for $3 per person. (Note: There are no flush toilets on the island.)

91 Epcot

CONTACT	http://disneyworld.disney.go.com; Orlando
PRICING	$$$$
BEST TIME TO VISIT	February and March (to avoid crowds); spring and fall (for best weather)
AGE RANGE	3 and older

Whatever your age, whatever your interests, it's next to impossible to be anything but impressed with the magical, entertaining, family-friendly environment Walt Disney created when he envisioned Disney World. This resort is massive and comprises nearly 50 square miles of central Florida real estate, within which are four theme parks, two water parks, a bevy of lovely themed hotels, and a downtown shopping and entertainment district.

But nowhere is Disney's legacy as a visionary more evident than the park known as Epcot. *Epcot* is an acronym for "Experimental Prototype Community of Tomorrow," and this park was Walt's baby: He imagined it as a utopian, technologically advanced community where people would actually live and work. Disney passed away before the park opened, and in the interim the plans changed to refocus it instead as an educational center that highlights scientific progress as well as worldwide culture. These two rather disparate goals are served by two distinct regions within the park: Future World, which houses the best of the theme rides and futuristic exhibits; and the World Showcase, which encompasses clever and convincing reproductions of the culture, art, and architecture of nearly a dozen countries from around the globe.

Future World

• **Innoventions:** This attraction is actually a large collection of hands-on exhibits that include technology and consumer electronics, arcade-style games, and interactive experiences. It can be a fascinating place to spend the better part of a day.

• **Mission: SPACE:** Climb aboard a small spacecraft, train for your mission to the red planet, and sit back to enjoy what seems to a nonastronaut to be a very convincing re-creation of space travel—including g forces during liftoff. Note that the sensations of flight are produced by a high-speed spinning pod, which will likely bother people prone to motion sickness.

• **Spaceship Earth:** Dominating the landscape of Epcot, this massive geodesic dome houses a gentle ride that carries guests through Animatronic scenes showing humankind's technological and educational progress throughout recorded history. The conveyance snakes up and around the inside of the dome (and then backs down somewhat awkwardly). Hint: Visit this attraction late in the day. Because it's so close to the entrance of Epcot, it is almost always overcrowded in the morning.

- **Test Track:** This thrill ride simulates a high-speed test drive of a racecar prototype that is put through the paces of a brake test, sharp turns, and near-crashes. Test Track is one of the most popular rides in the park and is subject to extremely long lines. Try to arrive first thing in the morning to avoid the worst congestion.

World Showcase

The World Showcase portion of Epcot showcases 11 pavilions that represent countries from around the world, and it's possible to experience the culture of the represented countries in a surprisingly authentic way. The architecture of iconic structures is re-created (for instance, the Eiffel Tower in "France" and the Campanile from St. Mark's Square in "Italy"), and within each pavilion guests will find import shops that sell wares from the country represented, artisans from the country demonstrating their crafts, indigenous entertainers, and truly wonderful restaurants that represent the cuisine of the area. You'll also find special attractions throughout, like the popular Maelstrom, within the Norway pavilion, a thrill ride that carries guests down fjords in a traditional longboat; within the Mexico pavilion, the Gran Fiesta Tour Starring the Three Caballeros, a lazy boat ride showing iconic Mexican scenes; within the China pavilion, the *Reflections of China* circle-vision film that offers a jaw-dropping view of the scenery of China; within America the patriotic *American Adventure*, a screen

and animatronic look at the United States through the perspective of famous Americans like Benjamin Franklin and Mark Twain; within the France pavilion, the film *Impressions de France* is shown on multiple screens and highlights the country's gorgeous countryside and charming cities; and within the Canada pavilion, the circle-vision film *O Canada!* is shown on nine screens that surround viewers with the sights and sounds of the lovely country up north.

There is live entertainment throughout the World Showcase section of the park day and night. Look for a band that re-creates the Beatles in the England pavilion, belly dancers in the Morocco pavilion, an oompah band in the Germany pavilion, and taiko drummers in the Japanese pavilion. Don't miss the nightly IllumiNations, a spectacular fireworks, laser, light, water, and music show at the World Showcase Lagoon.

92 Everglades National Park

CONTACT Ernest Coe Visitor Center, 305-242-7700, www.nps.gov/ever; 40001 State Rd., Homestead (there are many other park entrances)

PRICING	$
BEST TIME TO VISIT	December through April (the "dry" season, when insects are less intrusive)
AGE RANGE	7 and older

The Everglades National Park—the largest subtropical wilderness in the United States—preserves one of the most unique ecosystems on the globe, and offers a glimpse into a world that seems almost prehistoric. The park comprises more than 2,300 square miles (that's 1.5 million acres), but this represents only the southern fifth of the Everglades ecosystem, which is home to myriad plants (most notably the ubiquitous mangrove trees that grow in and around the waterways) and animals.

Bird-watching is a favorite activity in the park, and their relative abundance makes it easy for children to spot colorful and interesting individuals. More than 350 bird species have been identified in

The Disney World Resort is wildly popular and crowded year-round. To avoid the worst of the congestion, plan your visit so that it doesn't coincide with traditional school holidays, such as spring break and summer (which is a hot and sticky time to visit central Florida, anyhow). Weekends and Mondays are the most crowded days, so a visit from Tuesday through Thursday will mean shorter lines. Don't be tempted to sleep in: The first few hours in Epcot are vastly less crowded than later hours.

You might be surprised to learn that perhaps the most troublesome animal to humans in the Everglades is the vulture, a protected species that is drawn to rubber on vehicles, including tires and windshield wipers; vultures have been known to do surprising harm to these car parts. To minimize the chances of your vehicle being mistaken for a vulture snack, park in the full sun (where vultures are less inclined to congregate) and if possible cover rubber with tarps or wet towels. If you do find a vulture gnawing on your auto, do not attempt to harm the bird. Instead, make loud noises to shoo it away—or notify a park ranger.

the Everglades, including the ubiquitous white ibis, the diminutive ruby-throated hummingbird, the exotic yellow-billed cuckoo, the regal great horned owl, and the stunning greater flamingo. There are also more than 40 species of mammals in the park, most notably marsh rabbits, white-tailed deer, river otters, raccoons, and possums. The stars of the Everglades, however, are the reptiles: There are more than 50 kinds of reptiles in the park, including myriad snakes and lizards, several species of geckos, and dozens of species of turtles (including four endangered species). In addition to native species, there are many accidentally introduced invasive species of reptiles, such as the Burmese python, which threatens native species (and because of its large size, can be startling to witness in the wild).

The Everglades are famous for even larger reptilian residents, of course: the alligators and crocodiles that call this vast watershed home. Male American alligators can grow 15 feet long, and sighting one—

whether along an established land trail or via a boat or canoe—is an experience your family will not soon forget. Alligators are considered keystone species in the Everglades—meaning they are so important to the maintenance of the ecosystem that their loss would threaten the existence of many other species. Loss of habitat and hunting of these animals led to their listing as endangered species in 1967—but thankfully, prohibitions against poaching have allowed their numbers to rebound, and in 1987 they were removed from the endangered list. Crocodiles also live in the Everglades, and although they resemble alligators, you can tell them apart if you remember that their snouts are narrower; also, when its jaws are shut, a crocodile's fourth tooth on the lower jaw is visible.

There are several ways to get out into the park and see the wildlife and enjoy this unique preserve. Ranger-led activities include guided canoe tours, birding walks, car caravans, guided trail hikes, and "slough slogs" in which guests don waterproof boots and wade into the swamps. To really make the most of this "river of grass," take an airboat tour. These tours are available from park concessionaires, who are familiar with winding waterways and know the best places to find wildlife. Be aware: These exhilarating boat trips are noisy. Guests are provided headphones, but the sound might still be too intense for young children. Note also that the boats get close to some pretty scary-looking critters: The captains take every safety precaution, but if someone in your family is squeamish (or has an undue fear of reptiles), you might want to skip this experience.

93 Hemingway Home

CONTACT 305-294-1575, www.hemingwayhome.com; 907 Whitehead St., Key West

PRICING	$$–$$$
BEST TIME TO VISIT	Year-round
AGE RANGE	10 and older

Ernest Hemingway (1899–1961) was an American author and journalist who is often credited with rein-

Airboat in Everglades National Park   Courtesy Visit Florida

Polydactyl cats at Hemingway Home   Courtesy Visit Florida

Hemingway fans will also want to check out the Ernest Hemingway Memorial in Ketchum, Idaho. The author is buried at this site, and the nearby Ketchum/Sun Valley Heritage and Ski Museum offers a nice exhibit of photos and memorabilia from his days in Idaho.

venting the American novel genre with his lean style and disciplined narratives. In addition to writing classics like *The Sun Also Rises*, *The Old Man and the Sea*, and *For Whom the Bell Tolls*, "Papa" Hemingway is remembered for his adventurous life as a onetime war correspondent, his well-chronicled stint in Paris as an expatriate (with other literary luminaries like F. Scott Fitzgerald, Gertrude Stein, and Ezra Pound), his obsession with bullfighting, his African safaris, and his fascination with deep-sea fishing. Hemingway suffered the physical effects of years of alcoholism and from depression throughout his later years; he committed suicide in Ketchum, Idaho.

Nowhere is Hemingway's bigger-than-life personality evident more than at the Hemingway Home in Key West, where he lived with his second wife, Pauline, for 10 years. This restored home and museum is worth a visit even for children who haven't yet read his enduring works. The beautiful Spanish colonial house with wraparound porches upstairs and down is filled with antiques Hemingway and his wife collected, as well as artwork, original manuscripts, and first editions of his books. The structure is surrounded by serene tropical gardens. Kids who like animals will enjoy the many pets on property. Roaming the grounds are approximately 50 polydactyl cats.

These cats have six toes (cats generally have five front toes and four back toes). Many people in the area believe that during his lifetime Hemingway was given a polydactyl cat (he named it Snowball), and many of these cats are believed to be its descendants. (This is a fun story, but it is somewhat suspect: The author's son Patrick, who lived in the home, claims his father never had a cat in Key West.)

A highlight of the home tour is the sparkling inground swimming pool, which cost $20,000 to construct in 1938—quite a staggering luxury at the time. Hemingway is said to have complained to Pauline that construction of the pool was so expensive, she might as well take his last penny—and legend has it that with that harangue he tossed a penny onto the partially built pool patio. Guests with keen eyes will notice that there is a penny embedded in the concrete at the north end of the pool, supposedly to memorialize Hemingway's (somewhat comical) outburst. Overlooking the pool is the small workroom where the author penned *A Farewell to Arms* and the critically acclaimed short story "The Snows of Kilimanjaro."

94 Kennedy Space Center

CONTACT 866-737-5235, www.kennedyspacecenter.com; west of I-405, between Range Rd. and East Ave. SW, Cape Canaveral

PRICING	$$$$
BEST TIME TO VISIT	Year-round
AGE RANGE	3 and older

The John F. Kennedy Space Center has been the launch site for every U.S. manned space flight since

Launch at Kennedy Space Center   Courtesy NASA

insight into America's dedication to space exploration through the years. Hands down the most exciting attraction is the brilliant Shuttle Launch Experience, in which guests climb aboard a motion simulator ride that combines video and mild motion, giving visitors a real taste of what it must be like to blast off. Also on site are two large IMAX theaters, where movies about spaceflight surround guests via a five-story screen and 3-D effects; the films feature footage captured by NASA astronauts. The Apollo/Saturn V Center in the complex displays a real *Saturn V* rocket, plus numerous artifacts that tell the story of landing the first man on the moon; explore Atlas, Titan, and Redstone rockets like the ones that took the first astronauts into space; and then climb aboard Gemini and Mercury capsules to see the tiny quarters astronauts must endure. The Apollo Treasures Gallery exhibits equipment, uniforms, and other related items from Apollo moon missions.

Step outside to check out the dramatic Rocket Garden, a collection of NASA rockets that are displayed like sculpture (and are lighted patriotically in the evening). Also available for tour is the LC 39 Observation Gantry, a 60-foot-tall launch tower that allows for spectacular views of two shuttle launch pads. And kids 48 inches or less will not want to miss the Children's Play Dome, which offers youngsters the opportunity to crawl through rocket tunnels, climb a simulated moon rock wall, and step into miniature spacecraft.

If you're able, plan your visit to coincide with a rocket launch; tickets for viewing are additional, but witnessing a spacecraft blasting off into space is sure to be a lifelong memory for every family member.

1968. The NASA installation was created at a time when this country was in a fierce "race to space" competition with the Soviet Union, during the height of the Cold War. The facility was first commissioned under President Dwight D. Eisenhower in 1958. In recognition of his commitment to the U.S. space program, the center was renamed after President Kennedy, shortly after his assassination.

A visit to the center includes a 2.5-hour bus tour of the facility, which offers behind-the-scenes peeks at assembly stations and launch pads. Although much of the facility remains off limits to the public, the phenomenal Space Center Visitor Complex is a treasure trove of sights and activities that provide additional

Admission tickets to the visitor complex at the Kennedy Space Center include a second day free (if used within 7 days) that can be used at the nearby U.S. Astronaut Hall of Fame, which offers a collection of astronaut memorabilia, tributes to the astronauts, and the *Sigma 7* Mercury spacecraft.

95 Pelican Island National Wildlife Refuge

CONTACT www.fws.gov/pelicanisland; off A1A, south of Sebastian Inlet and north of Vero Beach

PRICING	$
BEST TIME TO VISIT	Late November through late July
AGE RANGE	5 and older

Pelican Island National Wildlife Refuge

Courtesy U.S. Fish and Wildlife Service

By the start of the 20th century, the Victorian-era craze of using exotic bird feathers to adorn ladies' hats had contributed to the near-obliteration of the extensive shorebird population on Pelican Island, which had been an important rookery for hundreds of years previously. At the urging of naturalist Paul Kroegel, President Theodore Roosevelt set aside the island as the first American wilderness preserve, to protect the breeding grounds of native birds like egrets and brown pelicans.

This small refuge today includes a 3-acre island and another 2 acres of surrounding water. The islands support 15 threatened and endangered species, including sea turtles, West Indian manatees, and two species of wood storks. Birders can also expect to see great blue herons, American white ibises, cormorants, snowy egrets, and American oystercatchers. The island is viewable by boat (either personal watercraft or via boat, canoe, or kayak tours).

96 Zora Neale Hurston Dust Tracks Heritage Trail

CONTACT	http://zorafest.org; St. Lucie County
PRICING	$
BEST TIME TO VISIT	Year-round
AGE RANGE	10 and older

Zora Neale Hurston (1891–1960) was a noted scholar and African American writer of the Harlem Renaissance period; eminent black American authors such as Toni Morrison, Alice Walker, and Ralph Ellison credit her as one of their most powerful influences. She's best remembered as the author of the 1937 novel *Their Eyes Were Watching God*. Her legacy is memorialized along the Zora Neale Hurston Dust Tracks Heritage Trail, which includes eight historical markers along a 3.6-mile trail that highlights the life of this remarkable author. Included along the trail is the Zora Neale Hurston House, where she lived for a time; the Lincoln Park Academy, a onetime segregated school where she taught; and the headquarters of the former *Fort Pierce Chronicle*, an African American publication for which Hurston wrote.

Zora Neale Hurston home

Courtesy Visit Florida

georgia

97 Andersonville National Historic Site

CONTACT 229-924-0343, www.nps.gov/ande; 496 Cemetery Rd., Andersonville

PRICING	$
BEST TIME TO VISIT	Year-round
AGE RANGE	12 and older

Visiting Andersonville National Historic Site, and the infamous Camp Sumpter prison it encompasses, is a reminder that war is a brutal, inhumane experience—and never more so in the United States than during the war that pitted brothers against brothers. This isn't an easy place to witness at any age; be prepared to answer tough questions that children inevitably will have about this black spot on the U.S. history books.

The original site at Andersonville was constructed as a stockade about 18 months before the end of the U.S. Civil War; it was built to hold Union prisoners captured by Confederate soldiers. The 25-acre facility was meant to house no more than 10,000 captives, but at its most crowded it held more than 30,000. These overcrowded conditions—and blatant disregard for the captives—bred horrific conditions. Most men held here were starving, infested with vermin, and suffering from overexposure to the elements and rampant infectious diseases. Of the nearly 45,000 prisoners who passed through this hellhole, more than 12,500 died (only to be buried in mass graves just beyond the prison walls). Indeed, many of the Confederate captors fared badly, too: Most were undernourished, and all suffered from unsanitary conditions.

The Andersonville National Cemetery that grew up alongside the prison holds the remains of nearly 14,000 Union troops who died in battle, in hospitals as a result of battle wounds, or from the intolerable conditions of prison camps both at Camp Sumpter and throughout the region. It remains a working cemetery. Visitors to the National Historic Site can tour the prison site, the adjacent cemetery, and the National Prisoner of War Museum, the latter of which was opened in the late 20th century as a memorial to

Andersonville National Historic Site   Courtesy National Park Service

U.S. prisoners throughout the country's history. The museum shows two films, one of which explains the Civil War history of Andersonville and another that focuses on the experiences of prisoners of war. Look for artifacts that tell the story of individual captives of Camp Sumpter, including some of the earliest photographs that chronicle the unfathomable brutality of life at this site.

98 Archibald Smith Plantation Home

CONTACT 770-641-3978, www.archibaldsmithplantation.org; 950 Forrest St., Roswell

PRICING	$$$
BEST TIME TO VISIT	Year-round
AGE RANGE	7 and older

There's really no better way to step back in time to experience the culture and mores of a bygone era than to visit house museums like the Archibald Smith Plantation Home, which perfectly encapsulates the gracious living enjoyed by well-to-do southerners during the 19th century. The home was owned for more than 150 years by the same family, the Smiths. Archibald Smith, his wife and children, and 30 slaves came to the area in 1838 to start a cotton farm. The lovely house and grounds survived the Civil War, and was occupied by the family until 1981. What is truly remarkable about this historic home is how well preserved are the Smiths's belongings, everything from

Savannah carriage tour   Courtesy Savannah Area Chamber of Commerce

PRICE KEY
$ free–$5
$$ $6–10
$$$ $11–20
$$$$ $21+

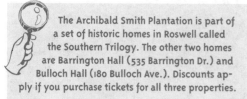

The Archibald Smith Plantation is part of a set of historic homes in Roswell called the Southern Trilogy. The other two homes are Barrington Hall (535 Barrington Dr.) and Bulloch Hall (180 Bulloch Ave.). Discounts apply if you purchase tickets for all three properties.

interior furnishings like an exquisite piano and several lovely bedroom sets, to cook pots and wooden spoons, to books and personal papers. The Smiths seemed to save everything: Even broken items were preserved here. When visiting, be sure to encourage children to contrast the genteel lifestyle of the wealthy property owner's home with the slave quarters housed in outbuildings. Also on site are a cookhouse, barn, carriage house, and springhouse.

99 Centennial Olympic Park

CONTACT 404-223-4412, www.centennialpark.com; 265 Park Ave. West NW, Atlanta

PRICING	$
BEST TIME TO VISIT	April through September
AGE RANGE	All ages

As early as the 8th century BC, ancient Greeks held regular athletic competitions in Olympia, Greece, when the fittest young men in the region showcased their physical skills. This practice was resurrected in the late 19th century by Pierre de Coubertin, who founded the International Olympic Committee. The Olympic Games are held every two years, alternating between winter sports and summer sports. The Games are an international sporting event, and one of the world's most prestigious competitions. Countries vie for the opportunity to host the Games, which bring with them hundreds of millions of dollars' worth of tourism and thousands of jobs to the locality to create the infrastructure that includes the athletic venues and the housing necessary for athletes, journalists, and spectators. The United States hosted the

Summer Olympics in 1996, in Atlanta, and the Centennial Olympic Park was at the heart of the ceremonies that mark this event.

The park was converted for public use after the Games were over, and today Centennial Olympic Park is a center for public festivals and point of pride in the downtown community. The focal point of the park is the Fountain of Rings, a series of water fountains in the shape of the Olympic symbol. The fountains are a great place for kids to play when it's hot (and Atlanta is known for its oh-so-hot summers). In addition, four times a day the fountains are the site of a water, music, and light show; the waterworks are timed to different tunes, like "Dancin' in the Streets" and the *1812 Overture*.

The park is also site to numerous free concerts, such as Music @ Noon, a midday concert held in the park's amphitheater every Tuesday and Thursday from April through October; and the Wednesday WindDown, another free concert held every Wednesday evening from April through September.

If you're in the area over the winter holidays, check out the Centennial Olympic Park's annual Holiday in Lights display, in which the park is transformed with thousands of lights. While you're here, don your skates at the park's outdoor ice-skating rink, the only outdoor rink in Atlanta.

100 Chickamauga and Chattanooga National Military Park

CONTACT 706-866-9241, www.nps.gov/chch; 3370 LaFayette Rd., Fort Oglethorpe

PRICING	$
BEST TIME TO VISIT	Year-round
AGE RANGE	7 and older

The Battle of Chickamauga (September 1863), named after the nearby West Chickamauga Creek, was a bloody Civil War conflict between Union forces led by

Chickamauga and Chattanooga National Military Park
Courtesy National Park Service

Major General William Rosecrans and Confederate forces led by General Braxton Bragg. Both sides wanted control over the region, because of the strategic importance of nearby Chattanooga. The battle ended in a Union defeat and was responsible for the second largest number of casualties in the war (behind only the Battle of Gettysburg); it was the last major Confederate victory of the war.

The Chickamauga and Chattanooga National Military Park—the first military park in the United States—commemorates this battle. Begin a visit here by checking out the visitor center, which houses several exhibits on the Civil War and offers an orientation film on the eponymous battle. The 5,000-acre park includes the hallowed Chickamauga Battlefield, which is most easily toured via a 7-mile automobile

route that is marked throughout by monuments, trails, and wayside exhibits. Use the "Dial and Discover" cell phone tour available in the confines of the park to further illuminate the scene.

101 Civil War Exhibit at the Atlanta History Center

CONTACT 404-814-4000, www.atlantahistorycenter.com/cms/Turning+Point%3A+ The+American+Civil+War/104.html; 130 West Paces Ferry Rd. NW, Atlanta

PRICING	$$$
BEST TIME TO VISIT	Year-round
AGE RANGE	7 and older

It's difficult to visit Atlanta without thinking of the Civil War: This southern city was the site of an infamous Union invasion and the subsequent burning of a majority of the city. The "War Between the States" was arguably the most important, most defining war in U.S. history—and it came at a staggering price: More than 3 million Americans participated, and from 1861 through 1865 more than 600,000 died (2 percent of the population at the time). The war ended slavery, all but ended the southern plantations the in-

Civil War Exhibit at the Atlanta History Center
Courtesy Atlanta History Center

> The Atlanta History Center comprises several other museums and historical sites, including the Swan House (see the description below), the Smith Family Farm, the Margaret Mitchell House (also below), six magnificent gardens, and the Kenan Research Center. There are money-saving bundle tickets available if you have time to visit several sites.

Etawoh Mounds   Courtesy Georgia Department of Natural Resources

stitution supported, and paved the way for modern industry and government.

Given the city's connection to this acrimonious war, it is fitting that it is home to one of largest, most comprehensive museum exhibitions on the Civil War. Turning Point: The American Civil War gallery is part of the large Atlanta History Center, a collection of museums, historic gardens, and historic homes (some of which are discussed elsewhere in this book). The exhibit displays more than 1,500 artifacts from both the Union and Confederate armies. Here you can see the flag that flew over Atlanta at the time of its surrender, original firearms used by the troops, uniforms, medical equipment used in the field, and photographs of the men who fought and often died to preserve their ideal America. Children will find numerous interactive exhibits, which include video stations and dioramas that will bring to life the history of this painful chapter in U.S. history.

102 Etawoh Mounds

CONTACT 707-387-3747, www.gastateparks.org/Etowah Mounds; 813 Indian Mounds Rd., SW, Cartersville

PRICING	$
BEST TIME TO VISIT	Year-round
AGE RANGE	7 and older

This site was once home to several thousand members of the Mississippian culture, a mound-building Native American civilization that was prevalent throughout the Southeast in the 9th through 16th centuries. The Etowah Mounds historic site (occupied

from about 1000 through 1500) preserves six distinctive earthen mounds built by the Mississippian people, as well as a defensive ditch (much like a moat) and a central plaza. It is the most intact Mississippian site in the region, and artifacts excavated here (and housed in an on-site museum) indicate that this was once a religious and political center. Other artifacts on display from the site include copper tools, brightly colored cloth woven with intricate patterns, sophisticated weapons, and numerous clay statues. It is intriguing to note that only 9 percent of the archaeological site has yet been excavated.

The largest mound on the site, a 63-foot earthen plateau, is believed to have been a platform for the home of the chief or a priest. Also on the site is a burial mound where important members of the clan were laid to rest in elaborate clothing and jewelry, accompanied by tools and weapons (should they need such items in the afterlife). The mounds were originally erroneously attributed to the Cherokee people until it was discovered that this Native group did not occupy the region until the late 18th century and thus could not have been responsible for the site.

In recent years, with the help of Native Americans from the area and numerous community volunteers, the Etowah staff fabricated a wattle-and-daub (cane and mud) house using an original floor plan from about 1250. The structure is quite elegant, and guests can come inside to see how members of the Mississippian culture might have lived when Etowah Mounds was an active community.

103 Fort Pulaski National Monument

CONTACT 912-786-5787, www.nps.gov/fopu; off Hwy. 80E, Cockspur Island

PRICING	$
BEST TIME TO VISIT	Year-round
AGE RANGE	7 and older

Although Fort Pulaski is most associated with the Civil War, it was actually built in reaction to the War of 1812, and was meant to serve as a coastline fortification against invading European forces. Robert E. Lee, straight out of West Point at the time, helped choose the location and designed the dike system to help control the tides and to facilitate drainage. The massive (and actually quite beautiful) structure was built with more than 20 million bricks, and construction lasted from 1829 to 1860. Walls are 11 feet thick, and at the time of construction were believed to be impenetrable. Despite its original intent, the fort did serve a pivotal role during the War Between the States, and in 1862 it was surrendered to the Union army, to prevent continued bloodshed that resulted from a massive onslaught. Visitors today can see cannonballs still embedded in the exterior walls.

The national monument incorporates most of Cockspur Island, including the fort and the adjacent McQueens Island. Begin your trip at the visitor center to view *The Battle for Fort Pulaski*, a 17-minute film

Fort Pulaski National Monument   Courtesy National Park Service

> Keep an eye out on Cockspur Island for alligators, which are native to coastal Georgia. They are partial to Fort Pulaski's moat and surrounding grassy areas. Keep a safe distance, and *never* feed alligators.

that explains the history of the fort's construction and the battle for its control during the Civil War. From there, explore the fort itself. There are a few reconstructed barracks to view, and the interior gives a sense of the massive undertaking that must have been necessary to build this large masonry structure. Scattered throughout the property are historic weapons that helped preserve the fort over its long history. There are several scenic hikes on the property, including the Lighthouse Overlook Trail that winds along a marsh and offers spectacular views of nearby Tybee Island. This trail also offers the best vantage point of the historic Cockspur Island Lighthouse. Another trail carries hikers past the historic dike system designed by Lee.

Children will not want to miss the fort's daily interpretive and living history programs, which include cannon and musket demonstrations and regular drills conducted by costumed interpreters. These demonstrations can be noisy, so beware if your kids are frightened by loud sounds.

104 Jimmy Carter Library and Museum

CONTACT 404-865-7131, www.jimmycarterlibrary.gov; 441 Freedom Parkway, Atlanta

PRICING	$–$$
BEST TIME TO VISIT	Year-round
AGE RANGE	7 and older

James Earl Carter Jr. (better known as Jimmy, b. 1924) was the 39th president of the United States, from 1977 to 1981. He was virtually unknown before receiving the nomination from the Democratic party, and became infamous for his previous experience as a peanut farmer (although he also served as governor of Georgia). He defeated Republican opponent Gerald Ford, the incumbent president who had assumed office after President Richard Nixon resigned in disgrace. During his one-term presidency, Carter brokered the Camp David Accords, the significant peace treaty between Israel and Egypt, and the SALT II treaty (an armament agreement) with the Soviet Union. He was defeated in his bid for a second term by Republican Ronald Reagan.

After Carter's presidency ended, he became a prolific author, publishing dozens of books on policy, history, and even a children's book and a collection of original poetry. He founded the Carter Center, a non-profit organization that champions peace, world health, and free elections throughout the globe; he is a volunteer and spokesperson for Habitat for Humanity (an organization that builds homes for low-income individuals); and in 2002 was recognized for his humanitarian efforts with the Nobel Peace Prize.

The Jimmy Carter Library and Museum includes a collection of Carter's papers (a reported 27 million pages' worth, plus 500,000 photos, not to mention films, videos, and audiotapes), as well as interesting and interactive exhibits focusing on the life of the president and his family. Start your visit with the informative orientation film, and then be sure to check out the eclectic collection of head of state gifts on display. Children will enjoy the re-creation of the Oval Office during Carter's administration (a well-done replica you can walk through). On most Mondays, the museum hosts a Book Nook event for preschoolers, when library staff read from storybooks about leadership, the presidency, famous Americans, and so on. And to work out the wiggles from story time, after-

Margaret Mitchell museum   Courtesy Atlanta History Museum

ward the kids are taken on a "garden safari" in the beautifully landscaped grounds.

105 Margaret Mitchell Museum

CONTACT	900 Peachtree St. NE, Atlanta
PRICING	$$–$$$
BEST TIME TO VISIT	Year-round
AGE RANGE	14 and older

Margaret Mitchell (1900–49) was the author of *Gone with the Wind*, one of the most beloved and best-selling novels of all time. The epic tale is a love story set in the South during the Civil War, and has sold more than 30 million copies around the world. In 1939 the long novel was translated into a major Hollywood movie of the same name, starring Clark Gable and Vivien Leigh. The movie version won 10 Academy Awards (a record total for many years) and remains one of the best-known American movie classics of all time.

The Margaret Mitchell House, which is part of the greater Atlanta History Center, preserves the apartment where she and her husband lived while she wrote her famous book. Although Mitchell nicknamed the apartment "The Dump," the restored space is quite beautiful, with classic architectural details and colorful period furniture. Look for her original typewriter on display, as well as personal mementos, an exhibit focusing on Mitchell's life, and an exhibit focusing on the big-screen adaptation of her greatest work. The Literary Center hosts regular programs at the museum throughout the year, including creative writing classes for children and adults.

If your children haven't read *Gone with the Wind* (some of the subject matter of which is a little racy for kids younger than 14) or seen the movie, they likely won't appreciate Mitchell's contributions to American culture. When they are old enough, do them a favor and encourage them to read the book first, then see the movie.

106 Martin Luther King Jr. National Historic Site

On Tuesday and Thursday mornings at 10, the MLK site presents a puppet show for young children that focuses on either Dr. King's life, the achievements of African Americans throughout the nation's history, or the Sweet Auburn neighborhood where Dr. King grew up.

CONTACT 404-331-5190, www.nps.gov/malu; various sites around Atlanta

PRICING	$
BEST TIME TO VISIT	Year-round
AGE RANGE	5 and older

Martin Luther King Jr. (1929–68) is revered around the world for his work furthering civil rights, and Atlanta proudly claims him as its native son. Dr. King modeled his campaign for social justice on the tenets of Christianity and the nonviolent example of the Indian activist Mahatma Gandhi. In 1957 King was elected to lead the Southern Christian Leadership Conference, a group dedicated to promoting the civil rights movement in the South. He worked tirelessly to promote the cause, traveling during his tenure more than 6 million miles to more than 2,500 speaking engagements. He is especially remembered for leading a protest against racial segregation in Birmingham, Alabama; his massive efforts to register black voters; and the largest-ever march on Washington, DC, at the time (1963)—a peaceful demonstration in which he delivered the inspiring "I Have a Dream" speech. He was awarded the Nobel Peace Prize at age 35—and donated the substantial cash that went along with it to support civil rights causes. Tragically, in 1968, on the eve of a protest march in sympathy with striking workers in Memphis, Tennessee, he was assassinated.

The Martin Luther King Jr. National Historic Site memorializes Dr. King's considerable contributions to America and preserves important sites in the neighborhood in which he lived and worked. The site comprises an interesting visitor center containing a museum that explains the American civil rights movement; a firehouse in the Sweet Auburn community that offers an exhibit on desegregation in the Atlanta Fire Department; the home where Dr. King was born; and the Ebenezer Baptist Church, where he and his father served as pastors. Plan ahead if you want to see the inside of the Birth Home, which can only be visited with a ranger-led tour. Register early in the day for these first-come, first-served tickets (free, but limited in number) at the Freedom Hall at The King Center. While at the center, check out rotating exhibits that highlight Dr. King's legacy.

Martin Luther King Jr. National Historic Site
Courtesy National Park Service

107 New Echota Historic Site

CONTACT 706-629-8151; 1211 Chatsworth Hwy. NE, Calhoun

PRICING	$
BEST TIME TO VISIT	Year-round
AGE RANGE	7 and older

In 1825 the Cherokee nation established a capital they called New Echota, just outside of present-day Calhoun. The site was home to the first Indian-language newspaper and an example of the earliest self-government among Native Americans. This planned community was designed by Cherokee surveyors and comprised a 2-acre town square and government buildings including the Cherokee Council House and

Print shop at New Echota Historic Site
Courtesy Georgia Department of Natural Resources

the Supreme Court; there were also private homes and a printing office. Sadly, it was here where the infamous "Trail of Tears" began. In 1838 a Cherokee removal fort called Fort Wool was built in the middle of New Echota; federal military and state law enforcement rounded up the Native Americans at gunpoint, and they were counted and "processed" before starting the long forced march to Indian Territory (now Oklahoma).

To memorialize the legacy of the Cherokee people who suffered and died, the township has been preserved as a state historic site. It includes 12 original and reconstructed buildings that offer a glimpse into what was once a thriving Native American settlement. Visitors can tour the Council House, the court, the print shop, a home once belonging to a missionary, and outbuildings like barns and smokehouses. Be sure to take the 1-mile nature trail that leads you to New Town Creek and a picturesque beaver pond.

108 Ocmulgee National Monument

CONTACT 478-752-8257, www.nps.gov/ocmu; 1207 Emory Hwy., Macon

PRICING	$
BEST TIME TO VISIT	Year-round
AGE RANGE	7 and older

The Ocmulgee National Monument is one of the most important archaeological and anthropological sites in North America. Evidence has been recovered from this site indicating that there has been continuous human habitation in the region for more than 17,000 years. The monument is a memorial to the people who lived in the Southeast over the millennia. The park includes 700 acres, including a visitor center and museum, earthen mounds constructed in about AD 900 by members of the Mississippian culture, a reconstructed ceremonial earth lodge built to mimic a 1,000-year-old excavated structure, earthenworks trenches, and a burial mound.

If your schedule allows, plan your visit around the annual Indian Celebration, held in mid-September. This annual festival is the largest gathering of Native Americans in the Southeast, and includes music, dancing, storytelling, living history demonstrations, and Native foods. (There is a small fee for admission.)

109 Pebble Hill Plantation

CONTACT 229-226-2344, www.pebblehill.com; 1251 U.S. Hwy. 319 S, Thomasville

PRICING	$–$$
BEST TIME TO VISIT	Early spring, when azaleas are in bloom
AGE RANGE	7 and older

Southern charm doesn't *begin* to describe the magnificent 3,000 acres and opulent structures that make up Pebble Hill Plantation, which dates to 1825. The original plantation grounds were converted in the late 1800s to a winter home for a wealthy family from Cleveland, Ohio, who made sure to gather every creature comfort for themselves and their guests. Come here to get a peek into the lives of southern aristocracy in the 19th and 20th centuries. The Main House of today, a Georgian beauty, dates to the early 1930s. You can tour the Main House, which is furnished with hunting art, Audubon prints, and priceless antiques. Visitors can also stroll a small chunk of the grounds (almost 80 acres are open to the public) to see impec-

👆 Children must be 6 years or older to enter the Main House at Pebble Hill. If you visit with younger kids, purchase the less-expensive ticket that affords access to the extensive gardens—which are apt to be more interesting to preschoolers, anyhow.

cably maintained gardens brimming with magnolias, camellias, crepe myrtle, showy azaleas, and an entertaining hedge maze. Kids will not want to miss the Noah's Ark building, near the pond. The ark-shaped structure was actually built as a bathhouse; inside is a mural depicting a collection of animals, each paired and each shown with the sort of food appropriate to that species. Also fun for children is the Log Cabin School, dating to 1901; this onetime schoolroom for the children of the plantation owners is filled with toys from the era. And for animal lovers, check out the Stable Complex, which houses a dozen friendly horses and mules that are available for petting.

110 Roosevelt's "Little White House"

🔔

CONTACT 706-655-5870, www.gastateparks.org/Little WhiteHouse; 401 Little White House Rd., Warm Springs

PRICING	$$
BEST TIME TO VISIT	Year-round
AGE RANGE	7 and older

Franklin D. Roosevelt (1882–1945) served as America's 32nd president, and he was the only chief executive to be elected to more than two terms. His first term in office began in 1933, during one of the most uncertain economic periods in U.S. history: the Great Depression. In his first 100 days in office, Roosevelt was responsible for legislation that created the New Deal, a wide-ranging series of programs designed to relieve the oppressive financial conditions of many Americans. Two major surviving institutions from this period are the Federal Deposit Insurance Corporation, which oversees banks, and the Social Security program. After the Japanese attack on Pearl Harbor

on December 7, 1941, Roosevelt entered the United States into World War II. He helped formulate the Allied strategy that eventually ended the war.

What many people don't know today—and almost no one knew during his administration—was that Roosevelt was disabled from a bout of polio that struck when he was in his late 30s. For several years after his illness, Roosevelt was paralyzed completely from his waist down. A few years after his affliction struck, a friend told FDR the story of a polio victim's recovery after swimming in the therapeutic waters at Warm Springs. Roosevelt hoped the waters would work similar miracles on him, and visited in late 1924 to bathe there. He immediately began to feel better, and for the first time in three years he was able to move his right leg. Although Warm Springs never cured FDR completely, he did gain physical and spiritual strength when visiting, and decided to buy the resort property encompassing the springs. He kept a small home on site and returned regularly, even during World War II. As the war was waning, however, Roosevelt's health began to fail again, and in 1945, while visiting Warm Springs, he died of a cerebral hemorrhage.

Visitors to the site—now a state park—can tour the grounds, see the small house FDR used when in Warm Springs, and view the therapeutic pools (which are open a very few times a year to the public, who can purchase tickets to swim here). This park is the site of several seasonal events, such as FDR Look-Alike Contests, holiday storytelling, and an Easter egg hunt for children.

Roosevelt's "Little White House"

Courtesy Georgia Department of Natural Resources

111 Swan House

CONTACT 404-814-4000, www.atlantahistorycenter.com; 130 W. Paces Rd., Atlanta

PRICING	$$–$$$
BEST TIME TO VISIT	Year-round
AGE RANGE	7 and older

This beloved Atlanta landmark is a stunning 1928 mansion designed by famed architect Philip Trammell Shutze. It was built for Edward H. Inman, heir to an enormous cotton fortune, and today offers a look into the lifestyle of the rich and famous in the early 20th century. Guests can take guided or audio self-guided tours of the jaw-dropping Second Renaissance Revival–style home, which is equally impressive inside and out. Explore the meticulously restored rooms, including the library, foyer, living and dining rooms, an impressive butler's pantry, and several opulent bedrooms and bathrooms. Step outside to see the lovely grounds, which include several perfectly maintained gardens and beautiful water fountains. There is plenty of lawn space here for kids to run off excess

Swan House　　　　　Courtesy Atlanta History Center

energy; in fact, if the mansion tours are booked for the day (the tickets are limited and sell out quickly during busy seasons), consider simply walking around the grounds. Hint: Ask your kids to look throughout the property and inside the house for the swan motifs after which the mansion was named.

112 World of Coca-Cola

CONTACT 404-676-5151, www.worldofcoca-cola.com; 121 Baker St., Atlanta

PRICING	$$$
BEST TIME TO VISIT	Year-round
AGE RANGE	All ages

The World of Coca-Cola is a museum dedicated to all things associated with the eponymous sugary drinks. Visitors to this colorful, entertaining new venue (relocated from a downtown site in 2007) will be treated to displays of Coca-Cola artifacts, exhibits focusing on the history of the wildly successful company, a working bottling line, a well-done six-minute animated feature on the product, a 4-D film chronicling the formation of the "secret formula," and a theater that shows Coke commercials from throughout the years. Children will most enjoy the *Taste It!* exhibit, where you can try a selection of beverages chosen from more than 60 Coca-Cola products sold around the world. Kids will be surprised at how different Coke formulations sold in, say, Japan, Zimbabwe, Chile, and Peru taste. You are welcome to sample all you like (a pleasant treat on a hot Atlanta summer day), and kids will enjoy mixing the formulas to come up with their own concoctions. The attraction is unabashedly commercial, offering a fun insight into an influential American product that is known across the globe. Don't miss the souvenir at the end of the tour: an 8-ounce bottle of Coca-Cola with a label and cap indicating that it was bottled on location.

Hawaiian island　Photo Tor Johnson, courtesy Hawaii Tourism Authority

Hawaii

113 Bernice Pauahi Bishop Museum

CONTACT 808-847-3511, www.bishopmuseum.org; 1525 Bernice St., Honolulu, Oahu

PRICING	$$$
BEST TIME TO VISIT	Year-round (closed Tuesday)
AGE RANGE	7 and older

Even if your family is not generally enamored with museums, do not miss this one: The stately, soaring main gallery, known as Hawaiian Hall, is worth the price of admission. Step into the impressive space and look up to see a life-sized model of a 55-foot sperm whale suspended overhead. This is the largest museum in Hawaii and offers the most extensive collection of Polynesian artifacts in the world. The museum was originally founded to showcase the collection of Hawaiian antiques, arts, and crafts owned by Princess Bernice Pauahi Bishop, a direct descendant of King Kamehameha I. It now also includes more than 6 million zo-ology specimens, 500 botany specimens, 13 million insects, and half a million cultural objects that represent both Hawaiian and other Polynesian cultures. Kids will not want to miss the interactive exhibits at the Science Adventure Center. Especially popular is the lava-making demonstration, where spectators have the opportunity to learn about volcanoes by witnessing rock and cinder melted to create lava.

114 Byodo-In

CONTACT 809-239-8811, www.byodo-in.com; 47-200 Kahekili Hwy., Kaneohe, Oahu

PRICING	$
BEST TIME TO VISIT	Year-round
AGE RANGE	All ages

Set in a contemplative, serene memorial park known as the Valley of the Temples, the astonishingly beautiful Byodo-In is a nearly perfect (but smaller-scale) replica of a 950-year-old temple of the same name in Uji, Japan. This replica temple was built in the 1960s to mark the 100-year anniversary of the first Japanese immigrants to Hawaii. In 1868, a group of 100-plus Japanese laborers arrived on the islands to work the sugarcane and pineapple fields. Although early immigrants from Asia were not always welcomed in Hawaii—for example, the "Bayonet Constitution of 1887" denied Hawaiian citizenship to any Asian—by 1902 there were more than 30,000 Japanese workers employed by plantations in Hawaii. Japanese culture continues to be a

Bishop Museum   Photo Tor Johnson, courtesy Hawaii Tourism Authority

Byodo-In   Photo Chuck Painter, courtesy Hawaii Tourism Authority significant influence through the Hawaiian islands, as this temple attests. Be sure to step inside the temple to see a 9-foot Lotus Buddha. Kids will want to roam the grounds to see the resident peacocks and the 10,000 gold koi that live in the on-site ponds.

115 Captain Cook Monument

CONTACT	Off Kealakekau Bay, Kona, Big Island
PRICING	$
BEST TIME TO VISIT	Year-round
AGE RANGE	7 and older

James Cook (1728–79) was a British explorer who conducted several expeditions throughout the world. On his last voyage, he left England in 1776 in search of a northwest passage to Asia across North America. After sailing to New Zealand, the Cook Islands, and Tonga, he landed in Hawaii on January 20, 1778, near the Waimea River on the southwestern coast of Kauai. Cook was the first known European to have set foot in Hawaii. He was killed in 1779 in Kealakekua Bay, on the Big Island, when he tried to kidnap a local chief as an inducement to Natives to return a stolen sailboat. At the foot of the bay where he was killed, the Captain Cook Monument marks the spot with a striking white obelisk. You can view the monument aboard a boat, or hike there via a 3-mile trail.

116 Diamond Head Volcano

CONTACT	
www.hawaiistateparks.org/parks/oahu/index.cfm?park_id=15; end of Waikiki Beach, Honolulu, Oahu	
PRICING	$
BEST TIME TO VISIT	Year-round
AGE RANGE	All ages

Waikiki Beach, with Diamond Head in the background   Photo Joe Solem, courtesy Hawaii Tourism Authority

One of the most photographed sites on the islands, Diamond Head crater is all that remains of a long-extinct volcano. The current glitzy name comes from calcite crystals (pretty but without value), which from a distance glittered like diamonds to 19th-century English sailors who visited the area. The Native Hawaiian name for the crater is Leahi, which means "brow of the tuna"—thanks to the crater's characteristic side profile. The nearly perfect bowl shape of the crater was formed about 300,000 years ago during one frightful (albeit brief) explosion. Geologists do not believe the volcano will ever erupt again. Today the iconic crater towers over the popular Waikiki Beach, reminding visitors of a series of volcanic eruptions that created many other geological landmarks on the island of Oahu, including Hanauma Bay, Koko Head, and Punchbowl Crater.

Visitors can climb the 760-foot summit to enjoy some of the most spectacular views on the island—both overlooking Waikiki and peeking into the belly of the volcano. The 1-mile hike along a paved surface is moderately strenuous, gaining more than 500 feet in elevation, and the latter portion of the trail includes stairs. It's necessary to pass through a 200-foot tunnel to reach the top. The trek is well worth the effort—but come early, to avoid the heat of the midday sun (there is no shade along the way) and to enjoy the greatest visibility. Look for Fort Ruger, a reminder of the crater's strategic location as a military outpost in the early 20th century. If you're visiting in the late fall and winter, Diamond Head summit is a great vantage point to spot the migrating humpback whales in the waters beyond that come to the island to mate.

PRICE KEY	
$	free–$5
$$	$6–10
$$$	$11–20
$$$$	$21+

117 Dole Pineapple Plantation

CONTACT 808-621-8408, www.dole-plantation.com; 64-1550 Kamehameha Hwy., Wahiawa, Oahu

PRICING	$–$$
BEST TIME TO VISIT	Year-round
AGE RANGE	All ages

The history of Hawaii is intertwined with two agricultural industries: sugarcane and pineapple. Spanish horticulturist Francisco de Paula Marín, a friend of King Kamehameha I, cultivated pineapples in the early 1800s—and some historians believe pineapples may have been grown on the islands even as early as the late 16th century. John Kidwell is the generally acknowledged founder of the pineapple industry in Hawaii; in 1885 he planted his first crops and found that they flourished in the volcanic soil, bright sun, and humid conditions. Later, James Drummond Dole got into the pineapple game with 60 acres of crops

Native pineapple   Photo Joe Solem, courtesy Hawaii Tourism Authority

planted in 1900. A year later, Dole officially started the Hawaiian Pineapple Company and began growing commercial crops in earnest. By the middle of the 20th century, there were eight pineapple companies on the islands, and Hawaii was the pineapple capital of the world. The more than 3,000 individuals employed in the industry at the time were responsible for 80 percent of the world's supply. At this time pineapples were the state's second largest industry (following sugarcane). In recent decades, however, the rising costs of labor in the United States, and soaring real estate and fuel prices in Hawaii, have significantly reduced the islands' influence in the pineapple market. (Top producers of the fruit today include Brazil, the Philippines, and Thailand.)

Come to the Dole Pineapple Plantation in central Oahu to get a glimpse of the crop that is synonymous with Hawaii. Check out the expansive fields of the truly beautiful pineapple plant, a bromeliad with a sculptural shape that is fascinating even without fruit. Kids will want to climb aboard the Pineapple Express, a small steam train that circles the complex; the short trip is narrated with a history of the pineapple plantation. Also fun is the world's largest maze here—3 acres of labyrinth created from more than 14,000 native Hawaiian plants: An aerial view of the maze reveals a pretty pineapple shape in the middle. Finally, don't miss the chance to sample the fruit: Unless you're from Hawaii, it is likely to be far superior to the pineapple you can purchase at home.

118 Haleakala National Park

CONTACT 800-572-4400, www.nps.gov/hale; off Hwy. 378, Mount Haleakala, Maui

PRICING	$
BEST TIME TO VISIT	Year-round
AGE RANGE	7 and older

There are few places on the globe that aren't reminiscent of others, but Haleakala is a notable exception: This is a landscape wholly unique. The vibrant colors, the fast-shifting cloudscape, and the sense of tran-

Haleakala National Park

Courtesy National Park Service

quility are almost otherworldly. Haleakala means "house of the sun" in Hawaiian. Legend has it that the demigod Maui stole the sun and held it captive at this site to make the day longer. Anyone who has ever gotten up early to see the awe-inspiring sunrises or equally transfiguring sunsets from the summit here will understand why even a mythical demigod would want just a little more time in this special place.

Haleakala National Park is divided into two quite different segments: the lush coastal Kipahulu region and the summit. The summit region boasts Maui's highest peak, at more than 10,000 feet above sea level, a remnant of the dormant volcano that shares the same name. The volcano erupted last around AD 1400, and the stark landscape still bears the scars. The Haleakala crater is nearly 7 miles across and nearly 3,000 feet deep. There are several trails that circle the rim of the crater and lead into the depths. There's no better way to get a good look at the geological formations called cinders than to take one of these unforgettable, strenuous hikes. But if you're not up for it—the sun is intense here, and the high altitude makes exercise even more challenging—you can drive to the top and enjoy the vistas along the way. The steep summit road, with its numerous switchbacks, climbs 10,000 feet in less than 38 miles.

The Kipahulu region is 12 miles past the quaint town of Hana, and a drive here gives you the chance

> The temperatures at the summit at Haleakala can be as much as 30 degrees cooler than at sea level. Be sure to bring a light jacket. Because the sun is particularly strong at high altitudes, you'll want to wear sunscreen and a hat as well.

to experience the infamous Hana Highway, surely one of the most scenic drives in the country. The coastal section of Kipahulu is easy to reach, and shows off the lush forests, sparkling streams, and stunning waterfalls Hawaii is known for. Be sure to hike to Waimoku Falls—one of the prettiest areas in the park. Kids will want to wear their bathing suits, to enjoy cooling off at the numerous shallow natural pools that can be found throughout this section of the park.

119 Hanauma Bay Nature Preserve

CONTACT 808-396-4229; 7455 Kalaniana'ole Hwy., Honolulu, Oahu

PRICING	$; additional fee for parking (Hawaiian residents gain free admission)
BEST TIME TO VISIT	Year-round; closed Tuesday
AGE RANGE	10 and older

Hanauma Bay presents a double whammy for nature lovers: This gently curved cove is a breathtaking masterpiece of blue water, white sand, and tropical vegetation, as well as a sanctuary for astonishing and unusual ocean life. Snorkelers will not want to miss a chance to swim alongside the surprisingly tame fish that not only tolerate humans but seem to enjoy them, gliding up curiously like friendly puppies. The bay was designated a marine life conservation area and underwater park nearly 50 years ago, and because no fishing is allowed here, the local wildlife have no learned fear of humans. Because of the high concentration of sea life, and because the water is shallow and relatively calm, this is a great place for beginning snorkelers—although more advanced snorkelers and even divers will also enjoy the expansive coral reef, especially in the areas where it extends into deeper water. The depth of water over the shallow coral ranges anywhere from 3 to 15 feet—so there is a lot to see from the surface. And even if you aren't up for donning a mask, you can enjoy the pretty beach and see a few large fish without even putting your face in the water: Just wade out and look down!

Hanauma Bay Nature Preserve

Photo Heather Titus, courtesy Hawaii Tourism Authority

Be sure to arrive early: The parking lot fills up quickly—once it's full, you'll be turned away—and the lines can be long at the ticket booth and snorkel rental concession. A decade ago Hanauma Bay was a victim of its own popularity, and the small beach and bay were regularly overrun with as many as 10,000 guests a day—many of whom did harm to the natural environment. Today visitors are limited to about 3,000 a day, and before you enjoy the bay you must watch a short video in the Marine Education Center on site to learn the rules. The biggest takeaway lesson: Make sure you never walk on or touch the fragile coral reef. Also note that although feeding the fish was once allowed, it is now illegal to bring any food into the water with you, for any purpose.

Once in the water here, guests are treated to some of the most beautiful, unusual, and colorful ocean creatures in the world. Snorkelers can expect to see a wide variety of coral and fish—there are more than 400 species inhabiting the bay—including the distinctive parrot fish, butterfly fish, tang, humu-huma (also known as triggerfish), surgeonfish, crabs, anemones, starfish, and "big eyes." This a great place to spot green sea turtles as well. Also at home in these waters are several varieties of moray eels—large, snake-like animals with extremely sharp teeth. Eels generally hide out in crevices and holes, and they are

> You can bring your own snorkeling equipment or rent gear at the park. To keep your mask from fogging up, spit into it and rub the spit around on the inside of the lens. A tiny bit of smeared toothpaste will also do the trick.

so well disguised you might not even notice them. They won't attack humans unless threatened, so avoid poking your fingers or toes into any covered spots. One more creature to watch out for is the stinging box jellyfish; these are sometimes in the vicinity. Check with lifeguards before diving in to see if jellyfish have been spotted recently.

120 Hawaii's Plantation Village

CONTACT 808-677-1100, www.hawaiiplantation village.org; 94-695 Waipahu St., Waipahu, Oahu

PRICING	$–$$
BEST TIME TO VISIT	Year-round; closed Sunday
AGE RANGE	7 and older

The sugarcane industry dominated the Hawaiian economy during the plantation era, which ran roughly from the mid-19th to the mid-20th century, and the thousands of men and women who toiled in the sugarcane fields made an indelible mark on the cultural makeup of the islands. In 1897 the Oahu Sugar Company located its mill in Waipahu, and the company shipped in workers from around the world to staff it. Few Native Hawaiians worked in the sugar plantations; laborers generally came from China, Japan, Korea, the Philippines, and Portugal, with the majority of the early workers being either Chinese or Japanese. Because of language barriers, each ethnic group was housed in separate living accommodations (called camps) on the

Hawaii's Plantation Village   Courtesy Hawaii Tourism Japan

plantations. During the height of the plantation era, more than 400,000 individuals migrated to the islands to work the sugarcane fields. Hawaii's Plantation Village is a living museum that memorializes the lives of these workers. Take an hour-long guided tour to see the re-created village—which includes 30 reproductions and restored plantation buildings like camp houses, a plantation store, religious temples, and a sumo-wrestling ring—and to hear the stories of the individuals who once called the plantation home.

121 Hawaii Volcanoes National Park

CONTACT 808-985-6000, www.nps.gov/havo; off Hwy. 11, 30 miles SW of Hilo, Big Island

PRICING	$
BEST TIME TO VISIT	Year-round
AGE RANGE	5 and older

Hawaiians have long looked at volcanoes as holy. According to ancient Hawaiian belief, Pele is the goddess of fire and volcanoes—and she is variously depicted as a beautiful young woman or a haggard old lady. Regardless of form, Pele and her volcanoes are considered sacred—and it is believed to be supremely bad luck to remove lava from the island because of this. Local post offices report that hundreds of lava rocks are returned anonymously every year by hapless tourists who picked up a souvenir while in Hawaii only to regret it later. It is no wonder volcanoes are so revered and respected here: Volcanoes built Hawaii, and continue to add to its landmass.

Hawaii Volcanoes National Park sits on the southeastern edge of the youngest volcanic island in the Hawaiian Archipelago (the Big Island), and more than 350 square miles are set aside at this park to protect Kilauea and Mauna Loa, two of the most active volcanoes in the world, as well as the unique flora and fauna that have taken up residence on this relatively new land. Start your visit to the park at the Kilauea Visitor Center, which offers exhibits and films that will help you and your family understand the geology of the area. While here, check in with park rangers to

Lava flowing into the sea

Photo Peter Garzke, courtesy Hawaii Tourism Authority

find out about any road closures due to volcanic activity; the rangers will also be able to tell you where you might see active lava flow (from a safe distance). Don't miss the chance to explore the summit of the volcano along the Crater Rim Drive, an 11-mile road that circles the caldera summit. Depending on the geological activity during your visit, there may be opportunities to see active lava flows from this road. Take a break from the wheel and hike the short Devastation Trail, a walk amid blackened, otherworldly landscapes that will give you a chance to see hardened lava up close. When hiking this trail or any other in the park, for your own safety *be sure to stay on the pathway*. Access the Jaggar Museum dedicated to volcanology from Crater Rim Road; you can see seismographs and other equipment used by scientists to monitor the park's volcanoes. The overlook at the museum offers a particularly good view into the caldera of Kilauea. To see massive and dramatic steam vents rise from what is believed by some to be the home of Pele, check out the Halemaumau Crater. And if you aren't shy of close enclosed places, no visit to the park would be complete without a walk through the Thurston Lava Tube (also known as Nahuku). This 500-year-old lava cave

If anyone in your family has asthma or other breathing challenges, check the current air quality in advance of your visit at www.hawaiiso2network.com. Sulfur dioxide and particulate levels can be high any time of the year here—and when volcanoes are particularly active, the volcanic gases can be dangerous for even those without health problems.

formed when an underground channel of molten lava created a hollow chamber and then cooled and hardened. The pathway through the tube is lighted, but you will be able to see the geological formations better if you bring along a supplementary flashlight.

122 Iolani Palace

Iolani Palace   Photo Joe Solem, courtesy Hawaii Tourism Authority

CONTACT 808-522-0822, www.iolanipalace.org; 364 S. King St., Honolulu, Oahu

PRICING	$–$$
BEST TIME TO VISIT	Year-round; closed Sunday
AGE RANGE	7 and older

Iolani Place was built in the late 19th century by the last king of Hawaii, King David Kalakaua, and was also later occupied by his sister and successor, Queen Lili'uokalani. The name translates to "hawk of heaven." It is the only royal palace in the United States, and it's as opulent and grand as one could hope a king's residence would be. The exterior construction is singular: The large structure is dominated by French-style mansard roofs, Greek columns, Victorian gingerbread, and distinctly Hawaiian lanais (verandas). This was the first building in Honolulu to have a telephone system, and it was wired for electricity even before the White House.

The impeccably restored first and second floors of the palace are open to the public. Guests can take self-guided audio tours or docent-led guided tours. Highlights include the magnificent koa-wood staircase in the Grand Hall, the dramatic gold Throne Room, the State Dining Room, the Music Room, and the king's and queen's private suites. Kids will get a kick out of seeing the bathrooms—which are proof that royalty like to live large. The copper-lined tubs are almost 7 feet long. Don't miss the imprisonment room, where Queen Lili'uokalani was kept under

The grounds of the Iolani Place are free and open to the public to explore during business hours.

house arrest for several months following the overthrow of her government.

There are free concerts on site every Friday afternoon at noon, and on the second and fourth Saturday of each month artisans demonstrate the art of lauhala plaiting. Note that children under 5 are not allowed on the docent-led Grand Tour.

123 King Kamehameha Statue

CONTACT 957 Punchbowl St., Honolulu, Oahu

PRICING	$
BEST TIME TO VISIT	Year-round
AGE RANGE	All ages

It's impossible to really understand the history of Hawaii without first understanding the importance of King Kamehameha I (also known as King Kamehameha the Great), whose legendary rule is commemorated with stories that rival those from Greek mythology. It was prophesied that a sudden and startling light in the sky would mark the birth of a great chief. Kamehameha is believed to have been born in 1758—the year Halley's comet passed over the islands. He was raised to be a leader, and trained from an early age as a warrior. He assumed power as was predicted, and he went on to conquer the various chiefs ruling the islands, formally establishing the Kingdom of Hawaii in the early 19th century. Kamehameha ruled Hawaii in 1778 when Captain James Cook arrived on the islands.

King Kamehameha statue

Photo Tor Johnson, courtesy Hawaii Tourism Authority

124 Kona History Center Museum

CONTACT Kona Historical Society, www.konahistorical.org; H. N. Greenwell Store: off Mamalahoa Hwy., 14 miles south of Kealakekua; Living History Farm off Mamalahoa Hwy., 15.5 miles south of Kailua-Kona, Big Island

PRICING	$–$$
BEST TIME TO VISIT	Year-round; closed Friday through Sunday
AGE RANGE	7 and older

The Kona Historical Society operates two living history sites that allow visitors to get a glimpse of life in late-19th-century and early-20th-century Hawaii. The first site, adjacent to a visitor center, is the H. N. Greenwell Store Museum. Costumed interpreters will guide you through the 1890s-era re-created store that once belonged to Henry and Elizabeth Greenwell, who sold wares here during the height of Kona ranching. This sort of store served the multiethnic community that farmed the region, and carried myriad supplies, from coffee beans to salted salmon, from canned

Kamehameha was considered to be powerful both in mind and body: Legend has it that as a teenager he lifted a 5,000-pound stone—the only person to have ever accomplished this feat. (This stone, called the Naha Stone, is on display in front of the Hilo Public Library on the Big Island.)

This well-known statue of Kamehameha, dating to 1883 and fabricated in Italy, sits in front of the Ali'iolani Hale, onetime grand palace and now home to government offices, just across from the Iolani Palace. Interestingly, this is the second statue to have been cast: The first was lost at sea en route, and what stands here is a replica. This is a fun photo-op year-round, but come here on King Kamehameha Day (June 11) to see the bronze statue draped with colorful, oversized leis.

Although this statue in Oahu is the most famous depicting Kamehameha, there are two other well-known sculptures of the famous king in Hawaii: On the Big Island, in North Kohala (near Kamehameha's birthplace at Kappau), you can see the original statue that was lost at sea but later recovered. In Hilo, also on the Big Island, see a different statue at Wailoa State Park; this is the tallest of the statues, at 14 feet. All three are decorated on June 11 with a plethora of flowers.

Kona History Center Museum   Courtesy Hawaii's Big Island Visitor Bureau

goods to fresh fruit. Customers could also buy tobacco, fabrics by the yard, denim trousers, woolen long johns, and curative oils and salves meant to heal a multitude of ailments. Just outside the store is an authentic Portuguese stone oven, where traditional bread-baking demonstrations are held.

The second site, 1.5 miles south of the Greenwell Store, is the Kona Coffee Living History Farm, a 5.5-acre historic site that preserves the first homesteaded farm dating to 1900 and depicts the life of coffee pioneers during the years 1926–45. Visitors will learn about the early Japanese immigrants who came to the Hawaiian islands to work on plantations. Stroll the coffee and macadamia nut orchards, view on-site animals, and tour the historic farmhouse. Throughout the property costumed interpreters demonstrate traditional cooking and crafts and tell stories about everyday farm life.

125 Mookini Heiau State Monument

CONTACT 808-974-6200; off Hwy. 270, 1.5 miles southwest of the sign for Upolu Airport, North Kohala, Big Island

PRICING	$
BEST TIME TO VISIT	Year-round
AGE RANGE	12 and older

Although this historic site is isolated and difficult to reach (you'll need to hike in from the highway or take a four-wheel drive over a muddy, unpaved road), it is one of the most important ancient religious and cultural places in Hawaii. The *heiau* is a sacred place of worship and dates to about 480. Priests worshipped here for several hundred years, and laypeople were forbidden to enter the sacred grounds. About 500 years after the temple's founding, a Tahitian high priest known as Pa'ao arrived on the island and assumed control of the religious community living

> Because of its chilling past, and because it is still considered a sacred place, remind children to treat Mookini Heiau with reverence.

there. Pa'ao instituted the practice of human sacrifice, and visitors can still see the large, flat stone where many people lost their lives. Because of this dark past, I'd recommend leaving younger children at home for this excursion; even adults will likely find the scene haunting. Pa'ao expanded the *heiau* significantly during his reign. Legend has it that the stones to enlarge the temple were passed to the site from 15 miles away, hand-to-hand among 18,000 warriors, in one evening.

126 Pearl Harbor: USS *Arizona* Memorial

CONTACT 808-422-3300, www.nps.gov/valr; 1 Arizona Memorial Place, Honolulu, Oahu

PRICING	$
BEST TIME TO VISIT	Year-round
AGE RANGE	7 and older

The attack by Japanese forces on American military sites in Pearl Harbor on December 7, 1941, was a brutal surprise. Strikes from the Japanese Imperial air force came in two waves, with the first planes hitting their targets just before 8 in the morning and the second just before 9. Within hours, the Japanese planes had left Pearl Harbor, and Japanese aircraft carriers were already returning to Japan. In the wake of the sudden strikes, more than 2,400 Americans were dead, more than 1,200 were wounded, close to 200 planes were destroyed, and eight battleships were either damaged or destroyed completely. Among the dead were close to 1,200 men aboard the battleship USS *Arizona*. The ship suffered four direct hits from enormous bombs dropped by high-altitude warplanes. The last bomb struck the ship's turret and detonated its powder magazine, which caused a massive explosion. The ship in essence cracked in half, and it sank within minutes. However, despite the chaos and utter shock the attacks provoked in Pearl Harbor that day, the Pacific Fleet's submarines, aircraft carriers, and fuel storage facilities were left unharmed. The next day the United States and its closest ally Britain declared war on Japan. In response, Germany and Italy declared war on the U.S. a

USS Arizona *Memorial, Pearl Harbor* Courtesy National Park Service

few days later, and at that moment the European and Southeast Asian wars coalesced into a global conflict. This was America's entry into World War II.

The USS *Arizona* Memorial is a tribute to the many Americans who lost their lives on this "day of infamy." A 184-foot-long structure spans the width of the sunken battleship—which rests on silt in shallow water beneath. Within the memorial there are three areas to visit: an entry room, an assembly room, and the shrine room where the names of every person killed on the USS *Arizona* are engraved on a marble remembrance wall. This is a haunting place, and it is all the more disturbing to see the oil slicks on the water near the memorial—fuel from the sunken ship still periodically bubbles to the surface. Some visitors bring flowers or leis to toss into the water as a tribute.

The memorial is only accessible by boat. You must start your tour at the Pearl Harbor Visitor Center; first-come, first-served tickets are available in the Aloha Court (although they may also be reserved online; see the Insider Tip below). While shoreside, explore the exhibit galleries that tell the story of the attack on Pearl Harbor and its aftermath. Especially moving are the personal stories relayed by eyewitnesses, the recordings of which are preserved in video kiosks. Across from the exhibit galleries is the Pearl Harbor Memorial Theater, which shows a 20-minute documentary that explains the events of the 1941 attack. After viewing the film, guests will be taken immediately by navy shuttle to the site. You may view the memorial at your leisure and then return via another regularly scheduled shuttle. Note that this is an extremely popular site in Hawaii, and the wait for a program to begin can be several hours. You are well advised to arrive as early in the day as possible to avoid delays and the worst of the crowds here.

In 1999 the USS *Missouri* was moved to Pearl Harbor, and now is docked near the *Arizona* memorial. It was on the deck of the USS *Missouri* in September 1945 that the Japanese unconditionally surrendered to U.S. Admiral Chester Nimitz and General Douglas MacArthur, which ended World War II. The *Missouri* offers a number of information tours (purchased tickets required).

127 Polynesian Cultural Center

CONTACT 800-367-7060, www.polynesia.com; 55-370 Kamehameha Hwy., Laie, Oahu

PRICING	$$$$
BEST TIME TO VISIT	Year-round; closed Sunday
AGE RANGE	All ages

Mormon missionaries settled in Oahu in the late 19th century, and in 1919 the first Mormon temple was

Hula in the Hawaiian Village, Polynesian Cultural Center

Courtesy the Polynesian Cultural Center

> You may reserve tickets to tour the USS *Arizona* Memorial and the USS *Missouri* in advance online at www.recreation.gov (for a minimal reservation fee). Print your tickets at the Pearl Harbor Visitor Center at least one hour before the reserved program time. There are also a limited number of tickets available for walk-up visitors.

built on the site of what is now the Polynesian Cultural Center. In the mid-20th century, the church opened the Polynesian Cultural Center as a way to celebrate the Native culture throughout the region. Now the center is on the tourist agenda, and although it has the aura of a theme park, the chance to see and be a part of Native culture is both educational and fun.

The entertaining, immersive experience offers seven themed villages to tour, representing the cultures of Fiji, Hawaii, the Marquesas, New Zealand, Samoa, Tahiti, and Tonga. Each "village" offers its own unique attractions. Come to Samoa and learn how to crack open a coconut—and then try to climb a 50-foot coconut palm to pick your own. Check out the drumming demonstrations in Tongo. Tour a six-story Fijian temple. And don't miss the Hawaiian village to learn hula and sample poi. Throughout the day you can enjoy myriad live entertainment, including dance and music; Native arts and crafts demonstrations; a canoe pageant every afternoon; and plenty of Polynesian food to try. Guests are always encouraged to participate.

Come to the center in the evening from 5 to 7 for the "Dinner and Luau" experience. Although you'll find luaus offered by many of the larger hotels throughout the islands, this is one of the most authentic. You'll be greeted with a flower lei, and enjoy Polynesian entertainment that includes music and lots of dance. Feast on traditional luau foods like kalua pork (a pit-roasted whole pig), poi, mahimahi, fresh pineapple, and coconut cake. No alcoholic drinks are served, making this one of the most family-friendly luaus on the island as well.

To view more rock art, check out the nearby Kaupulehu Petroglyphs at the Kona Village Resort (808-325-555). Call ahead for tour reservations.

Ancient Hawaiians carved art into volcanic stone throughout the islands, leaving arresting images to decipher for those of us who came later. They called these petroglyphs *k'i'i' pohaku*, or pictures in stone. Although more than 3,000 distinct designs have been identified—including animals, family groups, dancers, and deity symbols—archaeologists are not sure of their exact meaning or purpose. You'll find the largest collection of petroglyphs on the islands at the Puako Petroglyph Archaeological Preserve, 230 acres just north of the Mauna Lani Resort. There are approximately 1,200 petroglyphs open for public viewing, and all are easily accessed via a 1.5-mile trail just north of the resort. Stop by the lobby of the hotel to pick up a brochure and map, or sign up for a guided tour conducted by a Hawaiian historian. Remind kids to stay on the pathway—walking on the petroglyphs is not allowed. While you're at the resort, check out the Kalahuippua'a Fish Ponds, another preserved historic site on the grounds where ancient Natives once built inland ponds to trap fish at high tide.

128 Puako Petroglyph Archaeological Preserve

CONTACT Holoholokai Beach Park, near Mauna Lani Resort, Kohala Coast, Big Island

PRICING	$
BEST TIME TO VISIT	Year-round
AGE RANGE	7 and older

Petroglyphs carved in hardened lava

Punalu'u Black Sand Beach   © Debbie K. Hardin

129 Punalu'u Black Sand Beach

CONTACT 808-961-8311; off HI 11, Naalehu, Big Island

PRICING	$
BEST TIME TO VISIT	Year-round
AGE RANGE	All ages

Thanks to frequent volcanic activity on the Big Island, beach sand here is not only white (and in some cases green): It is also black. This surprising black sand is composed of basalt created when lava flows into the ocean from nearby volcanoes (Hawaii Volcanoes National Park is 30 miles away). Punalu'u is the most accessible black-sand beach in Hawaii, and the coal-black sands are stunning. When you first approach, the sand looks like a smooth field of lava rock, but walk on it with bare feet and you'll find it is as soft and fine as any white-sand beach. The park is pretty—fringed with coconut palms and punctuated by volcanic formations at the sea edge. It isn't the best place for swimming, but it makes for a nice picnic spot. Beware: Removing black sand (or any form of volcanic lava) from the islands is considered very bad luck. (Clean out your sandy shoes *before* heading home!)

130 Pu'uhonua o Honaunau National Historic Park

CONTACT 808-328-8251, www.nps.gov/puho; off Hwy. 160, Honaunau, Big Island

PRICING	$
BEST TIME TO VISIT	Year-round
AGE RANGE	7 and older

Pu'uhonua means "place of refuge"; there were pu'uhonua on every Hawaiian island during ancient times, and these were the sanctuaries sought out by breakers of the *kapu*, or sacred laws. These were also popular safe houses for conscientious objectors, the elderly, and women and children during times of war. This 180-acre site is believed to date back as far as 1200. Pu'uhonua o Honaunau is beautifully restored, and includes a *heiau*, a sacred temple where rituals were performed to absolve *kapu*-breakers of their crimes, and a Royal Grounds—onetime home to the chiefdom of Kona—and a collection of *kii*, fierce wooden images of gods meant to watch over the sacred space. It's a great place to learn about the ancient Hawaiian history and lifestyle that is still a major influence on the vibrant Hawaiian culture of today.

Children will enjoy playing *konane*, a Hawaiian game that was once popular among both the royalty and commoners who lived here. There is a stone playing surface in the Royal Grounds, and there are

Totems at Pu'uhonua o Honaunau   Courtesy National Park Service

printed rules available at the visitor center. This is also a great place to see Hawaiian cultural demonstrations, which might include traditional fishing techniques, weaving, and wood carving. On the first Friday of every month, the park is the site of authentic hula performances. The Ki'ilae Village on site includes the remnants of temples, ancient fishing ponds, and stone walls. Kids will get a particular kick out of the *holua* slides that are still in evidence: Chiefs rode high-speed sleds down their steep slopes.

131 Pu'ukohola Heiau National Historic Site

CONTACT 808-882-7218, www.nps.gov/puhe; 62-3601 Kawaihae Rd., Kawaihae, Big Island

PRICING	$
BEST TIME TO VISIT	Year-round
AGE RANGE	7 and older

This National Historic Site preserves one of the largest *heiau* (sacred temples) on the islands, and its origin is the stuff of legends. The great King Kamehameha I—the uniter of the islands and the ruler responsible for

Pu'ukohola Heiau

Courtesy National Park Service

establishing the Kingdom of Hawaii in the early 19th century—was told by his priest to build the Pu'ukohola Heiau to honor the war god Kukailimoku, which would (according to the prophecy) solidify his efforts to conquer the chiefs who ruled the islands before Kamehameha's kingdom. The fortress-style temple was completed by 1791, and as predicted Kamehameha went on to unite the islands successfully.

Visitors here will see the 224-by-100-foot structure, which has been meticulously restored. It was built of stones and is completely without mortar. It is thought to be the last sacred structure built on the islands before Captain James Cook came to Hawaii. Pu'ukohola means "hill of the whale," perhaps so named because this point is one of the best viewing sites of humpback whales as they migrate along the Kohala Coast in winter.

132 Queen Emma Summer Palace

CONTACT 808-595-6291, www.queenemmasummer palace.org; 2913 Pali Hwy., Honolulu, Oahu

PRICING	$–$$
BEST TIME TO VISIT	Year-round
AGE RANGE	7 and older

This onetime summer home to King Kamehameha IV and Queen Emma is tucked into the Nuuanu Valley—

Queen Emma Summer Palace

Photo Tor Johnson, courtesy Hawaii Tourism Authority

now adjacent to a highway, so not quite the tranquil getaway it probably was during Queen Emma's rule. The relatively small cottage is decorated with period antiques—both Native pieces crafted of koa wood and imported Victorian pieces—Native artifacts, and a collection of china that was a gift from Queen Victoria. As with any house museum, the fun here is in seeing how the residents lived in their time. Don't miss the adorable canoe-shaped cradle that was once the bed of Prince Albert (who tragically died as a toddler). Also on display are various Hawaiian royal regalia, such as feather cloaks and *kahili*, the feathered standards that mark the presence of Hawaiian *alii* (royalty).

133 Surfing at Waikiki Beach

Surfing in Hawaii   Photo Kirk Lee Aeder, courtesy Hawaii Tourism Authority

CONTACT	Various vendors; Waikiki Beach, Oahu
PRICING	$$$$
BEST TIME TO VISIT	Year-round
AGE RANGE	10 and older

Surfers are believed to have ridden the waves in Hawaii as long ago as the 4th century. Migrating Polynesians from the Marquesas and Tahiti brought the custom of board riding on *paipo* (belly) boards to Hawaii with them. The Hawaiians later called surfing *hee nalu*, and it was soon a popular athletic outlet for men on the islands. According to ancient stories and songs that preserved the Hawaiian history before written language was introduced, the strict cultural rules in Hawaii demanded that commoners and royalty swim and surf in different areas. Royalty were said to ride boards as long as 24 feet, whereas commoners surfed at different beaches and rode boards as long as 12 feet. By the time Captain James Cook's ship arrived in the islands, making the first known contact between Westerners and the Native Hawaiians, Cook's lieutenants wrote about their amazement at seeing surfing for the first time.

Duke Paoa Kahanamoku (1890–1968) is credited with introducing the Hawaiian sport of surfing to the world. He was an Olympic swimmer, winning a gold and silver in the 1912 games, and thanks to his good looks and athletic skills, he eventually found his way to Hollywood, where he appeared in more than two dozen films. Because California's waves were also ripe for surfing, the sport soon spread to the western mainland. Today, it is impossible to arrive at *any* beach that allows surfing (in Hawaii or California) without seeing hundreds of surfers trying their luck. It is a tough sport, requiring agility and a fair bit of innate athletic skill—and it is addictive. Hawaii is one of the best places to watch surfing: Beaches like Sunset Beach on the North Shore and Waimea Bay in Oahu continue to attract the best wave riders in the world—but the surf in these locales is incredibly dangerous for all but experts.

If you're game to grab a board and try surfing, crowded Waikiki Beach offers gentler rolling waves that are more suited to beginners. Dozens of surf schools operate from this beach, including Dane Kealoha Surf Academy (808-373-0805), Hans Hedemann Surf School (808-924-7778), and the long-operating Waikiki Beach Boys (800-939-8323). Expect group lessons to run about $50–75 per hour and private lessons to run about $125 per hour.

Before you prepare to hang 10, make sure everyone in your party is a strong swimmer. To avoid skin irritation from the salt water, sand, and board wax, put on a rash guard before you hit the waves.

134 Wailua Falls

CONTACT	Off Ma'alo Rd., Lihu'e, Kauai
PRICING	$
BEST TIME TO VISIT	Year-round (most dramatic after a heavy rainfall)
AGE RANGE	All ages to view; 10 and older to hike to the foot

Wailua Falls   Photo Tor Johnson, courtesy Hawaii Tourism Authority

The islands are places of incredible, incomparable natural beauty, and there are countless white-sand beaches, protected coves with aquamarine waters, lush green valleys, stark volcanic fields, and dramatic cliffs to make visitors appreciate that Hawaii is one of the most beautiful states in America. Perhaps the most iconic site on the island of Kauai is the stunning 80-foot tiered waterfall known as Wailua. The water flow varies by season, but the double falls are re-splendent year-round. You can hike to the falls via a slippery (somewhat treacherous) trail to the bottom of the falls and swim in the pool below. The falls are close enough to a roadside lookout that you can see them without the risk. It's said that ancient Hawaiians would jump from the top of the falls to prove their strength and bravery; it should go without saying that any such attempts by today's visitors would surely be fatal. Fans of classic TV will remember these falls from the opening shots of *Fantasy Island*.

IDAHO

135 Basque Museum and Cultural Center

CONTACT 208-343-2671, www.basquemuseum.com/visit/history; 611 Grove St., Boise

PRICING	$
BEST TIME TO VISIT	Year-round
AGE RANGE	7 and older

When you think of Idaho, you may not think about a European influence, but in fact the state is home to one of the largest Basque populations outside of Spain. Basques are thought to be the longest-surviving ethnic group in Europe. Although they are associated with Spain, Basques have never had a country of their own. Instead, Basque country in Europe consists of seven provinces stretching from the border of France and Spain, along the Atlantic coast. The region in Europe is a little more than 8,000 square miles. Basques came to America as early as the 16th century,

The Basque Museum also operates the Cyrus Jacobs-Uberuaga Boarding House (607 Grove St.), the oldest surviving brick building in Boise, once used as a boardinghouse for Basque immigrants. Other Basque sites nearby are the Fronton Building (619 Grove St.), another boardinghouse, famous for its Basque handball court, and Gernika (202 S. Capitol), a Basque pub and eatery that dominates "Basque Block" in Boise.

but the first Basques in Idaho came in the late 19th century, arriving first as miners during the gold rush era and then for several decades afterward earning their living as sheepherders. The immigrant Basques had a profound effect on the growth of the sheep industry in this region into the early 20th century. Likewise, the high demand for herders and the availability of inexpensive land in Idaho at the time was a boon to Basque immigrants, many of whom came to the area because they could not make their living in the mountainous terrain in Basque provinces in Spain due to limited farming options.

The Basque Museum and Cultural Center is a small, yet growing, museum dedicated to preserving and promoting Basque history and culture. Museum collections include oral history archives, a library, photographs, and an eclectic display of artifacts. The museum is also the site of several cultural festivals throughout the year, including the feast day of Saint Ignatius of Loyola (patron saint of Basques and founder of the Jesuit religious order), held on the last weekend of July; and the Sheepherder's Ball, an annual dance in December.

Basque Museum and Cultural Center
Courtesy Boise Convention and Visitors Bureau

136 Cataldo Mission

CONTACT 208-682-3814; 31732 S. Mission Rd., Cataldo

PRICING	$
BEST TIME TO VISIT	Year-round
AGE RANGE	All ages

Cataldo Mission

Photo Peg Owens, courtesy Idaho Tourism

The Jesuit religious order in Idaho dates to 1842, when Father Peter DeSmet first surveyed the region. It is believed that the first Catholic services were held on the Spokane River, near present-day Coeur d'Alene. As part of their efforts to convert the Native Americans, the Jesuits erected the Cataldo Mission in northern Idaho, and employed Coeur d'Alene Indians to build it, because they believed the Natives would take ownership of the church if they had a major hand in its construction. First named the Mission of the Sacred Heart, the Cataldo Mission was begun in 1850, under the supervision of Missionary Father Ravalli, and is now the oldest standing building in Idaho. The walls are a foot thick and were created using the wattle-and-daub method. Not a single nail was used; rather, pegs and adobe mud secure the walls and ceilings. The interior shows ingenuity in decoration, with chandeliers fashioned from tin cans, wood altars faux-painted to look like marble, and fabric purchased from the Hudson Bay Trading Company decorating the walls. Throughout the years the mission served as a worship site for the Coeur d'Alene tribe, a supply center for the gold-rush-era mining industry, and later a stop for railroad and pipeline workers. The mission today is part of the Old Mission State Park, which also includes an 1887 parish house, two cemeteries, and a visitor center with exhibits on Native American culture from the region.

137 Craters of the Moon National Monument and Preserve

CONTACT	208-527-1300, www.nps.gov/crmo; off Hwy. 20, southwest of Arco
PRICING	$
BEST TIME TO VISIT	Spring through fall (when Loop Rd. is open)
AGE RANGE	7 and older

Craters of the Moon National Monument and Preserve protects more than 1,000 square miles of otherworldly landscape created by molten magma that has coated the region and left this bit of Idaho looking like it belongs in the wake of a volcano on the Big Island of Hawaii. The park includes 60 lava flows and 25 volcanic cones, and together the Craters of the Moon lava field is the largest in the contiguous 48 states. It's so big it can be seen from space! The geological oddities that make up the lava field fall along the Great Rift of Idaho, which offers some of the largest rift cracks in the entire world, including—at 800 feet—the deepest known rift in the world. There are several other geological oddities to be seen here, most easily accessible via park roads or trails. There are more than 300 caves to explore—those created from lava flows (these caves are known as lava tubes), fissure

Craters of the Moon National Monument and Preserve

Courtesy National Park Service

PRICE KEY
$ free—$5
$$ $6—10
$$$ $11—20
$$$$ $21+

caves, and caves created by wind and water. Look for the impressive Indian Tunnel, a lava tube cave that is accessible for 800 feet.

138 Land of Yankee Fork State Park

CONTACT 208-879-5244, http://parksandrecreation.idaho.gov/; 24424 Hwy. 75, Challis

PRICING	$
BEST TIME TO VISIT	Memorial Day weekend through Labor Day weekend
AGE RANGE	7 and older

At about the same time the Sierra Nevadas and the Yukon were filling with prospectors hoping to strike it rich quick, gold and silver ore was found in the mountains at Yankee Fork. The biggest claim—named General George Custer—was discovered in 1876, and the new town of Custer quickly grew up around this mine and many others like it operating nearby. By 1896 Custer supported a population of 600 and included a jail, a school, a post office, and even a baseball team. It wasn't long before the mines played out, however, and within little more than a decade Custer became a ghost town.

Today the Land of Yankee Fork State Park is a historic district that memorializes Idaho's mining history. The park comprises museum exhibits on mining, interpretive performances, docents to conduct

Land of Yankee Fork State Park   Courtesy Idaho Parks

guided tours, and a gold-panning station. Custer, along with other ghost towns like Bonanza and Bayhorse, falls within its boundaries. Kids will enjoy walking through the old Custer schoolhouse, which is now used as a museum (open only from June to September), the Empire Saloon (whet your whistle with a cold sarsaparilla here), and the Custer Opera House. North of Bonanza is the Yankee Fork Gold Dredge, which was part of the mining industry of the mid-20th century.

139 Massacre Rocks State Park

CONTACT 208-548-2672, http://parksandrecreation.idaho.gov; 3592 N. Park Lane, American Falls

PRICING	$
BEST TIME TO VISIT	Spring and summer
AGE RANGE	5 and older

The 2,000-mile Oregon Trail is a historic wagon route that connected the residents of the Missouri River region to Oregon and locations in between in the days before the transcontinental railroad. The route (which breaks off into subtrails) crosses Kansas, Nebraska, Wyoming, Idaho, and Oregon. The route started out as passage for fur trappers who made their way west on horseback. Starting in the 1830s, and peaking in 1846–69, the Oregon Trail and its several side trails transported more than 400,000 pioneers who brought their families and generally meager belongings via wagon to settle in the West. The trip was grueling, physically and mentally, and took months, but hundreds of thousands of Americans gladly accepted the physical risks associated with the long trek in the search for a better life.

The focus of the park is an outcropping of boulders along the south bank of the Snake River, along the trail. The emigrants named the narrow passage Devil's Gate and Gate of Death because they found it unsettling to pass through the area of limited visibility, fearing ambush. Although many thousands of emigrants passed safely through this narrow passageway between the rocks for years, in 1862 a conflict

Massacre Rocks State Park   Photo Peg Owens, courtesy Idaho Tourism

broke out among four or five wagon trains and a group of Natives, and in the end 10 settlers were dead—and the rocks took on their current ominous moniker. Before and after this incident, the rocks were a popular way station where wagon trains camped for the night along the trail. Many carved their names in what is now known as Register Rock—and this early graffiti is viewable today (the rock is now surrounded by a picnic area). The park visitor center offers maps and a small display of pioneer artifacts. There are interpretive trails and a dozen miles of hiking trail. Children will be amazed to see that wagon wheel ruts are still visible along the trail. There is a nice campsite here, and the park often hosts living history demonstrations on pioneers cooking along the trail and wagon train camping.

140 Minidoka National Historic Site

CONTACT 208-933-4127, www.nps.gov/miin; off Hunt Rd., between Twin Falls and Jerome

PRICING	$
BEST TIME TO VISIT	Year-round
AGE RANGE	10 and older

After the surprise attack on Pearl Harbor by the Japanese Imperial Navy and America's subsequent entry into World War II in 1941, hostility toward Japan-

ese Americans took a particularly ugly turn. Hysteria and suspicion that Japanese Americans—even those born in the United States—were spies or lurking terrorists was rampant. In 1942 President Franklin Roosevelt signed Executive Order 9066, which mandated a forced removal of anyone of Japanese ancestry living on the West Coast; these individuals (men, women, children, and the elderly) were made to leave their homes and were incarcerated in one of 10 relocation centers built in remote regions of the West.

The Minidoka War Relocation Center was one such camp, and from 1942 to 1945 it was home to more than 10,000 internees. Those living in the camps worked as farm labor and also on construction of the nearby Anderson Ranch Dam. They existed in communal spaces, often in harsh conditions, and were sometimes separated from their families. In leaving their homes and possessions, most of them forfeited their wealth. In early 1945 the internees were finally allowed to return to their homes—or what was left of them—with little more than train fare in their pockets. Years later, in 1988, President Ronald Reagan signed the Civil Liberties Act that provided $20,000 in restitution to the survivors of these internment camps, and in 1989 President George H. W. Bush offered a formal apology to all those who lived through the relocations.

This relatively new National Historical Site has a temporary exhibit that commemorates the forced internment at Minidoka and offers educational services and historical displays to memorialize those who lived at this camp and the nine others that operated during the war. You can check out a temporary exhibit that tells the history of the camp at the nearby Hagerman Fossil Beds National Monument (208-933-4100, www.nps.gov/hafo). You can also return to the remains of the camp itself to see what is left of the entry guard station, waiting room, and a rock garden constructed by internees. This is a grim reminder of a dark spot in American history, and to be honest, there is a limited amount to see here—but Minidoka is an important historical remembrance and serves as a commemorative site for thousands of former internees and their descendants, who honor the wartime sacrifices by making an annual pilgrimage to the site.

141 Nez Perce National Historical Park

CONTACT 208-843-2261, www.nps.gov/nepe; 39063 Hwy. 95, Spalding

PRICING	Free
BEST TIME TO VISIT	Year-round
AGE RANGE	7 and older

The Nez Perce are Native Americans who live in the Pacific Northwest of the United States. The name was given to the people by Canadian fur trappers who frequented the original Nez Perce lands in the late 18th century: It translates to "pierced nose." The Nez Perce generally call themselves Nimíipuu, which translates to "the people."

The Nez Perce National Historical Park is a collection of 38 sites spread across four states (Idaho, Oregon, Montana, and Washington) that celebrates the history, legacy, and living culture of this Native American group. The Spalding visitor center is located on

Heart of the Monster, at the Nez Perce National Historical Park
Photo Peg Owens, courtesy Idaho Tourism

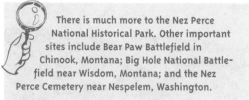

There is much more to the Nez Perce National Historical Park. Other important sites include Bear Paw Battlefield in Chinook, Montana; Big Hole National Battlefield near Wisdom, Montana; and the Nez Perce Cemetery near Nespelem, Washington.

the site of the 1838 Henry Spalding Mission, and contains an interpretive center that explains Nez Perce history. Other sites nearby include Canoe Camp, the site where Lewis and Clark and their "Corps of Discovery" worked in 1805 with the Nez Perce to carve canoes that carried them to the Pacific Ocean; and the Heart of the Monster, a sacred mound that is related to the Nez Perce creation story. (The creation story holds that a monster had eaten all of the animals, but the coyote had tricked the monster by carrying into its belly stone knives, which the coyote used to carve up the monster from inside to release all the eaten animals. The coyote discarded the monster bits around, and the drops of blood washed from the coyote's hands became the Nez Perce. The mound is said to be the resting place of the monster's heart.)

142 Sacajawea Interpretive, Cultural, and Educational Center

CONTACT 208-756-1222, www.sacajaweacenter.org; 200 Main St., Salmon

PRICING	$
BEST TIME TO VISIT	Year-round
AGE RANGE	7 and older

Sacajawea (1788–1812) was a Native American of the Shoshone tribe who acted as interpreter and guide to Meriwether Lewis and William Clark on their expedition throughout the American West. She traversed thousands of miles between North Dakota and Oregon—and during this period she was either pregnant or carrying her infant son. The explorers discovered her originally because they needed a guide up the Missouri River, and hired Sacajawea's husband, fur trader

Sacajawea Interpretive, Cultural, and Educational Center

Photo Ron Gardener, courtesy Idaho Tourism

Toussaint Charbonneau—largely because they believed his wife could act as translator and that her presence would also signify that their party meant no harm to the Native Americans. Sacajawea helped Lewis and Clark in myriad ways, primarily by interpreting for the Shoshone people they met along their route, but also by helping them find food when it was scarce and at times helping them find their way through the rough and isolated territory. Both men credited her with making their expedition a successful one, and Clark was so grateful that he eventually adopted Sacajawea's two children after she died.

The Sacajawea Interpretive, Cultural, and Educational Center, a 70-acre park on a site near the place where Sacajawea was born, memorializes this young woman's contribution to the Lewis and Clark expedition. The visitor center offers exhibits on Sacajawea and the Shoshone people and living history demonstrations. Be sure to check out the interpretive walking trail, which feature examples of Native-built

Sacajawea is a popular figure in American history and legend, and there are dozens of statues and memorials dedicated to her across the country. To name only a few of the others: A sculpture of Sacajawea and Pomp stands in front of the North Dakota State Capitol; there is a monument to her in Mobridge, South Dakota; and there is a sculpture of her at the Lewis & Clark College in Portland, Oregon.

dwellings, and don't miss the handsome bronze statue of Sacajawea and her infant son, who was nicknamed "Pomp."

143 Shoshone Falls

CONTACT	Off 3300E Rd., near Twin Falls
PRICING	$
BEST TIME TO VISIT	Spring (when water flow is greatest)
AGE RANGE	All ages

Prepare to be dazzled by what is often called the "Niagara Falls of the West"—at 1,500 feet wide and 212 feet high on the Snake River, it's an even longer drop than Niagara. Idaho Power controls the flow over the falls, harnessing hydroelectricity and water for irrigation as well. Because of the dam, and because of fluctuations in rainfall by seasons, water flow can vary greatly, but at its peak Shoshone Falls is breathtaking—and a vivid reminder that America has no shortage of natural beauty. You can get a good view of the falls from many vantage points within the park, including fenced overlooks that make for good photo ops. If you're lucky, you'll get to see a rainbow created by the mist from the falls. Kids will enjoy the playground equipment and a nearby swimming area.

Shoshone Falls

Photo Chris Ramsdell, courtesy Idaho Tourism

144 Three Island Crossing State Park

CONTACT 208-366-2394, http://parksandrecreation
.idaho.gov; 1083 Three Island Park Dr., Glenns Ferry

PRICING	$
BEST TIME TO VISIT	Spring through summer; August for Three Island Days
AGE RANGE	7 and older

Three Island Crossing was the most dangerous river crossing along the historic Oregon Trail. Pioneers moving west had to choose between crossing the Snake River via sandbars at this junction or heading along the south bank of the river, which was rocky and dusty. Taking their chances at Three Island Crossing meant a shorter route and more potable water along the way. About half of the wagon trains that passed through attempted the cross, but not all were successful and many lost their lives. Despite the danger, wagon trains used the river crossing until 1869, when a ferry was constructed upstream. The now-peaceful, beautiful site is home to the Oregon Trail History and Education Center, where visitors can

10 Tips for Hiking with Children

1. **Pick the right trail.** Consult trail maps and ask rangers to help choose a path that is the appropriate length and difficulty level for the slowest, least fit member in your party. Flat trails of no more than 1 or 2 miles are appropriate for young children; longer trails of 3 or 4 miles and with moderate changes in elevation are appropriate for older children and most adults. Save longer hikes, or trails that have extreme changes in elevation, until all members of the family are experienced hikers in good physical condition.

2. **Gear up appropriately.** Wear comfortable (worn-in) hiking shoes or thick-soled athletic shoes, preferably with ankle support. Don socks that wick away moisture, to prevent blisters. (If there's a chance you'll go near water or mud, bring along extra, dry socks.) Wear a hat for warmth and/or for sun protection. Dress in layers, to accommodate changing conditions. Bring along a hiking pole (or pick up an appropriate stick along the way, which will serve the same purpose). Don't forget sunscreen.

3. **Bring *plenty* of water.** For a full day's hike on a warm day, you ought to drink a gallon of water—and twice as much if it is particularly hot. Explain to your kids that if they feel thirsty, they are already dehydrated! Drink water before, during, and after a hike. Never drink from rivers or creeks along the way; even though the water might look pristine, there is a real chance it will be contaminated with microscopic organisms that could cause health problems.

4. **Bring along snacks** to replace energy supplies and electrolytes lost during hiking. Prepackaged nutrition bars work well, but so do homemade granola, GORP ("good old raisins and peanuts"), cheese and crackers, and fruit. If you're on a longer hike, plan 10- to 15-minute rest stops every hour to refuel with a snack and some water. Your exercising body will digest food better in small portions, over regular intervals, than it will a larger meal at one juncture.

Hiking with kids   © S. P. Gonzalez. Used with permission.

learn more about the pioneers who passed through this point and the Native Americans from the region who often helped them. Don't miss the interactive exhibits and the wagon replicas. The park maintains trails, a picnic area, and a campground; kids will go nuts over the opportunity to rent a tepee for an overnight stay.

Every August volunteers and park staff reenact the river crossing by driving wagons across the ford at this site. The reenactment is part of the larger Three Island Days Celebration, which includes a parade, a slow-water raft race along the Snake River, a knife-tossing competition, a chili cook-off, and live music.

Three Island Crossing State Park

Photo Peg Owens, courtesy Idaho Tourism

5. **Pack along a small first-aid kit** complete with antiseptic, Band-Aids, Ace bandage, bug bite treatments, ibuprofen (kids' and adults' formulations), and tweezers (to remove splinters, stingers, ticks, cactus spines, and the like). If allergies are a problem in your family, pack antihistamine or an EpiPen.

6. **Anticipate the weather.** Check the local forecast or ask the ranger on duty. Don't hike if thunderstorms are expected, and be prepared for precipitation. Rain ponchos are more practical on the trail than umbrellas. Be especially careful hiking in extreme weather—if it's too hot or too cold, you're inviting problems. During warm months, hike in the morning to avoid the worst of the heat. During cold months, avoid trails that are prone to ice and could be slippery.

7. **Be prepared if you get lost.** Trails are generally well marked in state and federal parks, but it isn't unusual to take a wrong turn and end up on a much longer hike than you expected. This means bringing extra food and water and emergency supplies like a rain tarp (which could be converted to shelter if need be) and something with which to start a fire. Stay together as a group—but make sure everyone in the family has a plan should you get separated. Equip each hiker with his or her own whistle, which can be used to signal others.

8. **Identify potential dangers before (and during) your hike.** Teach kids to identify poison oak and poison ivy—and emphasize the importance of staying away from them. Remind children that berries and mushrooms in the wild can be poisonous. Explain safety rules regarding wild animals (stay away from snakes, do not feed small rodents like squirrels, keep a safe distance from any large animals that might be encountered—even a seemingly docile deer can be dangerous if it feels threatened). If you're hiking on trails with steep drop-offs, explain the importance of careful footing and holding on to railings (or parents' hands). Let kids know you expect them to stay on the trails.

9. **Leave no trace.** Pack out whatever you pack in—including toilet paper, if that's an issue. (Bring along plastic bags to transport discarded paper.) Be sure to leave the natural environment intact: As tempting as it might be to pick wildflowers or collect pinecones, don't do it. Park regulations generally forbid collecting these sorts of items—and it is a crime in federal parks to remove any natural objects, including obsidian and petrified wood.

10. **Allow plenty of time.** Rushing through a hike is no fun, and could potentially overextend less fit members of your party. Especially when hiking with young children, leave space for distractions: Stop to smell the wild roses, observe a woodpecker in the forest, or look for pollywogs in a pond. These sorts of active interactions with nature are the best educational moments in the wilderness. Remember that hiking is less about getting from Point A to Point B than it is about reveling in the discoveries along the way.

ILLINOIS

145 Abraham Lincoln Presidential Library and Museum

CONTACT 217-782-5764, www.alplm.org; 212 N. 6th St., Springfield

PRICING	$$–$$$
BEST TIME TO VISIT	Year-round
AGE RANGE	7 and older

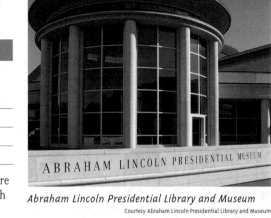

Abraham Lincoln Presidential Library and Museum
Courtesy Abraham Lincoln Presidential Library and Museum

Illinois is known as the Land of Lincoln, and there are myriad sites throughout the state related to the 16th president of the United States. Although Abraham Lincoln (1809–65) was the son of a Kentucky frontiersman, he settled in Illinois as a young lawyer and went on to become a member of the U.S. House of Representatives serving the state. It is fitting that the expansive Abraham Lincoln Presidential Library and Museum is located in Springfield, Lincoln's home for a quarter of a century. The facility is an impressive tribute to one of this country's most extraordinary leaders—a man who presided over the states at the very moment they were threatening to rip apart.

The museum is much more than a collection of dry documents and historical artifacts (although these items are in abundance as well): It's an interactive, immersive experience—entertaining, educational, and often deeply moving. Guests can view multidimensional films, attend live performances, see collections of period ball gowns worn by Mrs. Lincoln, peruse china and crystal from the White House, engage with interactive Civil War maps—even witness a "hologram" of Lincoln (an actor depicting him, of course) reading the famous Gettysburg Address. There are hundreds of personal items once belonging to the Lincolns on display here, including the president's famous stovepipe hat, a notebook he used as a child, and Mrs. Lincoln's music box.

Children will not want to miss the chance to be photographed with a life-sized mannequin of Lincoln and his family, with a re-created South Portico of the White House in the background. Another kid favorite at the museum is the exhibit called *Mrs. Lincoln's Attic*, a hands-on area where kids can dress up like Lincoln or his wife, play with the Lincoln home dollhouse, or practice their sums with an old-fashioned slate and bit of chalk, much like young Abe did. Families will also enjoy *Lincoln's Office in the White House* exhibit, an almost exact replication of the office Lincoln used while president.

Also on site is a massive noncirculating library collection that comprises papers, books, and artifacts related to Lincoln's life. There is an extensive collection of literature on the American Civil War, too. The library is open to the public.

146 Art Institute of Chicago

CONTACT 312-443-3600, www.artic.edu; 111 S. Michigan Ave., Chicago

PRICING	$–$$$
BEST TIME TO VISIT	Year-round
AGE RANGE	7 and older

The fabulous Art Institute of Chicago is a world-class facility, and the second largest art museum in the country (second only to the Metropolitan in New York City). In addition to hosting touring exhibits from the best museums around the world, the institute boasts

Abraham Lincoln House   Courtesy National Park Service

Art Institute of Chicago Courtesy Art Institute of Chicago

one of the finest permanent collections of impressionist and post-impressionist pieces outside of France. You'll find well-known works by luminaries like Vincent Van Gogh, El Greco, Georges-Pierre Seurat, Edward Manet, and Claude Monet. There are also hundreds of fine examples of American and European decorative arts, Asian art, American art, and modern and contemporary art.

It can sometimes be challenging to interest young children in fine art, but this museum makes the task easier. Start your visit at the Vitale Family Room, which offers a number of hands-on activities designed to coax youngsters into learning more about art in general and about the museum's offerings in particular. Kids can assemble puzzles based on the museum's masterpieces, make their own masterpieces using blocks or brightly colored magnets, and learn about art through interactive games and stories.

The museum offers self-guided tour brochures for families, as well as a fun Lions Trail audio tour for those traveling with children. If your kids are truly inspired by their visit, check out the free family workshops held in the Ryan Education Center. Kids 3 through 12 will especially enjoy the programs. (Some workshops require advance registration, so call ahead: 312-857-7161.)

147 Cahokia Mounds State Historic Site

CONTACT 618-346-5164, http://cahokiamounds.org; 30 Ramey St., Collinsville		
PRICING	$	
BEST TIME TO VISIT	Year-round (but closed some days, depending on season)	
AGE RANGE	7 and older	

The Cahokia Mounds State Historic Site preserves the archaeological ruins of a large, sophisticated city—what was one of the largest civilizations of the world during the 12th century. Researchers believe that Cahokia was inhabited from around 700 to 1400, at which point there were more than 120 structural mounds constructed, plus hundreds of homes and agricultural fields outside the city center. Its exact size through the years is unknown, but at its peak (around 1100) it is believed to have had a population of 20,000 people. The site's moniker came from a much later Illinois tribe, the Cahokias, that moved into the area sometime in the 17th century; historians named the archaeological site after these relatively recent arrivals—although there is no obvious connection between the later tribe and the Cahokia Mounds inhabitants. It is believed that by 1400 the site had been abandoned. There have yet been no clues unearthed to explain why the people left or where they went—although many historians suspect the resources dried up and that eventually the tribe was no longer able to sustain itself.

Cahokia Mounds Courtesy Cahokia Mounds State Historic Site

Visitors to the ancient city will find three kinds of mounds: conical and ridgetop mounds, some of which were used as burial sites, and the more prevalent and distinctive platform mounds—likely used for religious ceremonies—which may have been the site of important tribal structures or the foundations of homes to chiefs or priests. The most distinctive feature surviving is the largest earthenwork structure, called Monks Mound. It is 1,000 feet long and 800 feet wide—the largest such earthenworks mound in North America (although it has probably eroded significantly in the intervening years, so historians believe it was once even larger). The mound was likely built gradually, over several hundred years. It is believed that at one point there was a 2-mile-long fortress log wall surrounding the city center, complete with guard towers.

When visiting, be sure to pick up an audio tour from the information desk. The tape highlights three trails that wind through the plaza. Or purchase a booklet from the museum shop that will guide you through the more than 6 miles of trails, traversing both the cultural sites and the natural sites along the way.

148 Chaplin Creek Historic Village

CONTACT 815-456-2382, www.chaplincreek.com; 1715 Whitney Rd., Franklin Grove

PRICING	$
BEST TIME TO VISIT	June through September, weekends only
AGE RANGE	All ages

Step back in time and tour a mid-19th-century prairie settlement. The Chaplin Creek Historic Village is being developed with relocated restored period buildings. The evolving site includes a growing collection of re-sited structures, including an adorable saltbox house full of period furnishings, a country schoolhouse with the original cast-iron stove, an early settler's log cabin, a village jail (complete with two fearsome cells), and a road house. The replica log cabin is especially interesting to examine, because it was built using traditional techniques, including a limestone

Chaplin Creek Historic Village

foundation and a mortar mixture that was typical during the 1800s. The logs themselves were cut from a pine plantation near town, and then were hewn, notched, and chinked much as a pioneer home would have been constructed in the 19th century. There are demonstrations of period cooking and crafts here, and a musical festival the first weekend of every August. Nearby is the Franklin Creek Grist Mill (815-456-2718), the only water-powered gristmill still operating in Illinois.

149 Chicago Architecture Foundation

CONTACT 312-922-3432, www.architecture.org; 224 S. Michigan Ave., Chicago

PRICING	$–$$$
BEST TIME TO VISIT	Spring through early fall
AGE RANGE	7 and older

The Chicago skyline is one of the most beautiful, most recognized in the world, thanks to a lion's share of America's most impressive high-rises designed by

> Every Sunday the Chicago Architecture Foundation offers Family Studio workshops, created for kids 3 to 12 to learn about design, model building, and the basic principles of structural engineering.

Chicago skyline   Photo Carol M. Highsmith, courtesy Library of Congress

some of the most respected U.S. architects. Over the years the city was been home base to both Frank Lloyd Wright and Louis Sullivan. The Chicago Architecture Foundation is dedicated to architectural education and preservation of architecture, and in addition to offering free exhibitions on design (check out their scale model of downtown Chicago), lectures, and hands-on workshops, the institution is best known for its docent-led architectural tours. Although you can check out the sites by foot or by bus, a favorite way to explore the city is by the boat cruises along the Chicago River and Lake Michigan. Come to the Windy City in late spring and summer (when it's not so windy!) to enjoy the outside top deck of one of the many boats that ply the waters. Tour guides are knowledgeable, and this ends up being a great introduction to the city even for those who don't have a particular interest in architecture.

150 Field Museum of Natural History

CONTACT 312-922-9410, http://fieldmuseum.org; 1400 S. Lakeshore Dr., Chicago

PRICING	$$$–$$$$
BEST TIME TO VISIT	Year-round
AGE RANGE	All ages

The Field Museum of Natural History is one of the largest, most respected natural history museums in the United States—and one of the best places to teach children about the world around them. The Field Museum is an outgrowth of the World's Columbian Exposition, held in 1893 in Chicago. Today the museum contains more than 21 million natural specimens—the most famous of which is "Sue," the largest, most intact *Tyrannosaurus* skeleton ever discovered. There are other dinosaur remnants on display in the museum, as well as a comprehensive gems and minerals exhibit; a large collection of taxidermied animals; and an extensive display of Native American tools, jewelry, weapons, and clothing. Children will especially enjoy the Underground Adventure, which gives everyone in the family a *Honey, I Shrunk the Kids* experience: Walk through the display (scaled at 100 times larger than life-sized) to see a bug's-eye view of the world.

Be sure to pick up a Family Adventure Tour at the museum's information desk (or you can download one at the museum website beforehand—a good idea to help orient yourself in advance to this large facility). While exploring the museum, look for Interpretive Stations for hand-on activities like dissecting an owl pellet or printing Egyptian hieroglyphics. On weekends (and daily in July and August) the museum sponsors a story time and allows those 12 and younger to make a take-home art project. If you have a hard time prying your kids away from this fun, informative museum, consider the overnight program,

"Sue" at the Field Museum of Natural History
Photo John Weinstein, © The Field Museum. Used with permission.

Dozin' with Dinos. Held Friday nights from January through June, the program includes family arts and crafts, special tours of the museum, and the opportunity to spread out a sleeping bag and spend the night in the facility. (Hint: A self-inflating air mattress and a good pair of earplugs will make this slumber party more palatable for parents.)

151 Fort de Chartres State Historic Site

CONTACT 618-284-7230, www.illinoishistory.gov/hs/fort_de_chartres.htm; 1260 IL 155, Prairie du Rocher

PRICING	$
BEST TIME TO VISIT	Year-round (closed Monday and Tuesday)
AGE RANGE	7 and older

Before Illinois was a state, France governed the region in the 17th century, including an area that stretched from Lake Michigan and Lake Superior to the Missouri River. The French were trappers and miners, and by the 18th century the French colonial government had built three forts by the name of Fort de Chartres to safeguard the territory. The original fort—and all subsequent rebuildings—was named after Louis, the duke of Chartres. The remaining stone magazine—which survived the forces that destroyed most of the rest of the original site—is believed to be the oldest building in the state of Illinois.

Come to the park today to see a partially rebuilt fort, including the north wall, gatehouse, restored powder magazine, barracks, a government house, guards' houses, and the king's storehouse. Inside the storehouse you'll find the Piethman Museum, displaying archaeological artifacts uncovered from the site as well as period items that help interpret the French colonial period in the region. Fort de Chartres is the site of historical reenactments throughout the year. Especially popular is Kids' Day (held over the first weekend in May), with crafts, live entertainment, and kid-friendly 18th-century games and contests. The French and Indian War Assemblage reenactment is held the first weekend in October.

152 Frank Lloyd Wright Home and Studio

CONTACT 312-994-4000, http://gowright.org/home-and-studio.html; 951 Chicago Ave., Oak Park

PRICING	$$$
BEST TIME TO VISIT	Year-round
AGE RANGE	10 and older

Frank Lloyd Wright (1867–1959) has been recognized by the American Institute of Architects as the 20th century's greatest architect, and he is generally acknowledged to be the most forward-thinking, prolific designer ever in the United States. Over his 70-year career Wright designed more than 1,000 works, including homes, office buildings, and bridges. He also designed fabrics, wallpaper, dinnerware, and furniture. Wright is most associated with the Prairie School movement of architecture, a largely residential architectural movement that originated in Chicago and was prevalent throughout the Midwest.

The Frank Lloyd Wright Home and Studio was Wright's home for the first 20 years of his career; he raised his six children on the property, and built a studio in which he and his associates helped develop a new American architectural style. Visitors can tour the astonishingly beautiful home—which is furnished as it appeared in the early 20th century, when Wright lived and worked here. There are many options for family-friendly activities that will offer children the

Frank Lloyd Wright Home and Studio

Photo by Tim Long, courtesy Frank Lloyd Wright Preservation Trust

One of the most recognized Wright designs, the Robie House, was designed in Wright's Oak Park studio in 1908. The Prairie-style home is also open for tours Thursday through Monday (312-994-4000, 5757 S. Woodlawn Ave., Chicago).

chance for hands-on discovery. The Design Detectives Family Tour of the home and studio is an engaging, kid-friendly program that encourages family members of all ages to uncover the secrets of Wright's designs. This tour also offers some fun stories about the life of the Wright children who grew up on the property. In addition, there are numerous design workshops that allow kids to explore their own creativity, such as origami classes, Lego building, sun prints, and "stained-glass" window design (working with colored papers). In addition to tours of the home and studio, the museum offers walking tours of Oak Park, a historic district surrounding the Wright Home that comprises the largest collection of Wright-designed structures in the world. Tickets sell out quickly, so it's a good idea to purchase them in advance online (although there are a limited number of tickets for purchase on a first-come, first-served basis at the museum shop, starting at 10 AM).

153 Illinois Railway Museum

CONTACT 815-923-4000, www.irm.org; 7000 Olson Rd., Union

PRICING	$$–$$$ (depending on season)
BEST TIME TO VISIT	April through October
AGE RANGE	3 and older

There may be no happier place on earth for train lovers: The Illinois Railway Museum is the largest railroad museum in the United States, and offers a huge collection of trains, vintage streetcars, and railroad artifacts. The museum is dedicated to memorializing the role railroads played in the growth of Chicago and throughout the United States. There are more than

450 pieces of equipment on display. Look for highlights like the St. Louis–San Francisco Railway 2-10-0, a decapods steam engine; the Atchison, Topeka, and Santa Fe Railway 4-8-4 steam engine; the Milwaukee Road 4-8-4, the first diesel locomotive ever built by Fairbanks Morse; the Chicago Surface Lines 84, the oldest working trolley bus in the world; and a collection of 20 electric trolley buses from cities around the country. Best of all, visitors from April through October can ride a selection of the museum's antique diesel, steam, and electric trains. Children will not want to miss the annual Thomas the Tank Engine Festival, held in August, when families can climb aboard Thomas himself and take a ride.

154 Lewis and Clark State Historic Site

CONTACT 618-251-5811, www.campdubois.com; 1 Lewis & Clark Trail, Hartford

PRICING	$
BEST TIME TO VISIT	Year-round (closed Monday and Tuesday from September through April)
AGE RANGE	7 and older

In 1803, President Thomas Jefferson proposed an expedition to explore the uncharted wilderness of the North American continent west of the Mississippi River, in an effort to assess the commercial potential of the western regions. Jefferson selected Meriwether

Lewis and Clark State Historic Site   Courtesy National Park Service

Lewis to lead the expedition, and Lewis in turn selected William Clark to be co-commander. The Lewis and Clark State Historic Site commemorates one stop along this historic trek—Camp Dubois, a winter camp of Lewis and Clark. It was here that Lewis and Clark and the members of their Corps of Discovery readied for their trip onward to the Pacific Ocean. The site includes a large, comprehensive interpretative center that offers exhibits illuminating the expedition and Camp Dubois's role in the success of Lewis and Clark's endeavors. Don't miss the full-scale replica of the keelboat used by the explorers to traverse the Missouri River; one side of the boat is cut away to show how the vessel was jam-packed with provisions for the journey. There's also a theater on site that shows a 12-minute orientation video. Children will especially enjoy the reconstruction of the actual Lewis and Clark winter camp outside of the visitor center. This is the site of costumed reenactments throughout the year.

ToyMaker 3000 at the Museum of Science and Industry
Courtesy Museum of Science and Industry

155 Museum of Science and Industry

CONTACT 773-684-1414, www.msichicago.org; 57th St. and Lake Shore Dr., Chicago

PRICING	$$–$$$ (movies extra)
BEST TIME TO VISIT	Year-round
AGE RANGE	7 and older

The Museum of Science and Industry is the largest science museum in the Western Hemisphere. It is home to more than 35,000 artifacts and hundreds of exhibits, housed in the only remaining building from the 1893 World's Columbian Exposition. In addition to more displays than a family can explore in one day, the museum offers costumed program interpretations, daily science demonstrations, and spectacular Omnimax movies. Favorite permanent exhibits include the U-505 submarine, the only German U-boat to have been captured during World War II; a reproduction of an actual Illinois coal mine that will take you down 50 feet into the mineshaft; the extremely kid-friendly *ToyMaker 3000*, a toy factory that cranks out real toys with the help of a dozen robots; and *Science Storms*, a 25,000-square-foot-exhibit that lets you interact with weather by creating a miniature tsunami, triggering an avalanche, and controlling a tornado.

In addition to a huge array of permanent exhibitions, the museum hosts incredibly popular touring exhibits that offer hands-on possibilities. Past exhibits have included kid-friendly topics like the world of Harry Potter, Mythbusters (based on the Discovery channel series), and a hands-on exhibit highlighting artifacts from the *Titanic*. In addition to tapping into the natural inquisitive nature of children through its interactive approach, the museum also seeks to inspire and motivate kids to pursue science and technology education—but don't worry: This place is so much fun that most children will never realize how educational it really is.

The museum offers more than 50 free general-admission days every year; the facility is also one of five attractions included in the Chicago CityPass, a package that offers approximately 50 percent off the Museum of Science and Industry (or the John Hancock Observatory), the Shedd Aquarium, Skydeck Chicago, the Field Museum, and either the Art Institute of Chicago or the Adler Planetarium (www.citypass.com/chicago).

156 Naper Settlement

CONTACT 630-420-6010, www.napersettlement.org;
523 S. Webster St., Naperville

PRICING	$$–$$$
BEST TIME TO VISIT	April through October (closed Sunday); open November through March also, but building interiors are closed and self-guided tours are only available Tuesday through Friday
AGE RANGE	3 and older

Naperville is an immersive 13-acre village museum that interprets the evolution of a pioneer outpost from the years 1831 to 1907. Guests step into living history to experience costumed interpreters relating the histories of typical midwestern pioneers and to walk amid the 30 historic buildings—a few original to the site and many more relocated or reconstructed. At the heart of the park is the Martin Mitchell Mansion, an 1884 brick home lovingly furnished with what were at the time opulent and fashionable items. Also on site are the Log House (a rough-hewn timber reconstruction), the Copenhagen Schoolhouse (look on the southwest exterior for graffiti etched into the structure by children more than 100 years ago), and the Conestoga wagon (kids are encouraged to climb in and look around). Throughout the summer season there are artisans and reenactors demonstrating pioneer skills like blacksmithing, log-cabin construction, and hearthside cooking.

Also on site is a museum exhibition (part of the visitor center at the Preemption House) that displays a collection of folk art, artifacts, historic photographs, and oral histories. Children (3 through 10) will not want to miss the History Collection (located in the Meeting House), where they can try on period clothes, build a home with Lincoln Logs, or make a take-home art project. Other family-friendly programs on site include the Victorian Tea Party, a two-hour event (with plenty of sweet treats) that gives children the chance to learn about manners during the 19th century; and the History Scavenger Hunt, complete with activity book.

157 New Salem Historic Site

CONTACT 217-632-4000, www.lincolnsnewsalem.com;
15588 History Lane, Petersburg

PRICING	$
BEST TIME TO VISIT	Year-round (closed Monday and Tuesday from November through March)
AGE RANGE	7 and older

Abraham Lincoln, the 16th president of the United States, called New Salem home as a young adult. The reconstructed 1830s village is a faithful reenactment of the site where Lincoln studied law and began his life in politics, from 1831 to 1837. There are 23 historically furnished structures on site, including several small log homes, a cooper (barrel maker) studio, a blacksmith shop, a store in which Lincoln once owned a share, a tavern, a saw- and gristmill, and a wool-carding mill. Children will be especially interested in the "subscription school," in which parents were charged between 30 and 85 cents a month for their children's education, depending on their age and grade.

Abraham Lincoln   Courtesy Library of Congress

During the summer months, costumed interpreters are scattered throughout the village to explain the significance of the buildings, to discuss politics of the day, and to answer questions about Lincoln's life in New Salem. Be sure to stop by the visitor center to see *Turning Point*, an 18-minute video that explains Lincoln's early years.

158 Ulysses S. Grant Home

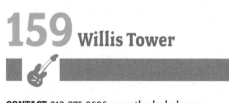

CONTACT 815-777-3310, www.granthome.com; 500 Bouthillier St., Galena

PRICING	$
BEST TIME TO VISIT	April through October (closed Monday and Tuesday)
AGE RANGE	7 and older

Ulysses S. Grant (1822–85) was the 18th president of the United States and a driving force behind the Civil War: Under Grant, the Union defeated the Confederate army, and Grant was a wildly popular war hero as a result, enjoying the equivalent of rock-star status in his day. On returning home to Galena after the Civil War, in 1865, a group of prominent (and wealthy) Galena citizens presented Grant with a fully furnished home to express their appreciation for his service.

Today the U.S. Grant Home operates as a historic house museum, faithfully preserved in its mid-1860s appearance. Ninety percent of the furnishings are original to the home in 1865—so this museum really does offer a nearly perfect window into the past. The charming five-bedroom home is relatively modest, lovingly maintained, and filled with the Grants' personal artifacts, like the china designed for Grant's daughter's White House wedding and the president's cigar holder. (Children might be interested to know that Grant smoked excessively before the dangers of tobacco were understood, and he ended up dying of lung cancer.) Tours are offered April through October by costumed interpreters, and the well-versed tour guides offer insight into Grant's history during the Civil War, his presidency, and his life as a family man.

159 Willis Tower

CONTACT 312-875-9696, www.theskydeck.com; 233 S. Wacker Dr., Chicago

PRICING	$$$ (audio tours additional)
BEST TIME TO VISIT	Year-round
AGE RANGE	All ages

If you have no fear of heights (I mean *zero* fear—or else, forget about it!), come to the Willis Tower (formerly known as the Sears Tower) to check out the

Ulysses S. Grant Home   Photo Carol M. Highsmith, courtesy Library of Congress

Willis Tower, downtown Chicago
Photograph in the Carol M. Highsmith Archive, Library of Congress, Prints and Photographs Division

tallest building in the United States and one of the top 10 tallest in the world. On its completion in 1973, this 108-story, 1,451-foot skyscraper surpassed the height of the World Trade Center towers in New York City. The structure boasts 16 double-decker elevators and one of the best lookout spots imaginable: Head to the Skydeck on the 103rd floor to get a dizzying view of Chicago in a glass box (with a glass floor that seems to disappear beneath you) that actually extends out 4 feet from the structure proper. On a clear day, this makes for some terrific photo opportunities—if you can manage it without losing your lunch.

Game at Wrigley Field   Photo Carol M. Highsmith, courtesy Library of Congress

160 Wrigley Field

CONTACT	1060 W. Addison St., Chicago
PRICING	$$$$ (for tours)
BEST TIME TO VISIT	Nongame days for a more extensive tour of the park; game days to see the retro ballpark in action
AGE RANGE	All ages

There's nothing more American than baseball, and the nostalgic love of the game is exemplified at this charming old ballpark, home of the Chicago Cubs since 1916. It is the oldest National League ballpark, beloved for its ivy-covered brick outfield wall and a scoreboard that is still operated manually. It was the last major-league ballpark to get lights, and it remains a favorite for sports fans throughout the country.

Even if your family doesn't root for the Cubs, you won't want to miss a behind-the-scenes look at the "Friendly Confines" (a popular nickname for Wrigley Field) with a tour of a ballpark. On nongame-day tours, you'll see the press box, bleachers, Cubs' clubhouse, Cubs' dugout, and get to step out on to the field. On game-day tours, you'll be slightly more limited—you'll likely still get to see the press box, bleachers, and indoor batting cage, but don't expect to get very close to the teams. An average tour takes about 90 minutes.

indiana

161 Benjamin Harrison Home

CONTACT 317-631-1888, www.presidentbenjamin harrison.org; 1230 Delaware St., Indianapolis

PRICING	$–$$
BEST TIME TO VISIT	Year-round (closed weekends except for June and July)
AGE RANGE	7 and older

Benjamin Harrison (1833–1901) was the 23rd president of the United States and the grandson of 9th president, William Henry Harrison—whose father, in turn, was one of the signers of the Declaration of Independence. In addition to boasting an impressively patriotic pedigree, Benjamin Harrison served in the Civil War with distinction, and then went on to hold office in Congress before his assumption of the presidency in 1889. The election of 1888 was memorable in large part because Harrison received 100,000 fewer popular votes than his opponent, Grover Cleveland (who served before and after Harrison as president), but Harrison won the Electoral College by a wide margin. Harrison was famous for his "front-porch campaign," in which he delivered short, informal speeches to delegations that came to see him at his home. At one of these impromptu rallies, a fervent supporter was so overcome that he famously snapped off a picket from the fence in front of Harrison's yard and carried it away.

Harrison lived in what is now known as the Benjamin Harrison Home from the 1870s until his death in 1901—minus the four years he called 1600 Pennsylvania Avenue in DC home. The beautiful, Italianate structure has 16 spacious rooms and is surrounded by lovely gardens and grounds (which are well worth exploring). Guided tours are offered on the hour, and you can see 10 of the rooms, beautifully restored and furnished with period antiques and original items owned by the Harrisons. When touring the home, be sure to admire the cut-crystal chandeliers and gold lacquered mirrors in the front parlor, which Harrison added during a redecoration for his second wife. You can see his law office on the second floor, and his master bedroom that holds an antique exercise machine and a cradle originally owned by Harrison's grandfather. Behind the home check out the reconstructed carriage house, which includes an exhibit on the First Ladies and a display outlining the women's suffrage movement.

The home is the site of a number of whimsical, educational living history performances throughout the year. On Presidents' Day the daily tours here include costumed actors who play the roles of Harrison family members and household staff—and you'll have a chance to hear them gossip about the news of the day from 1898. There are other regularly scheduled "Live from Delaware Street" historic performances in which guests will learn about life in the home after Harrison returned from the White House. There are also periodic Civil War Dinners, which in addition to offering a full meal include a chance to interact with an interpreter who acts as Benjamin Harrison himself.

Benjamin Harrison Home   Courtesy National Park Service

162 Conner Prairie Interactive History Park

CONTACT 317-776-6006, www.connerprairie.org; 13400 Allisonville Rd., Fishers

PRICING	$$–$$$ (depending on season and number of facilities open)
BEST TIME TO VISIT	April through October (outdoor experiences are closed November through March); closed Tuesday and Wednesday
AGE RANGE	3 and older

Conner Prairie Interactive History Park

Courtesy Conner Prairie Interactive History Park

163 Eiteljorg Museum of American Indians and Western Art

CONTACT	317-636-9378, www.eiteljorg.org; 500 W. Washington St., Indianapolis

PRICING	$–$$
BEST TIME TO VISIT	Year-round
AGE RANGE	7 and older

When children's imaginations are captured by a museum exhibit, it is tough for them to understand why they aren't allowed to touch. You'll have no such worries bringing kiddos to this open-air history park, where visitors are *encouraged* to touch, smell, taste, and participate. The Conner Prairie Interactive History Park stretches across 850 acres of prairie land that in the 1800s belonged to a fur trader named William Conner, and today is part 19th-century village, part amusement park, part history lesson.

Throughout the site costumed reenactors interpret the story of 19th-century Indiana by sharing personal narratives and carrying on the work of everyday life on the frontier. Don't be surprised if you and your children are invited to help with the chores!

You'll find five themed areas: the Conner Homestead, the Lenape Indian Campe, 1836 Prairietown, 1859 Balloon Village, and 1863 Civil War Journey. Everywhere you go, you will be encouraged to experience history by participating in such activities as fireside cooking, tending farm animals, making pottery and baskets, and chopping wood. There are numerous reenactments to witness—and often you can even join in the action. Children love the opportunity to do more than "look, don't touch," and this living history museum is one of the best interactive experiences of its kind—telling the story of the people of the past through their everyday routines and allowing visitors to feel like they've truly stepped back in time. Throughout the year the museum hosts seasonal events like a "Headless Horseman Ride" in the fall, a "Taste of the Past" banquet, "Hearthside Suppers," numerous Christmas events, and American Civil War reenactments.

The Eiteljorg Museum of American Indians and Western Art celebrates the legacy of the American frontier and the men and women who carved out their lives in this rugged, often dangerous environment. The museum offers an expansive collection of Native American art and artifacts along with western art, thanks to collector and founder Harrison Eiteljorg, whose personal collection constitutes the core of the museum.

The eclectic collection comes from Native artists throughout the United States, with a heavy emphasis on pieces indigenous to the Plains and the Southwest. On display you will find tepees, feathered head-

Eiteljorg Museum

Courtesy Indiana Office of Tourism Development

Visit the Eiteljorg Museum in mid-June to enjoy the colorful Indian Market Festival, where more than 100 artists from 50 tribes display their work. The festival includes live performances by musicians, singers, and dancers; artist demonstrations; and children's crafts. Don't miss a chance to sample the Indian tacos.

dresses, pottery, fine baskets, jewelry, beaded clothing, and totems. The western art collection includes sculptures and paintings by well-known western artists like Georgia O'Keeffe, Albert Bierstadt, Frederic Remington, and Charles Russell. The museum is also site to numerous traveling exhibits that focus on life in the West.

164 Grouseland

CONTACT 812-886-0400, www.grouselandfoundation.org; 3 W. Scott St., Vincennes

PRICING	$
BEST TIME TO VISIT	Year-round (closed Monday in January and February)
AGE RANGE	7 and older

William Henry Harrison (1773–1841) was the ninth president of the United States. He was the son of a wealthy landowner from Virginia, Benjamin Harrison, one of the signers of the Declaration of Independence, but William made his mark on the country serving as a military officer fighting Native American tribes (most notably in the Battle of Tippecanoe, from which he got his political nickname). He was appointed the first territorial governor of the Northwest Territory, and helped create legislation that established the Indiana Territory in 1800 (which at the time included what is now Indiana, Illinois, Michigan,

William Henry Harrison home   Courtesy National Park Service

part of Minnesota, and Wisconsin). Unfortunately, he is probably best remembered as being the first chief executive to die in office: He lived less than a month after he was inaugurated as president.

Harrison built this grand brick mansion on 300 acres and named it Grouseland because of the many game birds that lived on the site. Today visitors can tour the truly stunning home, beautifully decorated in period antiques, to learn more about Harrison, his life as a military man, his presidential campaign, and his brief stint as commander in chief. Children will not want to miss the nursery, which is furnished with miniature furniture and toys from the era.

165 Hoosier Valley Railroad Museum

CONTACT 574-896-3950, www.hoosiervalley.org; 507 Mulberry St., North Judson

PRICING	$ (train rides require a fee)
BEST TIME TO VISIT	Saturday only May through October (to enjoy train rides)
AGE RANGE	3 and older

Railroad travel opened up the West to Americans, and North Judson in Indiana was a railway hub: At its peak, more than 125 trains passed through the farmland community. The town was home to four major rail lines—the Chesapeake and Ohio, the Erie, the New York Central, and the Pennsylvania—and many of the residents at the time were employed by these railroads. But thanks in large part to air travel, passenger rail service collapsed in the mid-20th century, and depots were left abandoned by the 1980s. The Hoosier Valley Railroad Museum seeks to memorialize the contribution of the railways to the United States and to preserve the railroad history of this region. There is an interesting display of artifacts and photos to explore in the restored depot on site, and the grounds are overflowing with train equipment either on display or under restoration. But the real reason to visit is the chance to take a train ride on an antique diesel locomotive. Choose your favored conveyance: an open-air car or comfortable (air-conditioned) seating aboard a restored coach. The trains wind around the museum through bucolic farmland, and it doesn't take much imagination to picture yourself in an earlier era.

166 Indianapolis Motor Speedway

The Indy Racing Experience Two-Seat Ride offers you the chance to ride behind a professional driver circling the track at up to 180 miles per hour. There are a limited number of days in which this interactive experience is available, so be sure to call ahead (888-357-5002).

CONTACT 317-492-8500, www.indianapolismotorspeedway.com; 4790 16th St., Indianapolis

PRICING	$ for tours; gate admission varies by event
BEST TIME TO VISIT	Late May, late July, mid-August, to see racing events
AGE RANGE	7 and older

The Indianapolis Motor Speedway is the heart and soul of the racing world, and it's a must-see for die-hard adrenaline junkies and anyone who loves fast cars. The raceway hosts three major events throughout the year, but it's best known for the world-famous Indianapolis 500, a grueling 500-mile open-wheel event held in late May. You can visit the speedway even during noncompetition days to check out the Hall of Fame Museum, which includes 30,000 square feet of exhibit space. There are 75 vehicles on display on a rotating basis, which might include the Marmon "Wasp," the car that won the first Indianapolis 500 in 1911; the 1977 car driven by A. J. Foyt Jr. during his record-breaking fourth win of the Indianapolis 500;

and the Duesenberg #12 Murphy Special, the only car to ever win the Indianapolis 500 *and* the French Grand Prix at Le Mans. There is also a short orientation film showing footage of the Indy 500 races through the years, as well as behind-the-scenes tours at the track.

167 Johnny Appleseed Festival

CONTACT www.johnnyappleseedfest.com; Johnny Appleseed Park, 5800 Harry Baals Dr., Fort Wayne

PRICING	$
BEST TIME TO VISIT	Third weekend in September
AGE RANGE	All ages

Many of us grew up hearing the tales of Johnny Appleseed, who was said to roam the Midwest countryside during the 1800s sowing apple seeds to help feed his fellow pioneers. He was reputed to be an eccentric figure, wearing only raggedy clothes and a cook pot

Indianapolis 500   Courtesy Indiana Office of Tourism Development

Johnny Appleseed Festival   Courtesy Visit Ft. Wayne

Interior of Levi Coffin Home

on his head. This legendary figure was actually real-life missionary and nurseryman John Chapman (1774-1845), and he actually planted fenced-in orchards rather than scattering seeds willy-nilly. His efforts are credited with introducing apple trees to Indiana, Illinois, and Ohio. He sold trees to farmers for pennies each, but he gave away many more.

The annual Johnny Appleseed Festival commemorates the life and times of this U.S. icon. Come to this quintessentially American fair to enjoy crafts, historical reenactments, artisan demonstrations, live entertainment, and—yes—plenty of apples.

168 Levi Coffin Home

CONTACT 765-847-2432, www.indianamuseum.org/sites/leviplan.html; 113 U.S. 27, Fountain City

PRICING	$
BEST TIME TO VISIT	June through October (open days vary by season; call ahead for hours)
AGE RANGE	7 and older

The first African slaves in America were kidnapped from their homes and brought forcibly to the Jamestown colony in 1619. Slavery continued to grow in America as the new country grew, and through their forced labor slaves unwillingly contributed enormously to the economic success of farms and plantations across the young nation. Although there were always opponents to the institution of slavery, by the middle of the 19th century there was a vocal and growing movement that began to take action. Proponents of this burgeoning antislavery movement were known as abolitionists, and in part because of

their efforts the country eventually went to war with itself during the American Civil War (1861–65). After hundreds of years of cruelty and mistreatment that went hand in hand with the slave trade, and after the bitter and bloody conflict between the states, the Union victory finally freed the four million individuals who were held as property.

Before slaves were emancipated, abolitionists—including slaves and former slaves, as well as others—stood up against the disgraceful institution and exhibited tremendous bravery and moral fortitude: To free slaves one person at a time, the abolitionists devised the ingenious strategy of escape that came to be called the Underground Railroad. Runaway slaves were moved at night from one safe haven to another, often only a few miles at a time, toward free states—generally crossing through several points in Indiana. With the help of sympathetic individuals along the way, many eventually escaped slavery.

Levi Coffin and his wife, Catharine, were deeply religious Quakers who moved to Indiana from North Carolina because they opposed the slave trade in the South. In 1839 the Coffins built a home in Fountain City not only to serve as a residence for themselves and their children but also to be a safe house along the Underground Railroad. Indiana was a free state, but it was nevertheless illegal to aid runaway slaves—and so the Coffins took an incredible risk every time they opened their home to escaping slaves. It is believed that more than 2,000 slaves passed through the Coffin home to freedom; included among this number is Eliza Harris, the slave on whom Harriet

Beecher Stowe's *Uncle Tom's Cabin* was based. Coffin's role in the Underground Railroad was so pivotal that he is sometimes referred to as its "president."

Today visitors can tour the eight-room Federal-style brick home the Coffins created as a pivotal stop along the Underground Railroad. Informative docents tell the story of many of the slaves who passed through—much is known about the home and its various occupants because Coffin kept careful notes and eventually published the stories. You can even crawl into the small garrets throughout in which runaway slaves often had to hide for days. Although slavery was arguably the most horrific blot in the annals of American history, seeing this important historic site reminds us that as a rule Americans are resilient and dedicated to liberty, even under the most trying circumstances.

169 Lincoln Boyhood Home National Memorial

Lincoln Boyhood Home   Courtesy National Park Service

CONTACT 812-937-4541, www.nps.gov/libo; off IN 162, Lincoln City

PRICING	$
BEST TIME TO VISIT	Year-round (late spring through summer is best for viewing the historical farm)
AGE RANGE	7 and older

Before Abraham Lincoln became the 16th president of the United States—and before he led the divided Union into the bloody American Civil War and presided over the emancipation of the slaves in this country—he was a young boy living on the Indiana frontier with his family. From 1816 to 1830 (starting when he was only 7), Abe lived on this site, which is today preserved as a living history museum. His mother, Nancy Hanks Lincoln, is buried at the Pioneer Cemetery here, along with 27 other early settlers. The real fun at this attraction is the Lincoln Living Historical Farm, a homestead complete with vegetable gardens, crops, farm animals, and a log cabin that re-creates the original Lincoln home. Costumed interpreters in period garb work the

farm, tend the animals, cook meals, and perform myriad other activities that would have been typical in the 1820s. Guests can interact with the interpreters, and classes are sometimes offered in pioneer crafts. A short walk from the heart of the farm will take you to the ruins of the original Lincoln cabin, where the sandstone foundation is still visible.

There are more than 2 miles of easy hiking trails to explore, and you won't want to miss the nearby memorial building that features five panels depicting phases of Lincoln's life. There is a small theater here that shows a 15-minute orientation film about Lincoln's life in Indiana. Be sure to check out the exhibits that document Lincoln's life through artifacts, historic papers, and photos.

170 Marengo Cave

CONTACT 888-702-2837, http://marengocave.com/groups/directions; 400 E. IN 64, Marengo

PRICING	$$$$
BEST TIME TO VISIT	Summer
AGE RANGE	10 and older

There are more than 2,600 caves in southern Indiana, formed when acidic groundwater carved out sometimes massive passageways between the layers of limestone about a million years ago. Marengo Cave is one of the largest commercially operated caves in the area; it's 5 miles long and includes an upper, drier level and two underground rivers. Stalagmites and stalactites decorate the caves, and the constant drip-drip of mineral-rich water ensures that this place is ever-changing—albeit on an extremely slow time line.

There are multiple tours available, for various levels of experience and stamina—but be aware: Spelunking adventures at "wild caves" like this one are not for the faint of heart. Moving through the cave involves scrambling through tight spaces, in extreme dark; and it's likely you'll encounter critters like salamanders and bats. But for those who are game, cave exploring offers a chance to see another world. A good starter tour is the Underground Adventure (children must be 10 or older), in which you'll wade through the underground river and have multiple opportunities to crawl through the mud. The Waterfall Crawl (for children 12 and older) is an even muddier experience, and allows guests to see a portion of the cave that was only recently discovered. You'll exit

through a feature called Pig Pen, so called because of the slimy clay that you'll need to wriggle through to leave the cave. Expect to get very dirty—filthy, in fact. You'll need to wear old clothing (and bring towels and soap to shower off afterward, and a change of clean clothing). The tour operator will provide helmets, LED headlamps, and secondary lighting (you can keep the LED headlamp afterward). You might also want to don knee pads and gloves of your own, which will minimize the scrapes and bruises you'll likely pick up. Temps are a constant 52 degrees—and this includes the water you will often be crawling through—so dress in multiple layers.

For kids who are too young for wild cave exploration, check out The Crawl (requires a small fee), an indoor human-made winding maze that lets the little ones wriggle and squeeze through tight spaces of a more sanitized kind—all the while warm, dry, and well lighted. Kids can also pan for treasures here: Purchase a bag of sand full of gems or fossils and sift through them for treasures.

171 Tippecanoe Battlefield

CONTACT 765-476-8411, www.tippecanoe.in.gov; 200 Battle Ground Ave., Battle Ground

PRICING	$
BEST TIME TO VISIT	Year-round
AGE RANGE	7 and older

Chief Tecumseh (1768–1813) was an influential leader of the Shawnee people during the pioneer expansion days, and also led a union of multiple Native tribes of the northwest and southwest territories. Tecumseh's Confederacy, as it was known, opposed the U.S. expansion into traditional Indian territory, and in response the governor of the Indiana Territory at the time, soon-to-be-president William Henry Harrison, attacked the Shawnee settlement that served as Tecumseh's headquarters with a force of more than 1,000. When Harrison and his men marched into Prophetstown in late 1811, near the Tippecanoe and Wabash Rivers, Chief Tecumseh was actually not pres-

Marengo Cave   Courtesy Marengo Cave

ent. His brother, Tenskwatawa, a spiritual leader known as The Prophet, instead took charge and led the Native contingency into a surprise attack on Harrison's army. However, after several hours, the Native army ran low on ammunition and ultimately abandoned Prophetstown—before Harrison and his army burned it down. Some historians doubt that the battle was as decisive as is often believed, because although the defeat was a significant temporary blow for Tecumseh's Confederacy, they rebuilt Prophetstown and violence against pioneers soon increased. Regardless, Harrison was credited with a historic victory and soon picked up the nickname "Tippecanoe"; he even returned to the site of the battle in political rallies that were staged as part of his presidential campaign.

Today visitors can see the site of the Battle of Tippecanoe at the 100-acre park, the highlight of which is an 85-foot-tall obelisk that serves as a memorial. Check out the on-site museum for more information on the battle and on Tecumseh's Confederacy, as well as an exhibit of historic firearms, many of the kind used in the battle, and artifacts of Native American cultures. There are also several excellent hiking trails and picnic grounds on the site.

Iowa

172 Danish Immigrant Museum

CONTACT 800-759-9192, http://dkmuseum.org;
2212 Washington St., Elk Horn

PRICING	$
BEST TIME TO VISIT	Year-round
AGE RANGE	7 and older

Danish Immigrant Museum   Courtesy Iowa Tourism Office

The story of America is the collected story of a land of immigrants, and middle America is no exception. A number of small communities in the Midwest were settled in the 19th century by large numbers of formerly Danish citizens. Danish immigrants left their native countries by the hundreds of thousands for myriad reasons—to avoid religious persecution, to access better economic opportunities, and even to fulfill a sense of adventure. Most Danish immigrants originally settled on the East Coast in the 19th century. However, because the United States as part of the Homestead Act of 1862 promised any immigrant head of household who had declared his intent to became a U.S. citizen 160 acres of unoccupied government land for the purposes of homesteading (eventually earning the title in five years), immigrants who had come from around the world left the eastern cities to make their way to the American frontiers to claim a bit of the American dream for themselves. By the 1870s, Danes had moved westward to Wisconsin, Nebraska, North and South Dakota, California, and Iowa.

The Danish Immigrant Museum offers the largest collection of Danish American artifacts in the world, and is one of the best places to learn the story of Danish immigration. The 16,000-square-foot museum is a half-timbered structure housing a diverse collection of more than 35,000 pieces, including family heirlooms brought carefully from Denmark, like fine needlework quilts, jewelry, antique porcelain by Royal Copenhagen, household items like spinning wheels and teapots, and family photographs. The museum is the site of annual family-friendly festivals and a favorite stop for individuals researching their genealogy—the museum also houses tens of thousands of records on Danish Americans.

> While in Elk Horn, be sure to check out the Danish Windmill (712-764-7472; 4038 Main St.). The 60-foot mill was built in Norre Snede, Denmark, and shipped to Elk Horn to be restored in 1975. Guests can take guided tours to see the massive grinding stones, which still grind wheat and rye via wind power.

173 Grant Wood Studio

CONTACT 319-366-7503, www.crma.org/Content/Grant-Wood/Grant-Wood-Studio; 810 2nd Ave. SE, Cedar Rapids

PRICING	$
BEST TIME TO VISIT	May through December (often closed for winter season)
AGE RANGE	10 and older

A native of Iowa, Grant Wood (1891–1942) was an important American artist considered to be part of the Regionalist movement. His work is easily recognized because of his distinctive homey style and his preference for homespun subject matter, largely the people and landscapes of the rural Midwest. He's best known for the iconic painting *American Gothic*, which he painted in his Cedar Rapids studio in 1930. Today guests can get a glimpse into the artist's life and times by visiting the Grant Wood Studio. Begin your

Iowa State Capitol   ©Jeff Rivard/iStockphoto.com

For true Wood aficionados, the Cedar Rapids Museum of Art offers a map of the Grant Wood Trail (www.crma.org/Content/Grant-Wood/Visit-Iowas-Grant-Wood-Trail.aspx), which includes the Figge Art Museum in Davenport, the Dubuque Museum of Art, and half a dozen or so additional sites important to the life and career of this famous American painter.

Herbert Hoover National Historic Site

Courtesy National Park Service

tour in the visitor center, where you'll watch a video about Wood and about the structure he built. Afterward, docents will take you upstairs to the second-floor studio—filled with shelves and special niches that Wood used to display flowers and other objects he might be studying for a current project. Wood designed the studio himself, and it is a work of art on its own—reminiscent of a Parisian loft as much as a structure in middle America. Afterward, be sure to walk three blocks to the Cedar Rapids Museum of Art (319-366-7503, 410 3rd Ave. SE), with which the studio is affiliated. The museum displays the largest collection of Wood works in the world, including the well-known *Young Corn*. (His most famous piece, *American Gothic*, is housed at the Art Institute of Chicago; see the description under "Illinois.")

174 Herbert Hoover National Historic Site

CONTACT 319-643-5301, http://hoover.archives.gov; 210 Parkside Dr., West Branch

PRICING	$–$$
BEST TIME TO VISIT	Year-round
AGE RANGE	7 and older

Herbert Hoover (1874–1964) was the 31st president of the United States, and thus far the only chief executive to hail from Iowa. Hoover led a remarkable life: He was born in West Branch to Quaker parents, but was orphaned by the time he was 9. At that time he left Iowa for Oregon, to live with a maternal uncle, and managed to secure his education and fortune

very much as a self-made man. He attended law school at then-new Stanford University in California, worked as the U.S. food administrator under President Woodrow Wilson, was appointed the director of the American Relief Administration following World War I, and served as Secretary of Commerce under President Warren G. Harding. In 1928 Hoover won the Republican nomination for the presidency, and in the November general election won handily against Democratic opponent Alfred E. Smith.

The 187-acre Herbert Hoover National Historic Site comprises Hoover's birthplace cottage, a Quaker meetinghouse, a historic blacksmith shop, the grave site of President and Mrs. Hoover, and the Herbert Hoover Presidential Library. Begin your tour of the library and museum in the rotunda by checking out the 16-foot granite atlas that marks the nations where Hoover conducted his many food-relief efforts. Then move on to the thematically arranged galleries that progress throughout Hoover's lifetime. Don't miss the re-creation of the president's fishing cabin, the depiction of the Waldorf Towers suite where he lived in his last years, and a fun display of dresses belonging to the First Lady, Lou Henry Hoover. Kids will enjoy the diorama that depicts Mrs. Hoover—a longtime board member of the Girl Scouts of America—purchasing the first-ever box of Girl Scout cookies. The library has a voluminous collection of papers on Hoover and his presidency; also within the library is an extensive archival collection of papers on Laura Ingalls Wilder, author of the popular Little House on the Prairie novels.

175 Hitchcock House

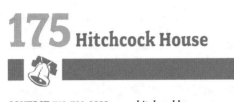

CONTACT 712-769-2323, www.hitchcockhouse.org;
63788 567th Lane, Lewis

PRICING	$
BEST TIME TO VISIT	Open May through September, closed Monday
AGE RANGE	7 and older

This unassuming red stone house played a pivotal role in the Underground Railroad, a system of safe houses throughout America that hid runaway slaves on their transit north. "Conductors" would guide the former slaves to each destination in secret—no records were kept and there were no written communications, because aiding runaway slaves was against federal law and punishable by imprisonment or, in some cases, by death. The Hitchcock House was built in 1856 by George B. Hitchcock, a reverend of the Congregational Church and a vehement abolitionist. When Hitchcock moved to Iowa, he built the home with the express purpose of providing sanctuary for escaped slaves. Visitors today can see the secret room Hitchcock built in the basement; the basement room is accessible from the stairs inside and also via a cellar door to the outside. The secret room was concealed from view behind a bookshelf that served double duty as a hidden door. Upstairs the structure is decorated with period pieces from the 19th century. Well-informed docents at this inspirational landmark will explain that because the home was relatively small, only a few men and women could be sheltered in the home at a time, and then usually only for a few nights; they generally moved from one station along the "railroad" to the next under the cover of nightfall, or sometimes during the day concealed in wagons under a load of hay—and just being on the property makes it possible to imagine the hardship slaves had to endure in their pursuit of liberty.

176 Iowa State Fair

CONTACT www.iowastatefair.org; E. 30th St. and E. University Ave., Des Moines

PRICING	$–$$ (midway rides, horse shows, and some grandstand entertainment additional)
BEST TIME TO VISIT	Held annually in mid-August
AGE RANGE	All ages

Many would argue that there's no better way to get a slice of American life than by attending a regional fair—and the folks in Iowa would agree with songwriters Rodgers and Hammerstein that their state fair is "dollars to donuts" the greatest. The annual fair takes place in Des Moines in late summer; it's the single largest event in Iowa and one of the largest and oldest agricultural expos in the United States. Every year more than a million people attend from around the world. There is a seemingly endless amount of things to do, including a midway—famous for its double Ferris wheel and dozens of other thrill rides and carnival games—more than 600 product and agricultural exhibits, livestock shows and sales, and more than 50 options for food on a stick. There is constant live entertainment—much of it free—including local dance troupes and musical performers and internationally recognized entertainers. There are dozens of wacky animal contests—like the biggest ram, the largest rabbit, the heaviest pigeon, the fluffiest cat, the smallest dog—and even more wacky human con-

Iowa State Fair   Courtesy Iowa Tourism Office

tests. Check out the lawn-chair-toss competition, the bubble-blowing contest, the horseshow-pitching contest, the arm-wrestling contest (men's, women's, and children's divisions), the beard-growing contest, the rubber-chicken-throwing contest, the pie-eating contest, the Big Wheel race, the yo-yo contest, the diaper derby, the mother–daughter look-alike contest, the turkey-calling contest, the wood-chopping contest, and the outhouse races (to name only a few). A highlight of every fair is the Butter Cow, a 100-plus-year tradition of sculpting a bovine from a dairy product. In recent years sculptors have added other butter art, including depictions of Elvis, Garth Brooks, and the scene from Grant Wood's *American Gothic*. The Iowa State Fair is an experience every family should share at least once: Don't miss it, don't even be late.

177 Mines of Spain Archaeological Site

CONTACT www.minesofspain.org; 8991 Bellevue Heights, Dubuque

PRICING	$
BEST TIME TO VISIT	Year-round
AGE RANGE	7 and older

The site of the Mines of Spain archaeological site was inhabited as long ago as 8,000 years. The earliest identified people to call the area home were the Mesquakie Natives, who traded furs with French trap-

Mines of Spain Archaeological Site

Courtesy Dubuque Area Convention and Visitors Bureau

pers who frequented the region. The first European to settle in what is now Iowa bears a familiar name: Julien Dubuque. Dubuque received a land grant in 1796 from the governor of Spain, giving him permission to mine the land for lead, and the Julien Dubuque Monument (built over Dubuque's burial site and overlooking the Mississippi River) is at the heart of the archaeological site today. Be sure to visit the E. B. Lyons Interpretive and Nature Center for maps and information on the park's 15 miles of walking and hiking trails and 4 miles of ski trails (several of which provide views of the Mines of Spain along old logging roads). The trails are a good place to spot wildlife: Look for river otters, beavers, mink, snapping turtles, flying squirrels, gray foxes, and white-tailed deer. Kids will especially enjoy the Betty Hauptli Bird and Butterfly Garden on site, which displays native prairie gardens and woodland flower gardens.

178 National Mississippi River Museum and Aquarium

CONTACT 563-557-9545, www.mississippiriver museum.com; 350 E. 3rd St., Dubuque

PRICING	$$–$$$; movie tickets additional
BEST TIME TO VISIT	Year-round
AGE RANGE	All ages

The Mississippi River is the longest river in the United States, and through the years served as the lifeblood first for Native Americans who called the land through which it flows home, then for westward-expanding pioneers who moved goods along its xpanse, and finally today as a continuing commerce route and recreational venue. The National Mississippi River Museum and Aquarium is a unique attraction that allows visitors to learn more about the culture, history, and natural ecosystems along the mighty Mississippi. The museum offers two centers to explore the significance of the Mississippi and other major rivers of the United States. The original Mississippi River Center features 12 aquariums, interactive exhibits, and galleries where families can learn more

National Mississippi River Museum and Aquarium
Courtesy Dubuque Area Convention and Visitors Bureau

about nature along the river. Look for frogs, turtles, ducks, sturgeon, and giant catfish on display. Outside you'll find a boatyard plaza with a working blacksmith shop and the historic steamboat *William M. Black*. The newer National River Center focuses on rivers throughout the United States, and includes exhibits like *Rivers to the Sea*, which showcases four saltwater aquariums full of sharks and fish native to the mouth of the Mississippi River; *RiverWays*, a gallery that highlights the culture, people, and artifacts indigenous to interior U.S. rivers; and *RiverWorks*, a hands-on area for kids where they can learn about rivers by crawling through a re-created beaver lodge and operating a pedal-powered water cycle. The center also includes a 3-D/4-D immersion theater that shows river-related films and includes special effects like mist and wind, as well as piped-in smells and seats that move with the motion of the movies.

179 Toolesboro Indian Mounds

CONTACT 319-523-8381; 6568 Toolesboro Rd., Wapello

PRICING	$
BEST TIME TO VISIT	Grounds are open year-round, but visitor center is available only from late May through October (call ahead)
AGE RANGE	7 and older

The Toolesboro Indian Mounds are the best preserved ruins of what is known as the Hopewell culture, a group of ancient Natives who lived along the Mississippi and Illinois Rivers from about 200 BC to AD 300. The culture left no written records, so we aren't sure what they called themselves, nor do we know precisely what the earthen mounds—which can be found throughout the United States—were used for. Researchers do know that the Hopewell people generally settled in wooded regions along rivers, where they trapped animals for food and fur and where they fished and hunted. And thanks to numerous artifacts uncovered at this site and others like it, we know they were skilled artisans who left behind precisely carved obsidian objects and stone tools. The site includes seven cone-shaped burial mounds on a hill overlooking the Iowa River. The mounds vary from 8 to 10 feet high and 30 to 80 feet in diameter. Archaeologists believe the earthenwork mounds were created around 100 BC as part of a village site. Visitors can walk through the woods to view all seven of the mounds—and two can be seen readily from the visitor center.

180 Western Historic Trails Center

CONTACT 712-366-4900; 3434 Richard Downing Ave., Council Bluffs

PRICING	$
BEST TIME TO VISIT	Year-round (closed Monday in winter)
AGE RANGE	7 and older

This interpretive museum preserves the legacy of four important pioneer wagon trails that passed through this region of Iowa: the Lewis and Clark Trail, from 1804 when Meriwether Lewis, William Clark, and their small Corps of Discovery set out from Illinois to explore uncharted wilderness en route to the Pacific Ocean; the Oregon Trail, which was the major route west for pioneers in the 1830s and 1860s; the Mormon Trail, which led members of the Church of Latter Day Saints from Nauvoo, Illinois, to Salt Lake City, Utah (settled by Brigham Young) in 1846; and the

California Trail, active starting in 1849 during the gold rush era. The completion of the transcontinental railroad in 1869 put an end to these trails, but they remain an important part of the story of westward ex-

pansion in America. The museum includes dioramas of pioneer life along the trails, maps and information for those wishing to follow the trails, and a beautiful nature pathway that runs from the center to the nearby river. Kids will enjoy the 15-minute film in the center theater that compares a cross-country trip of a modern-day family with that of a pioneer family 150 years earlier.

Western Historic Trails Center   Courtesy Iowa Tourism Office

While in Council Bluffs, be sure to check out the nearby Lewis and Clark Monument Park (19962 Monument Rd.), which commemorates the historic meeting between explorers Lewis and Clark and the Otoe and Missouria Native tribes.

Konza Prairie   Courtesy Kansas Division of Travel and Tourism

kansas

181 Carrie Nation Home

CONTACT	620-886-3553; 211 W. Fowler, Medicine Lodge
PRICING	$
BEST TIME TO VISIT	Year-round
AGE RANGE	7 and older

The Women's Christian Temperance Union (WCTU) was formed in 1873 and is best known for its efforts to reduce or eliminate alcohol consumption in the United States. Members of the WCTU saw their work as fulfilling both a moral imperative (most individuals involved in the organization believed it a sin to drink) and a social imperative. The WCTU was in fact one of the first vocal and influential advocates for women and children, who were often the victims of domestic abuse at the hands of husbands and fathers who drank in excess. In addition to efforts to ban alcohol use, the WCTU—with more than 120,000 members by 1879—worked to secure property and custody rights for women, protection for women in the workplace, and women's suffrage.

Perhaps the most colorful character to represent the temperance movement was Carrie Nation (1846–1911), a radical political activist in the days before Prohibition. Nation did more than protest and picket local watering holes: She is infamous for entering such establishments with a hatchet, vandalizing bar fixtures as she sang church hymns and prayed—some-

Carrie Nation Home   Courtesy Kansas Division of Travel and Tourism

The Carrie Nation home in Medicine Lodge is only one of two houses belonging to the temperance movement leader that is listed on the U.S. National Register of Historic Places: There is another (the Carry A. Nation House) in Lancaster, Kentucky.

times accompanied by a band of followers (whom she called "smashers") and sometimes alone. Nation aimed to destroy kegs of beer and whiskey, but she also often broke mirrors, tables, and windows—and occasionally even attacked the individuals who sold the liquor. Between 1900 and 1910, she was arrested more than 30 times for her so-called hatchetations.

The Carrie Nation House memorializes the small brick home where Nation lived from 1889 to 1902. The grounds for the museum site include a replica of a stockade once on the site, an 1877 pioneer cabin, and the preserved house. The home is furnished with period pieces and includes a display of Nation's personal belongings, including her writing desk, hats and purses, and a small pin in the shape of a hatchet—an example of a trinket she sold to help pay her legal fees.

182 Dodge City

CONTACT	www.dodgecity.org; Dodge City
PRICING	Prices vary by attraction
BEST TIME TO VISIT	May through September (many attractions are closed fall through spring)
AGE RANGE	7 and older

Dodge City is synonymous with the Wild West, and is remembered in the history books and popular culture for its often lawless past. It was established in 1872 to coincide with the coming of the Santa Fe Railroad, and it was a crossroads for massive cattle drives that took place across the Plains states. In the late 19th century the city was largely populated by cowboys, hunters, trappers, and those who catered to their transient lifestyle. Gambling, prostitution, gunfighting, and theft were common—and the general lawlessness of the area has often been immortalized on film. Today the city is a mecca for tourists who want a taste of this frontier past. Before you get out of Dodge, don't miss these attractions:

- **Boot Hill Museum** (620-227-8188; Front St.). This small, interactive museum highlights the infamous Boot Hill Cemetery (final resting place of notorious residents), and offers exhibits and displays that highlight the frontier Dodge City. Visit during the summer to see reenactors engage in faux gunfights or hear "Miss Kitty" entertain the crowd.
- **Gunfighters Wax Museum** (620-225-7311; 603 5th Ave.). If your kids like old western movies, they'll love the chance to "meet" some of the notorious gunslingers and heroic law enforcers in person—or at least via their wax facsimiles. Look for Davy Crockett, Buffalo Bill, Calamity Jane, Bat Masterson, and the notorious Wyatt Earp.
- **Santa Fe Depot** (620-225-1001; Central and Wyatt Earp). Check out the Santa Fe Depot, the largest train depot still standing in Kansas. Call ahead to arrange a guided tour of the facility.

Dwight D. Eisenhower boyhood home
Courtesy Dwight D. Eisenhower Presidential Library

183 Dwight D. Eisenhower Presidential Library and Museum

CONTACT 785-263-6700, www.eisenhower.archives.gov; 200 SE 4th St., Abilene

PRICING	$–$$
BEST TIME TO VISIT	Year-round
AGE RANGE	7 and older

Dwight D. Eisenhower (often known as "Ike") (1890–1969) was the 34th president of the United States and a five-star general in the U.S. Army. He served as supreme commander of the Allied Forces during World War II. As president Eisenhower oversaw civil rights legislation and the interstate highway system, and is often noted as being the first "television president." The Dwight D. Eisenhower Presidential Library and Museum comprises Ike's boyhood home, a mu-

seum, and the grave site of the former president and his wife, Mamie. The library houses more than 26 million pages of manuscript, more than 300,000 photographs, 1,100 hours of audiotapes, and nearly 70,000 artifacts relating to the Eisenhower presidency or to Ike himself. The museum includes five galleries that showcase Eisenhower's life from his childhood days in Abilene through his army years and presidency until his retirement. Be sure to check out the Mamie Eisenhower Gallery for a fun look at the First Lady's fashion style. The Military Gallery features objects and documents that interpret Eisenhower's role as supreme commander in World War II. Children will especially enjoy the Presidential Gallery, which includes a 1950s-era fallout shelter, a 1950s-style living room, and a re-creation of Eisenhower's retirement office.

184 El Cuartelejo

CONTACT 620-872-2061, www.kansastravel.org/scottstatepark.htm; within Lake Scott State Park; 520 W. Lake Scott Dr., Scott City

PRICING	$
BEST TIME TO VISIT	Summer
AGE RANGE	7 and older

El Cuartelejo is the site of the northernmost Native American pueblo in the United States—and the only

Learn more at the nearby El Quartelejo Museum (620-872-5912; 902 W. 5th St., Scott City). Displays here tell the story of the El Cuartelejo ruins and include temporary exhibits that focus on contemporary art and culture from the region. Guests can tour a re-creation of one of the rooms from the El Cuartelejo pueblo as it might have looked when the pueblo was occupied.

185 Fort Scott National Historic Site

CONTACT 620-223-0310, www.nps.gov/fosc; Old Fort Blvd., Fort Scott

PRICING	$
BEST TIME TO VISIT	Summer
AGE RANGE	7 and older

pueblo known to exist in Kansas. The adobe and stone remains of this small Indian village are unique to this region: Although pueblos such as this are common in Arizona and New Mexico, El Cuartelejo is hundreds of miles northeast of the vast majority of known pueblos in the U.S. Southwest. Archaeologists believe this isolated village was built in about 1650 by Taos Indians who fled their native New Mexico and Spanish colonial influence to seek refuge with the Plains Apache. The site has been extensively excavated, and visitors can see the remains when visiting the Lake Scott State Park, where the ruins are located. You will find that the pueblo was a seven-room dwelling—only large enough to house a small group of people. You can also see the remains of shallow channels running from nearby springs, which are believed to have been irrigation ditches for the Natives' nearby crop fields.

Fort Scott is located in the Osage cuestas—bluffs with one steep side and a gentle slope on the other side—in a lovely region of southeast Kansas. The cuesta on which the fort was built in 1842 overlooks the Marmaton River and Mill Creek, and partly because of this vantage point and the protection afforded by the natural geography of the cuesta, the fort never included a wall around it. Fort Scott was one in a line of forts from Louisiana to Minnesota created to keep the peace between Native peoples and white settlers on the Plains as well as protect pioneers moving through the region on their way to Oregon and California via the Santa Fe and Oregon Trails.

In addition to its significant role in opening up the American frontier, the fort was to play another pivotal role during the bloody Civil War. In 1854, under the Kansas-Nebraska Act, Congress created the Kansas and Nebraska Territories, which officially opened the surrounding lands for settlement. At this time slavery was a heated topic throughout the country, with three distinct opposing viewpoints about allowing slavery in the new territories: Proslavery individuals supported expansion of slavery into the western territories; abolitionists were against slavery throughout the country; and "free staters" fell somewhere in between—arguing that slavery should not extend westward but not taking a particular stand against slavery in states in which it was already

El Cuartelejo

Courtesy Kansas Division of Travel and Tourism

Check out the cell phone tour (620-921-3117) of Fort Scott, which includes 12 stops highlighting a building or area within the fort. The tour takes less than 15 minutes and is free.

Reenactors at Fort Scott National Historic Site
Courtesy Kansas Division of Travel and Tourism

186 Nicodemus Historic Site

CONTACT 785-839-4233, www.nps.gov/nico; 304 Washington Ave., Nicodemus

PRICING	$
BEST TIME TO VISIT	Year-round
AGE RANGE	7 and older

established. Because of these fractious viewpoints, and the violence that ensued because of the differences, the area came to be known as "Bleeding Kansas." Fort Scott was a proslavery town (although many free staters lived in surrounding areas), but in its turn the fort served as a supply depot for Union armies in the west, became a refuge for escaped slaves, and was the site of the swearing-in of the first African American regiment to engage Confederate soldiers during the war.

Today Fort Scott National Historic Site comprises 20 historic structures from the original fort, a parade grounds, and 5 acres of restored indigenous tallgrass prairie. Eleven of the historic buildings are open to the public and are furnished in original and reproduction period pieces. There are also three museums on the site, including the infantry barracks (which offers a 20-minute orientation film), the dragoon barracks museum, and the Wilson-Goodlander House. Guided tours are offered every day at 1 PM in the summer or by advance arrangement in other seasons. Kids will not want to miss event weekends in the summer when rangers and volunteers dress in period costumes and reenact historical events important in the fort's history. Throughout the year guests will find re-creations of Civil War encampments and living history demonstrations; in late fall the site hosts a popular candlelight tour.

In its heyday the small town of Nicodemus was the largest community established by freed slaves following the Civil War. Nicodemus was named after the first African American slave to purchase his own freedom in the United States; it was founded in 1877 during the Reconstruction period by the Reverend W. H. Smith (an African American minister) and W. R. Hill (a white land developer), plus five additional black men. Together these seven individuals formed the Nicodemus Town Company, and recruited residents for the new settlement by visiting black churches in Kentucky for the purpose of convincing folks to move to Kansas. Kansas had been a free state, and was thus believed to be receptive to African Americans; flyers distributed by the Nicodemus Company promised it to be a place for African Americans to form their own government and get a fresh start. Although life was hard for settlers in the small town, they managed to eke out a living, and by the mid-1880s Nicodemus boasted several general stores, three churches, two newspapers, a bank, and several small hotels. At its peak the town

Nicodemus Historic Site   Courtesy Kansas Division of Travel and Tourism

was home to more than 600 citizens. However, Nicodemus eventually floundered—largely because the railroad did not pass through and residents had to leave the area to find jobs. Today there are a scant several dozen residents. The townsite includes five buildings: the Township Hall (home to a temporary visitor center), the African Methodist Episcopal Church, the First Baptist Church, the schoolhouse, and the St. Francis Hotel. Pick up a walking-tour brochure at the Township Hall to help you find your way around this important historic site. Don't miss the Nicodemus Historical Society Museum (611 S. 5th St.), which offers an interpretive display on the development of the township and exhibits explaining the hardship settlers faced on the prairie.

187 Old Cowtown Museum

CONTACT 316-219-1871, www.oldcowtown.org; 1865 W. Museum Dr., Wichita

PRICING	$$
BEST TIME TO VISIT	Year-round (closed Sunday and Monday)
AGE RANGE	All ages

Old Cowtown is a living history museum that recreates a midwestern cattle town during the 1870s,

Old Cowtown Museum   Courtesy Kansas Division of Travel and Tourism

offering families a chance to experience life in the earliest days of Kansas. There are a number of themed areas within the park, each offering a unique insight into the historical period of the late 19th century. In the Hunter/Trader Area, check out the period

> ## Kids will enjoy hearing tales of the costumed buffalo hunters.

furnishings of the 1868 Munger House and Gardens, once a boardinghouse, home, church, and public gathering place. Nearby is the Trader's Cabin, relocated from its original location on the Chisholm Trail in Clearwater; kids will enjoy hearing the tales of the costumed buffalo hunters—and if they aren't squeamish, will be fascinated by the many animal pelts on display. The Drovers Camp area of the park is devoted to the cowboys, who relive the heyday of the Wichita cattle business. There are numerous demonstrations within this site, including cooking meals on the open range, roping, and branding cattle. The Industrial and Business Area includes a working blacksmith shop, a stocked drugstore from the era, a meat market, and a train depot. The Residential Street zone includes an 1874 middle-class home, complete with Victorian flower beds and period furnishings; and a "Story and a Half House," more typical for less affluent citizens of Kansas in the late 19th century. The highlight of the park is arguably the 1880 DeVore Farm, a 5-acre fully functioning farm that is stocked with animals (including longhorn steer) and equipment typical of the era. Costumed interpreters carry on the day-to-day chores of the farm, like feeding chickens, milking cows, and harvesting corn.

Throughout the year Old Cowtown hosts special events, like "Frozen in Time"—when events from a given day in the 1870s are re-created (based on the news stories culled from periodicals of the time); and "Civil War Day," an opportunity for guests to peek into the daily lives of Union and Confederate soldiers during a reenacted battle. And every day kids will enjoy watching cooking demonstrations, wagon rides, faux shootouts, and kicking back with an ice-cold sarsaparilla in the saloon.

188 Old Prairie Town Ward-Meade Historic Site

Visit the Old Prairie Town Ward-Meade Historic Site in early March (give or take a few weeks) to see the glorious tulips in the botanical gardens. You can purchase bulbs here to take home or just wander among the spectacular bursts of color.

CONTACT 785-368-3888, www.facebook.com/pages/Old-Prairie-Town-at-Ward-Meade-Historic-Site/179694758737279; 124 NW Fillmore, Topeka

PRICING	$
BEST TIME TO VISIT	Spring
AGE RANGE	All ages

A visit to the Old Prairie Town Ward-Meade Historic Site is like stepping into a Laura Ingalls Wilder novel. This 5.5-acre storybook-pretty living history museum is a re-creation of an idyllic pioneer town and includes a one-room schoolhouse where you can brush up on your spelling with the schoolmarm, an antique dentist's office complete with period instruments, a quaint log cabin, a general store, a church with lovely stained glass, a beautifully furnished (and some say haunted) 1870s Victorian Mansion, a charming small train depot, and the Potwin Drug Store with a real working soda fountain. (Don't miss the Green River Sodas.) There are also 2.5 acres of botanic gardens including more than 500 species of flowers and blooming trees, plus a romantic gazebo and a water garden. The real fun here are the costumed reenactments that staff and volunteers stage for events throughout the year, like the annual Apple Festival that includes

Old Prairie Town Ward-Meade Historic Site
Courtesy Kansas Division of Travel and Tourism

open-fire cooking demonstrations and games for children; the holiday meal in December that includes live period music and a costumed Father Christmas; hearth-cooked meals in the log cabin; and home-baked ginger and molasses cookies and apple cider treats shared with guests around an open fire.

189 Santa Fe Trail

CONTACT www.santafetrail.org; locations in Kansas run from Olathe in the east to Elkhart in the west

PRICING	Admission varies by site (most are free)
BEST TIME TO VISIT	Summer
AGE RANGE	7 and older

In the early to middle 19th century, before railroads made intercontinental travel relatively painless, there were several important trails used by westward-migrating Americans—perhaps none as important in opening up trade to the West as the Santa Fe Trail. The Santa Fe Trail ran from the Missouri River west to Santa Fe, New Mexico, and it was used more by traders and military personnel than by settlers. The 750-mile trail passes also through Missouri, Oklahoma, Colorado, and New Mexico—but two-thirds of it traverses the state of Kansas. The state boasts more than 130 attractions relating to the Santa Fe Trail, and for those looking to experience a little of what was an arduous pathway for folks pursuing Manifest Destiny there is no better place to explore. The Kansas portion of the trail stretches from Olathe, in the northeast, to Elkhart, in the southwest, taking approximately the same route as current U.S. 56. Ruts from the thousands of wagons that passed through can still be seen throughout, especially in Chase, Dodge City, and Wellsville.

If you're up for a road trip, consider crossing Kansas in the shadows of the Santa Fe Trail, and be sure to check out these stops along the way (listed in order, from east to west):

- **The Mahaffie Stagecoach Shop** in Olathe (1100 Kansas City Rd.) is open for tours, and marks the last remaining stop that is open along the Santa Fe Trail.
- **Black Jack Ruts** in Prairie Park in Douglas County (U.S. 56, 3 miles east of Baldwin City) are a collection of prominent parallel ruts—particularly pronounced because the geography of the region meant wagon trains had to stay on the proscribed pathway. Also in the park is an authentic log cabin that preserves artifacts from the Santa Fe Trail era.
- **Last Chance Store** (Main and Chautauqua) in Council Grove billed itself as the last stop for "bacon, beans, and whiskey" and remains a fun place to check out the supplies needed along the Santa Fe Trail.

Last Chance Store, along the Santa Fe Trail

- **Madonna of the Trail** (northeast side of the U.S. 56 and Hwy. 177 junction), also in Council Grove, is a monument dedicated to the "pioneer mothers of the covered wagon days."
- **Trail Days Café** (803 W. Main St.), another stop in Council Grove (part of a restored historic house called the Terwilliger Home), offers a chance to experience period food served in a museum-like setting. The fare includes Native American dishes and prairie-style American favorites, like ham and beans with corn bread and roast buffalo with Indian fry bread.
- **Maxwell Wildlife Refuge** (off Hwy. 86) in Canton offers fun covered-wagon rides (propelled with modern-day combustion engines) through the prairie, featuring great views of the resident bison.
- **Ralph's Ruts in Chase** display seven parallel trail ruts carved into the prairie by wagons, mules, and oxen more than 100 years ago.
- **The Santa Fe Trail Center** (1349 Hwy. 156) in Larned is an interpretive museum that includes artifacts and manuscripts relating to the trail and to the thousands of individuals who passed through the area.
- Nearby **Fort Larned National Historic Site** (off Hwy. 156) comprises nine restored military structures that date to 1859, including original barracks, a blacksmith shop, and a commissary. It is one of the best preserved frontier military posts in the region.
- **The Cimarron Crossing Park** in Cimarron marks the halfway point of the Santa Fe Trail, and includes a historical marker that relates the history of the region. The trail splits at this point, into the southern Cimarron Route—faster but considered more difficult because water was scarce—and the northern Mountain Route, longer but considered safer.

kentucky

190 Abraham Lincoln Birthplace National Historical Park

CONTACT 502-549-3741, www.nps.gov/abli;
7120 Bardstown Rd., Hodgenville

PRICING	$
BEST TIME TO VISIT	Summer (guided tours are available from Memorial Day to Labor Day)
AGE RANGE	All ages

Abraham Lincoln (1809–65), the 16th president of the United States, is remembered by historians as one of the greatest leaders of the nation—and is known by American schoolchildren as the president born of humble beginnings in a log cabin. His parents were from Virginia, but he was born in Kentucky, on a farm called Sinking Spring, and lived in the state in his young boyhood. Lincoln was a lover of learning and pursued his education with passion despite having little opportunity in his early life for formal schooling. As an adult he practiced law, and in 1858 ran against Stephen Douglas for senator of Illinois. Lincoln lost the election, but gained the fame necessary to win the Republican nomination for president two years later. He presided over a nation divided during the American Civil War; his most noteworthy accomplishment as commander in chief was the eloquent and extraor-

There are dozens of sites throughout the region dedicated to preserving the memory of Abraham Lincoln. If you're interested in exploring more, check out the Lincoln Heritage Trail (download a map at www.kentuckytourism.com/maps/lincoln-map.aspx), which follows the pathway of a series of highways throughout Kentucky, Illinois, and Indiana. This trail covers 2,200 miles, with more than 50 sites along the way marking the life and times of Lincoln.

dinarily powerful Emancipation Proclamation, which declared all slaves in the country to be free. On Good Friday in 1865, Lincoln was assassinated while watching a play in Ford's Theatre, just blocks from the White House.

The Abraham Lincoln Birthplace National Historical Park memorializes two farm areas where Lincoln spent his earliest days: the birthplace site of Sinking Spring and his boyhood home of Knob Creek Farm. Visit the birthplace site to see a representation of an early-19th-century log cabin like the one in which Lincoln was born; it is enshrined in the majestic Memorial Building. Be sure to stop by the visitor center to see a 15-minute orientation film and check out the Lincoln family Bible on display. The Knob Creek Farm site nearby—accessible from Sinking Spring via a trail—includes a log cabin and historic tavern. In summertime guests can walk through the pioneer garden to see crops like corn and pumpkin being cultivated.

Abraham Lincoln Birthplace   Courtesy National Park Service

191 Ashland: The Henry Clay Estate

CONTACT 859-266-8581, www.henryclay.org;
120 Sycamore Rd., Lexington

PRICING	$–$$
BEST TIME TO VISIT	Spring through fall; closed Monday and all of January; open February for larger groups by appointment only
AGE RANGE	7 and older

Henry Clay Estate

Courtesy www.kentuckytourism.com

Henry Clay (1777–1852) was an influential American Founder during the early years of the republic. Clay was a lawyer and statesman, and the Senate and the House of Representatives—serving in the latter for three terms as Speaker of the House. He also served as secretary of state. Clay is best remembered as the "Great Compromiser." With John Calhoun and Daniel Webster (who along with Clay made up what is remembered as the "Immortal Trio"), Clay negotiated the Missouri Compromise of 1820, in which antislavery and proslavery factions in the U.S. Congress agreed to prohibit expansion of slavery into the western territories, except within what is now the state of Missouri. Several decades later, Clay—working together with Stephen Douglas—was also responsible for the Compromise of 1850, a series of five bills that averted secession and reduced the threat of civil war for several years.

Ashland is the elegant 1809 Federal-style home Clay shared with his wife, Lucretia Hart, until his death. Clay named the property after its abundant ash trees, and was immensely proud of the grounds and the structure itself. It is interesting to note (given Clay's public stance on slavery) that he owned approximately 60 slaves to help manage the surrounding plantation and care for the large house, but upon his death he freed all of them in his will. The beautiful 18-room mansion is one of the finest house museums in the country, and is decorated and maintained with strict attention to historical detail. Begin your guided tour at the front door—you'll be welcomed warmly as any visitor to a southern country estate would expect. Highlights include the magnificent entryway, heady with ash woodwork; the formal drawing room, which includes a painting of George and Martha Washington given to Clay as a present from his wife; and the octagonal library with an impressive domed ceiling. After the tour, head outside to stroll through the outbuildings and check out the walking trails that crisscross the 17-acre grounds and formal garden (which is particularly fine during spring blooming).

192 Camp Nelson Civil War Heritage Park

CONTACT	859-881-5716, www.campnelson.org/foundation; 6614 Danville Rd., Nicholasville
PRICING	$
BEST TIME TO VISIT	Late September (for Living History Weekend); closed Sunday and Monday the rest of the year
AGE RANGE	10 and older

During the mid-19th century, Camp Nelson—a Civil War depot for the Union army—was akin to a small city, with nearly 400 structures. It was originally built in 1863, primarily using the labor of some 3,000 former slaves. Soon afterward Camp Nelson was Kentucky's largest recruitment and training center for African American troops—known at the time as "United States Colored Troops." More than 20,000 male African Americans were freed in exchange for enlistment in the Union military forces, and by an 1865 congressional decree their wives and children were freed as well. Often the soldiers brought their families with them to Camp Nelson, and encamp-

Camp Nelson

Courtesy www.kentuckytourism.com

PRICE KEY
$ free–$5
$$ $6–10
$$$ $11–20
$$$$ $21+

ments sprang up across the base to house the growing population.

Today the only building that remains from the Civil War era is the Oliver Perry House, an 1846 structure that was once a home. During the war, however, it was confiscated and converted to officers' quarters; it was often referred to as the "White House," and today serves as a museum for the park, housing artifacts that tell the story of Civil War soldiers. The park is the site of an incredibly popular Civil War reenactment, known as Living History Weekend (generally held over the third weekend in September). Although the life-like re-creation of battle scenes is too intense for some young children, it is a fascinating way to learn about 19th-century weapons, battle strategies, and the unspeakable horror of war.

Hensley Settlement at Cumberland Gap National Historical Park   Photo by Scott Teodorski, courtesy National Park Service

193 Cumberland Gap National Historical Park

CONTACT 606-248-2817; www.nps.gov/cuga; U.S. 25E S., Middlesboro

PRICING	$
BEST TIME TO VISIT	Spring through fall
AGE RANGE	All ages

When Americans first began moving westward in the late 18th and early 19th centuries to settle new territories, they faced the daunting task of crossing the Appalachian Mountains. Pioneers soon discovered a route carved over millennia by wind and rain—and used for almost as long by migrating animals—that passed through the Appalachians: Cumberland Gap. The Cumberland Gap became an important portal to U.S. expansion. From 1775 to 1810, nearly 300,000 people crossed the gap into Kentucky.

Cumberland Gap National Historical Park commemorates the importance of this site; it is located at the borders of Kentucky, Tennessee, and Virginia, and includes 70 miles of hiking trails (some easy enough for a family wielding a stroller and some multiday hikes designed for hard-core hikers); several scenic overlooks—don't miss Pinnacle Overlook, accessible

via a quarter-mile paved trail, that affords astonishing views of three states; interesting cave formations; and a tiny early-20th-century village known as Hensley Settlement. Children will enjoy walking through the rustic, charming log cabins and learning about life well away from civilization (the folks who called Hensley settlement home lived for decades without electricity, indoor plumbing, or paved roads).

For a small fee, schedule in advance a Gap Cave tour with a park ranger. The 1.5-mile tour covers four levels of the cave, which boasts sculptural stalagmites and flowstone cascades—and plenty of bats. Children must be 6 years old or older to take part.

194 Fort Boonesborough

CONTACT 859-527-3131; www.fortboonesborough livinghistory.org; 4375 Boonesborough Rd., Richmond

PRICING	$–$$
BEST TIME TO VISIT	April through October
AGE RANGE	All ages

Daniel Boone (1734–1820) was a frontiersman, explorer, and American folk legend, famous for his treks into and settlement of what is now Kentucky (which was outside of the settled 13 original colonies). Boone opened up what he called a "Wilderness Road" through the Cumberland Gap that cuts through the

Appalachian Mountains and forged into the wide-open spaces beyond. In 1775 Boone founded Fort Boonesborough, one of the first European settlements west of the Appalachians. The fort was important during the American Revolutionary War, and today serves as a living history interpretive museum, complete with costumed reenactors who bring history alive for children through storytelling, demonstrations, and exhibits.

The park offers a plethora of fun, family-friendly workshops and classes, which include artisan crafts like candle making, block printing, spinning, weaving, and hearth cooking. In addition, there are full-day and overnight "Frontier Life" programs that allow guests hands-on experience in cooking over a fire, working in a blacksmith shop, or building a rail fence. Other opportunities include "Tavern Nights" that comprise 18th-century tavern food, spirited discussions of the politics of the day, period music and dance, and tavern games; and the wonderful "Women on the Frontier" program, an interactive two-day adventure that allows visitors to learn skills necessary for frontierswomen—like how to roast a whole pig over a fire and how to put up vegetables for the winter.

Churchill Downs   Courtesy www.kentuckytourism.com

than might be expected—is PG-13: There is ubiquitous gambling, and alcoholic mint juleps are as much a part of the tradition of the Derby as the fancy hats many female spectators don. Nevertheless, for many horse lovers, this short race (it's only about two minutes) is a quintessential Kentucky experience. More family-friendly is the accompanying Kentucky Derby Festival, held the two weeks before the first Saturday in May. The festival includes the "Thunder over Louisville" display, billed as the largest annual fireworks display in North America; a parade; a balloon race; and numerous venues offering live entertainment.

195 Kentucky Derby

CONTACT 502-636-4400, www.kentuckyderby.com; Churchill Downs Racetrack, 700 Central Ave., Louisville

PRICING	Varies by seat
BEST TIME TO VISIT	First Saturday in May
AGE RANGE	13 and older

Horses are synonymous with Kentucky, and horse racing is a long-cherished tradition in the state, dating back to 1789 when the first racetrack was constructed in Lexington. The Kentucky Derby—the premiere horse-racing event in the United States—was first held in 1875, and is an annual event held at the historic Churchill Downs. It is often dubbed "The Run for the Roses" (because the winning thoroughbred is draped in a blanket of the flowers). To be honest, the atmosphere at the Derby—although more genteel

196 Louisville Slugger Museum and Factory

CONTACT 877-775-8443, www.sluggermuseum.org; 800 W. Main St., Louisville

PRICING	$$–$$$
BEST TIME TO VISIT	Year-round
AGE RANGE	3 and older

If baseball is America's favorite pastime, then the world-renowned Louisville Slugger baseball bat may very well be America's favorite piece of sporting equipment. The family-owned company that produces Louisville Sluggers has been crafting baseball bats since 1884, and has supplied some of the biggest names in the game throughout the past 100-plus years; today it is the official supplier to Major League

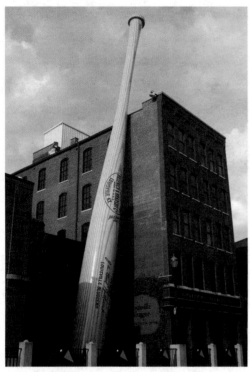

Louisville Slugger Museum and Factory

Courtesy www.kentuckytourism.com

Baseball. The Louisville Slugger Museum and Factory is housed at the corporate headquarters in downtown Louisville. You can't miss the building: Look for the world's largest baseball bat, seemingly resting against the side of the brick structure. The life-like sculpture crafted of steel weighs 68,000 pounds and reaches 120 feet tall; it is a scale replica of Babe Ruth's 34-inch Louisville Slugger.

Throughout the museum there are numerous artifacts to fuel a baseball fanatic's dreams for years—and the best part is that guests are allowed to interact with some of the memorabilia. You can try out your swing using bats from legendary Boys of Summer like Tony Gwynn, Ted Williams, and Derek Jeter—and step

For a good giggle, check out the mural facing the giant bat outside, on the wall of the Kentucky Mirror + Plate Glass building (822 W. Main St.), which shows a ball (in scale with the giant bat) shattering a window.

into a batting cage to test out new prototypes from the Louisville Slugger company as well. An on-site theater shows an emotional film called *The Heart of the Game*, featuring luminaries like Johnny Bench, Grady Sizemore, and Jim Thome.

Don't miss the chance to take a guided tour of the factory itself; tours take about 30 minutes, and bats are produced seven days a week (although sometimes the factory is offline for brief periods—in which case you'll be treated to a bat-making demonstration). Everyone on the tour receives a complimentary mini Louisville Slugger.

197 Mary Todd Lincoln House

CONTACT	859-233-9999, http://mtlhouse.org; 578 W. Main St., Lexington
PRICING	$–$$
BEST TIME TO VISIT	Spring through fall; closed Sunday and December through early March
AGE RANGE	10 and older

Wife to the 16th president of the United States, Abraham Lincoln, Mary Todd Lincoln (1818–82) was as controversial in her day as some recent First Ladies have been in our own: Mrs. Lincoln was perceived as an overspender, redecorating the White House during some of the bleakest days of the American Civil War to the tune of $20,000—$6,000 over budget (an enormous debt in 19th-century currency), purchasing expensive White House china, and dressing herself in lavish style. She was often criticized as being sympathetic to the Confederacy—several of her half brothers served in the Confederate army; she suffered from poor health most of her life, and battled bouts of depression and recurring migraine headaches. Despite her challenges and her critics, Mrs. Lincoln was a staunch political and social supporter of her husband, especially during his years as president; she volunteered as a nurse in Union hospitals, toured Union army camps as a way to boost morale, raised private funds to purchase blankets for woefully undersup-

Bring Along Younger Siblings

Throughout this book you'll see suggestions for minimum age ranges for all activities and sites. The National Holocaust Museum in Washington, DC, for example, is generally just too intense for very young children; and the Margaret Mitchell Museum in Atlanta isn't likely to hold appeal for kids who are too young to have read *Gone with the Wind*—and thus both are recommended for teenagers. Likewise, a majority of the historical sites will hold less interest for toddlers than they will school-aged children. But don't leave very young children out of the fun. Every new experience adds to a toddler's skill set, so if your older

Recreation break   Courtesy Mel Preimesberger

child has younger siblings who might not fully appreciate, say, the historical significance of the Mary Todd Lincoln House or the beauty of Cumberland Gap, they will revel in the smaller opportunities for learning and fun—like seeing a rabbit along a hiking trail or playing nine holes at a local miniature golf course. Likewise, it won't hurt an older sibling to tag along on a carousel ride or a trip to the petting zoo: Although older kids may think they're too cool for little-tykes adventures, they'll probably still end up enjoying the chance to relive their own toddlerhood.

plied Union troops, and engaged in vigorous fundraising for the Contraband Relief Association, which provided clothing, medical care, housing, and employment for recently free slaves. She considered her best friend to be her dressmaker, Elizabeth Keckley, a former slave. In her later years Mrs. Lincoln suffered enormous tragedy: In addition to the assassination of her husband, she endured the deaths of three sons. She was institutionalized in a mental hospital in 1875, and tried to commit suicide after being declared "insane" by a court. One of the country's first women lawyers, Myra Bradwell, believed Mrs. Lincoln was not mentally ill and that she was being held against her will—and after four months of confinement, Bradwell succeeded in getting Mrs. Lincoln released. After release from the hospital, Mrs. Lincoln lived abroad for several years, and then returned to the United States to live with her sister, until she died at 63 years old.

The Mary Todd Lincoln House museum preserves the childhood home of Mrs. Lincoln. The home was built between 1803 and 1808, and the young Mrs. Lincoln lived here until she moved to Springfield, Illinois,

Mary Todd Lincoln   Courtesy Library of Congress

in 1839, to live with her older sister. This house museum is the first in America to honor a First Lady. The house contains 14 rooms on three floors, each filled with period furnishings from the 1830s and 1840s, including many artifacts that once belonged to the Todd and Lincoln families. Children will enjoy seeing the doll collection in Mary's girlhood room—a surprisingly contemporary and feminine room; and the Gentleman's Parlor, which displays White House china and more toys.

198 Shaker Village of Pleasant Hill

CONTACT 800-734-5611, www.shakervillageky.org; 3501 Lexington Rd., Harrodsburg

PRICING	$$–$$$ (admission varies by season; some attractions are closed in the winter; wagon rides and riverboat cruises additional)
BEST TIME TO VISIT	Last Saturday in April through October, when riverboat rides are available
AGE RANGE	All ages

The Shakers were a religious group formed in 18th-century England who were known for communal, monastic living; exquisite clean-line furniture design; dedication to equality between men and women; and abhorrence of slavery. Pleasant Hill was the site of an active Shaker community from 1805 to 1910. The Pleasant Hill Shakers were known for their fine handcrafted brooms and their fruit preserves. The community grew over the years to include farms, orchards fenced in with lovely stone walls, and large communal living structures. Because of their religious beliefs, Pleasant Hill Shakers were staunch abolitionists, and routinely bought and then free slaves—a practice that incited an attack on Pleasant Hill by proslavery fac-

Quilting at Shaker Village of Pleasant Hill
Courtesy www.kentuckytourism.com

tions in 1825 that destroyed some of the buildings.

Today the Shaker Village of Pleasant Hill is the largest restored Shaker community in the United States, and includes 34 immaculately restored buildings and 3,000 acres of farmland. Visitors to this living museum can tour the extensive grounds, dine on period fare at the Trustee's House, attend concerts featuring Shaker music, and observe artisans at work using traditional 19th-century methods. It's even possible to lodge here overnight in some of the restored buildings. The site hosts festivals and educational exhibits throughout the year, many utilizing costumed interpreters who bring the history of this community to life. In late spring through early fall, you can cruise the Kentucky River aboard the *Dixie Belle*, Shaker Village's 115-passenger riverboat.

Alligator Bayou   Courtesy Louisiana Office of Tourism

Louisiana

199 Acadian Village

CONTACT 337-981-2364, www.acadianvillage.org;
200 Greenleaf Dr., Lafayette

PRICING	$$
BEST TIME TO VISIT	Year-round; closed Sunday and Monday
AGE RANGE	7 and older

In 1604 more than 10,000 individuals left their homeland in coastal France and set out for the New World to form a colony they called "La Cadie" (or Arcadia). Arcadia included part of Maine, Nova Scotia, New Brunswick, and Prince Edward Island, and it was one of the first European colonies in North America. Acadia existed for approximately 100 years in relative peace—they forged cooperative trade relationships with the Native Americans, largely because they did not have the propensity to acquire additional land, as did British colonies. British forces conquered Acadia in 1710, however, and the Acadians lived under British rule for almost 50 years. When Acadians refused to pledge their allegiance to the king of England—who openly opposed France and Catholics—British officers, along with New England rulers from the colonies, demanded that nearly 12,000 Acadians be deported. Estimates indicate that during what is remembered as the "Great Expulsion" of 1755, between a third and half of the deportees died from disease or drowning. The survivors scattered, some moving back to the original

Acadian Village   Courtesy Lafayette Convention and Visitors Bureau

Acadie colony, some returning to France, some migrating to the West Indies. Many subsequent Acadians who left France ended up in Louisiana, where they came to be called Cajuns.

The Acadian Village is a folk life museum that preserves the unique culture of the Acadians in a living history depiction of 19th-century life in south Louisiana. The village offers a collection of authentic, relocated homes situated along a picturesque bayou. The structures display the typical Acadian home-building construction of mud walls, hand-hewn cypress timbers, and wooden pegs; each is furnished with period pieces and artifacts from the era. Wander through buildings like the Barnard House, the oldest building in the village (dating to 1800)—and be sure to check out the entryway painting that depicts the exodus of the Acadians from Nova Scotia in 1755; the Billeaud House, directly on the bayou and today housing spinning and weaving equipment; the New Hope Chapel, a replica of an 1850s structure housing hand-carved Stations of the Cross; and the St. John House—a favorite with children—which is furnished as a schoolhouse, complete with inkwells, lunch pails, and old school textbooks.

200 French Quarter, New Orleans

CONTACT http://frenchquarter.com; running from Canal St. near the Mississippi River to Esplanade Ave. and then inland to N. Ramparts St., New Orleans

PRICING	Varies by attraction
BEST TIME TO VISIT	Year-round (although only sturdy types should visit during Mardi Gras in the weeks before Easter)
AGE RANGE	13 and older

The French Quarter is synonymous with New Orleans: The small historic district goes hand in hand with the annual Mardi Gras celebrations of the city, the ubiquitous jazz culture, and the renowned legacy of extraordinary food. Stroll through this beautiful neighborhood to see the well-known cast-iron balconies, authentic architecture, and a plethora of diverse

Bourbon Street, French Quarter, New Orleans
Photograph in the Carol M. Highsmith Archive, Library of Congress, Prints and Photographs Division

sounds, smells, and tastes: The French Quarter is a feast for the senses, and although some of the attractions are not exactly kid-friendly (beware of strip clubs on Bourbon Street and well-liquored tourists throughout), it is an experience older children—especially those who love music and food—will not soon forget.

The Quarter, known by many locals as Vieux Carré, was established in 1718 as the center of New Orleans. It is bounded by the Mississippi River from Canal Street to Esplanade Avenue and then inland to North Ramparts Street—comprising about 80 square blocks. Some of the structures date to the earliest days of the United States, and historic buildings throughout are strictly protected by law (no demolition or renovation is allowed without absolute adherence to the prevailing architectural style). The majority of the structures date to the time of Spanish rule over New Orleans—two devastating fires in the late 18th century all but destroyed the old French colonial architecture. There are dozens of sights to be seen in this small region. Here are some of the most family-friendly:

- **The Cabildo** (710 Chartres St.): This former city hall is the site of the signing of the Louisiana Purchase in 1803.

> If you're in the city during the annual Tennessee Williams Festival (a five-day celebration held in late March), don't miss the "Stella!" and "Stanley" shouting contests, held in the French Quarter and inspired by Williams's play (and more obviously the Hollywood adaptation starring Marlon Brando) *A Streetcar Named Desire*.

- **Café du Monde** (800 Decatur St.): Great food is easy to find in New Orleans, but a visit to the city is not complete without a stop at this coffee shop known for beignets (doughnut-style fried dough) and café au lait.

- **Jackson Square** (Decatur St.): This city-block-sized park is a bustling center of entertainment—live music, artists, street performers, tarot card readers—and home to an iconic equestrian statue of Andrew Jackson, the general who oversaw the victory of the Battle of New Orleans.

- **Pirates Alley** (off St. Peter's St., between Chartres and Royal): Officially named Ruelle d'Orleans, Sud, this alley dates back to 1831. It is most famous for the Faulkner House, where American writer William Faulkner wrote his first novel, *Soldier's Pay*.

- **St. Louis Cathedral** (615 Pere Antoine Alley): Next to Jackson Square, this beautiful Roman Catholic cathedral is the oldest operating in the United States and well worth a self-guided tour to see the magnificent painted ceilings and stained-glass windows throughout.

201 Frogmore Cotton Plantation

CONTACT 318-757-2435, www.frogmoreplantation.com; 11054 Hwy. 84, Frogmore

PRICING	$$–$$$
BEST TIME TO VISIT	Open mid-March to mid-November; closed Sunday year-round and Saturday and Sunday during the summer
AGE RANGE	7 and older

In the mid-19th century, cotton—a natural fiber that is grown as a crop—was America's biggest export. Most of the world's cotton in pre–Civil War days came from plantations scattered among southern states, including Louisiana. The invention of the cotton gin by Eli Whitney industrialized the process of separating cotton fibers from their seeds (a job that before had to be performed by hand); and because so

Frogmore Cotton Plantation   Courtesy Louisiana Office of Tourism

202 Magnolia Mound Plantation

CONTACT 225-343-4955, www.brec.org; 2161 Nicholson Dr., Baton Rouge

PRICING	$–$$
BEST TIME TO VISIT	Year-round
AGE RANGE	7 and older

There are dozens of historical plantations throughout Louisiana that preserve the legacy of the agrarian South, but Magnolia Mound Plantation House—although not as grand as some—stands as one of the few examples of architecture in the region influenced by French and West Indian settlers. Magnolia Mound is also one of the oldest structures in Baton Rouge, dating to 1791. The home was once surrounded by 900 acres of farmland that fronted the Mississippi River.

Today the house museum is dedicated to preserving and interpreting the culture of the French Creoles who continue to live in and influence the region. The main house is decorated with Louisiana-made objects and period antiques. Outbuildings open for tour include the Carriage House, which displays an exhibit of vintage tools; the Crop Garden, which in-season boasts cotton, sugarcane, tobacco, and indigo (traditional crops that were grown at Magnolia Mound during its heyday); the Open-Hearth Kitchen, filled with antique cooking tools like spider pots, sugar nippers, and an old-fashioned waffle iron; the Overseer's

much more cotton could be processed thanks to this new machine, much more cotton was grown—a farming process inextricably reliant on slave labor, an economic circumstance that arguably postponed the emancipation of slaves in the South.

The Frogmore Plantation is a unique attraction that combines a living history museum (complete with costumed interpreters) with an expansive 1,800-acre modern cotton plantation. Visit to contrast the working farm with the historic representation and come away with a greater understanding of the economics of agriculture and slavery during the pre–Civil War era. Guests can learn about cotton harvesting, the plantation system in early America, and slave life in the South from knowledgeable tour guides who tell stories based on extensive archives from the Frogmore Plantation, including slave narratives, handwritten journals, and logbooks. The site displays an 1884 Munger Cotton Gin and includes nearly 20 restored structures that date to the early 19th century. Visitors may tour the cotton mill, the old general store, slave quarters, the barn, and a plantation chapel. Don't miss the chance to attend a slave wedding reenactment that includes live gospel music and the "jumping of the broom" ceremony. Because slaves were not legally allowed to marry, this African wedding tradition was a way for slaves to mark their commitments to each other.

Magnolia Mound Plantation   Courtesy Louisiana Office of Tourism

House, operations-central for the business of the plantation; the Pigeonnier, a coop for game birds and now home to a collection of pigeons; and the Quarter House, a slave cabin dating to 1830 that includes an exhibit dedicated to slave life on a large plantation such as Magnolia Mound. Children will enjoy educational programs like *Grandmother's Attic*, in which costumed reenactors offer a guided tour through the plantation and engage in a take-home craft project; and *In the Quarter*, an examination of slave life in 1810 in which children explore a slave cabin and examine artifacts from slave life.

Mardi Gras parade float
Carol M. Highsmith's America, Library of Congress, Prints and Photographs Division

203 Mardi Gras in New Orleans

CONTACT www.neworleansonline.com/neworleans/mardigras; New Orleans

PRICING	$
BEST TIME TO VISIT	The 2 weeks preceding Fat Tuesday (which is 47 days before Easter)
AGE RANGE	13 and older

Mardi Gras celebrations date back to France in the 16th century—and possibly even further back, into the Middle Ages. The tradition of living it up in the days before Lent—which is observed starting on Ash Wednesday and then for 40 days before Easter (47 days counting Sundays)—is observed today in countries around the world with parades and hearty partying. At first blush, the annual bacchanalian festival in New Orleans (easily the most famous Mardi Gras celebration in the United States) to mark the coming of Lent doesn't sound suited to families traveling with children: The streets are often crowded with inebriated merrymakers, and it's become traditional for some folks on the parade route to go to extreme (and R-rated) lengths to get float riders to toss beads, "doubloons," and other trinkets to the crowd. In truth, children of any age are out of place in the French Quarter during the entire Mardi Gras season. But the good news is that there are numerous parades and celebrations throughout the city, so in some venues it is possible to avoid the debauchery while still indulging in the tradition. During the 12-day period before Fat Tuesday, there are approximately 70 parades held in the New Orleans area. Look for those that run down St. Charles Avenue, between First Street and Napoleon Avenue, which attract families with young children; the vibe is generally wholesome and festive without being overly rowdy or naughty. Allow your kids to get into the spirit of the event by dressing up and wearing masks—and a word to the wise: Bring along a pocketful of your own prepurchased baubles to distribute at the end of the parade, just in case your kids aren't able to snag their share of swag tossed from the floats.

204 New Orleans Jazz and Heritage Festival

CONTACT www.neworleansonline.com/neworleans/festivals/musicfestivals/jazzfest.html; French Quarter, New Orleans

PRICING	$$$$
BEST TIME TO VISIT	Late April and early May
AGE RANGE	13 and older

Jazz is often said to be one of America's only original musical genres—although fans of bluegrass and country-western might argue the point. But there is no disputing that jazz is one of the most influential art forms to come from the United States. Jazz originated in the early 20th century, and combines roots from blues to ragtime to big band. There are numerous subcategories of jazz today, but classical jazz is most readily identifiable with greats like Billie Holiday, Louis Armstrong, and Miles Davis.

The New Orleans Jazz and Heritage Festival is a remarkable music festival held over two weekends that celebrates all forms of jazz as well as numerous other popular forms of music, from zydeco to rock and roll, and it really is fun for the whole family (especially older kids who love music). There are nonstop performances throughout the four days spread out over 20-some outdoor stages set up around the French Quarter, as well as a few indoor stages. Over the years the festival has attracted some of the biggest names in music in the world, including Bruce Springsteen, John Mayer, Bonnie Raitt, Herbie Hancock, the Neville Brothers, Jimmy Buffett, the Foo Fighters, Al Green, and Tom Petty and the Heartbreakers.

In addition to music in the streets, there are dozens of opportunities to learn about the heritage and culture of the South through food and art demonstrations. Jackson Square in the French Quarter is one of the best places to go for local New Orleans fare like alligator, crawfish, and muffuletas. Children have their own activities, centered on the Kids' Performance Tent (along the riverfront), including live music, a chance to play in a jazz band, and various craft projects. In years past the tent has included an enormous mural children can add to, a kids' drum corps, and costumed performers from Mardi Gras parades. If your crew can stay up late enough, check out the fabulous fireworks show over the Mississippi River on the two Saturday nights of the festival.

Save as much as 30 percent on the gate price for adults by purchasing tickets for the New Orleans Jazz and Heritage Festival in advance online. (Children's tickets are only available for purchase at the gate, and anyone under 10 must be accompanied by an adult.)

205 Oak Alley Plantation

CONTACT 225-265-2151, www.oakalleyplantation.com; 3645 Hwy. 18 (also known as Great River Rd.), Vacherie

PRICING	$–$$$
BEST TIME TO VISIT	Year-round
AGE RANGE	7 and older

The wealth accumulated in pre–Civil War days from enormous plantations growing cotton, sugarcane, and tobacco allowed well-to-do agrarians in the South to build large, elaborate homes, and there are dozens of beautiful historic properties throughout the Mississippi Valley that bear witness to the luxurious lifestyle enjoyed by some of the richest Americans of the era. Oak Alley Plantation, on the Mississippi River, is one of the best-preserved examples. The plantation was originally called Bon Séjour, but came to be known as Oak Alley because of the 800-foot alley leading from the home to the river that is flanked by a double row of majestic—and enormous—live oaks. The alley was planted in the early 18th century, even before the current home was constructed.

The beautiful French Creole-style structure and the surrounding sugarcane fields survived the Civil War without damage, but the end of slavery marked the end of the plantation era—it took an enormous cash flow to maintain such large properties with paid labor, and by 1866 Oak Alley Plantation was in finan-

Oak Alley Plantation   Courtesy Louisiana Office of Tourism

If a tour of Oak Alley leaves you wanting to know more about Louisiana plantations, head to adjacent St. Joseph Plantation (3535 Hwy. 18, Vacherie). The property has been in the same family since 1877, and it's still maintained as a working sugarcane plantation. Visitors can tour the main house, slave cabins, and other outbuildings, and watch a short movie on sugarcane processing.

cial ruin. The place was sold at auction for little more than $30,000. Current owners have worked to painstakingly restore the home and grounds, and are working to restore slave quarters and outbuildings as well. Today guests are treated to tours of the mansion by guides dressed in period costumes; you can also arrange for tours of the outbuildings or sign on with a number of tour companies out of New Orleans that include Oak Alley in their city tours. Your family might just recognize the iconic whitewashed mansion from the big screen: The lovely property has been the backdrop of numerous movies, including *Interview with a Vampire* with Tom Cruise and Brad Pitt, and *Primary Colors* with John Travolta and Emma Thompson. Beyoncé even used the mansion in her music video "Déjà Vu." As with many of these historic plantation homes, Oak Alley also serves as a venue for weddings and other large events, and there is a restaurant on site.

206 Poverty Point State Historic Site

CONTACT 318-926-5492, www.crt.state.la.us/parks/ipvertypt.aspx; 6859 Hwy. 577, Pioneer

PRICING	$
BEST TIME TO VISIT	March through October
AGE RANGE	7 and older

It takes a little imagination to get the full import of this monument, which some archaeologists liken to the Great Pyramids in Egypt. Although the scale and the erosion that has occurred over millennia make it

Poverty Point State Historic Site   Courtesy Louisiana Office of Tourism

difficult to discern with the naked eye, on this site some 3,300 years ago a large, sophisticated civilization existed that created earthenwork mounds of proportions so large, they weren't rediscovered until the 20th century, when aerial photos revealed the massive site. The monument comprises some of the largest and oldest earthen mounds in North America, believed at one time to be home to as many as 5,000 people. The engineering feat required to bring this construction to fruition is said to have taken more than five million hours of labor. The complex includes a collection of mounds and ridges designed in six rows of concentric arcs, believed to be 4 or 5 feet high at one point. Archaeologists assume the ridges were the foundations on which dwellings and public buildings were constructed. Beyond the concentric ridges are two enormous mounds, one in the shape of a bird that is 700 feet across and 70 feet high (and at one time it was probably 100 feet high). It is estimated that this mound *alone* required more than 10 billion buckets of earth to be carried in to the site. In the center of the ridges is a 37-acre plaza that archaeologists think was the site of ceremonial and political activities. Although the mysteries of the site are just beginning to be unraveled, the cooperation and technical savvy required to complete such an undertaking have caused historians and archaeologists alike to rethink the roots of Western civilization. Excavation is ongoing (and is extremely interesting to observe). Visit the site to tour the small interpretive museum that includes a collection of artifacts and to catch a tram tour (conducted several times a day from March through October) that ferries guests to the remote corners of the monument.

207 World War II Museum

World War II Museum   Courtesy World War II Museum

CONTACT 504-528-1944, www.ddaymuseum.org; 945 Magazine St., New Orleans

PRICING	$$–$$$$
BEST TIME TO VISIT	Year-round
AGE RANGE	7 and older

World War II (1939–45) was a global conflict that involved most of the world's nations, which eventually split into two opposing military alliances known as the Axis powers and the Allies (of which the United States became a part when it joined the war in the aftermath of the Pearl Harbor attack in 1941). More than 100 million people fought in the war, and there were more than 50 million fatalities. A shocking percentage of the fatalities were civilians killed as part of the mass genocide known as the Holocaust. In addition, hundreds of thousands of Japanese civilians were killed during the detonation of nuclear weapons that effectively ended the conflict in the Asian theater.

The World War II Museum in New Orleans honors the legacy of the American soldiers and civilians who contributed to the Allies' success, and chronicles the story of the economic and political backdrop that precipitated the expansive war. It might seem as if New Orleans is an unusual choice for what is deemed the national museum documenting the war; in fact, the city was chosen largely because of Andrew Higgins, a New Orleans boat designer and manufacturer who built the vessels used by American troops during D-Day. President Dwight D. Eisenhower remarked of Higgins, "He is the man who won the war for us."

Guests to the museum can see large-scale exhibits like fighter planes, Sherman tanks, and the infamous Higgins boats; interact with touch-screen video displays that offer fascinating and poignant oral histories of men and women who lived through the war; and view a 4-D film (produced by Hollywood luminary Tom Hanks) on the war, which includes smoke that appears to flow from airplane engines hit by enemy fire and snow falling in the theater during the winter scenes depicted on screen. The recently expanded museum also includes a live-entertainment venue called the Stage Door Canteen, which features cabaret-style performances.

Mount Katahdin
Photo Chris Lawrence, courtesy Greater Portland Convention and Visitors Bureau

Maine

208 Acadia National Park

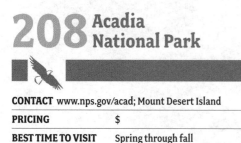

CONTACT www.nps.gov/acad; Mount Desert Island

PRICING	$
BEST TIME TO VISIT	Spring through fall
AGE RANGE	7 and older

The Wabanaki people, a cultural designation that comprises the Maliseet, Micmac, Passamaquoddy, and Penobscot tribes, lived in the coastal regions of what is now Maine as long ago as 12,000 years. These migratory tribes came to Mount Desert Island in the Atlantic in handcrafted birch-bark canoes to hunt, harvest clams, gather berries, fish, and trade with other tribes. Today the Acadia National Park preserves most of Mount Desert Island, as well as most of Isle au Haut and portions of Baker Island and the Schoodic Peninsula on the mainland. First named Lafayette National Park in the early 20th century, it was renamed Acadia in 1929 and become the first national park east of the Mississippi River. The stunning site is a feast for the senses, and includes spectacular rugged coastline, sparkling lakes, and mountains. Cadillac Mountain within the park is the tallest peak along the eastern coast of the United States; at the right time of the year this is the first site in the country to see the sunrise. In total there are more than 47,000 acres for visitors to explore.

From late June through early October, Acadia National Park runs bus shuttles among park attractions, trailheads, campgrounds, local lodging, and the Bar Harbor—Hancock County Regional Airport. Bus schedules are posted at stops, and the buses run frequently. Feel free to flag one down anywhere along the route; they will stop anywhere it is safe to do so.

Start off at the Hulls Cove Visitor Center to view *Gift of Acadia*, a 15-minute orientation video; this is also a good place to pick up maps and books on Acadia's natural wonders. Drive the picturesque 27-mile Park Loop Road to get your bearings. (Note that the road is closed December through mid-April every year.) There are several beaches in the park—including Echo Lake Beach and Sand Beach—but the temperatures are frigid enough for a wet suit (and often too cold for children even with wet suits). Tide pooling is a more temperate coastline activity. The intertidal zone along the coast of Maine is home to myriad creatures like anemones, crabs, barnacles, mussels, tiny fish, and small lobsters. Check the tide charts available in the park newsletter, the *Beaver Log*, or check the Internet, to determine the low tides that will enable the best exploration of the tide pools. Good places for access include Ship Harbor and Wonderland. (Hint: Wear appropriate footwear, because the rocks will be slippery; and remind children to watch where they step, lest they stomp on sea life.) If you've never gone tide pooling before, consider a ranger-led program (available in June, September, and October at Ship Harbor, and in July and August at Sand Beach).

Ranger program at the tide pools of Acadia National Park

Courtesy National Park Service

209 Colonial Pemaquid

CONTACT 207-677-2423, www.friendsofcolonialpemaquid.org; off Fort Rd., New Harbor

PRICING	$
BEST TIME TO VISIT	Summer
AGE RANGE	3 and older

Colonial Pemaquid preserves the site of one of America's earliest and most productive colonies. In the 1600s fishermen came to New England from Europe to fish for codfish, which were then salted, dried, and shipped back to Europe in barrels. The colony was formed perhaps as early as 1605, and was used for many years as a seasonal fishing station. A permanent village was settled on the site around 1629. Shortly thereafter, in 1677, the first of three forts (Fort Charles) was erected. Later forts included Fort Frederick and Fort William Henry, believed to be the first stone fort ever built in North America. What

> ## Fishermen came for codfish, which were then salted, dried, and shipped to Europe.

stands now is a 1908 re-creation of the impressive stone fortress, which at one time protected 60 soldiers and housed 20 cannons.

Visitors today can wander through the ruins, check out the reconstructed buildings (climb to the top of Fort William Henry for impressive views), and visit a small museum (open from Memorial Day through the end of August), which includes more than 75,000 prehistoric and colonial artifacts. Of particular interest is a 7,000-year-old arrowhead that was recovered by archaeologists' excavations of the site, as well as Native American currency (known as wampum), pottery, musket balls, early tools, bone dice, and glassware and ceramics (most imported from England, Germany, and Holland). A diorama on site shows guests what the buildings might have looked like in their heyday, based on foundations that have been excavated at Pemaquid. The museum also offers a 20-minute orientation film and a scavenger hunt brochure for kids.

The adjacent cemetery at Colonial Pemaquid includes gravestones dating from the 18th century. An on-site herb garden exhibits the kinds of plants 17th-century settlers would have cultivated for food and for medicine, like bee balm, chamomile, chives, dill, lavender, mint, thyme, and yarrow. In the summertime there are numerous living history demonstrations at the park, including pirate reenactors, battle reenactments, an 18th-century-style magician show, and demonstrations of cod processing.

210 Fort Knox

CONTACT	http://fortknox.maineguide.com; 740 Fort Knox Rd., Prospect
PRICING	$
BEST TIME TO VISIT	May through October (when the fort is open for touring)
AGE RANGE	7 and older

Because of its extreme northern location, in the early years of the Republic Maine was often forced to defend its territory during disputes with British Canada. In the American Revolution and the War of 1812, British ships sailed up Penobscot River and claimed the surrounding lands for Britain. Although the British occupations didn't last, Fort Knox was constructed in 1844 to protect the area from future squabbles. During the Civil War, when the fort was still being built, about 50 soldiers were garrisoned here—living in temporary buildings behind the fort walls. During the Spanish-American War, nearly 600 troops occupied the fort for a month. The fort was never seriously threatened during either of these wars, however, and the valley was never again invaded.

The finely crafted granite fort remains in extraordinary condition, and a tour of the historic attraction is great fun for military buffs. The fort is built on two levels, and its four batteries contain mounts for 135 cannons (although not that many were actually installed). The expansive, complexly designed facility includes a dry moat, separate quarters for enlisted men and officers, a cistern, a bakery, and in the interior of the fort a parade grounds. The fort is the site of numerous seasonal events (generally held on summer weekends), including cannon-firing demonstrations;

Adjacent to the fort is the Penobscot Narrows Bridge, which offers the highest bridge observation tower in the world. For a small fee, ride the elevator to the top to check out the views of the Penobscot River Valley and the fort from on high.

PRICE KEY
$ free–$5
$$ $6–10
$$$ $11–20
$$$$ $21+

Civil War reenactments complete with living history demonstrations of camp life; guided tours in search of paranormal activities; a pirate festival that includes swordfights and a mock pirate ship attack on the fort; and evening concerts.

211 Longfellow's Childhood Home

CONTACT 207-774-1822, www.mainehistory.org/about_visit.shtml; 489 Congress St., Portland

PRICING	$–$$$
BEST TIME TO VISIT	Open May–October
AGE RANGE	10 and older

Henry Wadsworth Longfellow (1807–82) was a famous poet and influential literary scholar in the United States, and is responsible for some of the most enduring American mythic poetry ever written. Schoolchildren still recite lines from his most famous pieces, like "Paul Revere's Ride" and "The Song of Hiawatha." His work was uniquely American—and the topics of his poems celebrated the history of this country and memorialized his countrymen. Longfellow was born in Portland, and grew up in a house built by General Peleg Wadsworth, a Revolutionary War soldier, U.S. congressman, and grandfather to Longfellow.

Visit Longfellow's Childhood Home today to tour the house museum, which has been painstakingly restored—preservationists did extensive research through journals and family letters, for example, when looking to replace bedroom wallpaper. Almost all of the furnishings and artifacts within the mu-

Another important Longfellow site is in Cambridge, Massachusetts. The Longfellow House—Washington's Headquarters National Historic Site (also known as the Vassall-Craigie-Longfellow House; 105 Brattle St.) was home to Longfellow for almost 50 years, and it was here that he wrote many of his most beloved epic poems. It was also a onetime headquarters of President George Washington.

Longfellow's Childhood Home
Photo Cynthia Farr-Weinfeld, courtesy Greater Portland Convention and Visitors Bureau

seum once belonged to the Wadsworth and Longfellow families. Don't miss the Longfellow Garden out back, which is particularly fine in the spring. The contemplative pathways and lush design might even bring out the inner poets in your family!

212 Maine Annual Lobster Festival

CONTACT 207- 596-0376, www.mainelobsterfestival.com; Harbor Park, Rockland

PRICING	$–$$
BEST TIME TO VISIT	Early August
AGE RANGE	All ages

Maine is well known for its succulent, reasonably priced lobster—and the region has been offering up the bounty of the sea for centuries. According to Indian lore, before the colonists arrived in the New World lobsters were even more plentiful along the coastline of Maine—so much so that Native Americans used to gather them to fertilize their crops. By the time the first colonists arrived, lobsters were still so abundant that they were harvested by collecting the crustaceans that had washed up on the beaches or were stranded in tide pools. During the 18th and 19th centuries, because of its oversupply in Maine, lobster was considered a cheap food—and was eaten by poor families and fed to servants. Today Maine remains the largest lobster-fishing state in the country, with more

Maine lobster fisherman

Photo by Carol M. Highsmith, courtesy Library of Congress

than 6,500 lobstermen making their living off the strange-looking creatures, which today are considered a luxury dining item.

To celebrate the legacy of lobster fishing, the Maine Annual Lobster Festival is held in early August (running from Wednesday to Sunday, starting before the first full weekend in the month). Come to experience some of the best lobster in the world (20,000 pounds of it are served over the course of five days), cooked in the world's largest lobster "pot." There's plenty of family-friendly entertainment at this all-American event, including the coronation of Miss Sea Goddess, a lobster-themed parade, live entertainment, cooking contests, and tours of U.S. navy ships. Visit the Children's Tent, which hosts special lobster-eating contests for kids, a diaper derby, a costume parade, and crafts. Another fun attraction is the Great International William Atwood Lobster Crate Race, in which contestants of all ages run along a course of 50 partially submerged lobster crates: Whoever covers the most crates before falling into the ocean wins.

213 Museums of Old York

🔔

CONTACT 207-363-4974, www.oldyork.org; 3 Lindsay Rd., York

PRICING	$–$$$
BEST TIME TO VISIT	June through Columbus Day weekend; closed Sunday
AGE RANGE	7 and older

British colonists settled along the York River in Maine in 1624, first naming their small village Agamenticus (and then renaming it over the years to Bristol, then Gorgeana, and finally York). As Gorgeana, the site became the first chartered city in 1641 and then the first incorporated city in 1642 in America (under King Charles I). Today the region is a favorite beach resort and the site of a fascinating living history museum that preserves the legacy of one of New England's earliest colonial settlements.

The Museums of Old York offer nine historic structures that comprise 37 rooms meticulously furnished in period pieces, as well as a collection of early New England art, artifacts, and decorative pieces. Living history demonstrations and costumed interpreters help tell the story of the men and women who built the settlement in the early 17th century, as well as the many people who lived and worked in this region of southern Maine after them. Families will particularly enjoy a tour through the following structures:

- **Jefferds' Tavern:** This structure dates to 1754 and highlights a cooking fireplace and beehive brick oven, as well as murals that illustrate historic York structures.
- **John Hancock Warehouse:** This 1740s structure is the only remaining commercial building from the colonial era, and as the name suggests it was once owned by Declaration of Independence signer John Hancock. Guests today can see examples of the

Museums of Old York

Courtesy Museums of Old York

wares that passed through the structure, including china, tea, grain, furs, tallow, and potatoes.

- **Old Schoolhouse:** This one-room schoolhouse was built in 1745, and it still bears the scars of colonial schoolchildren who scratched their marks into the walls. Kids will enjoy hearing from a costumed schoolmaster about how colonial children attended school for only three months a year, between harvest and planting season. Step out back to see an old privy.
- **Old Gaol:** The old jail housed prisoners from 1719 to about 1860, and remains one of the oldest British public buildings in the United States. Actors play the roles of the jailor and his wife, and guests can tour their quarters as well as a display gallery that elucidates the history of the building. Children will want to try out the pillory in front (or convince their parents to do so).
- **Virginia Weare Parsons Education Center and Remick Barn:** This structure, often used to host concerts and educational lectures, includes a replica hearth. Guests can watch reenactors bake bread and cook stews over the open fire, just as the earliest colonists might have done.

214 Portland Freedom Trail

CONTACT 207-591-9980, www.portlandfreedomtrail.org; Portland

PRICING	$
BEST TIME TO VISIT	Summer
AGE RANGE	All ages

The Underground Railroad was neither underground nor a railroad: Instead, it was a secret network of safe houses owned by abolitionists during the antebellum period organized to help escaped slaves find their way to free states in the North and sometimes beyond to Canada. "Conductors" who ferried slaves by night from one safe house to the next generally didn't know the full extent of the network: Rather, each member knew only the next stops on the route, in order to protect the entirety of the coalition should a segment of the network be discovered. For those traveling to Canada, Maine was often the last stop along the clandestine route to freedom. Historians believe there were approximately 75 Underground Railroad "stations," or overnight stops, in the state—although much of the exact history has been lost; to preserve secrecy, little documentation was kept.

The Portland Freedom Trail currently includes more than a dozen marked sites that trace the route of the Underground Railroad and commemorate the antislavery movement in the city. Download a free walking map at www.portlandfreedomtrail.org/images/PFT-walkingtour-map.pdf, then follow the granite and bronze markers to discover an unbelievably courageous group of people who risked their lives for the freedom of others. Along the way you'll learn about Jacob C. Dickson, a barber who supplied wigs and false beards to disguise escaped slaves (stop 2), Charles Frederick Eastman, a conductor on the Underground Railroad and an activist in the African American community in Portland (stop 5); and Lloyd Scott (stop 12), who was the vice president of the Portland Union Anti-Slavery Society and owner of a secondhand clothing store that supplied clean clothing for fugitives, among many others. The trail organizers promise to add markers every year until all of the 36 known Portland sites are identified.

215 Portland Head Light

CONTACT 207-799-2661, www.portlandheadlight.com; 1000 Shore Rd., Cape Elizabeth

PRICING	$
BEST TIME TO VISIT	Summer and early fall
AGE RANGE	7 and older

Maine is a state of rocky beaches, sparkling shorelines, and charming lighthouses—and Portland Head Light is a quintessential (and stunningly beautiful)

Kids must be 10 years old or older to climb the tower of the Portland Head Light.

Another spectacular lighthouse in Maine has a misleading name: The West Quoddy Head Lighthouse overlooking the Bay of Fundy is actually the *easternmost* lighthouse in the United States—and is distinctively marked with red and white horizontal stripes that make it one of the most photographed lighthouses in the world. This was one of the first stations in America to be equipped with a fog bell (eventually replaced with a steam whistle). The current lighthouse was built in 1858, to replace an original that dated to 1808. The tower is currently closed, but come anyhow to see the picturesque beacon and enjoy the trails in Quoddy Head State Park that run along the rocky coastline. This is a great backdrop for a picnic—there are tables available and plenty of open space for kids to run or fly a kite.

Portland Head Light
Photo Chris Lawrence, courtesy Greater Portland Convention and Visitors Bureau

representation of all of these attributes. Guarding the entrance of the shipping channel into Casco Bay, this whitewashed lighthouse is the oldest in Maine. It was constructed in 1791 (back when Maine was still part of Massachusetts), at the directive of George Washington. The first lighthouse keepers illuminated the lens using whale oil lamps. Check out the lighthouse from the water via boat tour or come here to climb the 85 steps to the top of the tower. There is a small on-site museum displaying artifacts and lenses open on weekends in late spring through early fall.

216 West Quoddy Head Lighthouse

CONTACT Off Boot Cove Rd., Quoddy Head State Park, near Lubec

PRICING	$
BEST TIME TO VISIT	Summer
AGE RANGE	7 and older

West Quoddy Head Lighthouse
Photo by Carol M. Highsmith, courtesy Library of Congress

217 Whaleback Shell Midden

CONTACT 207-563-1393, www.maine.gov/doc/parks; 109–110 Belvedere Rd., Damariscotta

PRICING	$
BEST TIME TO VISIT	Year-round (but note that the parking lot is not plowed in the winter)
AGE RANGE	7 and older

Come to this unique site to see one of the most interesting and historic trash dumps in the world. Shell middens are the remains of prehistoric people, generally along coastal areas, which are made up largely of discarded oyster shells, with bones and some ceramics thrown in for good measure. The shell piles are important to archaeologists because they offer evidence that migratory Indians harvested oysters in late winter and early spring, when they regularly visited the coastline. Because the shells are made largely of calcium carbonate, the resulting alkaline soil also preserves the remains of animals over longer-than-usual periods, so that researchers have been able to gain insight into hunting patterns and even weather conditions during the time when the sites were in active use. The eastern bank of the Damariscotta River is the site of one of the largest such middens in the world—in fact, it was once even larger, and the heap was so named because it resembled the back of a whale. It dates back at least 2,200 years. However, a good portion of the midden was mined in the late 19th century for use in chicken feed. Today visitors can still see the archaeological oddity and enjoy a scenic walking trail that includes interpretive signs to explain the early settlements and migrations of Native Americans in the region. If you look carefully across the river, you might catch sight of another prehistoric shell pile, called Glidden Midden.

MARYLAND

218 Antietam National Battlefield

"Bloody Lane," Antietam National Battlefield

Courtesy National Park Service

CONTACT 301-432-5124, www.nps.gov/ancm; 5831 Dunker Church Rd., Sharpsburg

PRICING	$
BEST TIME TO VISIT	Spring and fall
AGE RANGE	10 and older

Antietam National Battlefield has the dubious distinction of being the site of one of the deadliest battles in American history: On September 17, 1862, after only 12 hours of horrific combat, a staggering 23,000 soldiers were dead, seriously wounded, or missing in action. Both sides were nearly crippled from the extensive losses—at the end of the day more than 25 percent of the Union soldiers were gone, and 31 percent of the Confederates. Despite the heavy casualties, the battle was not a convincing victory for either side—although Union troops led by General George McClellan succeeded in rebuffing General Robert E. Lee's invasion of Maryland and President Abraham Lincoln was spurred to announce his plans for an Emancipation Proclamation. Such a declaration—freeing the slaves—meant there was no turning back from an all-out war between the North and the South.

Visit the battlefield today to explore the landmarks of the fight—like Burnside's Bridge, where Major General Ambrose Burnside eventually captured a small stone bridge from a group of Confederate soldiers from Georgia in what was an important turning point in the battle; Dunker Church, which was a focal point in several Union attacks (and mentioned extensively in battle reports by both sides); and Bloody Lane, also called Sunken Lane, which saw more than

> Antietam National Battlefield is the site of a well-attended battle re-creation, but be forewarned: This is a heady experience, and given the magnitude of the losses of life on this site, the battlefield is hallowed ground. Make sure children are sufficiently mature to respect the seriousness of both the site and any reenactments.

5,000 casualties during the battle. To get your bearings, start with a trip to the visitor center to see one of two films—a 30-minute introductory film that explains the significance of the battle and the sites throughout the park, or a more in-depth hour-long documentary (the longer film is shown once daily starting at noon). Then take the self-guided 8.5-mile car tour through the battlefield itself. Along the way the tour includes 11 stops. If you have the time, consider prescheduling a personalized tour with the Antietam Battlefield Guides (301-432-4329), who will drive with you in your vehicle and answer any questions your family might have about the battle or about life during the Civil War.

Don't miss the Pry House Field Hospital Museum, a relatively new attraction located in the structure used as Union General George B. McClellan's headquarters during the battle. Open Memorial Day through October (and weekends in May and November), the site includes a chilling re-creation of a Civil War–era operating room. There are also interpretive panels to explain the artifacts on display that were used in the care of wounded soldiers.

219 Babe Ruth Museum

CONTACT www.baberuthmuseum.com; 216 Emory St., Baltimore

PRICING	$–$$
BEST TIME TO VISIT	Baseball season (combine with a trip to Camden Yards)
AGE RANGE	All ages

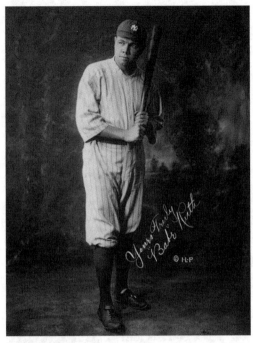

"Babe" Ruth   Courtesy Library of Congress

George Herman Ruth Jr. (1895–1948)—better known as Babe Ruth or "the Sultan of Swat"—is arguably the most famous baseball player in American history. Ruth spent his sports career playing for three teams (Boston Red Sox, New York Yankees, and Boston Braves) in Major League Baseball. Over 22 seasons, he set numerous records, won seven pennants and four World Series titles, and become one of the first players inducted into the National Baseball Hall of Fame. He is perhaps best remembered for being the first to hit 60 home runs in one season—1927—a feat that was not surpassed until 1961, when Roger Maris hit 61.

The Babe Ruth Birthplace and Museum is located in the row house in which Ruth was born, although he spent only a few years living in the home (his father signed over custody of Ruth when he was only 7 to a boys' reformatory and orphanage run by the Catholic Church). The site, fittingly, is only a few blocks from the new Camden Yards, the beautiful old-style Orioles baseball park that is the pride of Baltimore. The artifacts and furnishings on display were chosen by Ruth's family to best tell the story of his life in baseball. This small house museum is well worth the time for any baseball fan.

220 Baltimore and Ohio Museum

CONTACT	410-752-2490, www.borail.org; 901 W. Pratt St., Baltimore
PRICING	$$–$$$
BEST TIME TO VISIT	April through December, Wednesday through Sunday, when train rides are offered
AGE RANGE	3 and older

The Baltimore and Ohio Museum offers one of the most significant displays of trains and railroad artifacts in the world. The permanent exhibit includes the largest collection of 19th-century locomotives in the United States, as well as 15,000 related artifacts and four historic structures—including B&O's historic Mount Clare Station and adjacent roundhouse. Mount Clare was the site of the first regular passenger service via rail in the country, starting in 1830. The first 1.5 miles of tracks here are used for seasonal train rides to the spot where the first stone of the B&O Railroad was laid in 1828. In addition to the comprehensive collection of trains, the museum exhibits many small objects related to railroads, such as dining car china, signals, shop equipment, lanterns, and pocket watches used by early B&O employees.

Children who love trains will find endless possibilities for exploration at this museum, which dedicates several spaces to youngsters (best for kids 2 through 8). The Choo Choo Blue Kid Zone within the roundhouse offers regular story times, toddler crafts, and interactive educational activities. Don't miss the

Combine your visit to the Babe Ruth Museum with a trip to the relatively new Sports Legends Museum at Camden Yards (301 W. Camden St.); combination tickets for the two museums can be purchased at a discount at either location.

one-of-a-kind train carousel on site, a merry-go-round made entirely of miniature locomotives, cabooses, and stagecoaches. Another kid pleaser is Choo Choo Blueville, a miniature landscaped town with 12 buildings and water features; a kiddie train winds around the mini town during a three-minute ride.

While in Maryland, don't miss the Banneker-Douglass Museum (84 Franklin St.) in Annapolis, which celebrates the lives of influential African Americans Banneker and Frederick Douglass, a well-respected orator and statesmen of the 19th century.

221 Benjamin Banneker Historical Park and Museum

CONTACT 410-887-1081, http://catonsville.exploremd.us/oella/benjamin_banneker_historical_park; 300 Oella Ave., Baltimore

PRICING	$
BEST TIME TO VISIT	Year-round; closed Sunday and Monday
AGE RANGE	7 and older

Pierre L'Enfant, a Frenchman and contemporary of George Washington, was the architect of the capital city of Washington, DC, and along with his surveyors created the master plan for the city that included the placement of the U.S. Capitol Building and the White House. L'Enfant was responsible for the grand layout of what continue to be major thoroughfares in the city (Pennsylvania Avenue, Constitutional Boulevard, and others), as well as the predominance of parks and tree-lined streets. By most accounts, L'Enfant was not an easy person to work with, however, and President Washington eventually fired him for repeated conflicts with his supervisors before the real work of laying out the city could begin. L'Enfant was so disgruntled after his dismissal that he reportedly took all paper copies of his plans for the city with him, which left a surveyor who had worked with L'Enfant, free African American Benjamin Banneker (1731–1806), to reconstruct the plans from memory. For this service to the country, Banneker was dubbed "The Man Who Saved Washington." Banneker was in fact remarkable for many things: In addition to his work as a surveyor, he was a clockmaker, self-taught astronomer, mathematician, and successful farmer.

The 142-acre Benjamin Banneker Historical Park

and Museum, on the site of Banneker's home near Baltimore, commemorates Banneker's life as a man of science and as an influential black American during the earliest days of the Republic. Come to see exhibits at the visitor center that include a collection of Banneker's inventions, instruments used by Banneker, and numerous papers (including correspondence to Thomas Jefferson). Also on the site are a patio garden, a 225-square-foot replica of Banneker's log cabin, and numerous trails. Throughout the year there are educational and cultural presentations.

222 Clara Barton National Historic Site

CONTACT 301-320-1410, www.nps.gov/clba; 5801 Oxford Rd., Glen Echo

PRICING	$
BEST TIME TO VISIT	Spring and fall
AGE RANGE	7 and older

Clara Barton (1821–1912) was an academic and humanitarian and one of the most beloved women in American history. She was a trailblazer for women's rights in the workplace—she was a teacher at a time when most in the profession were men—and she was one of the first women to be employed by the federal government. She is most remembered for founding the American Red Cross, the organization that to this day brings medical and humanitarian aid to individu-

The Clara Barton home has no air-conditioning and poor heating; plan your visit during mild weather to avoid unpleasant conditions inside the structure.

Clara Barton House

Courtesy National Park Service

als in times of tragedy. Surprisingly, Barton never trained as a nurse. The genesis of her organization came shortly after the First Battle of Bull Run in Virginia, when she learned that many soldiers were dying because of inadequate medical supplies. She organized a relief effort to raise money for needed supplies, and began an independent organization to distribute goods like blankets, bandages, and basic medicines. For several years, throughout the Civil War, Barton followed battles in Virginia and into South Carolina to nurse the sick and provide critical supplies. For four years after the war, she also organized a program to locate men missing in action. She became an advocate for the women's suffrage movement and also an outspoken advocate for civil rights for African Americans.

Barton officially founded the American Red Cross in 1881 to carry on the work she began during the Civil War, and she based her operations in a large house in Glen Echo, which served as Red Cross headquarters, warehouse, and living quarters for Barton and her staff. The unique home is available for guided tours daily, and children can learn a lot about Barton and her

organization from the well-informed park rangers. The 35-room home contains an astonishing 60 closets—most of which were used to store supplies. The rooms throughout are furnished in period pieces and display items belonging to Barton, such as the Blue Willow china purchased on the day Barton was born; her roll-top desk; and an example of the *first* first-aid kit, compiled by Barton and her staff. When inside the property, be sure to check out the ceiling, which is covered in bandages: Barton was a frugal woman and chose to save the costs of plaster. Upstairs are the original stained-glass windows displaying two red crosses: Barton would light a candle behind the windows, so at night anyone looking for the Red Cross headquarters would find the building without difficulty.

223 Fort McHenry Monument and Historic Shrine

CONTACT	410-962-4290, www.nps.gov/fomc; 2400 E. Fort Ave., Baltimore
PRICING	$–$$
BEST TIME TO VISIT	Early September, for Defenders Day festivities
AGE RANGE	7 and older

The star-shaped Fort McHenry—named after the secretary of war under President George Washington, James McHenry—was built in 1798, after the Revolutionary War, to defend the port of Baltimore against

Fort McHenry

Courtesy Visit Baltimore

Enhance a trip to Fort McHenry by arriving via water taxi. These are readily accessible from Baltimore's Inner Harbor.

future foreign attacks. The fort is best known for its role in the War of 1812, in which the soldiers at Fort McHenry successfully prevented a British invasion by sea. During the ferocious attack on the fort, Francis Scott Key was moved to write a poem called "The Star Spangled Banner," which was eventually set to music and became our country's national anthem. The fort never came under attack again; during the Civil War the structure was used as a military prison.

Begin a visit to Fort McHenry with the 10-minute orientation film shown in the visitor center. Then take a self-guided tour of the well-preserved fort. The site is home to numerous festivals and historical reenactments, the largest of which are the Defenders Day ceremonies held annually in early September, to commemorate the fort's successful defense of the city during the Battle of Baltimore. The celebration includes special children's programs, battle recreations, and evening fireworks. During the summer you can enjoy daily ranger talks, and on weekends the Fort McHenry Guard performs drill, musket, and artillery demonstrations.

224 Historic St. Mary's City

CONTACT 240-895-4990, www.stmaryscity.org; 18571 Hogaboom Lane, St. Mary's City

PRICING	$$
BEST TIME TO VISIT	Open mid-March through mid-November
AGE RANGE	All ages

St. Mary's City was founded by Roman Catholic colonists from Britain in 1634. The settlers arrived in Maryland aboard small ships called the *Dove* and the *Ark*, and by 1649 the Maryland colony's legislative assembly passed the Maryland Toleration Act, considered to be the first legal protection of religious toler-

Historic St. Mary's City State House

Courtesy St. Mary's County Tourism

ance in what was to become the United States. The colonists settled into the New World, worshipping as they wished and trading with Natives to expand their livelihood, and the small village prospered during the colonial period.

Today guests to the outdoor living museum known as Historic St. Mary's City can enjoy costumed interpreters in a re-created 17th-century backdrop. Exhibits include a reconstructed State House from 1676; a town center complete with a 17th-century storehouse and coffeehouse; a working tobacco plantation; a Native American village; and along the waterfront a replica square-rigged ship known as the *Maryland Dove*. (Note that the *Maryland Dove* occasionally sails, so check the website in advance to ensure availability.) There are interactive opportunities throughout the site, and special events from March through December (the only time of the year the historic structures on site are open for tours). Kids can jump into the colonial lifestyle and churn butter, shoot a bow and arrow, and participate in a militia drill. There are also opportunities to work with archaeologists, who continue to excavate the carefully preserved colonial archaeological site. Special children's workshops throughout the season include A Pirate's Life for Me, in which kids climb aboard the *Maryland Dove* and become 17th-century pirates for the day—including acquiring a pirate name, making a pirate flag, and ferreting out buried booty; the Colonial Kids Workshop: Charting and Navigation, in which kids learn to navigate a ship using a chart and cross staff; and Manners: Past and Present, where very young kids (3 through 5) learn appropriate behavior for a 17th-century child through storytelling, crafts, and songs.

225 The Star Spangled Banner Flag House

CONTACT 410-837-1793, www.flaghouse.org; 844 E. Pratt St., Baltimore

PRICING	$$
BEST TIME TO VISIT	Year-round; closed Sunday and Monday
AGE RANGE	7 and older

After the Battle of Baltimore, a pivotal moment in the War of 1812, U.S. soldiers at Fort McHenry raised an immense American flag above the ramparts to celebrate their victory over the British would-be invaders. The flag was sewn by Mary Young Pickersgill, and it inspired Francis Scott Key to write a poem that became "The Star Spangled Banner," America's national anthem. The actual flag survives (and is a highlight to any visit to the National Museum of American History in Washington, DC). The legacy of the flag maker is also celebrated at the Star Spangled Banner Flag House (formerly known as the Flag House and Star-Spangled Banner Museum). The 1793 home of Pickersgill was the flag maker's workshop, and it was here that she created the large flag that has come to be so symbolic of American freedom. Guests to the house museum can see period furniture and antiques, as

The Star-Spangled Banner Flag House Courtesy Visit Baltimore

well as artifacts from the Pickersgill family. Next door to the home is a 12,000-square-foot museum, which displays exhibits on the War of 1812 and the Battle of Baltimore.

Children will love the interactive nature of this attraction. Costumed reenactors take the roles of Mary Pickersgill, Pickersgill's mother Rebecca Young, and African American apprentice Grace Wisher, and families can ask the actors questions about life in the early 19th century, help with the occasional chore, and get a real sense of what it must have been like to live during the period. While visiting, be sure to check out the Discovery Gallery for Kids in the Jean and Lillian Hofmeister Museum. Here children can design their own flags and then fly them on the gallery's flagpole, participate in a puppet show, or try out 19th-century games and toys.

226 U.S. Naval Academy Museum and Gallery of Ships

CONTACT 410-293-2108, www.usna.edu; 118 Maryland Ave., Annapolis

PRICING	$ (guided tour of the U.S. Naval Academy requires a fee)
BEST TIME TO VISIT	Year-round
AGE RANGE	7 and older

The U.S. Naval Academy and the 4,000 midshipmen who call the school their temporary home dominate the pretty waterside city of Annapolis; the university is open for guided tours, which include a trip to the beautiful chapel and offer a peek at the enormous pipe organ. (Underneath the chapel is the crypt of the Revolutionary War hero John Paul Jones, who declared "I have not yet begun to fight" during a battle with the British.) Don't miss the fun and educational Naval Academy Museum, which features more than 50,000 maritime artifacts and is the site of the astonishing Gallery of Ships, a collection of meticulous ship models. The collection includes more than 100 ships and boats built between 1650 and 1850 on a 1:48 scale. In most cases, the ships on which the models

U.S. Naval Academy Museum and Gallery of Ships
Courtesy Annapolis Convention and Visitors Bureau

USS Constellation
Courtesy Library of Congress

were created are no longer in existence—like the famous ship HMS *Brittannia*, a 100-gun warship, the original full-scale version of which has been destroyed. Look also for the *Minerva*, a British 38-gun frigate from 1780 that boasts tiny copper accents and intricately carved decorations; and the *Royal William*, a British ship from 1719 that includes an interior staircase with balustrades made of ivory and an exterior tiny golden equestrian figurehead.

227 USS *Constellation*

CONTACT 410-539-1797, www.historicships.org; 301 E. Pratt St., Pier 1, Inner Harbor, Baltimore

PRICING	$–$$$
BEST TIME TO VISIT	Year-round
AGE RANGE	5 and older

Part of the Historic Ships of Baltimore maritime museum collection, the USS *Constellation* was built in 1854 and is the last sail-only warship built by the U.S. Navy. The *Constellation*'s most notable contribution was as part of the U.S. Navy African Squadron. From 1859 to 1861 the ship's duty was to disrupt the African slave trade and release imprisoned Africans encountered along the way. The historic vessel is worth visiting because of the inventive and educational onboard programming that brings history alive, especially for children who love ships. The year-round events include daily cannon firings; hands-on demonstrations hosted by the ship's crew; and on weekends (at 1 and 3) the popular Powder Monkey Tour for Kids. Children are invited aboard the USS *Constellation* to learn about the youngsters who once served as "powder monkeys," usually 11- to 18-year-olds who were short enough to be easily protected behind the ship's gunwale from enemy fire and whose job it was to carry bags of gunpowder from the ship's hold to the gun crews. Young guests will be treated as recruits and learn how their 19th-century counterparts dressed, ate, and played. (No additional reservations are required for this program.)

Visitors wishing to tour all four historic ships that make up the Historic Ships of Baltimore Museum can save considerably by purchasing tickets that entitle the bearer to admission to the entire collection. For a few dollars, you can gain admittance to all ships on display, plus the Seven Foot Knoll Lighthouse.

Edgartown Lighthouse, Martha's Vineyard © MatthewBird/iStockphoto.com

massachusetts

228 Boston Museum of Fine Arts

America's Wing, Museum of Fine Arts

© Museum of Fine Arts. Used with permission.

CONTACT 617-267-9300, www.mfa.org; 465 Huntington Ave., Boston

PRICING	$–$$$$
BEST TIME TO VISIT	Year-round
AGE RANGE	7 and older

The Museum of Fine Arts in Boston is one of the greatest art museums in the country, and offers a brilliant collection of American art, including Gilbert Stuart's *Washington*, John Singleton Copley's *Paul Revere* (which is displayed near a silver Sons of Liberty bowl wrought by Revere), and a large collection of impressionist Mary Cassatt's paintings. The museum displays an impressive collection of European art, too, including one of the largest collections of work by Claude Monet outside of Paris. There are also great antiquities to be seen here, including Egyptian mummies, Asian ceramics, and Greek urns.

But what sets this museum apart are the *hundreds* of opportunities for hands-on art making, special family tours, and programming for children of all ages. Check in with the Family Art Cart (weekends only from October through June, and Wednesday, Thursday, and Saturday in July and August) to borrow a tote bag full of puzzles, art books, sketch books, colored pencils, and paper-and-pencil games that will engage children 4 through 10 in the MFA's permanent exhibits. Or if you are traveling with very young children (under 4), look into the MFA Play Dates, held the first and third Monday of the month: Toddlers enjoy story time, a special guided tour through select galleries, and an age-appropriate art-making project. (No preregistration is necessary—just show up at the Sharf Visitor Center.) Teenagers can take advantage

Admission to the MFA is by voluntary contribution every Wednesday after 4 PM. There are a handful of open-house days that are free all day, including Martin Luther King Jr. Day, Memorial Day, and the Fall Open House in early October.

of the incredible Art Engagement programs, offering studio art classes as part of one-day workshops or multiweek courses; older children can learn the techniques of painting, sculpture, glassblowing, welding, jewelry making, and comic-book illustration (to name only a few of the classes).

Visit during a traditional school vacation and even more family opportunities are available, like story hour for toddlers (with ASL interpretation in the afternoon session); special children's tours; historical dramatic presentations (in the Alfond Auditorium), with actors depicting characters like *Little Women* author Louisa May Alcott and George Washington's onetime slave Ona Maria Judge; and myriad hands-on art-making programs that include sketching, mixed-media collage, and sculpture.

229 Boston Tea Party Cruise

CONTACT 617-742-0333, www.libertyfleet.com; Liberty Fleet Tall Sailing Ships, 67 Long Wharf, Boston

PRICING	$$$$
BEST TIME TO VISIT	Summer
AGE RANGE	7 and older

The famous Boston Tea Party was an act of defiance by colonial rebels in reaction to the Tea Act that was passed by British Parliament in 1773. The act was loathed by colonists because they believed it constituted taxation without representation—and further, it seemed an especially egregious indignity that the

Don't rent a car in Boston: Parking is expensive and hard to come by (and the roadways can be confusing for out-of-towners). Instead use the inexpensive public transportation known locally as "the T," a comprehensive system of buses, subways, and trains that crisscross the Boston area. Individual tickets cost only a few dollars. For real savings, buy a Charlie Card, a reusable, reloadable ticket that permits access to the entire metro system. The Seven-Day Visitor Link Pass allows you unlimited trips, plus one free bus transfer per ride.

taxes would be levied on what many considered a *necessity* of life: tea. In reaction against the Tea Act and the East India Company that supplied tea to the colonies, protestors in three other colonies prevented tea from being unloaded from incoming ships; however, in Boston, the British governor Thomas Hutchinson refused to allow the shipment to his city to be returned to Britain. Rather than pay the tax, a band of angry colonists decided it would be better to destroy the tea. They boarded the ships disguised as Native Americans and dumped the tea into the Boston Harbor, igniting a firestorm of angry response. It wasn't long after this rather dramatic event that growing tension between the colonists and the British government escalated into the American Revolution.

A fun way to introduce children to the history of the Boston Tea Party and the principles behind the American Revolution is via a Boston Tea Party Reenactment Sail. Tall-ship tour operator Liberty Fleet takes guests back in time to experience the infamous act of civil disobedience firsthand. In warm months the *Liberty Clipper* (named after Founder John Hancock's ship) sails from the Boston Harbor with costumed actors aboard acting the part of raiders, who join with crew and guests to return to the site of the Tea Party. Actors explain the viewpoints of both the colonial dissenters and the British importers, and then guests vote on what they want to do about the shipment of tea. Not surprisingly, the result is usually that a crate of "tea" gets tossed overboard. (Crew discreetly pull up the crate after the exhibition.) This is an interactive experience—guests not only get to participate in the historical reenactment but also help hoist the sails and might even be invited to take the ship's wheel—and the relaxing sail is a good opportunity to see the lovely Boston skyline from the water.

230 Bunker Hill Monument

CONTACT 617-242-7511, www.nps.gov/bost/history culture/bhm.htm; Monument Square, Charlestown

PRICING	$
BEST TIME TO VISIT	Year-round
AGE RANGE	7 and older

On June 17, 1775, during the Siege of Boston that took place very early in the American Revolutionary War, a battalion of inexperienced and ragtag colonial army men stood their ground against highly trained and well-equipped British infantry men armed with muskets, guns, and bayonets. The battle took place at Breed's Hill, adjacent to Bunker Hill and just outside of Boston. American colonel William Prescott is credited with declaring the famous "Don't fire until you see the whites of their eyes" here. The victory ultimately went to the British—but their losses were significant, with more than 800 wounded and 225 killed, and the encounter proved that the scrappy colonial army could hold its own against its formidable foe.

Today the Bunker Hill Monument, a 221-foot granite obelisk, memorializes the battle and the colonists who fought in the early days of the Revolution. Visit during daytime hours and climb the 294 stairs to the top for a spectacular view. Across from the monument is the Battle of Bunker Hill Museum (43 Monument Square), which houses artifacts and

Liberty cruise on Boston Harbor Photo Ken Legler, courtesy Liberty Fleet

PRICE KEY
$ free–$5
$$ $6–10
$$$ $11–20
$$$$ $21+

Bunker Hill Monument   Photo Tim Graff, courtesy MOTT

Emily Dickinson's bedroom
Photo Jessica Mestre, courtesy Emily Dickinson Museum

exhibits that tell the story of the decisive battle. Both the monument and the museum are on the Freedom Trail (see below).

231 Emily Dickinson Museum

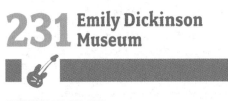

CONTACT 413-542-8161, www.emilydickinsonmuseum.org; 280 Main St., Amherst

PRICING	$–$$
BEST TIME TO VISIT	March through December (closed January and February; Monday and Tuesday)
AGE RANGE	10 and older

Emily Dickinson (1830–86) was an American poet who is remembered as a recluse and somewhat of an eccentric; more important, she is considered by historians and literary critics as among the finest 19th-century writers in the United States. The extremely influential poet penned more than 1,800 short works—but only a handful were published in her lifetime. Many of her poems focus on death, immortality, and nature and many are quite unconventional in style, especially considering the time period in which they were written.

The Emily Dickinson Museum comprises two homes: The Homestead, where Dickinson was born and lived most of her life; and The Evergreens, a home next door built by Dickinson's brother and his wife (who was one of Emily's best friends). The property is surrounded by 3 landscaped acres of gardens. For older children who've read Dickinson, take the 90-minute tour that includes both structures. This longer tour introduces guests to Dickinson's family life and the influences on her writing. Stroll through the homes to see the family library, Emily's bedroom (where she wrote many of her poems), a lavishly furnished dining room, the kitchen, a maid's room, and a nursery. The Evergreens is completely furnished with household items, artwork, and personal artifacts owned and displayed by the Dickinson family during the 19th century.

232 Fenway Park

CONTACT http://mlb.com/bos/ballpark; 4 Yawkey Way, Boston

PRICING	$$$ (games additional)
BEST TIME TO VISIT	Baseball season
AGE RANGE	All ages

Fenway Park   Photo by Carol M. Highsmith, courtesy Library of Congress

Sports fanatics will not want to miss a chance to see the home ballpark of the Boston Red Sox baseball team and the oldest Major League Baseball stadium in use (since 1912). The park is famous for the Green Monster, the landmark green-painted 37-foot left-field concrete wall (known for the difficulty of hitting a home run over it). Look for the lone red seat in the right-field bleachers, which marks the longest home run ever hit at the park—a 502-foot slam by Ted Williams in 1946. If you want to go to a game, plan well ahead: The Red Sox have sold out every home game for the past decade. On nongame days (or three hours before game time), guests can take a tour of the park, sit in the dugout, walk around the playing field, and drink in the baseball history.

233 Freedom Trail

CONTACT	www.thefreedomtrail.org; downtown Boston
PRICING	$
BEST TIME TO VISIT	Late spring through early fall
AGE RANGE	All ages

History buffs will not want to miss the chance to take a self-guided walking tour of Boston by following the red line (painted on the sidewalk or outlined in brick) that winds through the historical district downtown to view some of the most important sites in the city. The route is well marked, so there is no worry of getting

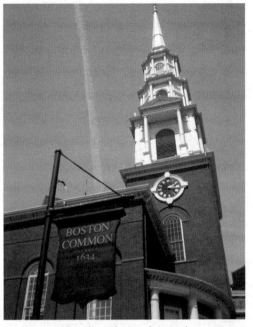

Boston Common, along the Freedom Trail   © Debbie K. Hardin

lost. The trail is 2.5 miles long and passes 16 sites. Pick up a brochure at your hotel concierge outlining the stops along the way, and catch the trail anywhere along the route (it starts at the Boston Common Visitor Information Center—although you can begin and end anywhere along the route). Highlights include Paul Revere's House (described below); the Old North Church (also detailed later in this book), where two lanterns

The Union Oyster House (617-227-2750, www.unionoysterhouse.com; 41 Union St.) along the Freedom Trail is the oldest continually operating eatery in the United States, and a stop here for lunch or dinner is an educational (and satisfying) way to relive history. The large restaurant has been in business for more than 250 years; in the early 19th century, this was a regular hangout for American statesman and senator Daniel Webster. In more recent years, it has been a favorite with Massachusetts politicians like the Kennedy clan and Bostonian senator John Kerry. Call ahead for reservations to sit at the Kennedy Booth, JFK's preferred seat when he was in town.

were hung to warn the colonists that British troops were coming by sea at the start of the American Revolution; the Old State House (below), the site of the Boston Massacre where the first bloodshed of the American Revolution occurred—five colonists were killed by the British in 1770; Faneuil Hall, known as the Cradle of Liberty because it was here where many of the most famous speeches calling for independence were made; and the USS *Constitution* (below), known as Old Ironsides, the oldest commissioned warship afloat in the world. In addition to being a fun, active way to explore the history of the city, the Freedom Trail is also a good way to see the charming neighborhoods that make up the cosmopolitan area.

234 Hancock Shaker Village

CONTACT 413-443-0188, www.hancockshakervillage.org; 1843 W. Housatonic St., Pittsfield

PRICING	$$–$$$
BEST TIME TO VISIT	Open April through October
AGE RANGE	3 and older

The Shakers are a religious group that dates to the 18th century; they exist today (albeit in *very* small numbers) and believe in pacifism, communal living, celibacy, and the necessity of working toward utopia on earth. They originally called themselves the United Society of Believers in Christ's Second Appearing, but they earned the nickname of Shakers from their style of worship, which includes singing, dancing, and

Hancock Shaker Village   © Debbie K. Hardin

To protect the antique wooden floors in the dwelling and several other buildings at Hancock Shaker Village, the museum requests guests wear shoe protectors while inside certain structures. These are somewhat awkward and generally too large for children's feet, so plan ahead and wear a sturdy pair of socks, so you can instead just slip off your shoes and pad around without disturbing the woodwork.

shaking. In their earliest days, they were persecuted for their beliefs in their native England, so leader Ann Lee (known as Mother Ann) brought a small group of followers to America in 1774.

Hancock Shaker Village was founded shortly afterward, in the late 1780s, when 100 Shakers began to create a community on land donated by local farmers who converted to the Shaker movement. (Because the religion called for celibacy, Shakers relied on converts for continued propagation.) By the 1830s more than 300 Shakers lived in the communal village, on more than 3,000 acres. They constructed communal dwelling houses, workshops, and barns; they tended livestock and created large and productive gardens. They called their small slice of heaven The City of Peace.

Today the village serves as an outdoor history museum, and visitors can tour 20 buildings scattered throughout the property, including the Round Stone Barn (dating to 1826) and the beautiful and spare dwelling structure (which features separate doorways and stairs to keep the sexes segregated). Throughout costumed interpreters tend to vegetable and herb gardens; farmers care for livestock; and craftspeople demonstrate wood crafting, wool dying, and spinning. Children will not want to miss the Discovery Room, which is filled with opportunities to dress up, play games, and try out crafts like weaving and knitting. Throughout the season the museum offers a large number of specialty tours that allow you to customize your visit around your own interests: You can learn a Shaker dance, cook a traditional Shaker recipe, take an in-depth tour of the medicinal herb garden, take a traditional Shaker school lesson in a one-room schoolhouse, tour the library to examine voluminous letters and manuscripts, or—for kids—don a bonnet or straw hat and re-create a typical day in the life of a Shaker child.

235 Harvard University

For prospective student tours, book online in advance—as much as a month ahead if you plan to visit during the busy spring break and summer seasons.

CONTACT 617-495-1573, www.harvard.edu/visitors/tours; Harvard Information Center, 1350 Massachusetts Ave., Cambridge

PRICING	$
BEST TIME TO VISIT	Spring through fall; closed Sunday
AGE RANGE	All ages (but high schoolers will get the most from a visit)

A college tour is a rite of passage for many American teenagers, and there's no more famous mecca of higher learning in the country than the esteemed Harvard University, the oldest institution of its kind in the United States. The school was established in 1636—at the time admitting only men (and then only rich white men from prominent families). Today the school educates close to 7,000 undergraduates a year; the vast library (comparable only to the Library of Congress in Washington, DC) contains 17 million volumes; and the proverbial ivy-covered halls have been home to 44 Nobel laureates and an impressive number of U.S. presidents.

You can prearrange a tour for prospective students that begins at the admissions office; a current student will lead a small group around the lovely campus and discuss student life. You can also arrange for a public tour that highlights the history and architecture of the venerable institution, take an audio tour via your handheld mobile device (at yardtour.harvard.edu), download an audio tour for your MP3 player (www.harvard.edu/visitors/audio-tours), or download a campus map (www.harvard.edu/sites/default/files/visitors/tours/Harvard-Yard-Tour-Map.pdf) and take your own self-guided tour. However you visit, be sure to rub the foot of the statue of Harvard's namesake for good luck. And while on campus, check out the Harvard Museum of Natural History (617-495-3045, www.hmnh.harvard.edu; 26 Oxford St., Cambridge). Young kids will enjoy the chance to see the 42-foot *Kronosaurus*, the only such prehistoric skeleton on display in North America. There are also hands-on opportunities to touch meteorites. And don't miss the garden of Glass Flowers, a collection of blown-glass flowers executed with perfect anatomical proportions (they are beautiful and educational).

Harvard University © Debbie K. Hardin

236 The House of the Seven Gables

CONTACT 978-744-0991, www.7gables.org; 115 Derby St., Salem

PRICING	$$–$$$
BEST TIME TO VISIT	Year-round
AGE RANGE	10 and older

Nathaniel Hawthorne (1804—64) is one of the most famous American novelists and short-story writers of

> If you have the chance, visit The House of the Seven Gables museum during the winter holiday season, when scores of designers are invited in to re-create Christmas decorations from history.

237 John F. Kennedy Presidential Library and Museum

all time, and his works are still widely read. Few students in the United States pass through high school *without* reading his *Scarlet Letter*. Another famous Hawthorne novel, *The House of the Seven Gables*, focuses on similar themes of guilt and retribution. The story was inspired in part by a home in Salem where Hawthorne's cousin, Susanna Ingersoll, lived, and in part by Hawthorne's ancestors, who participated in the infamous Salem witch trials in the late 17th century.

The home was built in 1668 by John Turner, a sea captain whose family lived on the property for three generations before selling the place to Captain Samuel Ingersoll in the late 18th century. In the early 20th century the home was restored as a museum. Today visitors can take guided tours through the grand old home to look for details described in Hawthorne's novel, like the wooden closet with a false back that leads to a secret staircase to the attic. By the mid-20th century the birthplace home of Hawthorne, originally located on nearby Union Street, was moved on site as well, and this more modest structure is also open to visitors. The charming garden offers beautiful views of the Salem harbor.

CONTACT 617-514-1600, www.jfklibrary.org; Columbia Point, Boston

PRICING	$$–$$$
BEST TIME TO VISIT	Year-round
AGE RANGE	7 and older

John F. Kennedy (1917–63) was the 35th president of the United States. At 43, he was the youngest person to be elected as chief executive, and he was the first Roman Catholic elected to the office. JFK was a member of one of the wealthiest families in America, and was educated in the best institutions in the country. He distinguished himself early in life as a hero in World War II, as a commander of a PT boat in the South Pacific. Despite his privileged status, he dedicated his life to public service; he was first elected to the U.S. House of Representatives and then served in the U.S. Senate.

Atrium of the John F. Kennedy Presidential Library and Museum   © Debbie K. Hardin

House of the Seven Gables   © Debbie K. Hardin

Kennedy became the Democratic nominee for the presidency in 1960, and defeated then vice president Richard Nixon for the office. During his short administration, he inspired greater efforts in the space race, made enormous strides in the civil rights movement, and commanded the earliest stages of the Vietnam War. Including his fashionable wife Jacqueline and his photogenic young children Caroline and John Jr., the Kennedy family was much admired while in the White House; historians continue to rank JFK as one of the most successful presidents of all time. Tragically, Kennedy was assassinated on November 22, 1963, during a visit to Dallas, Texas, by Lee Harvey Oswald.

On the campus of the University of Massachusetts (and a bit of a trek from the central part of the city—grab a free shuttle from the subway to avoid a long, confusing walk), the John F. Kennedy Library and Museum allows visitors to relive the 1,000 days of the Kennedy presidency. A tour begins with a 40-minute film about Kennedy's life, narrated in his own words. Guests then walk through dozens of multimedia exhibits, including a collection of campaign buttons, numerous documents written in JFK's hand, a re-created Oval Office, and fun displays of Jackie Kennedy's dresses, jewels, and correspondence. The exhibit terminates in a moving display dedicated to Kennedy's assassination, and guests leave the building through a soaring atrium that looks out over Kennedy's beloved Boston Harbor.

238 *Mayflower II*

CONTACT 508-746-1622, www.plimoth.org; Plymouth Waterfront, across from 74 Water St., Plymouth

PRICING	$$
BEST TIME TO VISIT	Open late March through Thanksgiving
AGE RANGE	All ages

Children learn about the *Mayflower* from their earliest days in school: Most will know all about the voyage in 1620 that brought Pilgrims seeking religious freedom to the coast of what is now Massachusetts, and

Mayflower II   Photo by Debbie K. Hardin, with permission of Plimoth Plantation

many will probably have some sense of the hardships the newcomers endured. What kids might not know is that the 102 passengers and crew were aiming for a settlement in Virginia, but the *Mayflower* was hit with bad weather that caused them to drift north of their intended stop—and by the time they arrived, the New England winter had already set in and the Pilgrims had little choice but to stay in Massachusetts.

To get a taste of what the voyage was like for the first intrepid colonists, check out the *Mayflower II*, a full-scale replica of the original ship built in England in the middle of the 20th century with strict attention to historical accuracy, complete with oak timbers and tarred hemp rigging (although the replica includes some innovations necessary to make the vessel safe for modern visitors). Children will probably be shocked at how small the ship is—especially when they climb belowdecks to see where the Pilgrims slept. On board are costumed reenactors portraying original *Mayflower* passengers (on weekends and holidays, there are often costumed young children). Visitors can interact with the reenactors, hear tales of the perilous transatlantic voyage, check out the accommodations of the sailors who served as *Mayflower* crew, and examine the tools used to navigate in the 17th century. There are historical reenactments held throughout the season, and special living history programming on weekends.

Purchase combination tickets to visit the *Mayflower II* and the Plimoth Plantation (see below) on the same day and save nearly 20 percent.

239 Minute Man National Historical Park

CONTACT 978-369-6993, www.nps.gov/mima; 174 Liberty St., Concord

PRICING	$
BEST TIME TO VISIT	May through October (when the greatest number of structures are open)
AGE RANGE	7 and older

Minuteman Statue, Minute Man National Historic Park

Photo Tim Graff, courtesy MOTT

Tensions between citizens in the colonies and the British government increased in the early 1770s as the British Crown sought to raise taxes on the Americans and the Americans increasingly chafed under the yoke of colonial rule. In what was described by writer Ralph Waldo Emerson as "the shot heard round the world," the April 19, 1775, battle at Lexington and Concord between British regulars and colonial minutemen (volunteers who were armed at all times so they could be ready to fight at a "minute's" notice) was the official start of the American Revolutionary War. A few days before the battle, British military governor of Massachusetts, General Thomas Gage, was tasked with destroying the colonists' military stores in Concord, in an effort to avoid rebellious armed resistance. On the night of April 18, some 700 British troops left Boston for Concord with this goal in mind. Patriots, however, learned of the plan and sent two emissaries—Paul Revere, during his famous midnight ride, and William Dawes—to the towns of Lexington and Concord to warn the citizens there. By the time the British troops arrived, there was an ample showing of minutemen waiting to rebuff their attack.

Minute Man National Historical Park commemorates both the battle that started the War for Independence and the spirit of revolution embodied by the Americans who dared to imagine a new sort of government. Start your visit at the Minute Man Visitor Center to view *The Road to Revolution*, a multimedia presentation that offers a good historical introduction to the battle and to the war in general. The park features a 5-mile interpretive trail (good for biking or walking) known as the Battle Road Trail that allows guests to trace the pathway that the minutemen took between Lexington and Concord and includes a monument at the site where Revere was captured. Along the way is Hartwell Tavern, a preserved period home where from May through October costumed reenactors interact with patrons and demonstrate arts and crafts. Also preserved within the park is the North Bridge, where the colonial minutemen were first ordered to fire on British troops (and where the first British soldiers of the war were killed). Nearby is a British Grave Site monument and a minuteman statue by Daniel Chester French, as well as The Wayside, onetime home to influential American writers Amos Bronson Alcott, his daughter Louisa May Alcott, and Nathaniel Hawthorne. There are numerous festivities and living history demonstrations throughout the park, especially in the warmer months. The Whittemore House, a historic property in the park, offers family activities Thursday through Monday in the summer that include demonstrations on spinning yarn, the opportunity for hands-on garden tending, and hat making. In mid-April, Patriot's Day—a Massachusetts state holiday commemorating the battle at Lexington—is celebrated at the park with a weekend of parades, commemorative ceremonies, and historical reenactments.

240 New Bedford Whaling Museum

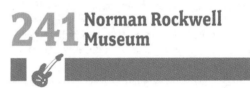

CONTACT 508-997-0046, www.whalingmuseum.org; 18 Johnny Cake Hill, New Bedford

PRICING	$$–$$$
BEST TIME TO VISIT	Year-round
AGE RANGE	7 and older

One of the most economically viable industries in 19th-century America was whaling. An enormous whaling fleet, based largely in New England, sailed the globe in search of whales, which provided raw materials used for lighting and heating oil and in the manufacture of other products like candles. Although several seaports supported the industry, by the mid-19th century New Bedford was the world's most prolific whaling seaport, with more than 400 whaling vessels calling the port home. Because of the extensive use of whale oil to power lanterns (for home use and for the dozens of lighthouses that dotted the New England coastline), New Bedford was nicknamed "The City That Lit the World."

The New Bedford Whaling Museum documents the international whaling industry, particularly as it relates to the rich "old Dartmouth" region along the south coast of Massachusetts. The museum is located within the New Bedford Whaling National Historical Park, which itself is a monument to the legacy of whaling and its enormous economic impacts on this small seaside village. The museum comprises more than 200,000 artifacts pertaining to whales, including 3,000 examples of scrimshaw (artwork carved from whale bones) and 2,500 handwritten logbooks of whaling expeditions—the largest collections of both items in the world.

Permanent collections also include fine and decorative art, folk art, books, maps, charts, textiles, whaling prints, and maritime artifacts. Children will not want to miss the chance to climb aboard the *Lagoda*, the world's largest ship model, built at half scale (and fully rigged in its indoor location). The museum is home to what is believed to be the longest painting in the world, at 1,275 feet: the 1848 *Whaling Voyage Around the World*, which documents the 19th-century maritime world in panoramic detail. Whale skeletons are on display as well (although the museum is quick to note that these whales died naturally—they were not hunted for the purposes of displaying them).

New Bedford Whaling Museum

Photo John Robson, courtesy National Park Service

241 Norman Rockwell Museum

CONTACT 413-298-4100, www.nrm.org; 9 Rt. 183, Stockbridge

PRICING	$–$$$
BEST TIME TO VISIT	Year-round
AGE RANGE	10 and older

Twentieth-century painter and illustrator Norman Rockwell (1894–1978) created some of the most recognizable, iconic artwork in American history. He is most famous for illustrating countless covers for the *Saturday Evening Post* magazine depicting idealized American life, including the well-loved *Freedom from Want* showing a typical midwestern family sitting down to a Thanksgiving turkey, and *Doctor and the Doll*, showing an elderly physician examining a broken doll at the request of a young girl. Although he was known for such charming themes, Rockwell also explored the issues of his time, including race discrimination and religious intolerance. Regardless of subject matter, Rockwell's art is evocative, often humorous, and sure to spark discussion.

Norman Rockwell Museum   Courtesy Berkshire Visitors Bureau

The Old North Church in Boston was made famous in a poem by Henry Wadsworth Longfellow, commemorating the "midnight" ride of patriot Paul Revere; it was from the steeple of this church that Robert Newman, the church caretaker sympathetic to the revolutionary cause, at Revere's request hung two lighted lanterns to signal that the British were moving toward Lexington and Concord by sea in an attempt to destroy the colonists' ammunition stores. Revere, along with William Dawes, delivered the same message in person, but the lantern signaling was the easiest way to let their backups in nearby Charlestown know the whereabouts of the British in case these alternates had to ride into Lexington and Concord if Revere and Dawes were arrested before spreading the news. Newman hung the signal lanterns for a very brief period—maybe less than a minute—but that was long enough to arouse the suspicion of British troops, who saw the signal. British soldiers were at the front doors of the church to investigate even before Newman was down the stairs. To avoid capture, Newman escaped through a window on the right of the altar—

The Norman Rockwell Museum has the largest collection of Rockwell paintings and illustrations in the world, sited on the property that was once Rockwell's home. Guests can still stroll past his lovely stone house (although it is not open for visitors) and tour the barn-like structure in the back that he used as his studio. In addition to the Rockwell paintings, the museum often hosts traveling exhibits, generally with multigenerational appeal. An added bonus for families: There are extensive programs for children here, including a summer sketch club for kids 7 and older and a parent–child interactive experience that introduces children 4 and older and an adult companion to various art media and techniques.

242 Old North Church

CONTACT 617-523-6676, www.oldnorth.com; 193 Salem St. (on the Freedom Trail), Boston

PRICING	$
BEST TIME TO VISIT	Year-round (although closed Monday in January and February; not open for tours during Sunday-morning and Thursday-evening worship services)
AGE RANGE	7 and older

Old North Church   © Debbie K. Hardin

now called the "Newman window." Today a replica of the famous lantern Newman used to signal the patriots hangs above the window.

Guests to the site, which is still a working church, can sit in the box pews and listen to a five-minute lecture on the role of the Old North Church in Revolutionary War history. If you'd like a more in-depth look at the structure, schedule a Behind the Scenes Tour that will take you to the second-floor gallery, to the bell-ringing chamber in the church's steeple where Revere worked as a teenager; you'll also tour the crypt beneath the church, where more than 1,000 people are entombed.

Site of the Boston Massacre Courtesy Jon Preimesberger

243 Old State House

CONTACT 617-357-8300, www.thefreedomtrail.org; along the Freedom Trail, 30 State St., Boston

PRICING	$
BEST TIME TO VISIT	Year-round
AGE RANGE	7 and older

Redcoat soldiers stationed in Boston in 1770 were tasked with enforcing the unpopular British laws and keeping a lid on increasingly rebellious actions from Bostonians. However, on March 5 of that year, tensions erupted into bloodshed. On this late-winter day, a British guard at the Custom House left his command post and assaulted a young Bostonian with the butt of his musket—after the British soldier endured a good bit of harassment from the young American, it should be noted. A crowd gathered, and the guard was soon surrounded by a hysterical mob. When word of the incident reached the British regimental commander, eight more British soldiers were dispatched to reinforce the guard. By the time the Redcoats arrived, there were several hundred angry people on site—who assailed the British with rocks, clubs, and even snowballs. The mob continued to attack until the soldiers fired shots into the assembly. Five men were killed immediately. Patriot Samuel Adams organized elaborate public funerals for the victims and branded the action a "massacre." The event—although hardly constituting a massacre by today's standards—heralded the beginning of the Revolutionary War five years later. Today the spot of the incident is marked by a circle of cobblestones, located in a traffic circle across from the beautiful Old State House downtown. Reenactments are held every year on the anniversary of the massacre.

244 Old Sturbridge Village

CONTACT 508-347-0395, www.osv.org; 1 Old Sturbridge Village Rd., Sturbridge

PRICING	$$–$$$$
BEST TIME TO VISIT	Spring
AGE RANGE	3 and older

Old Sturbridge Village (formerly known as simply Sturbridge Village) is an expansive living history museum that interprets a New England town from 1790 to 1840. Costumed reenactors populate the village and tell the stories of life in this part of the country during the late 18th and early 19th centuries. Guests here have numerous opportunities to learn from the knowledgeable staff, participate in craft making, and tour the period-furnished buildings. There are more than 40 original reconstructed structures (most brought to the museum site from towns elsewhere in New England), including the Cider Mill, which uses

Hands on at Old Sturbridge Village

Photo Erika Sidor, courtesy Old Sturbridge Village

Paul Revere (1734–1818) was a successful gold- and silversmith and an early supporter of the American Revolution. Revere served as an intelligence gatherer for the colonists before the war, and volunteered as a courier running correspondence between Boston and the Continental Congress in Philadelphia. He is most famous, of course, for spreading the word that British forces were advancing before the Battles of Lexington and Concord (the start of the war)—and from the lyrical poem by Henry Wadsworth Longfellow that immortalized this midnight ride and turned Revere into a folk hero. During the war Revere served as a lieutenant colonel in the Massachusetts artillery. Today Revere's home in the North End of Boston is a landmark both because of its onetime famous owner and because the structure is the oldest surviving building in Boston, dating to 1680. Revere bought the wooden home in 1770. Today guests can take a self-guided visit and tour the interior; two rooms upstairs are furnished with items once belonging to the Revere family.

horsepower to press apples; the Fitch House, a modest cottage that is displayed as the home of the local printer; the Freeman Farm, a 70-acre homesite that includes a barn and outbuildings—young children will enjoy coming here in the spring to see the baby lambs and pigs; the Parsonage, a lean-to that is re-created as the home of a Congregational minister and his family; the Pottery House, where you can watch skilled artisans throw mugs, milk pans, and crocks; the Printing House, where you can see books printed and bound; Salem Towne House, depicting the domestic life of a successful farmer; and the Tin Shop where you can watch everyday tin items being manufactured. There is also a working blacksmith shop, a gristmill, a sawmill, and a carding mill.

The museum offers interactive exhibits that include opportunities to dip candles, churn butter, bake bread, ride in a horse-drawn carriage, play old-time games, pick vegetables from the garden, and try your hand at weaving.

Fans of Paul Revere should consider visiting the nearby Concord Museum (978-369-9609, www.concordmuseum .org; Lexington Rd. and Cambridge Turnpike, Concord), a small but intriguing collection that includes a lantern hung at Revere's request in the steeple of the Old North Church the night of his infamous "midnight ride" to warn Lexington and Concord that the British were coming.

245 Paul Revere's House

CONTACT 617-523-2338, www.paulreverehouse.org; along the Freedom Trail, 19 North Square, Boston

PRICING	$
BEST TIME TO VISIT	Year-round
AGE RANGE	7 and older

Paul Revere's House

Courtesy MOTT

246 Peabody Essex Museum

CONTACT 978-745-9500, www.pem.org; 161 Essex St., Salem

PRICING	$–$$$
BEST TIME TO VISIT	Year-round; closed Monday
AGE RANGE	7 and older

The recently renovated Peabody Essex Museum is the oldest continuously operating museum in the country. The origin of what is now the museum was founded in 1799 by mariners and merchants of the East India Marine Society—originally based on the society's collections from world voyages—and is well known for its oceanic and maritime collection as well as a diverse collection of Asian art. Included among the 1.8 million pieces in the permanent collection are paintings, ceramics, sculptures, textiles, decorative objects, and photographs, as well as original court documents from the Salem witch trials of 1692 (which are exhibited on a rotating basis). Children will especially enjoy touring the Yin Yu Tang House, a 200-year-old Chinese house from the Anhui province that was disassembled and removed from its original site, then reconstructed within the museum.

Atrium courtyard, Peabody Essex Museum © Debbie K. Hardin

247 Peacefields

CONTACT 617-770-1175, www.nps.gov/adam/history culture/places.htm; Adams National Park Visitor Center, 1250 Hancock Street, Quincy

PRICING	$
BEST TIME TO VISIT	Open late April through early November
AGE RANGE	7 and older

John Adams (1735–1826) was the second president of the United States and vice president to first commander in chief, George Washington. He was immensely influential in the earliest days of the Republic, and is widely recognized as one of the most important Founders of the country. He was a contributor to the Declaration of Independence and served in the Continental Congress. His family connections are equally impressive: He was married to Abigail Adams, one of the most respected early first ladies; and he was father to the sixth president of the United States, John Quincy Adams. In 1800 Adams lost his bid for reelection to the presidency to Thomas Jefferson and retired to private life. He continued to write and publish on government and politics and carried on a prolific correspondence with his onetime nemesis, Jefferson. On the 50th anniversary of the adoption of the Declaration of Independence—July 4—Adams died at his beloved home in Quincy. Coincidentally, Thomas Jefferson died on the same day, a few hours earlier.

Peacefields is the home to which Adams retired

John Adams home   Courtesy National Park Service

after he left the President's House (which wasn't called the White House for another decade). The Massachusetts home, which Adams also called the Old House, was built in 1731, and was kept in the Adams family from 1788 to 1927. It was also home to John Quincy Adams and several generations of Adams afterward, all of whom were remarkably accomplished individuals. Peacefields is part of the Adams National Historical Park, which also includes the John Adams and John Quincy Adams birthplace houses. Also on site is the Stone Library, a structure that holds more than 14,000 books, built as a fireproof repository at the request of John Quincy. Peacefields and the other structures at the park can only be visited by tour—and be aware that tickets can sell out quickly. Come to the park visitor center to arrange for tours, park at the site, and take a trolley to the historic buildings. Look for Abigail's 17th-century clock, which still keeps time. And don't miss the chance to tour the beautiful grounds. Abigail was an avid gardener, and it's said that a rosebush she planted on the property herself still blooms.

248 Pilgrim Hall Museum

CONTACT 508-746-1620, www.pilgrimhall.org; 75 Court St., Plymouth

PRICING	$–$$
BEST TIME TO VISIT	Closed in January
AGE RANGE	7 and older

The Pilgrim Hall Museum is dedicated to the story of the Pilgrims and the Plymouth Colony, which it tells through an impressive collection of Pilgrim possessions that include furniture, books, armor, and textiles as well as artwork. Included in the permanent collection are leader of the Plymouth Colony William Bradford's Bible, the cradle of the first English baby born in New England (Peregrine White), a wooden beer tankard owned by Myles Standish, and an embroidered sampler by Loara Standish (Myles's daughter). In addition, the museum includes a library and archives.

249 Plimouth Plantation

CONTACT 508-746-1622, www.plimoth.org; 137 Warren Ave., Plymouth

PRICING	$$$–$$$$
BEST TIME TO VISIT	Open early April through late November
AGE RANGE	All ages

New Plymouth was the first settlement of the Plymouth Bay, an English colony sited at a location originally surveyed by Captain John Smith. The venture was one of the earliest successful British colonies in North America—thanks in part to the initial support of the Native peoples, who introduced the colonists to local agricultural techniques.

Plimoth Plantation today is a living history museum comprising a small reconstructed farming and fishing village from the year 1627 and staffed by costumed interpreters who work and speak the way Pilgrims would have more than 350 years ago. You can step back in time here to discuss religion, gardening, home building, and the politics of the day with the actors who portray real individuals, and unlike some living history museums that invite guests to step back and observe—as if watching a play—the folks at Plimoth invite guests to participate. You and your family might be invited into one of the timber-framed homes to chat with the lady of the house while she prepares a typical meal; you might stroll through the gardens with a reenactor to learn about medicinal herbs; or your kids might pitch in with chores like gathering eggs or sweeping the dirt floors. The reenactors are enthusiastic, well informed, and highly entertaining to speak with—encourage your kids to ask questions about how children of their own age lived in the early 17th century.

Located along the Eel River on site is the Wampanoag Homesite, a 17th-century Native village that illuminates the traditional way of growing crops, fishing, boat making, and cooking. The small village features Native homes and common houses; this portion of the exhibit is staffed by Native people—many Wampanoag—and they are *not* historical reenactors but true representatives of the still-living culture. The Natives at this village are dressed in period clothing (mostly made of animal skins), and will happily engage you in traditional games, storytelling, and Native dancing. In addition, kids will not want to miss the Nye Barn, where Plimoth Plantation's heritage-breed animals are raised, including rare Arapawa goats, Tamworth swine, and Wiltshire Horned sheep.

For a completely immersive experience, consider an overnight visit at Plimoth Plantation. Families will dress up in reproduction colonial clothing, learn historic songs and dances, play games, chop wood—in fact, the experience can be catered to whatever your family is most interested in. A museum staff member will teach you everything you need to know for an enjoyable and productive overnight visit. At the end of the day, everyone will pitch in to prepare a hearth-cooked meal, and then spend the night in reproduc-

Plimouth Plantation

Photo by Debbie K. Hardin, with permission of Plimoth Plantation

tion colonial homes at a nearby education site. (These homes were originally built by Plimoth Plantation artisans at another location, for a PBS reality television show called *Colonial House*.) Or you could choose to spend the night on the *Mayflower II* (see above), a full-scale reproduction of the original vessel that brought the Pilgrims to the colony, where you can learn to tie knots, try foods the Pilgrims would have eaten on their voyage from England, make a model of the ship to take home, or just swab the decks. The overnight adventures are a bit pricey, but sure to make lasting memories.

250 Plymouth Rock

CONTACT Plymouth waterfront, across from the *Mayflower II*, Plymouth

PRICING	$
BEST TIME TO VISIT	Year-round
AGE RANGE	All ages

Don't come here expecting a metaphorical rock—like the sturdy New England bedrock on which the Pilgrims landed—or even a grand and impressive literal rock. The Plymouth Rock that is said to mark the point of disembarkation of the original *Mayflower* Pilgrims in Massachusetts is actually just a small and rather unimpressive stone with the year "1620"

Guests are asked to refrain from visiting the Plimoth Plantation in costume. Also, remind children when touring the Wampanoag Homesite that the individuals dressed in Native American clothing *are* Native Americans of the present day, not actors representing historical figures (as in the Plimoth settlement). The costumed staff at both sites are happy to answer questions and interact with guests—especially curious kids—but children should be advised that some people will speak with unfamiliar accents or use words they may not know, and nevertheless should be treated with respect and courtesy.

Plymouth Rock   © Debbie K. Hardin

It's worth noting that the first written record of the rock doesn't appear until 121 years after the Pilgrims landed in Plymouth; it is not mentioned in the journals of the original Pilgrims. So it could be the rock is a bit of historic nostalgia—perhaps the product of an 18th-century imagination that wanted to memorialize the *Mayflower* landing in a concrete way. Nevertheless, kids will likely get a kick out of seeing the rock—and its picturesque site makes it worth a stroll down the waterfront to view it.

carved in its face; today it sits opposite the re-created *Mayflower* docked in the Plymouth Harbor. Although the physical representation is somewhat anticlimactic to visitors, the symbolic meaning of the stone is as heavy and important as we might want it to be; the rock is a piece of American folklore that memorializes the determined men and women who made their way to the shores of the New World in search of religious freedom and a new political order.

251 Salem Witch Museum

CONTACT 978-744-1692, www.salemwitchmuseum.com; 19½ Washington Square N., Salem

PRICING	$$
BEST TIME TO VISIT	Year-round
AGE RANGE	10 and older

Salem Witch Museum   © Debbie K. Hardin

Although this quaint town was once a major seaport for ships en route to the East Indies and China, Salem is now infamously known as the "witch city." In 1692, hundreds of citizens of Salem were accused of being in league with the devil and practicing witchcraft. The accusers were teenage girls, whose fervor and paranoia were contagious. After the pretense of trials—in which spectral evidence (from dreams) was used to present a case against the innocent individuals— 19 people, men and women, were sentenced to death. The Salem Witch Museum commemorates this sad history with 13 somewhat creepy dioramas that tell the stories in dramatic detail. Although the presentation is overly dramatized, the story of the Salem witch trials offers important lessons for modern Americans about tolerance. (Note that this is an intense experience and might not be suitable for even older children who are particularly sensitive.)

For a lighter look at witchcraft in Salem, look for the statue of Samantha from TV's *Bewitched* in Lapin Park, at the corner of Essex and Washington Streets.

252 Sojourner Truth Memorial

CONTACT www.sojournertruthmemorial.org; corner of Park and Pine Sts., Florence

PRICING	$
BEST TIME TO VISIT	Year-round
AGE RANGE	7 and older

Sojourner Truth was the name Isabella Baumfree (c. 1797–1883) gave herself as a symbol of her religious awakening. Truth was an African American women's rights activist and abolitionist. She was born into slavery in New York, and was sold several times before reaching adulthood—suffering physical, psychological, and sexual abuse throughout her days as a slave. She escaped slavery with an infant daughter in 1826, and soon became an evangelist in the Pentecostal faith. She lived in Florence, Massachusetts, and preached and lectured widely; she also published a detailed account of her treatment as a slave. When the Civil War began, Truth advocated for black troops in the Union army and became increasingly involved in the women's suffrage movement. Today she is remembered with a small memorial in western Massachusetts. Visit to see the bronze statue erected on site; there are periodic events held at the memorial, including theatrical performances and annual celebrations of Truth's contributions to American life.

Sojourner Truth   Courtesy Library of Congress

253 USS *Constitution*

CONTACT www.history.navy.mil/ussconstitution; along the Freedom Trail, Pier 1, Bldg. 5, Charlestown Navy Yard, Charlestown

PRICING	$
BEST TIME TO VISIT	Year-round
AGE RANGE	All ages

Also known as Old Ironsides, the USS *Constitution* is the oldest commissioned navy vessel in the world. The grand old ship was named by President George Washington, and launched in 1797 as one of the six original frigates authorized by the Naval Act of 1794. The ship was originally used to defeat the Barbary pirates in the First Barbary War, but it is probably best known for its involvement in the War of 1812, when the ship's crew captured and defeated numerous British merchant and warships. Free guided tours are given most days by active-duty navy personnel. For a special treat, take your chances on the annual lottery;

USS Constitution   Photo Tim Graff, courtesy MOTT

For security reasons, visitors to the USS *Constitution* who are 18 and older may be asked to present a valid federal or state photo ID before gaining admittance to the ship. Expect that all bags you carry on will be inspected at the security checkpoint. During high season, arrive at the checkpoint 15 minutes early, to allow ample time to get through the inspection.

150 people are chosen by drawing to sail on the USS *Constitution* for a yearly Fourth of July turnaround cruise. Enter at constitution.events@navy.mil. (Winners must be between the ages of 8 and 70, and be able to climb up and down ladders without assistance; they may bring along one guest.)

254 Walden Pond

CONTACT 978-369-3254, www.massgov.dcr; 915 Walden St., Concord

PRICING	$
BEST TIME TO VISIT	Summer
AGE RANGE	All ages

Henry David Thoreau (1817–62) was a poet and philosopher identified with the American transcendentalist movement and a disciple of Ralph Waldo Emerson, another immensely influential intellectual and writer in early America. Thoreau is perhaps best known for his two-year "experiment": In 1845 he bowed out of society and went to live on Walden Pond (on property owned by his friend and mentor Emerson), where he meant to "live deep and suck all the marrow of life." His experiences while living on the pond resulted in his most famous publication, *Walden*, which chronicles his interactions with nature and his personal growth during this period. Visitors today can visit the Walden Pond State Reservation; the pond is open to kayaks and swimming in the warmer months, and remains a lovely, contemplative site. Fans of Thoreau will not want to miss the re-creation of his *tiny* cabin just off the shores.

Walden Pond   © Debbie K. Hardin

MICHIGAN

255 Colonial Michilimackinac

Colonial Michilimackinac   Courtesy Mackinac State Historic Parks

CONTACT 231-436-4100, www.mackinacparks.com; 102 W. Straits Ave., Mackinaw City

PRICING	$$–$$$
BEST TIME TO VISIT	Open early May through early October
AGE RANGE	3 and older

The Great Lakes region was a popular Indian hunting and trading site for decades before the arrival of French colonists, who first came seasonally in search of pelts and later set up permanent encampments along the waterfront. By the early 18th century, the fur trade in the area was an important economic venture and a bellwether for colonial–Native relations in America. French hunters came to make their fortunes on the animal furs—and in short order began trading with the Native Americans to increase their stock, sometimes exchanging baubles and alcohol for valuable pelts. Despite an often inequitable economic arrangement, the two cultures coexisted in the region near what is now Mackinaw City for decades, with periodic military interference from British troops who were ever on the lookout to expand the territory of Britain.

Colonial Michilimackinac, in the Lower Peninsula, is an outdoor living history museum that interprets the 1770s era of a fort and fur-trading community. The reconstruction is based on historical maps and more than 50 years of archaeological excavations. There are more than a dozen reconstructed buildings furnished with period pieces to explore, and lots of opportunities for children to get hands-on ex-

perience of what life must have been like at the 18th-century outpost: They can participate in drills with the King's Army; play *baggatiway*, a traditional Native American game that was a precursor of lacrosse; witness cannon- and musket-firing demonstrations; learn to make Native American crafts; help reenactors do chores like washing laundry, preserving foods, or working in their gardens; or help prepare a colonial meal on an open hearth using historic recipes. Also on site is a re-creation of a Native American summer encampment where Ojibwa and Odawa peoples came annually to fish, trade, and smoke fish.

In the summertime, don't miss the reenactment of a French wedding that took place in St. Anne's Church in 1775; after the ceremony, you'll be invited to dance at the reception. The attraction offers special Children's Tours in which a historic reenactor will guide families through Colonial Michilimackinac with an eye to explaining how kids lived at the fort in the 18th century. On this tour, kids and parents alike will pitch in with typical children's chores like hauling water from the lake, pulling carrots from the garden, and piling wood for the hearth. Afterward children will learn old-fashioned games like hoop-and-stick and cup-and-ball. The *Treasures from the Sand* collection on site exhibits thousands of artifacts excavated here—the ongoing excavation is one of the oldest continuous digs in the United States, beginning in 1959. Look for rosary beads, tools, coins, buttons, and cooking utensils. And if the urge to blow off steam is irresistible after a few hours of history lessons, check out the Kids' Rendezvous Interpretive Playground, which includes an oversized map of the Great Lakes, climbing structures, and a mini fort palisade.

The Mackinac Triple Choice ticket offers significant discounts for those who want to explore all that the region has to offer. The seven-day combination ticket offers admission to any three of five sites: Colonial Michilimackinac, Fort Mackinac (below), Historic Hill Creek Discovery Park, Old Mackinac Point Lighthouse, and The Richard and Jane Mannogian Mackinac Art Museum.

256 Fort Mackinac

Note that Mackinac Island—a popular summer resort since the 19th century—does not allow cars; the only options for getting around are to walk, bike, or take a horse-drawn carriage. To reach the island, guests can fly in on small private jets, boat in, or take a ferry service from either St. Ignace or Mackinaw City.

CONTACT 906- 847-3328, www.mackinacparks.com; 7127 Huron Rd., Mackinac Island

PRICING	$$–$$$
BEST TIME TO VISIT	Open early May through early October
AGE RANGE	3 and older

Mackinac Island (pronounced *mack-i-naw*) is just off the northern tip of the lower peninsula of Michigan, at the juncture of Lake Michigan and Lake Huron, in what was once prime trapping and trading territory. French colonists built the first fort on the Straits of Mackinac in the late 17th century, and followed up with new and larger forts for several decades afterward, both to shore up their military defenses and to serve as trading posts for the burgeoning fur business. In 1715 the French built Fort Michilimackinac (see the description above) in what is now Mackinaw City, on the mainland. The fort served as a depot in the fur trade and as a military post, first under French rule and then, in 1761, under British rule after the French relinquished the fort and the surrounding territory following the French and Indian War. But during the American Revolution, the British worried that the original fort on the mainland would be vulnerable and relocated to Mackinac Island starting in 1779. Americans won the Revolutionary War and took control of the fort in 1796. The fort soon played an important role in the next American–British conflict: The first land engagement in America in the War of 1812 took

place at the site, when the British gained control of the fort and held it until after the war. It remained an active fort until the late 19th century.

Today the Officers Stone Quarters, the south sally port, and the stone ramparts are all that remain of the original structure; the rest of the buildings date from the late 1790s to just before the turn of the 20th century, but have been restored to their historical origins. Visitors today can tour the grounds and see interiors like the soldiers' barracks, the officers' quarters, the commissary, the bathhouse, the schoolhouse, and a guardhouse. Families can participate in several interactive historical reenactments, such as cannon firings and military drills. Children will especially enjoy the Kids' Quarters, with a fun interactive video that lets kids see themselves on screen as soldiers in a military drill and offers plenty of dress-up options; and the Post Hospital, which features a large children's area with an oversized stethoscope and microscope for them to experiment with—to say nothing of the hologram of a doctor attending to 19th-century patients in a re-created hospital room. Seasonal programs include a special children's tour of the fort led by a costumed interpreter that ends with Victorian games; and a music and dance program in which guests learn the steps to a historic dance and then perform it to live music.

Fort Mackinac and harbor
Courtesy Mackinac Island Convention and Visitors Bureau

257 Gerald Ford Museum

CONTACT 616-254-0400, www.fordlibrarymuseum.gov; 303 Pearl St. NW, Grand Rapids

PRICING	$–$$
BEST TIME TO VISIT	Year-round
AGE RANGE	7 and older

PRICE KEY
$ free–$5
$$ $6–10
$$$ $11–20
$$$$ $21+

Gerald Ford Museum Courtesy The Gerald R. Ford Presidential Library and Museum

Gerald R. Ford (1913–2006) assumed the presidency in a tumultuous and discontented period of the 20th century, stepping in after fellow Republican Richard Nixon resigned the office in disgrace. Ford first came to the White House as vice president, when Nixon appointed him to replace Vice President Spiro Agnew after Agnew resigned in 1973 as part of a plea bargain in a tax evasion charge. Less than a year later, Nixon himself resigned as a result of the Watergate debacle, a scandal involving an illegal break-in at Democratic National Headquarters during Nixon's reelection campaign and the subsequent cover-up that took down many prominent politicians. Ford was sworn in as chief executive to replace Nixon, and thus became the first person ever to serve as president of the United States who was never elected to either the presidency or the vice presidency. Before his ascension to the office of the vice president, Ford had served in the U.S. House of Representatives for more than 20 years. As his first act as president Ford pardoned former president Nixon. He was defeated in his bid for a second term in 1976 by Jimmy Carter.

The Gerald R. Ford Museum is part of the larger Gerald R. Ford Presidential Library (734-205-0555; 1000 Beal Ave., Ann Arbor), which is housed at the University of Michigan, Ann Arbor. The library is home to thousands of documents and audiovisual materials pertaining to Ford's career as the 38th president. Unlike others in the presidential library system, the museum is at a separate site in Grand Rapids, in Ford's hometown. The Grand Rapids site offers interactive exhibits on Ford's early life, his

Prepping Kids for a Trip

Have your kids do their homework before any trip, to make the most out of educational possibilities—just don't tell them that it's homework! A few weeks in advance of any adventure, head to the library to find books on the site (or the person or event the site commemorates). Send away for travel brochures from local visitor bureaus (these are always free and usually beautifully illustrated). Rent and watch documentaries that highlight the attraction or tell the history of the site. Look up online field guides and print out a list of species to look for. Spend family time talking about the things you plan to see and do—and make an itinerary that includes everyone's preferences. Encourage school-aged kids to write down five questions that they will investigate once you arrive. Then once you're at your destination, look for more information: National parks have wonderful newspapers and printed brochures, for example, that will teach kids about the flora and fauna they are likely to encounter, the history of the park, and its natural features. The more you can expose children to the story behind the adventures they're about to experience, the more meaningful the experience will be—and the more likely they will learn something that sticks.

Research literature on the road   © Debbie K. Hardin

naval career, his work in Congress, and his presidential tenure. Included is a Watergate gallery that offers a six-minute film illuminating the 1972 break-in; the tools used during the burglary are on display. Children will enjoy seeing the faithful re-creation of the Oval Office as it was during Ford's era, as well as a re-creation of the Cabinet Room. Don't miss the 1970s Gallery, a collection of multimedia pop-culture artifacts of the time that includes music and distinctive fashions like tie-dyed shirts and bell-bottoms.

258 The Henry Ford

Model T Village, The Henry Ford

Photo by Michelle Andonian, Michelle Andonian Photography, courtesy of The Henry Ford

CONTACT 313-982-6001, www.hfmgv.org; 20900 Oakwood Blvd., Dearborn

PRICING	$$$
BEST TIME TO VISIT	Year-round
AGE RANGE	5 and older

The Henry Ford, named after the automotive industrialist who helped inspire the original museum collection, is an enormous complex that comprises The Benson Ford Research Center, Greenfield Village, The Ford Rouge Factory Tour, the Henry Ford Museum, and the Henry Ford IMAX Theater. The sprawling attraction is the repository for 26 million artifacts that celebrate the innovation and spirit of invention in America. It could take several days to see the full extent of the exhibits here—and you might be surprised to find more than just cars to see. There *are* vintage automobiles—lots of them—on display in a cavernous warehouse space, as well as trains (full-scale and model), planes, bicycles, helicopters, and just about every other kind of conveyance you can imagine. But the museum complex is more than a tribute to the auto industry: It is an American history museum that chronicles the Industrial Age and the political and popular culture of the 20th century. Look for the chair Abraham Lincoln was sitting in at Ford's Theatre when he was assassinated; engineer Buckminster Fuller's Dymaxion House, a futuristic-looking home designed in the midcentury that would make modern-day green architects proud; John F. Kennedy's presidential limousine; an Oscar Mayer Wienermobile; the actual bus on which civil rights activist Rosa Parks refused to give up her seat; and an astonishing collection of 17th-century violins.

The Greenfield Village section of the complex holds almost 100 historical buildings that were moved to the site from their original locations and rearranged in a village setting that documents how Americans have lived and worked through the decades. Notable structures include the courthouse where Abraham Lincoln practiced law; Henry Ford's birthplace; Noah Webster's Connecticut home; Thomas Edison's Menlo Park laboratory; and the Wright brothers' bike shop from Dayton, Ohio. Visitors can also check out the Ford Rouge Factory Tour (board buses at the Henry Ford Museum, for transport to the working River Rouge Plant and the Dearborn Truck Plant). On select days, you can watch the assembly line in action.

The attraction is the repository for artifacts that celebrate the spirit of invention in America.

259 Model T Automotive Heritage Complex

CONTACT 313-872-8759, www.tplex.org; 461 Piquette Ave., Detroit

PRICING	$$
BEST TIME TO VISIT	Open April through October; closed Monday and Tuesday
AGE RANGE	5 and older

Detroit is often referred to as the "Motor City," thanks to its dominance of the automotive industry for decades. In the early 20th century, businessmen like Henry Ford capitalized on the industrial prowess that already existed in the city and began producing assembly-line cars. The Ford Piquette Plant is the site where Ford designed and built the first 12,000 Model T's, as well as other early Ford models, from 1904 to 1910. The plant was sold in 1910 to the Studebaker company, which manufactured its automobiles here until 1933. Today this is the only early Detroit automobile factory open to tours. The site is maintained as the Model T Automotive Heritage Complex, and you can tour the factory floor and see a fun collection of "Tin Lizzies" and other early-20th-century Fords on display. Interpretive panels throughout illuminate the history of the Ford plant and the workers who built America's very first cars.

There are historic sites commemorating Detroit's considerable role in automobile manufacturing throughout the city (see The Henry Ford and the Walter P. Chrysler Museum, for instance, both described below). For a highbrow look at the influence of the car industry, check out world-renowned artist Diego Rivera's frescoes at the Detroit Institute of Arts (5200 Woodward), commissioned by Edsel Ford in 1933. The panoramic works focus on scenes Rivera reproduced based on his experiences visiting a later Ford plant.

260 Motown Historical Museum

CONTACT 313-875-2264, http://www.motown museum.org; 2648 W. Grand Blvd., Detroit

PRICING	$$
BEST TIME TO VISIT	Year-round; closed Sunday in the summer and Sunday and Monday throughout the rest of the year
AGE RANGE	10 and older

The Motown sound of rhythm and blues is synonymous with Detroit, and the genre remains a uniquely American art form. The Motown Record Corporation in its heyday in the 1960s had 450 employees and more women vice presidents than any other company in America. The distinctive music had a profound impact on American culture and the American civil rights movement, and included world-famous performers like Diana Ross and the Supremes, Smokey Robinson and the Miracles, the Temptations, Marvin Gaye, Stevie Wonder, and the Jackson 5. Today you can tour the original offices and studios of "Hitstown U.S.A." at the Motown Historical Museum, which includes owner Berry Gordy's upstairs apartment, decorated in the groovy style in which it appeared in the 1960s, plus instruments and costumes worn by Motown artists. The original recording equipment is on display as well, and exhibits tell the story of the music industry when Detroit was at its epicenter.

261 Walter P. Chrysler Museum

CONTACT 248-944-0001, http://wpchryslermuseum.org; 1 Chrysler Dr., Auburn Hills

PRICING	$–$$
BEST TIME TO VISIT	Year-round, closed Monday
AGE RANGE	5 and older

Walter Chrysler was an automotive industrialist of the early 20th century and founder of the Chrysler Corporation. The museum that bears his name showcases three floors with more than 65 antique, concept, and custom vehicles, as well as interactive exhibits that chronicle Chrysler's contributions to automotive innovation. Step into the two-story atrium and you'll immediately be drawn to a rotating tower that displays a changing exhibit of spectacular concept cars. The first floor houses antique vehicles that date to the early 1900s and include pristine DeSotos, Plymouths, and Ramblers. The second floor is dedicated to vehicles produced in the latter half of the 20th century. The attraction offers several short films on Walter Chrysler and his company.

Walter P. Chrysler

Courtesy Library of Congress

minnesota

262 Charles Lindbergh Boyhood House

CONTACT 320-616-5421, www.mnhs.org/places/sites/lh/index.html; 1620 Lindbergh Drive S., Little Falls

PRICING	$$
BEST TIME TO VISIT	Open Memorial Day through Labor Day, Thursday through Sunday
AGE RANGE	7 and older

Charles Lindbergh (1902–74) was an internationally recognized American aviator who made the first successful solo nonstop transatlantic flight. In 1927, aboard a small plane named *The Spirit of St. Louis*, Lindberg left New York City in the morning and landed in Paris the next evening, flying for more than 33 hours straight across 3,600 miles. Lindbergh spent his life working in aviation, but he was a groundbreaking inventor and engineer as well. He is remembered, too, for a tragic personal event: His infant son was kidnapped five years after Lindbergh's historic flight; the toddler was found dead several months later. The case was so sensationalized in the press that Lindbergh and his family were eventually driven to leave the United States and live in Europe for many years.

Although Lindbergh was born in Detroit, he spent most of his childhood in Little Falls. Today you can tour his boyhood home, which is meticulously furnished with original family items that include his snowshoes,

Lindbergh's plane, Spirit of St. Louis, *National Air and Space Museum*
© Debbie K. Hardin

a family piano, china, an interesting collection of travel souvenirs, a collection of campaign buttons, and hundreds of family photos. The on-site visitor center includes a full-scale re-creation of the *Spirit of St. Louis* cockpit, which kids can climb into, as well as the 1959 VW Bug that Lindbergh drove across four continents (including Africa). "Lucky Lindy"—a nickname that historians note was quite inappropriate, given his personal tragedies and his relatively taciturn nature—was at times a controversial figure, holding unpopular views about American involvement in World War II, for example, and environmental and conservationist ideals that were ahead of his time. This museum explores the whole person, "warts and all," and offers insight into an American hero whose image was largely out of sync with who he really was.

263 Fort Snelling

CONTACT 612-726-1171, www.historicfortsnelling.org; 200 Tower Ave., St. Paul

PRICING	$$–$$$
BEST TIME TO VISIT	Open May through Labor Day; closed most Mondays
AGE RANGE	7 and older

Fort Snelling was the farthest outpost of the U.S. government in the 1820s and the first fort in Minnesota; the compound overlooks the Minnesota and Mississippi Rivers, and at one time was in the deepest reaches of the midwestern frontier. In the mid-19th century, Dred Scott and his wife, Harriet, lived at the fort. Scott and his wife were slaves belonging to the fort's doctor; Scott is remembered for his role in the landmark *Dred Scott v. Sanford* case, in which he unsuccessfully sued for his freedom and that of his family. Scott based his case on the fact that he and Harriet were being held as slaves in Minnesota (then part of what was the Wisconsin Territory), where slavery was illegal. The U.S. Supreme Court, however, ruled that because Scott was a slave he didn't enjoy the rights of an American citizen and thus could not bring a suit in federal court.

Minnesota Boundary Waters Canoe Area © YinYang/iStockphoto.com

PRICE KEY
$ free–$5
$$ $6–10
$$$ $11–20
$$$$ $21+

Reenactment at Fort Snelling   Courtesy Visit St. Paul

Today you can tour the well-preserved fort, including Dred Scott's quarters, barracks for enlisted men and officers, and weapons storage facilities. Children will enjoy visiting the schoolhouse building, which was used both as a school for the children of soldiers and as a chapel. Costumed reenactors often pose as teachers to offer 19th-century lessons. It's also fun to tour the Sutler Store, a post office and commissary combined where you can see period merchandise on display as it might have been in the early days of the fort. The facility offers special programs throughout the season, such as the Independence Day Celebration, which includes reenactments, fife-and-drum corps, and military parades; Civil War Weekends, which include living history demonstrations and family-interactive opportunities; and "Cradle to Grave" programs that explore 19th-century life at the fort, including how babies and young children were cared for, how families lived on a daily basis, and how deaths were handled on the frontier.

264 Grand Portage National Monument

CONTACT 218-475-0123, www.nps.gov/grpo; 170 Mile Creek Rd., Grand Portage

PRICING	$
BEST TIME TO VISIT	Summer (historic structures open mid-May through mid-October)
AGE RANGE	7 and older

Grant Portage National Monument along the shores of Lake Superior in northeastern Minnesota preserves the legacy of the fur trade in the region and the Native American heritage of the Ojibwe people. As early as 2,000 years ago, Native Indians used a pathway they called "the Great Carrying Place" to migrate annually from their summer homes on the Great Lakes to winter hunting grounds in Canada. Thanks to the abundance of fur-bearing animals in the region—and the growing demand for fur pelts in Europe during the 18th century—the region continued to be a vital link in the fur trade industry for hundreds of years. In the late 18th and very early 19th centuries, the Scottish North West Company was the most successful fur-trading operation in the Great Lakes area and maintained its headquarters at this site. Native Americans and Europeans traveled to the headquarters to sell pelts (mostly beaver furs). To reach the site, voyageurs (rugged individuals who were employed to transport pelts) carried heavy packs over the 8.5-mile trail they renamed the Grand Portage. The footpath bypasses a spectacular series of rapids and waterfalls on the Pigeon River that made the usual transportation by traditional birch-bark canoe impossible.

The monument comprises more than 700 spectacularly beautiful acres that include the historic depot on Lake Superior, the site of Fort Charlotte, a canoe warehouse, and the Grand Portage trail. Start your visit at the Heritage Center, which displays archaeological artifacts and screens several excellent orientation films on the fur trade, canoe building, and Native peoples. Next check out the reconstructed fur-trade depot, historic heirloom gardens, and an exhibit displaying a typical Ojibwe village. Throughout the summer season there are craft demonstrations and historical reenactments, including lessons on working with birch bark, fur-treating demonstrations, and open-fire cooking classes. The park offers several excellent ranger programs (each lasting about an hour), which can include walking tours, historic weapons

Visit nearby Grand Portage State Park (9393 Hwy. 61 E.) to see Minnesota's tallest waterfall, known as High Falls, which tops out at about 120 feet.

Encampment at Grand Portage National Monument
Courtesy National Park Service

Nearby, off U.S. 169, is the Mille Lacs Indian Museum (43411 Oodena Dr., Onamia), which offers educational exhibits on the Mille Lacs area from the late 17th century onward.

firing demonstrations, bagpipe demonstrations (recall the Scottish connection), and lectures on Native American life. The highlight of the park is a hike along the Grand Portage, a relatively flat footpath that runs from Lake Superior to Fort Charlotte and back, past waterfalls and along the river. In the spring the wildflower show here can be stunning. The full route is 17 miles round-trip—so plan on a full day of hiking if you want to see it all. However, it is easy to break the trail into a shorter segment for a quicker hike as well.

265 Mille Lacs Kathio State Park

CONTACT 320-532-3523,
www.dnr.state.mn.us/state_parks/mille_lacs_kathio/
index.html; 15066 Kathio State Park Rd., Onamia

PRICING	$
BEST TIME TO VISIT	Summer
AGE RANGE	7 and older

Mille Lacs Kathio State Park preserves 19 separate archaeological sites believed to date from approximately 3000 BC to AD 1750. Native peoples lived here continuously for 9,000 years, from one of the earliest cultures identified that made copper tools to the bands of Sioux who lived in the region until moving to the southern prairies in the 18th century. Loggers

came to the site in the mid-19th century, taking advantage of Mille Lacs Lake to float large numbers of trees to sawmills where they could be processed. Westward-expanding pioneers soon followed.

Today visitors can learn about the many people and cultures that called the area home by participating in ranger programs at the interpretive center, as well as from exhibits of artifacts uncovered at the several archaeological sites in the park. On display are arrowheads, finely crafted clay pots, beads, and historical photographs and documents. Every year, on the last Saturday in September, the Minnesota Archaeological Society hosts an archaeology day at Petaga Point, an active archaeological dig in the park. The event includes hands-on family activities such as pottery-making demonstrations, spear throwing, and children's crafts. The region offers incredible natural beauty as well, with a pretty swimming beach on the lake, hiking trails, and good bird-watching: Look for ospreys, loons, and bald eagles.

266 Sinclair Lewis Boyhood Home

CONTACT 320-352-5201; 810 Sinclair Lewis Ave., Sauk Centre

PRICING	$
BEST TIME TO VISIT	Open for tours June through August; closed Monday
AGE RANGE	10 and older

Sinclair Lewis (1885–1951) was one of the best-known writers in the United States in the early 20th century, and the first American ever to win the Nobel Prize for Literature (in 1930). He is best remembered for well-received books like *Babbitt* and *Elmer*

Sinclair Lewis Boyhood Home   Courtesy Sinclair Lewis Foundation

Ice sculpture at St. Paul Winter Carnival   Courtesy Visit St. Paul

Gantry. He was born in Sauk Centre and spent his childhood in the small town that would become inspiration for his novel *Main Street*, many characters in which were quite obviously based on real-life figures in the town. Visit his boyhood home (which stands across the street from the home in which he was born) to see the house where he spent his early years. The home has been restored with period antiques and artifacts, some of which belonged to the Lewis family—including Lewis's boyhood bed and a radio the writer purchased as a gift for his father, the town's doctor. Children will enjoy this visit (and a tour of Sauk Centre) ever so much more if they have first read Lewis's books: They are likely to recognize parts of the home from descriptions in *Main Street*.

267 St. Paul Winter Carnival

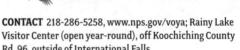

CONTACT 651-223-4700, www.winter-carnival.com; citywide throughout St. Paul

PRICING	Fees vary by event
BEST TIME TO VISIT	Held late January through early February
AGE RANGE	All ages

Although many people try to get out of the bitter cold of winter, hearty Minnesotans embrace it during the St. Paul Winter Carnival. Billing itself as the oldest and largest winter festival in the United States, the carnival celebrates Minnesota's northern climate with plenty of all-American and family-friendly attractions

that center on ice and snow. Legend has it that in the late 19th century, a smug newspaperman described the city as akin to "Siberia," and to prove him wrong the locals have been putting on a two-week festival every year that includes an elaborate royal court, ice hockey, marathons, fireworks, and intricate and ethereal ice sculptures. There's also a stunning Torchlight Parade downtown, snow-sculpting exhibits, dogsled races, and plenty of food and spirits. If you're in town for the long haul, don't miss the annual Medallion Treasure Hunt. The local newspaper prints a clue a day for 12 days running, all pointing to the location of a hidden special medallion; the lucky one to claim the medallion wins $10,000 and a chance to ride in the closing parade.

268 Voyageurs National Park

CONTACT 218-286-5258, www.nps.gov/voya; Rainy Lake Visitor Center (open year-round), off Koochiching County Rd. 96, outside of International Falls

PRICING	$
BEST TIME TO VISIT	Summer
AGE RANGE	7 and older

This unique watery ecosystem comprises four major lakes, 26 interior lakes, and more than 650 miles of coastline. The mosaic of water and land includes more than 500 islands, and spans the U.S.–Canada border. The park was named after the voyageurs, the French Canadian fur traders and trappers who were the first European settlers in the region. But Native peoples inhabited the area long before the European lust for beaver pelts brought the fur industry to this northern outpost. Archaeologists believe that people were living in the region thousands of years before, just after the last of the glaciers melted from the previous ice age. The Assiniboine, Cree, and Monsoni tribes fished and hunted here during summer migrations at the time when the first European—believed to be French explorer Jacques de Noyon—arrived in the late 17th century. A generation later these tribes had left the area to the Ojibwe, who became the primary inhabitants of the border lakes region.

The Ojibwe were instrumental to the European fur trade, helping the early voyageurs as guides and trading pelts and other goods that ensured the Europeans' economic success. Voyageurs were rugged in-

Rainy Lake ice road, Voyageurs National Park
Courtesy National Park Service

Campsites at Voyageurs National Park are free, and available on a first-come, first-served basis (although a free permit is required; 218-875-2111). Note that there are no drive-in campsites; all individual sites are accessible by boat only.

dividuals who paddled birch-bark canoes along the extensive waterways in the area, carrying heavy loads of furs and living off the land. The extensive woodlands eventually brought loggers as well, and soon miners and commercial fishermen came to the region. Today the expanse of unusual wilderness is a prime spot for recreation, and visitors to the national park will find excellent opportunities to canoe, kayak, and fish. Indeed, most of the park is accessible only by boat, making a visit peaceful, serene, and generally uncrowded. In warm months, the park offers rental boats, kayaks, and canoes; and there are concessionaires that rent houseboats by the week. In the summer the park provides a free shuttle service to interior lakes, and there are ranger-led boat tours as well.

MISSISSIPPI

269 Beauvoir

CONTACT 228-388-4400, www.beauvoir.org; 2244 Beach Blvd., Biloxi

PRICING	$–$$
BEST TIME TO VISIT	Year-round
AGE RANGE	7 and older

Jefferson Davis home   © Christina Carter. Used with permission.

Jefferson Davis (1808–89) was a U.S. senator from Mississippi, the secretary of war serving under President Franklin Pierce, and the only president of the Confederate States of America during the Civil War. Some historians attribute the Union victory in part to mismanagement of the Confederacy by Davis, especially his apparent inattention to economic concerns. After Union troops captured him in Irwinville, Georgia, at the end of the war, Davis was tried for treason and imprisoned in Fort Monroe. He was paroled several years later, in 1867, and returned to Mississippi to live out the rest of his days writing his memoirs. Many viewed him as a disgraced figure, but he has come to be seen as a hero to some who admire his dedication to the South. Although initially he stubbornly resisted the Reconstruction, by the late 1880s he urged his fellow southerners to pledge their loyalty to the United States.

Beauvoir (which fittingly translates to "lovely view") is a small yet elegant raised cottage-style plantation home on the waterfront, with stellar views of the Mississippi Sound and the Gulf of Mexico. When Davis came to Biloxi in search of a place where he could retire in peace, his friend Sarah Dorsey, who owned Beauvoir, invited him to stay in a cottage on the grounds. Davis eventually planned to buy the home, but Mrs. Dorsey passed away before he could do so and left the property to him and Davis's daughter in her will. The main house, and an adjacent library (which at one time held more than 12,000 volumes), were both all but destroyed in Hurricane Katrina in 2005. The library is being rebuilt at a new site, and the home has been painstakingly restored to its former glory and is once again open for public tours. The interiors are a peek into true southern gen-tility: the beautiful decorated ceilings and plaster-work, along with polished wood furniture and smatterings of fine silver and china, all paint a picture of a charming, gracious lifestyle. Many of Davis's original belongings are on display, including a piano that was nearly destroyed by Katrina: It was carried out of the house by the floods and later found at the top of an oak tree. The grounds are also beautiful, and on a hot summer day a restful place to sit and enjoy the coastal breezes and water views. Events are held on the site throughout the year, including a Confederate Memorial Day in April, a Fall Muster in October, and a Candlelight Christmas in December.

270 Brices Cross Roads National Battlefield

CONTACT 800-305-7417, www.nps.gov/brcr; off Rt. 370, 6 miles west of Baldwyn

PRICING	$
BEST TIME TO VISIT	Summer; the Visitor and Interpretive Center is closed Sunday and Monday
AGE RANGE	7 and older

It has often been said that an army travels on its stomach—because without food and other vital sup-

State Capitol in Jackson Courtesy U.S. Fish and Wildlife Services

PRICE KEY
$ free–$5
$$ $6–10
$$$ $11–20
$$$$ $21+

Brices Cross Roads National Battlefield

Courtesy National Park Service

routes explain where the fighting took place. Also worth a visit is the Bethany ARP Church Cemetery, the burial site for the Confederate soldiers who perished in the battle.

271 Eudora Welty House and Gardens

CONTACT 601-353-7762, www.eudorawelty.org; 1119 Pinehurst St. in Jackson

PRICING	$
BEST TIME TO VISIT	Spring
AGE RANGE	10 and older

plies (weapons, ammunition, first aid), military success is impossible. This idea was tested during the Battle of Brices Cross Roads during the Civil War. Major General Nathan Bedford Forrest commanded the Confederate army during an 1864 battle that was largely meant to destroy the Union supply lines between Nashville and Chattanooga. The much smaller Confederate force defeated General William Sherman's Union troops, ultimately disrupting Sherman's

> Without food and other vital supplies, military success is impossible.

railroad supply route that brought in food, guns, artillery, and wagons. The Union suffered great losses—for every Confederate man who fell, three Union soldiers were killed. Despite the decisive battle, of course, the Confederate victory did little to slow the Union forces, who went on to win the war.

Today the 1-acre site at Brices Cross Roads National Battlefield preserves a small portion of the battlefield and includes a memorial to the men who were killed and wounded. It is worth noting that half of the more than 200 Union troops who were killed during the battle were part of the U.S. Colored Troops forces. There are two interpretive trails on site that will allow you to look over the battlefield; signs posted along the

Eudora Welty (1909–2001) was a beloved American author whose novels and short stories were largely set in the South. Her style is often described as Southern Gothic, which is identified both by its setting in the American South and by its exploration of tragic, sometimes macabre, events that are intertwined with the cultural issues of the day. Welty won the Pulitzer Prize for *The Optimist's Daughter* in 1973; won the National Book Award for the paperback version of *The Collected Works of Eudora Welty*; and was awarded both the Presidential Medal of Freedom and the French Legion of Honor medal.

The Eudora Welty House and Gardens preserves the Tudor-style home where she lived for most of her life. Her father built the home when she was a teenager, and Welty remained a resident until she died. You can tour the home to see period furnishings and many belongings from the Welty family, including Welty's writing desk in her upstairs bedroom, complete with an old typewriter; a telescope her father purchased in the sitting room; and the family's large collection of novels in the boys' bedroom (once belonging to Welty's brothers). Don't miss a tour of the gardens, which have been restored to be historically correct for the period of 1925–45. If possible, visit the home in April to see a stunning display of camellias, dogwoods, cornflowers, and sweet alyssum in bloom.

272 Natchez Trace Parkway

CONTACT 800-305-7417, www.nps.gov/natr; milepost zero of the Old Trace is off Liberty Rd., Natchez

PRICING	$
BEST TIME TO VISIT	Spring and summer
AGE RANGE	All ages

The Natchez Trace Parkway is a roadway that follows the path of the 444-mile Old Natchez Trace trail running from Natchez, Mississippi, to Nashville, Tennessee. The ancient pathway was first used by Native Americans, who followed the existing bison and deer pathways during hunting forays. The best-known travelers along the Old Natchez Trace were boatmen from Kentucky, Ohio, and Pennsylvania who floated crops, coal, livestock, and other products down the Ohio and Mississippi Rivers to ports like Natchez and New Orleans. These sturdy individuals (called Kaintucks) dismantled their boats and sold the timber once the goods were delivered, and then walked back home via the Natchez Trace. The trip took about 30 days by foot or 20 days on horseback; it is believed that more than 10,000 Kaintucks took the Old Trace route in 1810.

Today the parkway follows the route through beautiful scenery and past dozens of historical sites.

Natchez Trace Parkway   Courtesy National Park Service

From Natchez to Jackson, the pathway passes prehistoric mound sites; from Jackson to Tupelo, there are numerous archeological sites that explore ancient civilizations in the region. Also on the Trace are the Tupelo National Battlefield and Brices Cross Roads National Battlefield (both near Tupelo, Mississippi).

273 Rowan Oak

CONTACT 662/234-3284, www.rowanoak.com; Old Taylor Rd., Oxford

PRICING	$
BEST TIME TO VISIT	Year-round; closed Monday
AGE RANGE	10 and older

William Faulkner (1897–1962) was an American Nobel Prize–winning writer of novels, short stories, and screenplays. He is considered one of the greatest U.S. writers of the 20th century, and is arguably the first to explore the modern South, often delving into the dark side of humanity. His literature is set almost exclusively in a fictional county of Mississippi modeled on his hometown of Oxford, where he grew up. Faulkner was awarded two Pulitzer Prizes for fiction—for *A Fable* and *The Reivers*—but he is probably better known for the novels *As I Lay Dying* and *The Sound and the Fury*, both of which are still widely studied today.

Rowan Oak was home to Faulkner and his family for more than 40 years. The Greek Revival structure was built in 1844 on 29 acres. The home is now a museum, owned and operated by the University of Mississippi, and is open for tours by appointment. For book lovers there are several treats in store. The rooms are arranged as they were in Faulkner's later years, and you can see personal items belonging to the famous author, like his spectacles, his pipe, and a beautiful old piano. Also on exhibit are the tools of his trade: a desk and his portable Underwood typewriter. Perhaps the most intriguing sight are the walls of Faulkner's study: He outlined the novel *A Fable* in pencil directly on the plaster, where it is still visible today.

274 Vicksburg National Military Park

CONTACT 601-636-9497, www.nps.gov/vick; 3201 Clay St. (also known as U.S. 80), Vicksburg

PRICING	$
BEST TIME TO VISIT	Summer
AGE RANGE	7 and older

Vicksburg was the site of one of the most important events of the American Civil War. From May 18 to July 4, 1863, the city was under siege. Union general Ulysses S. Grant and his troops attacked Confederate fortifications around the city and forced Confederate general John C. Pemberton and his troops to take up defensive positions. Initial assaults by the Union early in the battle were unsuccessful, and there were heavy casualties, so Grant decided to wait out the Confederates, whom Grant knew were running short on supplies. The Confederates held out for 47 days,

Vicksburg Visitor Center   Courtesy Library of Congress

but finally surrendered on Independence Day. Grant's victory in large part helped to secure the Mississippi River for Union forces, splitting the Confederacy and cutting off vital communications among the commanders of the southern forces. The Union troops were able to keep control of the important waterway throughout the rest of the Civil War—an action Abraham Lincoln himself described as key to a Union victory. The drawn-out action is often considered to be one of the turning points of the war. It's interesting to note that the residents were so distraught about the Confederate defeat that the city of Vicksburg refused to observe Fourth of July celebrations for almost a century afterward.

The Vicksburg National Military Park is a collection of sites that encircle the modern city along a 16-mile road. Along the route are 15 marked stops to commemorate and preserve the historic Siege of Vicksburg. Begin your trip at the visitor center, which offers exhibits and displays of Civil War artifacts that tell the story of the 47-day siege, as well as an informative 18-minute film that provides historical context. Outside the center you can check out a fortification exhibit and cannon display. Next visit the USS *Cairo* Museum and Gunboat, which includes exhibits highlighting the naval operations of the Civil War as well as an interesting collection of artifacts that once belonged to the sailors aboard the *Cairo*. Pemberton's Headquarters, in downtown Vicksburg, is the site of the Confederate commander's operations, and it's open for tours as well.

Throughout the summer (from the first week in June through the first week in August), the park presents several living history programs, including interpretive talks on the lives of everyday soldiers during the Civil War; artillery and rifle drills; and ranger programs that delve into what life must have been like for ordinary citizens during the siege.

MISSOURI

275 Gateway Arch

CONTACT 314-655-1600, www.stlouisarch.com/experience/the-gateway-arch; 200 Washington Ave., St. Louis

PRICING	$–$$ (for tram ride up)
BEST TIME TO VISIT	Spring and fall
AGE RANGE	All ages

The iconic Gateway Arch is part of the Jefferson National Expansion Memorial. The 630-foot Arch was built from 1963 through 1965; it weighs 17,246 tons and took more than 900 tons of stainless steel to construct. This is the tallest national monument in the United States, and was built to commemorate the leadership role of President Thomas Jefferson and of the city of St. Louis in the westward expansion of the country. Start your visit with the half-hour film *Monument to the Dream*, shown daily at the Tucker Theater

Gateway Arch

Courtesy National Park Service

As with all high-profile national monuments these days, expect to pass through a security checkpoint before visiting the Gateway Arch. Needless to say, no weapons are allowed—even small pocketknives. Allow at least 30 minutes before your scheduled tram ride to get through the bag check.

Visitor Center, which explains how the arch was constructed. Take a memorable tram ride to the top for a spectacular view of the Mississippi River and St. Louis.

276 The Griot Museum of Black History

CONTACT 314-241-7057, www.thegriotmuseum.com; 2505 St. Louis Ave., St. Louis

PRICING	$–$$
BEST TIME TO VISIT	Year-round; open Wednesday through Saturday
AGE RANGE	7 and older

The Griot Museum of Black History is a tiny museum dedicated to a big ideal: preserving the history and stories of African Americans through the centuries. It started life in 1997 as the Black World History Wax Museum, and it continues to feature life-sized wax sculptures of well-known African Americans. The new name is derived from the African term *griot* (pronounced *gree-oh*), the title of a respected community member who collects and preserves stories. The exhibits are in many ways strollable dioramas that tell the stories of legends like Josephine Baker, Dred Scott, Clark Terry, and Martin Luther King Jr. There's an exhibit on scientist George Washington Carver (who is often attributed with inventing peanut butter) that includes a reproduction of his laboratory; and a display on jazz musician Miles Davis that includes a re-creation of his club. Although the museum celebrates the legacy of African Americans in this country, a visit is a sobering reminder of the shameful practices of slavery and lingering racism. Two of the most striking displays include a slave cabin—an original structure built in Jonesburg, Missouri, disman-

The Griot Museum of Black History

Courtesy Missouri Division of Tourism

tled, and then rebuilt on site—and a replica of a portion of a slave ship, which shows the unbelievably inhumane conditions aboard. The museum also sponsors community education programs throughout the year, including gallery talks and cultural celebrations.

277 Harry Truman Library and Museum

CONTACT 816-268-8200, www.trumanlibrary.org; 500 W. Hwy. 24, Independence

PRICING	$–$$
BEST TIME TO VISIT	Year-round
AGE RANGE	7 and older

Harry S. Truman (1884–1972) stepped into the presidency after Franklin D. Roosevelt died in office; Truman had served only 82 days as vice president before assuming the mantle of commander in chief in the waning days of World War II. The war in Europe was all but over—German leader Adolf Hitler committed suicide only a few weeks into the Truman administration—but the war in the Pacific showed signs of continuing indefinitely. As part of a secret plan that had been in the works under the Roosevelt administration, the first nuclear device was tested in the summer of 1945, and President Truman ordered the new technology to be used against Japan. On August 6 the U.S. military dropped an atomic bomb on Hiroshima; and three days later dropped a second one on Nagasaki, instantly killing more than 100,000 people. Researchers believe at least twice that number died later from the radiation poisoning the bombs caused. The emperor of Japan, Hirohito, surrendered a few days later, thus ending the war. During his terms in office, Truman also oversaw the creation of the United Nations and the Marshall Plan and saw the start of the Korean War and the Cold War.

Truman was a native son of Missouri, and the Harry S. Truman Library and Museum in his hometown of Independence celebrates his historic contributions as a world leader and commemorates his early life in the state. The museum includes numerous exhibits on the political and military events of Truman's presidency, including displays on his difficult decision to drop atomic bombs on Japan, the recognition of Israel, and the increasingly tense relations with Indochina. Explore an exact replica of Truman's Oval Office, see love letters that Truman wrote to his wife, Bess (his childhood sweetheart), and view a display on American life in 1952. Throughout there are hands-on activities for children, including several audiovisual stations, a chance to write a letter and make a campaign button for Truman, and a fun and interactive station that lets kids race one another to

Harry Truman Library and Museum

Courtesy Missouri Division of Tourism

PRICE KEY
$ free–$5
$$ $6–10
$$$ $11–20
$$$$ $21+

see whether it was faster for Truman to drive or to take the train from his farm in Grandview to visit his then girlfriend Bess in Independence.

278 Mark Twain's Boyhood Home and Museum

CONTACT 573-221-9010, www.marktwainmuseum.org; 120 N. Main St., Hannibal

PRICING	$$
BEST TIME TO VISIT	Year-round
AGE RANGE	7 and older

The Mark Twain Boyhood Home and Museum preserves the early dwelling of beloved humorist and author Samuel Langhorne Clemens (1835–1910), who published under the pen name of Mark Twain. The attraction comprises nine sites that preserve the

Mark Twain's Boyhood Home and Museum
Courtesy Missouri Division of Tourism

Hannibal, Missouri, has a wealth of sites dedicated to the legacy of one of its favorite sons, Mark Twain (aka Samuel Clemens). Explore the Mark Twain Cave (573-221-1656; 300 Cave Hollow Rd.) to tour the site that Twain featured in several of his novels; ride the Mark Twain Riverboat (573-221-3222; 100 Center St.) for a sightseeing tour of Twain's boyhood city; or listen to the author in *Mark Twain Himself* (573-231-0021; 319 N. Main St.), in which an actor portrays the famous humorist in a one-man play that runs during the summer months. If you're willing to go farther afield, Hartford, Connecticut, preserves another of Twain's homes (described earlier in this book).

legacy of Twain's early life: He lived in the city along the Mississippi River from the ages of 4 to 17.

The fun of this museum is the chance to step inside the novels of Mark Twain and experience his youth, which was the inspiration for novels like *Tom Sawyer* and *The Adventures of Huckleberry Finn*. Start your visit at the interpretive center, which includes several hands-on exhibits that present a time line of Twain's childhood. Next move on to Mark Twain's Boyhood Home and Garden, to see the wood-siding-clad home where Twain spent his earlier days. Be sure to check out the adjoining picket fence, which Twain was sentenced to whitewash by his mother when he skipped school; this incident, of course, became a memorable scene in *Tom Sawyer*. Nearby is the Huckleberry Finn House, where Twain's boyhood friend Tom Blankenship grew up; Finn's character was modeled on Blankenship. Across the street is the Becky Thatcher House, home of the real-life Laura Hawkins on whom Twain based the character of Becky. You can also tour the J. M. Clemens Justice of the Peace Office, where Twain's father worked. Don't miss the Tom and Huck statue (at the end of Cardiff Hill). The Museum Gallery (at Main and Cedar) is another highlight: The first floor offers opportunities to walk through interactive exhibits on Twain's books, including a reconstructed pilothouse and a cave. Upstairs houses artifacts once belonging to Twain, including one of the many white suit coats he favored. The museum also includes 15 paintings by artist Norman Rockwell that illustrate Twain's beloved novels.

279 Museum of Westward Expansion

CONTACT www.nps.gov/jeff/planyourvisit/muse um-of-westward-expansion.htm; Gateway Arch, St., Louis

PRICING	$–$$
BEST TIME TO VISIT	Year-round
AGE RANGE	7 and older

The Jefferson National Expansion Memorial comprises the Gateway Arch (see above), the Old Courthouse where African American slave Dred Scott sued for his freedom, and the Museum of Westward Expansion. The museum highlights the expedition commissioned by President Thomas Jefferson to explore the western United States—Meriwether Lewis and William Clark's Corps of Discovery, which set out on its historic journey near this site. The museum is located beneath the iconic Gateway Arch, within the visitor center, and is accessed from a ramp at the base of either end of the archway. The exhibits are old school—expect to see a good number of taxidermied bison, bears, and other frontier animals, along with animatronic figures that tell the story of westward expansion and Native Americans who were encountered along the way—although there are plans to renovate and update the offerings in the near future. Within the subterranean site there are also some of

Old Courthouse, Museum of Westward Expansion
Photo by JNEM Media Services, courtesy of National Park Service

the rarest artifacts from the Lewis and Clark expedition. Look for an American Indian tepee made of hide and a life-sized wagon, along with displays that tell the stories of miners, buffalo hunters, and farmers during the era. The highlight is arguably a permanent exhibition of 33 photo murals, each 15 feet high, showing the campsites and other places visited by Lewis and Clark during their journey. The murals extend 500 feet on the back wall of the museum.

280 National World War I Museum at Liberty Memorial

CONTACT 816-888-8100, www.theworldwar.org; 100 W. 26th St., Kansas City

PRICING	$$–$$$
BEST TIME TO VISIT	Year-round; closed Monday fall through spring
AGE RANGE	10 and older

World War I (which was called simply the World War until the outbreak of the *Second* World War) was a conflict in the early 20th century (1914–18) that began in Europe and spread rapidly across the globe, ultimately involving 36 countries representing all of the world's most powerful nations, including the United States, which sent two million soldiers overseas to fight. The forces were divided into the Allies (predominantly the United States, Britain, France, and Russia) and the Central Powers (predominantly Austria-Hungary and Germany). The conflict lasted more than four years, and more than nine million people were killed.

The National World War I Museum at Liberty Memorial commemorates the individuals who lost their lives in the "Great War," and seeks to explain the causes of the conflict—and the reverberations of both the enormous loss of life and the war's political aftermath. Visitors enter the museum by crossing a dramatic depiction of a poppy field on the Western Front: There are 9,000 poppies, each representing a thousand deaths. Throughout are moving collections of myriad artifacts from the war, including diverse objects like a child's dress-up German soldier uniform,

National World War I Museum at Liberty Memorial
Courtesy Missouri Division of Tourism

281 Pony Express Museum

CONTACT 800-530-5930, www.ponyexpress.org;
914 Penn St., St. Joseph

PRICING	$
BEST TIME TO VISIT	Year-round
AGE RANGE	7 and older

The Pony Express was a much-romanticized mail line that transported communications from the Missouri River region across the nation to California and other western states during the mid-19th century. The organization was conceived when it became clear that the Civil War would create the need for faster, more reliable communication with the western territories than was possible before. Men riding horses undertook a kind of relay race across the 2,000-mile trail, passing off saddlebags full of mail at interchanges

personal letters written home by an American nurse, a full-sized tank complete with artillery damage; an enormous collection of guns, from rifles to Howitzers; propaganda posters; photographs; a wide collection of uniforms from forces around the world; and a 1918 Model T ambulance. An interactive exhibit depicts a series of six trenches that visitors can walk through to get a sense of the views combatants faced; along the way there are recorded statements from participants in various battles, and battle sounds are piped in, giving this a particularly eerie ambience.

There is a lot to see at the museum, and even more to absorb: World War I was a cataclysmic conflict, and it's difficult for adults to understand; it can be overwhelming for children. To make the experience more accessible for kids, get a free copy of the *Family Guide*, a 14-page booklet that will lead children through the collections via a scavenger hunt. The booklet is available at the museum store, which will supply an answer key as well.

> *World War I was a cataclysmic conflict, and it can be overwhelming to understand.*

Pony Express Museum
Courtesy Missouri Division of Tourism

Check out the nearby Patee House Museum (1202 Penn St.), which was the Pony Express headquarters from 1860 to 1861. The former luxury hotel now offers exhibits like an 1860 train car, a stagecoach, a blacksmith shop, a jail, and a vintage carousel.

Scott Joplin bust at the state capitol

Courtesy Missouri Division of Tourism

along the way. The first trip west took just under 10 full days. At its height, the Pony Express staffed nearly 200 stations; employed more than 80 riders at a time; and kept nearly 500 horses. The service was extremely reliable—only one bundle of mail was reported to have been lost. The Pony Express became obsolete when the Pacific Telegraph line was completed in 1861.

The Pony Express Museum is housed in Pikes Peak Stables, the first station from which westbound riders struck out on the route to Sacramento, California. The small museum features exhibits that commemorate the Old West institution, and include a harness and tack room display; a blacksmith and wheelwright shop; an extensive coin collection from the 1860s; and a 60-foot diorama that illustrates the hazards of riding the Pony Express. The original stable is well preserved and includes hundreds of original artifacts.

282 Scott Joplin House State Historic Site

CONTACT 314-340-5790, http://mostateparks.com/park/scott-joplin-house-state-historic-site; 2658 Delmar, St. Louis

PRICING	$
BEST TIME TO VISIT	Spring through fall; closed November through January, as well as all Sundays and some Mondays (depending on season)
AGE RANGE	7 and older

Scott Joplin (circa 1868–1917)—remembered as "The King of Ragtime"—was an American composer and pianist who pioneered the jaunty, bluesy style of music for which he is famous. Although Joplin died in his 40s, he wrote nearly 50 ragtime compositions and two operas. "Maple Leaf Rag," one of his first musical efforts, is considered one of the finest rags ever written. He is probably best known today for his composition called "The Entertainer," which was used as a theme song for the popular 1970s film *The Sting*.

Joplin was born in Texas and grew up in Texarkana, where he showed musical talent from a very early age. He began moving through the South as a traveling musician, landing in Missouri in 1894 to earn his living by teaching piano and by playing in saloons and brothels throughout the low-rent district of the city. Although he enjoyed a good bit of fame in his day, he had financial and health difficulties throughout his short life.

The Scott Joplin House preserves an upstairs apartment where he lived with his wife from 1901 through 1903; it is believed that this was his home when he wrote "The Entertainer." The gaslit rooms are furnished as they would have been in Joplin's time, with household items like a foot-powered sewing machine, a washboard, and an apple peeler. The most interesting artifact is the authentic player piano housed here, which families can play themselves: Pick a piano roll (many of which feature compositions by Joplin) and sit down in front of the ivories to enjoy. Adjacent to the apartment is the New Rosebud Cafe, a replica of a nearby bar where Joplin used to perform.

283 Ulysses S. Grant National Historic Site

CONTACT 314-842-1867, www.nps.gov/ulsg; 7400 Grant Road, St. Louis

PRICING	$
BEST TIME TO VISIT	Spring and fall
AGE RANGE	7 and older

Ulysses S. Grant (1822–85) was the 18th president of the United States, serving two distinguished terms in office. But his popularity (and the large number of memorials in his honor today) are in part thanks to his decisive role in the Union victory in the American Civil War. Abraham Lincoln appointed Grant general in chief of the Union forces in 1864, and Grant led his Army of the Potomac to defeat General Robert E.

Ulysses S. Grant National Historic Site
Courtesy Missouri Division of Tourism

Lee's Army of Northern Virginia. Lee ultimately surrendered to Grant at the Appomattox Court House (see the description under "Virginia"), ending the bloody conflict.

The Ulysses S. Grant National Historic Site—which was named White Haven during Grant's time—preserves the legacy of Grant, commemorating his personal life, military career, and role as president. The park includes 10 acres that house five historic buildings at the site of the childhood home of Grant's wife, Julia Dent Grant. Julia and Ulysses lived on the once-1,100-acre plantation from 1854 to 1859. Grant bought the property from his father-in-law, and kept it until shortly before his death. Visitors today can tour the main house (a two-story residence with inviting porches), a barn, and stone buildings that were likely quarters to Frederick Dent's slaves. A museum in the barn displays interesting artifacts that were owned by the Grants. The visitor center shows an introductory film on Grant's life. There is also an accessible walking path that rings the property and includes interpretive signs to help guests navigate a self-guided tour. Guests must acquire free timed tickets from the visitor center for a ranger-led tour of the home; these are held every half hour.

284 Wilson's Creek National Battlefield

CONTACT 417-732-2662, www.nps.gov/wicr; 6424 W. Farm Rd. 182, Republic

PRICING	$
BEST TIME TO VISIT	Summer
AGE RANGE	7 and older

On August 10, 1861, a battle raged on Wilson's Creek that determined the fate of Missouri during the Civil War: After five hours of bloody fighting, in which 2,500 soldiers were killed or wounded, the Confederates emerged victorious. The battle at Wilson's Creek was the first battle in the Civil War west of the Mississippi River and only the second major clash in the war.

The Wilson's Creek National Battlefield commemorates the battle and preserves historic sites

played a pivotal role in the war. Start with a 27-minute film on the battle that is shown at the visitor center. Then take a 5-mile self-guided road tour that will lead you to battle sites like the appropriately named Bloody Hill and the historic John Ray House, the latter of which served as a temporary field hospital for Confederate soldiers. (The Ray House is open for tours, led by costumed interpreters, on weekends from Memorial Day through Labor Day.) The park is the site of living history programs throughout the year, including cavalry drills, artillery demonstrations, and talks on surgery and first aid during the war. The Wilson's Creek Civil War Museum at the park contains interesting artifacts and exhibits that explain the significance of the battle.

When driving the 5-mile battle road, check out the Wilson's Creek National Battlefield Cell Phone Tour, which offers interesting stories about the people who fought and died in the battle. Use your phone to call 417-521-0055, and then at each stop along the roadway, push # and the corresponding stop number to hear facts about the site.

Reenactment at Wilson's Creek National Battlefield
Courtesy National Park Service

montana

285  Bannack State Park

CONTACT 406-834-3548, www.bannack.org; 4200 Bannack Rd., Dillon

PRICING	$
BEST TIME TO VISIT	Summer
AGE RANGE	3 and older

Bannack State Park Courtesy Montana Office of Tourism

Bannack State Park preserves one of the most intact ghost towns in the country. The town was the site of Montana's first major gold discovery: In 1862 John White found his first nugget in Grasshopper Creek. He soon realized that deposits were easy to uncover, and all that was needed were simple tools like gold pans and sluice boxes. White's discovery set off a gold rush that brought fortune seekers to the region in droves. At its heyday, in 1863, there were more than 3,000 residents living in what was a thriving town full of saloons, restaurants, and boardinghouses. However, it wasn't long before gold prices fell—and the easy deposits of precious ore were picked over—and the population of Bannack began to dwindle. A small contingent of hydraulic and dredge miners remained, but the town's vitality was drastically reduced. By the early 1940s, nonessential mining was prohibited in the region, and the few remaining residents left soon after.

Today there are more than 50 buildings on Main Street, built in a charming log-and-frame style that is distinctively from Montana. It is fascinating to walk down the streets to see the structures—which have been lovingly preserved rather than re-created or restored, as with many such Old West locales. Feel free to walk into any of the structures that aren't locked—so long as they aren't marked as private residences. There are seasonal events that include historic displays and costumed reenactments held throughout the summer. Summer weekends are also prime for gold panning. Visitors sift through pay dirt dug from a river basin near the infamous Grasshopper Creek. The park concession provides a shovel, screens, and gold pans—and guests can keep whatever they find. (Note, however, that gold panning and rock collecting are prohibited elsewhere in the park.) On weekend nights in October, Bannack Ghost Walks are a popular and spooky chance to walk through the town by candlelight. And in the winter, starting December 26 and running through early March (weather permitting), you can rent skates (or bring your own) and glide along the park's frozen dredge pond.

286 Crow Fair and Rodeo

CONTACT 406-638-1800, www.crow-fair.com; Bighorn River, north of Crow Agency, off I-90 near Hardin

PRICING	$
BEST TIME TO VISIT	Third week of August
AGE RANGE	All ages

The history of America is inextricably intertwined with the cultures of the Natives who occupied the land for millennia before European colonists arrived, and nowhere is Native American culture so keenly present as in the U.S. West, which continues to be home to many sovereign Indian nations. For more than 100 years, leaders from the Crow Nation have organized what they term a "giant family reunion under the Big Sky," which calls Native Americans from around the country to celebrate Native culture in the enormous expanse of Montana grasslands. The eclectic gathering attracts close to 50,000 participants and guests from around the world. It is considered to

Glacier Valley © Debbie K. Hardin

PRICE KEY
$ free–$5
$$ $6–10
$$$ $11–20
$$$$ $21+

Crow Fair and Rodeo   Courtesy Montana Office of Tourism

287 Dinosaur Trail

CONTACT	www.mtdinotrail.org; throughout Montana
PRICING	Admission varies by attraction
BEST TIME TO VISIT	Summer
AGE RANGE	5 and older

Several hundred million years ago the prehistoric terrain of what is now Montana was the perfect mix of swamp and jungle to attract dozens of species of dinosaurs, which lived for millennia and then died off suddenly. Modern-day Montana in turn has attracted paleontologists from around in the world to search for the abundant remains of these prehistoric creatures. Hundreds of well-preserved fossils have been found here and subsequently shipped to prestigious collections like the Smithsonian Institution and the Natural History Museum in New York City. The Montana Dinosaur Trail was established to allow guests to enjoy the fossils in their place of origin. The trail comprises 15 museums, field stations, and interpretive exhibits throughout 10 communities in the central and eastern portion of the state. Each site includes dinosaur fossil displays, and several allow guests to participate in fossil excavation during field-dig programs.

Download a map of the trail from www.mtdinotrail.org, jump in your car, and head off for an adventure that dinosaur-loving children will never forget. Favorites along the way include the Fort Peck Inter-

be the largest northern Native American encampment. In fact, the gathering is also known as the tepee capital of the world, thanks to the approximately 1,500 tepees used as temporary shelters during the festivities.

Drumbeats signal the beginning of the fair, which is held the third week of August near the Little Big Horn River. The celebration is a colorful and exuberant venue that includes Native foods, art and crafts, and contests for activities like woodcutting, singing, and traditional games. The fair includes a daily morning parade that highlights beautiful and handmade traditional clothing; an evening powwow in which all nations attending display different dance and music styles; an "all-Indian" rodeo; pari-mutuel horse racing; and Indian relay horse races. The fair closes with the "dance through camp," or parade dance, which is a spiritual blessing of the Crow Tribe. The fair is an exciting and joyful way to introduce children to the rich cultural heritage of American Natives from around the country.

Fort Peck Interpretive Center, along the Dinosaur Trail   Photo Donnie Sexton, courtesy Montana Office of Tourism

Pick up a *Prehistoric Passport* booklet, for sale for a few dollars at each of the Dinosaur Trail sites, which describes the displays along the trail and provides field notes and additional information on the dinosaur species that have been found in Montana. The passport includes space for a dinosaur stamp, available from each of the sites. Once you've got stamps from all 15 of the attractions, you'll receive a certificate of completion and a Montana Dinosaur Trail Prehistoric Passport T-shirt. (You have five years from purchase date to complete the trail and collect the T-shirt and certificate.)

First People's Buffalo Jump   Courtesy Montana Office of Tourism

pretive Center and Museum in Fort Peck (406-526-3493), which offers a full-sized cast skeleton of a *Tyrannosaurus rex*; Makoshika State Park in Glendive (www.makoshika.org), where 10 different dinosaur species have been found, including *T. rex* and *Thescelosaur*; the nearby Makoshika Dinosaur Museum (www.makoshika.com), which includes a large display of fossils found in the local region, along with a working fossil preparation laboratory and programs in which museum guests can dig for fossils on local ranches; the Museum of the Rockies in Bozeman (www.museumoftherockies.org), which houses a large collection of fossilized dinosaur eggs; the Phillips County Museum in Malta (www.phillipscountymuseum.org), home to "Elvis," a 33-foot-long *Brachylophosaurus*; and the Two Medicine Dinosaur Center in Bynum (www.tmdinosaur.org), which offers an extensive fossil preparation class and field digs to the public, as well as the world's largest earth-shaker lizard—a 137-foot *Seismosaurus halli*.

288 First People's Buffalo Jump

CONTACT 406-866-2217, http://stateparks.mt.gov; off I-15 at Ulm Exit, Ulm

PRICING	$
BEST TIME TO VISIT	Summer
AGE RANGE	7 and older

The wide-open ranges, grasslands, and buttes of what is now Montana were once home to as many as 13 million bison. (*Bison* is the proper common name of the American animal many people know as the buffalo.) Bison are enormous animals—a mature individual is about the size of a typical mini van and weighs up to a ton. These impressive animals provided meat for food, fur and hides for shelter and clothing, and bones and sinews for tools for early Plains Indians. Before horses were introduced to Native Americans by Spanish explorers in the 18th century, bison hunters employed an ingenious—albeit shocking—means of hunting the huge animals: Hunting parties rounded up entire herds and slowly and surely drove them over the edge of cliffs, where the bison plunged to their deaths. The animals were then butchered at the base of the cliffs, and meat and hides were shared among the community. The sites at which such hunts took place are termed buffalo jumps, and there are more than 300 throughout Montana.

The First People's Buffalo Jump (which until recently was known as Ulm Pishkun State Park) is one of the largest prehistoric buffalo jumps in this country. The cliffs over which the bison were herded here are more than a mile long. Archaeologists believe the site was in use for at least 2,000 years; bison remains 18 feet deep have been found at the base of the cliff, and tools and weapons have been found at the site that have been carbon-dated to AD 500. It is believed that the Native peoples preserved the bison meat into pemmican, a kind of jerky that is made from ground meat and dried fruit mixed with fat, and this food was used throughout the year, sustaining the Native peoples until the next hunting event.

The site is considered a sacred place by Native Americans. Today a small visitor center displays arti-

Camping Checklist

Want to save a bundle on accommodations while traveling? Consider camping. Tents are available for purchase for under $100 new (and can be found at a fraction of this price at garage sales); camping sites generally run from $10 to $25 per night (and most backcountry camping is free). A typical site (zoned for tents rather than RVs) generally includes a picnic table, a water spigot, and sometimes an electrical outlet. Most campgrounds include a nearby public restroom with running water and pay showers (with hot water), so "roughing it" can be kept to a minimum. And it's a rare kid (and I'm talking about those who haven't hit puberty) who doesn't enjoy sleeping under the stars. If you're game to give it a try, keep these tips in mind:

Tent assembly is for all ages   © Debbie K. Hardin

- You'll need a good, waterproof tent. Practice pitching it in the backyard or in a local park before taking it out for an official run.
- Sleeping bags are handy—but if you're traveling in warm weather, blankets and sheets work fine, too. Parents will appreciate an air mattress (or even a yoga mat) to cushion the lumps.
- Bring a mallet or hammer to drive in the stakes that will secure the tent. Extra stakes are a good precaution.
- A large bucket can serve as a receptacle to wash dishes, brush teeth, or soak tired feet.
- Keep food preparation simple: PB&J sandwiches, canned tuna, crackers and cheese, and so on. If you're camping at a site with a power source, bring along an electric teakettle to heat water for instant oatmeal and coffee—if you want to get fancy, camping stores sell dehydrated meals that will plump back to life with a little hot water. (If your campground does not provide potable water, bring bottled water for drinking and cooking.)
- If you're camping where there are no fire restrictions, bring along matches, kindling, and firewood. Most campsites include either a fire ring or a fire barrel. (The old Girl Scout trick of using premade nuggets of candle wax and sawdust is an easy way to start a roaring blaze.)
- In addition to a fully stocked first-aid kit, bring along bug repellent. There are a number of products on the market that are safe for young children—but don't tempt fate: Also pack long pants and long-sleeved shirts, and then change into them at dusk, when the mosquitoes come out to feast. If you

can stand the smell of it, a lighted citronella candle will help ward off the pests, too.
- For every family member, bring along a pair of shoes that is easily slipped into, and before you go to sleep every night line them up by the tent flap. This will make midnight trips to the restroom less frantic.
- Speaking of midnight trips to the restroom: If you're traveling with very young children, think about bringing a portable toddler potty to keep inside the tent for emergencies.
- Let there be light—and lots of it. Pack a lantern (battery powered is easier to manage than kerosene, and the battery-powered versions have nightlights). Also be sure that each family member has his or her own flashlight.
- Prepackaged wipes are a must—disinfectant hand wipes are nice, but baby wipes work, too. Liquid hand sanitizer is also welcome.
- An old bath mat or small rug placed just outside the tent exit will keep the tracked-in dirt to a minimum. You may appreciate a broom and dustpan to tidy up the tent floor as well. (A broom works well to clean the outside of the tent before you pack it away, too.)
- Keep clothing simple and disposable. Bring along old, comfortable items that you won't mind tossing should they become irreparably stained. Choose items that can be layered, because it can get colder in the elements at night than you might expect.
- Finally, ease up on the grooming rules. A kid's teeth will not fall out if she skips brushing them for one night. And maybe a daily shower isn't strictly necessary, either. Embrace the wilderness and it will embrace you!

facts, archaeological finds, a storytelling circle, and Native art that preserves the legacy of the traditional bison hunts. The park includes interpretive trails, which offer stunning views. Rangers offer seasonal classes on Native American games.

289 Glacier National Park

CONTACT 406-888-7806, www.nps.gov/glac; Glacier National Park, West Glacier

PRICING	$
BEST TIME TO VISIT	Summer
AGE RANGE	7 and older

There are very few places in the world more beautiful than Glacier National Park, which has been called the Swiss Alps of the United States. Don't let the name fool you into expecting an abundance of glaciers. Global climate change is quickly shrinking these icy remnants from the last ice age—scientists expect all the glaciers will have melted by 2025. This shouldn't discourage you from visiting, however: Glacier got its name because millions of years ago ancient glaciers carved the peaks and valleys of this magnificent landscape, leaving in their wake hanging valleys with ethereal waterfalls; powder-blue lakes cloudy with "glacier flour" (suspended particles deposited by glaciers that give the water a milky quality); and dramatic peaks that are topped with snow even in August.

Although Glacier National Park is open year-round, it's really only possible to get around in summer. Facilities and roads are generally open from late May through early September. And the lyrically named Going-to-the-Sun Road, the mountain pass that cuts through the heart of the park, isn't completely plowed until mid-June. A drive along this 50-mile stretch of road—a curvy mountain pass straddling precipitous drops—is the highlight of any visit. Expect to see dozens of waterfalls, shimmering blue lakes, lovely mountaintop meadows, and nearly ubiquitous rainbows arching up from the valleys far below. White-knuckle drivers will want to check out the Red Bus Tours, which can be booked at any park hotel

or ranger station. Climb aboard one of the restored 1930s-era red buses and let someone else deal with the gear jamming. Highlights along the Going-to-the-Sun Road include the following:

- **Bird Woman Falls** is a ribbon-like waterfall that stretches nearly 500 feet and is visible from several miles of the road. The falls are fed by snowmelt and can dry up in late summer, but in the flush of late June and early July the water tumbles down in flowing veils of white froth.

- **Garden Wall** is a knife-edged slice of cliff honed by two glaciers that ground down both sides. The ridge is part of the Continental Divide—a geological division where waters on the west flow into the Pacific Ocean and waters on the east flow to the Atlantic Ocean.

- **Jackson Glacier**, one of the easiest glaciers to view in the park, is visible from the road about 4 miles beyond Logan Pass.

- **Logan Pass**, the highest point on the road, lies along the Continental Divide. Park here and catch the Highline Trail (a scenic path along the cliffs that overlooks frightening drops—save this for children 10 and older) or the easier Hidden Lake Nature Trail, a 3-mile round trip that begins modestly on a boardwalk and increases in difficulty before it culminates in a stunning view of Hidden Lake. Look for mountain goats traipsing through the wildflowers and patches of snow (often piled up just off the pathway well into July).

- **Weeping Wall** is a whimsical waterfall that seems to seep out of the pores of a cliff that is only feet from the Going-to-the-Sun Road. Depending on temperatures and snowmelt, the wall alternately sobs gently or wails wildly. Children will love driving by this fea-

A moose in Glacier National Park

© Debbie K. Hardin

Glacier has a sister park across the Canadian border, known as Waterton Lakes, and the two sites are managed cooperatively. If you decide to drive into Canada for the day, be sure to bring valid passports, even for children.

Little Bighorn Battlefield   Courtesy National Park Service

ture with the windows rolled down (or better yet, in a convertible with the top down) to get the full force of the waterworks.

Also well worth visiting in the park are the Many Glacier region, featuring snowcapped mountains surrounding a valley filled with pristine lakes and a shoreline accented with chalets; St. Mary Valley, east of Logan Pass, along the Going-to-the-Sun Road, a high-elevation location that offers tremendous views of snowy peaks; Lake McDonald, a 10-mile-long and nearly 500-foot-deep lake ideal for fishing and wildlife viewing; and Two Medicine Valley, in the southeastern section of the park, an area surrounded by commanding peaks and full of huckleberry meadows, colorful geological formations, crystalline lakes, and dramatic waterfalls.

290 Little Bighorn Battlefield

CONTACT www.nps.gov/libi; off U.S. 87 (I-90), within the Crow Indian Reservation, near Hardin

PRICING	$
BEST TIME TO VISIT	Spring through fall
AGE RANGE	7 and older

Native warriors called the bloody battle "Greasy Grass"; U.S. Army troops called it "Custer's Last Stand." The 1876 conflict, memorialized in history books as the Battle of Little Bighorn, after the nearby river of the same name, was a historic clash between Cheyenne, Arapaho, and Lakota Indians joined together against American military forces to resist continued incursions of white settlers into Indian reservations and sacred sites in the Black Hills (where gold had been discovered). The tribes formed a coalition

and gathered with the intent of fighting the U.S. Army. In an effort to quash the Indian resistance, Lieutenant Colonel George Custer, leading the 7th Cavalry, attempted a surprise attack on Lakota chief Sitting Bull's encampment, but thanks to bad intelligence and—some historians argue—bad judgment, Custer greatly underestimated the number of Native warriors involved. Native forces, led by Crazy Horse and others, dealt the U.S. Army a crushing defeat. Custer himself was killed during the battle, along with 267 other American troops. The battle proved to be the beginning of the end for the Native resistance, however. In response to the battle outcome, the United States redrew boundary lines in the Montana territory so that the Black Hills were not included within the confines of the Indian reservation, which officially opened up what the Natives considered sacred lands to settlement.

The Little Bighorn Battlefield memorializes the legacy of the Native warriors and the U.S. Cavalry soldiers who fought and were killed or wounded during the decisive battle. Start at the visitor center, which offers an orientation film on request, and hosts seasonal programs such as interpretive talks. The on-site museum displays artifacts and interpretive exhibits on the Battle of Little Bighorn, including weapons, a history of the battle, and the life of Plains Indians. Next to the visitor center is the Custer National

The memorial offers a free cell phone tour of Little Bighorn Battlefield. Dial 406-214-3148, and then enter the number you'll find at more than a dozen sign posts along the roadway. The audio tour includes Native accounts of the battle as well as history of the battle sites.

Cemetery, which includes the final resting places of known and unknown combatants, both U.S. Army soldiers and Native warriors, as well as pioneers who were early non-Native settlers of the region. Perhaps more haunting than the official cemetery, however, are the gravestones scattered throughout the battlefield; the spots where army personnel perished have white stone markers and the spots where Native warriors died, red granite. In addition, a large-scale white granite marker was erected on Last Stand Hill, where Custer was killed; nearby is an Indian Memorial that shows an artistic rendering of Native warriors.

Although you can tour the memorial by foot, via interpretive trails, or by automobile, consider joining a guided tour led by a Native guide. The one-hour tours are offered from Memorial Day through Labor Day, and tickets must be purchased from the visitor center in advance.

291 Virginia City

CONTACT 800-829-2969, www.virginiacity.com; Virginia City

PRICING	Fees vary by attraction
BEST TIME TO VISIT	Summer
AGE RANGE	7 and older

In 1863 a group of prospectors looked for gold near a small stream in Alder Gulch, hoping for enough of the precious ore to buy tobacco. They soon found that the area contained a good deal more riches than they had expected. Thanks to the epidemic of gold fever that had struck throughout the West in the mid-19th century, it wasn't long before word got out that gold had been discovered, and soon the hillsides were blanketed with tents and other crude shelters housing thousands of hopeful fortune hunters. At one point the "fourteen-mile city"—so called because of the string of settlements that lined the gulch—was home to more than 10,000 people. Virginia City (the official name of the new settlement) was an honest-to-goodness boomtown, and the population grew much more quickly than the city's infrastructure. Because there was little

Another gold-rush-era boomtown, Nevada City, is less than 2 miles away, and includes more than 100 original or relocated historic buildings. The town hosts living history weekends throughout the summer, and includes the Nevada City Music Hall, which showcases player pianos and music boxes from the Victorian era.

law enforcement in the burgeoning region, the city attracted more than its fair share of criminals and ruffians—and soon acquired a reputation as a rough-and-tumble settlement, with bars and brothels aplenty (although it also attracted pioneer families, and was the site of the first public school in Montana). Alder Gulch ultimately yielded an estimated $120 million in gold flakes and gold nuggets. But eventually the gold ran out, and many of the residents moved on, leaving their homes and businesses behind, frozen in time.

Today the gold-mining town is a preserved and restored Old West ghost town, but with Victorian structures set aside for their historic significance standing next to modern homes and businesses (most of which cater to the modern-day tourist industry). There are more than 100 historic homes, most furnished with period pieces and artifacts. In addition to strolling through the preserved town, you can take a stagecoach tour; ride a historic train from Virginia City to nearby Nevada City (see above); witness historic reenactments; attend theater programs that focus on the gold rush era; or try your own hand at panning for gold. Don't be surprised to see a few faux gunfights break out on the wooden sidewalks.

Virginia City   Courtesy Montana Office of Tourism

NEBRASKA

292 Ashfall Fossil Beds State Historical Park

CONTACT 402-893-2000, http://ashfall.unl.edu; 86930 517 Ave., Royal

PRICING	$ for entry fee, plus $ for the required Nebraska Park Entry Permit
BEST TIME TO VISIT	Open April through mid-November
AGE RANGE	7 and older

More than 12 million years ago, a massive volcanic eruption centered in what is now Idaho spewed ash over an enormous area of the Midwest; several feet of the ash coated the grasslands of northeastern Nebraska. Most of the animals living in the region at the time died several weeks after the eruption because of compromised air quality and contaminated food and water. Many of these animals came to a watering hole on the property that is now preserved as Ashfall Fossil Beds State Historical Park; they were looking for potable water but ended up dying here. There are no dinosaur fossils on site—the volcanic event happened after the age of the dinosaurs had passed—but 17 species of vertebrates have been found, including ancient species of horses, camels, deer, dogs, birds, and rhinoceroses; currently more than 200 skeletons have been exposed. The fossils are especially fragile,

New Barn at Ashfall Fossil Beds State Historical Park

Photo R. Neibel, courtesy Nebraska Tourism

so unlike most archaeological excavations, the animals here have not been removed to a museum. Instead, they are being uncovered but left intact where they were found. Indeed, the fossils are so delicate that they can't be exposed to rain or extreme temperatures, so an enormous structure called the Hubbard Rhino Barn was built over the site. Guests can visit to see the fossils in place and watch archaeologists' ongoing efforts to discover more animals. Start out a trip to see the fossil preparation laboratory and view interpretive displays that will help your family understand how paleontologists do their work. There are also regularly scheduled educational programs in-season to discuss new discoveries and explain the significance of the animals found thus far.

293 Fort Kearny

CONTACT 308-234-9513, www.nps.gov/oreg/planyourvisit/site4.htm; Rt. 4, Kearney

PRICING	$
BEST TIME TO VISIT	Summer
AGE RANGE	7 and older

The 2,000-mile Oregon Trail that runs westward from the Missouri River to the Pacific Coast was heavily trafficked in the mid-19th century by California 49ers seeking their fortune in gold and pioneers looking to settle along the route in the Midwest. Tensions were high between the increasingly large wagon trains that brought more and more settlers into Indian territory and the Natives who were living in these regions—often after having been pushed out from other lands farther east. In an effort to stave off the flow of emigrants, some Native tribes attacked the wagon trains along the Oregon Trail, which in turn prompted the U.S. Army to establish forts along the route to protect the many Americans passing through. Fort Kearny was built in 1848 for just this purpose. The outpost was situated at the point where several smaller trails converged into one larger trail that followed the Platte River west to Fort Laramie. Military escorts joined wagon trains at this juncture and escorted

Covered wagon at Scotts Bluff National Monument
© Dave Sucsy Photography/iStockphoto.com

PRICE KEY	
$	free–$5
$$	$6–10
$$$	$11–20
$$$$	$21+

Fort Kearny   Photo R. Neibel, courtesy Nebraska Tourism

them through to the next way station. In addition, the fort served as an outpost for the Pony Express and an outfitting depot for Indian campaigns. Shortly after the transcontinental railroad was completed, less than 30 years after the fort was established, the Oregon Trail fell into disuse; Fort Kearny was decommissioned, disassembled, and moved.

None of the original sod and adobe buildings remains at the site, but guests today can tour two reconstructed fort buildings—the stockade and the blacksmith shop. Ongoing archaeological digs have uncovered the foundations of the original structures, which are also interesting to view. A tiny on-site museum offers displays of artifacts, period cannons, and original equipment. Visitors may view a 20-minute video history of the fort. The park is the site of several reenactments on national holidays, which includes a cannon firing every Fourth of July.

294 Fort Robinson

CONTACT 308-665-2900, www.stateparks.com/fort_robinson.html; 3200 W. Hwy. 20, Crawford

PRICING	$
BEST TIME TO VISIT	Spring and summer
AGE RANGE	7 and older

Fort Robinson was established in 1874 to oversee the Red Cloud Agency—akin to a Native American reservation—which was home to 13,000 Ogalala Indians, who were sometimes hostile to the pioneers pushing westward through the Great Plains. Unlike many western forts established to protect settlers from Native attacks—which were dismantled soon after the overland trails fell into disuse and a military presence was no longer required to protect emigrating wagon trains—Fort Robison persisted through World War II, and eventually grew to become one of the largest military outposts on the northern Plains. Over the years the fort was the site of many historic events, including the imprisonment in 1878 of close to 150 Cheyenne—part of a larger group of kinsmen who had broken away from Indian territory in what is now Oklahoma to move into Kansas and Nebraska. In an effort to contain the Cheyenne—and curtail the occasional violence that broke out among the Natives, settlers, and army troops—the group was held at Fort Robinson. After several months of increasingly restrictive confinement, the Cheyenne used hidden weapons to help them escape from the fort; most escapees were eventually either captured and sent back to their reservation to the south or were killed. Less than a decade later, in 1885, at a time when the U.S. Army was segregated by race, African American soldiers were stationed at the fort, which served as the 9th Cavalry ("Buffalo Soldiers") headquarters from 1887 through 1898. In 1942 the fort hosted a K-9 Corps training center, which oversaw the training of more than 14,000 dogs used for military and civilian agencies. From 1943 to 1946, the fort was a POW camp during World War II.

Today guests can tour several historic buildings that have been preserved from the fort's earliest days, including an 1875 guardhouse, the 1887 officers' quar-

Fort Robinson   Photo R. Neibel, courtesy Nebraska Tourism

ters, a blacksmith shop, and the post cemetery. The 1905 headquarters building serves as the Fort Robinson Museum, which features exhibits that illuminate the fort's varied history. There is plenty to explore here, because the state park that preserves the fort is an extremely beautiful one, with rugged scenery, bison herds, and bike and hiking trails. The fort management offers guided horse trails, fireside programs, and pancake breakfasts throughout the year.

295 Homestead National Monument

Homestead National Monument

Photo R. Neibel, courtesy Nebraska Tourism

CONTACT 402-223-3514, www.nps.gov/home/index.htm; off NE 4, Beatrice

PRICING	$
BEST TIME TO VISIT	Summer
AGE RANGE	7 and older

Perhaps no piece of legislation in American history has had a more profound effect on the expansion of the country than the Homestead Act of 1862. This remarkable law, signed by President Abraham Lincoln after the secession of the southern states from the Union, granted to any person 21 years or older 160 acres of land in the Midwest and West practically free for the taking: All that was required to make an initial claim was an $18 filing fee. Men and women—including former slaves and new immigrants who came to the country for the purpose of claiming the free land—were entitled to keep the land for good after they had lived on the property for five years and made improvements including building a home and clearing soil to plant crops. More than 1.6 million people made claims on more than 270 million acres, which represents 10 percent of the land in the United States. Surprisingly, the Homestead Act was in effect until it was repealed in 1976, except for provisions for homesteading in Alaska, which were active until as recently as 1986.

Daniel Freeman was one of the first people to file a claim under the Homestead Act—reportedly 10 minutes after midnight on January 1, 1863, the first day the act was law. He settled in southeast Nebraska, and his homestead is today the site of the Homestead

National Monument of America. The monument memorializes the act and preserves the legacy of the pioneers who had a lasting effect on westward expansion and the landscape of the Midwest. Start your visit at the Heritage Center, which offers interactive exhibits that help visitors understand the Homestead Act's immense influence on agriculture, on Natives who had been living on the land before the settlers, and on immigration. Be sure to check out the Living Wall, a series of sculptures arrayed along the sidewalk entrance to the center that show the percentage of successfully homesteaded land in each state. Another highlight of the park is the Palmer-Epard Cabin, built in 1867 by homesteader George W. Palmer. The original log structure was 14 by 16 feet and home to a family with 10 children. Kids will also enjoy touring the Freeman School, a one-room brick schoolhouse that is furnished with period desks and supplies. (Note that access to the inside of the schoolhouse is limited to ranger-conducted tours, which are available year-round during business hours.) The 244-acre monument is also the site of a 100-acre restored tallgrass prairie, which is home to varied wildlife. The extensive trail system is a great way to discover the many species of plants and animals that call the area home. From Memorial Day through Labor Day there are regularly scheduled living history demonstrations that can include hearth cooking, agricultural demonstrations, and log-cabin construction.

296 Pioneer Village

CONTACT 308-832-1181, www.pioneervillage.org; 138 E. U.S. 6, Minden

PRICING	$$–$$$
BEST TIME TO VISIT	Summer
AGE RANGE	3 and older

The 1862 Homestead Act brought thousands of settlers—many of them German and Scandinavian immigrants—to the plains of Nebraska to claim their 160 acres of land, and these immigrants had an enormous impact on the culture of the region. The Pioneer Village is a historical attraction that showcases original structures and collections of artifacts that explain the everyday lives of the early pioneers. The site includes 12 historic buildings arrayed around a circular green, as well as a dozen-plus structures that house an enormous collection of American memorabilia. Included among the re-created or restored sites are a Pony Express station (look for Buffalo Bill's saddle), a small cottage made of 3-foot-thick sod (indicative of the earliest shelters on the prairie), a general store complete with a glass cat on the cracker barrel to scare away mice, the 1869 Elm Creek fort that was used during the Indian wars, and a one-room schoolhouse that is full of original furnishings. A charming China House showcases a collection of pottery, glass, and china items that were carried lovingly in covered wagons across the nation; look for the sugar bowl once owned by Abraham Lincoln. Museum warehouses are home to large-scale items that include more than 100 antique tractors and 350 antique cars. You can also

tour five intact period kitchens that include a traditional hearth for cooking, a Franklin stove, and an iron cookstove. Don't miss the 1879-era merry-go-round, rides on which still cost only a nickel.

297 Willa Cather House

CONTACT 866-731-7304, www.willacather.org; 413 Webster, Red Cloud

PRICING	$–$$
BEST TIME TO VISIT	Year-round (open days are seasonal)
AGE RANGE	10 and older

Willa Cather (1873–1947) was an important American writer best remembered for novels about frontier life on the Plains, including *O Pioneers!* and *My Ántonia*. Cather was born in Virginia, but moved to Nebraska—to a farm in Red Cloud—when she was only 9, amid the first wave of early homesteaders. She was presented with the Pulitzer Prize for Literature in 1922 for a World War I novel called *One of Ours*. Today her childhood home in Red Cloud is preserved as a museum, open for public tours and furnished with period pieces, many of which belonged to the Cather family. Perhaps most interesting is Cather's bedroom, which still bears the original wallpaper that she herself hung; also on display is a seashell collection and several items of clothing. The kitchen houses the original Cather china, which the family brought from Virginia wrapped in Confederate money; and the dining room showcases Cather's antique high chair.

Nevada

298 Chollar Mine Tour

CONTACT 775-847-0155, www.visitvirginiacitynv.com; 615 S. F St., Virginia City

PRICING	$–$$
BEST TIME TO VISIT	Open late spring through October; call ahead for hours, which vary seasonally
AGE RANGE	10 and older

Growth of many western cities was fueled by discoveries of gold and silver ore. The Comstock Lode, a tremendous cache of silver first found in 1859, was responsible for the growth of Virginia City, which became the mining district's capital, at one point boasting a population of 25,000. When ore production slowed, so did population growth in Virginia City—by 1930 the town was a shadow of its former self, with only several hundred people claiming to be residents. Today the charming preserved Victorian mining town offers a remarkable glimpse into the heyday of the Chollar Mine. The half-hour tour through the mine makes it clear how difficult and dangerous the conditions were for miners during the late 19th century; guests walk through the main haulage tunnel and have the chance to see silver ore, rock drills, and the bucket conveyance apparatuses used during the era. Guides explain about cave-ins, and this combined with tight quarters means that this attraction should be saved for folks who have no issues with claustrophobia.

299 Hoover Dam

CONTACT 866-730-9097; www.usbr.gov/lc/hooverdam; off NE 172, Boulder City

PRICING	$–$$$$
BEST TIME TO VISIT	Fall through spring
AGE RANGE	8 and older

Despite the palm trees, lush lawns, and rambling golf courses that might lead you to believe otherwise, the Southwest is an extremely dry desert. Precious little rain falls in Nevada, Arizona, and Southern California, yet populations in these regions have been expanding for generations, taxing the limited natural resources. An early solution that brought water and power to the remotest parts of the desert (and made possible modern-day Las Vegas) was the construction of the Hoover Dam, the highest concrete dam in the Western Hemisphere (725 feet aboveground), conceived to harness the water and the hydroelectric power of the mighty Colorado River, which runs along the border of Nevada and Arizona. Construction of the dam began in 1931, and it was completed in five years—remarkably, two full years ahead of schedule and significantly under budget. Oasis-like Lake Mead on the other side of the dam was created as a result; the lake took more than six years to fill completely, but today is a favorite recreational spot for fishing, waterskiing, and houseboating.

The Hoover Dam is a huge tourist draw (and a favorite excursion from nearby Las Vegas), especially in the summer. (Note: The heat can be oppressive in the

> *A solution that brought water and power to the remotest parts of the desert was the Hoover Dam.*

warm months—topping out at more than 115 degrees—and crowds are worst from June through August.) There are two tours available to the public: a Power Plant Tour that includes admission to the visitor center and a 30-minute guided tour of the power plant; and a Dam Tour that includes a one-hour guided visit to the power plant and other passageways within the dam. Tours are offered on the half hour on a first-come, first-served basis—no reservations are taken. Inside the power plant, you'll get to see a 30-foot-diameter pipe that carries nearly 100,000 gallons of water per second to the dam's generators; check out the enormous generators themselves; and navigate the massive tunnels that run through the heart of the dam. Be sure to step out onto the observation deck, which of-

United States. It's especially well known for its sapphire-blue waters. The lake is more than 20 miles long and 10 miles wide; about a third falls in Nevada and the rest, in California. The lake is further divided into northern and southern portions, the latter of which is generally more crowded and offers more resorts and amenities. The Nevada side, both north and south, is notorious for its abundance of casinos—many of which are literally steps from the California border. Although the Nevada portion of the shoreline offers plenty of glitzy entertainment, gambling, and inexpensive buffet food, there is abundant natural beauty wherever you go on this jewel-like lake.

The region averages 40 feet of snowfall a year, so winter sports like cross-country and downhill skiing are immensely popular throughout Lake Tahoe. Popular family-friendly ski resorts include Diamond Peak (www.diamondpeak.com), Heavenly (www.skiheavenly.com), and Mount Rose (www.mtrose.com). In the warmer months fishing, kayaking, and swimming are popular pastimes. Don't miss the pretty Sand Harbor Beach on the Nevada side—although it can get crowded on busy weekends, it's a good place for families to swim and lounge on the sand. Also look for Cave Rock, a 75-foot outcropping that is part of an extinct volcano. Legend has it that Tahoe Tessie (a mythical creature akin to the Loch Ness Monster) lives in a cave at the base of Cave Rock. (Lest your kids be tempted to look for Tessie, be aware that it is forbidden to climb up to the cave, because it is a sacred site for the Native Washoe people.) A fun outing that will get you out on the water is a ride aboard one of two

Hoover Dam
Courtesy Las Vegas News Bureau

fers spectacular views of the dam, the Colorado River, and Lake Mead. You can also stroll along the top of the dam to see extraordinary views, including the art deco intake towers and other surprisingly artistic features of this impressive engineering marvel.

300 Lake Tahoe

CONTACT Southwest of Reno, straddling the border of Nevada and California

PRICING	Fees vary by attraction
BEST TIME TO VISIT	Winter and early spring for winter sports; summer for water sports
AGE RANGE	All ages

Lake Tahoe is surrounded by towering mountains and forests and is one of the deepest, purest lakes in the

Lake Tahoe
© Debbie K. Hardin

If you're into downhill skiing and snow-boarding, don't miss the enormously popular Squaw Valley resort (530-583-6985, www.squaw.com; between Tahoe City and I-80), which falls on the California side of the lake. This former Olympic Village offers varied terrain, so there's a run that's appropriate for every skill level in the family. Be sure to purchase lift tickets in advance, because this well-known resort gets crowded quickly.

Las Vegas Strip   Courtesy Las Vegas News Bureau

authentic Mississippi paddle wheelers that ply the waters of Lake Tahoe throughout the year—and each visits the spectacular (and aptly named) Emerald Bay, on the California side. Pick up the MS *Dixie II* at Zephyr Cove Resort, which is 4 miles east of the state line, in the southern portion of the lake; there are two-hour guided tours, as well as dinner and brunch cruises. Hop aboard the *Tahoe Queen* at Ski Run Marina, off U.S. 50 (also in the southern part of the lake), which offers sunset cruises and narrated tours.

301 Las Vegas Strip

CONTACT	S. Las Vegas Blvd., Las Vegas
PRICING	Varies by attraction
BEST TIME TO VISIT	Spring and fall
AGE RANGE	10 and older

At first blush, Las Vegas hardly seems like a family-friendly destination. Indeed, the plethora of casinos, bars, nightclubs, and other adult entertainment can make it a challenging locale for parents looking for wholesome activities for the entire brood—but there are a surprising number of fairly remarkable kid-appropriate attractions in Sin City, if you know where to look. Be forewarned: It's just about impossible to stay or travel along the Las Vegas Strip without exposing children to a certain amount of gambling (most of the hotels are also casinos, so to get to the majority of accommodations, attractions, and restaurants, it's necessary to walk through gambling sites, which serve

alcohol and are generally very smoky from tobacco fumes). There are also some racy establishments that aren't shy about advertising their services on enormous billboards and in local newspapers and flyers that are ubiquitous street side. But these naughty venues do not *have* to be the focus of a visit to the Las Vegas Strip.

The glitz and lights of the Strip—a 4-mile length of casinos and mega-hotels that runs along South Las Vegas Boulevard—are pretty irresistible to viewers of all ages, especially at night. In recent years the city has re-created some of the world's most iconic architecture here, such as a smaller-scale version of the Eiffel Tower and the New York skyline, so a drive down the traffic-laden Strip is an unforgettable sightseeing opportunity. Some of the over-the-top entertainment offered by large casino resorts is ideal for children, like the water-fountain extravaganza in front of the Bellagio Hotel (3600 S. Las Vegas Blvd.), with more than 1,000 fountains choreographed to music (shown daily on the half hour); the volcano eruptions at the Mirage (3400 S. Las Vegas Blvd.), which spew fire and smoke on the hour from 5 to 11 PM; *CSI: The Experience* at the MGM Grand (3799 S. Las Vegas Blvd.), an interactive exhibit that allows guests to investigate a faux crime scene; and the Secret Garden and Dolphin Habitat, also at the Mirage (3400 S. Las Vegas Blvd.), a free-flowing zoo that is home to leopards, tigers, and dolphins. Several family-friendly resorts offer jaw-dropping pools and other kid-pleasing amenities for their guests: The Mandalay Bay Resort (3950 S. Las Vegas Blvd.) boasts a mini water park, complete with wave pool and lazy river, as well as an on-site aquarium with an intriguing walk-through shark tank; the Venetian (3355 S. Las Vegas Blvd.) dazzles with an indoor lagoon with real gondola rides; the Bellagio (3600 S. Las Vegas Blvd.) includes an indoor botanical garden and world-class art museum; Circus Circus (2880 S. Las Vegas Blvd.) offers daily free circus performances like high-wire acrobats; and the Flamingo Resort (3555 S. Las Vegas Blvd.) is home to a flock of real flamingos, as well as a collection of other exotic birds guests can admire.

There are a handful of exciting amusement attractions on the Strip as well, offering thrills that are quintessentially Las Vegas in style: Don't miss Adventuredome (2880 S. Las Vegas Blvd.), an indoor park that will appeal to youngsters and teenagers alike, with wild roller coasters, a 4-D theater experience, plenty of kiddie rides, and laser tag; The Rollercoaster at New York, NY (3790 S. Las Vegas Blvd.), a 67-mile-per-hour thriller that includes two inversions and a drop of more than 200 feet; and the Stratosphere Tower (2000 S. Las Vegas Blvd.), a spectacularly daring amusement park that offers thrill rides atop a 1,000-foot observation tower.

302 Rhyolite

CONTACT	Off Hwy. 374, 4 miles west of Beatty
PRICING	$
BEST TIME TO VISIT	Late fall through early spring
AGE RANGE	All ages

When you drive through the remains of Rhyolite, you enter into complete desolation. This ghost town on the edge of Death Valley is not a Disney-fied version of an Old West mining town: This is the real deal, or what's left of it, and a reminder of the dashed dreams of so many people who emigrated west to make their fortunes in gold and silver. The original town sprang up in 1905, as a mining camp to support the thousands of miners and prospectors who rushed to the Bullfrog Mining District in the surrounding hills. In its heyday, as many as 5,000 people called the place home—and the two-story schoolhouse for the chil-

dren of mine workers indicates that they meant to stay. But by 1911, the Montgomery Shoshone Mine, the region's biggest ore producer, was closed, and the unemployed miners left town as quickly as they had come. Today the ruins are all that is left. Rhyolite was named after a pinkish igneous rock, much like granite, and the crumbling facades of the structures are in fact beginning to return to the earth like crumbling rocks. There are no concessionaires making money off tourists, no modern-day trappings to make a trip to Rhyolite comfortable: All you'll find is an uneasy quiet and the inescapable sadness of decay. Yet the place is fascinating—almost apocalyptic—and a quick drive through will ignite children's imaginations. You can even pull over to the side and peer through the windows of some of the ruins—but be careful, as most of these buildings are extremely unstable. Be sure to look for the famous Bottle House, constructed with more than 30,000 bottles by miner Tom Kelly (and a miniature bottle village wrought by Kelly as well); the old railroad depot; and the skeleton of the schoolhouse.

Miniature bottlehouse village in Rhyolite
Courtesy Travel Nevada

303 Virginia and Truckee Railroad

Virginia and Truckee Railroad   Courtesy Travel Nevada

CONTACT 775-847-4386, www.visitcarsoncity.com;
off Flint Dr., Carson City

PRICING	$$$$
BEST TIME TO VISIT	Year-round (hours and routes vary seasonally)
AGE RANGE	3 and older

During the fever pitch of the gold rush era, the Comstock Lode of silver ore was discovered in Virginia City, Nevada, in 1859, which brought prospectors clambering to the area to look for the pricey silverish gray deposits. To serve the burgeoning mining communities that soon sprang up throughout northwestern Nevada, the Virginia and Truckee Railroad (V&T) was built. During its heyday, the V&T ran from Reno to Carson City, where the mainline then split into two routes—one that led to Virginia City and one to Minden.

Today a small portion of the original line is preserved as a historic route, which is served by antique steam locomotives. Guests board near the Carson River Canyon, and within a few miles of departure the train runs along the historic Comstock-era route. You'll pass American Flat, a onetime gold- and silver-mining town; travel through Tunnel No. 2, a 566-foot-long pass-through; and end up at the F Street Depot in Virginia City. You can then hop aboard a free shuttle to downtown Virginia City for some sightseeing (see the description above) before the train ride back. There are numerous special holiday train rides, like patriotic trips on the Fourth of July, Christmas events for children, and many trips that include historical reenactors who interpret the silver rush days of Nevada. Keep your eyes peeled for wild mustangs en route.

NEW HAMPSHIRE

304 American Independence Museum

CONTACT 603-772-2622, www.independencemuseum.org; 1 Governors Lane, Exeter

PRICING	$–$$
BEST TIME TO VISIT	Open Wednesday through Saturday, mid-May to last Saturday in October
AGE RANGE	5 and older

In 1623 Captain John Mason directed English colonists to settle a fishing village near the Piscataqua River in what is now New Hampshire. The Province of New Hampshire was so named in 1629, after the English county of Hampshire (Mason's hometown). It was officially organized as a royal colony in 1691. As one of original 13 colonies of America, New Hampshire and its citizens played a crucial role in the earliest government charters in the colonies, and eventually helped establish the American system of government. To recognize the contributions of these Founders, and to

New Hampshire was named after the English county of Hampshire.

help further the study of the American Revolution, the American Independence Museum in historic Exeter teaches visitors about the birth of the nation and the everyday lives of many of the patriots.

The museum comprises two historic structures in downtown Exeter: The Folsom Tavern, a 1775-era institution that played host to President George Washington; and the Ladd-Gilman House, dating to the early 18th century and once home to successful merchants from the city who were heavily involved in the American Revolution. (Nicholas Gilman Jr., of the same Gilman family, signed the U.S. Constitution.) The Ladd-Gilman House exhibits an original (out of 200 copies) Dunlap Broadside printing of the Declaration of Independence, as well as two drafts of the Constitution. Also on display are early American furniture, silver sets, and china; as well as letters by luminaries such as President Washington and Major Pierre Charles L'Enfant (who designed the layout of Washington, DC).

305 Canterbury Shaker Village

CONTACT 603-783-9511, www.shakers.org; 288 Shaker Rd., Canterbury

PRICING	$$–$$$
BEST TIME TO VISIT	Open late May through October
AGE RANGE	3 and older

Shakerism was founded by Englishwoman Ann Lee, who in the 18th century led a handful of followers to America to spread the religion throughout the New World. Adherents called themselves the United Society of Believers in Christ's Second Appearing—but they came to be known as the Shakers, because of their practice of shaking and dancing during worship. They were a celibate group—and therefore relied on converts to propagate their faith—and they were advocates for gender and social equality long before these ideals fully took hold in America. At the zenith of the faith, in the mid-19th century, there were more than 6,000 believers spread across 19 communal villages throughout the United States. (The religion continues today in a very tiny community in Maine.)

Canterbury Shaker Village is an outdoor museum dedicated to preserving the legacy of the Shaker community that lived in New Hampshire for some 200 years. The site comprises 25 original Shaker structures, four reconstructed buildings, and almost 700 acres of gardens, fields, and forests. Shaker architecture, furniture, and everyday objects are greatly admired today for their simplicity in design and their sturdy construction, and this is one of the best places to appreciate the Shakers' efficiency and dedication to utilitarianism. Stroll through the beautiful vegetable gardens in summer, tour the simply furnished living quarters, and step back in time with many hands-on opportunities to experience another era. Don't miss the Power House Family Activity Center, where children can dress up like 19th-century Shakers, play games common to the time, and make period crafts. The site offers a Family Tour (recommended for children 3 and older; available daily in the summer and on weekends in the fall) that includes singing and dancing and offers kids the chance to try out the kinds of chores their 19th-century counterparts were responsible for. There are also opportunities to watch—and often participate—in traditional crafts, such as box making, broom making, rug braiding, spinning, and weaving. Seasonal parent-and-child classes include gingerbread house making and cooking from freshly harvested garden produce.

306 Daniel Webster Birthplace Site

CONTACT 603-934-5057, www.nhstateparks.org/explore/state-parks/daniel-webster-birthplace-state-historic-site.aspx; off Rt. 127, Franklin

PRICING	$–$$
BEST TIME TO VISIT	Open late June through early September, weekends only
AGE RANGE	7 and older

Daniel Webster (1782–1852) was a prominent American statesman, serving in the U.S. House of Representatives, as a senator, as secretary of state, and as a presidential candidate. He spent 40 years as a public servant, and was a strong advocate for states' rights. The Daniel Webster Birthplace State Historic Site memorializes the 140-acre farm on which Webster was born and spent his early years; the property includes the original Webster home, the remains of an early fort, and a historic cemetery. His parents sold the property in part to help pay for his Dartmouth University education, and it was later used as an orphanage for children who lost their parents during the Civil War; several buildings survive from the orphanage and the convent associated with it. In addition to serving to preserve the legacy of Webster, the farm also demonstrates what life on a 1700s farm

would have been like. The site sponsors living history programs throughout the season, and the extended property offers an inviting countryside to explore.

307 Fort at Number 4

CONTACT 603-826-5700, www.fortat4.org; 267 Springfield Rd., Charlestown

PRICING	$–$$
BEST TIME TO VISIT	Open mid-May through October
AGE RANGE	7 and older

The Fort at Number 4, now in the historic community of Charlestown, was the northernmost British settlement in New Hampshire until after the French and Indian War. The wooden fort was founded in the 1740s, and laid out so that a series of interconnected houses formed a square settlement that eventually included a stockade with a guard tower. The fort has been reconstructed and today is a living history museum that portrays the life of early settlers and town militia. There are several examples of lean-to homes, avail-

> The Fort at Number 4 has faced some funding challenges in recent years and has in turn presented curtailed hours in some seasons. Be sure to call ahead for hours and open dates.

Fort at Number 4   Photo David Lawyer, courtesy Fort at Number 4

able for tour, and in the summer the fort reenacts battles from the French and Indian War and the American Revolution. In addition, there are demonstrations throughout the season, such as open-hearth cooking, a blacksmith weekend, and a harvest dinner. Don't miss the chance to see another 60-plus historic structures on nearby Main Street in Charlestown, all listed on the National Register of Historic Buildings.

308 Franklin Pierce Homestead

CONTACT 603-478-3165, www.nps.gov/history/nr/travel/presidents/franklin_pierce_homestead; 301 2nd NH Turnpike, Hillsborough

PRICING	$–$$
BEST TIME TO VISIT	Open weekends late May through June and September to mid-October; daily July and August
AGE RANGE	7 and older

Franklin Pierce (1804–69) was the 14th president of the United States. He started his political career in the U.S. House of Representatives and the Senate, and in 1852 was nominated as the presidential candidate for the Democratic party. Pierce and his running mate, William King, defeated the Whig party by a large margin in the electoral college in Pierce's first and only presidential bid. However, Pierce was not a popular president: Although he was a northerner—born in New Hampshire—he was accused of having southern sympathies. His administration oversaw the Kansas-Nebraska Act, which repealed the Missouri Compromise and reopened slavery in the American West—a move that arguably accelerated the Civil War. Pierce served only one term; in fact, he failed to secure his party's nomination for the next election.

The Franklin Pierce Homestead preserves 13 acres at the site of Pierce's boyhood home, where he lived until he was married. The lovely Federal-style home was built in 1804 by Pierce's father, and is a testament to Pierce's affluent upbringing. The structure includes a ballroom that takes up the entire second floor; the Pierce family used the space for entertaining other prominent families in the region. Today guests can tour the lovingly restored home to see period furnishing and artifacts. It is possible to prearrange private tours for a small fee.

309 Robert Frost Homestead

CONTACT http://robertfrostfarm.org; 122 Rockingham Rd., Derry

PRICING	$–$$
BEST TIME TO VISIT	Grounds open year-round; farmhouse and barn open mid-May through mid-October (days and hours vary by season)
AGE RANGE	7 and older

Robert Frost (1874–1963) was one of the most well-known and influential American poets of the modern era. He was born in California but moved to New Hampshire as a child, and a good deal of his writing explored farm life in New England. He enjoyed popular and critical success in his lifetime, and was awarded four Pulitzer Prizes for poetry. When he was 86 years old, Frost read his poem "The Gift Outright" at President John F. Kennedy's inauguration.

The Robert Frost Farm was home to the poet and his family from 1900 to 1911, and it was here that he wrote many of his most beloved poems, including "Tree at My Window" and "Mending Wall." The two-story clapboard farmhouse is open for guided tours.

Franklin Pierce Homestead   Courtesy National Park Service

There is also a children's garden on site, a summer lecture series—generally focused on Frost—and poetry readings on many Sundays. In warmer months, don't miss a stroll along the bucolic Hyla Brook Trail on site.

310 Strawbery Banke Museum

Lowd House, Strawbery Banke Museum

Courtesy Strawbery Banke Museum

CONTACT	603-433-1100, www.strawberybanke.org; 14 Hancock St., Portsmouth
PRICING	$$–$$$
BEST TIME TO VISIT	Open May through October
AGE RANGE	3 and older

The Strawbery Banke Museum is a living history site that showcases life across four centuries in this New England town that started out as an English settlement. In 1630 a small outpost along the Piscataqua River was named Strawbery Banke after the huge numbers of wild berries the settlers found growing along the riverbanks. By the mid-17th century the same neighborhood had become a bustling seaport that was renamed Portsmouth. And by the 19th century it morphed into a neighborhood popular with immigrants, who nicknamed it Puddle Dock. The outdoor museum comprises more than 40 historic buildings that tell the story of the hundreds of people—famous and otherwise—who passed by here through the generations, including Paul Revere, John Paul Jones, and George Washington, and portrays life in the community from the late-17th through the mid-20th centuries. The 10-acre attraction includes restored homes and shops, antique gardens, and costumed interpreters who present living history programs throughout the season. There are plenty of hands-on opportunities for kids. Come to the Discovery Center to learn period games, crafts, and help with chores; the Victorian Children's Garden, which features a beautiful tree house and a butterfly garden; and the Wheelright House, where kids can try on period clothing.

NEW JERSEY

311 Atlantic City Boardwalk

CONTACT www.atlanticcitynj.com/boardwalk.aspx; oceanside in Atlantic City

PRICING	$
BEST TIME TO VISIT	Summer
AGE RANGE	All ages

Even if you've never set foot in New Jersey, your kids will likely be familiar with Atlantic City: It was the inspiration for the board game Monopoly, and property names like Marvin Gardens (which is actually a misspelling of Marven Gardens) and Boardwalk were taken from the city and used in the game. Today Atlantic City is synonymous with high rollers and glitzy casinos—but at its heart it is still an oceanfront resort whose iconic boardwalk offers nostalgic businesses, entertaining piers, and a chance to walk along the waterfront with sand-free feet. The first boardwalk in Atlantic City (and the first in the United States) was little more than its name implies: literally a wide sidewalk made of boards. It was first built in 1870, in response to complaints by hotel owners that their guests were tracking in too much sand from the beach. A decade later the original boardwalk fell apart, so a new one was built—slightly wider and much longer. But a storm in 1884 ripped out the second boardwalk, and so a third was built, this time 20

"Rolling chairs" on the boardwalk
Courtesy New Jersey Division of Travel and Tourism

Holgate Beach
Courtesy U.S. Fish and Wildlife Service

feet wide, 2 miles long, and atop pilings, so that the tidal surges did not claim it for the ocean. Finally, in 1916, after a storm destroyed it yet again, the current version was erected. Now the boardwalk runs for 4 miles, from Absecon Inlet along the beach to the city limit. There are plenty of adult attractions in the city today, but a stroll along the boardwalk can be good family fun for everyone, and is accessible for strollers and wheelchairs. If you don't have the energy to walk the length, look for the ubiquitous "rolling chairs," a unique conveyance that allows guests to sit and be pushed in comfort. And be sure to check out the free Water Show on the Boardwalk at The Pier Shops (a retail complex connected to Caesar's Atlantic City); the entertaining waterworks are featured at the top of every hour.

312 Boxwood Hall

CONTACT 908-282-7617, www.visitnj.org/boxwoodhall; 1073 E. Jersey St., Elizabeth

PRICING	$
BEST TIME TO VISIT	Year-round; closed Sunday
AGE RANGE	5 and older

As far as historic houses go, Boxwood Hall boasts about as impressive a pedigree as can be imagined in America. In the late 18th century the Federal-style structure was home to Elias Boudinot (1740–1821), a delegate to the Continental Congress who eventually served as its president (1782–83), and was later the director of the new U.S. Mint. While Boudinot was in residence at Boxwood, he often entertained the first U.S. secretary of the treasury, Alexander Hamilton. And later, he hosted a lunch for George Washington before accompanying the soon-to-be first president to New York City for his inauguration. Boudinot sold the home to Jonathan Dayton (1760–1824), who was the youngest signer of the U.S. Constitution. Dayton served in Congress, first as a member of the U.S. House of Representatives, later as the fourth Speaker of the House, and eventually as a senator. While living at Boxwood, Dayton entertained Marquis de

PRICE KEY
$ free–$5
$$ $6–10
$$$ $11–20
$$$$ $21+

Lafayette—the French general who served in the Continental army under General Washington during the Revolutionary War.

Today the residence is maintained as a historic museum property, and is open for public tours. The main house, floors, and interior paneling are original. Guests can tour the first-floor sitting and dining rooms as well as the drawing room and library. Look for elaborately carved mantels over the fireplaces and ornate molding flourishes—and remind children while they are at Boxwood Hall that they are walking in the footsteps of America's Founders.

313 Fort Lee Historic Park

CONTACT 201-461-1776, www.njpalisades.org/flhp.htm; Hudson Terrace, Fort Lee

PRICING	$
BEST TIME TO VISIT	Spring through fall; visitor center open Wednesday through Sunday
AGE RANGE	7 and older

This remarkable park is doubly attractive: Fort Lee offers one of the most spectacular views of the Hudson River, the expansive George Washington Bridge into New York, and the skyline of Manhattan. In addition, it holds historical significance as the site where General George Washington's army was encamped during the Revolutionary War battle to defend New York City. Washington was forced to order the Continental army to retreat as British general Lord Charles Cornwallis advanced on the fort with some 6,000 soldiers. Patriot Thomas Paine described the maneuver with the famous phrase, "These are the times that try men's souls."

In the southern part of the park, guests can meander along pathways that wind past a reconstructed blockhouse, 18th-century soldiers' huts, a woodshed, and a wood-burning bread oven. Historical reenactments and patriotic celebrations are held here throughout the summer and on weekends. Don't miss the visitor center, which offers displays commemorating Washington's evacuation from the area in 1776

and his so-called retreat to victory across New Jersey. Kids will enjoy the miniature soldiers that display various styles of uniforms worn throughout the Revolutionary War, as well as weapons displays and a collection of antique medical equipment used to attend to wounded troops.

314 Monmouth Battlefield State Park

CONTACT 732-462-9616, www.nynjtc.org/park/monmouth-battlefield-state-park; 347 Freehold-Englishtown Rd., Manalapan

PRICING	$
BEST TIME TO VISIT	Summer
AGE RANGE	5 and older

In the summer of 1778, British troops aimed to march into New York and claim it as a stronghold for the Crown. General George Washington learned of the maneuver and moved some 5,000 of his men to intervene. The Continental army and the Redcoats clashed a little more than a week later, and what ensued was one of the largest battles of the American Revolutionary War. Washington and his soldiers eventually forced the British forces to retreat and claimed the battle as an American victory. It was during this prolonged fight that an American legend was born. During an artillery battle, Mary Hays—the wife of a Conti-

Reenactment at Monmouth Battlefield State Park

Photo Richard Wilber, courtesy New Jersey Division of Travel and Tourism

nental army soldier—brought water to the troops, for which she earned the nickname Molly Pitcher. When her husband was wounded during the battle, Molly Pitcher took his position of loading the cannon. It is said that General Washington himself was impressed with her bravery.

Visitors to the state park that preserves the Monmouth Battlefield will find a beautiful, peaceful expanse of rolling hills that comprises numerous horseback and hiking trails. Guests can tour the site of the important battle and also visit the Craig House, a restored Revolutionary War farmhouse, which was used as a field hospital by both armies. The newly restored visitor center is perched on a hill overlooking the battlefield, and offers a collection of artifacts from the battle, as well as a fiber-optic map that helps explain the troop movements. The battle is reenacted annually on the fourth weekend of June.

315 Morristown National Historical Park

Wick House at Morristown National Historical Park

Courtesy National Park Service

CONTACT 908-766-8215, www.nps.gov/morr; 30 Washington Place, Morristown

PRICING	$
BEST TIME TO VISIT	Spring through fall
AGE RANGE	5 and older

The Morristown National Historical Park is the two-time site of General George Washington's winter encampment during the American Revolution—and incidentally the first National Historical Park in America. The park comprises Jockey Hollow, the remains of Fort Nonsense (on a hilltop overlooking Morristown), and the Jacob Ford Mansion. Jockey Hollow is a 1,200-acre expanse that was home to 10,000 Continental army soldiers during the exceedingly harsh winters of 1777 and later 1779–80. Unfortunately, the army did not expect the especially frigid weather, and the soldiers were not trained properly in creating appropriate shelter—nor were they adequately equipped with warm clothing and food. Although they built wooden huts to protect them, an estimated 3,000 soldiers died from exposure and

disease (largely because of improper sanitation). Today at Jockey Hollow guests can view five of these reconstructed drafty huts, along with the Wick House, headquarters to General Arthur St. Clair, commander under Washington of the 3rd Pennsylvania Regiment.

General Washington fared better than his troops: He was housed safely inside the Ford Mansion—at the time the largest home in the county. Jacob Ford's widow and her four children shared the home with Washington, Alexander Hamilton, and his other staff. The general's wife, Martha Washington, spent the winter of 1779–80 here with her husband as well. Visitors today can tour the mansion, which is decorated with items of the era of Washington's encampment, including original Chippendale and Queen Anne furniture.

The park visitor center offers a collection of firearms that date to the American Revolution, as well as an auditorium that features a film explaining the significance of Morristown and the harsh winter conditions that tested General Washington's leadership skills. The park offers seasonal programs and

Tours of the Ford Mansion are offered several times a day. Tours are limited to no more than 20 people, and are available on a first-come, first-served basis. Be sure to arrive early at the contact desk inside the museum to secure your preferred time. Also note that the extensive trail system at Jockey Hollow is sometimes closed throughout the winter for deer hunting. Call ahead (973-326-7600) to determine open dates.

reenactments. A favorite with kids is Spies, in which guests take on the role of a spy during the American Revolution and learn about how Washington used espionage in his wartime strategizing.

316 Old Barracks

CONTACT 609-396-1776, www.barracks.org; 101 Barrack St., Trenton

PRICING	$$
BEST TIME TO VISIT	Year-round; closed Sunday
AGE RANGE	5 and older

The Old Barracks was built in 1758 to house British soldiers during the French and Indian War. It is best remembered as the site of the December 26, 1776, Revolutionary War Battle of Trenton, which took place after General George Washington crossed the Delaware River and led the Continental army in a clash against Hessian soldiers stationed here. Most of the forces garrisoned at Trenton were captured, and the relatively quick victory was a significant win for the Continental army. The barracks were also used as a hospital during the Revolution.

Today the living history museum is open for tours, and is the site of numerous hands-on educational activities that include military reenactments (the famous December 26 battle is re-created annually), family workshops on barracks life, living history programs that provide insight into the women of the Old Barracks, a lecture series, and summer history day camps for kids. The museum also sponsors the Colonial Times concert series, which includes an authentically costumed fife-and-drums corps.

> Nearby is the Princeton Battle Monument (adjacent to town hall in Princeton) and the Princeton Battlefield State Park (609-921-0074), where in early 1777 soldiers of General Washington's Continental army defeated a troop of British regulars.

317 Thomas Edison National Historical Park

CONTACT www.nps.gov/edis; 211 Main St., West Orange

PRICING	$–$$
BEST TIME TO VISIT	Year-round; open Wednesday through Sunday
AGE RANGE	7 and older

Thomas Alva Edison (1847–1931) was one of the most prolific American inventors in history, and today his name is synonymous with U.S. ingenuity. We have Edison to thank for innumerable items that make life a little easier and a little more enjoyable, like the phonograph (tell the kids this was a precursor of the iPod!), the motion picture camera, and a long-lasting electric lightbulb. Edison enjoyed great success during his lifetime, earning 1,093 U.S. patents—a record number for an individual that still holds. Edison also earned several hundred foreign patents from European countries.

The Thomas Edison National Historical Park preserves Edison's lab and his home. Visit the Laboratory Complex for a self-guided tour to see the inventor's library, chemistry lab, machine shop, and drafting room, and well as a collection of artifacts Edison used in his work. Kids will enjoy watching *The Great Train Robbery*, one of the earliest silent movies (dating to 1903), an innovation possible because of Edison's

Thomas Edison's laboratory   Courtesy National Park Service

work. Be sure to pick up tickets at the visitor center for a tour of nearby Glenmont, the elegant home Edison shared with his second wife, Mina. The magnificent 29-room Queen Anne Revival structure was originally built with more than 150,000 bricks, 10,000 pounds of iron, 91 windows, and seven chimneys, and today is furnished with period pieces. Look for Mina's collection of stunning ruby glassware, as well as extensive artwork throughout the home.

 You must take a guided tour through the Walt Whitman House to see the property; hours are subject to change, so call ahead to ensure that a staff member is available as guide.

318 Walt Whitman House

CONTACT 856-964-5383, www.state.nj.us/dep/parksand forests/historic/whitman; 330 Mickle Blvd., Camden

PRICING	$
BEST TIME TO VISIT	Year-round; closed Monday and Tuesday
AGE RANGE	10 and older

Walt Whitman (1819–92) was an American poet who is today remembered as the "father of the free verse" and whom critics hail as one of the most influential

Walt Whitman   Courtesy Library of Congress

figures in literary history. He self-published the first edition of his most famous collection of poetry, *Leaves of Grass*, a volume that is still studied in high schools and colleges throughout the United States (despite occasional complaints that the material is in parts overtly sexual).

Late in his life, Whitman purchased the only house he ever owned: a small two-story structure where he lived until his death. Whitman had attained an international reputation, and as a result entertained some of the most important writers of the time in this modest home, including Charles Dickens and Oscar Wilde. You can tour the personal world of the great poet at the Walt Whitman House, which contains Whitman's personal artifacts, the bed in which he died, and an enormous collection of his handwritten letters.

319 Washington Crossing State Park

CONTACT 609-737-0623, www.state.nj.us/dep/parksand forests/parks/washcros.html; 355 Washington Crossing–Pennington Rd., Titusville

PRICING	$
BEST TIME TO VISIT	Year-round
AGE RANGE	5 and older

General George Washington's crossing of the Delaware River was immortalized by artist Emanuel Leutze, who painted the romantic scene for posterity. (See the painting in person at the Metropolitan Museum of Art in New York City, described below.) Leutze took some artistic license, however: The crossing was at night, not during the day as painted; the weather was dreadful, so it isn't likely Washington would be standing at the helm of the boat (which was probably

Keeping a Travel Journal

Travel journals are a terrific way for children to chronicle their experiences—and a good way to create a meaningful souvenir that costs next to nothing. Pick up an inexpensive composition book and let your child decorate it with stickers—or spring for a beautiful bound blank journal (bookstores have dozens of options). Then set aside 10 to 15 minutes every day you're away to let them gather their thoughts and create entries. This is a good time filler when waiting for a meal at a restaurant, or an effective cool-down exercise before bed. But if your kids aren't into writing (or haven't learned how to write yet), there are other

Postcards to be assembled into a scrapbook later
© Debbie K. Hardin

options. Journaling needn't be a formal, prescribed process: Creating a journal can be as simple as keeping a running list of all the birds spotted in a forest or the state license plates seen on the road. Or sketching the interesting architecture in a city. Or collecting postcards of sites visited and sending them home to be collated later into a booklet. Or photographing fun memories along the way and then gathering them into a scrapbook. The very act of journaling will focus children—they know they will be writing/sketching/photographing important details of the trip, so they will be more inclined to pay attention along the way. And the process of compiling these details allows children to reflect on what they have seen and learned in a way that will help them make meaningful memories about what interests them most. Tip: Kids will be more inclined to keep a travel journal if they see their parents doing the same thing—so bring along blank notebooks for everyone!

getting tossed around pretty badly); and Washington himself was not then the white-haired statesmen he is remembered as from his later years as president but rather a 44-year-old who probably commanded less presence than Leutze depicted. Nevertheless, the crossing was an immensely important real-life event in the Revolutionary War: Troops from the Continental army rowed across the icy Delaware River on Christmas night 1776, landed at Johnson's Ferry (now Washington Crossing State Park), and then marched into Trenton, where they defeated the Hessian troops garrisoned at the Old Barracks. After a long, demoralizing winter, this victory was a turning point in the war, and foreshadowed Washington's successes at the Second Battle of Trenton and at Princeton.

The Washington Crossing Park in New Jersey, to-gether with the Washington Crossing Historic Park on the Pennsylvania side of the Delaware, make up the Washington's Crossing National Historic Landmark. Every Christmas dedicated reenactors re-create the historic crossing by rowing three replica boats across the river. At other times of the year, you can visit the Johnson Ferry House, an 18th-century farmhouse and tavern that General Washington and his officers used as their headquarters during the time of the 1776 crossing. The rooms are furnished with local period pieces similar to what was likely in the farmhouse during Washington's era. On weekends, this structure is the site of historic reenactments. A visitor center on site explores the military campaign dubbed "the ten crucial days," of which Washington's Delaware River crossing was a part.

Pecos National Historic Park © daveparsons.com/iStockphoto.com

NEW MEXICO

320 Albuquerque International Balloon Fiesta

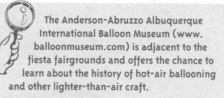

The Anderson-Abruzzo Albuquerque International Balloon Museum (www. balloonmuseum.com) is adjacent to the fiesta fairgrounds and offers the chance to learn about the history of hot-air ballooning and other lighter-than-air craft.

CONTACT 505-821-1000, www.balloonfiesta.com; Balloon Fiesta Park, 5000 Balloon Fiesta Pkwy. NE, Albuquerque

PRICING	$$
BEST TIME TO VISIT	Early October
AGE RANGE	All ages

What started out as a humble community event has *literally* ballooned into a world-renowned extravaganza that epitomizes the beauty and wide-open spaces of the southwest United States. The annual Albuquerque International Balloon Fiesta, held over nine days in early October, is the largest hot-air balloon festival in the world and arguably the most photographed single event in the country. More than 750 balloons take part in an unforgettable display of piloting, sights, and sounds.

Many days begin with a "mass ascension" in which massive numbers of hot-air balloons are launched simultaneously, in two waves. Be on the fiesta grounds before the 7:15 AM launch to see the lead balloon flying the American flag and hear the playing of "The Star Spangled Banner." Kids will enjoy the Balloon Glows, in which collections of brightly colored balloons are lighted at night by their propane burners; the balloons remain on the ground during these events, and special "glowdeos" are held to highlight

unusually shaped balloons like bumblebees, dinosaurs, and animals. Afterward there are evening fireworks. Families will enjoy walking amid the balloons throughout the days' events and having the chance to talk to balloon crews. There are also more than 200 booths on the grounds, which offer displays of New Mexico history and culture, as well as plenty of food and live entertainment.

321 Aztec Ruins National Monument

CONTACT 505-334-6174, www.nps.gov/azru; 84 County Rd., Aztec

PRICING	$
BEST TIME TO VISIT	Fall through spring
AGE RANGE	7 and older

In the 12th century ancient people in what is now northwest New Mexico began building an elaborate pueblo village crafted from mud, stones, timbers, and sandstone. During the three decades of construction, the ancient peoples cleared more than 2.5 acres of land, harvested and carried log beams from forests miles away, and laid out handcrafted blocks to create solid perimeter walls. Included within this settlement near the Animas River was a great house that reached three stories high and contained as many as 500 rooms and a 40-foot-diameter kiva (a structure used for religious and ceremonial purposes), as well as several smaller structures. The site was used over a 200-year period. Historians believe that the Ancestral Puebloans eventually left the area because water was scarce or land they used for agriculture became infertile.

Like many other ancient Native archaeological sites, the Aztec Ruins were misnamed by early set-

Albuquerque International Balloon Fiesta
Photo Mike Stauffer, courtesy New Mexico Tourism Department

Aztec Ruins National Monument Courtesy National Park Service

tlers, who stubbornly refused to believe that the ancestors of the modern-day Indians they encountered were capable of creating such a sophisticated settlement. Instead, they attributed the remains of the pueblo to people of the Aztec Empire in Mexico. These days the sacred site is protected as a national park, and guests can explore the pueblo via an easy 700-yard interpretive trail that winds through to the West Ruin, the excavated great house. While here, encourage your children to look for the fingerprints of the workers who built this construction, which are still preserved in the handmade bricks. The park offers ranger talks through the year, as well as demonstrations of Native arts and crafts. A visitor center on site includes a museum of excavated artifacts and a theater that screens a 25-minute video exploring the pre-Columbian history of the region.

322 Bandelier National Monument

CONTACT 505-672-3861, www.nps.gov/band; 15 Entrance Rd., Los Alamos

PRICING	$
BEST TIME TO VISIT	Fall through spring
AGE RANGE	7 and older

Bandelier National Monument is a hidden gem, offering pristine views of deep canyons, verdant mesas, and exceptionally blue sky (something about the light in New Mexico seems to make natural colors pop in a way they don't elsewhere in the country). But the 23,000-acre monument also preserves several thousand Ancestral Pueblo dwellings, strewn throughout the park and remarkably accessible to the curious tourist, as well as petroglyphs, a form of early rock art. Ancestral Puebloans lived here starting around 1150, and occupied the region for about 400 years. They hunted and farmed the land and built homes carved into the very cliffs—which is actually volcanic tuff and thus relatively easy to sculpt.

Because of the incredible natural beauty, and because of the somewhat haunted sense you get from treading through the now-abandoned structures of an ancient culture, a visit to this national monument is a quiet revelation. It takes some perseverance to see the sights here, however. There are dozens of trails that will take you past the most impressive sites. The Main Loop Trail is arguably the best for families; this 1.2-mile loop trail is partially paved, with some steep stone steps, and will take you past the Big Kiva, Long House, Talus House, and Tyuony dwellings. There are ladders along the trail that will allow guests to climb up into the carved structures—although beware if anyone in your party is afraid of heights: It's a lot scarier coming down these wooden ladders than it is going up. The Tsankawi section of the park offers several short trails that also pass by intriguing sites, like the Ancestral Puebloan village of Tsankawi, cavates (caves initially carved by the elements and then augmented by human excavation), and several fine examples of petroglyphs. Once again, expect to climb steep ladders to get the best views of the cliff structures.

Petroglyphs at Bandelier National Monument
Courtesy National Park Service

Don't miss the charming visitor center, which exhibits a collection of contemporary Pueblo art, including pottery and paintings. The center provides a 10-minute video that introduces the history of the monument.

323 Bradbury Science Museum

CONTACT 505-667-4444, www.lanl.gov/museum; 1350 Central Ave., Los Alamos

PRICING	$
BEST TIME TO VISIT	Year-round
AGE RANGE	10 and older

Well before the United States's involvement in World War II, American and Allied leaders feared German chancellor Adolf Hitler's government would sponsor and build an atomic bomb. Even Albert Einstein, who was an outspoken opponent of war, urged President Franklin Roosevelt to spearhead the development of an American atomic bomb to address the possibility of a Nazi force wielding atomic weapons. Roosevelt agreed that it was vital that the United States be the first to develop atomic capabilities, and undertook a top-secret mission—code-named the Manhattan Project—for just this purpose.

There were sites around the country involved in the Manhattan Project. In the early 1940s, the U.S. government appropriated a private school in a remote section of New Mexico and converted it into the headquarters for the research and development of the atomic bomb. The resulting Los Alamos National Laboratory was populated by some of the most influential scientists in the world, including Einstein, physicist J. Robert Oppenheimer, Enrico Fermi, and Harold Urey. The mission was so secret that employees at the facility simply referred to Los Alamos as "the Hill," and the infrastructure that grew up around the lab was largely anonymous—the streets were unnamed, houses were unnumbered, and even the personnel were identified by numbers rather than names on documents like income tax returns and bank accounts. Within a few years, the Manhattan Project comprised close to 40 facilities and employed 200,000 people. Together this secret coalition discovered how to convert the power of fission into a nuclear weapon. The first atomic bomb was assembled and tested about 200 miles from Los Alamos (in Alamagordo, New Mexico) in the summer of 1945. Within a few weeks, then president Harry Truman authorized that the new bombs be used against Japan: The 9,000-pound bomb code-named Little Boy was dropped on Hiroshima on August 6, 1945, killing more than 60,000 people instantly and obliterating the landscape 1 mile in diameter. A few days later, an even larger bomb, nicknamed Fat Man, was dropped on Nagasaki, with similarly devastating effects. The Japanese Empire surrendered shortly afterward, effectively ending the conflict in the Pacific Theater and ending World War II.

The Bradbury Museum (named after a scientist who worked at the lab, not the science-fiction writer) is on the site of the Los Alamos National Lab and offers more than 40 hands-on exhibits that chronicle the Manhattan Project and educate visitors about the lab's contemporary focus on life sciences, space, and energy. Visit the Demo Stage for live lectures and demonstrations by science staff, and then join in to participate in experiments and interactive exhibits in the TechLab. Be sure to visit the History Gallery to view the 15-minute film that tells the story of *The Town That Never Was*, a fascinating video that focuses on the extreme secrecy maintained in Los Alamos during the Manhattan Project. The museum offers a number of artifacts and declassified documents from World War II, including full-sized replicas of the Little Boy and Fat Man atomic bombs.

324 Carlsbad Caverns National Park

CONTACT 505-785-2232, www.nps.gov/cave; 3225 National Parks Hwy., Carlsbad

PRICING	$–$$
BEST TIME TO VISIT	Year-round
AGE RANGE	5 and older

Carlsbad Caverns National Park is an underground fantasy world, full of whimsical geological formations that are sure to excite the imagination. This park in southern New Mexico comprises 113 underground caves, formed some 200 million years ago when percolating sulfuric acid dissolved the surrounding limestone. In the years since, stalagmites (those geological features that rise from the floor of the caverns) and stalactites (those features that hang from the ceilings of the caves) slowly took shape as the by-product of dissolving stone. The end result is a collection of evocative natural sculptures that have a surprising amount of personality. Kids will get a kick out of the feature names, many of which are silly and descriptive, like Witch's Finger, Caveman, Longfellow's Bathtub, Texas Toothpick, Christmas Tree, and Queen's Draperies.

Guests can take self-guided walks or ranger-led tours through a series of caves. First-timers (and anyone who is a bit claustrophobic) should start out with the hour-long Big Room Tour, which begins with an 800-foot descent by elevator. The tour follows a paved and lighted pathway (which can be slippery; be sure to wear appropriate shoes) and ends up in the largest cave room in the park, which is roughly the size of six football fields. It's here where you'll find the largest formations, including the 62-foot stalagmite called Giant Dome. To see evidence that the cave is still a work in progress, check out the Crystal Spring Dome, an active stalagmite that grows a little bit with each mineral-laden drop of water that splashes over it.

True spelunkers should try the Slaughter Canyon Tour for a more authentic experience. Or for those who have no problems with dark spaces and who want to wriggle and crawl through tight quarters, the Spider Cave Tour is a favorite. (Expect to get very dirty on this adventure.)

If you visit in the summer, don't miss the nightly exodus of bats from the Natural Entrance: At twilight, nearly 400,000 resident bats swarm the skies every minute as they begin their nocturnal feeding routine. Park rangers conduct an evening talk to coincide with

Tours of Carlsbad Caverns book up quickly, especially for the less developed caves. Call ahead to 877-444-6777 to make advance reservations.

"Dolls Theater," Carlsbad Caverns   Courtesy National Park Service

the bat flight. In late October and into November, the bats migrate to Mexico for the winter; they return in midspring. The largest grouping of bats leaving the caves is normally seen in July and August. If you want to beat the sunrise, come to the cave entrance before dawn to see the bats as they reenter the caves.

325 Chaco Culture National Historical Park

CONTACT 505-786-7014, www.nps.gov/chcu/index.htm; off U.S. 550, Nageezi

PRICING	$
BEST TIME TO VISIT	Spring and fall
AGE RANGE	7 and older

Chaco Culture National Historic Park preserves one of the most important pre-Columbian historical and archaeological site in the United States. The extensive ruins of the Ancestral Puebloan culture that existed from the mid-800s through about 1100 show a remarkable level of sophistication for such an early civilization and paint a portrait of a highly articulated society with a complex community structure. The area is noteworthy because of its unique building structure and the massive scale of the public and ceremonial buildings, as well as many notable petroglyphs. Many of the buildings are oriented to the cardinal directions, or are otherwise arranged to mimic the patterns of the sun and the moon. A total of 150

Chetro Ketl, Chaco Culture National Historical Park
Courtesy National Park Service

Georgia O'Keeffe Museum
Photo Robert Peck, © Georgia O'Keeffe Museum. Used with permission.

Great Houses—enormous stone buildings that contain hundreds of rooms—are interconnected with an extensive road system, and include astronomical markers, water transportation systems, and protective earthen mounds. Visiting these ancient sites is a remarkable opportunity to get a glimpse into the long-ago past and the stark beauty of the surroundings.

Take the 9-mile loop drive through the park to access the most important sites in Chaco Canyon, including Casa Rinconada, Chetro Ketl, and Pueblo Bonito. Pueblo Bonita is the largest Great House in the park, spanning nearly 2 acres and including 650 rooms. The 3-foot masonry walls stretched to four stories high. The sites are extremely fragile and are remarkably open to visitors, so tread lightly in this ancient place.

If you're here at night, don't miss a visit to the Chaco Observatory, which offers superlative views of a relatively light-free environment—ideal for stargazing. Come during May and September for "Star Parties" sponsored by the Albuquerque Astronomical Society.

Georgia O'Keeffe (1887–1986) was an artist who redefined American style with a unique vision and a staggering work ethic: In her long life O'Keeffe is known to have completed 2,029 painting and sculptures. She is best remembered for her abstract, close-up depictions of flowers. In her later years she fell in love with and moved to New Mexico, and came to focus her attention on the southwestern imagery that surrounded her, including the stark landscape and the lyrical architecture. The Georgia O'Keeffe Museum boasts the largest collection of O'Keeffe's work in the world, with close to 1,200 pieces by O'Keeffe herself and nearly 2,000 by artists who were her contemporaries. The museum sponsors family art workshops that include collage making, watercolor painting, and rain stick construction.

326 Georgia O'Keeffe Museum

CONTACT 505-946-1000, www.okeeffemuseum.org; 217 Johnson St., Santa Fe

PRICING	$–$$$
BEST TIME TO VISIT	Year-round
AGE RANGE	7 and older

327 Palace of the Governors

CONTACT 505-476-5100, www.palaceofthegovernors.org; 105 W. Palace Ave., Santa Fe

PRICING	$–$$
BEST TIME TO VISIT	Year-round; closed Monday except in summer
AGE RANGE	All ages

Vendors outside Palace of the Governors

Photo Chris Corrie, courtesy Santa Fe Convention and Visitors Bureau

For millennia the American Southwest was populated by a rich and highly sophisticated Native population. A large portion of this area, including the region now known as New Mexico, was colonized by Spain in the late 16th century and later became part of Mexico in 1821. The territory was ceded to the United States in 1848 via the Treaty of Guadalupe Hidalgo, and become a state in 1912. This rich and varied history makes the city of Santa Fe one of the best places in America to see a blending of cultures—and this is especially in ev-

Also on or nearby the Santa Fe Plaza are three historic churches worth exploring: Check out the beautiful Cathedral Basilica of St. Francis Assisi (131 Cathedral Place) built by Archbishop Jean Baptist Lamy in the late 19th century on the site of a destroyed adobe church that dates to 1626. Also nearby is the smaller but equally lovely Loretto Chapel (207 Old Santa Fe Trail), famous for its helix-shaped spiral staircase that seems to defy all laws of physics—the construction of which is sometimes attributed to a miracle. Finally, the San Miguel Mission (401 Old Santa Fe Trail) dates to 1600, and is believed to be the oldest surviving church in the country. Despite many repairs and restorations over the years, the adobe walls are largely original.

idence at the Palace of the Governors, on the highly popular and historic Santa Fe Plaza. The Palace of the Governors is the oldest continuously occupied building in the United States, dating to 1610. It was built by the first Spanish governor of the region. The low-slung adobe structure served as a territorial capital and the governor's residence until America's assumption of control in the mid-19th century. Today the elegant building is part of the Museum of New Mexico, and offers exhibits that tell the story of both the city of Santa Fe and the now-state of New Mexico. There are more than 15,000 items on display that chronicle the Spanish colonial, Mexican, U.S. territorial, and current eras. Among the most interesting items in the collection are the Segesser Hide Paintings, which represent the earliest known depictions of colonial life in America. Outside the building contemporary Native American artisans display and sell handmade jewelry, exquisite pottery, sand paintings, and other artifacts beneath the covering of the portal (or porch).

328 Pecos National Historical Park

CONTACT 505-757-6032, www.nps.gov/peco; off Hwy. 63, Pecos

PRICING	$
BEST TIME TO VISIT	Summer
AGE RANGE	7 and older

The Pecos Pueblo, near what is now Santa Fe, was the largest Native American pueblo in the Southwest, home to more than 2,000 people and an integral part of the trade route between the farming Puebloans and the hunters of the Great Plains. The pueblo was also a supply stop along the Santa Fe Trail. During the Spanish colonial era, missionaries built a church here, the remains of which are still in evidence. The pueblo was active for more than 400 years, but was abandoned in the 19th century.

Today the Pecos National Historical Park preserves the ruins of the Pecos Pueblo and what's left of its Spanish mission. A 1.25-mile self-guided trail winds through the expansive pueblo and mission

Pecos Pueblo Photo Mike Stauffer, courtesy New Mexico Tourism Department

Petroglyph National Monument
Courtesy National Park Service, Petroglyph National Monument

grounds. The visitor center offers an introduction video on the pueblo, as well as an interpretive exhibit that explains the time line of the settlement. Although the summertime weather in this area can be brutal—expect temperatures over 90 degrees—the season offers the best chance to view fascinating cultural demonstrations in the park. Past events have included classes in bread making, pottery, medicinal herbs, and musical-instrument crafting.

329 Petroglyph National Monument

CONTACT 505-899-0205, www.nps.gov/petr; 6001 Unser Blvd. NW, Albuquerque

PRICING	$
BEST TIME TO VISIT	Year-round
AGE RANGE	7 and older

The Petroglyph National Monument preserves more than 20,000 ancient petroglyphs—images carved into the face of rock. Hundreds of years ago Native peoples etched the images of animals, human figures,

The entrance pass purchased for Pecos National Historical Park is also good also for a visit during the same seven-day period to the Fort Union National Monument (www.nps.gov/foun) in Watrous.

and geometric shapes into the "desert varnish"—a patina of clay particles that give the exterior coat of rocks a much darker color than the stone beneath. The majority of the images were carved by Ancestral Puebloans between 1300 and 1650. Some 5 to 10 percent were carved by Spanish sheepherders who came to the region as colonists; these petroglyphs often take the shape of crosses or cattle brands. The meanings of the images created by Ancestral Puebloans are less clear: Some believe that these are sacred symbols that mark the movement of the soul of a departed individual.

The park also preserves five volcanic cones and hundreds of archaeological sites. There are several excellent trails, of varying difficulty, that allow close examination of the park's features. Be sure to pick up a trail guide at the visitor center—and carry *lots* of water. Even in cooler months, the low humidity in the region can lead to dehydration during physical exertion.

330 Puye Cliff Dwellings

CONTACT 888-320-5008, www.puyecliffs.com; NM 30 and Santa Clara Canyon Rd., Espanola

PRICING	$$$–$$$$
BEST TIME TO VISIT	Spring (closed the week before Easter and periodically for other holidays)
AGE RANGE	7 and older

Puye Cliff Dwellings © Debbie K. Hardin

Puye Cliffs was the mountainside home to 1,500 Ancestral Puebloans, who lived here from about 900 until 1580. Multiroom homes were carved out of the sheer face of a mile-long cliff, and timber was brought in for support beams. The fascinating site includes two levels of cliff and cave dwellings carved into the soft tuff stone and also the ruins of freestanding structures at the top of the mesa. The Ancestral Puebloans carved stairways into the rock to access the cliff dwellings, and included toe- and fingerholds. Today visitors can access the charming structures via numerous pathways as well as by wooden ladders. The kiva at the top of the mesa—a sacred ceremonial site—is open to visitors as well. You can explore the area via the somewhat steep Cliff Trail, which can be picked up at the visitor center, and follow it up to the cliff dwellings and the 700-room Community House at the top of the mesa, or drive directly to the top of the mesa and walk from the parking area. Descendants of the Puye Puebloans, the Santa Clara Indians, own and manage the site, and also offer informative guided tours that provide historical and cultural details. Visit during spring to see a riot of wildflowers. As with many of the southwestern attractions that include cliff dwellings, it is important to overcome any fear of heights you might have to make the most out of a visit to Puye; you're absolutely going to want to climb up to the cliff dwellings, so make sure everyone in your party is up to the task.

331 Salinas Pueblo Missions National Monument

CONTACT	505-847-2585, www.nps.gov/sapu; visitor center at the corner of Ripley and Broadway, Mountainair
PRICING	$
BEST TIME TO VISIT	Year-round
AGE RANGE	7 and older

The history of American colonization is inextricably bound to the newcomers' interference with the Native cultures already occupying the land—even when the newcomers' intentions were good. Throughout the Southwest, including the region that is now New Mexico, ancient peoples lived off the land, some leading nomadic hunter-gather lifestyles and, later, cultivating crops and learning to harness the available water. Complex cultures called the region home for thousands of years before Europeans arrived. At the site of what is now known as the Salinas Pueblo Missions, Tiwa- and Tompiro-speaking Ancestral Puebloans were involved in a sophisticated trade system here. They lived in communal dwellings—pueblos—which are a little like modern-day apartments, with many families sharing the larger space. In the early 17th century, Spanish missionaries moved into the area with the goal of bringing Christianity to the Natives. Their successes were equivocal: Some Natives converted to Roman Catholicism by choice, and some by coercion. Others fled their homes to avoid the mis-

Salinas Pueblo Missions National Monument
Photo Mike Stauffer, courtesy New Mexico Tourism Department

sionaries, and still others succumbed to diseases the missionaries brought for which the Natives had no immunity. By the late 1670s the region was abandoned, by both the Spanish missionaries and the Puebloans.

The Salinas Pueblo Missions National Monument preserves the remains of three missions and accompanying Native structures, and provides insight into the lifestyle and ambitions of the Spaniards who came to what for them must have seemed like a very desolate landscape. The haunting ruins of their mission churches at Abó, Gran Quivera, and Quarai, along with the partially excavated pueblo at Gran Quivira, are a reminder of the earliest contact between southwestern Natives and Europeans bent on enlightening them. Start your exploration at the visitor center in Mountainair, which offers trail maps and information on the individual sites. The Abó Ruins are 9 miles west of the visitor center; you can view the beautiful church architecture here, as well as an unexcavated pueblo. The Gran Quivira Ruins are 26 miles south of the visitor center, and comprise two churches, excavated Native dwellings, and interpretive exhibits at a small on-site museum. The Quarai Ruins are 8 miles north of the visitor center and boast the most intact church in the region. There are easy trails that loop past the partial buildings and offer views of the austere scenery.

332 Taos Pueblo

CONTACT 505-758-9593, www.taospueblo.com; 120 Veterans Hwy., Taos

PRICING	$–$$ (plus camera fees should you wish to take photographs)
BEST TIME TO VISIT	Late spring, fall; the pueblo closes to the public for 10 weeks in the late winter and early spring, and periodically for sacred ceremonial days
AGE RANGE	All ages

Unlike many pueblos throughout the Southwest, which are abandoned and in various stages of ruin,

Taos Pueblo   Photo by Cameron Martinez Jr., courtesy Taos Pueblo

the Taos Pueblo is beautifully intact and home to a vibrant community made up of Puebloan people whose ancestors have lived here for close to 1,000 years. The pueblo is sited on a reservation that is close to 100,000 acres and is inhabited by nearly 2,000 individuals. It is the largest surviving Pueblo structure in the world.

The Taos Pueblo represents an opportunity to learn about Native American culture firsthand: On feast days, it is possible to witness performances of ancient songs and dances. It is important to help children understand that such performances are not entertainment but rather sacred and traditional ceremonial dances: Such events should not be photographed or videotaped; outsiders should not attempt to join in, nor should they applaud. This is also an excellent place to view and perhaps purchase finely crafted art pieces, such as mica-flecked pottery, exquisite silver jewelry, and handcrafted moccasins. Guests may also visit the San Geronimo Chapel, which dates to 1850; the active Catholic church was built to replace a church from 1619 that was destroyed.

> When visiting the Taos Pueblo, keep in mind that you should not photograph residents without first asking (and receiving) their permission, and you may not photograph inside San Geronimo. Also, the ruins of the old church and the cemetery are off limits to guests.

NEW YORK

333 9/11 Memorial

CONTACT 212-266.5211, www.911memorial.org; 1 Albany St., New York City

PRICING	$
BEST TIME TO VISIT	Year-round
AGE RANGE	All ages

On the morning of September 11, 2001, America awoke to a nightmare: In a series of suicide terrorist attacks undertaken by members of the extremist organization al Qaeda, for the first time since the Japanese attacks on Pearl Harbor during World War II Americans were under siege in our own country. In coordinated attacks, two hijacked passenger jets piloted by al Qaeda militants flew into each of the Twin Towers of the World Trade Center in Lower Manhattan; another jet crashed into the Pentagon in Washington, DC. A fourth was thwarted in an attempt to destroy yet another target in the nation's capital: Passengers aboard the fourth jet learned of the hijackers' plot and overpowered them; the plane crashed in a field near Shanksfield, Pennsylvania. Close to 3,000 people were killed in the attacks, including the passengers aboard all four planes as well as the 19 hijackers. The audacity and brutality of the terrorist events shocked Americans and citizens of countries around the world and changed—perhaps forever—our perception of our own vulnerability.

> ## For the first time since the attacks on Pearl Harbor Americans were under siege in our own country.

Emblematic of the attacks were the smoldering remains of the World Trade Center, the two 110-floor towers of which collapsed within hours of the initial attack. Rescue crews, and soon recovery crews, worked tirelessly in the days and weeks afterward to find victims. For several years the site was dubbed Ground Zero, and the scorched earth itself became a memorial to the thousands of victims. After some political disagreements about how best to commemorate the tragedy, a design contest for a permanent memorial was held. The memorial ultimately chosen is titled *Reflecting Absence*, which consists of a pair of black granite craters dug into the footprints of the Twin Towers. The dramatic voids create human-made waterfalls that plunge into reflective pools. Engraved on 76 bronze plates attached to the memorial are the names of the 2,977 victims who were killed on 9/11—in New York; in Arlington, Virginia; and in Pennsylvania—as well as six individuals who were killed in an earlier 1993 World Center bombing. As part of the greater 9/11 Memorial, there will also be a museum chronicling the events, as well as a park.

In addition, it was decided almost immediately that a new skyscraper would be built here. The result is the new building once called Freedom Tower and now called One World Trade Center (or 1 WTC), a 104-story structure that sits adjacent to the memorial. Once the final floors were in place, it was among the tallest buildings in the Western Hemisphere: It stretches to 1,776 feet from ground level, a symbolic nod to America's year of independence.

Ground Zero under construction

Carol M. Highsmith's America, Library of Congress, Prints and Photographs Division

> Additional memorials to the victims of the September 11, 2001, terrorist attacks are in the works or have already been constructed, including the Flight 93 National Memorial (2 miles north of Shanksville) in Pennsylvania and the Pentagon Memorial in Arlington, Virginia.

334 Apollo Theater

CONTACT 212-531-5300, www.apollotheater.com; 253 W. 125 St., New York City

PRICING	Varies by performance
BEST TIME TO VISIT	Year-round
AGE RANGE	12 and older

The world-famous Apollo Theater in the Manhattan neighborhood of Harlem (historically a predominantly African American area) is one of the premier music venues in the country. The Apollo was especially important during the Harlem Renaissance, a prolific time beginning in the 1920s, after World War I, and continuing into the 1930s, for artists of all genres. The movement included musicians, authors, and visual artists in Harlem, and had far-reaching influences, including French-speaking black writers living in Paris. Despite the burgeoning art scene and the incredible talent this artistic era spawned, racism had a stronghold in America in the early 20th century, and thus African American artists had limited venues in which to exhibit and perform. The Apollo Theater was for many years the only theater in New York City that would hire African Americans.

The roster of musical artists who built the foundations of their career at the Apollo is astonishing: Ella Fitzgerald debuted in 1934 at only 17 years old at the Apollo; other notables who performed here over the decades since include James Brown, Mariah Carey, Aretha Franklin, Jimi Hendrix, Diana Ross, Luther Vandross, and Stevie Wonder.

Guests can schedule a tour (212-531-5337) daily, to see the interior of the theater and to hear countless stories of the stars who have performed here. To experience the venue in all its glory, attend a performance or check out the very popular Amateur Night—a precursor to TV shows like *American Idol* and *America's Got Talent*.

Apollo Theater   Courtesy NYC and Co.

335 Baseball Hall of Fame

CONTACT 888-HALL-OF-FAME, http://baseballhall.org/; 25 Main St., Cooperstown

PRICING	Adults $20, children $7
BEST TIME TO VISIT	Year-round
AGE RANGE	All ages

Baseball has long been considered "America's pastime," even though it's likely the game evolved from sports played in other countries, including an English game called rounders. As early as the 18th century, however, Americans were playing some version of baseball: There's a 1791 Massachusetts statute that prohibited anyone from playing the game within 80 yards of the meetinghouse in Pittsfield. The earliest game rules (known as the Knickerbocker Rules) were written in 1844 by Alexander Cartwright (*not* Abner Doubleday, as is often believed). The first baseball game that was ever recorded in the United States was between the semiprofessional Knickerbockers and the New York Baseball Club. The first all-professional team was the Cincinnati Red Stockings. Today nearly every major American city boasts a professional baseball team, each of which has an avid following.

The National Baseball Hall of Fame and Museum chronicles the history of baseball in America and offers a huge display of baseball artifacts. Start off your visit at the Grandstand Theater to see a 12-minute film in a venue with reproduction stadium seats that is designed to look like Comiskey Park, the former ballpark where the Chicago White Sox played for

PRICE KEY
$ free—$5
$$ $6—10
$$$ $11—20
$$$$ $21+

National Baseball Hall of Fame Library

Courtesy National Baseball Hall of Fame Library, Cooperstown, NY

TKTS booths (in Duffy Square, in Times Square, in Lower Manhattan, and in Brooklyn) sell same-day tickets (and sometimes next-day matinee tickets) for selected Broadway shows. These tickets are generally sold for between 25 and 50 percent less. If you go to the theater box offices directly, also, you'll find that many Broadway venues offer student rates, standing-room-only tickets, and even same-day "rush" tickets, also at significant discounts.

decades. On the second floor, check out the immense collection of historical items, arranged in a time line. Special exhibits include a display dedicated to women in baseball, an exhibition solely on Babe Ruth, and an exhibit on the so-called Negro Leagues. Kids will enjoy the *Today's Game* exhibit, which is designed to look like a baseball clubhouse. Guests can peek into glass-enclosed lockers, one representing each major-league team; inside are jerseys and a team history. On the third floor, the Records Room houses the stats for every baseball category you can imagine. The *Sacred Ground* exhibit examines ballparks around the country, including computer tours of three now-extinct parks (Boston's South End Grounds, Brooklyn's Ebbets Field, and Chicago's Comiskey Park).

336 Broadway Theaters

CONTACT Websites and addresses vary by venue; between W. 40th St. and W. 54th St., between 6th Ave. and 9th Ave., New York City

PRICING	Tickets vary by venue
BEST TIME TO VISIT	Year-round (theaters are generally closed on Monday)
AGE RANGE	7 and older

"The Great White Way," the eclectic and exciting theater district in the Manhattan borough of New York City, is the heart of theatrical arts in the United States. Theater has its roots in the city as far back as the 1700s, when the first theater was built on Massau Street; grand theaters were built starting shortly after the American Revolution, and Broadway grew in

prominence well into the 20th century. Starting in the early 1900s, Broadway theaters lit up the night with dazzling white lights as a way to advertise their shows, and today a stroll through the district at night is an impressive sight. There are now 40 professional theaters in the district (each must have 500 or more seats to be considered "on Broadway"), although only a handful are actually on Broadway street, and they stage a variety of genres, from the ubiquitous musicals to drama to one-person shows. With a little research, it's easy to find family-appropriate live entertainment on Broadway—and the revitalization of the area in the late 20th century means that the atmosphere is generally family-tolerant.

Most theaters offer evening performances Tuesday through Saturday, with matinee shows on the weekends and sometimes on Wednesday. Theaters are generally "dark" (closed) on Monday. Most curtain times are 8 PM, but some kid-oriented shows start at 7 PM. There are a couple of strategies for securing tickets to a Broadway show: To ensure the best seats, and to guarantee you see the show of your choice, purchase tickets as early as possible online (often this

Times Square

Photo Jen Davis, courtesy NYC and Co.

means planning months in advance). But if you wind up in New York City *without* tickets, there are still a couple of options: Top-ranked hotels often hold tickets for their guests to purchase (although be prepared to pay top dollar), and there are often tickets available at the box office a few days before a performance (or even the day of), especially if the show has been running for some time—although don't expect to get premier seating. If you are traveling with older children, consider sitting in single seats for the best opportunity to squeeze in at the last minute. There are also TKTS booths throughout the city that sell same-day seats at a discount (see above).

Central Park   Photo Alex Lopez, courtesy NYC and Co.

337 Central Park

CONTACT www.centralparknyc.org; bounded by W. 110th St., W. 59th St., 8th Ave., and 5th Ave. (along the park's borders, these streets are known as Central Park North, Central Park South, and Central Park West respectively; 5th Ave. along the park's eastern border keeps its name)

PRICING	$
BEST TIME TO VISIT	Year-round
AGE RANGE	All ages

Central Park in Manhattan is the most recognized city park in America, and a familiar sight from movies and television shows. The expansive public park in the heart of New York City is 2.5 miles long and half a mile wide, and the beautiful and naturalistic landscaping includes bridle paths, two ice-skating rinks (one of which converts to a swimming pool in the summer), walking and jogging trails, a 100-acre reservoir encircled with a running track, several smaller lakes and ponds, streams traversed by lovely stone bridges, seven major lawns, meadows, sports fields, and 21 playgrounds and tot lots.

In addition to providing a charming spot of green in an otherwise concrete-glass-and-steel borough, the park has numerous cultural and recreational highlights, including the following:

- **Alice in Wonderland Sculpture** (East Side at 75th St.): This charming bronze sculpture of the Lewis Carroll character and her friends is a favorite with children.
- **Belvedere Castle** (mid-park at 79th St.): This whimsical structure looks over the Great Lawn and the reservoir, and is a favorite photo op.
- **Central Park Carousel** (mid-park at 64th St.): This historic merry-go-round is one of the largest in the United States, with 58 hand-carved horses and two chariots. Although it was installed in 1951, it dates to the turn of the 20th century and was originally sited at nearby Coney Island in Brooklyn.
- **Central Park Zoo** (East Side between 63rd and 66th Sts.): This popular zoo is home to an indoor rain forest, a polar bear pool, and a penguin house, among many other attractions.
- **Cleopatra's Needle** (East Side at 81st St.): This ancient obelisk was constructed in Egypt in about 1450 BC to commemorate a pharaoh's anniversary, and moved to Central Park in the late 19th century.
- **Conservatory Garden** (East Side at 104th through 106th Sts.): This formal garden comprises three smaller gardens, each with its own style: English, French, and Italian. Come during the early spring and be dazzled by blooms.
- **Delacorte Theater** (mid-park at 80th St., on the southwest corner of the Great Lawn): This lovely outdoor amphitheater is the site of live performances in the summer, particularly the Shakespeare in the Park summer festival.
- **Heckscher Playground** (West Side at 79th St.): This 3-acre playground is the largest in Central Park, and well populated in all but the wettest, coldest New York weather.

- **Model Boat Pond** (East Side from 72nd to 75th Sts.): This pretty pond is home to wooden model boats that are steered via radio or wind power, and is reminiscent of the *bateaux* ponds in the gardens in Paris. Rent miniature vessels at the Kerbs Memorial Boathouse nearby from April through October.
- **Shakespeare Garden** (West Side at 79th and 80th Sts.): This pretty garden is planted with the flowers and herbs mentioned by the English poet and playwright in his extensive published works.
- **Swedish Cottage Marionette Theater** (West Side at 79th St.): The Swedish Cottage structure that is home to marionette shows in the park was built as a model schoolhouse in Sweden, and expertly crafted of pine and cedar. Landscape architect Frederick Law Olmsted disassembled the building and rebuilt it at the present site in 1877.

338 Coney Island

CONTACT www.coneyisland.com; Coney Island peninsula, between W. 8th and W. 24th, from Surf Ave. to the Atlantic, New York City

PRICING	Prices vary by attraction
BEST TIME TO VISIT	Summer
AGE RANGE	5 and older

We have Coney Island to thank for the modern American amusement park: "America's Playground," as it has been called, is an entertainment zone comprising more than 50 attractions, sited on a small peninsula that extends from the south edge of the borough of Brooklyn. Although the misnamed "island" includes residential sections, Coney Island is best known for the amusement attractions that run from West 8th to West 24 Streets, from Surf Avenue to the ocean.

> Check out the tiny Coney Island Museum (1208 Surf Ave.), open Thursday through Sunday, which proudly exhibits artifacts salvaged from the historic rides in Coney Island.

Cyclone Rollercoaster, Coney Island

Photo Bami Abedoyin, courtesy NYC and Co.

Coney Island attractions go back to the early 1800s—and the attractions are myriad. It's said that the American hot dog was invented here (still for sale here at Nathan's Famous). Today the amusement area includes a 3-mile beachfront boardwalk, several individually managed amusement parks and rides, the New York Aquarium, a minor-league baseball park, the Abe Stark skating rink, the antique B&B Carousel, the Coney Island Arcade, and even a collection of circus acts at Sideshows by the Seashore. Thrill seekers will not want to miss the Cyclone, a wooden coaster that dates to 1927; this classic roller coaster includes an 85-foot drop and plenty of shimmying and shaking to remind you that this ride has been around for almost 90 years.

339 Ellis Island

CONTACT www.nps.gov/elis; Liberty Island, New York Harbor (south of Lower Manhattan, New York City); ferries depart from Battery Park, 1 Battery Place, New York; and Liberty State Park, 1 Audrey Zapp Dr., Jersey City, NJ

PRICING	$$–$$$ (for ferry tickets)
BEST TIME TO VISIT	Year-round
AGE RANGE	All ages

Throughout the nation's history, immigration has been vitally important to the United States. For much of our past, immigration was a major contributing factor to population growth as well as cultural change—and immigration has always been a hot-button issue for politicians. Ellis Island is symbolic of the ebb and flow of immigrants to the United States, and remains a fascinating link to the ancestry of many Americans. It is estimated that as many as 40 percent of us can trace at least one of our ancestors back to immigrants who passed through Ellis Island.

The facilities at Ellis Island were collectively the largest immigration inspection station in the United States from 1892 until 1954. More than 20 million Americans were processed at the site; a typical inspection took from three to seven hours, and included a basic physical and an interview. About 2 percent were turned back—leading some to nickname the site the "Island of Tears." The island sits in New York Harbor, in the Upper New York Bay, and includes nearly 28 acres—most of which was created through land reclamation. Although the original 3.3 acres of land that the island included is part of New York City, the reclaimed land is actually part of Jersey City, New Jersey.

Today guests can visit the site, although it is accessible by ferry only—no private boats are allowed to dock at the island for security reasons. The 45-minute audio tour allows visitors to experience the facility as an immigrant might have, guiding them through the stations in the order an immigrant would have gone through. (If you're visiting with young kids, check out the children's tour, which is offered in five languages.) Be sure to tour the Ellis Island Immigration Museum, which is sited in the main building of the former immigration station complex. The self-guided exhibits within the museum include a plethora of photo-

Ellis Island Courtesy Aramark Parks and Destinations

graphs, oral histories, artifacts, and interactive displays. And don't miss the Wall of Honor, which looks out over the nearby Statue of Liberty; this is the longest wall of names in the world and contains more than 700,000 inscriptions; families can request inclusion of their own ancestors on this memorial. If you're looking to trace your roots, the American Family Immigration History Center at the museum is invaluable: Here you'll find passenger records for those who passed through the center.

340 Empire State Building

CONTACT 212-736-3100, www.esbnyc.com; 350 5th Ave., New York City

PRICING	$$$–$$$$
BEST TIME TO VISIT	Clear days in spring and fall
AGE RANGE	All ages

The Empire State Building is an icon of New York City and of metropolitan America—and has been a star player in movies, TV shows, and novels. (You may remember the role the massive structure played in *Sleepless in Seattle*; your kids will probably know about the building from the Percy Jackson children's book series.) It reaches 1,454 feet in height (including its TV antenna and lightning rod), comprising 102 floors of office space. It was the world's tallest building for 40 years, from its opening in 1931 until the New York City's World Trade Center's North Tower

Statue Cruises is the only sanctioned concessionaire for ferry service to Ellis Island. During spring and summer months, congestion is highest on the island—so be sure to make advance reservations by calling 877-523-9849 or online at www.statuecruises.com. Same-day tickets can be available at the ferry ticket box office in Castle Clinton in Battery Park or at Liberty State Park. And be sure to leave plenty of time for security clearance at the start of your trip and board times at the end. During peak season (April through September and all school holidays), wait times to board the ferry can be more than 90 minutes.

View from the Empire State Building

Photo Jen Davis, courtesy NYC and Co.

too, which can be found on the 80th floor. Here you'll see displays of photographs and documents chronicling the history of the Empire State Building, as well as a specially decorated window that allows you to look out on modern-day New York but also see the structures of the historical city.

341 Erie Canalway National Heritage Corridor

CONTACT	www.nps.gov/erie; from Whitehall south to Waterford, from Waterford west to North Tonawanda
PRICING	$
BEST TIME TO VISIT	May 1 through November 15 (when waterways are navigable)
AGE RANGE	5 and older

was finalized in 1972. The structure has 6,500 windows, 1,860 steps from the ground floor to the 102nd floor, and a total footprint of close to 2 acres. The Empire State Building is *so* big it even has its own zip code.

Surprisingly, construction of the building was finished in record time: Excavation began in January 1930; construction moved forward at an astonishing pace (an average of 4.5 stories per week), and the building officially opened in May 1931. Because of its massive size, you can see the distinctively art deco Empire State Building from many vantage points in Manhattan—although the top of the structure is often hidden behind clouds. To get the full effect of this engineering marvel, purchase a (somewhat pricey) elevator ticket to check out the view from two observatories. The 86th-floor deck has an open-air terrace that runs around the full perimeter of the building; the deck is equipped with binoculars, and on a clear day there is simply no better view of the city. The 102nd-floor observatory is the highest public point in New York City; the observation deck is fully enclosed, which means you can enjoy it even in very chilly weather. The price of your admission ticket entitles you to visit the New York City's Skyscraper Museum,

Lines can be horrifyingly long, both to purchase tickets and to board the elevators of the Empire State Building. Buy tickets online and skip the ticket queue at the entrance; you can also purchase express tickets (for a premium) and cut to the front of the elevator lines.

The 363 miles of the Erie Canal that run roughly from Albany to Buffalo was the first waterway shipping and transportation system that serviced the eastern seaboard and the Great Lakes that didn't require portage—in other words, didn't require that vessels or cargo be carried overland to avoid obstacles along the waterway. Lake Erie is 570 feet higher than the Hudson River in Albany, and thus an elaborate system of locks was required to lift and lower boats along the route. The Erie Canal includes 35 locks—think of these like waterborne elevators for ships. Once the canal was completed in 1825, shipping was substantially faster and cheaper (cutting freight costs by as much as 90 percent). A route that had taken two weeks via stagecoach or wagon from the eastern border of New York to the western was trimmed to five days via the Erie Canal. This savings in time and money afforded by the canal meant that commerce exploded—which helped New York City become the major center for industry and finance that it is today. In turn the canal was responsible for opening up western New York State and areas farther west to settlement; it was used for years to transport products like crops and lumber produced in the Midwest to markets in the east.

Explore America's most important human-constructed waterway by car, bicycle, or foot. The historic corridor spans the width of the state of New York, roughly paralleling I-90, but it's possible to get a sense of the history and beauty of the canal by visiting only a portion or two of the Erie Canal. One of the most enjoyable ways to experience the waterway today is via a boat or pontoon that navigates along a portion of the canal and uses the ingenious lock system. There are dozens of concessionaires along the canal that operate such vessels, which generally provide narrated tours to explain the history and the mechanisms of the locks. When visiting the Erie Canalway National Heritage Corridor, you'll also find dozens of historic cities and towns that grew up alongside the waterway. Don't miss the Erie Canal Park and Sims Store Museum in Camillus (http://eriecanalcamillus.com); the Sims Museum is a re-creation of a canal-side store of the kind that would have been found in the mid-19th century. In Rome, the Erie Canal Village (www.eriecanalvillage.net) offers an outdoor living history museum that reconstructs the 19th-century village where excavation was first begun on the canal, in 1817.

Federal Hall Memorial   Courtesy National Park Service

now known as Federal Hall marks the spot where he stood as he became the first commander in chief. This is also the site where the Bill of Rights was first introduced. Three successive buildings have claimed the same address. The current Greek Revival structure was built as a customhouse in 1842; it later became the U.S. Sub-Treasury. The architecture is reminiscent of what you'll find in Washington, DC, today—and although elegant is frankly dwarfed in its Manhattan home by the skyscrapers that surround it. Self-guided as well as guided tours are available during weekdays. Tour the lovely interior—the dome in the Main Hall will remind you of the current U.S. Capitol. And look for the Bible used in Washington's swearing-in, which is sometimes (but not always) displayed at the Washington Inaugural Gallery.

342 Federal Hall Memorial

CONTACT 212-825-6990, www.nps.gov/feha/index.htm; 26 Wall St., New York City

PRICING	$
BEST TIME TO VISIT	Year-round; closed weekends
AGE RANGE	7 and older

When we think of Wall Street in New York City, we're apt to conjure visions of the stock exchange long before we think about the history of the federal government. But the Wall Street site on which Federal Hall stands, in the midst of the most powerful financial district in the world, actually marks the spot where the U.S. government first took shape. This original structure on site was once the home of the offices of the Continental Congress, the Supreme Court, and the executive branch. In 1789 George Washington was inaugurated on its second-floor balcony; a bronze statue of Washington on the front steps of what is

343 Fort Ticonderoga

CONTACT 518-585-2821, www.fortticonderoga.org; 30 Fort Ti Rd., Ticonderoga

PRICING	$$–$$$
BEST TIME TO VISIT	Open mid-May through mid-October
AGE RANGE	7 and older

The 18th-century star-shaped fort on the picturesque southern end of Lake Champlain, known today as Fort Ticonderoga, was originally a French outpost called

Fort Ticonderoga

© Debbie K. Hardin

Fort Carillon. The large fort was constructed by the French and Canadians during the French and Indian War, in part to control shipping access across the nearby La Chute River, between Lake Champlain and Lake George—protecting the waterway that connected New France in what is now Canada with Britain's colonies in America. The fort was captured by the British in the French and Indian War, but then in 1775 came under American control early in the Revolutionary War, in the well-chronicled battle co-led by patriot Ethan Allen and the infamous traitor Benedict Arnold.

Today the surprisingly beautiful structure, set amid the grandeur of upstate New York, is a living history museum. Guests can tour the facilities of the fort, including barracks, powder magazine, and officers' quarters. The facility offers a host of interpretive programs, led by costumed historians who interact with visitors and demonstrate how soldiers lived in the 18th century. Expect to see daily musket and cannon demonstrations; fife-and-drum concerts; arts and crafts demonstrations; and hands-on family programs that will allow children to participate in everyday 18th-century chores and dress up like soldiers. Throughout July and August, the on-site Deborah Clarke Mars Education Center offers additional craft activities for children; there are historic games on the parade grounds; and visitors can join in a military drill. An on-site museum displays historic weapons, uniforms, and other artifacts from the era, along with annual special exhibitions. Starting in early June, don't miss the spectacular King's Garden, re-created at the site of the original Fort Garrison Garden. The

walled garden includes 32 geometric beds that flank a lawn and reflecting pool. And in late summer through the end of the fall season, check out the 6-acre Heroic Maze, a fun and challenging corn labyrinth.

344 Harriet Tubman Home

CONTACT 315-252-2081, www.harriethouse.org; 180 South St., Auburn

PRICING	$
BEST TIME TO VISIT	Year-round; November through January by appointment only; closed throughout the year Sunday and Monday
AGE RANGE	7 and older

Harriet Tubman (1820–1913) was a remarkable American who is remembered for her pivotal role in the Underground Railroad, a network of secret safe houses that ferried escaped slaves from one stop along the "railroad" to another, eventually moving them northward, to Canada and U.S. states and territories that prohibited slavery. She was born into slavery as Araminta Ross in Dorchester County, Maryland. In her early 20s she married John Tubman, a free African American man, and took his last name; she later changed her first name, after her mother. She escaped from slavery shortly after marrying—believing she was about to be sold and thus separated from her husband—and took refuge in Philadelphia. In 1850 she journeyed to Baltimore, where her mother and two sisters lived as slaves, and she helped them escape. Thereafter, she made more than a dozen additional trips to Maryland and helped some 300 slaves escape into Canada. Although the specifics of the Underground Railroad were a well-kept secret, Tubman became recognized for her abolitionist ef-

> The birthplace of Harriet Tubman (Green Briar Rd., Cambridge, MD) is also preserved as a historic landmark.

forts, and at one time slaveholders offered a bounty of $40,000 for her capture. Legend has it that during one of her trips to help fugitive slaves she overheard two people discussing her MOST WANTED poster, which noted that she was illiterate. Tubman grabbed a newspaper and pretended to read it, which was enough to fool her would-be captors. During the Civil War she served as a spy for the Union and worked as a nurse as well; in her later years she worked for women's suffrage.

The Harriet Tubman Home in Auburn preserves her last home. The property includes 26 acres and four structures, two of which were used by Tubman. Tubman deeded the property to the AME Zion Church, and the church continues to operate the facility. The property is open for self-guided tours, and special events are held each Memorial Day weekend. Note that the opening hours are subject to change, so it's a good idea to call ahead to ensure the availability of tours.

Interacting with Eleanor and Franklin   © Debbie K. Hardin

345 Home of Franklin D. Roosevelt National Historic Site

CONTACT 845-486-7770, www.fdrlibrary.marist.edu; 4079 Albany Post Rd., Hyde Park

PRICING	$–$$$
BEST TIME TO VISIT	Year-round
AGE RANGE	7 and older

Franklin Delano Roosevelt (1882–1945) was the 32nd president of the United States, and the only chief executive to have been elected for more than two terms. FDR led the country through the Great Depression and World War II, and is well remembered for his many social programs that he dubbed part of his New Deal—programs that included the Civilian Conservation Corps, which rebuilt roads and created much of the infrastructure we see today at national parks, as well as programs that survive today, such as the Federal Deposit Insurance Corporation and Social Security. His wife, Eleanor, was a beloved public figure herself and is considered the first modern American First Lady; Eleanor took an active role in her husband's administration, holding weekly press conferences and writing a syndicated newspaper column. She was an outspoken advocate for civil rights and a particular champion of women's rights.

The Franklin D. Roosevelt Presidential Library and Museum, on the extensive grounds of FDR's familial home in Hyde Park, honors the memory of the president and First Lady with exhibits of artifacts and documents that chronicle their lives in public office, as well as their early years. One of the most fascinating items on display is FDR's custom wheelchair: Many Americans of his day did not know that the president was disabled from a bout with polio; he was careful to be photographed in situations that did not require him to walk, in the dated notion that citizens might fear a disabled individual would not be strong enough to lead the country through the tough times it was facing in the early 20th century. Children will particularly enjoy the re-creation of the Oval Office, which features the actual desk that President Roosevelt used during his time in office, as well as his 1936 Ford Phaeton, outfitted with hand controls so that he could drive it despite his disability. Because the library is built on the grounds of the Roosevelt home, the museum also offers the chance to see FDR's actual study, used during his lifetime: It is furnished exactly as it was at the time of his death in 1945. After a tour through the library, be sure to walk the grounds to see the burial site of Franklin and Eleanor. In addition, kids can pose with a life-sized sculpture of the president and First Lady, located just outside the main entrance of the museum.

346 Lake George

CONTACT www.visitlakegeorge.com/home; off I-87, near Ticonderoga, northeastern New York

PRICING	$
BEST TIME TO VISIT	Summer
AGE RANGE	All ages

The storied Adirondack region is a 6-million-acre area in northeastern New York famous for stunning mountains, forests, and lakes. Winter sports are popular in the mountains in colder months—the Adirondacks are home to Lake Placid, the site of the Winter Olympic Games in 1980. And in the summer, weary city dwellers flock to the lakes to beat the summer heat and enjoy water sports like fishing, kayaking, and water skiing.

Lake George falls on the southeast border of the Adirondacks. The long and skinny body of water is especially deep and clear, and is characterized by "the Narrows," a 5-mile section of water surrounded by mountains and filled with islands. In total, Lake George has 395 islands, which run the gamut from tiny sand spits to the larger Long Island and Vicar's Island, which are popular camping sites. The lake is 200 feet at its deepest, and offers some of the finest boating opportunities in the area. From late spring through early fall, families can launch their own vessels, charter small yachts (check out Indian Pipers Charter Cruises in Bolton Landing; www.lakegeorgenewyork.com/

Boating on Lake George   © Debbie K. Hardin

The nearby Fort William Henry Museum (48 Canada St., Lake George) is a restored colonial fortress that was built during the French and Indian War. The fort features living history demonstrations and family-friendly activities that can include Native American storytelling, hands-on crafting opportunities, and the chance to join in re-created military drills.

indianpipes), or climb aboard historic steamships for narrated cruises (try the Lake George Steamboat Company, www.lakegeorgesteamboat.com).

347 Lower East Side Tenement Museum

CONTACT 212-982-8420, www.tenement.org; 103 Orchard St., New York City

PRICING	Varies by experience
BEST TIME TO VISIT	Year-round
AGE RANGE	Kids must be 5 years and older for Meet the Resident Programs and 8 years and older for neighborhood tours

It isn't unusual to visit the restored and preserved homes of rich and famous individuals from earlier times—this book is filled with examples of luxurious houses open for tours that were once owned by presidents and captains of industry, as well as comfortably furnished homes formerly belonging to successful authors and artists. The Lower East Side Tenement Museum offers a different experience: the unique opportunity to tour the former homes of everyday people who lived in humble—even squalid—circumstances. The 1863 apartment building at the heart of this museum was home to almost 7,000 working-class Americans over the years, most of them recent immigrants. The structure was shut down in 1935, and its residents moved elsewhere, when it was deemed a fire hazard. Remarkably, the doors were sealed shut and the interior remained untouched until 1988. When this accidental time capsule was rediscovered,

Levine Kitchen, Lower East Side Tenement Museum

Photo Baltman Studios, courtesy Lower East Side Tenement Museum

348 Macy's Thanksgiving Day Parade

CONTACT Route: 77th St. and Central Park West through to Macy's Herald Square, New York City

PRICING	$
BEST TIME TO VISIT	Thanksgiving morning, starting at 9
AGE RANGE	All ages

museum curators realized they had found a gold mine of cultural information about the way immigrants without means experienced their new country and how they lived and struggled on a day-to-day basis.

Guests can take guided tours of this fascinating structure and tour apartments that have been restored to their late-19th- and early-20th-century conditions, along the way learning the personal histories of actual residents of the apartments uncovered through painstaking research. The apartments are small, cluttered, and often in disrepair (as they would have been while still occupied). No detail is left out of the tour experience: Look for dishes in the sink, a coffeepot on the stove, dolls and other toys strewn about, laundry drying on inside lines, common cleaning products and canned foods from the era, and even family heirlooms carried to New York City from the immigrants' home countries, like lace tablecloths and porcelain curios. Costumed reenactors take on the roles of the residents, and special augmented tours through the apartments allow guests to interact with the actor-historians. For example, in a tour designed for families, visitors meet resident Victoria Confino, a 14-year-old girl from a Greek Sephardic family who explains how she and her parents adjusted to life after immigrating. There are also neighborhood tours that guide visitors through the Lower East Side to learn more about how immigrants shaped the culture of the neighborhood. A favorite of such walking tours is the Foods of the Lower East Side, in which guests explore the ethnic grocery stores and restaurants of the neighborhood and learn about the immigrant influence on American food while sampling traditional fare.

Thanksgiving is a uniquely American holiday, one that commemorates the earliest colonists and the Native Americans who helped them celebrate their first harvest festival. And the holiday is celebrated in a uniquely American way as well: In addition to feasting on turkey and pumpkin pie—and watching the ubiquitous televised football games that have marked the holiday season in the last several decades—many of us observe the day by watching the Macy's Thanksgiving Day Parade, either in person or on TV. The annual parade dates to 1924, when department store employees dressed up like clowns and cowboys and marched from Harlem to Herald Square in New York City, to celebrate the holiday season and to drum up a little business for Macy's. The inaugural event drew close to 250,000 people, and thus it was decided it would be an annual event. In 1927 the first cartoon balloon was included in the parade; after the festivities, the balloon (a depiction of Felix the Cat) was released into the air, where it promptly popped. The next year more balloons were added to the parade,

Macy's Thanksgiving Day Parade

Courtesy NYC and Co.

and they, too, were released into the air, this time with return labels sewn inside and the promise that anyone returning the balloons would receive a gift certificate from Macy's. This practice proved dangerous, however (the freed balloons tended to drift into power lines), and was soon discontinued. The parade itself was briefly discontinued during World War II: From 1942 to 1944, the balloons that had been used in previous parades were recycled into 600 pounds of rubber that was donated to the war effort.

Today the two-hour event includes the famous balloon characters, floats, marching bands, performances from current Broadway shows, performing artists from around the world, and Santa Claus (who pulls up the rear of the parade and marks the official start to the holiday season). Close to 4 million people show up in person to see the parade; another 50 million households will view it on television.

Seeing the parade in person is a once-in-a-lifetime opportunity—and it's best to plan in advance if you are an out-of-towner, because hotels book up quickly. Public viewing areas are located along the parade route, including 6th Avenue, between 34th and 58th Streets; 34th Street, between Broadway and 7th Avenue; and Central Park West, from 70th Street to Columbus Circle. Arrive before 6 AM to claim your spot. (Some zealous fans camp out overnight—but this is not advised with children, because of frigid weather and a host of other reasons that go without saying.) Another fun way to experience the parade—without enduring the worst of the crowds—is by checking out the balloons as they are inflated the day before, in a staging site between 77th and 81st Streets, off Central Park West.

> Manhattan offers some of the finest art museums in America. In addition to the largest—the Metropolitan Museum of Art—nearby is the Guggenheim Museum (1071 5th Ave.), the structure of which is itself a masterpiece of architecture (created by Frank Lloyd Wright); the Museum of Modern Art (MoMA; 11 W. 53rd St.), offering one of the most extensive collections of modern and contemporary art in the world; and the Whitney Museum of American Art (945 Madison Ave.), which chronicles the story of American art and culture through the years.

The Metropolitan Museum of Art (comprising the Main Building on 5th Avenue and the Cloisters—featuring medieval collections—on 99 Margaret Corbin Dr.) boasts one of the largest permanent collections of artwork in the world. Included in the more than 2 million pieces are 26,000 ancient Egyptian artifacts—the largest collection of Egyptian art outside of Cairo; 2,500 European paintings—including highlights like Johannes Vermeer's *Young Woman with a Water Pitcher*, Jacques-Louis David's *The Death of Socrates*, and Vincent Van Gogh's *Self-Portrait with Straw Hat*; and the most extensive collection of American artwork in existence. Other museum holdings include African, Asian, Byzantine, Islamic, and ancient Greek and Roman art; a huge collection of musical instruments; and a plethora of weapons and armor from all around the world.

The exhibit halls are vast, and navigating the displays can be daunting. Pick up one of several themed

349 Metropolitan Museum of Art

CONTACT 212-535-7710, www.metmuseum.org; 1000 5th Ave., New York City

PRICING	$–$$$$
BEST TIME TO VISIT	Year-round; closed Monday
AGE RANGE	7 and older

Metropolitan Museum of Art   Photo Marley White, courtesy NYC and Co.

family guides at the information desk, which will pique the interest of children and help you discover the items that excite them the most. For kids 6 to 12, check out the *Family Audio Guide*, which will lead you through thematic tours of the museum's permanent collection. But the real fun comes in drop-in hands-on family programs, like Storytime in Nolen Library (for youngsters 18 months to 7 years), which culminates in a scavenger hunt through the collections; Sunday Studio, which offers sketching stations within the museum galleries for children and parents; and Drop-in Drawing classes, in which instructors offer tips to recreating the masterpieces on display in the museum.

350 Niagara Falls

CONTACT 716- 278-1796, www.niagarafallsstatepark.com, Niagara Falls

PRICING	$ to view; $$$$ to tour
BEST TIME TO VISIT	Summer
AGE RANGE	3 and older

Niagara Falls is one of the natural wonders of the world. The astonishingly beautiful waterworks are actually made up of three separate waterfalls sited along the international border with Canada. Horseshoe Falls is the largest—and arguably the most spectacular; this aptly named falls sits on the Canadian side of the attraction. American Falls and Bridal Veil Falls are on the American side. Together the falls account for 1,360 tons of water per second moving over a vertical drop (at the highest point) of more than 165 feet. Something about the power of nature on display here tends to inspire people to find ways to try to tame it. Through the years various daredevils have gone over the falls in barrels: Some survived, and some did not. Likewise, tightrope walkers have been drawn here with a desire to inch across the falls from above, also with mixed results. In mid-2012 Nik Wallenda (a seventh-generation acrobat) became the first person to walk across the falls in 116 years (after receiving special permission from U.S. and Canadian authorities to do so).

Niagara Falls Courtesy Kevin Legg

You can get a good look at the falls on this side of the American border from walkways along Prospect Point Park in Niagara or from Goat Island, which can be accessed by foot or car via bridge. An even better way to get a premier view of the falls is via a trip aboard the *Maid of the Mist*, a ship that ferries guests close enough to the waterfalls that they are apt to get drenched from the overspray. (The boat kindly provides yellow rain slickers.) In the evening high-powered spotlights illuminate the falls with different shades of color, making the natural beauty of the attraction even more ethereal. In the summertime look for nighttime fireworks on Friday, Sunday, and certain holidays.

351 Pollock-Krasner House and Studio

CONTACT 631-324-4929, http://sb.cc.stonybrook.edu/pkhouse; 830 Springs-Fireplace Rd., East Hampton

PRICING	$
BEST TIME TO VISIT	Open June and July, Thursday through Saturday only (open in May, September, and October by appointment)
AGE RANGE	10 and older

Of all the modern artists in America, Jackson Pollock (1912–56) is perhaps the most accessible to kids: His exuberant style, huge-scale paintings, and almost

Paint-splattered floors, Pollock-Krasner House and Studio   Photo Helen A. Harrison, courtesy Pollock-Krasner House and Studio

child-like style are generally appealing even to people who don't necessarily understand the intent of the artwork. Among art critics, Pollock is considered one of the most influential American painters of the abstract expressionist movement. He is most identified by his unique drip paintings, in which he spread large canvases on the floor and poured streams of paint directly on to the surfaces.

In 1945 Pollock married artist Lee Krasner (1908–84), and the couple moved to a small home on Long Island's East End. (The artists financed their property by trading a Pollock painting to famed art dealer Peggy Guggenheim, who in turn made the down payment.) Although the marriage was rocky, the couple lived in the home until Pollock's death in a car crash in 1956, only a mile from the house. Today the Pollock-Krasner House and Studio is open for tours. Guests can stroll the bucolic grounds, tour the home, and then don a pair of foam slippers and step into the studio (a barn the artist converted for the purposes) where Pollock painted many of his most important works. The floors themselves resemble a Pollock painting, thanks to numerous paint splatterings. Look for Pollock's old paintbrushes, stored in paint cans along his studio walls.

The site continues to be an active arts center, hosting exhibits of contemporary artists throughout the season. In summer there are opportunities for children to try their hand at drip painting outside the Pollock's studio. This is also the site of numerous Pollock exhibits and lectures.

352 Sagamore Hill

CONTACT	516-922-4788, www.nps.gov/sahi; 12 Sagamore Hill Rd., Oyster Bay
PRICING	$
BEST TIME TO VISIT	Year-round in the summer; closed Monday and Tuesday in other seasons
AGE RANGE	7 and older

Theodore Roosevelt (1858–1919) was the 26th president of the United States—and the youngest man ever to hold that office. Roosevelt was 42 when then president William McKinley was assassinated, and vice president Roosevelt was sworn in as commander in chief. (John F. Kennedy remains the youngest president to have been *elected* to office.) Roosevelt had a bigger-than-life personality, and is well remembered for his boisterous family, his love of the outdoors, and his penchant for hunting. Before assuming the presidency, Roosevelt served at the city, local, and federal levels of

Theodore Roosevelt's home   Courtesy National Park Service

government from a very early age. As president, he created a series of domestic policies that came to be known as the Square Deal, an attempt to level the playing field for Americans of modest wealth. His international policies were best characterized by his famous slogan, "Speak softly and carry a big stick." He was awarded the Nobel Peace Prize for negotiating an end to the Russo-Japanese War—making him only one of three sitting presidents to have received the honor. (The others are Woodrow Wilson and Barack Obama.)

Shortly after marrying his first wife, Alice, Roosevelt purchased a property in Long Island and proceeded to build a home. Sadly, Alice died shortly after childbirth—before construction was completed. Two years later Roosevelt married his second wife, Edith, and together they moved into the Long Island home and raised six children in the place they called Sagamore, where they both resided for the rest of their lives. The property includes 95 acres of forest, a salt marsh, and a beach on the bay. The home itself is a lovely Victorian, with 23 rooms, including an impressive grand room measuring 30 feet by 40 feet in which Roosevelt showcased his artwork, hunting trophies, and numerous artifacts presented to him by heads of state.

In late 2011 the home closed for a multimillion-dollar renovation, although the expansive grounds, an on-site Theodore Roosevelt Museum, and the visitor center remained open. Guests can schedule guided tours of the grounds and enjoy a nature trail that leads to a national wildlife refuge on Cold Spring Harbor.

Neilson House, Saratoga National Historical Park

Courtesy National Park Service

353 Saratoga National Historical Park

CONTACT 518-664-9821, ext. 224, www.nps.gov/sara; 648 Rt. 32, Stillwater

PRICING	$
BEST TIME TO VISIT	Summer (tour road open April through November; Schuyler House and Saratoga Monument open Memorial Day through Labor Day Wednesday through Sunday)
AGE RANGE	7 and older

The Battle of Saratoga in the fall of 1777 is considered the first decisive victory of the Continental army during the American Revolutionary War. In this confrontation, the colonial forces clashed with, and bested, the British army—an outcome that was in part responsible for France's recognition of American independence and eventual entry into the war as a major military ally of the Americans. The Saratoga National Historical Park preserves the battlefield, the Saratoga Monument (in nearby Victory, New York), and the General Philip Schuyler House (in nearby Schuylerville)—Schuyler was a general in the Revolutionary War and a U.S. senator. Also here is the infamous Boot Monument to Benedict Arnold. The memorial is meant to commemorate General Arnold's service during the Battle of Saratoga—but Arnold's name does not appear anywhere on the memorial, in recognition of the fact that Arnold later defected to the British army.

Start your trip at the visitor center, which shows a 20-minute orientation film and has a fascinating fiber-optic map that illustrates troop movements during the battle. Guests can then take a self-guided tour of the battlefield or arrange for a guided tour, conducted by costumed historians who provide informative background. (Call 518-664-9821, ext. 2985 for advance reservations.) The John Neilson Farmhouse is also open for tours; this farmhouse was the only building on the battlefield in 1777, and came to be used by the Continental army as one of their headquarters. The park is the site of reenactments and living history demonstrations through the summer months.

354 Statue of Liberty

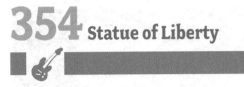

CONTACT www.nps.gov/stli; Liberty Island (off New York City); ferry departure points in Battery Park (1 Battery Park Place, NYC) and Liberty State Park (1 Audrey Zapp Dr., Jersey City, NJ)

PRICING	entrance: $; ferry $$–$$$
BEST TIME TO VISIT	Year-round
AGE RANGE	All ages

There is perhaps no more recognized symbol of America than the Statue of Liberty, which stands watch over the New York harbor and for decades was one of the first sights new immigrants saw when arriving by boat to nearby Ellis Island. The statue was a gift to the United States from the country of France, designed by Frédéric Bartholdi and dedicated in 1886. When it was shipped from Europe, the statue came in 350 pieces—which took some four months to assemble. The artwork depicts a robed woman representing the Roman goddess of freedom, Libertas, who carries a torch raised in one hand and a tablet inscribed with the date July 4, 1776, the date of the American Declaration of Independence, in the other. The Statue of Liberty is an impressive site because of its massive girth: The statue stretches 151 feet high; Liberty's head is more than 17 feet tall—her nose is 4.5 feet long; her index finger is more than 8 feet long. More than 60,000 pounds of copper and more than 250,000 pounds of steel were used to construct the colossal figure.

If you want to get an up-close peek at Lady Liberty, take a ferry from either New York or New Jersey aboard Statue Cruises (the only sanctioned concessionaire—private boats are not allowed to dock on Liberty Island). You can purchase ferry tickets in person at the two departure points, by phone (201-604-2800), or online (www.statuecruises.com); advance ticket purchase is highly recommended in the spring and fall, when crowds are typical. (Note that the ferries also stop at Ellis Island—see above—so it's possible to visit both sites in the same day.) Expect long lines for security screening regardless.

After the 9/11 terrorist attacks in New York, the inside of the statue was closed for several years. It was reopened briefly in 2009, then closed again for renovation work, and finally reopened again. Those wishing to enter the base and pedestal of the statue can secure free tickets to do so when purchasing ferry tickets. An extremely limited number of people per day are allowed to climb the 354 stairs to the crown of the statue; these tickets can be reserved a year in advance.

Statue of Liberty   Courtesy National Park Service

355 Susan B. Anthony House

CONTACT 585-235-6124, http://susanbanthonyhouse.org; 17 Madison St., Rochester

PRICING	$–$$
BEST TIME TO VISIT	Year-round; closed Monday
AGE RANGE	7 and older

Susan B. Anthony (1820–1906) was a vocal advocate for civil rights, and especially influential in the women's suffrage movement. With Elizabeth Cady Stanton, Anthony founded the first Women's Temperance Movement in the United States, in part as an effort to reduce violence against women and children. She published and lectured widely on women's rights and the need for a national right to vote. She was famously arrested and tried for voting in the 1872 presidential election. Her trial was held in Canandaigua, New York, before Justice Ward Hunt, who refused to allow Anthony to testify on her own behalf. The jury—on explicit orders from the justice—found her guilty and she was fined $100 (a fee she refused to pay for the rest of her life). Anthony did not live to see the passage of the 19th Amendment to the U.S. Constitution in 1920, which provided federal voting rights for women of age.

The National Susan B. Anthony Museum and House preserves the home of Anthony, who lived here for 40 years, until her death. (Her famous arrest took place in the parlor.) The site offers exhibits on the women's suffrage movement in the 19th century, as well as displays of artifacts belonging to Anthony. A visitor center next door (19 Madison St., onetime home to Anthony's sister) is a learning center that offers regular lectures and symposia.

356 Vanderbilt Mansion National Historic Site

CONTACT 845-229-9115, www.nps.gov/vama; 4097 Albany Post Rd., Hyde Park

PRICING	$$$
BEST TIME TO VISIT	May through October (tours are limited in late fall through early spring)
AGE RANGE	7 and older

The Vanderbilt Mansion National Historic Site preserves remnants of the opulent lifestyle enjoyed by extraordinarily wealthy industrialists during the Gilded Age. The spectacular mansion, which is sited

The well-manicured lawns are a lovely site for a picnic.

on 211 acres of the original larger property that was historically known as Hyde Park, was first owned by Frederick William Vanderbilt (1856–1938), who owed his financial success in part to his role as director of the New York Central Railroad and in part to his connections to his famous family. The prominent Vanderbilts inherited much of their wealth from patriarch Cornelius Vanderbilt, who built a massive shipping and railroad empire. The family was a social force well into the early 20th century—and even today prominent descendants such as designer Gloria Vanderbilt and her son, television journalist Anderson Cooper, continue to make their mark on American culture.

The historic site includes the stunning 54-room mansion, beautiful formal gardens, woodlands, and breathtaking views of the Hudson River. Guests today can tour the grand home and its outbuildings—furnished in opulent period pieces—as well as enjoying the extensive grounds. The well-manicured lawns are a lovely site for a picnic, and allow plenty of free space for little ones to run off excess energy.

Although tours of the structures on this site require a fee, admission to the extensive grounds and gardens of the Vanderbilt Mansion is free.

Vanderbilt Mansion National Historic Site

Courtesy David Preimesberger

357 Women's Rights National Historical Park

CONTACT 315-568-2991, www.nps.gov/wori; 136 Fall St., Seneca Falls

PRICING	$
BEST TIME TO VISIT	Year-round
AGE RANGE	7 and older

The 1848 Seneca Falls Women's Rights Convention is considered the beginning of the women's rights movement in the United States and the origin of the women's suffrage movement—a struggle that persisted until the passage of the 19th Amendment in 1920 that granted women of age the vote. The nexus of the idea for the convention came at another early civil rights symposium: the 1840 World Antislavery Convention held in London, in which the women delegates were not allowed to participate in the debates. Activists Lucretia Mott and Elizabeth Cady Stanton were forced to sit behind a partition during the abolitionist convention while their husbands spoke—and it was this shoddy treatment that spurred the idea of a convention to discuss social and civil rights of women.

In preparation for the convention, Stanton wrote her Declaration of Sentiments, a document modeled on the Declaration of Independence, which included resolutions to prevent men from taking women's property and to allow for women to vote. More than 300 participants attended the convention, held in the summer over two days, during which period they revised Stanton's document and ultimately voted their support.

The Women's Rights National Historical Park in Seneca Falls preserves four properties central to the early women's movement and the Seneca Falls convention. Begin your visit with a trip to the visitor center, which offers an excellent orientation film that introduces the central figures in the convention, as well as exhibits that explain the early history of women's rights. Don't miss the statue titled *The First Wave*, which illustrates the planners of the Seneca Falls convention. Adjacent to the center is a waterfall memorial in which the Declaration of Sentiments is engraved along a 100-foot stone wall. Next door is the Wesleyan Chapel, a reconstruction of the site where the convention was held. Nearby (32 Washington St.) is the Elizabeth Cady Stanton House where Stanton lived with her family; the home has been restored to its 1848 appearance and is open for guided tours.

Declaration of Sentiments Waterwall, Women's Rights National Historical Park   Courtesy National Park Service

North Carolina

358 Bentonville Battlefield

CONTACT 910-594-0789, www.nchistoricsites.org/bentonvi; 5466 Harper House Rd., Four Oaks

PRICING	$
BEST TIME TO VISIT	Spring and summer
AGE RANGE	7 and older

The 1865 Battle of Bentonville was the largest Civil War conflict in North Carolina. The skirmish began when the Confederate army attacked a flank of the Union army in an effort to stop General William T. Sherman's march into the Carolinas—and on the first day of the conflict the Confederate army was able to subdue two divisions. On the second day, however, another group of Union soldiers arrived and held back the Confederates. The result, just more than a month later, was that Confederate general Joseph Johnston surrendered to General Sherman. This event, along with General Robert E. Lee's surrender a few weeks earlier, marked the final gasps of the war.

Visitors to the Bentonville Battlefield can survey the battlefield grounds, tour a Civil War field hospital (enshrined within the restored Harper House), and check out exhibits at the visitor center that explain the troop movements and offer historical background on the generals who figured prominently in this battle. Also look for re-created battle trenches, a mass grave used by the Confederate army, and a field fortification exhibit. Seasonal events are held at the battlefield from March through December, including the Bentonville Battlefield Anniversary Reenactment, held the third week in March every fifth year; a living history series focusing on the lives of Civil War soldiers and their families, held June through August; and a Christmas Holiday Open House that features costumed interpreters and Civil War—era holiday decorations, held the first Saturday in December.

359 Biltmore Estate

CONTACT 828-225-1333, www.biltmore.com; 1 Lodge St., Asheville

PRICING	$$$$
BEST TIME TO VISIT	Year-round
AGE RANGE	7 and older

George Vanderbilt II (1862–1914) was the grandson and heir of Cornelius Vanderbilt, an extremely wealthy American industrialist and head of the famous Vanderbilt family. The summer estate George built modeled on a French château is as close to a castle as mainland America can boast. The 250-room

Conservatory, Biltmore Estate   Photographs in the Carol M. Highsmith Archive, Library of Congress, Prints and Photographs Division

Reenactment at Bentonville Battlefield   Courtesy VisitNC.com

mansion is sited among the remaining 8,000 acres (there were originally 125,000) of magnificent grounds and gardens, which were designed by famed landscape architect Frederick Law Olmsted (designer of Central Park in New York City). The home was constructed between 1889 and 1895, and at 175,000 square feet it is the largest privately owned home in the United States. Descendants of the Vanderbilts still own the property, although they haven't lived in the mansion since 1956.

Guests can take a self-guided tour of the magnificent and opulent mansion to see an indoor swimming pool, a two-story library, a private bowling alley, and museum-quality artwork. Amble through the lush gardens, tour farming exhibits at the Antler Hill Village site, sample wine at the on-site winery (kids will receive grape juice), and ride horses along 80 miles of trails. An on-site Outdoor Adventure Center rents bikes, offers fly-fishing and river float trips, and hosts Segway tours. Seasonal events are held year-round; favorite times to visit include spring, when the azalea garden bursts into color, and the holidays, which include luxurious Christmas decorations. The property also hosts an evening concert series in the late summer and into early fall.

360 Blue Ridge Parkway

CONTACT 828-298-5330, www.blueridgeparkway.org; visitor center for Blue Ridge National Heritage Park at 195 Hemphill Knob Rd., Asheville

PRICING	$
BEST TIME TO VISIT	Spring through fall
AGE RANGE	All ages

In recognition of the stunning scenery through which it winds, the Blue Ridge Parkway has been designated an All-American Road and is protected and maintained by the National Park Service. The roadway skirts the Blue Ridge Mountains, starting in Rockfish Gap, Virginia, at the end of the Skyline Drive within Shenandoah National Park (see the description under "Virginia") and terminates at Oconaluftee, North Carolina, in the Great Smoky Mountains National Park (see "Tennessee"). This lovely road proves that the trip *is* as important as the destination—it's well worth a drive even if you don't plan to visit the national parks it connects.

Construction of the 469-mile-long parkway began in 1935, under President Franklin D. Roosevelt. Work was completed by New Deal public works agencies like the Works Progress Administration, which did some of the roadway construction; and the Civilian Conservation Corps, which helped with roadside cleanup and beautification; and conscientious objectors from World War II, who helped build roadside pull-offs. In all, the parkway took 52 years to complete and includes 26 tunnels, 168 bridges, and six viaducts.

Many visitors drive the parkway in the last two weeks or so of October to see the explosion of autumnal color: If you plan to do so, arrive as early in the day as possible—and expect crowds. The rest of the year, however, the roadway is generally blissfully free of congestion and offers a bucolic experience, even if you never leave your automobile. Come early in the morning, as the mist and fog lift off the mountains, and you're sure to see white-tailed deer and perhaps even black bears along the roadway (and often crossing it—drive with care!).

The parkway is marked throughout with numbered mileposts, beginning at 0 in Rockfish Gap. There are hundreds of sights to be seen along the road, but there are a few don't-miss stops:

- **Mile 294, Flat Top Manor House:** The Moses H. Cone Memorial Park includes trout and bass fishing in sparkling lakes and streams; horseback riding and hiking; and cross-country ski trails in the winter. The highlight is the Flat Top Manor, a 13,000-foot mansion built by a wealthy textile manufacturer during the Gilded Age. (The mansion is open for tours spring through fall.)

There are dozens of scenic overlooks along the Blue Ridge Parkway—but it's permitted to pull off and enjoy the scenery from anywhere along the roadway wherever it is safe to do so; just be sure to pull off the road completely. Unless signs warn against it, parking is permitted along the shoulders.

Blue Ridge Parkway   Courtesy VisitNC.com

- **Mile 316, Linville Falls:** This 90-foot stepped waterfall gushes in the spring into the Linville Gorge. Hike to five viewpoints along two trails that originate at the visitor center (which is 1.5 miles off the parkway).

- **Mile 382, Southern Highland Folk Art Center:** The Folk Art Center is a great place to view (or purchase) fine handcrafted art of the Southern Appalachians. The center hosts a series of events throughout the year, including crafting demonstrations every day from March through December and a permanent exhibit of museum-quality artifacts.

- **Mile 384, Blue Ridge Parkway Visitor Center:** Stop by the visitor center to see a 25-minute film on the parkway, as well as a 22-foot interpretive map of the road. This is a good place to pick up trail maps as well.

- **Mile 451.2, Waterrock Knob:** Waterrock Knob is a favorite viewpoint; the visitor center is at 6,000 feet elevation, and it is one of the best spots along the parkway to view the sunset. There is a hiking trail here, too, if you want to stretch your legs before heading into the Great Smoky Mountains beyond.

361 Cape Hatteras Lighthouse

CONTACT	www.nps.gov/caha; off NC 12, Nags Head
PRICING	Climbing fee: $–$$
BEST TIME TO VISIT	Late April through early October
AGE RANGE	7 and older (and at least 42 inches tall)

Nicknamed "the Big Barber Pole" for its distinctive diagonal striping, the Cape Hatteras Lighthouse on the Outer Banks is the tallest brick lighthouse in the United States. For more than 100 years the light from its beacon stretched up to 20 miles out to sea to warn ocean navigators away from the Diamond Shoals, a series of shallow, shifting sandbars that reach out almost 15 miles off the coast of Cape Hatteras. Before the lighthouse was built, numerous ships, large and small, wrecked off the coast because of these treacherous sandbars, including the Civil War vessel the USS *Monitor*. The seas were so dangerous before the lighthouse that the waters were called the Graveyard of the Atlantic. It took more than 1,250,000 bricks to build the 6,250-ton, 208-foot structure. Beach erosion and ever-present hurricanes on the Outer Banks prompted officials to move the lighthouse slightly inland in the summer of 1999—so today it continues to look over the Atlantic, but at a more discreet distance.

For unparalleled views and the chance for a good workout, consider climbing the stairs to the top of the Cape Hatteras Lighthouse. The structure is open from the third Friday in April through Columbus Day. Tickets are required, and must be purchased on site the day of

Cape Hatteras Lighthouse   Courtesy National Park Service

There are four other lighthouses well worth visiting on the Outer Banks: the Bodie Island Lighthouse, near the Oregon Inlet; the Currituck Beach Lighthouse, in Corolla; the Ocracoke Lighthouse, on Ocracoke Island (see below); and the Roanoke Marshes Lighthouse, in Manteo.

the climb (starting at 8:15 AM). Beware: The climb is tough. There are 248 iron stairs that spiral inside the cylindrical lighthouse; there is a hand railing only on one side; and the lighting is poor. Furthermore, there is no air-conditioning in the hot and humid North Carolina summers. Kids have to be 42 inches tall, and anyone under 12 must be accompanied by an adult.

362 Carl Sandburg Home

CONTACT 828-693-4178, www.nps.gov/carl; 1800 Little River Rd., Flatrock

PRICING	$
BEST TIME TO VISIT	Summertime
AGE RANGE	10 and older

Carl Sandburg (1878–1967) was an influential American writer and recipient of three Pulitzer Prizes, including one for his autobiography of Abraham Lincoln. He is best remembered for his collections of poetry, including *Chicago Poems* and *Cornhuskers*, as

Carl Sandburg Home

Courtesy VisitNC.com

well as for a beloved collection of children's tales called *Rootabaga Stories*.

The Carl Sandburg Home preserves the house where Sandburg lived with his wife, Lilian, from 1945 through his death in 1967. The 1838 Greek Revival home sits on 264 acres, which includes gardens, walking trails, and a working goat farm (once run by Lilian Sandburg). Guests can tour the property and take a 30-minute guided tour of the house, which the family called Connemara. The home is furnished with Sandburg's original furnishings, including a massive 10,000-volume library. The site often presents summertime live performances on the property, including readings of Sandburg's poetry and performances of *Rootabaga Stories*.

363 Duke Homestead and Tobacco Factory

CONTACT 919-477-5498, http://dukehomestead.org; 2828 Duke Homestead Rd., Durham

PRICING	$
BEST TIME TO VISIT	Spring and summer, closed Sunday and Monday
AGE RANGE	7 and older

Tobacco has played an important role in the politics and economy of North Carolina since the antebellum period, and the state continues to be a major manufacturer of tobacco products today, despite the acknowledged serious health risks associated with tobacco use. The Duke Homestead and Tobacco Factory is an opportunity to learn about the agricultural heritage of the South in general—and in particular to learn about the influence tobacco has had on the United States over the years.

Washington Duke owned the extensive farmland in the 19th century. He started out farming cotton, but when that crop failed he switched to tobacco in 1859. After the Civil War interrupted their farming pursuits, the Duke family converted their tobacco-farming operation into a tobacco-processing operation, establishing what was to become the American Tobacco Company in 1890—which at its height was

Duke Homestead and Tobacco Factory   Courtesy VisitNC.com

the largest tobacco company in the world, until it was broken up in 1911 by an antitrust suit. The Duke family enjoyed enormous financial success as a result, and donated huge sums to philanthropic causes—such as an endowment that became Duke University.

Today guests can visit the restored 1852 homestead, which includes four period-furnished rooms in the main house, a curing barn, a pack house, and an 1869-era factory. There is also a Tobacco Museum on site that offers exhibits on tobacco farming and the history of tobacco. Although the focus of the property is antithetical to most families, the attraction offers the opportunity to step back in time and understand a cash crop that was (and continues to be) economically important to this part of America.

364 Guilford Courthouse National Military Park

CONTACT 336-288-1776, www.nps.gov/guco; 2332 New Garden Rd., Greensboro

PRICING	$
BEST TIME TO VISIT	Year-round
AGE RANGE	7 and older

In a decisive Revolutionary War battle that occurred in the spring of 1781, Redcoat general Charles Cornwallis and his force of 1,900 soldiers defeated a group of 4,500 colonial soldiers led by Major General Nathanael Greene at the site of the Guilford Courthouse. But ironically the victory seriously weakened Cornwallis's forces—he lost 25 percent of his men during the battle; he was nevertheless encouraged to march his remaining troops into Virginia, which in turn allowed Major General Greene to pick apart British control in a largely unguarded South. Just seven months later Cornwallis met his final defeat in Yorktown, Virginia, where he surrendered to Major General George Washington and Lieutenant General Comte de Rochambeau.

Today the Guilford Courthouse National Military Park stands as a memorial to the patriots who served in the Revolutionary War. Start your trip at the expansive visitor center, which screens a 30-minute orientation film on the battle as well as a 10-minute animated battle map program. Within the park are 28 monuments to honor soldiers and statesmen, accessible via a roadway that can be driven, biked, or hiked. Also on site are the grave sites of two signers of the Declaration of Independence: William Hooper and John Penn. A highlight is the equestrian statue of General Green. On the anniversary of the battle, an annual event is held in mid-March that includes military encampments, battle re-creations, fife-and-drum corps, living history demonstrations, and a lecture series.

Guilford Courthouse National Military Park
Courtesy National Park Service

365 Ocracoke Island

CONTACT www.ocracokevillage.com; Ocracoke Island, in the Outer Banks

PRICING	Fees vary by attraction
BEST TIME TO VISIT	Spring through fall
AGE RANGE	All ages

The small island of Ocracoke in the Outer Banks is one of the most isolated spots in North Carolina—it can be reached only via a public toll ferry or by private boat. In part because of this remote locale, Ocracoke became infamous as a onetime pirate hideout. From 1716 through 1718, Blackbeard (aka Edward Teach) and his crew preyed on passenger and cargo ships on the Atlantic Ocean and Caribbean. The pirates came upon unsuspecting ships, attacked them with firepower, and then boarded the ships and stole anything of value—often taking food and sometimes even the clothing worn by their victims. Blackbeard's favorite hiding spot was off Ocracoke Island, which proved an ideal vantage point from which to watch ships traveling between the colonial settlements.

In late 1718 Blackbeard returned to Ocracoke Island to celebrate a particularly successful raid by hosting a pirate party, complete with bonfires, music, and dancing; the bacchanal went on for days, and word of Blackbeard's get-together reached the governor of Virginia, Alexander Spotswood. Spotswood sent Lieutenant Robert Maynard of the Royal Navy to stop Blackbeard and his gang for good. Maynard brought two ships with him, and they closed in on Blackbeard's vessel under cover of nightfall. At dawn, the factions faced off along the coast of Ocracoke, and after prolonged fighting in which both sides suffered losses, Maynard succeeding in shooting Blackbeard; although reportedly shot and stabbed repeatedly, the pirate refused to die immediately—but ultimately he was finished off by one of Maynard's men, who slashed his throat. As a warning to other pirates to stay away from the region, Blackbeard was decapitated and his head was suspended from the bow of Maynard's ship.

Visitors today to Ocracoke Island can see

Lighthouse on Okracoke   © Debbie K. Hardin

Springer's Point Nature Preserve, the pirate hangout that in Blackbeard's day was called Teach's Hole. There is also a small Blackbeard museum and gift shop combination nearby called Teach's Hole Blackbeard Exhibit (935 Irvin Garrish Hwy.). Check out the life-sized re-creation of the fearsome pirate, as well as a collection of pirate flags, antique bottles, and models of Blackbeard's ships.

366 Roanoke Island

CONTACT 252-473-2127, http://thelostcolony.org; 1409 National Park Dr., Manteo

PRICING	$$–$$$
BEST TIME TO VISIT	Plays are staged throughout the summer season
AGE RANGE	7 and older

The Lost Colony Players
Courtesy VisitNC.com

Sir Walter Raleigh (1554–1618) was an English explorer who hoped to establish a financially successful endeavor in the New World. In 1587 Raleigh hired John White to lead more than 100 individuals to establish a self-sufficient colony on Roanoke Island. After White departed from the settlement to procure additional supplies, the group planted crops, built shelters, and celebrated the first English child to be born in America (the baby was named Virginia Dare). White was delayed in his return for three years. When he finally made it back to Roanoke Island, he found no trace of the settlers. All 117 people had disappeared—with only the clue the word CROATAN scrawled on a post. To this day the settlers' fate is unknown: Some believe they were attacked by Native Americans; some believe they were wiped out by a horrific storm. In recent years, tree-ring analysis has turned up evidence that the region suffered a terrible drought during the period, which could have driven the colonists out to find better farming land.

Today the Fort Raleigh National Historic Site

Say Cheese!

There's a saying that encapsulates the experience of raising kids: The days are long but the years are short. Chronicle your adventures through the years with photography, so that children—and you—have tangible evidence of the vacations and day trips you've taken throughout their childhood. Here are a few tips for taking good travel photos with your kids:

- **Take multiple candid shots of kids in action.** Plan to take *lots* of pictures at once, so that you can go back through and find the one or two that tell the story best.

- **Catch kids at their happiest.** Don't wait until they're tired and cranky after a long day to line them up in front of a monument and expect them to smile. Instead photograph them early in the day, while the adventure is still fresh and exciting.

- **Photograph kids with the postcard shots** at their backs—in other words, instead of taking a photo of, say, the steps up to the Lincoln Memorial, photograph *your* child climbing the steps.

- **Take photographs during the "golden hours"**— the first and last hour of sun in which everything is bathed in a warm, soft light and glare is at a minimum.

- **Turn off your flash and use natural light whenever possible:** This will make photographing children less obtrusive, and you're likely to get more candid shots.

- **Don't insist that kids pose and look straight at the camera.** Many children (and adults) get stiff and uncomfortable when a camera lens points their way, so taking profile shots occasionally can ease their discomfort.

- **Let children be silly in pictures.** These photographs will always be joyful and capture their true personalities.

Capture the fun in photos
Courtesy Emilee Legg

(www.nps.gov/fora) memorializes the colony and inhabitants; visitors can tour the restored earthworks that surrounded the settlement and try to imagine what could have happened to the Roanoke Island colonists. In addition, in the summertime the Lost Colony Players stage a two-hour theatrical presentation that interprets the events of the founding of the colony, which includes lavish costumes and a large number of actors. This popular presentation has been ongoing for more than 75 years.

Tryon Palace gardens   Courtesy VisitNC.com

367 Tryon Palace

CONTACT 800-767-1560, www.tryonpalace.org; 610 Pollock St., New Bern

PRICING	$$–$$$
BEST TIME TO VISIT	Spring and fall
AGE RANGE	All ages

Tryon Palace is an interactive, engaging living history museum that re-creates North Carolina's first capital, circa 1770, in a unique, hands-on way that is sure to be fun and immersive for children. Start out your visit at the North Carolina History Center (529 S. Front St.) to purchase tickets, view orientation films, visit gallery exhibits, and participate in active group adventures. The museum is designed to use the latest technology to help guests experience the past in an entertaining, collaborative way. And throughout visitors are encouraged to participate in activities like gardening, quilting, cooking, and printmaking.

Tryon Palace includes seven re-created buildings, three galleries, and 16 acres of gardens. Throughout, costumed interpreters will explain life in the 18th century, from various perspectives: Children can learn about how their counterparts lived, as well as discover how African American slaves, women, and others carried on their day-to-day chores. The highlight of the site is the Governor's Palace, the original version of which was considered the most luxurious public building in all of the colonies. The palace was the site of the first sessions of the general assembly for North Carolina from after the Revolutionary War until 1798,

when a fire destroyed the original structure. Adjacent to the palace are several reconstructed, historically accurate homes and dozens of colorful gardens. Guests can take guided tours of the palace and self-guided tours of the other structures, each of which is a faithful reproduction of 18th-century life.

368 USS *North Carolina*

CONTACT 910-251-5797, www.battleshipnc.com; 1 Battleship Rd., Wilmington

PRICING	$$–$$$
BEST TIME TO VISIT	Year-round
AGE RANGE	5 and older

The USS *North Carolina* was the first newly constructed American battleship designed for duty during World War II, and it was considered a state-of-the-art fighting machine. The vessel participated in every major naval offensive in the Pacific Theater during the war, eventually earning 15 battle stars—

There are narrow corridors and multiple levels accessed without elevators throughout, so visiting the USS *North Carolina* with a stroller or wheelchair is not recommended. Furthermore, the quarters are tight—and the structure of the ship presents numerous tripping hazards. Be prepared to climb steep stairs and watch your step.

USS North Carolina   Courtesy VisitNC.com

making it the most decorated American battleship of the era. The *North Carolina* was decommissioned after the war, and is now moored at the seaport in Wilmington, open as a museum for self-guided tours. Climb aboard to check out the enormous vessel, including the bridge, hospital, bunk rooms, engine rooms, and the galley. The museum allows children to interact with the site by sitting down in the dining hall or climbing into bunks. Throughout there are immersive exhibits that tell the stories of the many sailors who called the battleship home.

369 Wright Brothers National Memorial

CONTACT 252-473-2111, www.nps.gov/wrbr; at milepost 7.5, off U.S. 158, Kill Devil Hills

PRICING	$
BEST TIME TO VISIT	Spring through fall
AGE RANGE	3 and older

Brothers Wilbur (1867–1912) and Orville (1871–1948) Wright were American inventors credited with the design and construction of the first successful airplane. The Wright brothers made their first powered and controlled human flight on December 17, 1903, off the windy dunes of Kitty Hawk, in North Carolina's Outer Banks. After testing more than 200 wing and airframe designs, and after making several attempts over three years, the Wright Flyer, a wooden-framed biplane covered with fabric and powered by two pro-

pellers and a 12-horsepower engine, flew for the first time for 12 seconds and a distance of 120 feet. It is worth noting that the Wright brothers were not the first to experiment with and build aircraft, but they were the first to invent controls that made fixed-wing powered flight viable.

Visit the Wright Brothers National Memorial Visitor Center to see a full-scale replica of an early-1900s-era glider built by the Wrights; a full-scale reproduction of the 1903 powered Wright Flyer; and a version of a wind tunnel the Wright brothers built to test their designs. Outside the center you can walk to the top of Big Kill Devil Hill. Here a 60-foot marker commemorates the site where the aviators conducted their first flight experiments. The adjacent Paul E. Garber First Flight Shrine also memorializes the groundbreaking experiments conducted by the Wrights. Don't miss the chance to walk the Flight Line, where a granite boulder marks the takeoff point for the first powered flight and smaller stone markers note its path; and tour the reconstructed buildings where the Wright brothers and their staff set up shop. There are kids' programs and special events throughout the warmer months, including ranger talks about the Wright brothers and demonstrations in kite making.

Wright Brothers National Memorial   Courtesy National Park Service

Badlands   Photo by Bruce Wendt, courtesy of North Dakota Tourism

NORTH DAKOTA

370 Bonanzaville USA

CONTACT 701-282-2822, www.bonanzaville.com; 1351 W. Main Ave., West Fargo

PRICING	$–$$
BEST TIME TO VISIT	Open Memorial Day through the end of September
AGE RANGE	3 and older

Bonanzaville USA is an expansive outdoor museum complex dedicated to commemorating life on the prairie during the pioneer era. The museum sprawls across 12 acres and includes nearly 50 buildings, with more than 400,000 historical artifacts. Many of the structures are historic and have been moved to the site and arranged to form a village; others are faithful reconstructions. Visitors are welcome to stroll through the grounds, tour the period-furnished buildings, and interact with costumed reinterpreters. Included within the museum you'll find a blacksmith shop with original hammer and forge; a courthouse; a drugstore; several historic homes, including the first permanent structure built in Fargo; several styles of log cabins; a jail; a newspaper press, complete with a hand-operated linotype machine; a saloon; and school, furnished as it might have been 100 years ago. The site features seasonal events throughout the summer, including a popular Fourth of July celebration and the well-attended Pioneer Days celebration in August.

371 Fort Abraham Lincoln

CONTACT 701-663-4758, www.fortlincoln.com; 401 W. Main St., Mandan

PRICING	$–$$
BEST TIME TO VISIT	Interpretive sites open from the end of April through October
AGE RANGE	7 and older

Fort Abraham Lincoln Photo by Jason Lindsey, courtesy of North Dakota Tourism

The U.S. military expanded west along with settlers, to ensure the steady progress of the railroads and to protect the homesteads and small towns growing up on the otherwise isolated Plains from attacks by the displaced Native Americans from the region. And with the military came a string of forts. In 1872, Fort McKeen was built on the banks of the Missouri River as an infantry post; it was soon renamed Fort Abraham Lincoln. The outpost eventually garrisoned six companies of the 7th Cavalry, commanded by Lieutenant Colonel George Custer. Within a few years of its establishment, the fort was the largest in the state, and key to continuing the expansion of the frontier into Dakota Territory. In 1876 Custer and his cavalrymen left the fort and attempted to return Native Americans in the area to their reservations. At the infamous Battle of Little Bighorn, Custer and more than 250 of his men were killed in the effort. The fort was abandoned in 1891.

Today visitors have the opportunity to see the restored fort, Custer's home, and a reconstructed Native American village, together providing a picture of 19th-century Dakota life. On-a-Slant Village was originally established in the late 16th century by the Mandan tribe, along with more than half a dozen other villages sited along the Missouri River. On-a-Slant was the farthest south and included almost 90 earthen lodges. It got its name because the village was built on ground that slopes toward the river valley. Guests can view six reconstructed lodges in an interpretive tour that tells the story of the Mandan people. Custer's home is open for touring as well; this is the house he lived in with his wife, Libbie, until his death. Other historic structures from the fort include a barracks, a stable, several blockhouses, and a theater, all of which are open for viewing in-season.

372 Fort Mandan

Historical reenactors at Fort Mandan
Photo by Jason Lindsey, courtesy of North Dakota Tourism

CONTACT	www.fortmandan.com; off 8th St. SW, Washburn
PRICING	$–$$
BEST TIME TO VISIT	Year-round
AGE RANGE	7 and older

The explorers Meriwether Lewis and William Clark, along with their Corps of Discovery—a small group of individuals accompanying them—undertook the first transcontinental expedition in the United States. By commission of President Thomas Jefferson, Lewis and Clark journeyed to the Pacific Coast from 1804 to 1806 to study the geography and flora and fauna along the way, as well as to determine how the western frontier could be developed economically. During the especially severe winter of 1804–05, the expedition set up camp along the Missouri River, near Washburn, North Dakota, to shelter themselves from the severe weather and to prepare for their journey to come. They constructed a rough triangular fort of cottonwood, and surrounding the quarters and storage rooms they included 16-foot pickets, designed to de-

> Nearby Fort Mandan is the Lewis and Clark Interpretive Center (at U.S. 83 and ND 200A, near Washburn). The center includes exhibits that explain how the Corps of Discovery interacted with Native Americans throughout their journey. Kids can try on a buffalo robe or a cradle board like the kind Sacajewea used to carry her baby on the journey to the Pacific.

fend against hostile Native Americans, most especially the Sioux tribe, which had threatened to attack the local Mandan tribe with which Lewis and Clark had been trading, as well as the Corps of Discovery explorers. It was at this fort that Lewis and Clark met Sacajawea, the Native woman who would serve as interpreter and guide for the expedition. Once the thaw of spring arrived, Lewis and Clark moved on; when they returned in the summer of 1806 they found that the fort had burned to the ground. The exact location of the original site is now uncertain—it's believed the eroding banks of the Missouri River caused the river to shift and flow over the site.

Today a reconstruction of the encampment sits near the river. Guests can tour the fully furnished quarters and participate in living history programs led by costumed reinterpreters. Look for Lewis's field desk on display, Clark's mapping tools, equipment and provisions the explorers carried with them, and a makeshift blacksmith's forge.

373 Fort Union Trading Post

CONTACT	701-572-9083, www.nps.gov/fous; 15550 Hwy. 1804, Williston
PRICING	$
BEST TIME TO VISIT	Late spring through early fall
AGE RANGE	7 and older

Fort Union Trading Post

Photo by Gene Kellogg, courtesy of North Dakota Tourism

Fort Union on the border of North Dakota and Montana was the largest and most prosperous fur-trading post in the region during the 19th century. The fort was established in 1828 by the American Fur Company, owned by John Jacob Astor, a wealthy investor and merchant, to facilitate commerce between the company and several Northern Plains Native American tribes. It operated until 1867; over the years more than 25,000 bison hides were traded, as well as thousands of pelts from smaller animals. In its heyday more than 100 people were employed at the fort. In exchange for the furs, the Native American trappers were given tobacco, cloth, firearms, and other small gifts. The exchanges were an exercise in diplomacy, requiring protracted negotiations that included speeches by both sides, a meal or two, and sometimes ceremonial pipe smoking—and it was a generally satisfactory relationship for both sides. There is no recorded incidence of violence between the American Fur Company personnel and the tribesmen with whom they did business. Today the fort has been partially reconstructed, and includes the Trading House where guests can learn about the transactions from costumed reinterpreters and handle the furs, as well as the Bourgeois House, now a visitor center.

> The Fort Union Trading Post is sited in two different time zones, but it operates on central time.

374 Knife River Indian Villages National Historic Site

CONTACT 701-745-3300, www.nps.gov/knri; off County Rd. 37, just north of Stanton

PRICING	$
BEST TIME TO VISIT	Summer
AGE RANGE	7 and older

The Knife River, which flows into the Missouri River near what is now Stanton, was once home to several Native American villages belonging to the Hidatsa and Mandan Indians. At its height some 5,000 individuals lived in the region, which in the 19th century served as a major trading center for Native Americans and settlers as well. Meriwether Lewis and William Clark visited the villages on their expedition west; in addition to trading for supplies, the explorers gained valuable information about the route that awaited them. Unfortunately, as a result of trading with non-Natives, the Mandan and Hidatsa peoples were hard hit by a series of smallpox outbreaks, which raged through the Plains from 1837 to 1840 and killed 90

Artifact from Knife River Indian Villages

Courtesy National Park Service

percent of the individuals infected. The Knife River villages were abandoned as a result, and the few survivors migrated north.

Today the Knife River Indian Villages preserve the remains of round earthen dwellings used by the Native peoples, as well as fortification ditches and hunting trails. An on-site museum boasts a remarkable collection of Indian crafts and other artifacts. Outside the center there is a reconstructed full-scale Earthlodge available for touring, as well as a traditional Hidatsa garden. Every year, on the last full weekend in July, the site hosts the Northern Plains Indian Cultural Fest, which includes archaeology lectures; demonstrations of beadworking, porcupine quill work, and flint knapping; and live entertainment, including Indian flute music, cultural demonstrations, and crafts and games for children.

375 Ronald Reagan Minuteman Missile Site

CONTACT 701-797-3691, http://history.nd.gov/historic sites/minutemanmissile; 555 113-1/2 Ave. NE, Hwy. 45, Cooperstown

PRICING	$–$$
BEST TIME TO VISIT	Open May through October; November through February by appointment only
AGE RANGE	7 and older

Following World War II, when defeat of the Nazis effectively left the United States and its NATO allies and the Soviet Union and its communist allies as world superpowers, a prolonged period of military and political tension arose between the two that lasted from the mid-1940s until the collapse of the Soviet Union in 1991. The period has been termed the Cold War, because although there were a number of diplomatic clashes and close calls through the years, the friction between the United States and the Soviet Union never involved direct military intervention. Both sides possessed enough nuclear weapons to ensure mutual annihilation, so each refrained from attacking

the other. Because of the ongoing possibility of confrontation, however, the U.S. military was on constant alert. To ensure the United States was prepared to respond to an attack if and when necessary, in the 1960s the U.S. Air Force deployed Minuteman missiles in bases across less populated states like Missouri, Montana, and North Dakota.

The Ronald Reagan Minuteman Missile State Historic Site—named after the U.S. president who was most vocally critical of the Soviet Union—preserves two such sites that together commemorate the history of the men and women who worked in such facilities during the Cold War. The Oscar-Zero Missile Alert Facility and the November-33 Launch Facility, the last launch control center with its topside facility left intact, are what is left of the 321st Missile Wing that was scattered at sites around the Grand Forks Air Force Base. Visitors today can tour the topside facilities to learn about how security forces and facility personnel went about their lives at the site; it's also possible to take the elevator down to the underground Launch Control Equipment Building and Launch Control Center to see the equipment that stood ready should a watch crew be required to launch the nuclear missiles. During tours of the facilities, guests will learn about the two-person crews who worked 24-hour shifts, every three days, for an average of eight shifts a month; these crews were charged with monitoring the missiles continuously and being prepared 24/7, every day of the year, to launch an attack if ordered, and guests will also learn about the considerable support team that kept the facility secure. Touring the facility is a fascinating look

Blast door at Ronald Reagan Minuteman Missile Site

into what until very recently was a super-secret operation—and it's a sobering reminder of the fearsome power wielded by the U.S. military.

376 Theodore Roosevelt National Park

CONTACT 701-842-2333, www.nps.gov/thro; South Unit, off I-94, near Medora; Elkhorn Ranch, off U.S. 85 near Fairfield; North Unit, off Hwy. 85, south of Watford City

PRICING	$
BEST TIME TO VISIT	Summer
AGE RANGE	5 and older

America's 26th president, Theodore Roosevelt, is remembered as a conservationist president—and the beginning of his concern with the natural world is sometimes attributed to his first trip to the badlands in 1883. Badlands are stretches of heavily eroded landscape that is sparsely vegetated and generally not suitable for cultivating—but in the case of the badlands of the Dakotas, their unusual geographic formations and bright mineral colorations make them stunning, if not immediately useful. Roosevelt came here to shoot big game, but by the time he arrived the huge herds of bison that used to roam the region had already been wiped out by overhunting. He fell in love with the region nevertheless, and in time came to purchase two cattle ranches in the area. During his visits to these ranches he began to notice how overgrazing

Theodore Roosevelt National Park   Courtesy National Park Service

adversely affected the extensive grasslands and as a consequence destroyed the habitats of small mammals and birds. By the time he became president in 1901, Roosevelt was keenly interested in conserving and preserving the landscape of America: He created the USDA Forest Service, established four national game preserves, five national parks, 51 federal bird reservations, and 150 national forests. In total, Roosevelt was responsible for protecting more than 230,000,000 acres of what became public land.

It is therefore fitting that a national park that preserves a portion of the badlands in western North Dakota—and the animals that call it home—is named after Theodore Roosevelt. The park comprises three sections—the North Unit, the South Unit, and the Elkhorn Ranch Unit—and includes 110 square miles.

• **South Unit:** The South Unit visitor center at the park entrance is in Medora, and features Roosevelt's Maltese Cross Cabin, the rough-hewn structure used by Roosevelt as home base when he was visiting his ranch. Don't miss the 36-mile Scenic Loop Drive that offers spectacular views; interpretive signs on multiple pullouts explain the park's history and geological features. Another must-see is the view from the Painted Canyon Visitor Center, which overlooks panoramic scenes of the badlands.

• **Elkhorn Ranch Unit:** The site of Roosevelt's second cattle ranch in the region is another 35 miles beyond the South Unit entrance. The structures have long since deteriorated or been torn down, but there are interpretive panels to explain how Roosevelt used the land.

• **North Unit:** Near Watford City, the North Unit visitor center is open daily from April through mid-October and on weekends throughout the rest of the year; it offers ranger programs, exhibits, and an orientation film. Don't miss the 14-mile Scenic Drive that runs from the north entrance to Oxbow Overlook; along the way are multiple self-guided hiking trails.

All three sites offer some of the best wildlife viewing in the country. There are more than 186 species of birds that live in or migrate through Theodore Roosevelt National Park. In addition, the park is home to numerous mammals, including bison herds (which have been restored to the area since Roosevelt's time), elk, longhorn sheep, deer, pronghorn antelope, wild horses, and ubiquitous prairie dogs.

Columbus skyline   © anharris/iStockphoto.com

OHIO

377 Dayton Aviation Heritage National Historic Park

Dayton Aviation Heritage National Historic Park

Office of Tourism Ohio, www.discoverohio.com

CONTACT www.nps.gov/daav; sites located in and around Dayton

PRICING	Dayton History Center: $–$$; Paul Laurence Dunbar House: $–$$; Hawthorn Hill: $$$; other sites $
BEST TIME TO VISIT	Year-round
AGE RANGE	5 and older

The Dayton Aviation Center commemorates the lives of three of Dayton, Ohio's, native sons: aviation pioneers Wilbur and Orville Wright and author and poet Paul Laurence Dunbar, who was a neighbor and friend of the Wright brothers since childhood. The park comprises five units throughout the Dayton area that were important to the three men:

- **Dayton History at Carillon Historical Park** (937-293-2841; 1000 Carillon Blvd.): Come to this expansive 65-acre complex that includes 25 exhibition buildings to see the 1905 Wright Flyer III, built by Orville and Wilbur and flown at Huffman Prairie Flying Field. Also here is a large collection of vintage automobiles, bicycles, train cars, and the largest carillon in Ohio.

- **Hawthorn Hill** (937-293-2841; 901 Harmon Ave., Oakwood): This beautiful Georgian Revival mansion (so grandiose it resembles the White House), just outside of Dayton, was the home of several members of the Wright family for many years. Orville lived at the residence until his death in 1948, along with his younger sister, Katharine; Wilbur, however, died before the home was completed. The home is not open to the public, but private tours (limited to 10 individuals) may be arranged Wednesday and Saturday through the Dayton History Museum.

- **Huffman Prairie Flying Field** (937-425-0008; Gate 16A off OH 444, Wright-Patterson AFB): Now located on an active military base, the Huffman Prairie Flying Field allows guests to walk in the flight paths where the Wright brothers tested their earliest planes. The nearby Huffman Prairie Flying Field Interpretive Center (937-425-0008; 2380 Memorial Rd., Wright-Patterson AFB) offers exhibits that explain the Wrights' significance in aviation history.

- **Paul Laurence Dunbar House** (937-313-2010; 219 N. Paul Laurence Dunbar St.): Dunbar was the son of former slaves and the first African American poet to be recognized internationally. Although he lived only 33 years, he published more than 400 poems, six novels, short stories, and lyrics for musicals. Reservations are required to tour his onetime home, where he lived with his mother, Matilda, from 1904 until his death in 1906. Come here to see beautifully restored period decorations and to learn more about the writer who is credited with inspiring the Harlem Renaissance many years later.

- **Wright Cycle Company Complex** (937-225-7705; 16 S. Williams St.): The Wright Cycle Company Complex includes the Wright Cycle Company building (the fourth, and only surviving, bicycle shop owned by the Wrights), a plaza, and the Wright-Dunbar Interpretive Center. Also within this complex is the Wright and Wright Job Printers building, owned and operated by Orville and Wilbur Wright from 1890 to 1895. Many people do not realize that the Wright brothers were also publishers: They printed the *Dayton Tattler*, written by Paul Laurence Dunbar.

378 First Ladies National Historic Center

CONTACT 330-452-0876, www.nps.gov/fila; Saxton McKinley House: 331 S. Market Ave., Canton; Education and Research Center: 205 S. Market Ave., Canton

PRICING	$–$$
BEST TIME TO VISIT	Year-round; open Tuesday through Saturday, and Sunday in the summer
AGE RANGE	7 and older

First Ladies throughout the years have served myriad roles, from hostesses in chief to spokespeople for their own causes to advocates for their husbands' administrations. Recent First Ladies have maintained rigorous schedules and agendas of their own, serving—in effect—as unpaid presidential advisers. So integral was Hillary Clinton to his campaign and administration that President Bill Clinton once campaigned that a vote for him was a "buy-one get-one-free" proposition. First Lady Michelle Obama speaks out against childhood obesity, advocates for healthier food in the nation's schools, and is an active supporter of military families; Laura Bush supported literacy causes; and Nancy Reagan was famous for her anti-drug campaign. First Ladies from earlier centuries certainly made their marks as well: Dolley Madison was an active social director, serving as stand-in First

Saxton House, First Ladies National Historic Center
Courtesy National First Ladies Library

Lady for widowed President Thomas Jefferson and later officially for her own husband, President James Madison. Eleanor Roosevelt was an outspoken supporter of her husband President Franklin D. Roosevelt's New Deal program, as well as an advocate for civil rights. Lady Bird Johnson undertook the considerable task of beautifying America's highways.

For their contributions to America—in what is an unpaid full-time job—it is fitting that the First Ladies National Historic Center honors the accomplishments of the women who have lived in the White House alongside their powerful husbands. The site includes two properties, the home of First Lady Ida Saxton McKinley and the Education and Research Center, housed in the historic 1895 City Bank Building. The Saxton McKinley house was home to President William McKinley from 1878 to 1891, when he served in the U.S. House of Representatives. The home has been painstakingly restored to the McKinley era and is furnished lavishly with period furniture, carpets, and historic wallpaper. The museum complex includes 500 artifacts, including a fun exhibit of more than 150 dresses and fashion accessories once owned by First Ladies; a research library that includes a collection of books replicating First Lady Abigail Fillmore's collection; and a small theater that hosts documentaries and lectures on First Ladies throughout history.

379 Fort Meigs

CONTACT 800-283-8916, www.fortmeigs.org; 29100 W. River Rd., Perrysburg

PRICING	$–$$
BEST TIME TO VISIT	Open April through October; closed Monday and Tuesday
AGE RANGE	7 and older

Only a few decades after Americans defeated the British in the 1781 Battle of Yorktown and thus won the Revolutionary War, the United States again declared war on its old patriarchical nemesis, Great Britain. June 18, 1812, marked the start of what is now known as the War of 1812; the conflict was precipi-

PRICE KEY
$ free–$5
$$ $6–10
$$$ $11–20
$$$$ $21+

Reenactment at Fort Meigs   Office of Tourism Ohio, www.discoverohio.com

tated by residual resentment between the two nations, Britain's interference with America's role in international trade, and America's unease over the British involvement with Native American tribes. Despite a strong start by the Americans in early battles in the Atlantic and on Lake Erie—largely because Great Britain was preoccupied with Napoleon and his armies in Europe—it soon became clear the United States would have to expand its military resources if it was to defeat Great Britain once again.

To shore up its defenses, the United States constructed several forts, both to serve as defensive positions for American troops and to aid in supplying them for battle. In early 1813 General William Henry Harrison oversaw the construction of a fort in what is today Perrysburg, Ohio, which was designed to be a supply depot and mustering point for war maneuvers in Canada and to protect northwest Ohio and Indiana from invasion. The expansive fort was enclosed with 15-foot logs and an earthen embankment; when it was completed, the fort was the largest walled wooden fort in America. The fort saw action during two sieges undertaken by British and Canadian troops—with the help of Native Americans under the command of Chief Tecumseh. Both sieges were unsuccessful.

Today guests can visit the reconstructed 10-acre Fort Meigs, which includes re-creations of historic structures along with a museum and education center. The museum offers a fascinating collection of artifacts from the war, including letters and diaries written by soldiers stationed at the fort; original maps; and a large collection of swords and guns. Don't miss the detailed diorama of the original fort, as well as a full-size display of a soldier's tent.

Throughout the season costumed interpreters present living history demonstrations to teach families about camp life. Fort Meigs hosts several battle reenactments every year as well, including a reenactment of the Siege of Fort Meigs in May 1813; a reenactment of the Fourth of July as celebrated in the fort in 1813; and a special Halloween tour of the fort in which guides regale guests with ghost stories.

380 Lawnfield

CONTACT	440-255-8722, www.nps.gov/jaga; 8095 Mentor Ave., Mentor
PRICING	$
BEST TIME TO VISIT	Open May through October daily; November through April on weekends only
AGE RANGE	7 and older

James Garfield (1831–81) was the 20th president of the United States, a post he served only 200 days: He was shot by an assassin on July 2, 1881, and eventually perished from his wounds on September 19. During his brief time in the White House, President Garfield sought reforms to end political corruption, and particularly sought to revamp the U.S. Post Office.

Lawnfield—as it was dubbed by journalists—was the onetime home of President Garfield and his family and the site of his successful 1880 campaign for the presidency. Instead of traveling across the country to meet with voters, as modern-day candidates do,

Park rangers provide special guided tours twice a month. Every first Saturday the "Behind the Scenes" tour offers a more extensive look at the home, including the servants' quarters, the basement, and the 1870s barn. Every third Saturday the "Garfield and the Civil War Tour" takes guests to the third-floor suite to learn about Garfield's brother-in-law, Civil War general Joe Rudolph. Both tours begin at the visitor center. Reserve the $15 tickets in advance.

Garfield invited people to hear his speeches from the front porch of this home—making his one of the first "front-porch campaigns." Garfield purchased the house in 1876 and immediately added 11 rooms to create space for his family. Today guests can tour the restored home to view the period furnishings and enjoy the beautiful grounds, which include walking paths and gardens.

To learn more about the Underground Railroad in Ohio, check out the Clermont County Ohio Freedom Trail (get maps at the Convention and Visitors Bureau, 800-796-4282, 410 E. Main St., Batavia). The trail comprises 33 sites tracing a trail along the Underground Railroad.

381 National Underground Railroad Freedom Center

CONTACT 513-333-7500, www.freedomcenter.org; 50 E. Freedom Way, Cincinnati

PRICING	$$–$$$
BEST TIME TO VISIT	Year-round; closed Monday
AGE RANGE	12 and older

The National Underground Railroad Freedom Center preserves the history of the Underground Railroad in America before the Civil War and commemorates the struggle for freedom around the world in the modern era. The Underground Railroad refers to a covert network of safe houses and abolitionists, both black and white, who ferried escaped slaves from the South into the free states in the North (and sometimes beyond to Canada). Cincinnati and the Ohio River Valley were the hubs of much of this activity. Step into the lovely structure, with windows looking out to the river and beyond, and it's impossible to miss the slave pen, placed in a central location in the atrium. The 21-foot-by-30-log structure was built in 1830 to house slaves before they were shipped to auction. Often dozens of slaves were crammed into the tiny structure, some manacled; individuals could be enslaved in pens like this one for months, awaiting the next slave sale. Be sure to check out the permanent exhibit titled *Slavery Today*, which examines human trafficking in contemporary society. Because of the subject matter, visiting this museum is a moving, sometimes disturbing experience, and thus should be reserved for mature children.

Slave pen, National Underground Railroad Freedom Center   Office of Tourism Ohio, www.discoverohio.com

382 Rankin House Abolitionist Site

CONTACT 937-392-1627; 6152 Rankin Rd., Ripley

PRICING	$
BEST TIME TO VISIT	Open May through October, Wednesday through Sunday
AGE RANGE	7 and older

By the mid-19th century, slavery was illegal in Ohio, but under the Fugitive Slave Law of 1850 slave owners were allowed to pursue their escaped slaves, even when those escaped individuals were living in free states. So to ensure their liberty, slaves had to run away as far as Canada. The Underground Railroad, the informal and secret network of safe houses and abolitionists who were committed to helping former slaves make their way north, had stops throughout Ohio and running north to the Canadian border. The Rankin House in southern Ohio was an important

Rankin House   Office of Tourism Ohio, www.discoverohio.com

early stop along the Underground Railroad. John Rankin was a Presbyterian minister and teacher, and together with his wife, Jean, was an active and vocal abolitionist. He published *Letters on American Slavery*, an antislavery volume, in 1826. In 1834 Rankin founded the Ohio Anti-Slavery Society. But Rankin had perhaps his greatest impact between the years of 1825 and 1865, when he helped more than 2,000 slaves escape to freedom. Rankin boasted that he never lost a "passenger" at his stop. He sheltered as many as a dozen slaves at a time, in a house already filled with 13 of his own children. He kept a lantern lighted in the window of his home, to indicate to slaves approaching that his was a place of sanctuary.

The home is sited at the top of a steep hill overlooking the river; guests today can climb the 100 stairs to the structure, just as escaped slaves did. Arrange to tour the home to see many of Rankin's personal items, including his family Bible, and to learn more about the antislavery movement in Ohio.

The Rock and Roll Hall of Fame is the kind of museum that people who don't love musuems love.

The Rock and Roll Hall of Fame and Museum is the kind of museum that even people who don't normally enjoy museums tend to love. The gorgeous glass-and-steel structure on the shore of Lake Erie commemorates all things related to rock music: Archived here are the histories and extensive artifacts of influential musicians, producers, and songwriters, and it's enormous fun for music lovers to stroll the multiple levels to discover treasure after treasure. Look for Paul McCartney's handwritten arrangements, Lady Gaga's stage outfits, the original reel-to-reel recordings done by the Doors, Janis Joplin's wildly painted 1965 Porsche, Joey Ramone's black leather jacket, Stevie Wonder's harmonica, Mick Jagger's Union Jack flag cape, John Lennon's acoustic guitar complete with Lennon's signature and a doodled self-portrait alongside Yoko: The collections go on and on. The Rock and Roll Hall of Fame has movie theaters, too, that screen a rotating collection of films, like a Rolling Stones concert, Elvis on Tour, and a 3-D U2 concert. The museum opened its doors in 1995, and every year inducts a select group into its Hall of Fame. The first inductees included Elvis Presley, Fats Domino, Chuck Berry, Jerry Lee Lewis, and Buddy Holly. Recent inductees have included Guns N' Roses, the Red Hot Chili Peppers, and the Beastie Boys.

383 Rock and Roll Hall of Fame

CONTACT 216-781-7625, http://rockhall.com; 1100 Rock and Roll Blvd., Cleveland

PRICING	$$$–$$$$
BEST TIME TO VISIT	Year-round
AGE RANGE	7 and older

Rock and Roll Hall of Fame   Office of Tourism Ohio, www.discoverohio.com

384 Rutherford B. Hayes Presidential Center

CONTACT 419-332-2081, www.rbhayes.org/hayes; Spiegel Grove, Fremont

PRICING	$–$$
BEST TIME TO VISIT	Year-round; closed Monday
AGE RANGE	7 and older

Rutherford B. Hayes (1822–93) was the 19th president of the United States, and was elected in one of the most hotly contested elections in American history. An Electoral Commission was called in to resolve what were otherwise too-close-to-call results; Hayes was ultimately declared the victor by only one electoral vote. Hayes was born in Ohio (a state that boasts being the birthplace of seven U.S. presidents). Before assuming the office of president, Hayes had a distinguished military career as a union officer in the Civil War, served in Congress, and was governor of Ohio for three terms. His wife, Lucy Webb Hayes, is well remembered as the First Lady who forbid liquor to be served in the White House.

The Rutherford B. Hayes Presidential Center comprises the Rutherford B. Hayes Museum and Library along with Spiegel Grove, the estate and home that belonged to Hayes and several generations of his family. Visitors can tour the lovely 31-room mansion, use the resources of the expansive Hayes library, pay respects at Hayes's burial site, and stroll through the 25 acres of grounds. The museum displays some 2,000

Rutherford B. Hayes House   Office of Tourism Ohio, www.discoverohio.com

artifacts out of its collection of more than 19,000, many originally belonging to Hayes and his family. Look for Civil War weapons, White House china, 19th-century toys, and a collection of military uniforms.

385 Serpent Mound Archaeological Site

CONTACT 937-587-2796, http://arcofappalachia.org/visit/serpent-mound.html; 3850 OH 73, Peebles

PRICING	$ (parking fee additional)
BEST TIME TO VISIT	Open daily June through October; open weekends the rest of the year (with closings during the winter holiday season)
AGE RANGE	7 and older

The Serpent Mound in southwest Ohio presents a mystery to visitors: The 1,340-foot-long, 3-foot high prehistoric effigy mound winds through the natural features of the locale, forming a distinct and stylized shape of a snake with an open mouth encircling an oval. It is considered the largest and finest such structure in the world. Many researchers have interpreted the design as a snake eating an egg—although some researchers have hypothesized that the oval in the snake's mouth is meant to represent the sun, and the whole piece is a representation of an eclipse. The head of the serpent is aligned to the summer solstice sunset, and the coils point to the winter solstice and equinox sunrises. The precise date of the mound's construction, the builders of the effigy, and its exact purpose are unknown. Archaeologists originally attributed the mound to the Adena culture, which dates back as far as 1000 BC. The Adena were an early agricultural and gathering people that lived from the Midwest to the Atlantic coast of what is now the United States; it has been posited that the mounds were used to bury and preserve the dead of the Adena. Recent research has suggested that the mound was actually constructed by people of the Fort Ancient culture, which dates to AD 900. These people lived in the central Ohio Valley and are known to have built large earthen structures. Today, visitors can follow a trail that winds alongside the mysterious (and beautiful)

Serpent Mound   Office of Tourism Ohio, www.discoverohio.com

construction, view the mound from an overlook, or—for the best view—climb to the top of the Observation Tower.

386 Warren G. Harding Home

🔔

CONTACT 800-600-6894, http://hardinghome.org; 380 Mount Vernon Ave., Marion

PRICING	$–$$
BEST TIME TO VISIT	Open Memorial Day to Labor Day, Thursday through Sunday; open weekends only in September and October
AGE RANGE	7 and older

Warren G. Harding (1865–1923) was the 29th president of the United States. He started his career as a newspaper publisher, then served in the Ohio Senate, as lieutenant governor of Ohio, and as a U.S. senator before being elected to the presidency. His administration pledged a return to "normalcy" and was staunchly against the League of Nations, but is probably best remembered for a rash of political scandals. He died in office of a heart attack.

Two miles from the Harding home is the marble tomb that is the final resting place for President Harding and his wife (OH 423 and Vernon Heights Blvd.)

Guests today can visit the beautiful Queen Anne home President Harding shared with his wife, Florence Kling DeWolfe. The couple arranged for the design and construction of the home in 1890 and were married in its completed front hallway in 1891. Tour the parlor, library, dining room, and several bedrooms, including Harding's, all of which are decorated in period furnishings, most of which originally belonged to the president and his wife. Look for the "haunted clock"—an eight-day clock that reportedly stopped at the exact moment when President Harding died on August 2, 1923. The clock was repaired, but docents claim that it stops some years on the anniversary of Harding's death.

387 William McKinley Library

🔔

CONTACT 330-455-7043, www.mckinleymuseum.org; 800 McKinley Monument Dr. NW, Canton

PRICING	$$
BEST TIME TO VISIT	Year-round
AGE RANGE	7 and older

William McKinley (1843–1901) was the 25th president of the United States, best remembered as commander in chief during the Spanish-American War. He was a strong advocate of American industry and maintained the gold standard during his administration. He was assassinated in 1901, during his second term in office, while standing in a receiving line at the Pan-American Exposition in Buffalo. A mentally unstable individual shot him twice, and he died a week later.

The William McKinley Presidential Library and Museum is an eclectic homage to the fallen president, and includes multiple family-friendly attractions, such as Discover World; the Hoover-Price Planetarium, which hosts shows as part of the admission price (for kids 5 years and older); the Keller Gallery; the McKinley Gallery, in which animatronic figures of the president and First Lady greet visitors; the Street of Shops, a life-sized replica of a historic town that includes a horse-drawn fire engine and a fire pole kids can slide down; and the McKinley National Memorial, the burial site of President McKinley and his family.

Bricktown Canal, Oklahoma City   © chrispo/iStockphoto.com

OKLAHOMA

388 Centennial Land Run Monument

CONTACT www.okc.gov/landrun/index.html; south end of Bricktown Canal, Oklahoma City

PRICING	$
BEST TIME TO VISIT	Year-round
AGE RANGE	All ages

The Indian Appropriations Bill of 1889 opened up unoccupied lands in Indian Territory (what is now Oklahoma). This in turn allowed President Benjamin Harrison to open 2 million acres to settlement for Americans eager to migrate west. The existing Homestead Act of 1862 provided that settlers could claim 160 unoccupied acres without cost. In exchange, the settlers agreed to live on the land for five years continuously and make improvements, such as adding structures and plowing fields—and there was plenty of interest in homesteading the new lands. It was determined that to be fair, no one could enter the region until noon on April 22, 1889. This caused enormous excitement throughout the country: More than 50,000 people poised on the edges of the soon-to-be-open territory to claim fewer than 12,000 homesteads. The "Land Run," as it was later called, began when cannons were fired to mark 12 PM, at which point hopefuls raced on horseback and in wagons to grab their piece of the American dream. Not everyone played by the rules, however: A number of individuals snuck into the territory early and hid until the legal time of entry, so that they could be the first to arrive at the best homesteads. These folks have been given the nickname "Sooners," and there were dozens of legal disputes resulting from their shenanigans.

The in-progress Centennial Land Run Monument in Oklahoma City commemorates this important event in the history of western America. Artist Paul Moore was commissioned to create a dramatic and truly monumental sculpture group that captures the excitement and promise of the Land Run. The first installations were put into place in 2003. When complete, the collection of sculptures will feature depictions of 45 Land Run participants, rendered in bronze at one and a half times life sized. The total collection will stretch 365 feet long, 36 feet wide, 16 feet high, and span a waterway. The monument includes a soldier firing the cannon that alerted participants to the start of the Land Run; a woman riding her horse sidesaddle; an eager pioneer aboard a buckboard; and a startled rabbit watching from a safe distance. Throughout, the piece presents a moment in time that is full of life: Look for the chair falling from the back of a bouncing buggy; children peeking through the canvas of their covered wagon; and a cowboy desperately trying to maintain his mount as the horse he is riding falls amid the chaos. The amazing piece is set to be complete in 2015, and when it is it will be one of the largest such statuary collections in the world.

389 Chisholm Trail Heritage Center

CONTACT 580-252-6692, www.onthechisholmtrail.com; 1000 Chisholm Trail Parkway, Duncan

PRICING	$–$$
BEST TIME TO VISIT	Year-round
AGE RANGE	5 and older

The Chisholm Trail was a well-worn route used from 1867 through 1884 to drive cattle from Texas northward through what was then Indian Territory, into Kansas. The cattle industry depended on the route—some states had closed their borders to Texas cattle drives as a result of diseases the cattle carried, so this was one of the few routes that allowed Texans to get their cattle to eastern markets. And the Texas economy depended on the cattle industry. The trail is named after Jesse Chisholm, who was famous for driving cattle from a southern trading post along the Red River in Texas to a northern trading post near Kansas City. Chisholm built several trading posts along the way in what is now Oklahoma.

The Chisholm Trail Heritage Center in Duncan is located near the old trail, and offers an interactive experience that tells the story of the cowboys who were responsible for epic cattle drives. Guests are encouraged to do more than look at the displays: Kids can try

Pint-sized cowboys, Chisholm Trail Heritage Center
Courtesy Chisholm Trail Heritage Center

their hand at lassoing, don on a cowboy hat, or design their own cattle brand. The small museum features an animatronic "Jesse" that regales visitors with a campfire tale from the trail. There's also a 4-D Experience Theater featuring a film on the cattle drives that allows viewers to feel the earth move during a stampede and smell wildflowers on the prairie. Don't miss the Garis Gallery of the American West, housed here, which exhibits work by some of the best western artists in the country, including George Catlin and Frederick Remington.

390 Fort Gibson

CONTACT 918-478-4088, www.okhistory.org/sites/fort gibson; Fort Gibson

PRICING	$
BEST TIME TO VISIT	Open mid-April through mid-October, Tuesday through Sunday; open late October through early April, Thursday through Sunday
AGE RANGE	7 and older

In the early 19th century Fort Gibson was the westernmost post of the U.S. military. The fort was built to protect the "Five Civilized Tribes" from other Native peoples in the area as well as from pioneers pushing westward into Indian lands. *Five Civilized Tribes* was the name given to the Cherokee, Chickasaw, Choctaw,

Creek, and Seminole peoples, whom the earliest European settlers considered civilized because they were generally friendly to colonists and adopted many of the European mores (such as wearing European-style clothing). The fort also served as a staging area for military expeditions heading west and for campaigns seeking peace between warring tribes in the region.

The original fort burned down and very little remained after the Civil War. In the 1930s, the Works Progress Administration rebuilt the primitive log fort. Visit the reconstruction to see archaeological ruins, as well as re-created and period-furnished original buildings, including enlisted men's barracks, officers' quarters, a stockade, and a carpenter's shop. The visitor center includes interpretive exhibits on the history of the fort, and the site hosts living history events throughout the year.

391 National Cowboy and Western Heritage Museum

CONTACT 405-478-2250, www.nationalcowboymuseum.org; 1700 NE 63rd St., Oklahoma City

PRICING	$$–$$$
BEST TIME TO VISIT	Year-round
AGE RANGE	7 and older

The National Cowboy and Western Heritage Museum celebrates the heritage of the Old West and exhibits cowboy history and culture from the earliest Spanish colonial vaqueros to the cattle ranchers of today. With more than 28,000 works of art and cultural artifacts, the world's most extensive collection of American rodeo paraphernalia, and interactive areas for families, the museum has something for everyone interested in learning about the real American West. The complex includes three halls of fame: The Hall of Great Western Performers, which pays homage to movie cowboys like John Wayne and Clint Eastwood; the Hall of Great Westerners, which commemorates the lives of real cowboys; and the Rodeo Hall of Fame, which memorializes the greatest rodeo stars in America.

PRICE KEY
$ free–$5
$$ $6–10
$$$ $11–20
$$$$ $21+

National Cowboy and Western Heritage Museum

Oklahoma City Convention and Visitors Bureau

Visitors are greeted with outdoor sculptures scattered across the 18-acre site, and welcomed indoors by the massive *End of the Trail* sculpture by James Earle Fraser that sits in the atrium. There are a number of galleries inside to visit, each offering a glimpse into the American West:

- **American Cowboy Gallery:** This exhibition includes the largest exhibition on the working cowboy in this country. Look for a diorama of a chuck wagon, a collection of branding irons, and an extensive collection of cowboy wear—from 10-gallon hats to hand-tooled boots to studded chaps.

- **Art of the American West Gallery:** Within this museum space you'll find extraordinary paintings and sculptures—more than 2,000 pieces—that tell the story of the American West. Look for Albert Bierstadt's romanticized *Emigrants Crossing the Plains.*

- **Children's Cowboy Corral:** This hands-on gallery allows young children to explore the life of a cowboy by dressing up in authentic gear, climbing aboard pint-sized saddles (resting atop "log ponies"), and setting up a play campfire and chuck wagon. Toddlers will enjoy the oversized puzzles and the generous collection of books about the Old West.

- **Native American Gallery:** There are almost 200 cultural items on display that explain Native culture and traditions. Look for extraordinary textiles, hand-beaded clothing, and baskets.

- **Osborn Studio:** This whimsical gallery re-creates the studio of an itinerant photographer. Guests can stroll through to see a vintage camera, photo portrait back-drop, and other equipment before entering an exhibit on the history of photography.

392 Oklahoma City National Memorial

CONTACT 405-235-3313, www.oklahomacitynational memorial.org; 620 N. Harvey Ave., Oklahoma City

PRICING	$$–$$$
BEST TIME TO VISIT	Year-round
AGE RANGE	10 and older

April 19, 1995, marked what was the deadliest and most destructive terrorist act in the United States until the September 11, 2001, attacks. Domestic terrorists used a massive truck bomb to destroy the Alfred P. Murrah Federal Building in downtown Oklahoma City, killing 168 people, including 19 young children who were in a day care facility on the property. More

Oklahoma City National Memorial

Courtesy Oklahoma National Memorial and Museum

than 680 people were injured, and 324 buildings were either destroyed or damaged.

The Oklahoma City National Memorial at the site of the bomb blast honors the memories of those killed and celebrates those who survived. The Memorial Museum offers a chronological, interpretive history of the event. Galleries include exhibits on terrorism, a collection of artifacts rescued from the building, pieces of the building itself, and a heartbreaking collection of personal items left behind. The extensive outdoor memorial includes a reflecting pool; the Field of Empty Chairs, 168 separate sculptures each inscribed with the name of a victim of the bombing; the Survivor Wall, built from salvaged pieces of granite from the Murrah Building, which includes the names of those who survived the attacks; and the Survivor Tree, an elm on the property that survived the blast and continues to grow. Take kids to the Children's Area, which includes a wall of tiles painted by children from around the country and chalkboards and buckets of chalk and chalkboards built into the ground, so that kids can express their feelings after touring the solemn monument.

393 Oklahoma Route 66 Museum

CONTACT 580-323-7866, www.route66.org/index2.html; 2229 W. Gary Blvd., Clinton

PRICING	$
BEST TIME TO VISIT	Year-round
AGE RANGE	5 and older

In much the way the Santa Fe and Oregon Trails allowed pioneers to emigrate westward in the 19th century in search of a better life, Route 66 allowed Americans to traverse the country for the pleasure of travel and to keep moving ever westward in the early 20th century. U.S. Route 66, which has been nicknamed the Mother Road, was one of the original U.S. highways, crossing Illinois, Kansas, Missouri, Oklahoma, Texas, New Mexico, Arizona, and California. It was built in 1926 and ran from Chicago to Los Angeles, covering 2,448 miles. The roadway became vitally im-

There are dozens of Route 66 museums in the West and myriad remaining roadside attractions still to see. In Oklahoma look for the *Golden Driller* at the Tulsa Expo Center, a 76-foot-tall statue of an oilman. In Foyil, check out the world's largest totem pole, which includes 200 carved illustrations that run up the base and is topped with four 9-foot statues of Native Americans representing four different tribes. *Pops* in Arcadia is a relative newcomer: A 60-foot-tall pop bottle illuminated at night by hundreds of LEDs that change colors marks a soda shop.

portant to the economies of the communities along its route, and hundreds of businesses sprang up to support the Route 66 traffic, including gas and service stations, restaurants, inexpensive motels, and unusual and quirky roadside attractions. To appeal to travelers and to outdo their competition, such businesses often sought to attract guests through flashy neon signs, oversized sculptures, large and colorful billboards—just about anything that might catch the eye of someone passing through. The iconic roadway became so popular it inspired songs and TV shows. But by mid-century the Interstate Highway System, which was faster because it bypassed the small communities along Route 66, had all but replaced the historic route. In 1985 Route 66 was officially removed from the U.S. highway system.

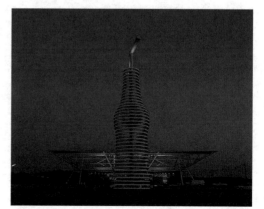

Pop's Restaurant, Arcadia, along Route 66
Carol M. Highsmith's America, courtesy Library of Congress, Prints and Photographs Division

Route 66 lives on, however, including more than 400 miles that run through Oklahoma. In Clinton, the Oklahoma Route 66 Museum is a neon-clad homage to the route and to the roadside stops it inspired. Visitors will find an operating trading post at the Mohawk Indian Lodge, the world's largest curio cabinet (which houses trinkets collected along Route 66), a drive-in theater, and the tiny 1950s Valentine Diner. The museum has been recently renovated to include interactive exhibits, such as audio conversations that might have been overheard in a bus station along Route 66 in the 1940s and interactive kiosks that relay news from the 1930s.

394 Red Earth Festival

CONTACT 405-427-5228, www.redearth.org/red-earth-festival; Oklahoma City (venue can vary yearly)

PRICING	$$
BEST TIME TO VISIT	Early June; check website for annual dates
AGE RANGE	All ages

The Red Earth Festival held annually in Oklahoma City is a three-day celebration of Native American culture at which more than 1,200 American Indian artists and performers from around the country gather to share their heritage. Everyone is welcome at the event, which includes a wide array of visual arts created by some of the finest Native artists in North America. Attendees can view juried exhibits and purchase examples of beadwork, baskets, fine jewelry, handmade pottery, paintings, and sculpture. Dance exhibitions and competitions are colorful and offer a glimpse into the distinct tribal dress and customs that are represented by more than 100 tribes that at-

Visit the Red Earth Museum (6 Santa Fe Plaza, Oklahoma City) year-round to see Native American artwork and artifacts and watch cultural demonstrations.

tend the festival. Don't miss the grand parade, which kicks off the celebration on the first morning of the festival: Participants dressed in full tribal regalia march down the streets of downtown Oklahoma City, along with high school marching bands, drum groups, and floats.

395 Washita Battlefield

CONTACT 580-497-2742, www.nps.gov/waba; off Hwy. 47A, Cheyenne

PRICING	$
BEST TIME TO VISIT	Spring and fall
AGE RANGE	7 and older

The history of U.S. westward expansion is inextricably tangled and messy: The admirable pioneering spirit that spurred independent individuals to leave their homes in established eastern communities and move westward to build the country and to create new lives for themselves and their families is inseparable from the unjust, often brutal treatment that Native peoples already living on the lands Americans hoped to claim suffered at the hands of the U.S. government. As in any conflict in which opposing parties seek the same territory, there were inevitable clashes between the pioneers and the Indian tribes, and over many years there were numerous bloody encounters incited by both sides. To contain the conflict—and to retain the right to take the prairies of what is now the Midwest—the United States forcibly removed the Natives to reservations in regions in which the United States had no interest (at the time) in settling. Over the history of U.S.–Native conflict, many tribes were forcibly removed from their homelands, and many others were coerced to sign treaties agreeing to such relocations.

One such treaty was the Medicine Lodge Treaty, in which the Arapaho and Southern Cheyenne peoples were made to leave what is now Kansas and Colorado for Indian Territory—now Oklahoma. A move to Oklahoma meant giving up the roaming grounds of bison, their main source of meat and an important symbol in Native culture. Once in Indian Territory, the tribes also found little arable land—and as a result Natives fought back in an effort to regain their traditional territories in the prairies. In summer 1868 war parties of the Cheyenne as well as allied tribes, including the Oglala, Lakota, and Pawnee, repeatedly attacked pioneer settlements in parts of Colorado, Kansas, and Texas. At least 15 white settlers were killed and several others wounded. Several deadly skirmishes followed among the U.S. military and Native tribes. In an effort to contain the Cheyenne, the 7th U.S. Cavalry, led by Lieutenant Colonel George Armstrong Custer, surprised the Southern Cheyenne village of Chief Black Kettle by attacking before sunrise on November 27, 1868. At least 100 Natives were killed—perhaps many more. In addition, Custer ordered his men to shoot Indian horses: As many as 800 animals were slaughtered. This battle, known now as the Battle of Washita, was pivotal in U.S.–Native relations. The U.S. government counted the battle as a significant victory against Indian raids, but many Natives along with contemporary historians view the battle as a massacre.

> *As in any conflict in which opposing parties seek the same territory, clashes were inevitable.*

Snow on the Washita River, Washita Battlefield
Courtesy Washita Battlefield National Historic Site

The Washita Battlefield preserves the site along the Washita River where the controversial clash occurred. Begin your trip at the visitor center to view the 30-minute film *Destiny at Dawn: Loss and Victory on the Washita*, to learn more about the U.S.-Indian wars in the 19th century and, specifically, about Custer's infamous attack on the Cheyenne. Tour the battlefield via the 1.5-mile self-guided trail; or sign up for a ranger-led tour that will provide background on the battle. Be sure to check out the Washita Native Garden. The garden is shaped like a medicine wheel and is separated into four sections that include medicinal herbs and vegetable plants.

oregon

396 Crater Lake National Park

CONTACT 541-594-3000, www.nps.gov/crla; off Rt. 62, Crater Lake

PRICING	$
BEST TIME TO VISIT	Year-round (come prepared for massive snows in winter)
AGE RANGE	All ages

Crater Lake National Park   Courtesy National Park Service

Scenic Crater Lake in southern Oregon is the deepest lake in the United States—and the second deepest in the world. The lake was created after the enormous volcanic eruption of Mount Mazama some 8,000 years ago caused the mountain to collapse in on itself. What was left was a deep caldera (a volcanic basin), which after thousands of years filled with rain and snowmelt. The lake is 5 miles by 6 miles, and at its deepest it is 1,943 feet. Perhaps the most astonishing feature of the lake is its crystal-clear, deep sapphire-blue color—which is even more breathtaking when viewed against a backdrop of heavy snowfall and evergreen forests.

Crater Lake National Park comprises the gorgeous lake, along with 183,224 acres of wilderness that includes multiple elevations, a diverse collection of wildlife, and numerous trails that are ideal for hiking in the short summer season and even better for snowshoeing and cross-country skiing in the winter.

Crater Lake National Park is open year-round, but note that it gets an average of 533 inches of snow per year, which all but ensures a winter wonderland most months. Note that accessibility can be challenging in the colder months: Roads are subject to closure starting in mid-October and continuing well into summer. Highway 62 and Munson Valley Road (the road to the rim) are plowed; plowing of the Rim Drive and the North Entrance Road begins in April. The North Entrance Road and the West Rim Drive generally open in June. The Pinnacles Road and East Rim Drive usually don't open until as late as July.

Rim Drive is one of the best ways to see the lake; it follows the rim of the caldera and offers spectacular views from on high. Get out of the car and hike part of the Pacific Crest Trail—a 2,650-mile long-distance hiking trail that runs from Mexico to Canada—to experience the tranquility of the lake and its surrounds. In addition to viewing one of the loveliest lakes on the planet, while visiting be sure to check out the adjacent Pumice Desert, an accumulation of ash and pumice north of Mount Mazama that is almost completely free of plants because of the poor soil conditions in the aftermath of the volcanic eruption thousands of years ago. Another interesting geological feature attributed to volcanic activity is the Pinnacles, otherworldly pumice and ash spires created from erosion of the volcanic outpourings.

397 Fort Clatsop National Memorial

CONTACT 503-861-2471, www.nps.gov/lewi/planyourvisit/fortclatsop.htm; 92343 Fort Clatsop Rd., Astoria

PRICING	$
BEST TIME TO VISIT	Spring through fall
AGE RANGE	5 and older

It was one of the most ambitious American adventures in history: Under the orders of President Thomas Jefferson, Meriwether Lewis and William Clark set out to explore the unknown wilderness of the Louisiana Purchase and beyond, to the West

Oregon Caves   Courtesy National Park Service

PRICE KEY
$ free–$5
$$ $6–10
$$$ $11–20
$$$$ $21+

Fort Clatsop National Memorial Courtesy National Park Service

Coast. The expeditioners, along with a small group they dubbed the Corps of Discovery, journeyed 8,000 miles from St. Louis to the western coastline, chronicling the natural wonders—and economic possibilities—they encountered along the way. The Corps of Discovery began their trek in 1804 and finished in 1806, throughout suffering physical hardship because of unusually harsh winters. Trapper Toussaint Charbonneau and his Native American wife, Sacajawea, served as guides and translators, and contributed greatly to the success of the expedition (and the survival of the explorers).

The explorers found themselves in northwest Oregon in the winter of 1805–06, and they built Fort Clatsop as a winter encampment, where they stayed from December 1805 to March 1806. The fort was named after a local Native tribe who were especially helpful to the Corps of Discovery. Visitors today can see the site of the encampment and tour a reconstruction of the fort, built to specifications recorded

in journals kept by the explorers. The fort comprises two parallel rows of wooden cabins, separated by a parade ground 20 feet by 48 feet. The reconstruction of the buildings and furnishings has been undertaken by hand, using the kinds of tools that would have been available to the Corps of Discovery, so the recreation is quite authentic. Peek inside the sleeping quarters, a room the explorers used to store and cure meat, and observe interpretive living history displays that can include preparing animal skins and making bullets. Summer ranger programs can include lectures and guided hikes along adjacent trails.

398 John Day Fossil Beds National Monument

CONTACT 541-987-2333, www.nps.gov/joda; Clarno Unit: off Hwy. 218, west of Fossil; Painted Hills Unit, off Hwy. 26, northwest of Mitchell; Sheep Rock Unit, off Hwy 19, between Dayville and Kimberly

PRICING	$
BEST TIME TO VISIT	Year-round
AGE RANGE	5 and older

The John Day Fossil Beds National Monument offers the most extensive fossil beds from the Cenozoic era, which has been dubbed the Age of Mammals. Colorful layers of volcanic tuff encasing the fossils span more than 40 million years of history, which makes the

Fort Clatsop is part of the expansive Lewis and Clark National Historic Park, which includes several hiking trails that trace the route of the Corps of Discovery. Check out the Clatsop Loop Trail, where you can climb to Tillamook Head just like Clark and Corps of Discovery members, who hiked to see a whale that had washed ashore. Also worth checking out, the Fort to Sea Trail from Fort Clatsop to Sunset Beach passes through what was the traditional homeland of the Clatsop Natives, winding through forests and coastal rivers and offering beautiful views of the Oregon wilderness.

John Day Fossil Beds National Monument
Courtesy National Park Service

John Day beds one of the most complete records of evolution in the world. Paleontologists have discovered and cataloged species dating back as long as 54 million years. The park comprises more than 14,000 acres, within three distinct units: Clarno Unit, Painted Hills Unit, and Sheep Rock Unit. All of the units fall within the John Day River Basin, a tributary of the Columbia River. The semi-arid region has sparse vegetation and spectacularly colorful badlands. The Painted Hills Unit in particular includes layered geological formations with extremely vivid shades of green, red, orange, and yellow.

As pretty as the unusual landscape is, the real draw are the fossils that continue to be found at the site. These include more than 100 species of mammals, among them saber-toothed tigers, prehistoric horses, camels, dogs, cats, pigs, and turtles. There are also more than 60 plant species fossilized in the layers of hills, including hydrangea, mulberry, and hawthorn. Hike one of the many trails accessible from any of the three units, and encourage kids to keep their eyes open for fossils. If you *do* find a fossil, *don't* try to remove it: Instead, carefully note its location, then tell a ranger at any of the visitor centers. The fossil will be carefully removed, cataloged, and then put on display at the wonderful Thomas Condon Paleon-

For a Happy Kid, Just Add Water

Beach trips are a recipe for family fun, but there's a lot to be learned along the coastlines of the United States, too. Next time you're at the shore, consider these educational activities:

- **Go tide pooling:** Check the local papers for low tide, wear nonslip shoes, and head out to rocks along the coastline that harbor myriad underwater species. You're likely to see urchins, sea stars, small fish, crabs, and maybe a tiny octopus. Be careful about what you touch—some of the creatures you encounter will sting, bite, or pinch—but if you do pick something up, be sure to put it back exactly where you found it.

- **Spot wildlife:** There are a wide variety of shorebirds along the coastlines of the United States, and these are readily observable. If you're in the right place at the right time, you might be able to spot larger wildlife in the ocean, like migrating whales or groups of dolphins. Do a little research online before your visit to find out the local animals you're likely to see.

- **Measure the tides:** On arrival at the shore, encourage kids to mark the high-water line with a stick. Then have them check the stick in a few hours. In this way they can determine if the tide is moving in or moving out. This is a good excuse to explain what causes tides (the gravitational pull of the moon on the earth).

- **Pick up trash:** Okay, cleanup isn't exactly a day at the beach, but taking an hour or so to remove

Water play
Courtesy Ann Passantino

pollution that others have left behind is a good opportunity to teach kids about treating the planet with care. They will be amazed at the things they find. Bring along a trash bag and gloves—and have a chat with kids beforehand about the kinds of things you *don't* want them to pick up.

- **Learn a new water sport:** Prearrange for a lesson for the whole family to learn how to surf, how to sail, how to kayak, or the like. Getting out onto the water will help children appreciate the natural beauty of American coastlines and expand their skill sets. This will also expand the opportunities for wildlife viewing.

tology Center. Even if you aren't lucky enough to find a prehistoric animal or plant, don't miss this museum, which features interactive displays, hundreds of well-preserved fossils, and audiovisual presentations. Check out the window that peeks into the paleontology lab to see scientists studying recent finds.

399 Kam Wah Chung Company Building

CONTACT 541-575-2800; 125 NW Canton St., John Day

PRICING	$
BEST TIME TO VISIT	Open May through October
AGE RANGE	7 and older

The gold rush era of the mid-19th century brought people to the West Coast from all around the world. Chinese immigrants came to Oregon in search of their share of the wealth, and small "Chinatowns" grew up around the new immigrants. In John Day, the Kam Wah Chung Company Building was constructed in one such Chinatown, and stands today as the sole survivor of the once-thriving Chinese community. Kam Wah Chung translates to "golden flower of prosperity." The structure was erected in 1866 as a commercial trading center that served both the Chinese population and non-Chinese citizens (mostly miners), and has been preserved as a historic landmark to commemorate the contributions of Chinese immigrants to the culture, economy, and infrastructure of the American West.

Tour the slightly ramshackle structure and its seven rooms to see an enormous collection of artifacts from the period, including a fascinating display of medicinal herbs, household merchandise imported for Chinese immigrants, and period furniture. The fully stocked shelves of the storeroom and shop overflow with period provisions in their original packaging, such as soap, coffee, candles, tobacco, candy, incense, and firecrackers. Take the audio tour to understand the significance of the collection and the importance of the store, which also served as a medical facility, a post office, and an employment office. Guests can also tour the kitchen and tiny bedrooms occupied by the store's owners.

Goods displayed at Kam Wah Chung Company Building

Courtesy National Park Service

400 National Historic Oregon Trail Interpretive Center

CONTACT 541-523-1843, www.blm.gov/or/oregontrail; 22267 OR 86, Baker City

PRICING	$
BEST TIME TO VISIT	Spring through fall
AGE RANGE	5 and older

Manifest destiny was a 19th-century notion that was generally interpreted to mean that Americans had the right to expand into the entire North American continent. This idea was spurred on by the Homestead Act, which provided 160 acres of free land to aspiring homesteaders—the only requirement was that claimants improved their land by building structures and farming for at least five years. The Oregon Trail

The Oregon Trail was the major artery west, running 2,000 miles from Missouri to Oregon.

Wagons, National Historic Oregon Trail Interpretive Center — Courtesy of the Bureau of Land Management

was the major artery west, running 2,000 miles from Missouri to the Willamette Valley in Oregon. The historic trail started off as a series of footpaths used by Native Americans during their seasonal migrations, and was improved on by fur traders and missionaries traveling the same route. The first large-scale migration using the route took place in 1843, when a wagon train of 120 wagons, more than 800 people, and close to 5,000 cattle set out on the five-month trek. During the trail's heyday, some 300,000 people made the journey.

The National Historic Oregon Trail Interpretive Center memorializes the thousands of pioneers and at the same time offers a chance to step back in time to learn about life on the Oregon Trail. The on-site museum displays artifacts and interactive exhibits, including a life-sized wagon train re-creation, as well as multimedia presentations and more than 4 miles of interpretive trails, one of which leads from the center to still-visible ruts left by the wagon trains. Throughout the year (especially in summer) there are a number of entertaining interpretive programs, which in the past have included the chance to join a wagon train and sing pioneer songs and listen to stories of the trail; storytelling in traditional Native American Sign Language; and lectures on the wildlife encountered regularly along the Oregon Trail.

Pennsylvania

401 Benjamin Franklin National Memorial

Statue of Benjamin Franklin at the Franklin Memorial
Courtesy National Park Service

CONTACT 215-448-1200, www.nps.gov/inde/benja min-franklin-national-memorial.htm; rotunda of the Franklin Institute; 222 N. 20th St., Philadelphia

PRICING	$$$
BEST TIME TO VISIT	Year-round
AGE RANGE	5 and older

Benjamin Franklin (1706–90) was one of the most influential people in early American history—and arguably the most powerful Founder to have never served as U.S. president. Franklin was a true Renaissance man: In addition to being a gifted politician and diplomat, he was a philosopher, political theorist, musician, scientist, postmaster, and extraordinarily successful inventor. He famously invented bifocal glasses, the Franklin stove, and the lightning rod (with which he made significant discoveries about electricity). Franklin was a successful writer and publisher—famous for his *Poor Richard's Almanack* and *Pennsylvania Gazette*; he was the first president of the American Philosophical Society; the governor of Pennsylvania; and the first American ambassador to France. He was an outspoken critic of the British colonial government before the American Revolution: Franklin was behind the push to repeal the Stamp Act of 1765 (the first direct British tax on American colonies). In his older years, Franklin became an abolitionist, and freed his own slaves.

The Benjamin Franklin National Memorial remembers the accomplishments of this remarkable American. The 20-foot-tall, 30-ton marble sculpture sits in the rotunda of the Franklin Institute. The institute itself speaks to Franklin's legacy as an inventor and scientist: This science museum and education center includes hundreds of interactive displays to help children learn about the natural world. Inside the expansive complex there are also flight simulators, a "sky bike" that guests can ride 28 feet in the air, an IMAX theater, and a planetarium. The museum also has an extensive "Frankliniana" collection, which is on rotating display, including one of Franklin's original lightning rods, an odometer Franklin used to measure postal routes in Philadelphia, and coins from around the world bearing his likeness.

Save money on admission to the Franklin Institute and other attractions in Philadelphia with a CityPASS. For about $60 per adult and $40 per child, you'll receive admission to the Franklin Institute, the Philadelphia Zoo, the Adventure Aquarium, and the National Constitution Center (among others). Purchase your CityPASS at the box office of any of the attractions. The pass is good for nine days after purchase.

402 Betsy Ross House

CONTACT 215-686-1252, http://historicphiladelphia.org/ betsy-ross-house; 239 Arch St., Philadelphia

PRICING	$
BEST TIME TO VISIT	Open daily March through November; closed Monday, December through February
AGE RANGE	5 and older

Valley Forge Courtesy National Park Service

PRICE KEY	
$	free–$5
$$	$6–10
$$$	$11–20
$$$$	$21+

The flag included 13 stars arrayed in a circle.

Elizabeth Griscom Ross (1752–1836), better known as Betsy, is an American icon remembered for having created the first American flag. Many historians dispute the story of Ross's contributions, and it is unlikely we will ever know for certain who stitched the first version of the Stars and Stripes. Nevertheless, Ross is a plausible candidate because she was a seamstress from Philadelphia who had worked for George Washington through the years. If the legend is to be believed, Washington arrived at Ross's home in June 1776 with congressional representatives Colonel Ross and Robert Morris. The group presented her with a rough design of the first flag, which she reportedly embellished (changing what were six-point stars to five-point stars, supposedly because they were easier to cut). The flag that resulted—from whoever executed the final design—included 13 stars arrayed in a circle, to represent the idea that no colony was to be held more important than another.

Visitors today can tour the 1740-era colonial-style home, which is blocks from the Liberty Bell and Independence Hall. Ross is believed to have rented the structure from 1773 to 1785. Climb the compact staircases and peek into the small, period-furnished rooms (including two bedrooms and a tiny kitchen) to get an idea of how a working-class woman lived in 18th-century America. The house displays items once belonging to the Ross family, including her Bible and snuff box. Throughout the summer there are a number of living history demonstrations carried on by costumed interpreters. Children will not want to miss the chance to meet "Betsy" herself; they can watch her sew and work in her 18th-century upholstery shop and ask her questions about her life and work in colonial Pennsylvania. Another interesting program here demonstrates how 18th-century households concocted their own medications.

403 Carpenters' Hall

CONTACT 215-925-0167, www.carpentershall.org/; 320 Chestnut. St., Philadelphia

PRICING	$
BEST TIME TO VISIT	Year-round
AGE RANGE	7 and older

The creation of the First Continental Congress marked the unofficial beginning of the American Revolution, and the first session was the opening act of the coalescing American government. The event was actually a convention of delegates from 12 of the 13 original colonies. On September 5, 1774, 56 members appointed by the colonies (excluding Georgia) met to protest and formulate an official response to the so-called Intolerable Acts, a bundle of laws passed by the British Parliament that proved the tipping point for the outraged American colonists; among these laws were retributive rules to punish Boston for the Boston Tea Party. The attendees considered options that included an economic boycott of British goods and peti-

Betsy Ross House   Photo George Widman, courtesy Historic Philadelphia

Carpenters' Hall

Courtesy National Park Service

tioning King George III to repeal the offending laws. When it became clear that Britain would not abolish the Intolerable Acts, the delegates called for a Second Continental Congress the next year to determine America's options.

Carpenters' Hall in Philadelphia hosted the First Continental Congress. The lovely Georgian structure was built for the Carpenters' Company, founded in 1724 as a trade guild—in fact, the Carpenters' Company continues to hold meetings, making it the oldest such trade organization in America. The historic hall has also been home to the American Philosophical Society, Benjamin Franklin's Library Company, and the First and Second Banks of the United States. During the Revolutionary War the structure served as a hospital for colonial soldiers. Guests today can tour the building (now part of the Independence National

> Before checking out any of the sites the Independence National Historic Park comprises, visit the Independence Visitor Center (at the corner of 6th and Market Sts., Philadelphia). Watch the 30-minute film *Independence* to get an overview of the events that make Philadelphia one of the most historic cities in America. Note that you can pick up tickets to visit Independence Hall at the center.

Park) to see the space that was once occupied by the likes of famous early Americans George Washington, Samuel Adams, and Patrick Henry.

404 Declaration House

CONTACT	215-965-2305, www.nps.gov/inde/declaration-house.htm; 701 Market St., Philadelphia
PRICING	$
BEST TIME TO VISIT	Year-round (open noon–4)
AGE RANGE	7 and older

Representatives from the Second Continental Congress determined by June 1776 that the American colonies needed to declare a formal break with England, and it was decided that a document was required to spell out in no uncertain terms America's determination to be free of King George III. A congressional representative from Virginia, Richard Henry Lee, submitted a resolution to declare independence, and the Continental Congress set to vote on the matter three weeks later, once an official document could be prepared. Several individuals were chosen to formulate the declaration—including Benjamin Franklin and John Adams—but it was decided that Thomas Jefferson would write the first draft.

However, Jefferson found he could not concentrate on his work in the city, so he moved to rent rooms from a bricklayer named Jacob Graff, who lived on the outskirts of Philadelphia, in a bucolic home Jefferson judged to be more suitable for the task at hand. Jefferson wrote his first draft in less than three weeks, basing it somewhat on the Virginia Constitution. In his original draft, Jefferson included a repudiation of the slave trade taking hold in the colonies; had his original declaration been ratified, slavery would have been outlawed from that point forward in America. However, the language about slavery was cut from the final draft. The approved version was adopted by the Continental Congress on July 4, 1776, and with it the 13 colonies announced their determination to be independent from Britain.

Graff's home has since been destroyed, but in 1975

a reconstruction of the house where the Declaration of Independence was written was built. Today visitors can tour the small home, view a film about Jefferson, and see a copy of Jefferson's first-draft declaration (with his abolitionist sentiments intact). The house reproduces the tiny rooms Jefferson rented, and they are furnished much as they would have been in Jefferson's day. Look for the original key to the front door—the only surviving relic from the original Graff house.

405 Franklin Court

CONTACT 215-965-2305, www.nps.gov/inde/frank lin-court.htm; 318 Market St., Philadelphia

PRICING	$
BEST TIME TO VISIT	Year-round
AGE RANGE	5 and older

Philadelphia was home to statesman, inventor, publisher, and Founder Benjamin Franklin while he served in the Continental Congress and the Constitutional Convention. Franklin and his wife, Deborah, had a large brick home built to serve their needs in the city; Franklin died in the home in 1790. Within 20 years, the house had been torn down. Visitors to the site today can view a steel "ghost structure" that out-

Ghost structure at Franklin Court   Courtesy National Park Service

lines the area where Franklin's house stood. Stroll around the structure to see flagstones engraved with correspondence between Ben and Deborah about the design and decor of the house. Look for a costumed interpreter who portrays Franklin and occasionally roams the grounds, ready to answer questions or discuss the "latest" news of the 18th century. Belowground is a newly renovated museum that documents the life and enormous contributions of Franklin: Look for Franklin's glass harmonica, a musical instrument he invented. (Famous composer Wolfgang Amadeus Mozart even wrote a piece for the instrument.) Kids will enjoy the Franklin Exchange, a room that includes a phone bank where guests can listen to actors read the opinions about Franklin written by famous Americans like George Washington and John Adams. There's also an intriguing orientation film on Franklin's life. Adjacent to the ghost structure, on Market Street, are restorations of several buildings associated with Franklin, including an 18th-century printing office, an operating post office, and a postal museum. (Get your postcards hand-canceled at the Benjamin Franklin Post Office.)

406 Gettysburg Battlefield

CONTACT 717-334-1124, www.nps.gov/gett; 1195 Baltimore Pike, Gettysburg

PRICING	Battlefield: $; admission to Gettysburg Museum Experience, tickets to the film *A New Birth of Freedom*, and the Gettysburg Cyclorama program: $$–$$$
BEST TIME TO VISIT	Fall through spring
AGE RANGE	7 and older

The small hamlet of Gettysburg was the site of the largest, deadliest battle ever waged in North America—and it was the turning point of the Civil War. From July 1 to July 3, 1863, more than 160,000 soldiers engaged in a fierce and bloody struggle that would determine the fate of the United States. The Union's Army of the Potomac, under the command of Major General George G. Meade, sought to hold back

Gettysburg　　　　Courtesy Commonwealth Media Services

the Confederacy's Army of Northern Virginia, led by General Robert E. Lee, which was slowly moving northward, threatening Union cities like Philadelphia and Baltimore. Lee's army went into the battle with much momentum, and the Confederates were largely successful for the first two days of the skirmish. However, the battle turned on July 3, and Lee had little choice but to order his army back into Virginia. When the smoke cleared, 23,049 Union soldiers were either killed, wounded, or missing; as were 28,063 Confederates. The Battle of Gettysburg, along with the Confederate loss in Vicksburg, Mississippi, almost immediately afterward, signaled the beginning of the end for Confederate dreams of independence (although the war waged on for another two years).

Nearly five months later, President Abraham Lincoln visited the site for the dedication of the Soldiers' National Cemetery, where many of the casualties from the Battle of Gettysburg were laid to rest, and delivered one of the most famous speeches in American history: the Gettysburg Address. Although the speech was relatively short (delivered in less than two minutes), Lincoln's eloquence reminded Americans of the foundations on which the United States was built: freedom, equality, and self-determination.

A visit to the Gettysburg Battlefield is a solemn experience, and it is important that children understand that the area is hallowed ground. Begin your exploration of the site at the National Park Service Museum and Visitor Center to see an orientation film and view interactive exhibits that explain the battle and its significance within the greater context of the Civil War. Next, tour the battlefield. A self-guided auto tour map and guide is available in the visitor center, and will point you to stops at important sites

on the battlefield. Interpretive exhibits on the field explain the significance of each stop. You can also prearrange a battlefield guide, who will ride with you in your automobile to explain the battle, provide context at each stop, and answer questions. There are special battlefield walks led by park rangers held in the summer. Don't miss the Soldiers' National Cemetery, which in addition to being the final resting place for many of the Union soldiers killed at the Battle of Gettysburg is also the burial site for soldiers from 1865 onward.

407 Hersheypark

CONTACT 800-HERSHEY, www.hersheypark.com; 100 W. Hersheypark Dr., Hershey

PRICING	$$$$
BEST TIME TO VISIT	Year-round
AGE RANGE	5 and older

Milton S. Hershey (1857–1945) was an American entrepreneur best remembered for his candy making—but he was also a philanthropist who built an entire community around his chocolate factory in his hometown of Derry Church, Pennsylvania (a town that was renamed Hershey to honor his contributions) and then kept its citizens employed through the Great Depression.

Hershey founded his candy company in 1894, and by 1905 it was the largest chocolate manufacturing plant in the world. To repay his employees for the company's enormous success, Hershey began investing in the community around the plant. He built

Save money on the entrance fees to Hersheypark by purchasing sunset admission tickets, which are sold at about a 50 percent discount. Enter the park after 4 pm on the days when the park closes at 8 and after 5 pm when the park closes at 10 and 11. Or consider the three-day flex pass, which allows three visits in any one season for a little less than the price of two visits purchased separately.

Ready for chocolate   Courtesy Jo Legg

- **Hershey Gardens** (717-534-3492, www.hershey gardens.org): This serene botanical display offers dozens of themed gardens, a butterfly house, and a children's garden with chocolate-scented blossoms. Visit in late spring to see the more than 5,000 rose-bushes in bloom.
- **The Hershey Story: The Museum on Chocolate Avenue** (717-534-3439, www.hersheystory.org): This hands-on museum honors the legacy of Milton Hershey and offers the chance for guests to take hands-on chocolate-making classes.
- **ZooAmerica** (717-534-3900, www.zooamerica.com): This 11-acre zoo is home to more than 200 animals and 60 different species; admission to Hersheypark includes admission to the zoo.

408 Independence Hall

CONTACT 215-965-2305, www.nps.gov/inde/independ ence-hall-1.htm; 5th and Chestnut Sts., Philadelphia

PRICING	$ (timed tickets are required from March through December)
BEST TIME TO VISIT	Year-round
AGE RANGE	7 and older

If walls could talk: Independence Hall has been the site of some of the most historic events in American history, and can arguably be considered the birth-place of the United States. Aside from the winter of 1777–78 (when Philadelphia was occupied by British

---

homes, created an accessible public transportation system, and included entertainment venues like a large park, a pool, a carousel, and a bowling alley. By the 1930s Hershey had added a water flume ride, a roller coaster, a penny arcade, and a fun house. In the 1970s the park expanded to become the full-fledged amusement park that it is today. Today Hersheypark sits on more than 100 acres and includes more than 65 rides, including some of the most thrilling roller coasters in the country and dozens of waterslides to cool off in the summer. There are also plenty of op-tions for smaller children, like oversized slides and water-play zones.

While you're in Hershey, don't miss the other chocolate-themed attractions, including:

- **Hershey Chocolate World** (717-534-4900, www.hersheyschocolateworld.com): Adjacent to the amusement park is Hershey's Chocolate World, a chocoholic's fantasy: Here you can eat chocolate, shop for chocolate, watch chocolate being made, and even bathe in chocolate (the on-site spa at the adja-cent Hotel Hershey offers cocoa baths and chocolate facials).This attraction offers insight into chocolate making with tours, 3-D shows, and tastings. Kids will enjoy the chance to create their own candy bar here.

Independence Hall is a popular place, and during the spring and summer months, it can be extremely crowded. Timed tour tickets are mandatory from March through Decem-ber. Same-day passes are available on a walk-up basis from the Independence Visitor Center, starting at 8:30 pm . One person may request up to 10 tickets for family or friends. To ensure access, plan to arrive as early as possible. You can also purchase timed tickets by phone (877-444-6777) or online (www.recreation.gov) for a small processing fee.

military), the building was the meeting site from 1775 to 1783 for the Second Continental Congress. George Washington was appointed commander in chief of the Continental army in the assembly room here in 1775. The Declaration of Independence was voted on and adopted here on July 4, 1776. The Articles of Confederation were also ratified under this roof in 1781, and the U.S. Constitution was drafted here in 1787 and approved in 1789. The U.S. Constitution, of course, is the guiding document that continues to shape American government and law. It was conceived of from May to September 1787, and debated and framed by delegates from 12 of the original 13 colonies. The document is now the oldest federal constitution in the world.

The impressive Georgian structure was designed by Andrew Hamilton to house the Assembly of the Commonwealth of Pennsylvania; it was constructed between 1732 and 1756. When complete, it was topped with a steeple holding a 2,000-pound bell—

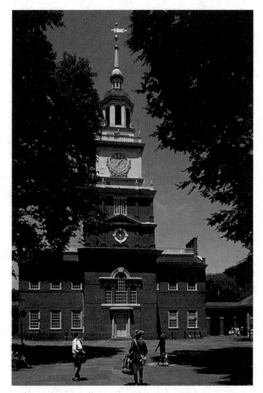

Independence Hall   Photo Bob Krist, courtesy Commonwealth Media Services

now known as the Liberty Bell—which cracked almost immediately (and now is housed separately; see below); a replica bell now hangs in the steeple. The original bell was rung to call lawmakers to legislative sessions and to summon citizens to public forums.

Public tours of Independence Hall are led by national park rangers, and free timed tickets are required. (See the tip below for more information on securing tickets.) You will see the courtroom and the Assembly Room in your tour, both of which are furnished as they were in the late 18th century. Look for the "Rising Sun" chair in the Assembly Room, the chair George Washington used when presiding over the constitutional debates. In the West Wing, check out the original inkstand used to sign the Declaration of Independence. You can also see an original draft of the Constitution.

409 Liberty Bell

CONTACT	215-965-2305, www.nps.gov/inde/index.htm; 600 Chestnut St., Philadelphia
PRICING	$
BEST TIME TO VISIT	Year-round
AGE RANGE	7 and older

The Liberty Bell is one of the most recognized American icons, and a favorite tourist attraction in Philadelphia. The bell is 12 feet in circumference and weighs 2,080 pounds; inscribed at the top is a Bible verse that reads "Proclaim liberty throughout all the land unto all the inhabitants thereof." It was originally hung in the Pennsylvania State House, what is now known as Independence Hall, in 1753. Sadly, the 44-pound clapper cracked the bell the first time it was rung. Local artisans repaired the bell on two different occasions. It was used to call lawmakers to legislative sessions and to alert citizens to public forums.

The bell has long since been removed from Independence Hall, and it is now housed in a new separate structure nearby. It isn't necessary to secure tickets to view the Liberty Bell, but visitors must pass through a rigorous security screening, the line for

Liberty Bell   Photo Bob Krist, courtesy Commonwealth Media Services

which can be oppressively long. Once inside the Liberty Bell Center, be sure to check out the X-rays of the bell, which show the bell's crack and its insides.

410 National Civil War Museum

CONTACT 717-260-1861, www.nationalcivilwarmu seum.org; 2 Lincoln Circle at Reservoir Park, Harrisburg

PRICING	$$
BEST TIME TO VISIT	Year-round
AGE RANGE	7 and older

Located near the Gettysburg Battlefield—site of the largest conflict in the American Civil War—the National Civil War Museum is dedicated to telling the story of the War Between the States from the viewpoint of the soldiers and average citizens of the day, without favoring one side or the other. The relatively

new museum includes more than 4,400 artifacts, some from famous names of the war but most recovered from everyday Union and Confederate soldiers. The museum is the largest such display dedicated solely to the Civil War, and offers 17 themed galleries to explore that cover the period from 1850 to 1876. Displays include *A House Divided: 1850–1860*, which explores the events that led to the Civil War; *American Slavery: The Peculiar Institution, 1850–1860*, which examines the way 19th-century Americans viewed slavery; *First Shots 1861*, focusing on the events at Fort Sumpter, where the war officially began; *Civil War Music*, which includes an interesting display of antique instruments and recorded music; *Gettysburg 1863*, an in-depth look at the most pivotal battle in the war; and *Women in the War*, which explores women's roles as nurses, as wives, and in other vocations during the war. Throughout various galleries, segments of a video titled *We the People* are shown that focus on 10 individuals and their lives before, during, and after the war; the video concludes in an on-site theater. Look for the chair captured from the Confederate White House by Union soldiers; a lock of hair belonging to General George Pickett (famous for the ill-fated Pickett's charge at the Battle of Gettysburg), and lead bullets given to wounded soldiers to bite down on during surgery. (You can still see the teeth marks.) This is an easily accessible museum, and not overwhelming in presentation, which makes it an ideal introduction to the Civil War: If you have the chance, visit this museum first, and *then* make your visit to Gettysburg Battlefield.

411 National Constitution Center

CONTACT 215-409-6600, http://constitutioncenter.org; 525 Arch St., Philadelphia

PRICING	$$$
BEST TIME TO VISIT	Open daily
AGE RANGE	7 and older

The National Constitution Center is a relatively new museum and educational facility dedicated to exploring the far-reaching effects the U.S. Constitution has had on this country and nations all around the globe. The state-of-the-art museum invites visitors to explore what it means to be American through active participation with the interactive exhibits and multimedia presentations. The heart of the museum is a permanent exhibit called *The Story of We the People*, which includes a star-shaped theater that presents a 20-minute production called *Freedom Rising*, an entertaining and stirring presentation that includes a live actor and video projection on a 360-degree screen. The *American Experience* display provides a history of the U.S. Constitution, telling the story through 100 interactive exhibits. Signers' Hall houses a collection of 42 life-sized bronze statues of 39 signers of the Constitution as well as three individuals who chose not to sign. Throughout, children have the chance to be active participants—for example, deciding opinions on important Supreme Court cases, deciding to sign (or not) the Constitution, and even repeating the presidential oath of office. Look for a rare first public printing of the Constitution, on display in an alcove adjacent to Signers' Hall.

Steamtown National Historic Site Courtesy National Park Service

412 Steamtown National Historic Site

CONTACT 570-340-5200, www.nps.gov/stea/index.htm; 150 S. Washington Ave., Scranton

PRICING	$–$$; excursions additional
BEST TIME TO VISIT	Spring through fall
AGE RANGE	3 and older

The Steamtown National Historic Site is a must-see for train lovers and anyone looking to learn more about the influence of railway travel in America. This national park is dedicated to steam railroading, and features an extensive collection of coal-fired steam locomotives, diesel-electric locomotives, freight cars, passenger cars, cabooses, and a plethora of maintenance equipment. The expansive site includes a roundhouse with an operating turntable, a locomotive repair shop, a museum complex, and a 250-seat theater. The attraction is located at the site of the for-

mer Scranton yards of the DL&W Railroad. Many of the locomotives and passenger cars have open compartments that allow visitors to walk through. Even better than touring the magnificent trains on display is taking a ride on a restored train; short rides are included in the price of admission. Long excursions are available to guests at additional cost. (Note that routes are determined seasonally, and no rides are offered in the winter.)

You'll also find a range of tours to help you learn about how railroads functioned in the late 19th- and early 20th centuries. You can tour a locomotive shop to see work being done on an original engine. There are also demonstrations of the train turntable daily. Don't miss *Steel and Steam*, a 20-minute film on the history of railroads shown in the comfortable Steamtown theater.

413 Valley Forge National Historical Park

CONTACT 610-783-1099, www.nps.gov/vafo; 1400 N. Outer Line Dr., King of Prussia

PRICING	$
BEST TIME TO VISIT	Year-round
AGE RANGE	7 and older

Students of U.S. history will recognize the name Valley Forge: It is well associated with the deprivation and desperation of the early Continental army. The site served as a military encampment for General George Washington's army for six months, starting in December 1777. When the soldiers marched into the camp, they were cold, poorly fed, ill equipped, lacking essential military training, and vastly dispirited. Although no battles were fought at Valley Forge, more than 2,000 soldiers died here from disease—and many deserted. Despite the struggle against the cold and against hunger, what remained of Washington's army marched out of the encampment in mid-June, ready and eager to fight—and what's more, they were at last *prepared* to fight.

The transformation of the ragtag army into a disciplined fighting machine can be attributed in large part to Friedrich Wilhelm von Steuben, who had previously served under Frederick the Great, king of Prussia. Von Steuben presented himself to General Washington, via an introduction from Benjamin Franklin, early in 1778, and Washington immediately assigned him to train the soldiers at Valley Forge. To begin the task, von Steuben wrote an original training manual for the men: Because he spoke no English, he wrote the manual in French, then had aides translate it to English and distribute it to the regiments. He marched the soldiers parade-style, taught them to move column by column, and drilled them in loading muskets and fighting at close range with bayonets. At the same time the soldiers were undergoing training, General Nathanael Greene was appointed to head the Commissary Department, and ensured that food and supplies began to flow into Valley Forge. Together von Steuben and Greene built the men into a determined, capable fighting force.

Start your visit to the park by viewing the 18-minute orientation film at the park theater. Then tour the rows of cannons in Artillery Park, view the earthen fortifications, and stroll past the reconstructed log huts—faithful representations of soldiers' barracks that on summer weekends are populated by costumed reenactors who interpret life in the camp. The highlight of the park is a tour of the lovely restored colonial home that General Washington used as his headquarters; a visit here makes palpable the contrast between the relatively comfortable life of the officers and that of the soldiers, who struggled just to stay alive. While visiting the park, don't miss the Memorial Arch, the statue of von Steuben, and the Monument to Patriots of African Descent. The park

Soldier cabin, Valley Forge National Historical Park

Courtesy National Park Service

sponsors a number of interactive activities for children throughout the year, including a chance for kids 6 to 12 to "join" the Continental army and learn drills and parade skills. For a real sense of the difficult conditions the soldiers faced, visit Valley Forge in the winter months, to see how everyday soldiers managed to keep warm and healthy in the primitive conditions of the camp.

414 Washington's Crossing

CONTACT 215-493-4076, www.nps.gov/nr/travel/delaware; 1112 River Rd., Washington Crossing

PRICING	$
BEST TIME TO VISIT	Christmas Day; closed Monday
AGE RANGE	7 and older

On Christmas Day, 1776, General George Washington led 2,400 soldiers across the Delaware River from McConkey's Ferry, Pennsylvania, to Trenton, New Jersey, where his small band of Continental soldiers attacked a Hessian garrison. The surprise battle was a victory for General Washington's army, and provided the morale boost they needed for subsequent victories at Princeton and the Second Battle of Trenton. Every year the historic river crossing is reenacted by costumed interpreters, including an actor portraying

Currier and Ives print of Washington Crossing the Delaware

Courtesy Library of Congress

Washington. Three replica boats are launched in the early afternoon and rowed across the river. If you can't attend on December 25, check out the dress rehearsal of the event, which is held approximately two weeks before.

Throughout the rest of the year, the 500-acre park is open to visitors to enjoy the spectacular scenery and to explore the historic significance of the region. There are two distinct sections. The lower park in the town of Washington Crossing comprises 13 historic buildings, including the McConkey Ferry Inn, a tavern that served as a guard post during the Continental army's encampment here; legend has it that General Washington ate his supper here before making the famous river crossing. Also here is a barn that houses five Durham boats, replicas of the vessels used to transport soldiers, equipment, and even horses across the river in 1776. These same boats are used in the Christmas reenactment. Don't miss the Hibbs House, a 19th-century home restored and furnished as it might have been during Washington's time: This is the site of open-hearth cooking demonstrations. The Frye House is another 19th-century home open for tour; it is believed to have been owned by a blacksmith, and the property features a re-

If you can't attend on December 25, check out the dress rehearsal.

created blacksmith shop that is used for historic demonstrations throughout the year.

The upper park comprises the Thompson-Neely House, a onetime military hospital, and the unmarked graves of about 50 soldiers who died in the makeshift hospital. There are 23 memorial headstones to remind visitors that the area is a grave site, although the exact burial locations are unknown. Also here is Bowman's Hill Tower, a 125-foot stone memorial built in the early 20th century to commemorate the American Revolution. The tower is open seasonally, and guests can travel to the top via an elevator and an additional 20-some steps, to see magnificent views of the Delaware River Valley.

415 Wheatland

CONTACT	717-392-4633, www.lancasterhistory.org; 230 N. President Ave., Lancaster
PRICING	$–$$
BEST TIME TO VISIT	January and February, open for tours by appointment only; March, open Friday and Saturday; April through October, open Monday through Saturday; November, closed; December, open for Yuletide tours (call ahead for hours)
AGE RANGE	7 and older

James Buchanan Jr. (1791–1868) was the 15th president of the United States and the only chief executive to hail from Pennsylvania. Before moving into the White House, Buchanan served five terms in the House of Representatives, was appointed briefly as minister to Russia and later as minister to Great Britain, served for 10 years in the Senate, and was secretary of state under President James Polk. As president he presided over the executive branch when the divisive 1857 *Dred Scott v. Sandford* case was decided—in which an African American slave unsuccessfully sued for his own freedom and the freedom of his wife and children. Reaction to the court decision from the South was predictably euphoric, but northerners responded quite differently. From

James Buchanan House

Courtesy Pennsylvania Dutch Convention and Visitors Bureau

early in his presidency, Buchanan missed the significance of slavery and misunderstood how deeply divided the country had become. As a result, he left the question of slavery for the 16th president, Abraham Lincoln, to decide. Buchanan was the only chief executive who remained a lifelong bachelor; his niece, Harriet Lane, served the role of First Lady during his years as president.

Wheatland was the home Buchanan retired to after leaving the White House. The brick, Federal-style home was built in 1828, on little more than 20 acres. The structure contains 17 rooms, a Doric-columned porch, and three stories. Guests can tour the home to see the interior decorated much as it would have been in Buchanan's time; aside from the addition of lighting and heating, very little has been done to the structure since the president lived here in the 19th century. Period-costumed docents will lead you through the structure, including the library where Buchanan wrote his presidential memoirs and inaugural speech and the bedroom where he died. Be sure to check out the carriage house, the icehouse, and the beautiful gardens. Kids will not want to miss the frog pond. Throughout the year the property offers living history programs, which include Life Below the Stairs, a presentation that examines the lives of servants during the Victorian era; and Sweet 16, an exploration of what 16-year-old Buck Henry, Buchanan's adopted orphaned nephew, did for fun on the grounds.

RHODE ISLAND

416 Block Island National Wildlife Refuge

CONTACT www.fws.gov/blockisland; about 12 miles off the coast of Charlestown, on Block Island

PRICING	$ (ferry tickets required to reach the island are additional)
BEST TIME TO VISIT	Fall
AGE RANGE	All ages

Aspiring birders and youngsters who love animals will appreciate a visit to the Block Island National Wildlife Refuge. Block Island is about 12 miles off the coast of Rhode Island, within the Block Island Sound. The small, sparsely populated island falls within the Atlantic Flyway; about 40 percent is conserved for wildlife, including the 95 species of songbirds, 70 species of neotropical migratory birds, and 40 species of shorebirds. Look for bald eagles, black-crowned night herons, piping plovers, snowy egrets, and yellow-crowned night herons. The fall is an especially good time to experience the biodiversity of the island, thanks to the many migratory birds that land here briefly before continuing their annual journey south. The site is also home to the endangered American burying beetle—this is the only known population of the species east of the Mississippi River.

Block Island Refuge comprises two regions: One is in the northernmost point of the island, on a former U.S. Coast Guard light station, and it is accessible via easily traversed dunes. The other is 3 miles south, on West Beach—but this portion of the refuge is not open to the public, to avoid disturbing nesting birds. You can get regular ferry service from the Port of Galilee in Galilee and from Point Judith (off Rt. 108) in Narragansett.

Crescent Beach, Block Island

417 First Baptist Meeting House

CONTACT 401-454-3418, www.firstbaptistchurchin america.org; 75 N. Main St., Providence

PRICING	$
BEST TIME TO VISIT	Guided tours available Memorial Day through Labor Day; closed Saturday
AGE RANGE	All ages

What is now Rhode Island was founded as one of the original American colonies (then known as the Colony of Rhode Island and the Providence Plantation) by Roger Williams (circa 1600–83), a Protestant theologian who left England to pursue his ideals of religious freedom and separation of church and state. Williams originally landed in the Massachusetts Bay Colony, but was soon banished for his outspoken opinions on religion. He then founded Providence Plantation in 1636, which soon drew other settlers who wished to worship as they saw fit, without interference from colonial government. Williams is also remembered as the first to organize an effort to ban slavery in the 13 colonies.

In 1638 Williams established what is now the oldest Baptist church in America in Providence. The existing church structure was built in 1775; it held 1,200 people—a third of Providence's population at the time. With its 185-foot steeple, the meetinghouse is

While in town, check out the Roger Williams National Memorial (401-521-7266; 282 N. Main St.) to learn more about the founder of Rhode Island and his views on religious freedom.

the first in New England to have such an architectural embellishment. The church remains an active parish. When visiting, don't miss the Waterford crystal chandelier, which dates to 1792.

418 General Nathanael Greene Homestead

CONTACT 401-821-8630, www.nathanaelgreenehomestead.org; 50 Taft St., Coventry

PRICING	$
BEST TIME TO VISIT	Open April through October, Saturday through Monday
AGE RANGE	7 and older

Nathanael Greene (1742–86) was a general in the Continental army during the American Revolutionary War, and a close friend to General George Washington. He served for several terms in the colonial legislature and was made major general in 1776. Greene is remembered for his contributions to the Battles of Trenton, Brandywine, and the Guilford Courthouse.

His 18th-century home (called Spell Hall) overlooking the Pawtuxet River is open for tours, and the 13 acres of grounds are a lovely place for children to burn off a little steam. Greene lived in the home from 1770 to 1776; afterward, the house passed to his brother Jacob. Eight rooms of the structure are furnished with period pieces and Greene family artifacts. Look for Greene's wooden desk, complete with a

General Nathanael Greene Homestead

Photo by Lydia Rapoza, courtesy General Nathanael Green Homestead

handwritten letter and an ink well Greene once owned. Kids will also enjoy touring the winter kitchen, which is furnished with antique cooking utensils like a fireplace toaster and manually operated rotisserie. A children's bedroom, once belonging to General Greene's grandniece, includes a trundle bed beneath an elaborate wooden-framed bed, as well as furnishings that were common in 18th-century nurseries. Note: This house museum is off the beaten track, so it's advisable to call in advance to confirm that tours are indeed available on the day you intend to visit.

419 Museum of Work and Culture

CONTACT 401-769-9675, www.woonsocket.org/workandculture.htm; 42 S. Main St., Woonsocket

PRICING	$$
BEST TIME TO VISIT	Year-round; closed Monday
AGE RANGE	7 and older

The interactive Museum of Work and Culture chronicles the story of French Canadian immigrants who left failing farms in Quebec to work in factories and mills in Rhode Island, often enduring horrific conditions, long hours, and poor pay. Start your tour by walking through a re-creation of a Quebec farm house and listen to the ersatz residents debate a potential immigration. Then progress through to the shop floor of a textile mill to see the sights and hear the sounds typical of a 19th-century factory, peek into a three-family tenement to see how factory workers lived, and get a glimpse at a parochial school as children of factory workers might have experienced in Woonsocket. The hands-on museum offers films, audiovisual presentations, and walk-through dioramas to tell the story of the American factory worker into the 20th century. Kids will be especially interested in the exhibit on child labor: Young children often worked in factories for 12 to 14 hours a day, doing demanding physical labor in exchange for pennies (or often just small bags of candy). The museum is housed in a former textile mill (belonging first to the Barnai Worsted Company and later the Lincoln Textile Company).

420 Newport Rhode Island Mansions

CONTACT 401-847,1000, ext. 111, www.newportmansions.org; Preservation Society of Newport County, 424 Bellevue Ave., Newport

PRICING	Admission to 1 property $$–$$$; admission to any 5 properties: $$–$$$$
BEST TIME TO VISIT	Spring and summer
AGE RANGE	7 and older (although young children will appreciate the Green Animals Topiary Garden)

American author and wit Mark Twain called the late 19th century the "Gilded Age," a term that criticized the period from the 1860s into the early 1900s, which Twain and many others argued was marked by political corruption and excessive displays of financial success. This period was dominated by extraordinarily wealthy industrialists, who'd made their considerable fortunes through railroads, heavy industry, and financing. Families led by still-recognizable names like Andrew Carnegie, J. P. Morgan, and John D. Rockefeller, as well as the Astor and Vanderbilt clans, reveled in ostentatious displays of their money—although it must be said that many of these same so-called robber barons greased the wheels of the American economy *and* were extraordinary philanthropists, using portions of their amassed fortune to fund colleges, museums, libraries, and various other charities.

During this period, many of America's super wealthy flocked to the oceanside at Newport for a brief summer social season. They built enormous, lavish "cottages" that included bejeweled and literally gilded ballrooms, palatial dining rooms, and grand gardens with sweeping views of the sea. Today the Preservation Society of Newport County maintains 14 of the historic properties, 11 of which are open for public tours. Each home is well worth touring: They are immaculately kept and furnished with museum-quality art and antique furnishings. When here, don't miss these sites:

- **The Breakers:** To my mind, this 70-room estate of Cornelius Vanderbilt II, president of the New York Central Railroad, is the most spectacular property in the collection. It faces the sea, and interiors are particularly over the top, with alabaster walls, an abundance of gilding, and rich furnishings worthy of a French castle. The audio tour for The Breakers includes re-created first-person accounts by servants and children that offer interesting insight into the lives of the people who kept these ostentatious mansions in tip-top shape.

- **The Elms:** Once belonging to coal magnate Edward Julius Berwind, the French-inspired château has an impressive collection of art, including Chinese lacquer panels and museum-quality Venetian paintings. The audio tour for this cottage includes entertaining tips on the rigid table manners of the day. ("One must not smack one's lips, *ever*.")

- **Green Animals Topiary Garden:** This leafy menagerie will capture the imagination of young children, especially, who will be amazed at shrubs trimmed to the shapes of elephants, bears, lions, teacups, ships, and fanciful spirals. The topiary garden is a bit off the beaten path—about 10 miles from Newport—but well worth a visit.

- **Marble House:** Alva Vanderbilt designed this glittering "temple to the arts" after Versailles. It contains more than 500,000 cubic feet of marble. Children will not want to miss the Chinese Tea House at the back of the property, which overlooks stunning ocean views and offers a good chance to refuel on sandwiches, salads, and sweets.

- **Rosecliff:** Built in 1902 for Tessie Oelrichs, heiress to the famous Comstock lode silver and gold for-

Newport Rhode Island mansions Courtesy Rhode Island Tourism Division

tune, Rosecliff was designed with inspiration from the Grand Trianon, the playground of French royalty at Versailles. The interiors are so sumptuous that they were used in the Robert Redford film *The Great Gatsby*.

421 Slater Mill Historic Site

CONTACT	401-725-8638, www.slatermill.org; 67 Roosevelt Ave., Pawtucket
PRICING	$$–$$$
BEST TIME TO VISIT	Open May through June, Tuesday to Sunday; July through October, daily; November, weekends only
AGE RANGE	7 and older

The Slater Mill in Pawtucket was the first successful cotton-spinning mill in the United States—and is today sometimes considered a birthplace of the Industrial Revolution in America. Slater Mill is also historically important because it was one of the first factories in the United States to employ women and children—a practice that was copied in factories throughout the country (until child labor was prohibited in 1938 by the Fair Labor Standards Act, signed into law by President Franklin D. Roosevelt during the Great Depression).

Visitors to the mill can tour the factory, check out exhibits explaining the shift from farm to factory in the surrounding Blackstone River Valley, and watch demonstrations and lectures on cotton milling and factory organization. Exhibits focus on the life of laborers, women's rights (and workers' rights more generally), and the history of the textile industry in this region. You'll visit three structures: At the Slater Mill, see the factory machines that enabled countless workers to turn raw cotton into cloth. At the Brown House, get a glimpse into a 19th-century artisan's home and watch demonstrations of hand spinning and weaving (which contrast starkly with the industrial processes illustrated in the Slater Mill). At the Wilkinson Mill, an early-19th-century machine shop, see a 16,000-pound waterwheel turn the huge gears in the machine shop.

422 Touro Synagogue National Historic Site

CONTACT	401-847-4794, www.nps.gov/tosy; 85 Touro St., Newport
PRICING	$–$$$
BEST TIME TO VISIT	Hours vary seasonally; call ahead for schedule
AGE RANGE	All ages

The Touro Synagogue is the oldest synagogue in the United States, and stands as a testament to the founding principles of the original Rhode Island colony (and its founder, Roger Williams) of religious tolerance. The synagogue was dedicated in 1763, but the congregation goes back as far as 1658, to descendants of Jewish families who escaped the religious inquisitions in Spain and Portugal; these individuals originally fled to the Caribbean, but eventually immigrated to America to enjoy the greater religious freedom that Rhode Island offered.

Guests can tour the working synagogue to see the ethereal interior, which is dominated by a series of 12 Ionic columns that support airy balconies. The columns are meant to represent the 12 tribes of ancient Israel, and each was carved from a single tree. Look for the sacred Holy Ark, which houses a 500-year-old scroll, and don't forget to look up to see the ornate antique brass chandeliers.

Interior, Touro Synagogue Courtesy National Park Service

SOUTH CAROLINA

423 Boone Hall Plantation

CONTACT 843-884-4371, www.boonehallplantation.com; 1235 Long Point Rd., Mount Pleasant

PRICING	$$–$$$
BEST TIME TO VISIT	Closed January
AGE RANGE	7 and older

Boone Hall Plantation

Courtesy South Carolina Department of Parks, Recreation, and Tourism

Preserving the legacy of the Old South, the magnificent Boone Hall is a fabulously maintained plantation first established in 1681 by Major John Boone. One of the most outstanding characteristics of the property is the mile-long "Avenue of Oaks," a spectacular driveway bordered by trees dating to 1743. The site includes a palatial Colonial Revival home (built in 1935) that replaces the original home, which was destroyed; nine original brick slave cabins; lush flower gardens; and a stable (among other outbuildings). Take the 30-minute tour of the mansion conducted by a guide in a historically appropriate costume. Next move on to "Slave Street" for a presentation on the living quarters and lives of the slaves that lived at Boone Hall; historical records indicate that as many as 40 slaves worked on the plantation at any one time. You can explore the many gardens on the front lawn on your own; look for rosebushes that are more than 100 years old. In-season, kids will enjoy the Butterfly Pavilion, featuring dozens of species of butterflies. Don't miss the Plantation Coach Tour: An open-air coach will pick guests up at the Butterfly Pavilion for a 40-minute motorized tour around the plantation, offering views of the crops that still grow on the property. (Boone Hall is one of the oldest working plantations in the United States: It has been growing crops continuously for more than 300 years. The site offers you-pick fields in-season for strawberries, pumpkins, and other fruits and vegetables.)

The plantation is the site of a number of special events throughout the year including the world's largest oyster roast, held every January; more than 70,000 pounds of oysters are served each year at this popular food festival. And every November, hundreds of reenactors relive the Battle of Secessionville, a battle that took place on June 16, 1862, when Confederate soldiers fought to keep Charleston from being taken by the Union army.

424 Burt-Stark Mansion

CONTACT 864-366-0166, www.burt-stark.com; 400 N. Main, Abbeville

PRICING	$$
BEST TIME TO VISIT	Year-round; open Friday and Saturday only
AGE RANGE	7 and older

Although the surrender of General Robert E. Lee at Appomattox (see the description under "Virginia") is generally considered the end of the American Civil War, Confederate president Jefferson Davis wasn't ready to abandon his cause. Less than a month after the events at Appomattox, on May 2, 1865, Davis met with his Council of War at the home of his friend, Major Armistead Burt. Davis was determined to continue to fight the Union army, but his advisers and staff were unanimously against this. Eventually, Davis was convinced to release the Confederate troops from service and officially admit defeat. Because of this final confabulation, Abbeville is remembered as the "grave of the Confederacy." Guests today can tour the small home, which contains many original furnishings that were in place during Davis's visit—including

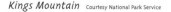

Kings Mountain Courtesy National Park Service

Burt-Stark Mansion   Courtesy Abbeville Historic Preservation Commission

Charles Towne Landing
Courtesy South Carolina Department of Parks, Recreation, and Tourism

the bed he slept in. Although subsequent owners added on a modern kitchen to the historic home, the original cookhouse remains on the property and is available for tour as well. Check out the 10-foot fireplace and the interesting collection of iron kettles and pots that date to Davis's era.

425 Charles Towne Landing

CONTACT 843-852-4200, www.charlestowne.org; 1500 Old Towne Rd., Charleston

PRICING	$–$$
BEST TIME TO VISIT	Year-round
AGE RANGE	3 and older

Charleston is one of the most beautiful cities in the South, with plentiful historical architecture, massive old trees, and southern charm to spare. To get a sense of where the city—indeed, the state of South Carolina (one of the original 13 colonies)—started, visit his-

toric Charles Towne Landing. Europeans came to the region as early as 1540, but it wasn't until 1670 that the English colony of the Province of Carolina was established on Albermarle Point, at the confluence of the Ashley and Cooper Rivers. About 150 colonists settled here, and they named the area after King Charles II.

The refreshingly uncommercial Charles Towne Landing re-creates life in colonial Charleston, and the living history department is committed to teaching guests what life was really like for colonists more than 300 years ago. Interpretive reenactors festooned in 17th-century fashions engage visitors with stories of life in early America and with living history demonstrations like candle making, woodworking, and open-hearth cooking. Don't miss the Experimental Crop Garden, which follows the instructions regarding agriculture given to the leader of the Carolina expedition, Captain Joseph West, in 1670. Crops here vary by season, but look for the ubiquitous indigo and sugarcane—two plants that were particularly successful (and profitable) for the early colonists. The Fortified Area within the attraction marks the boundaries of the settlement with sharpened logs and a ditch dug in front, to discourage hostile Native Americans or any other European expeditions that might seek to attack the settlement. Kids will enjoy touring the reproduction of a 17th-century cargo vessel—the *Adventure*—fashioned after similar ships that carried commodities and provisions between the colonies and the West Indies.

426 Cowpens National Battlefield

CONTACT 864-461-2828, www.nps.gov/cowp; 4001 Chesnee Hwy., Gaffney

PRICING	$
BEST TIME TO VISIT	Year-round
AGE RANGE	7 and older

From 1779 to 1780, during the American Revolutionary War, the British army swept through the American South, defeating much of the relatively ill-prepared Southern Continental Army and capturing cities like Savannah and Charleston. The British grew cocky from these victories, however, and U.S. commander Nathanael Greene was able to take the Redcoats by surprise in a number of backcountry skirmishes. The Battle of Cowpens, on January 17, 1781, is often regarded as the turning point of the Revolutionary War in the South, eventually leading to American success at Yorktown.

Cowpens National Battlefield commemorates the victory and memorializes the soldiers who fought for independence. (*Cowpens* refers to pastureland.) Begin at the visitor center, which includes displays of Revolutionary War artifacts and hands-on exhibits. The on-site theater shows an 18-minute orientation film, and there is a fiber-optic map that illustrates the Southern Campaign of the war, including the maneuvers at the Battle of Cowpens. Walk the 1.3-mile trail along the 500-yard-square battlefield and see the Washington Light Infantry Monument. Or take the 3.8-mile (one-way) loop road that skirts the perimeter of the battlefield. This roadway will take you past the Robert Scruggs House, a log cabin that was built several decades after the Battle of Cowpens. The interior of the cabin is indicative of the type of furnishings that might have been used in the 1850s. Throughout the year there are living history demonstrations at the Scruggs House, as well as seasonal battle reenactments. The grounds are lovely, and in the spring and fall, when the weather is mild, this is a fine site for a picnic.

Reenactment at Cowpens National Battlefield Photo by Tony Smith Photography.com, courtesy South Carolina Department of Parks, Recreation, and Tourism

427 Drayton Hall

CONTACT 843-769-2600, www.draytonhall.org; 3380 Ashley River Rd., Charleston

PRICING	$$–$$$ (family packages $$$$)
BEST TIME TO VISIT	Year-round
AGE RANGE	7 and older

Drayton Hall is a superbly preserved 18th-century plantation just northwest of Charleston; it is the only plantation along the Ashley River to survive the Revolutionary and Civil Wars (not to mention a number of hurricanes that have swept through the South Carolina low country). The Palladian-style home and grounds were owned for seven generations by the Drayton family, who preserved the property as closely as possible to its original condition.

Drayton Hall   Courtesy South Carolina Department of Parks, Recreation, and Tourism

Guests can take a guided tour of the historic mansion—which is remarkable in its architectural detail. Especially fine is the Great Hall, which features intricate plasterwork on the ceiling and an ornate mantelpiece. Outside, stroll the grounds, which are also preserved much as they were during the 18th century. Walk along the salt river marsh on a trail that affords views of 18th-century rice fields. Look for the "ha-ha," a ditch that served as a barrier to keep grazing animals from the vicinity of the house without disrupting the views as a fence would have. The property pays homage to the slaves who helped build and maintain the property in the early years through a program called *From Africa to America*, which documents the journey of Africans to America and their struggles through slavery and emancipation. Be sure to visit the African American cemetery on site—the oldest such cemetery in America that is still in use.

South Carolina offers myriad plantations to explore, some—like Drayton Hall—preserved much as they were in the antebellum period and some restored and reconstructed to serve as modern-day entertainment venues and luxurious bed & breakfasts. If your family can't get enough of the Old South, check out Magnolia Plantation and Gardens (3550 Ashley River Rd.) and Middleton Place (4300 Ashley River Rd.), also in Charleston; Hopsewee Plantation (494 Hopsewee Rd.) and Mansfield Plantation (1776 Mansfield Rd.) in Georgetown; and Radcliff Plantation (181 Radcliff Rd.) on Beech Island (among dozens of other worthy destinations).

Drayton Hall offers a museum collection including historical artifacts that have been found through archaeological surveys of the property, as well as an impressive collection of fine and decorative arts. Look for the poignant and rare slave tag: Copper badges such as the one displayed at Drayton Hall were carried by slaves when they journeyed to Charleston. Slaves were required to wear the badges at all times—or else risk arrest and a stiff fine for the plantation owner.

428 Fort Hill

CONTACT 864-656-3311, www.clemson.edu/about/history/properties/fort-hill; off I-85, near the intersection of Fort Hill St. and Calhoun Dr., on the Clemson University campus, Clemson

PRICING	$
BEST TIME TO VISIT	Year-round (but closed during university holidays)
AGE RANGE	7 and older

John C. Calhoun (1782–1850) is arguably the most recognized 19th-century statesman from South Carolina, and is remembered as part of the "Great Triumvirate," a trio of influential early congressional leaders that also included Henry Clay and Daniel Webster. During his expansive political career Calhoun served in the state House of Representatives, the U.S. Congress, as secretary of war under President James Monroe, as vice president alongside Presidents John Quincy Adams and Andrew Jackson, and as secretary of state under President John Tyler. Calhoun instituted a gag rule to prevent resolutions in Congress that threatened the institution of slavery, and although he was aware that the divisive subject threatened the Union he was against the idea of secession.

Pick up visitor parking passes for Clemson University at the University Visitor Center on Alumni Circle.

John C. Calhoun home

Courtesy South Carolina Department of Parks, Recreation, and Tourism

Don't miss a trip to the Fort Sumter Visitor Education Center (340 Concord St.) on mainland Charleston, which offers an expansive museum with exhibits that chronicle the escalating sectionalism between the North and the South that eventually led to the Civil War. Also nearby is the Patriots Point Maritime Museum (40 Patriots Point Rd.) in Mount Pleasant, the largest naval and maritime museum in the world.

Fort Hill was Calhoun's home from 1825 until his death 25 years later. The estate was built on property originally owned by Calhoun's mother-in-law. After Calhoun's death, his wife, Floride, passed the estate to her three children, one of whom (Anna Maria) was married to Thomas Green Clemson. Thomas Clemson bequeathed the property in his will to the state of South Carolina to build an agricultural college—the institution that today is known as Clemson University. The antebellum plantation home remains intact in the center of campus as a museum, furnished with family artifacts.

429 Fort Sumter

CONTACT 843-883-3123, www.nps.gov/fosu; located on a small island in Charleston Harbor

PRICING	$; ferry ride additional
BEST TIME TO VISIT	Spring through fall
AGE RANGE	7 and older

More than 600,000 soldiers died in the gruesome American Civil War—the epic conflict that pitted brothers against brothers to settle the question of states' rights, end slavery, and ultimately strengthen the United States as a force to be reckoned with on the international scene. But the battle that started it all was nearly bloodless: The first shots of the war rang out on April 12, 1861, when Confederate artillery attacked Fort Sumter, in an effort to drive out federal forces from the borders of South Carolina, which had seceded months earlier (on December 20, 1860). Union forces were low on ammunition, and after 34 hours under siege the federal troops surrendered. Only two Union soldiers were killed in the skirmish.

The site of Fort Sumter is preserved as one of the most historically significant of the Civil War. Visitors today can explore the fort and check out a collection of period weapons. Fort Sumter is located on a small island just off the coast of Charleston, and it is accessible only by boat. Guests can arrive via their own boat for free or take a ferry service run by the park's concessionaire (800-789-3678). Ferry departures are from Liberty Square in Charleston or the Patriots Point Maritime Museum in Mount Pleasant; the ride takes about 30 minutes, and includes a narrated tour that will explain the events of the Battle at Fort Sumter and discuss its significance in American history.

Fort Sumter

Courtesy National Park Service

430 Old Slave Mart Museum

CONTACT 843-958-6467, www.nps.gov/nr/travel/charleston/osm.htm; 6 Chalmers St., Charleston

PRICING	$–$$
BEST TIME TO VISIT	Year-round; closed Sunday
AGE RANGE	10 and older

Ridding the United States of slavery was a long, slow process that began as far back as 1807, when President Thomas Jefferson signed a law prohibiting further importation of slaves into the country. However, the legislation allowed for many loopholes, and the ban didn't take effect officially until January 1, 1808.

Because slave labor had become integral to the economic success of the plantation system in the South, this ban on the international slave trade increased the demand for domestic slave trading. In the first half of the 19th century, before the Civil War put an end to slavery once and for all in America, more than a million U.S.-born slaves were sold away from their plantations of origin. During the antebellum era, Charleston, South Carolina, was a center of the plantation economy of the South, and thus a major center of the domestic slave trade. Slaves were originally sold on the north side of the Custom House (what is now the Exchange Building) in town, but an 1856 ordinance forbid slave trading in public, and so a collection of slave "marts" sprang up. The Old Slave Mart, once known as Ryan's Mart, is the only existing building known to have been used as a slave auction gallery in South Carolina. The structure is preserved as a museum today, and focuses on Charleston's role in the slave trade and chronicles the slave sales that took place on site.

Walking through the small museum is a visceral experience: Knowing what took place within these walls is a reminder of the atrocities of the slave trade. For example, visitors will learn that slaves were made to stand on 3-foot-high tables, so that potential owners could better inspect them. While here, don't miss the audio exhibit that records the voice of a former slave who was interviewed about his life before and after emancipation. As you wander through the displays, you will learn how slaves were priced (by age, gender, and special skills) and discover how slaves lived with forced labor and frequent poor treatment by plantation owners. The experience of the Old Slave Mart can be chilling and might be disturbing to young children—although this is a chapter in American history that must be understood, both in the context of the Old South that is evident throughout South Carolina and in the context of modern-day cultural diversity in America.

Old Slave Mart Museum
Courtesy South Carolina Department of Parks, Recreation, and Tourism

SOUTH DAKOTA

431 Badlands National Park

CONTACT 605-433-5361, www.nps.gov/badl; 25216 Ben Reifel Rd., Interior

PRICING	$
BEST TIME TO VISIT	Spring through fall
AGE RANGE	5 and older

Badlands National Park   © Charles Arensman. Used with permission.

In historic times, Lakota Sioux Indians lived on inhospitable, quickly eroding land in what is now southwestern South Dakota, giving it the name *mako sico*, which translates to "land bad." But when European fur trappers and American homesteaders came on the scene, the Natives of the region were slowly (and brutally) forced out. After the battle between the Lakota Sioux and the U.S. Army in the Wounded Knee Massacre of 1890—considered the last battle in the conflict between the American military and Natives, in which more than 200 Native men, women, and children were killed—soldiers forced the remaining Lakota Sioux off the badlands and onto reservations.

Today the Badlands National Park is jointly administered by the Lakota Sioux Tribe (who live on the Pine Ridge Reservation, on which half of the park is located) and the National Park Service. Visitors come to see the unusual geological formations, the colorful mineral deposits, and one of the world's most expansive fossil beds. Start your trip with a tour of the Ben Reifel Visitor Center, which screens a short film called *Land of Stone and Light* that explains the natural and historical significance of the area, and includes interactive museum exhibits. Kids will not want to miss the chance to assemble a virtual skeleton on a computer screen. Next, get out and drive the Highway 240 Badlands Loop Road (accessed from I-90) that runs through the north end of the park and affords great views and numerous scenic turnouts; or hike one of the many trails that will take you through the spires, eroded plateaus, pinnacles, and other formations created by natural erosion. During the summer, the park offers a Night Sky Program that includes a 40-minute multimedia presentation about the universe, followed by a ranger-led star viewing. Because the park

is so far away from the light pollution of big cities, the views at night are remarkable: An estimated 7,500 stars are visible through a state-of-the-art telescope accessible during the program.

The park is also the site of the largest assemblage of late Eocene and Oligocene mammal fossils. Check out the Saber Site fossil quarry, adjacent to the Ben Reifel Visitor Center, from early June through late August, to observe paleontologists at work. Guests can also tour the fossil prep lab to learn about current discoveries within the park.

The Badlands is a great place to view living wildlife, too. Thanks to wildlife introduction efforts, the once nearly exterminated American bison species boasts a population close to 800 within the park boundaries. Other reintroduced species include the rare black-footed ferret, swift foxes, and Rocky Mountain bighorn sheep.

432 Crazy Horse Memorial

CONTACT 605-673-4681, http://crazyhorsememorial.org/; 202 Ave. of the Chiefs, Custer

PRICING	$$
BEST TIME TO VISIT	Summer
AGE RANGE	All ages

The Crazy Horse Memorial is a monument both to the Oglala Lakota leader who fought the U.S. federal government in protest of encroachments onto the terri-

Crazy Horse Memorial

Several generations of children have grown up reading the beloved *Little House on the Prairie* series of juvenile novels by American author Laura Ingalls Wilder (1867–1957). Ingalls Wilder was born in Wisconsin, but as a young child emigrated with her family to what was still Indian Territory, in Kansas. The family quickly moved on to Minnesota and then the Dakota territory, where Ingalls Wilder's father homesteaded in De Smet. Her exciting, often harrowing, experiences of living on the Plains as a pioneer are the basis of her books, which chronicle her life as a young girl. Ingalls Wilder's books have been translated and sold in more than 40 countries around the world, and they were the inspiration for a popular television series.

De Smet was featured in Ingalls Wilder's novels *By the Shores of Silver Lake*, *The First Four Years*, *The Little Town on the Prairie*, *The Long Winter*, and *These Happy Golden Years*. Today guests can visit the site of "Pa Ingalls's" homestead and get a glimpse into pioneer life. Tour re-creations of the family's two homestead buildings—*Ma's Little House* and the *Hay-Roof Barn*, which have been reconstructed in their original locations. Also check out the *Dugout Home*, a version much like the underground shelter Laura and her family lived in on the banks of Plum Creek, in Walnut Grove, Minnesota. Children will love the chance to don bonnets, straw hats, and calico pinafores in the Little Prairie School on site, which is decorated as a one-room schoolhouse would have been in the 1880s. A costumed reenactor playing the part of schoolmarm will conduct a brief lesson for visitors, who might get to practice their sums or partake of a spelling lesson. The attraction features a covered-wagon ride across the

tories of the Lakota Natives and led warriors to victory at the Battle of Little Bighorn in 1876—*and* to Korczak Ziolkowski, the sculptor who gave the better part of his adult life to realizing the memorial. The massive sculpture is carved on the face of a mountain in the Black Hills, and depicts the Native American hero riding a horse. The sculpture was commissioned by Henry Standing Bear, a Lakota leader, who chose Ziolkowski to design and execute the memorial. He began the project in June 1948 with a box of dynamite, a sledgehammer, and a drill bit; he spent the next 36 years chiseling his vision into millions of tons of granite. When Ziolkowski died in 1982, only the vaguest outline was evident. He left plan books and scale models behind, however, and his children took up where he left off. Work continues on the 60-story-high figure, which is now more than halfway completed. Crazy Horse's face has emerged, and the horse is beginning to take shape.

433 Ingalls Homestead

CONTACT 800-776-3594, www.ingallshomestead.com; 20812 Homestead Rd., De Smet

PRICING	$$
BEST TIME TO VISIT	Open Memorial Day to Labor Day
AGE RANGE	5 and older

Walking in the steps of Laura Ingalls Wilder

PRICE KEY
$ free–$5
$$ $6–10
$$$ $11–20
$$$$ $21+

prairie and hands-on pioneering activities like grinding wheat, making rope, and crafting a corncob doll. For a true *Little House* experience, consider overnighting on the property in a covered wagon. For $50 per night, families can rent a large wagon with a double bed and two small roll-out mats, and then fall asleep to the wind rustling through the prairie grasses.

434 Mammoth Site

CONTACT 605-745-6017, www.mammothsite.com/location.html; 1800 U.S. 18 Bypass, Hot Springs

PRICING	$$
BEST TIME TO VISIT	Year-round
AGE RANGE	3 and older

Columbian and woolly mammoths roamed what is now South Dakota more than 26,000 years ago. At one point, a sinkhole opened up near a well-visited pond, and the large mammals that were drinking there at the time were trapped and eventually died. The bones lay buried for millennia, until a construction worker uncovered one of the fossils by accident when preparing a new housing subdivision. The site was quickly investigated and set aside instead for research. As of this publication, 59 mammoths have been unearthed, along with the fossils of a wolf, camel, short-faced bear, llama, and prairie dog. The fossils have been left displayed in the dry pond sediments, and a climate-controlled building has been constructed over them for protection. Guests can stroll along an elevated walkway to get a good look at the fossils and watch ongoing paleontological excavations. Admission to the museum includes a 30-minute guided tour and a 10-minute orientation video.

On select summer days, there are three fun and interactive programs for children. Kids ages 4 through 12 can sign up for the Junior Paleontologist Excavation Program and dig for fossil replicas. For youths 13 and older, the Advanced Paleontolgist Excavation Program teaches participants excavation and bone-identification techniques. And also for children 13 and older, the Atlatl Throwing Experience teaches

kids an ancient Native hunting technique. (Note that an adult is required to accompany children 16 years older or younger.)

435 Minuteman Missile National Historic Site

CONTACT 605-433-5552, www.nps.gov/mimi; 21280 SD 240, Philip

PRICING	$
BEST TIME TO VISIT	Year-round
AGE RANGE	7 and older

In the aftermath of World War II, tensions grew between the world's emerging superpowers: the United States and the Soviet Union. The hostility escalated into what came to be known as the Cold War, an era marked by a mutual arms race that threatened

Minuteman Missile National Historic Site

atomic warfare. In an effort to amass a sufficient stockpile of weapons, both countries accumulated enough nuclear weaponry to destroy life on earth—and then some. As part of this arms buildup, in 1961 the U.S. Air Force began burying intercontinental ballistic missiles in the plains of South Dakota. This endeavor was top secret, and at its height there were 150 missiles and 15 launch control facilities in the state. Thankfully, none of the weapons was ever deployed. On July 31, 1991, U.S. president George H. W. Bush and Soviet leader Mikhail Gorbachev signed the Strategic Arms Reduction Treaty, which called for the reduction of nuclear weapons. As a result, the United States began deactivating much of its missile stockpile, including the sites in South Dakota.

The Minuteman Missile National Historic Site was established in the late 20th century to chronicle the importance of the Cold War and its concurrent arms race. The site comprises a launch control center and a missile silo launch facility. Together the sites represent the only remaining portions of the nuclear missile field that once stretched across 13,500 square miles of South Dakota. Rangers will guide visitors through the living area and security control center in the topside launch control facility and then down an elevator to the underground launch control center. Peek into a silo to see an inactive Minuteman II missile within.

Mount Rushmore   Courtesy National Park Service

more than 90 percent of the crafting was executed using dynamite, which blasted away nearly 500,000 tons of granite from the side of the mountain. The sculpture took 14 years to complete—and cost a mere $1 million. Today the site is an iconic American attraction, drawing viewers from around the world.

Arrive at the Grandview Terrace (the most accessible vista) via the Avenue of Flags, which includes representations from each U.S. state and territory. The sculpture is grand by day but perhaps even more impressive at night, when the mountainside is illuminated for several hours. In the summertime take a ranger-led walk along the Presidential Trail that leads to the base of the sculpture to hear about the natural and cultural significance of Mount Rushmore and the surrounding Black Hills. Or to learn more about the actual construction of the massive art piece, attend the Sculptor's Studio Talk, which includes demonstrations of the tools used and the artist's working model.

436 Mount Rushmore

CONTACT 605-574-2523, www.nps.gov/moru; 13000 Hwy. 244, Keystone

PRICING	$; parking $$
BEST TIME TO VISIT	Spring through fall
AGE RANGE	All ages

Mount Rushmore is an epic-scale sculpture chiseled into the Black Hills that features the likenesses of four beloved American presidents: George Washington, Thomas Jefferson, Abraham Lincoln, and Theodore Roosevelt. These 60-foot-high faces peer out to onlookers from a height of 500 feet. The massive sculpture was begun in 1927 by artist Gutzon Borglum;

437 Wounded Knee Memorial

CONTACT Located at the junction of BIA Hwy. 27 and BIA Hwy. 28, south of Porcupine

PRICING	$
BEST TIME TO VISIT	Spring through fall
AGE RANGE	10 and older

The press of homesteaders into the western Plains and the resistance from Native Americans already liv-

Wounded Knee Memorial   Courtesy South Dakota Tourism

ing there resulted in tensions that often erupted in violence, instigated by both sides. As a way of containing the violence, the U.S. government set about relocating Native peoples, usually with little regard for their culture and traditions. After a military intervention, in 1877 the Lakota Sioux were forced to move from their historic hunting grounds throughout the badlands of South Dakota to the Pine Ridge Reservation, where they were no longer able to hunt bison, which was a driving force in their culture in the pre-reservation era. The U.S. government was not content at relocation, however, and attempted to force the Native people to give up their very way of life and assimilate into white culture. Their language was banned, and American-style boarding schools were built to indoctrinate young Lakota Sioux.

At the same time—perhaps in response to the unease the Native Americans felt—a religious ceremony called the Ghost Dance arose among tribes in the Southwest. Settlers feared the Ghost Dance, because the ceremony was intended to drive out the white homesteaders and thereby allow the tribes to return to their Native lands. When the Ghost Dance arrived at the Pine Ridge Reservation, the authorities panicked. The U.S. military planned to arrest Lakota Sioux leader Sitting Bull, who was reputed to be ready to join the Ghost Dancers, but in the process of his apprehension he and several of his warriors were killed. Soon after, on December 29, 1890, cavalry raided a camp of Ghost Dancers to search for and seize weapons. The group, having heard about Sitting Bull's death, was reportedly ready to surrender. Before the U.S. military entered the camp, however, soldiers set up machine guns along the ridge, pointing to the camp below. When a shot was fired within the camp, the U.S. military retaliated by firing the machine guns into the crowd. At least 200 people were murdered—including individuals found as far as 2 miles away, who had obviously been killed as they were running away. Although the details of the encounter are sometimes disputed, the incident is remembered as a massacre and the last important clash in the West between the U.S. military and Native people.

The Wounded Knee Memorial is a small, unremarkable cemetery fenced in by chain link, with a stone marker engraved with the names of Lakota Sioux who were killed in the incident. There is little to see here, but the site offers a chance to reflect on the events that took place nearby more than 100 years ago and help children put into perspective the price Native peoples paid for the American dream of Manifest Destiny.

Great Smoky Mountains   Courtesy U.S. Fish and Wildlife Service

tennessee

438 Andrew Johnson National Historic Site

CONTACT 423-683-3551, www.nps.gov/anjo; 121 Monument Ave., Greenville

PRICING	$
BEST TIME TO VISIT	Year-round
AGE RANGE	7 and older

Andrew Johnson (1808–75) was the 17th president of the United States, succeeding President Abraham Lincoln after Lincoln was assassinated. Johnson had the misfortune of presiding over the nation as a contentious Congress struggled through the Reconstruction following the Civil War. Historians and his contemporaries alike criticized Johnson for not rigorously upholding the rights of newly freed slaves, and attacks from the legislative branch ended in his impeachment by the U.S. House of Representatives, making Johnson the first American president to have been impeached. (Johnson was only one of two presidents to have been impeached to this date; President Bill Clinton was impeached in the late 20th century, and was acquitted.) Johnson was acquitted by the U.S. Senate, in 1868, and was thus not removed from office.

The Andrew Johnson National Historic Site comprises four components. The visitor center includes a tailor shop owned by Johnson in his early years (children can try on 19th-century clothing here), as well as a presidential museum. Guests to the museum are given replicas of the original tickets to Johnson's impeachment, and at the end of their visit are given the opportunity to render their own opinion; the visitor votes are tallied every year, on May 26, the anniversary of the Senate vote that acquitted the president. Move on to Johnson's Early Home, which includes an exhibit on Johnson's slave-owning history and an interesting family photo album. The highlight of any trip is a tour of the Homestead, a two-story brick Greek Revival home where Johnson and his wife lived from 1869 to 1875. During the Civil War, the house was occupied by soldiers and sustained enough damage that it had to be renovated before the couple returned. Today the home is decorated in period furnishings, with many belongings dating to the Johnson family. Johnson's final resting place is within the on-site cemetery; his grave is marked with a 27-foot obelisk topped with a sculpture of an American eagle.

Grandchild's bedroom, Andrew Johnson National Historic Site   Courtesy National Park Service

439 Davy Crockett Birthplace

CONTACT 423-257-2167; 1245 Davy Crockett Park Rd., Limestone

PRICING	$
BEST TIME TO VISIT	Year-round
AGE RANGE	7 and older

David Crocket (1786–1836), better known as Davy, was a soldier, politician, and frontiersman; in the years since his death he has morphed into an American folk hero, and has been the subject of popular songs, movies, and TV shows that painted him as a mythic figure. In real life, Crockett grew up in Tennessee, and had the reputation for being a crackerjack hunter and a master storyteller. He was a colonel in the Tennessee militia and served a stint in the Tennessee state legislature. He moved on to Washington, DC, as a representative in the U.S. House. When he lost a reelection bid, Crockett left for Texas, where he fought in the Texas Revolution and died at the Battle of the Alamo (see the description under "Texas").

Crockett's birthplace has been preserved as a state park. The attraction comprises more than 100 acres along the Nolichucky River, and includes a replica of the log cabin where Crockett was born. The site is a popular place for picnics, and includes an extensive campground.

440 Graceland Mansion

Graceland gates
Carol M. Highsmith's America, courtesy Library of Congress, Prints and Photographs Division

CONTACT 901-332-3322, www.elvis.com/graceland; 3734 Elvis Presley Blvd., Memphis

PRICING	$$$$
BEST TIME TO VISIT	Year-round
AGE RANGE	10 and older

Elvis Aaron Presley (1935–77) was one of the most influential American popular entertainers in the 20th century. The "King of Rock and Roll" had a unique voice, a sexy stage presence, and a musical style that proved irresistible to the masses—especially teenage girls, who swooned over their television sets when Elvis appeared on the iconic *Ed Sullivan Show*, flocked to his live concerts, and bought his records by the armloads—including classics like "Jailhouse Rock," "Hound Dog," "Blue Suede Shoes," "Don't Be Cruel," and "Love Me Tender." He went on to star in movies and eventually became a staple of the Las Vegas entertainment industry. His later years were marked by drug addiction and poor health, and he died unexpectedly at age 42.

Partly because of his death at such an early age and partly because of his epic fame, his former home, Graceland Mansion, has become a kind of shrine to Presley. The property has been converted to a museum, and visitors can take self-guided audio tours including the kitchen, pool room, dining room, living room, several bedrooms, and the infamous Jungle Room—a themed space with green shag carpeting and ornately carved animal-adorned furniture. The home is a time capsule for over-the-top 1970s decor. Visitors can also tour Elvis's trophy building, which houses an astounding collection of his gold and platinum records. The Automobile Museum displays more than

30 vehicles once owned by the King, including a pink Cadillac, a Mercedes Benz limousine, and even a John Deere tractor. There are also two jets on the property, one custom jet named *Lisa Marie* (after his only daughter) that includes gold-plated seat belts, suede chairs, and leather-covered tables; and a smaller one used to transport Elvis's manager and staff during concert tours. The Meditation Garden on the property is the final resting place of Elvis and his parents.

441 Grand Ole Opry

CONTACT 615-871-OPRY, www.opry.com; 2804 Opryland Dr., Nashville

PRICING	Tour and performance prices vary
BEST TIME TO VISIT	March through December
AGE RANGE	10 and older

The Grand Ole Opry is a legendary music hall that has launched some of the biggest names in American country music, including Hank Williams, Patsy Cline, and Minnie Pearl; more recently, it has served as a place for young established stars like Garth Brooks, Carrie Underwood, and Brad Paisley to shine. Although the Opry moved to its current locale in the 1970s, the institution dates back more than 80 years; a live show has been broadcast from the Opry stage several times a week since its founding. If your family likes country music, there's no better place to be from March through December, when there are live shows

PRICE KEY
$ free–$5
$$ $6–10
$$$ $11–20
$$$$ $21+

Stage at Grand Ole Opry

Courtesy Grand Ole Opry

every Tuesday featuring big-name acts and up-and-comers alike. If you'd just like to get a look at a place that has hosted world-renowned artists, take a daytime tour of the theater, which allows guests to walk backstage, view the artist entrance, and hear tales from the venue's storied past.

442 Great Smoky Mountains National Park

CONTACT www.nps.gov/grsm; park entrances in Gatlinburg (off U.S. 441) and Townsend (off TN 73); additional entrance in Cherokee, NC (off U.S. 441)

PRICING	$
BEST TIME TO VISIT	Spring through fall
AGE RANGE	5 and older

The Great Smoky Mountains National Park is one of the most heavily visited national parks in the United States. At more than 500,000 acres, it is also one of the largest protected areas in the eastern United States. The park falls within the Appalachian Mountain chain. The area was originally inhabited by the Cherokee, who called the mountains *Shaconage*, which translates to "place of the blue smoke," referencing the bluish fog that hangs on the mountains and valleys. It is a place of great beauty and enormous biodiversity—and there is no shortage of things for families to do.

In addition to hiking the many trails, fishing, camping, touring by automobile, horseback riding, and biking, this is one of the best places on the East Coast for wildlife viewing. The largest mammals in the park are elk, herds of which can be easily spotted in the Cataloochee Valley (especially in the early-morning and twilight hours). Also making their home in the Great Smokies are black bears, white-tailed deer, bobcats, and 27 species of rodents. If you have a family member who loves bug-watching, this is the place to be in mid-June. The Great Smoky Mountains is home to synchronous fireflies—the only North American species that can synchronize their light-flashing patterns (a mating display), a behavior that is most apt to be seen in late spring and early summer.

There are dozens of spectacular waterfalls to view in the park, including the 90-foot Hen Wallow Falls within a rhododendron forest, popular Laurel Falls, Mingo Falls—the tallest waterfall in the Southern Appalachians, at 120 feet—and Rainbow Falls, which as the name suggests produces ubiquitous rainbows on sunny days. For more examples of nature at its colorful best, visit the park in autumn, when foliage displays are spectacular: Look for mountain maples, hobblebush, American beech, and yellow birch. At the park's highest elevations, leaves start to turn in mid-September. In mid-October, lower elevations reach their peak color: Look for sugar maple, red maple, hickory, and sweetgum, which are readily viewed along the Blue Ridge Parkway that runs through the park.

The Great Smoky Mountains National Park is one of the few places in the eastern United States where black bears live in the wild. Rangers estimate that as many as 1,500 bears live in the park, at all elevations. As tempting as it is to approach the beautiful animals, don't do it: Laws prohibit visitors from getting closer than 50 yards—because, bottom line, these animals can be dangerous. If a bear approaches *you*, don't run: Back away slowly. If the bear continues to move toward you, shout at it and try to look as large as possible (group together with companions, climb to higher ground). Remember: Running away is prey behavior announcing to bears that you are a potential meal.

Great Smoky Mountains National Park   Courtesy Linda Frandsen

If you're interested in human-made beauty, the Great Smokies has that, too: The park boasts one of the largest collections of historic, finely crafted log structures in the East. More than 90 cabins, barns, churches, schools, and gristmills have been preserved or restored within the park boundaries. The greatest concentration of such structures is in Cades Cove, which is accessible via an 11-mile one-way loop road.

Families will also find extensive ranger programs in the park, including disparate activities like guided night hikes, classes on salamandering (finding the 13 species of salamanders that live in the park), performances of mountain music indigenous to the Appalachians, guided wagon rides, bat tours, craft demonstrations like basket making and candle dipping, blacksmithing demonstrations, art classes, bear awareness programs, photography classes—the list goes on. There is no danger of running out of activities, but one of the most satisfying pastimes is arguably watching the sunset in this magnificent natural place.

443 Hermitage

CONTACT 615-889-2941, www.thehermitage.com; 4580 Rachel's Lane, Nashville

PRICING	$$$
BEST TIME TO VISIT	Year-round
AGE RANGE	7 and older

Andrew Jackson (1757–1845) was the seventh president of the United States. He was a soldier and an attorney in his younger years, and as president managed to make some powerful enemies in Congress. He dismantled the Second Bank of the United States, and is probably best remembered for signing the Indian Removal Act of 1830—the forced relocation of Native Americans from their traditional grounds to Indian Territory (what is now Oklahoma). The relocation is often referred to as the Trail of Tears. Personally, Jackson was a tough customer: Nicknamed "Old Hickory," he was a wealthy slaveholder prone to brawls. In one instance, he killed a man in a duel after the man had insulted his wife, Rachel.

This tough, aggressive image of the man contrasts sharply with the genteel lifestyle he enjoyed, which is memorialized at the magnificent, surprisingly luxurious Hermitage, a historical plantation that was owned by Jackson from 1804 until his death more than 40 years later. Guests begin a visit at the Andrew Jackson Visitor Center to watch an introductory 20-minute film on the former president and his extensive plantation. Just beyond the center is the Hermitage Mansion, which has been faithfully re-

Andrew Jackson's tomb   Courtesy Brinda Deaton Taylor

stored to its 1837 appearance. Throughout are personal objects like weapons and books that belonged to the Jackson family, along with a large collection of family portraits on display. The beautiful grounds include a vegetable garden, extensive herbs and flowers, and Jackson's tomb. If you have the chance, take the outdoor tour that explores the history of farming and slavery on the property.

444 Shiloh National Military Park

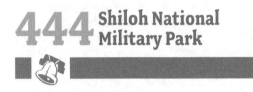

CONTACT 731-689-5696, www.nps.gov/shil;
1055 Pittsburgh Landing Rd., Shiloh

PRICING	$
BEST TIME TO VISIT	Year-round
AGE RANGE	7 and older

The two-day Battle of Shiloh in Hardin County was one of the first important battles in the Western Theater of the Civil War, and it proved to be one of the bloodiest: Approximately 24,000 soldiers were either seriously wounded, killed, or missing in action. On April 6, 1862, Confederate troops surprised their opponents early in the morning. (In fact, reports have it that the Union troops were still eating breakfast, and as Confederate troops arrived at the Union camps they stopped to eat the remainders of the meal.) Although Union troops commanded by General Ulysses S. Grant held the battlefield, the battle did not end with a decisive tactical victory. The event did, however, begin a six-month struggle for control over adjacent Corinth, which was strategically important as a transportation and communications center.

The site of the battle is now known as Shiloh National Military Park (which is also home to the Corinth Civil War Interpretive Center). Shiloh and Corinth battlefields are preserved, along with the small town of Shiloh. There are 151 monuments in this site, as well as 217 cannons and more than 450 historic markers. Begin a trip here at the visitor center, which screens an interpretive film, *Shiloh—Fiery Trial*, that plays on the hour and offers a contextual introduction to the battle. There are also numerous artifacts on display in the visitor center that were recovered from the Shiloh battlefield. The best way to see the entirety of the park is via a 12.5-mile auto tour route that includes 20 stops at infamous sites from the battle, including Bloody Pond (which was reputedly turned red with human blood during the battle), surviving fortifications, and homes used as command posts by Civil War generals. Don't miss the Iowa Monument, the tallest monument to the fallen within the park. In addition, pay your respects at the Shiloh National Cemetery, the final resting place for more than 3,500 Union soldiers (as well as two Confederates). The park also preserves prehistoric Indian mounds that date to the Mississippian era. Living history demonstrations are held throughout the year, including battle reenactments near the anniversary of the battle, and interpretive programs that can include rifle firing and re-creations of camp life.

Shiloh National Military Park   Courtesy National Park Service

texas

445 The Alamo

CONTACT 210-225-1391, ext. 34, www.thealamo.org; 300 Alamo Plaza, San Antonio

PRICING	$
BEST TIME TO VISIT	Year-round
AGE RANGE	7 and older

The structure that is known today as the Alamo was founded as Mission San Antonio de Valero in 1718 by Spanish Franciscans as part of their efforts to convert to Christianity and to educate Native Americans. By the late 18th century, the mission was abandoned, and within a decade it was taken over by the Second Flying Company of San Carlos de Parras of the Mexican army, the members of which probably renamed the mission the Alamo (which means "cottonwood" in Spanish). Today the Alamo is one of the most revered historical sites in Texas because of the Battle of the Alamo, a turning point in the Texas Revolution. The Texas Revolution was a conflict between Texas colonists and the government of Mexico. After a 13-day siege in which the Mexican army cut off the water supply to the Alamo complex where nearly 200 Texas defenders (including American legends Jim Bowie and Davy Crockett) were barricaded, Mexican troops commanded by General Antonio Santa Ana attacked the Alamo garrison in 1836. After a valiant effort against overwhelming odds, all but two of the Texian

The Alamo   Courtesy Texas Tourism

defenders were killed. In part because of the battle—and the outrage it caused among Texas settlers—the Texians defeated the Mexican army at the Battle of San Jacinto less than two months later, and the Republic of Texas was established.

Visitors to the Alamo today can start by viewing exhibits in the old church, which includes artifacts once belonging to the Texian defenders—including a buckskin vest worn by Crockett and a Bowie knife. Outside the church are the Alamo Gardens and an outdoor exhibit named the Wall of History, which chronicles the time line of the mission and the infamous battle on site. Don't miss the Long Barrack Museum, which houses exhibits on the mission and shows a 20-minute film on the battle. If you're visiting with kids ages 5 to 10, check out the Alamo Young Courier Program. Purchase an educational activity book, complete fun activities like calculating how many shots a single musket can fire, and then return to the museum to claim a Young Courier badge.

446 Dinosaur Valley State Park

CONTACT 254-897-4588, www.tpwd.state.tx.us/state-parks/dinosaur-valley; off Park Rd. 59, west of Glen Rose

PRICING	$–$$
BEST TIME TO VISIT	Summer
AGE RANGE	3 and older

More than 110 million years ago, dinosaurs roamed vast tracks of earth, including the region around what is now Glen Rose, Texas—and they left their marks, making enormous footprints in the mud. Over the years, silt and sediment filled in the tracks, preserving them for millennia. More recently, the Paluxy River washed away the sediment and uncovered the tracks (and in the 1930s paleontologists excavated the area to expose even more). Scientists believe that the 100-some tracks in what is now preserved as Dinosaur Valley State Park were made by a theropod and a sauropod. The 30- to 50-foot-long dinosaurs left prints that are more than a yard long. Come in the summer, when the river level is usually low, to get the best view of the tracks. Kids will enjoy the two fiberglass sculptures of dinosaurs on site: the 70-foot apatosaurus and the 45-foot *Tyrannosaurus rex*. The sculptures were commissioned for the New York World's Fair in 1964–65, and were relocated near the parking lot entrance to catch the attention of passing motorists. The park is also a beautiful place to picnic, hike, fish, and swim.

447 El Paso Mission Trail

CONTACT 915-534-0630, www.visitelpasomissiontrail. com; along 8 miles of I-10, southeast of downtown El Paso

PRICING	$
BEST TIME TO VISIT	Fall through spring
AGE RANGE	7 and older

Archaeologists estimate that the area that is now El Paso was inhabited as long ago as AD 400, when Native migrant hunter-gatherers began building small villages. In time, the Native tribes began cultivating crops, and this more sustainable food supply allowed them to stay put. By 1200 the Natives were living in larger villages and constructing pueblos; they also began to trade with other tribes in the Southwest and northern Mexico. However, for reasons that are unclear, by 1450 the region was abandoned and the Natives again began a migratory lifestyle.

More than 100 years later the first Spanish expedition came through the area. In 1595 Don Juan de Oñate was appointed by King Philip II of Spain to conquer the territory of New Mexico. Oñate traveled northward through Mexico to what is now Santa Fe, New Mexico, in the process crossing the desert in search of "el paso" (a pass) through the mountains. After considerable hardship through the rough terrain, the expedition eventually found the Rio Grande and traced it northward to what is now San Elizario, Texas. On reaching the site, the expedition held a ceremony to claim a chunk of the American Southwest for Spain—the start of more than 200 years of Spanish rule in New Mexico (of which El Paso was then a part). The settlement that came to be known as El

Paso became an important trade route to Santa Fe. It was soon proposed that because the Spanish were in the region for the long haul, missions and presidios should be built among the Native peoples, both as a way to pacify them and as a way to provide a kind of fortress along the thoroughfare to New Mexico.

The El Paso Mission Trail comprises three remaining Spanish missions from the 17th and 18th centuries:

- **Mission Socorro** (328 S. Nevarez Rd.) dates to the late 17th century. The original adobe chapel was destroyed in a flood in the 18th century; it was rebuilt and then destroyed again in the 19th century. The current structure dates to 1843 and boasts an intricately painted interior and beautiful wooden ceiling beams.
- **Mission Ysleta** (131 S. Zaragosa Rd.) was established in 1744. Look for the distinctive silver dome that marks the exterior of this vibrant mission.
- **Presidio Chapel San Elceario** (1521 San Elizario Rd.) dates to 1789. This is the largest of the three structures, with lovely pressed-tin ceilings. During the Civil War, U.S. troops were garrisoned in the presidio in 1850.

All three missions remain active parishes, so be sure to plan visits around worship services.

448 George H. W. Bush Library and Museum

CONTACT 979-691-4000, http://bushlibrary.tamu.edu; 1000 George Bush Dr. West, College Station

PRICING	$–$$
BEST TIME TO VISIT	Year-round
AGE RANGE	7 and older

George H. W. Bush (b. 1924) was the 41st president of the United States. In his youth, he served in the navy, flying 58 combat missions during World War II. He later served as a U.S. congressman, the director of the Central Intelligence Agency, and vice president of the United States under President Ronald Reagan. He has the unique distinction of being only the second com-

George H. W. Bush Library and Museum
Courtesy Bush Library and Museum

449 Lyndon B. Johnson Presidential Library

CONTACT 512-721-0200, www.lbjlibrary.org; 2313 Red River St., Austin

PRICING	$
BEST TIME TO VISIT	Year-round
AGE RANGE	7 and older

mander in chief to see one of his children become president as well. Bush Sr.'s son, George W. Bush, served as 43rd president. (John Adams was the second U.S. president, and *his* son, John Quincy Adams, was the sixth.)

The George H. W. Bush Library and Museum (part of a 90-acre complex on Texas A&M's West Campus that is also home to the Bush School of Government and Public Service and the Annenberg Presidential Conference Center) is dedicated to preserving memorabilia and official records pertaining to President Bush. The site's archives include more than 44 million pages of documents, two million photographs and videos, and 100,000 artifacts. Guests can peruse changing exhibits that focus on the culture and politics of the late 20th century in America, and can check out replicas of the White House Situation Room and President Bush's Camp David Office. Children won't want to miss the chance to get their photos taken in the library's faithful re-creation of the Bush administration's Oval Office.

Lyndon B. Johnson (1908–73) was the 36th president of the United States, a role he succeeded to from the office of vice president after the assassination of President John F. Kennedy in 1963. Johnson completed Kennedy's term, and waged a successful bid for reelection in the following presidential season. But as a result of his growing unpopularity—largely because of the increasing American involvement in the Vietnam War under his watch but also because of Johnson's polarizing personality—he chose not to run for a second elected term. He is remembered for his "Great Society" legislation that included expansive policies to uphold civil rights, strengthen public education, and protect the environment, along with welfare programs as part of his so-called War on Poverty.

The Lyndon B. Johnson Presidential Library is home to 45 million pages of historic documents pertaining to this president and his administration. The library displays a 7/8-scale replica of the Johnson Oval Office, which includes a desk the president used when he was in the Senate, a rocking chair from the White

The George W. Bush Presidential Library and Museum opened in 2013 on the campus of Southern Methodist University in Dallas (214-346-1558, www.gwbush.library@nara.gov; 2943 SMU Blvd.); exhibits spotlight important issues and events during the Bush 43 administration, and a kids' program offers hands-on opportunities for children to learn about the presidency.

Lyndon B. Johnson Presidential Library
Photo Charles Brogel, courtesy Lyndon B. Johnson Presidential Library

House, and three original televisions once belonging to Johnson. LBJ's black stretch limousine is also on display; guests will learn about the car's standard equipment, including a TV, reserve gas tank, and special communication system (and discover that the vehicle was surprisingly *not* bulletproof). The library facility has recently been renovated, and new exhibits include interactive audiovisual displays, touch-screen exhibits, a handheld mobile tour device, and an animatronic President Johnson that "talks."

450 San Jacinto Battleground State Historic Site

CONTACT 281-479-2431, www.tpwd.state.tx.us/state-parks/san-jacinto-battleground; 3523 Independence Parkway S., La Porte

PRICING	$
BEST TIME TO VISIT	Year-round
AGE RANGE	7 and older

The expansive San Jacinto Battleground State Historic Site comprises the battlefield of San Jacinto, site of the famous conflict in which Texian troops led by General Sam Houston won Texan independence from Mexico against Mexican army General Antonio Lopez

Monument at San Jacinto Battleground State Historic Site
Courtesy Texas Tourism

de Santa Ana in 1836; a monument to the battle; the USS *Texas*, a decommissioned battleship that served in both world wars and is now a museum; and a lovely preserved marshland that is good for hiking and birding. Visitors can walk the battlefield to learn more about the strategy of the conflict, or take an auto tour that includes interpretive markers. During business hours, take the elevator 489 feet to the top of the San Jacinto Monument Observation Deck, which offers amazing views of the Houston harbor. Be sure to check out the San Jacinto Museum of History at the base of the monument to see 250,000 documents, and artifacts and dioramas that tell the story of more than 400 years of Texas history.

451 Sixth Floor Museum at Dealey Plaza

CONTACT 214.747.6660, www.jfk.org; 14 Elm St., Dallas

PRICING	$$$
BEST TIME TO VISIT	Year-round
AGE RANGE	10 and older

When John F. Kennedy was sworn in as commander in chief in 1961, he was the youngest person (43) to have been elected president of the United States; a little more than 1,000 days later, he became the youngest president to die in office. President Kennedy was assassinated on November 22, 1963, while traveling with his wife, Jacqueline, and Texas governor John Connally and his wife in a presidential motorcade through Dealey Plaza in Dallas. Although there were (and continue to be) conspiracy theories regarding the number of people involved in planning the assassination, the Warren Commission determined that

> While in Dallas, visit the John F. Kennedy Memorial Plaza (646 Main St.). The plaza—one block east of Dealey Plaza—includes a memorial to the fallen president that was designed to be an open tomb. The square, roofless structure is constructed from 72 concrete columns that seem to float 2 feet off the ground.

Sixth Floor Museum at Dealey Plaza   Courtesy Sixth Floor Museum

Space Center Houston   Courtesy Space Center Houston

Kennedy was killed by Lee Harvey Oswald, a lone sniper acting from the sixth floor of what was then known as the Texas School Book Depository. The sixth and seventh floors of the structure are today a museum with exhibits pertaining to the Kennedy assassination as well as other important social and political milestones of the era. A permanent exhibit offers more than 40,000 photographs, films, living history audios, and artifacts that tell the story of President Kennedy's life and death. Note: Although the exhibits are wide-ranging and touch on more than the assassination, a visit here is sobering and might be too intense for some children.

452 Space Center Houston

CONTACT 281-244-2100, www.spacecenter.org; 601 NASA Parkway, Houston

PRICING	$$$
BEST TIME TO VISIT	Year-round
AGE RANGE	5 and older

This educational and *entertaining* attraction will make everyone in the family dream of becoming an astronaut when they grow up. Space Center Houston is a public outreach component of the Lyndon B. Johnson Space Center, NASA's center for human spaceflight. The enormous complex houses full-sized, actual spacecraft, including the *Gemini 5* capsule, the

Apollo 17 command module, a Lunar Rover vehicle trainer, and the *Mercury 9* capsule. Also on display is a full-scale replica of the space shuttle *Explorer*, a 122-foot model that offers the chance for visitors to stroll through the spacecraft to get a sense of life on board (note how cramped the accommodations are!).

Start your visit with a tram tour of the Johnson Space Center, which takes guests behind the scenes to see historic sites like the Apollo Mission Control Center and cutting-edge facilities that are developing space robotic technologies of the future. Guests will also be taken to the Saturn V complex, and (depending on availability) may also visit training facilities—it's sometimes possible to see astronauts preparing for upcoming missions.

Additional attractions at Space Center Houston include the Northrop Grumman Theater, which features a five-story screen that highlights films on spaceflight; the Blast-Off Theater, a full-sensory experience that gives guests the chance to feel as if they are launching into space; the Starship Gallery, a museum that includes space artifacts like moon rocks, the largest collection of space suits in the world, and a full-scale Skylab mockup; and the Kid's Space Place, an interactive play zone for kids 10 and younger.

Save $5 each off gate admission prices by pre-purchasing tickets to the Houston Space Center online. If you plan to visit more than once in a year, consider an annual Membership Pass, which is just a few dollars more than an adult gate ticket. Membership also comes with a 10 percent discount off food and souvenir purchases at the center.

UTAH

453 Bryce Canyon National Park

CONTACT 435-834-5322, www.nps.gov/brca;
P.O. Box 640201, Bryce Canyon

PRICING	$
BEST TIME TO VISIT	Spring (snow is possible into June) and summer
AGE RANGE	5 and older

Bryce Canyon National Park   © Debbie K. Hardin

This geological fairyland in southern Utah owes its spectacular scenery to the relentless eroding effects of rain: The hoodoos—the natural pinnacle formations for which the park is famous—have been carved out over the millennia by falling water and ice, which slowly erode the spectacularly colorful limestone into sculptural formations that defy description. These formations remind the visitor of familiar sites—Roman ruins, fantastical castles, modern art—but Bryce Canyon is like no other place. Indeed, a hike through the hoodoos is otherworldly. Children will enjoy the fanciful names given to many of the formations, and the unusual surroundings are sure to spark their imaginations.

The park is small, and encompasses several amphitheaters that house the famous hoodoos. It's possible to visit the sights in a day or two, taking in a drive to catch the best views and perhaps a hike or two. The park road is less than 40 miles round-trip, and offers 13 very pleasant viewpoints. Among the prettiest is Bryce Point: The clear air and impossibly blue sky make this overlook irresistibly photogenic. Also lovely are Sunset and Sunrise Points, stunning at any time of the day. Rainbow Point, at the termination of the park road, offers long-range views and, as the name implies, some of the brightest-hued cliffs.

There are dozens of trails that wind along the tops of the amphitheaters and in and among the hoodoos, and these are accessible to most children in good shape. Beware: Many of these hikes start out with what seems like an easy stroll into a canyon and end with a rigorous hike back up, made even more strenuous because of the high elevation. Be sure to pick a hike that fits the fitness level and attention span of your party. One of the easiest hikes, even for parents pushing strollers, is the paved rim trail that runs about a mile from Sunrise Point to Sunset Point and rewards you with ever-changing viewpoints of the largest amphitheater in the park. The 1.8-mile Queen's Garden Trail is said to be the easiest of the trails that descend into the amphitheaters—although it is still a little challenging to climb up and out. Catch the trailhead just beyond Sunrise Point.

Another good choice for a family day hike is the moderate 1.3-mile Navaho Loop Trail, which begins at Sunset Point and winds through the slot canyon named Wall Street, offering a good view of the iconic structure known as Thor's Hammer. This can be combined with the Queen's Garden hike via a short connector trail that is well marked among the hoodoos. This trail is steep, and there can be lots of falling rocks, so best save this for older children who are experienced hikers.

454 Golden Spike National Historic Site

CONTACT 435-471-2209, ext. 29, www.nps.gov/gosp;
off Hwy 83, west of Brigham City

PRICING	$
BEST TIME TO VISIT	May through September
AGE RANGE	5 and older

Americans have always sought to push boundaries and to meet the challenges of new adventures, and this was especially evident during the era of westward expansion in the 19th century. Whether driven by a quest for gold and silver, motivated by the promise of free homesteading land, or guided by a restless spirit, Americans pushed into the midwestern prairies and eventually to the West Coast to fulfill their Manifest Destiny—first setting off in wagon trains and then riding the increasingly vital railway lines. In these early days, railways were revered because they brought increased mobility and opened up trade and communications. So important were the rails that on May 10, 1869, when the Union and Central Pacific Railroads joined their lines at Promontory Summit, dignitaries gathered to drive in four ceremonial spikes to cap the engineering feat—including two spikes that were solid gold.

The Golden Spike Historic Site memorializes the site of the railway junction, and every May 10 (and Saturdays thereafter through October) it is the site of a historic reenactment of the ceremony. To explore this park, check out the Big Fill Loop Trail, which allows guests to see drill marks where rock was blasted away. Children will not want to miss the chance to take a short ride on one of the working replicas of the 1860s steam locomotives Jupiter and 119 (which generally run from May through September).

455 Temple Square

CONTACT 801-240-3323, www.visittemplesquare.com; 50 W. North Temple, Salt Lake City

PRICING	$
BEST TIME TO VISIT	Spring and summer
AGE RANGE	All ages

Beautiful Temple Square in Salt Lake City is at the heart of the Mormon community, and offers stunning religious shrines and historical sites that include the following:

- **Beehive House:** The Beehive House is a mansion once belonging to Mormon leader Brigham Young. Free tours are available Monday through Saturday, year-round.
- **Brigham Young Historic Park:** The land on which the park sits once belonged to Young. Come to the lovely community venue during the summer for free concerts on Tuesday and Friday nights.

Reenactment at Golden Spike National Historic Site
Courtesy National Park Service

Salt Lake Temple
Photo in the Carol M. Highsmith Archives, Library of Congress, Prints and Photographs Division

PRICE KEY
$ free–$5
$$ $6–10
$$$ $11–20
$$$$ $21+

- **Deuel Pioneer Log Home:** This preserved log cabin is typical of the homes built in early Salt Lake City. This structure is named after the first such home, built by William Henry Deuel.
- **Salt Lake Tabernacle:** Home to the famous Mormon Tabernacle Choir, the structure houses an impressive 11,623-pipe organ. The acoustics of the hall are said to be so spectacular that a pin dropped at the front of the building can be heard at the back. Choir rehearsals are open to the public on Thursday nights, and the tabernacle is generally open for tours during weekdays and Saturdays.
- **Salt Lake Temple:** The temple is a beautiful neo-Gothic granite structure surrounded by serene gardens. Only members of the Church of Jesus Christ of Latter-Day Saints are permitted to enter the building, but the grounds are open to the public and the exterior is quite spectacular.

Blacksmith at This Is the Place Heritage Park

Courtesy This Is the Place Heritage Park

456 This Is the Place Heritage Park

CONTACT 801-582-1847, www.thisistheplace.org; 2601 E. Sunnyside Ave., Salt Lake City

PRICING	$$ (admission varies by season)
BEST TIME TO VISIT	Old Deseret Village is open from Memorial Day through Labor Day, Monday through Saturday, plus seasonal events in October and December
AGE RANGE	5 and older

Mormon pioneers who belonged to the Church of Jesus Christ of Latter-Day Saints migrated en masse from Illinois to Utah in search of religious freedom starting in April 1847, after founder Joseph Smith (1805–44) was killed in Illinois. More than 70,000 Mormons trekked across the western Plains in well-organized wagon trains, under the guidance of Smith's successor, Brigham Young (1801–77). After the arduous 1,300-mile journey, the pioneers saw Salt Lake Valley for the first time at the site of what is now called This Is the Place Heritage Park. The park includes more than 1,600 acres that comprise part of the historic Mormon Trail, a granite and bronze memorial, and Heritage Village, a living history museum that includes original buildings and reproductions that re-create a pioneer village of the mid-19th century. Costumed reenactors encourage visitor interaction: Guests can take a ride in a 19th-century-style wagon, visit a barbershop typical of the era, or watch a blacksmith at work.

457 Zion National Park

CONTACT 435-772-3256, www.nps.gov/zion; Springdale

PRICING	$
BEST TIME TO VISIT	Spring and fall for cool temperatures; summer for the chance to hike The Narrows
AGE RANGE	5 and up

This stunning park in southwestern Utah has as its focus Zion Canyon, a 15-mile-long gash through impossibly red sandstone cliffs, rugged mountains, and a bucolic green valley. It is a place of peace and contemplation, with nearly limitless opportunities for families to explore nature and take in the clean air and vast scenery.

From April through the end of October, visitors may not drive the expanse of the scenic parkway through the park. This means no parking hassles, no roadway congestion, and almost no traffic noise. Park at the Zion Canyon Visitor Center to board the comfortable free shuttles, the wait for which is never more than 10 minutes. The buses run from early morning until nighttime, and make eight stops along the way; you can get on and off as much as you like. You can also hop a shuttle to the visitor center from six locations in nearby Springdale, which is a good option if you plan to arrive after 10 AM, when the main parking lot is usually full.

Start your trip at the Zion Canyon Visitor Center, where you'll find a topographic map to help get your bearings. If your kids are interested in wildlife, consider purchasing a field guide here before setting out. There are 207 species of birds, 68 species of mammals, 29 kinds of reptiles, nine varieties of fish, and six species of amphibians living in the park, including some rare and endangered species like the California condor and the tiny Zion snail. Easier to spot are mule deer that graze throughout the park, and the magnificent desert bighorn sheep that clamber over what is called slickrock on the Zion's east side.

Another good stop early in your visit is the Zion Human History Museum, which runs a free informative movie that tells the story of the human inhabitants of the area (from Native Americans to early Mormon settlers) as well as giving a good overview of the geology. There is also a small collection of artifacts from early inhabitants, with informative panels that explain the collection. Head outside, to the back of the museum, for some of the finest views in the park. You can also catch the trailhead for Pa'rus Trail, an easy, flat hike that meanders through the valley floor.

Be a Junior Ranger!

National parks are among the greatest resources in America: They preserve places of spectacular natural beauty; they promote species diversity; they protect sites of archaeological, geological, historical, or cultural importance. And they are some of the best nontraditional classrooms around. Each national park, large and small, is staffed by park rangers, who in addition to maintaining safety for visitors within the parks also are invaluable teachers. Visit any national park and you'll find a host of ranger-led activities, from guided hikes to photography classes to history lectures, and many programs are designed especially for families. Most national parks also offer a comprehensive Junior Ranger program, which encourages kids to participate in hands-on activities that will help them learn more about the park. School-aged

Up a tree Courtesy Jo Legg

children pick up an activity book (available for purchase for usually no more than $5—and in some parks they are free) from participating ranger stations, complete a series of activities during their park visit—including paper-and-pencil lessons, interactive ranger programs designed just for kids, and active pursuits like climbing a tree or going fishing. A typical ranger program at Yosemite National Park (see the entry in "California"), for instance, has children complete puzzles, draw pictures, and read about the natural wonders of the park; kids will also complete at least one ranger-led class and fill a bag with trash they pick up from public areas of the park. Junior Rangers then return to share their workbooks with a "senior" ranger, who will present them with a badge or patch and conduct an impromptu "swearing-in" (which makes for a good photo op). Most Junior Ranger programs are geared to two age groups: very young school-aged children (5 to 7) and older school-aged children (8 to 12).

Other great hiking options include:

- **Riverside Trail**, an easy 2-mile out-and-back path that traces the Virgin River through red polished canyon walls, past waterfalls, hanging gardens, and more photo opportunities than you can count.
- The most famous hike in the park is called **The Narrows**, which is 16 miles long (although it is not necessary to hike the whole distance), beginning at the termination of Riverside Trail. Intrepid adventurers don special gear (waterproof shoes, walking sticks, insulated clothing—available for rent from a number of local outfitters or for purchase in most camping gear stores) and hike down the middle of the river itself, through increasingly narrowing canyon sides that rise up along the river like massive, polished cathedral walls. Because of the frigid waters and the ferocity of the current in other seasons, The Narrows is open for hiking only in summer.
- The **Lower Emerald Pools Trail** is good for kids 7 and older; it is 1.2 miles round-trip, and the paved trail leads to a charming pool fed by numerous waterfalls. Connect to the much more challenging trail (extending another mile) leading to the **Upper Emerald Pools** (a larger pool protected by a grotto

Zion National Park   © Debbie K. Hardin

and fed by a pretty seasonal waterfall). Beware: The climb to the upper pool is up stone stairs, which are steep and uneven. This is recommended for kids 10 and older who are in good shape.

- For younger children, consider the easy hike to **Weeping Rock**. A paved (but steep) walkway leads a quarter mile from the shuttle stop to an overhanging cliff that drips with water year-round (and features a stunning waterfall in the spring); look for wildflowers that magically sprout from the wet rocks, especially the lovely purple columbine that blooms in mid-spring.

Zion offers extensive ranger-led programs, including guided walks, lectures, nighttime stargazing, wildlife-spotting tours, and campfire programs. From Memorial Day to Labor Day, there are a number of activities designed just for kids, including photo safaris, butterfly walks, and geology hikes.

The National Park System offers a free week for all its parks in April, during which families and groups can visit without paying the $25-per-week entrance fee. The freebie week is a welcome budget-saving option, but it also brings considerable crowds.

Vermont

458 Ben and Jerry's Factory

CONTACT 802-882-1240, www.benandjerrys.com;
1281 Waterbury-Stowe Rd., Waterbury

PRICING	$
BEST TIME TO VISIT	Year-round, Monday through Friday (tours are available on weekends, but the factory produces ice cream only on weekdays)
AGE RANGE	All ages

Just outside of Montpelier, in central Vermont, the Ben and Jerry's factory offers a peek into modern American industry and highlights the story of two extremely successful entrepreneurs, who got their start with a $5 correspondence course on ice cream making. The popular factory tour takes guests from "cow to cone," starting with an entertaining, educational video that introduces visitors to the company's socially conscious mission statement, which includes a commitment to fair-trade practices and sustainable growth that benefits the company's employees and its shareholders. From the "moovie" theater, guests progress through a glass enclosure that overlooks the factory line. A tour guide will explain the ice cream–making process, which is fascinating for young kids, especially. The tour then moves to the Flavoroom, where in the early days Ben and Jerry

Make your own ice cream label at Ben and Jerry's Factory
© Debbie K. Hardin

created new flavors of frozen treats. It's at this point that guests get a sample of the latest flavor.

After the tour, head to the back of the property, where there is a large children's play area, and the Flavor Graveyard, a faux cemetery complete with silly tombstones marking the demise of once-popular flavors like Rainforest Crunch and Oh, Pear. The factory is set amid the Green Mountains, and is a bucolic, restful place for a picnic.

459 Calvin Coolidge Homestead District

CONTACT 802-672-3773, www.nps.gov/nr/travel/presidents/calvin_coolidge_homestead.html;
3780 Rt. 100A, Plymouth

PRICING	$–$$
BEST TIME TO VISIT	Open late May through mid-October
AGE RANGE	7 and older

Calvin Coolidge Jr. (1872–1933) was the 30th president of the United States, and was known as being a man of few words. An anecdote from his time has it that at a dinner party he sat next to a woman who said she bet she could get him to say more than three words. Coolidge's response was: "You lose." Although Coolidge was born and raised in Vermont, he began his political career in Massachusetts, at the state level, and eventually served as governor. Not long after he was elected vice president under Warren G. Harding, whom he succeeded in 1923 when Harding died in office. Coolidge became a popular president, and was reelected on his own ticket in 1924. Despite his popularity, Coolidge did not to run for reelection in 1928.

Coolidge took the oath of office in his childhood home in Vermont, while he was visiting his father. His father was a notary public and administered the oath in the wee hours, by the light of a kerosene lamp. This home is preserved, along with several buildings associated with Coolidge and his family, at the Calvin Coolidge Homestead District. Guests can tour Coolidge's childhood home, a re-created general

Calvin Coolidge Homestead

store, a post office, a church, barns displaying tools of the time, and a dance hall that doubled as the summer White House. Don't miss a tour of the still-active Plymouth Cheese Factory, once owned by President Coolidge's father; after looking around at the production process you can sample the chewy cheese curds.

460 Ethan Allen Homestead Museum

CONTACT 802-865-4556, www.ethanallenhomestead.org; 1 Ethan Allen Homestead, Burlington

PRICING	$–$$
BEST TIME TO VISIT	Open early May through mid-October, Thursday through Monday
AGE RANGE	7 and older

Ethan Allen (1738–89) was an American Revolutionary War hero, one of the founders of the state of Vermont, a farmer, and a writer. He was born in Connecticut, but in his early adulthood purchased land in what is now Vermont, as part of the New Hampshire Grants. However, the ownership of the territory was disputed, and legal challenges to the legitimacy of many of the land purchases encouraged Allen to form a paramilitary group known as the Green Mountain Boys, who engaged in acts of intimidation to drive out any would-be challengers to the property. Allen and the Green Mountain Boys are best remembered for capturing Fort Ticonderoga in New York in 1775, during the American Revolution—with the help of Benedict Arnold. (Both larger-than-life personalities subsequently sought to claim credit for seizing the fort.)

The Ethan Allen Homestead Museum preserves the restored 1787 farmhouse once belonging to Allen. The rustic structure is sited on the Winooski River, and offers a glimpse into what life was life during the late 18th century in rural Vermont. Guests can explore the home, view artifacts that chronicle Allen's military life, and explore the extensive grounds. Kids can dress up in period costumes and try out reproductions of antique toys.

461 Maple Sugaring in Vermont

CONTACT 800-242-2740, www.morsefarm.com; 1168 County Rd., Montpelier

PRICING	$
BEST TIME TO VISIT	Early spring, during sugaring time
AGE RANGE	Toddlers through age 12

Native people living in New England were the first to learn how to produce maple syrup and maple sugar from the sap of trees: They cut incisions into the trunk; inserted reeds through which the sap could flow; and then gathered the sap, which was concentrated through boiling. Maple syrup production was

Maple sugaring in Vermont

thus one of the first agricultural processes in North America that did not originate in Europe. Early colonists learned the process from the Algonquin people; these colonists were involved in sugaring as early as 1680.

There are dozens of sugarhouses throughout the state of Vermont, many of which provide tours of their operations. If you're near the Vermont capital of Montpelier, check out Morse Farms, a seventh-generation sugaring farm that produces delicious maple syrup, maple candies, and maple soft-serve ice cream (a cone is known as a creemee). Young children are fascinated by the production process, in which maple trees are tapped after the freeze of winter to capture sap, which is then boiled down to make syrup. It takes about 40 gallons of sap to make 1 gallon of syrup. One tap in any given tree produces about 15 gallons of sap: A little math will show kids that it takes three maple trees to produce 1 gallon of the sweet pancake elixir. In early spring the sugarhouse at Morse Farm boils off the sap and allows visitors in to see the process. Visitors can taste the four grades of syrup the farm produces. The farm is also home to sheep, alpacas, a herd of cattle, and a pet goat.

462 Shelburne Museum

CONTACT 802-985-3346, http://shelburnemuseum.org; 6000 Shelburne Rd., Shelburne

PRICING	$$–$$$
BEST TIME TO VISIT	Open mid-May through October
AGE RANGE	7 and older

The Shelburne Museum offers one of the most extensive collections of American folk art and crafts in the country as well as interactive experiences that engage visitors in the act of creating art. The unconventional museum is actually a complex of nearly 40 exhibition buildings—including barns, a one-room schoolhouse, a jail, a lighthouse, and the 220-foot steamboat *Ticonderoga*—many of which are historic structures that have been relocated to the site. The total collection comprises more than 150,000 arti-

Ticonderoga, *Shelburne Museum*
Photo Natalie Shultz, courtesy Shelburne Museum

facts, including a remarkable collection of textiles—exquisite quilts, hand-hooked rugs, antique samplers, intricate lace, and nearly 3,000 costumes. Guests will also discover a huge exhibit of wildfowl decoys; extensive decorative arts, including scrimshaw, pewter, and glass; more than 1,000 antique dolls and more than 1,200 doll accessories; and myriad American and European toys that date to the early 19th century. There is an extensive circus collection, with memorabilia, antique posters, and an extraordinary 4,000-piece hand-carved mini circus. There are numerous opportunities for families to create art together, including mobile carts positioned outdoors, and recurring craft workshops. Artisans demonstrate blacksmithing, printing, and weaving throughout the season. The outdoor gardens are also lovely, and are likely to inspire younger artists to create their own masterpieces.

463 Simon Pearce Glass Factory

CONTACT 802-295-2711, www.simonpearce.com; 1760 Quechee Main St., Quechee

PRICING	Free
BEST TIME TO VISIT	Year-round
AGE RANGE	7 and older

Glassmaking was America's first industry: German and Polish immigrants brought the craft to

Blowing glass requires highly skilled practitioners.

Jamestown in 1608 and had an operating shop shortly after the first settlers arrived in the new country. Although this first attempt at American glassmaking was unsuccessful—largely because there were too few craftsmen in the new colony—a second, more successful venture was undertaken 12 years later, this time staffed with Italian artisans. Blowing glass requires highly skilled practitioners, and most glass in the United States today is mass produced in factories.

In Quechee, Vermont, the art of glassblowing lives on at the fascinating Simon Pearce factory and showroom, where visitors can stroll through the workshops and see artists at work creating lovely goblets, vases, pitchers, and bowls. Children are mesmerized by the process, which begins with molten glass heated in furnaces that keep the workshops at toasty temperatures year-round, and ends with artists blowing, clipping, and shaping the pieces, which are then displayed for sale upstairs in the expansive showroom. (The handcrafted pieces are pricey, and obviously highly break-able, so a trip through the showroom is best reserved for older children.)

Also on site is a pottery workshop where kids can watch craftsmen throw pots and then have an opportunity to mold their own creations with lumps of clay. At the back of the property is a small waterfall and a lovely covered bridge spanning the width of the Ottauquechee River (rebuilt after being destroyed in the floods that accompanied Hurricane Irene in 2011). There are a handful of picnic spots along the river, and the quaint town of Quechee is fun to explore further.

View from Simon Pearce Glass Factory   © Debbie K. Hardin

virginia

464 American Civil War Center

CONTACT 804-780-1865, www.tredegar.org; 500 Tredegar St., Richmond

PRICING	$–$$
BEST TIME TO VISIT	Year-round
AGE RANGE	7 and older

Richmond was the site of several major skirmishes in the American Civil War. Indeed, much of the city burned down during the occupation in 1865. The Richmond National Battlefield Park commemorates four major episodes of the American Civil War and includes 13 sites along an 80-mile driving route through the area. Of the remaining structures is the Chimborazo Hospital, which treated the many casualties of the battlefield and is now a museum of the war's medical history. At the heart of the park is another original structure that is home to the new American Civil War Center. The interactive museum chronicles the War Between the States from three perspectives: the Union, the Confederacy (of which Richmond was at the heart), and the slaves. The historic structures are part of the 1861 Tredegar Gun Foundry complex, a munitions factory during the war. Three floors of exhibits include interactive maps relating to important Civil War battles, collections of artifacts from the era, examples of Confederate bills, and changing exhibitions that tell the story of the war from personal perspectives. The museum does a good job of tackling the differing opinions on the war and presents the issues without obvious bias. There are several interactive video displays that will engage kids. The grounds display more than 100 years of iron making at the site.

465 Appomattox Court House National Historical Park

CONTACT 434-352-8987, ext. 226, www.nps.gov/apco/index.htm; off VA 24, Appomattox

PRICING	$
BEST TIME TO VISIT	Year-round
AGE RANGE	7 and older

The American Civil War was a four-year bloody encounter that was waged to settle the secession of the Confederate states in the south as well as to determine the future of slavery in America. Eleven states attempted to declare their independence from the United States as a whole, but the other 25 existing states at the time supported the Union—and from 1861 to 1865, brother often fought brother to resolve the national crisis.

Finally, on Palm Sunday, 1865, Confederate general Robert E. Lee surrendered at the village of Appomattox Court House in Virginia, which was the effective end of the war—although the conflict didn't subside officially until May 26, when General E. Kirby Smith surrendered the Trans-Mississippi Department in New Orleans. The federal government was strengthened as a result of the Union victory, and slavery was abolished in the United States. The Appomattox Court House National Historical Park has been preserved, along with many structures from the era as well as several reconstructions. The highlight of the park is the Wilmer McLean House, site of the actual surrender. Although the three-story home is re-created, it has been designed and furnished to be faithful to the original. The parlor of the home—where the surrender meeting took place—has items from the mid-century as well as reproductions. The home's outbuildings are also available for tour, in-

American Civil War Center

Courtesy Richmond Convention and Visitors Bureau

Skyline Drive Courtesy Aramark Parks and Destinations

PRICE KEY	
$	free—$5
$$	$6—10
$$$	$11—20
$$$$	$21+

Appomattox Court House   Courtesy National Park Service

Arlington House   © Debbie K. Hardin

cluding the outhouse, outdoor kitchen, and slave quarters. Throughout the summer months, the park offers myriad living history programs, with actors portraying actual people who were in Appomattox Court House at the time the war ended. The reenactors are well versed in the history, manners, and speech of the era—and they will *not* break character. It is interesting to note that although the reenactors will acknowledge the same day and month as your visit, they maintain the year is still 1865. Visit the onsite museum to see the pencil Lee used to map out the terms of surrender.

466 Arlington House: The Robert E. Lee Memorial

CONTACT 703-607-8000, www.arlingtoncemetery.org; west end of Memorial Bridge, Arlington

PRICING	$
BEST TIME TO VISIT	Year-round
AGE RANGE	7 and older

Arlington Cemetery (see below) is home to the Arlington House (the Robert E. Lee Memorial), onetime home of the famous Confederate general. Lee didn't actually own the house—it was the ancestral home of his wife, Mary Custis—but the family lived in this yellow Virginia sandstone home overlooking the Potomac for many years, and Lee was said to have been extremely fond of the property. When Lee left the home to fight for the South in the Civil War, the house was surrounded by more than 1,000 acres of plantation. In his absence, Union forces confiscated Arlington House for back taxes and then buried soldiers very close to the house itself—all but ensuring the mansion would never be used as a residential property again. Soon the federal government took over the property altogether for the national cemetery. Lee never returned to the home after the war, and judging by what he wrote in personal letters, he remained bitter about his loss until the day he died. Visitors can tour the interior of the home, which appears much as it did when Lee left it. Be sure to tour the Robert E. Lee Museum on the grounds, which displays original artifacts from the Lee and Custis families. In addition, walk through the Lee slave quarters to learn about the lives of the enslaved families that once worked on the extensive property.

467 Arlington National Cemetery

CONTACT 703-607-8000, www.arlingtoncemetery.org; off Rt. 27, Arlington

PRICING	$
BEST TIME TO VISIT	Spring through fall
AGE RANGE	7 and older

Arlington National Cemetery dates to the American Civil War; it was established on the grounds of an estate formerly belonging to Confederate general Robert E. Lee's in-laws. More than 300,000 American soldiers are buried on this hillside cemetery just across the river from Washington, DC, and the symmetrical rows of small, white marble tombstones seem to stretch endlessly over the peaceful hills. The most famous grave is likely that of John F. Kennedy, whose final resting place is marked with an eternal flame. Nearby are two of his brothers, Senator Robert Kennedy and Senator Edward Kennedy, whose graves are marked with simple white crosses. Four state funerals have been held at the site: Presidents William Howard Taft and Kennedy; General John Pershing; and Senator Edward Kennedy. Also here is the Tomb of the Unknown Soldier, patrolled 24/7 by a dress guard; every hour on the hour (and every half hour in the sweltering summer months), witness the precise changing of the guard.

Start by looking through the visitor center, which has exhibits and displays that explain the history of the site and will help orient you. Then walk upward (the grade is quite steep in spots) to the Lee House (see above), along the way taking in the incredible sight of the orderly graves. While here, pay your respects at the many monuments on site, including the Space Shuttle Challenger Memorial that honors the seven astronauts killed during a shuttle launch in 1986; the Pan Am Flight 103 Memorial that commemorates the 270 lives lost during a terrorist attack on a jetliner that subsequently went down over Lockerbie, Scotland; and the Civil War Unknowns Memorial, dedicated to the more than 2,000 unknown soldiers who were recovered from the Battle of Bull Run. It

Arlington National Cemetery   Courtesy Juliane Preimesberger

goes without saying that this is a somber setting, and children should be reminded to be respectful. Funerals are still held here during weekdays—generally more than 25 a day.

468 Ash Lawn

CONTACT	434-293-8000, www.al-h.us; 1000 James Monroe Parkway, Charlottesville
PRICING	$$–$$$
BEST TIME TO VISIT	Year-round
AGE RANGE	7 and older

Virginia is sometimes known as the "Mother of Presidents": The state boasts more native sons in the office of commander in chief than any other. (In order, the eight presidents born in the state are George Washington, Thomas Jefferson, James Madison, James Monroe, William Henry Harrison, John Tyler, Zachary Taylor, and Woodrow Wilson.) Of this group, President Monroe (1758–1831), the fifth president of the United States, was the last of the original Founders to serve in the office. Monroe was a soldier in the American Revolutionary War—he carried a battle scar from a musket ball in his shoulder from the Battle of Trenton. He studied law with none other than Thomas Jefferson, and then went on to serve as a delegate in the Continental Congress. (Monroe was actually an Anti-Federalist who initially opposed ratifying the U.S. Constitution, on the grounds that it created an overly large and overly powerful central government.) Once the new federal government was established, however, Monroe jumped in feetfirst: He was a governor of Virginia, was elected to the U.S. Senate, held the positions of secretary of state and secretary of war under President James Madison, and helped negotiate the Louisiana Purchase. His administration is remembered as part of the "era of good feelings," a period of history that was relatively unmarked by partisan struggles, and was responsible for the Monroe Doctrine, a policy that was meant to discourage further efforts by European nations to colonize North America.

In 1799 Monroe moved his family to a plantation

adjacent to Thomas Jefferson's Monticello (described below). The lovely surviving home is open for tours, and has been refurbished to period accuracy after painstaking research. Children will especially enjoy seeing the dining room, in which a lovely Hepplewhite dining table is piled high with a feast typical of Monroe's era; and the children's room, which includes a large canopy bed and toys, like a small table set for a tea party of dolls. The home's study is also a highlight of the tour; it includes a Louis XVI desk and a collection of Monroe's books.

The extensive grounds comprise a 535-acre working farm (complete with animals, including a flock of peacocks), reconstructed slave quarters, and beautiful gardens. Look for the white oak—20 feet in circumference—that was on site during Monroe's lifetime, set among beautiful boxwood gardens. Throughout the year the property offers fascinating hands-on classes like candle making, tin lantern making, rope making, and open-hearth cooking (most of which are open to children and parents). The site is also a popular local venue for events like the annual Ash Lawn Opera Festival, the Virginia Wine Festival, and special Christmas celebrations.

469 Chincoteague and Assateague Islands

CONTACT www.chincoteague.com; off the coast of Virginia, east of Crisfield, MD

PRICING	$
BEST TIME TO VISIT	End of July, during pony penning
AGE RANGE	All ages

Chincoteague and Assateague are small islands off the coast of Virginia, near the Maryland border (in fact, Assateague is partly in Virginia and partly in Maryland). Chincoteague is a small resort area with charming modest hotels, plentiful seafood restaurants (don't miss the blue crab in-season), and family-friendly beaches. Assateague is accessible by bridge, and is home to the Chincoteague National Wildlife Refuge, nearly 40 glorious miles of pristine beach along the Atlantic Ocean. The refuge is sanctuary to

Prime your children (especially those age 7 through 10) for a visit to the islands by suggesting they read Marguerite Henry's 1947 novel *Misty of Chincoteague*, a beloved work of fiction that tells the story of pony penning on the islands. There's also a (less satisfying) movie version of the story that dates to 1961.

hundreds of species of birds and several mammals, including the endangered Delmarva fox squirrel, deer, and two small herds of wild ponies (separated by a fence on the Virginia–Maryland border).

Wild ponies have lived on Assateague Island for hundreds of years; the most famous explanation of their habitation is that they are descendants of ponies that survived the wreck of a Spanish galleon off the coast of the island. Some argue that the ponies can be traced to domesticated horses that were released by early settlers. No matter their origins, the ponies have adapted to the island vegetation and thrive here. These small, shaggy ponies graze on dune grasses and can be seen roaming the beaches throughout the year. The Virginia herd is managed by the Chincoteague Volunteer Fire Company, which every July thins out the herd by swimming the horses across the narrowest portion of the Assateague Channel at low tide. Some of the animals are then auctioned, and the proceeds help fund the volunteer fire department. The wildly popular pony penning event is held on the last Wednesday and Thursday of every July, and it's a sight that must be seen to be believed.

Assateague ponies   Courtesy Maryland Office of Tourism

470 Colonial Williamsburg

CONTACT 757-229-1000, www.history.org; P.O. Box 1776, Williamsburg

PRICING	$$$$
BEST TIME TO VISIT	Spring, fall
AGE RANGE	3 and older

Governor's Mansion, Colonial Williamsburg © Debbie K. Hardin

Williamsburg dates to 1699, when Virginia named it the capital of the colony. This compact, surprisingly lush city brimming with tidy southern gardens came to be home to many of the nation's Founders, and the city and its citizens played a vital role in the American Revolution. Today in America's premier living history museum, guests to Colonial Williamsburg encounter an entertaining, historically accurate re-creation of life in 1700s America, complete with hundreds of original buildings and many more reconstructed public structures, private homes, and shops, as well as acres of period-accurate gardens and bucolic pastures full of grazing animals.

The real fun is that Colonial Williamsburg lets visitors indulge in a trip back in time. Here it's possible for your children to meet great people from history, like Thomas Jefferson, who might be discussing slavery in one of the general stores; or Patrick Henry, who might be arguing the evils of the Virginia Stamp Act outside the Capitol. It's necessary to suspend disbelief in these encounters because—of course—these luminaries are actually costumed reenactors.

Just walking through the historic area is a treat: Kids will especially love the stocks adjacent to the courthouse, where they can "lock up" their parents or siblings. Also fun for the whole family are opportunities to dine in historic inns, watch artisans like wig makers and bakers ply their trades, and take in the lovely colonial architecture. With paid admission, you will gain access to a number of entertaining attractions:

- The Geddy House offers children the chance to play on a big rope swing in the back garden, roll wooden hoops with youth reenactors, and try their hand at a game of ninepins (an outdoor version of bowling).
- The Peyton Randolph House offers insight into the lives of less fortunate colonial children. After touring the fashionable home—one of the grandest in Colonial Williamsburg—head to the backyard and outbuildings to see how children born to slaves and indentured servants lived. Kids can pitch in and help reenactors here with chores like washing laundry by hand or churning butter.
- Check out the Cabinet Maker's Shop, which is built spanning the width of a charming creek; encourage musically minded kids to play a tune on the pianoforte in the entryway.
- The Governor's Mansion has boxwood mazes in the back gardens to explore and an open-hearth working kitchen in which kids can help out by grinding spices or grating lemon peel for pies.
- Head to the Printer and Bookbindery to watch artisans set type and print newspapers and broadsides, which can be purchased throughout the colonial district as unique souvenirs.

Most of the historic buildings close their doors at 5 PM, but there are plenty of evening programs throughout the city. Check out Cry Witch, a mock trial held at the Capitol Building in which colonial citizens testify

Although tickets are required to enter the living history museum exhibits at Colonial Williamsburg, no fee is required for admittance to the exterior venues. You can wander through most of the gardens, stroll the charming streets, and pop into the historically themed shops and restaurants for free.

against an alleged witch and those in attendance serve as members of the jury. In Ghosts Among Us, guests walk the streets with candles and lanterns to hear scary tales that date to colonial times. (Some of these stories are too intense for young children. Save this activity for kids 10 and older.)

471 Fredericksburg and Spotsylvania Battlefields Memorial

CONTACT www.nps.gov/frsp/index.htm; 120 Chatham Lane, Fredericksburg

PRICING	$
BEST TIME TO VISIT	Spring through fall
AGE RANGE	7 and older

Fredericksburg and Spotsylvania Battlefields Memorial
Courtesy Virginia Tourism Corporation

Nowhere in the country does the devastation of the American Civil War remain in sharper focus than the expansive Fredericksburg and Spotsylvania Battlefields Memorial, the second largest military park in the world. Battle scars are still visible on the landscape and in the remaining structures. The park preserves four important battlefields: the sites of the Battle of Chancellorsville, the Battle of Fredericksburg, the Battle of Spotsylvania Court House, and the Battle of the Wilderness. Also within the boundaries of the national park are four historic buildings that were important to these battles. The region that is protected and preserved by the park is described as one that witnessed some of the bloodiest conflicts in North America: There were more than 100,000 casualties as a result of these battles, which took place over a span of 18 months.

The scope of the park can be overwhelming, so to

The battlefields are authentically preserved, and at various sites throughout the Fredericksburg and Spotsylvania Battlefields Memorial there are limited facilities (at some sites there is no running water). Bring drinks and snacks, and plan restroom breaks around stops at the main visitor centers.

orient yourself begin a trip here at either the Chancellorsville Battlefield Visitor Center or the Fredericksburg Battlefield Visitor Center. Both offer overview films and exhibits. These centers are also the place to pick up trail maps and driving-tour information. During late spring through early fall, the park offers guided walking tours that explain the battles and their importance both to the overall war and to the local citizens who lived through a prolonged campaign that in many cases drove them from their homes.

Among the historic buildings on site, don't miss the Chatham Manor, an 18th-century Georgian home built by William Fitzhugh, who served in the House of Burgesses with his friend George Washington before the American Revolution. By the Civil War era, the home was owned by James Horace Lacy and his wife, a plantation owner sympathetic to the Confederate cause. Ironically, the lovely mansion came to be occupied by the Union army for more than a year. Today the home and 85 acres of the original property are open to the public; five rooms in the 12,000-square-foot structure are open for tours; the gardens and outbuildings are also available for viewing.

Another sight worth seeking out at the park is the General Stonewall Jackson Memorial. Jackson (1824–63) was a legendary commander in the Confederate army, serving as corps commander in the Army of Northern Virginia. He was mistakenly shot by his own troops during the Battle of Chancellorsville, and although he survived for a time, he eventually succumbed to complications after an arm was amputated. He died in the small town of Guinea Station, and the memorial preserves the home where he perished. The structure is open Saturday through Monday from May through October.

472 Gadsby's Tavern

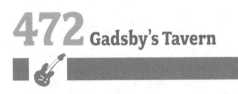

CONTACT 703-838-4242, www.gadsbystavern.org; 134 N. Royal St., Alexandria

PRICING	$
BEST TIME TO VISIT	Year-round
AGE RANGE	10 and older

Many sites in America make dubious claims that George Washington ate, slept, or drank there, but Gadsby's Tavern, just down the river from the first president's home, is the real deal. Many founding luminaries—including Washington, Thomas Jefferson, John Adams, and James Madison—lifted their steins on this site just across the street from the Alexandria Court House. Today the tavern, which dates to 1785, and an adjacent hotel (circa 1792) are restored to the appearance of their heyday, when they served as an important gathering place for folks visiting the capital city, as well as the site of many important celebra-

Dining room, Gadsby's Tavern   © Debbie K. Hardin

tions. (In the 18th century Washington's annual "Birthnight Ball" was held here, and the president himself attended in 1798 and 1799.) Guests today can tour the restored inn to see what a hotel during colonial times might have looked like. (Suggest to children they ask the tour guide to explain where the phrase *Sleep tight, don't let the bed bugs bite* came from—they'll get a memorable story.) Or treat the family to an elegant meal here to dine on colonial favorites like ham biscuits, peanut soup, or Washington's favorite: grilled duck breast with corn pudding.

473 Jamestown

CONTACT Historic Jamestowne: 757-229-1733, www.historicjamestowne.org, 1368 Colonial Parkway, Jamestown; Jamestown Settlement: 888-593-4682, www.historyisfun.org, Rt. 31 S., Jamestown

PRICING	Historic Jamestowne: $$; Jamestown Settlement: $$–$$$
BEST TIME TO VISIT	Year-round
AGE RANGE	7 and older

In 1607, 104 English citizens settled at the tip of a small peninsula just off the James River in Virginia, and together they built the first successful English colony in North America. Within a year, the Virginia Company sponsoring the colony brought additional colonists from Poland and Holland. And in 1619, the first documented Africans brought to the United States came to Jamestown. But there were already an estimated 14,000 Native peoples living in the Chesapeake area when the new settlers arrived. This Powhatan Confederacy, as they came to be known, at first welcomed the newcomers, but the alliance with the Natives didn't last long.

Despite the efforts of leader Captain John Smith, who was famously assisted by Native princess Pocahontas, the majority of colonists died within the first five years. In 1622 the chief of the Powhatan Confederacy tried to wipe out the rest of the colony. Natives attacked plantations and communities along the James River, killing more than 300 settlers. Nevertheless, the colony survived the onslaughts and became the capital of the region—but more than 50 years later, during Bacon's Rebellion in 1676, Jamestown was burned. The capital was moved to Williamsburg, and soon after Jamestown faded from prominence. In the 20th century the area was rediscovered as a tourist and cultural attraction, portions of which are designated as national park land.

Today visitors will find two distinct sites in Jamestown, located near each other. Note that each requires separate admission fees.

Historic Jamestowne

Historic Jamestowne is the original site of Jamestown Colony, and is operated by the National Park Service. It's possible to walk among the foundations and ruins of colonial America's earliest buildings at this location. There are ongoing excavations of the original James Fort, and curious children can get a close look at this painstaking work. Archaeological finds from Jamestown include tobacco pipes, cooking vessels, agricultural tools, weapons, coins, and armor; many of these artifacts are on display at the Dale House, home of the governor of Virginia in the early 1600s and now an exhibition gallery. Kids will also want to check out a popular bronze statue of Pocahontas, Captain John Smith's Native American guide to the New World.

When in the historic area, don't miss the Glasshouse, where guests can watch costumed interpreters blow red-hot glass into bottles, vases, and bowls much the way colonists did. The current building was constructed near the site of the original

Fort reconstruction at Jamestown   © Debbie K. Hardin

Jamestown Glassworks, the first industrial site in English America. It's also fun to explore the island via the wilderness loop of Jamestown, which is accessible by car, bicycle, and foot. The loop—which you can take for 5 miles or a shortened route of 3 miles—passes through swamps and tideland forests, and is a good place to spot wildlife like deer and rabbits, especially early in the morning.

Jamestown Settlement

Nearby Jamestown Settlement offers a re-created version of the early colony, with faithful reconstructions and costumed interpreters. Begin exploring at the Jamestown Settlement visitor center and gallery, which offers a film on the founding of Jamestown and myriad exhibits on colonial artifacts, such as early toys, tools, and weapons. Once outside the visitor center, wander through a Powhatan Indian Village, which showcases several Native dwellings fashioned out of saplings and furnished with reed mats and furs. Kids can walk inside these dwellings to get a real sense of how Native Americans lived in the colonial days. Throughout the day (depending on the season) there are hands-on opportunities for children to harvest vegetables and grind corn, much as Pocahontas would have done as a child.

The James Fort is a re-created representation of the colonial settlement between the years 1610 and 1614. Inside tall, protective walls are several colonial homes—crafted beautifully from wood, mud, and straw; a storehouse; the governor's house; and a blacksmithing forge. Historical interpreters engage in military training exercises, teach handicrafts like rope making and sewing, and demonstrate meal preparation. Kids will enjoy trying on child-sized armor similar to what the colonial soldiers of the fort wore.

A favorite section of Jamestown Settlement is the Riverfront Discovery Area, where reproductions of the three (small) ships that brought the early settlers across the Atlantic are docked. Guests can walk on board each vessel, and friendly interpreters will explain early navigation principles and answer questions about colonial cruising. Kids will be surprised at how tiny the ships are, and will learn quickly that sea travel in the 17th century took physical strength, cunning, and an urge to survive.

474 Manassas National Battlefield Park

CONTACT 703-361-1339, www.nps.gov/mana; Henry Hill Visitor Center site, 6511 Sudley Rd., Manassas

PRICING	$
BEST TIME TO VISIT	Year-round
AGE RANGE	7 and older

Battlefield marker, Manassas National Battlefield
© Debbie K. Hardin

The First Battle of Bull Run (sometimes also called First Manassas) was the first major land battle of the American Civil War—and it was a wake-up call to both sides that settling the issues of secession of the southern states and slavery in America was going to be anything but quick and easy. On July 16, 1861, Union general Irvin McDowell's 35,000-person-strong army marched out of Washington, DC, and into Richmond, in the hope of capturing the Confederate stronghold of Richmond and ending the war in short order. But the Union troops were ill prepared: In fact, they were known as "90-day volunteers," called to arms by President Abraham Lincoln after the events at Fort Sumter began the war, and they themselves didn't expect to be soldiers for very long. In preparation for the first major battle of the war, many soldiers and everyday citizens were excited at the prospect of what they expected to be a quickly settled skirmish. So unconcerned (and naive) were some of the troops that they stopped to pick berries on their march to the battlefield. And so unconcerned (and misguided) were many of the civilians and congressional representatives from DC that spectators showed up at the battlefield with picnic baskets, ready to snack as they watched what they expected to be an entertaining scene. The scene was anything but entertaining. Although the Confederate forces, led by Brigadier General P. G. T. Beauregard, were also ill prepared for the fight, the bloody battle ended with heavy casualties on both sides and Union troops fleeing and spectators running for their lives. More than a year later, on August 28–30, 1862, Confederate and Union forces met on the battlefield in Manassas for a second time—and the outcome was the same: a Confederate victory.

Manassas National Battlefield Park preserves the site that was home to both the First Battle of Bull Run and the Second Battle of Bull Run (also known as the Second Battle of Manassas). The bucolic site is haunting—the lovely setting *does* seem more suited to picnics than warfare. The cannons strewn across the otherwise peaceful setting are the first clue that this isn't just a lovely bit of wilderness. Start at the Henry Hill Visitor Center to view the fascinating film *Manassas: End of Innocence*, a 45-minute orientation to both battles. The center also displays a fiber-optic map that explains the battle strategy (or lack thereof) and exhibits equipment and battle memorabilia. In the warmer months there are interpretive living history programs that can include weapons-firing demonstrations and battle re-creations. Tour the battlefield of First Bull Run via a 1-mile self-guided trail; then take the 13-mile driving tour of the Second Battle of Bull Run. Be sure to visit the Stone Bridge—the very structure that carried Union troops in their retreat after both battles—and Stone House, a home that was used as a hospital during the war.

475 Marine Corps War Memorial

CONTACT www.nps.gov/gwmp/planyourvisit/usmc_memorial.htm; on Marshall St., off U.S. 50, Arlington

PRICING	$
BEST TIME TO VISIT	Summer
AGE RANGE	7 and older

Marine Corps War Memorial Courtesy National Park Service

One of the deadliest battles during World War II was the Battle of Iwo Jima (1945), in which the United States captured airfields from the Japanese island of Iwo Jima in the Pacific Theater over 35 days of intense fighting. More than 6,000 marines died in the protracted encounter. The Marine Corps War Memorial (also known as the statue of Iwo Jima) is just north of Arlington Cemetery, and was erected to commemorate marines who have died in battle since 1775. The 100-ton sculpture is one of the largest bronze statues in the world; it re-creates the scene of five marines and one navy corpsman raising the U.S. flag on Iwo Jima (a scene originally captured in an iconic photograph taken by war correspondent Joe Rosenthal). On Tuesday nights in the summer, the marines present free concerts on the site by the U.S. Marine Drum and Bugle Corps, and the Marine Corps Silent Drill Platoon performs precision drills. Guests are welcome to bring lawn chairs and blankets, and picnics are permitted on site.

Thomas Jefferson (1743–1826) was the third president of the United States, and one of the most influential individuals in the formation of the American political system. Jefferson was the primary author of the Declaration of Independence; served as a representative of Virginia in the Continental Congress; was the U.S. minister to France; acted as the first U.S. secretary of state under President George Washington; and was vice president to President John Adams. As president Jefferson approved the purchase of the Louisiana Territory from France, and was the force behind the Lewis and Clark expedition that subsequently mapped and surveyed the newly acquired land. In addition to his considerable talents as a politician and a political philosopher, Jefferson had extensive intellectual skills and a broad array of talents: He spoke several languages, studied sciences (and kept his own museum of sorts that included an impressive collection of fossils), was an inventor, and was a gifted architect. He founded the University of Virginia and designed the old campus himself; he also designed a spectacular mansion on a 5,000-acre plantation overlooking his beloved UVA.

Jefferson named his home Monticello, and today it is arguably the finest historic presidential property in America. Guests can tour the magnificent structure to see period-furnished rooms that include the entrance hall, adorned with archaeological artifacts meant to educate visitors while they waited to be invited in; the sunny and cheerful tea room; the bright yellow dining room, where for efficiency's sake a table was only set up during mealtimes; and Jefferson's combination bedroom and study, which is demarcated by a bed built within a cabinet that separates the spaces.

476 Monticello

CONTACT 434-984-9800, www.monticello.org; 931 Thomas Jefferson Parkway, Charlottesville

PRICING	$$–$$$
BEST TIME TO VISIT	Spring and summer
AGE RANGE	7 and older

Thomas Jefferson home © Debbie K. Hardin

The gardens of Monticello are a riot of color in the spring and summer. Thousands of flowers spill over the West Lawn gardens, and in-season this is a delightful place to view exotic tulips and myriad annuals. In late spring through summer, the extensive vegetable gardens overflow with well-tended vegetables and herbs of the kind grown by Jefferson, as well as meticulously tended fruit tree orchards. Jefferson himself was an avid horticulturist and experimented with hybrids and imported seeds; in his day he grew 250 varieties of more than 70 species of vegetables (and kept painstaking notes on their success). The property even offers summer tastings of crops grown on the property, like heirloom tomatoes and peaches. Be sure to visit Mulberry Row, the hub of slave life on Monticello. During his life, Jefferson owned more than 600 slaves—and employed several free white craftsmen and workers who together kept the plantation nearly self-sufficient. Mulberry Row was both the site of slave quarters and workshops and storehouses, and tours through this portion of the plantation offer insight both into the nature of slavery and into the complicated psyche of one of the most brilliant Americans.

James Madison home   Courtesy Virginia Tourism Corporation

477 Montpelier

CONTACT www.montpelier.org, 11407 Constitution Hwy., Orange

PRICING	$$–$$$
BEST TIME TO VISIT	Spring through fall
AGE RANGE	7 and older

James Madison (1751–1836) was the fourth president of the United States and one of the most instrumental Founders of the country. Madison was an important force behind the U.S. Constitution and the author of the Bill of Rights. He collaborated with early American leaders Alexander Hamilton and John Jay to publish the *Federalist Papers*, a series of influential essays that advocated the ratification of the Constitution. After ratification, Madison helped in the organization of the federal government—and then he broke off, with Thomas Jefferson, to form the Democratic-Republican Party, in opposition to the Federalists. Madison served as President Jefferson's secretary of state before assuming the office of commander in chief himself. He presided over the nation during the War of 1812, and famously fled the White House when British troops tried to burn down Washington, DC. (His lively wife, Dolley Madison, is famous for having rescued a number of important political and cultural artifacts from the Executive Mansion, including the famous Gilbert Stuart portrait of George Washington, only moments in advance of looting British troops.)

Montpelier was the only home James Madison ever knew; he was raised on the expansive plantation, lived here after he married, returned to the estate after his days in the White House, and died in his study. The lovely property includes the Madison mansion, thousands of acres of forest and garden, and active archaeological sites. There is a great deal to explore here and myriad hands-on opportunities for children to learn. In addition to more than 2,500 acres of beautiful grounds—with views of the Blue Ridge Mountains and old-growth forests—other favorites include:

- **Archaeology Laboratory:** Archaeologists are still at work uncovering the remains of slave quarters and Madison's kitchen work yard. Guests can watch the archaeologists at work, and scientists are available to answer questions. Kids can also participate in a dig using real tools, then wash and identify any artifacts they find.

- **Children's Getaway** (open weekends, April through October): In homage to the many children who visited Montpelier during Madison's day, the property has a space dedicated to pint-sized visitors, who will find books to read, artwork to color, miniature furniture, and lots of reproduction period dolls and toys. Kids will enjoy creating their own postcard to send back home.

- **Dolley's Kitchen and Outdoor Cooking Demonstrations:** On the north yard off the mansion, the outdoor kitchen is the site of cooking demonstrations that encourage guests to help prepare food in the style of the early 19th century. Kids can grind spices, knead dough, and churn butter.

- **Gilmore Cabin, A Freedman's Farm:** This small cabin and 16-acre farm was built by George Gilmore, a former slave from Montpelier; a trip here offers insight into the lives of former slaves during the Reconstruction era.

- **Hands-On Tent** (open Friday through Sunday, April through October)**:** This interactive venue is the site of living history demonstrations and participative programs: Learn to make a brick, saw a log using period tools, or mend a basket.

- **Madison Mansion:** The stunning mansion is the highlight of any tour of Montpelier. The interior and exterior were painstakingly restored several years ago, and many furnishings are original to the Madison family.

478 Mount Vernon

CONTACT 703-780-2000, www.mountvernon.org; 3200 Mount Vernon Memorial Hwy., Mount Vernon

PRICING	$$$
BEST TIME TO VISIT	Spring, winter holidays
AGE RANGE	7 and older

First president of the United States George Washington (1732–99) said of his Mount Vernon home, "No estate in United America is more pleasantly situated than this." Visitors will soon agree that the 500 acres that remain of Washington's original 8,000 are indeed breathtaking, sited on a bucolic bend of the

George Washington home   © Debbie K. Hardin

Potomac River and surrounded by old-growth trees, many of which have been on the property since the 18th century. After passing through a slick visitor center that shows an optional 15-minute orientation film, guests move on to the genteel old home, furnished much as it was during President Washington's era.

A highlight of the tour is Washington's personal office, a manly wood-paneled library where he is said to have spent the earliest hours of the day catching up on his voluminous correspondence. On display is a letter press where Washington was able to make an early "Xerox" by pressing still-wet ink on his original document against onionskin copy paper. Guests during the hot summertime months will marvel at his fan chair, a contraption that allowed him to sit back and read or work while pedaling a foot treadle that drove a wooden fan blade suspended over the top of the chair.

Upstairs half of the 10 bedrooms in the house are on display, all featuring authentic 1799 decorations (although not all of the furnishings on display actually belonged to the Washingtons). Kids will want to see the baby crib in the "Nelly Custis" bedroom—a gift from Martha to her daughter. Guests can also peek into the room where the Marquis de Lafayette stayed when he visited—one of the grandest bedrooms in the home, festooned with rich carpets, bright paint colors, and ornately patterned fabrics. George and Martha's bedroom, at the end of a private hallway, is much more subdued, with white walls, white bed linens, simple wooden desks and tables, and only a touch of color on the painted moldings.

Step outside the mansion and enjoy the Washingtons' phenomenal view of the back lawn and the river beyond. A row of wooden chairs on the rear-facing porch invites guests to rest a spell before moving on to the extensive gardens. Be sure to visit the poignant slave quarters, a slave memorial and burial ground, the kitchen, the clerk's quarters, the smokehouse, a washhouse, a coach house, stables, various "necessaries"—what we now call outhouses—and Washington's tomb, set on a site he selected himself.

On the way out of the property, visitors will pass through the Donald W. Reynolds Museum and Education Center, housing original letters to and from Washington, an original key to the Bastille that Lafayette gave to GW, and artifacts that belonged to Washington, such as china and weaponry. The adjacent education center was designed to engage younger visitors in the hope that they leave Mount Vernon understanding Washington better. Here are life-sized wax creations of the general during various stages of his career, interactive exhibits about Washington's occupations, and several theaters that show films depicting the most important events in his public life—including a full-sensory experience with vibrating theater chairs and special effects like fog and "snow."

Mount Vernon offers a number of seasonal activities, including holiday tours throughout December in which the mansion is decorated with natural greenery and the third floor (normally closed to the public) is available for touring; a Revolutionary War encampment in late September in which reenactors act as soldiers, camp in authentic colonial tents, and demonstrate military maneuvers; and a patriotic Fourth of July celebration that includes live music along with "Happy Birthday, America" cake for guests.

White House of the Confederacy Courtesy Virginia Tourism Corporation

479 Museum of the Confederacy

CONTACT 804-649-1861, www.moc.org; 1201 E. Clay St., Richmond (secondary site in Appomattox)

PRICING	$$–$$$
BEST TIME TO VISIT	Year-round
AGE RANGE	7 and older

The Confederate States of America was a government of southern states that originated in 1861, with their secession from the United States at the start of the Civil War, and terminated in 1865, when Union forces defeated the Confederacy. The interesting Museum of the Confederacy has the largest, most wide-ranging collection of artifacts, manuscripts, books, and photographs from the Confederate States. The museum comprises three sites in two locations: The museum proper and the adjacent White House of the Confederacy, both in Richmond, and the Appomattox Museum in Appomattox.

The Richmond site offers collections of weapons, uniforms, and personal belongings of famous Confederates like Jefferson Davis, J. E. B. Stuart, and Stonewall Jackson. Look for General Robert E. Lee's fully stocked field tent on display, complete with eating utensils. The provisional Confederate Constitution is on display here, as well as the Great Seal of the Confederacy. There are more than 500 wartime battle flags exhibited that were carried by Confederate soldiers into battle, many of which have been donated by veterans and their descendants. The White House of the Confederacy, just next door, was the executive mansion for Confederate president Jefferson Davis, his wife Varina, and their children, who lived in the elegant quarters from summer 1861 through the end of the war. The elaborately decorated, opulent mansion is furnished with reproduction pieces as well as original pieces that were here in Davis's time. A guided tour through the mansion offers insight into Civil War Richmond and into the lives of the Confederates' first family. (Abraham Lincoln himself is said to have toured the mansion after the war—declining to go upstairs, in the families' quarters, because he believed it was indecorous to invade another man's home.)

480 Pentagon

CONTACT 703-697-1776, http://pentagontours.osd.mil; Army and Navy Dr. and Fern St., Arlington

PRICING	$
BEST TIME TO VISIT	Year-round, Monday through Friday
AGE RANGE	7 and older

Headquarters for the secretaries of defense, army, navy, and air force, the Pentagon is one of the ten largest buildings in the world: There are 17.5 miles of corridor inside the building, but because of the clever box-in-a-box design, it is said to take no more than 10 minutes to walk from any given point in the building to another (provided you know where you're going). The iconic building was the site of the September 11, 2001, terrorist attack in the DC area: A hijacked airliner crashed into the western side of the building, which housed the Naval Command Center, among

9/11 Memorial, Pentagon
Carol M. Highsmith's America, courtesy Library of Congress, Prints and Photographs Division

other offices, and the subsequent explosion caused a fire that spread through the three outer rings of the building. One segment of the structure collapsed completely; 125 people perished, along with all passengers and crew aboard the aircraft. The damage to the building was repaired quickly, and there is an on-site memorial to the victims.

One-hour walking tours of the building are conducted by active-duty military personnel, and tickets must be requested from your state congressional representative at least a week in advance (and as much as 90 days in advance), or via an online service on the Pentagon website. Expect purses and handbags to be x-rayed and be sure to leave battery-operated devices, cameras, and backpacks at home. Children 12 and younger do not require ID to enter the Pentagon; children 13 through 17 must bring a photo ID and be accompanied by a parent or guardian; adults must bring two forms of ID, one of which must be a photo ID.

481 Red Hill

CONTACT 434-376-2044, www.redhill.org; 1250 Red Hill Rd., Brookneal

PRICING	$–$$
BEST TIME TO VISIT	Year-round
AGE RANGE	7 and older

Patrick Henry (1736–99) was an influential Founder of America and an important force in the American Revolution. He is often remembered as the "voice of the Revolution" because of his extraordinary oratory skills. He worked as an attorney and as a farmer, and served as the governor of Virginia for two nonconsecutive terms. Henry led the opposition to the Stamp Act of 1765—and he famously stated, "Give me liberty, or give me death!"

Red Hill was Henry's final home; he moved to the small house and tobacco plantation overlooking the beautiful Staunton River Valley in 1794 with his second wife, and lived there until his death. He is buried on the property. Guests start with a 15-minute orientation video on Henry's life and career, and then move

Patrick Henry National Memorial
Courtesy Virginia Tourism Corporation

on to the Red Hill Museum, which contains the largest collection of Henry memorabilia and artifacts in the world. The property also includes seven historic structures that are open for tours, including Henry's reconstructed home—a modest building with three rooms downstairs and two upstairs, furnished with some 18th-century pieces that belonged to Henry. Also open for viewing is a building Henry used as his law office. The attraction is the site of several seasonal events, including a spectacular Fourth of July Revolutionary reenactment and a fireworks show at night.

482 Shenandoah National Park

CONTACT 540-999-3500, www.nps.gov/shen; off U.S. 340 at Front Royal; off U.S. 211-Luray at Thornton Gap; off U.S. 33-Elkton at Swift Run Gap; off U.S. 250 at Rockfish Gap

PRICING	$
BEST TIME TO VISIT	Fall
AGE RANGE	5 and older

Shenandoah National Park in northeastern Virginia encompasses part of the Blue Ridge Mountain chain, as well as the Shenandoah River on the west and the Virginia Piedmont on the east. The long, narrow park is bisected by the famous Skyline Drive, one of the most beautiful scenic drives in the United States. The 105-mile road runs along the ridge of the mountains and offers access to dozens of wilderness trails and absolutely breathtaking views. The Appalachian Trail runs through the park as well, roughly paralleling Skyline Drive. The park is a favorite destination for seasonal leaf-peepers. During the peak of autumn color (usually the last two weeks of October), Skyline Drive can be bumper-to-bumper—but the views are so dramatic, it's still worth the effort. Visit any other season of the year, however, and experience solitude and panoramic views from dozens of dramatic Skyline Drive overlooks.

There are 500 miles of foot trails and 180 miles of horse trails (guests can bring their own horses or rent one for the day from the park's concessionaire) that wind past waterfalls, along streams, and past the remains of former pioneer homesteads. One of the most popular hikes in the park is along Old Rag Mountain Trail, although this can be dangerous in spots and is not recommended in its entirety for young children. Whether you drive through the park, hike the trails, or horseback ride, you're sure to see the abundant wildlife in the park, including a huge population of white-tailed deer and some of the more than 200 species of birds that call the park home; other residents are shy of visitors, but it's still possible to spot black bears, bobcats, and shrews. For the best chances to see wildlife, arrive at the park at dawn, before the traffic on the parkway increases.

Shenandoah National Park
Courtesy Aramark Parks and Destinations

There are four established campgrounds in Shenandoah National Park that are available for about $20 a night. But for real adventure—and the chance to enjoy free accommodations—consider backcountry camping. Most of the park is open for camping; a permit is required, but it is available at no charge.

Yorktown Victory Center   Courtesy National Park Service

If you are up for a little history, check out Rapidan Camp in the park, the former summer retreat of President Herbert Hoover and his wife, Lou Henry Hoover. The house President Hoover once owned is furnished in period style, and there are exhibits on site that chronicle the Hoover administration. You can hike in via the 4-mile round-trip Mill Prong Trail; catch the trailhead at the Milam Gap parking lot.

483 Yorktown Victory Center

CONTACT 757-253-4838, www.historyisfun.org/Yorktown-Victory-Center.htm; 200 Water St., Rt. 1020, Yorktown

PRICING	$$
BEST TIME TO VISIT	Year-round
AGE RANGE	7 and older

In the autumn of 1781, General George Washington led American and allied French troops into Yorktown to battle British general Charles Cornwallis's army. On October 19 Cornwallis surrendered; this last major battle of the Revolution is considered by historians as the end of America's war for independence—although sporadic fighting continued elsewhere in the country for nearly a year afterward.

Today the Yorktown Victory Center is a living museum that chronicles the story of the American Revo-

Save as much as $5 per individual on admissions to Yorktown Victory Center and nearby Jamestown Settlement by purchasing a combination ticket, available at either site or online.

lution and offers the chance for visitors to experience life as it might have been in colonial days. The outdoor museum includes historic reenactments—especially popular is the Continental army encampment, where actors re-create the daily life of American soldiers at the end of the war—and costumed interpreters throughout the attraction, who remain in character to answer any questions visitors might have about colonial life. Children will enjoy the 1780s-era farm, which includes a small house, herb and vegetable garden, crop fields, a tobacco barn, and a kitchen. During warmer months kids can help weed or water the garden, learn about how herbs were used in cooking and for medicine, and comb cotton flax into fiber in preparation for weaving cloth. Don't miss a trip to the Discovery Room, where kids can try on 18th-century-style clothing: The center has a huge collection of kid-sized costumes, from tricorn hats to buckle shoes and everything in between.

The Yorktown Victory Center is near the site of the actual Yorktown National Battlefield (www.nps.gov/yonb), which is preserved as a national park. A visitor center in the park shows an orientation film on the historic battle; guests can then explore the battlefield via one of two self-guided auto tours. Look for original and reconstructed earthworks and siege lines used by both American and British troops; guest can also see the site of Washington's Headquarters (off the 9-mile Encampment Tour Road).

Mount Rainier   Courtesy National Park Service

WASHINGTON

484 Fort Vancouver

CONTACT 360-816-6230, w-w.nps.gov/fova; 612 Reserve
St., Vancouver

PRICING	$
BEST TIME TO VISIT	Year-round
AGE RANGE	7 and older

Fort Vancouver (which straddles Oregon and Washington) started out as a 19th-century fur-trading outpost along the Columbia River. The fort was the headquarters of the Hudson's Bay Company, the oldest commercial corporation in North America. The company began by English royal charter in 1670 as the Governor and Company of Adventurers of England Trading Into Hudson Bay, and enjoyed huge economic success trapping and trading animal pelts for export to Europe. The fort served as the primary supply depot for the company's fur-trading operations in the Pacific Northwest. Later, the U.S. Army occupied a post, Columbia Barracks, at the site, with the mission of maintaining peace (and suppressing Native uprisings) during the pioneer settlement of Oregon Country. Today at Fort Vancouver, a replica of the fort is open for public tours. There are also ongoing archaeological excavations that continue to uncover historical artifacts, some of which are on display at the fort. The Oregon portion of the site includes the McLoughlin House, home to John McLoughlin, often known as the Father of Oregon; the restored,

McLaughlin House, Fort Vancouver   Courtesy National Park Service

period-furnished home gives a glimpse into life in the region during the 19th century.

The fort also offers a number of cultural demonstrations, varying by season. Reenactors in period costumes demonstrate blacksmithing skills, carpentry skills using reproduction antique tools, and cooking and baking. In the summer there are a number of special programs designed for kids, including hourlong programs that teach children 1800s-era games. There are also hands-on archaeology programs (with classes designed for ages 8 through 12 and also for younger children) that give kids the chance to extract artifacts with trowels, screen dirt, and clean and catalog their finds.

485 Mount St. Helens National Volcanic Monument

CONTACT 360-449-7800, www.fs.usda.gov/mountst
helens; Johnson Ridge Observatory, 24000 Spirit Lake
Hwy., Toutle; Park Headquarters, 42218 NE Yale Bridge Rd.,
Amboy

PRICING	Fees vary by entry point
BEST TIME TO VISIT	Late spring through fall
AGE RANGE	5 and older

On the morning of May 18, 1980, what had been a quiet, peaceful mountain scene some 100 miles south of Seattle literally exploded into the most destructive volcanic eruption the modern United States has ever seen. Mount St. Helens is part of the Cascades Ridge, and is one of the youngest volcanoes in the country. An earthquake measured at 5.1 on the Richter scale hit it, triggering an avalanche of debris, which was followed by a massive eruption. Pre-eruption the mountain measured 9,677 feet; afterward it measured 8,365 feet—and in its wake a 1-mile-wide crater was formed. Fifty-seven people were killed, nearly 200 miles of highway was destroyed, and approximately 250 homes were lost. The monument was created to preserve the region for future study.

Remarkably, the vegetation has started to return to Mount St. Helens, but the scene is still reminiscent of a moonscape. There are numerous activities within the monument grounds available to visitors, including incredible (and pricey) helicopter tours, horseback riding over the ash flows, and miles of hiking trails with unique glimpses into the aftermath of the eruption. Check out the Johnston Ridge Observatory for incredible views of the lava dome—which is still steam-ing today. This is also a good place to peer into the crater and see the landslide deposit. The visitor center on site includes a 300-seat theater, video terminals that provide information on volcanoes around the world, and rangers who lead guided walks. You can catch the trailhead to one of the most popular trails at the site—Boundary Trail #1—from here as well.

Roadside Attractions

Road trips offer the chance to see the landscape: Kids can really get a sense of how big America is, and long driving trips across states (or better yet, across the country) provide a sense of how different the various regions in the United States are. If you have the time, pick a route that includes at least some portion *off* the freeways. The highways and byways will take you through cities and towns and past countless interesting sights that you would otherwise miss speeding by on a freeway (or flying over in an airplane). Make the most of these driving adventures: Stop for "the world's best cherry shake"; pull over at the farm stand promising freshly picked tomatoes; get out and take a photo of kids standing next to a "welcome to the state" sign. These small moments are often the stuff of the most indelible travel memories for children.

And if you find yourself near any of the following roadside oddities, don't miss them:

- **Cadillac Ranch (Amarillo, Texas):** This brightly colored, oversized sculpture is constructed from 10 partially buried cars, slanted just so, in an otherwise bucolic cow pasture.
- **Carhenge (Alliance, Nebraska):** Because one monument constructed out of old cars just isn't enough, check out this artistically arranged collection of 38 old cars (painted stone gray) meant to evoke England's ancient Stonehenge.
- **Catoosa's Blue Whale (Catoosa, Oklahoma):** Along historic Route 66, this giant, friendly blue whale beckons families, who can enjoy an adjacent reptile zoo and picnic area.
- **Corn Palace (Mitchell, South Dakota):** Every year since 1892, the exterior of this monument to maize has been redesigned to create murals using more than 275,000 ears of corn.
- **Idaho Potato Museum (Blackfoot, Idaho):** It's hard to drive by this homage to carbs without noticing the *many* signs announcing you're approaching. It's a fun reminder to kids that museums aren't always *serious*.
- **Lucy the Elephant (Margate, New Jersey):** This crazy animal-shaped structure is actually a 65-foot building that was once a vacation home.

- **Randy's Donuts (Inglewood, California):** Not too far from the LA International Airport, a giant doughnut, several stories high, calls out to hungry pastry lovers. (Bonus: The doughnuts here are *awesome*.)
- **World's Largest Ball of Twine (Darwin, Minnesota):** This oversized cat toy is housed in a Plexiglas gazebo—and is worth pulling off the road for a good giggle.
- **World's Largest Buffalo (Jamestown, North Dakota):** This buffalo statue stands 26 feet tall and 46 feet long—and is a real eye catcher along I-94.

Randy's Donuts, a roadside attraction that's a sweet treat Courtesy Jon Preimesberger

PRICE KEY
$ free–$5
$$ $6–10
$$$ $11–20
$$$$ $21+

486 Museum of Flight

CONTACT 206-764-5720, www.museumofflight.org;
9404 E. Marginal Way, Seattle

PRICING	$$–$$$
BEST TIME TO VISIT	Year-round
AGE RANGE	5 and older

The Museum of Flight at the King County Airport south of downtown Seattle is one of the largest aviation museums in the country. The permanent collection includes more than 150 historically important airplanes and spacecraft, as well as an expansive aviation and space archive and library. Displays include the first presidential jet (which was active from 1959 through 1996)—kids will enjoy the chance to walk through the plane; a sleek British Airways Concorde, also open for guests to step into; and the first fighter plane, which served during World War I. Guests can also explore a re-created air traffic control tower, climb inside a replica of a full-scale International Space Station research lab, or check out an expansive collection of World War II fighter planes. For die-hard aviation fans, the museum offers a great vantage point from which to watch planes take off and touch down at the adjacent two-runway airport. Children will not want to miss the numerous flight simulators here (for an additional fee): The two-seat X-Pilot simulators let riders engage in a World War II–like aerial dogfight or choose one of three modern jets that can race for speed or be maneuvered to roll and loop. Other simulators provide 3-D projectors that will allow guests to experience the sensation of flying an F-18 Hornet, pilot a hand glider, or take the controls of an Apollo lunar lander.

> Discount tickets for the Museum of Flight are available for AAA members and Boeing employees. Active military personnel and their families can receive free admission (up to five guests). And every first Thursday of the month admission is free from 5 to 9 PM.

487 Olympic National Park

CONTACT 360-565-3130, www.nps.gov/olym; off Hwy. 101, Port Angeles

PRICING	$
BEST TIME TO VISIT	Spring through fall
AGE RANGE	5 and older

Olympic National Park is a cornucopia of geographic and species diversity, and one of the most stunning and undeveloped sites on earth. The national park, which is also designated a World Heritage Site, offers three distinct regions: craggy, undeveloped coastline; dense rain forests thick with flora and fauna; and high country that includes perpetually snowcapped and glaciated mountains. The variety of terrain allows for a huge variety of animals and plants, too, and the remoteness of many of the sights—and the relative difficulty of getting to them—all but ensures a visit to this rugged park will be a complete wilderness experience. Access to the park is via Highway 101, but there are no roads that bisect the large peninsula, which makes exploring the area challenging—yet immensely rewarding.

The coastline protected within the park is the longest undeveloped stretch of coast in the Lower 48, and includes more than 60 miles of oceanside to explore: Look for massive, sculptural rock formations

Olympic National Park   Courtesy National Park Service

just off the coast, richly populated tide pools, long stretches of sandy beach, glorious beachcombing, and a huge collection of native and seasonal shorebirds. A favorite hike within this section of the park is the 9-mile Ozette Loop. Catch the trailhead at Ozette Lake; the first 3 miles of the trail includes boardwalk through cedar swamplands. Once the trail hits the ocean, there are alternative inland loops hikers can take to avoid getting stranded on the beach at high tide. During high season, and especially on weekends, hikers must register and reserve access to the trail, to avoid overcrowding.

At the center of the park are the majestic Olympic Mountains, dotted with glaciers. Mount Olympus rises to nearly 8,000 feet and has the largest concentration of glaciers in the park—more than 60, which is a remarkable number given the relatively low altitude compared with other glaciated sites that remain in America and elsewhere. A good way to see the mountain ridges and their beautiful glaciers is to visit Hurricane Ridge, which offers stunning views of the peaks and terrific hiking opportunities through subalpine meadows. Visit the area in spring and the wildflower display is breathtaking. In the winter Hurricane Ridge is the site of a wildly popular alpine skiing and snowboarding center.

The isolated nature of the park, and its status as a protected reserve, equates to excellent wildlife-viewing opportunities. The park is home to populations of the endangered northern spotted owl, bull trout, and marbled murrelet. There are 15 animals that evolved in this region that are found nowhere else on earth, including the Olympic Mazama pocket gopher, the crescent trout, and the Olympic mud minnow. In addition, many other interesting species call the park home, including the mountain beaver, the trumpeter swan, the boreal toad, the North American porcupine, and massive herds of elk and nonnative mountain goats.

Because of its rugged nature and the expanse of wilderness that is not accessible via roadways, the most satisfying way to tour Olympic National Park is via a backpacking trip. Local concessionaires offer guided trips for less experienced campers and hikers. Be aware, however, that the ubiquitous fog, heavy rainfall, and dense undergrowth make this a challenging place to hike, so venture into the interior only if everyone in your family is up for the physical rigors of the experience.

488 Seattle Space Needle

CONTACT 206-905-2100, www.spaceneedle.com, 400 Broad St., Seattle

PRICING	$$$
BEST TIME TO VISIT	Year-round (when visibility is good)
AGE RANGE	All ages

The Space Needle is an architectural icon of the Pacific Northwest, and a favorite tourist site in Seattle. The 605-foot tower was built for the 1962 World's Fair, and at the time it was completed it was the tallest structure west of the Mississippi River. It was designed to withstand an earthquake of up to 9.1 on the Richter scale and 200-mile-per-hour winds. Visit on a clear day and the views from the observation deck (at 520 feet) are worth the price of admission: From the top of the Space Needle you can see the pretty skyline of downtown Seattle as well as the magnificent nearby mountain ranges and even a handful of the islands off the coast of Washington. Kids will enjoy the 41-second ride to the top; elevators travel at a speedy 10 mph—fast enough to produce a queasy stomach for those inclined to motion sickness. If you want to enjoy the views at a leisurely pace, consider eating at the pricey restaurant at the top of the Needle—but reserve this for kids 10 and older, who will appreciate the experience and be able to sit through a long, expensive meal.

Seattle Space Needle
Courtesy Carol M. Highsmith's America, Library of Congress, Prints and Photographs Division

west virginia

489 Beckley Exhibition Coal Mine

CONTACT 304-256-1747, www.beckley.org/exhibition_coal_mine; 513 Ewart Ave., Beckley

PRICING	$$$
BEST TIME TO VISIT	Open April through October
AGE RANGE	7 and older

Coal mining was an important economic venture in West Virginia even before the region became a separate state; mining began in the early 1800s, when the area was still part of Virginia. There are vast reserves of coal here—53 of 55 of the counties in West Virginia have supplies of the natural resource. Coal is an organic substance that forms over thousands of years, as plant life decomposes and sandstone and shale layer on top, compressing the matter into a burnable fuel. Mining for the valuable substance is notoriously difficult, dangerous work, and the hardscrabble industry has defined much of the state for decades.

The Exhibition Coal Mine offers a chance to peek inside a typical early-20th-century historical coal-mining operation. The site includes a coal museum

> ## Coal is an organic substance that forms over thousands of years.

with an extensive collection of mining artifacts and tools, as well as geological specimens that have been recovered during mining operations. The real adventure here is a tour that goes belowground. Under the supervision of a veteran coal miner, guests will journey 1,500 feet below the surface via "man cars" that run from the mine entrance to the former working areas of the coal mine. Guides will explain the history of mining, from the days when coal was loaded by hand and carried out by carts to the modern era marked by mechanization. After the tour, check out the historical coal camp on the grounds, which includes a re-created coal miner's home, a coal camp school, a church, and the superintendent's home. The structures are furnished with 1940s-era antiques.

490 Grave Creek Mound Archaeological Complex

CONTACT 304-843-4128, www.wvculture.org; 801 Jefferson Ave., Moundsville

PRICING	$
BEST TIME TO VISIT	Year-round; closed Monday
AGE RANGE	7 and older

Grave Creek Mound is one of the largest conical-shaped burial mounds in the United States: It measures 62 feet high and 240 feet in diameter. The ancient earthenworks dates to 150 BC, when representatives of the Adena culture carried more than 60,000 tons of dirt in baskets to construct it. Archeologists believe that at one time there were hundreds of Adena mounds in the region, but only a few survive to the present day—and most are considerably smaller than they were originally, thanks to thousands of years of erosion. The Adena culture was a pre-Columbian Native group that lived throughout the midwestern and eastern United States, including West Virginia, Kentucky, Ohio, Indiana, Pennsylvania, and New York, as far back as 1000 BC. Archaeologists have discovered that the mound was constructed in various stages, over approximately 100 years, and burials have been found at different levels within the mound. At one time a moat about 40 feet wide and 5 feet deep ringed the mound. Visitors today can view the mound, as well as visit the adjacent Delf Norona Museum, which displays 450,000 artifacts recovered from the site and offers exhibits on the Adena culture.

> No matter how hot (or cold) it is outside, it is always 58 degrees in the heart of the Beckley Exhibition Coal Mine. Bring a sweater!

View from Harpers Ferry   Courtesy National Park Service

PRICE KEY
$ free–$5
$$ $6–10
$$$ $11–20
$$$$ $21+

491 Harpers Ferry National Historical Park

 Harpers Ferry is a small, popular destination—especially on warm weekends—and the parking is extremely limited. Avoid the congestion and park at the visitor center at the Cavalier Heights entrance, and then take a six-minute shuttle ride to the town.

CONTACT http://historicharpersferry.com; off U.S. 340 alt., Harpers Ferry

PRICING	$
BEST TIME TO VISIT	Year-round
AGE RANGE	7 and older

Harpers Ferry is a lovely, well-preserved historic town nestled among the rocky hills of West Virginia, at the confluence of the Potomac and Shenandoah Rivers. The natural setting is one of the most beautiful in the country—and a self-proclaimed favorite of President Thomas Jefferson, who visited the site as a young man. And the town itself is charming: The Harpers Ferry Historic District includes 100 historic structures, including 19th-century houses built for the Harpers Ferry Armory, the Harpers Ferry Train Station, and the picturesque U.S. Armory Potomac Canal.

The town is best remembered for abolitionist John Brown's raid of the armory in the mid-19th century. Brown was a notorious personality in the region: He aimed to arm slaves so that they could stage a rebellion that would ultimately lead to their freedom, and his methods were often bloody. On October 16, 1859, Brown and 19 men (including 2 of his sons and 5

African Americans, among them Dangerfield Newby, who was motivated to rescue his enslaved wife) raided the federal arsenal at Harpers Ferry. Another famous abolitionist, Frederick Douglass, was against the plan: Douglass argued that the isolated town, surrounded by mountains and two major rivers, would be difficult to subdue with such a small force—and Douglass proved to be correct. Brown and his tiny band did manage to capture the arsenal; they expected that with this victory slaves in the region would join their rebellion and thus increase their numbers, but the slave insurrection Brown imagined never materialized. It wasn't long before Brown and his men were barricaded in the arsenal's firehouse. U.S. military forces stormed the building and captured the rebels; Brown was then tried and hanged for "conspiracy" with slaves and for treason and murder. Many historians argue that Brown's bold maneuver accelerated the country's move toward civil war.

A trip to Harpers Ferry National Historical Park today offers the chance to meander the narrow (hilly) streets to explore restored structures housing antiques stores and cafés. There are 4 miles of trails that ring the outlying wilderness; kayaking and rafting are popular on the rivers as well. Don't miss the chance to see the slightly kitschy John Brown Wax Museum (on High Street), an exhibit on the abolitionist and his infamous raid. Also visit the Harper House, at the top of stone stairs above High Street; this is the oldest structure in Harpers Ferry (dating to 1775) and was a onetime tavern that hosted George Washington and Thomas Jefferson.

The Harpers Ferry Historical Association (304-535-6881) hosts a number of excellent living history workshops throughout the year; these require advance registration and payment (about $10–15 per person), and most welcome children when accompanied by an adult. Learn to bake bread in a beehive oven, craft tin tableware, or take part in an heirloom seed sale and gardening demonstration.

Harpers Ferry National Historical Park

492 New River Gorge National River

CONTACT 304-465-0508, www.nps.gov/neri; off Rt. 19, near Beckley

PRICING	$ (rafting excursions additional)
BEST TIME TO VISIT	Spring through fall
AGE RANGE	5 and older (for whitewater rafting, ages 10 and older)

The spectacular, wild New River Gorge National River Park comprises 53 miles of the New River in West Virginia, from Bluestone Dam to Hawk's Nest Lake. The whitewater river is one of the oldest on the planet, and it continues to be the force behind the creation of the deepest and longest river gorge in the Appalachian Mountains. The waterway is surrounded by a rich forest ecosystem that fosters enormous species diversity. Habitats include uninterrupted forest, cliffs, wetlands, and mature bottomlands, all of which are home to endangered animals like the Virginia big-eared bat, the Allegheny woodrat, and many examples of rare amphibians, birds, mammals, and reptiles.

In addition to being a repository and preserve for flora and fauna, the New River offers myriad outdoor sporting opportunities, including fishing, camping, horseback riding, rock climbing, hiking, mountain biking, and extremely popular whitewater rafting.

Rafting on the New River Gorge National River

Courtesy National Park Service

The Lower Gorge is renowned as one of the best whitewater rafting sites in the world, with rapids ranging in difficulty from Class III to Class V (which are best from April through October). The upper river offers Class I to Class III rapids (depending on conditions and season). The river is open to experienced paddlers to explore, but families should not miss the chance to prearrange a guided rafting tour with an experienced concessionaire. Guided tours will provide equipment, wet suits, and (depending on the danger involved) helmets. Wear water shoes or diving booties—and reserve this adventure for fearless family members. Rafting on this exciting river can be exhilarating for some and terrifying for others.

Among the many sites along the river, don't miss the chance to see the New River Gorge Bridge, the longest steel bridge in the Western Hemisphere and the second highest in the United States. On the third Saturday of every October, the bridge is open for pedestrians to cross. If you are able to take part in "Bridge Day," expect to see hundreds of parachutists who base jump the nearly 900-foot drop to the river. Also, check out the Sandstone Falls, the largest waterfall on the New River. The river drops 10 to 25 feet in a pretty tiered waterfall that is punctuated by several islands. The falls are a little more than 8 miles north of Hinton, off Route 26 (also called the River Road), and are easily accessible via a boardwalk that leads to observation decks over the falls.

493 Prickett's Fort State Park

CONTACT 304-363-3030, www.prickettsfortstate park.com; off I-79, Fairmont

PRICING	$–$$
BEST TIME TO VISIT	Open late April through October; closed Monday and Tuesday after Labor Day
AGE RANGE	5 and older

Prickett's Fort State Park is a re-creation of a 1774-era fort, which was originally built by pioneers as a refuge from Native American war parties on the edge of

Prickett's Fort State Park

Photo by Steve Shaluta, courtesy Prickett's Fort State Park

494 Washington Heritage Trail Byway

CONTACT www.washingtonheritagetrail.org; western end near Paw Paw, along WV 9 east to Berkeley Springs; here the trail splits in two, with the southern branch heading along U.S. 522 and WV 51 and the northern branch along WV 9, WV 230, and WV 480; the two branches rejoin west of Harpers Ferry

PRICING	Attraction fees vary
BEST TIME TO VISIT	Spring through fall
AGE RANGE	All ages

what was then the frontier of colonial Virginia (and is now part of West Virginia). American settlers lived in the surrounding countryside, but when Indian uprisings threatened their safety, as many as 80 families fled to the fort to wait out the violence, which could last for a few days or a few weeks. The accommodations within the fort were cramped and primitive, but they were tolerated as a necessity for survival during the late 1700s.

The modern-day re-created 100-by-100-foot construction is today a living history site that hosts demonstrations of the 18th-century lifestyle. The fort is surrounded by 12-foot-high log walls, and is anchored on each corner by a blockhouse. Along the stockade walls there are 16 small log cabins, a meetinghouse, and a storehouse, all open for exploration. Costumed interpreters perform everyday chores like weaving, spinning, and blacksmithing; there's also a gun shop on site that offers demonstrations of 18th-century firearm manufacturing. Just south of the fort is the Job Prickett House, an 1859-era home that is now a museum, housing original furnishings and tools typical of a 19th-century farmhouse.

The natural surroundings are lovely, and the Prickett's Fort Nature Trail is an excellent way to enjoy the scenery and learn about the animals and plants indigenous to the region. There are 25 interpretive stations along the way to introduce hikers to the diverse life in this part of West Virginia. There's also a rails-to-trails converted path, the 3-mile MC Trail, that is open to walkers and cyclists.

Before George Washington became the Father of the Country, he was a great admirer of the landscape. One of his first jobs was as surveyor for Culpepper County, which allowed him the chance to enjoy the beauty of the Shenandoah Valley and beyond. He loved the eastern panhandle of West Virginia so much that he purchased several acres of land in the region, and spent numerous holidays "taking the waters" at the natural mineral springs in what is now Berkeley, West Virginia. Another president admired the natural scenery here, too: Thomas Jefferson once remarked that the view of the Potomac River from Harper's Ferry was "one of the most stupendous scenes in nature." The Washington Heritage Trail is a 136-mile loop through three West Virginia counties (Berkeley, Jefferson, and Morgan) that traces the footsteps of Washington and includes historic sites like railroad landmarks, Civil War sites, and favorite sites of the early U.S. presidents. The majority of the trail follows the Potomac River and the historic road that ran from Alexandria, Virginia, to Warm Springs, West Virginia. Included in the byway is Harpers Ferry National Historical Park (see above), the site of abolitionist John Brown's unsuccessful raid on the town's arsenal in his attempt to arm slaves in the South so that they could be the agents of their own revolution.

There is much to see and do along the byway—it makes a lovely weekend drive, even with few stops. But if you have the chance to get out and explore, check out these highlights:

In Berkeley County

- **Belle Boyd House** (126 E. Race St., Martinsburg): This 1853 home was built by the father of Isabella (Belle) Boyd, a onetime Confederate spy and confidante of General Stonewall Jackson. In addition to ferrying information, she once shot and killed a Union soldier. Today the home hosts a museum with artifacts from the Civil War.
- **Mount Zion Episcopal Church** (WV 9, Hedgesville): This beautiful brick church built in 1818 is on the site of the Hedges Chapel where George Washington worshipped in the early 18th century.

In Jefferson County

- **Claymont Court** (off Huyett Rd., northwest of Berryville): This grand estate was built by George Washington's grandnephew Bushrod Corbin Washington, and at the time of its construction it was the largest in the region. It was destroyed completely by fire shortly after its construction, but was rebuilt and refurbished.
- **Jefferson Rock** (within Harpers Ferry National Historical Park, near St. Peter's Church): A mound of sedimentary rock adorned with four stone pillars marks the spot where Thomas Jefferson stood in 1783 to admire the confluence of the Potomac and Shenandoah Rivers. This view is a stunning one, and well worth the steep climb.

- **Peter Burr House** (Kearneysville): The Peter Burr house is the oldest wooden frame structure in the state, and offers a glimpse into a pre-1760 settlement homestead. Peter Burr was the brother of Aaron Burr Sr., who was the president of Princeton University (then known as the College of New Jersey) and father of Aaron Burr Jr., the third vice president of the United States.

In Morgan County

- **Bath Historic District** (Berkeley Springs): This small town was established in 1776, years after George Washington and other colonial luminaries pitched tents and took the waters in mineral spring pools.
- **George Washington's Bathtub** (within Berkeley Springs State Park): Don't miss the chance to see this monument to presidential ablutions. The stone tub on display is actually much fancier than what was available to George Washington during his visits in the mid-1700s: He likely bathed in pools lined with sand and smooth stones.
- **Roman Bath House and Museum of the Berkeley Springs** (corner of Fairfax and Wilkes, in Berkeley Springs State Park): Preserved here are nine historic bathing chambers that continue to soothe the ailments of visitors who come to soak in the 102-degree waters. It has been in continuous use for bathing since 1815. The second floor of the bathhouse is home to the Museum of Berkeley Springs.

WISCONSIN

495 Aztalan State Park

CONTACT http://i94.biz/aztalan/aztalan.html;
1213 S. Main St., Lake Mills

PRICING	$
BEST TIME TO VISIT	Year-round
AGE RANGE	7 and older

The Aztalan State Park preserves an ancient archaeological site occupied from about 1000 to 1200 by people of the Mississippian culture. Mississippian people built earthen platformed pyramids used for religious and ceremonial purposes. This interesting site reconstructs two of the pyramids and a protective stockade, to give visitors an idea of the ancient constructions. Although not the first people in the area (there were ancients who lived along the Crawfish River in Wisconsin's Jefferson County as long ago as 900), the Mississippian people established a sophisticated society that was based on agriculture, hunting, and fishing. Today the park is open for visitors, and includes open prairie, oak woodlands, and picnic shelters. The Crawfish River is a popular site for fishing for northern pike and walleye.

496 Madeline Island Historic Museum

CONTACT http://madelineislandmuseum.wisconsin history.org; 226 Colonel Woods Ave., La Pointe, Madeline Island

PRICING	$–$$
BEST TIME TO VISIT	Open daily May through September; Friday and Saturday for select weekends in October
AGE RANGE	7 and older

French explorers and fur traders who came to the region from Canada via the Great Lakes were the first

> Madeline Island in Lake Superior can be reached via a 20-minute ferry ride from the Madeline Island Ferry dock; it runs from Bayfield every hour or so, depending on the season, starting at 7:30 am. Rates start at $25 per vehicle or $13 per person for a round trip. Access the docks from Washington Avenue, off Highway 13 in the northeast side of Bayfield.

Europeans to settle in the territory that eventually became Wisconsin. Traders soon discovered that there were enormous populations of beaver in the area, and starting in the mid-1600s and for another 200 years, the fur industry thrived here. Beaver pelts were converted into pliable felt, which was made into coveted hats worn in Europe and throughout the colonies—and because the demand for felt was so high, the trade in furs was economically rewarding. Enterprising traders from Montreal and elsewhere began stocking up on trade goods like steel flints, guns and ammunition, wool blankets, and glass beads, which they then traded for beaver pelts with Native American hunters in posts scattered along the coasts of the Great Lakes.

Tiny Madeline Island, one of the Apostle Islands in Lake Superior, was the site of one such fur-trading post. The community of La Pointe was first established in 1693 as a fur-trading post, and in the 19th century the American Fur Company also opened a post here. Today the Madeline Island Historical Museum preserves the legacy of the Native Ojibwe hunters and the French and Canadian traders who settled the region. The museum comprises historic buildings like the former La Pointe Jail and the American Fur Company's regional headquarters, an old log barn, and the Old Sailor's Home (built as a memorial to a drowned sailor). Displays within the structures tell the story of the Native American tribes who hunted for beaver pelts, the European fur traders who helped settle the region, early missionaries who visited Madeline Island, and the maritime history of the small island. Outside the structures larger artifacts are on display, like a bell and foghorns from a lighthouse, an antique boat winch, and a maple-sugaring kettle. Be sure to watch the 20-minute orientation film at the visitor center, to get a good overview of the early days of the island.

Milwaukee skyline © Rudy Balasko /iStockphoto.com

PRICE KEY
$ free–$5
$$ $6–10
$$$ $11–20
$$$$ $21+

497 Pabst Mansion

CONTACT 414-931-0808, http://pabstmansion.com;
2000 W. Wisconsin Ave., Milwaukee

PRICING	$$
BEST TIME TO VISIT	Year-round
AGE RANGE	7 and older

Captain Frederick Pabst (1836–1904) was a German immigrant who discovered that the path to his American dream was paved in beer bottles. Pabst came to the United States in 1848, married, and soon went into business with his father-in-law, who was a brewer. Pabst revolutionized production at the family brewery, converted the company into a public offering, and eventually became president—and in short order the brewery, renamed from Best Brewery to the Pabst Brewing Company, had enormous influence on the Milwaukee economy. To celebrate his wealth, and to create a showpiece for the city, Pabst and his wife, Maria, built a stunning mansion, designed by Milwaukee architect George Bowman Ferry, in the Flemish Renaissance Revival style. The Pabst family lived in the magnificent structure from 1892 until 1908. After the deaths of Pabst and his wife, the house was sold to the Archdiocese of Milwaukee, and for the next 70-some years five archbishops used the mansion as their home, as did Franciscan sisters and priests.

Today the palatial monument to the Gilded Age is open as a house museum. It has been meticulously refurbished and contains many original furnishings—most of which were designed and built by local craftsmen (an unusual circumstance; many wealthy Americans of the time imported furnishings from Europe rather than employ local craftsman). Look for

Purchase the Magnificent Three Pass for $12 per person for hugely discounted admission to the Pabst Mansion along with the Villa Terrace Decorative Arts Museum (2220 N. Terrace Ave.) and Charles Allis Decorative Art Museum (1801 N. Prospect Ave.) in Milwaukee.

Pabst Mansion   Courtesy Captain Frederick Pabst Mansion, Inc.

the 6-foot-wide chandelier made from three pairs of elk antlers in the entryway, the gilded rococo fireplace in the parlor, and modern conveniences that included 10 bathrooms, a battery-powered burglar alarm, and central air. The home also showcases fine art, decorative art, and the archives of Captain Pabst.

498 Taliesin

CONTACT 608-588-7090, www.taliesinpreservation.org; at the intersection of Hwy. 23 and County Rd. C, Spring Green

PRICING	$$$–$$$$
BEST TIME TO VISIT	Open May through October
AGE RANGE	12 and older (younger children are not allowed on most tours)

Frank Lloyd Wright (1867–1959) was one of the most influential American architects in history. Wright designed more than 1,000 structures in a style he dubbed "organic." The buildings were meant to exist in balance with their natural environment, and each unique Wright structure sits in harmony with its site. Taliesin was Wright's summer home and studio for 48 years, and it is here where he designed some of his most famous structures, including Fallingwater and the Guggenheim Museum. The site today is a privately owned complex that includes Wright's home, a drafting studio and office, guest quarters, a working farm, orchards, and its own hydroelectric plant.

The site was notorious in Wright's time for a series of fires and murders on the property. Wright started tongues wagging when he moved to Taliesin in 1911 with Mamah Borthwick Cheney, the former wife of a client with whom he had been having an affair. Within a few years, while Wright was in Chicago for work, a servant at the estate set fire to Taliesin and then killed seven people with an ax as the fire burned. Among the dead were Mamah and her two children. Afterward, Wright rebuilt the living quarters, renaming it Taliesin II. Incredibly, the structure was destroyed again by fire in 1925, as a result of a lightning strike that was believed to have surged through the telephone system and sparked the flames. Wright responded by building Taliesin III.

Today the final iteration of the home and the sprawling complex that grew up around it as part of the Taliesin Fellowship—an on-site apprenticeship program Wright founded to mentor younger archi-

tects and artists—is open seasonally for guided tours. The informative tours vary considerably in length and in price, and include studio tours, tours of the home, and a full estate tour. The fascinating tours provide a glimpse into the creative life of one of the most recognized American artists in the world.

Taliesin   Photo Pedro E. Guerrero, courtesy Taliesin Preservation Inc.

WYOMING

499 Buffalo Bill Historical Center

CONTACT 307-587-4771, www.bbhc.org; 720 Sheridan Ave., Cody

PRICING	$$–$$$
BEST TIME TO VISIT	Year-round
AGE RANGE	5 and older

The remarkable Buffalo Bill Historical Center preserves the legacy of infamous American soldier, showman, and Wild West celebrity William "Buffalo Bill" Cody (1846–1917) and also memorializes the spirit of the American West within a complex of five fascinating museums. This is one of the best sites in the country to learn about western culture, and it makes a fine introduction to the region for guests coming to experience the awe-inspiring national parks (Yellowstone and Grand Tetons) nearby.

- The flagship of the complex is the **Buffalo Bill Museum**, which chronicles the legacy of Buffalo Bill Cody and includes more than 9,000 artifacts that illustrate the impact Cody and his Wild West shows had on the American perception of the region; it also tells the stories of the cowboys, farmers, and

> *This is one of the best sites in the country to learn about western culture.*

settlers who made their home in the West. Look for the resited boyhood home of Cody, as well as full-scale wagons and stagecoaches on display.
- The **Cody Firearms Museum** displays the most comprehensive collection of American firearms in the world. Look for weapons that range from a 16th-century hand cannon to modern guns. At the heart of the collection is the extensive Winchester collection.
- The **Draper Museum of Natural History** offers wide-ranging, interactive exhibits on the geology,

Buffalo Bill Historical Center
Photo Sean Campbell, courtesy Buffalo Bill Historical Center, Cody, Wyoming

wildlife, and anthropological history of the Greater Yellowstone region (of which Cody is a part). Children will enjoy the life-sized dioramas that focus on grizzly bears, bighorn sheep, moose, and the many other spectacular animal species that call the area home.
- The **Plains Indian Museum** concentrates on objects that chronicle the history of the Plains Indians, telling their cultural and traditional history as well as showcasing their modern-day lives. Artifacts on display include ceremonial clothing used by Lakota and Cheyenne people, bear-claw jewelry, tepee furnishings, peace medals, and eagle feather bonnets.
- The **Whitney Gallery of Western Art** showcases paintings and sculptures of the American West, spanning the time period of the 19th century through the present day. Among an expansive collection of art are also the reconstructed studios of American western artists Frederic Remington, Joseph Henry Sharp, and Alexander Phimister Proctor.

The center hosts the Plains Indian Museum Powwow in mid-June every year, a colorful festival that includes Native American dancers, musicians, and storytellers. Visitors are welcome to view the dance competitions and experience the vibrant cultural traditions on display. Look for the Learning Tipi, which houses an educational program that teaches guests about the traditions of a powwow.

Serene rafting Courtesy U.S. Fish and Wildlife Service

PRICE KEY
$ free–$5
$$ $6–10
$$$ $11–20
$$$$ $21+

500 Cheyenne Frontier Days Rodeo

CONTACT 307-778-7200, www.cfdrodeo.com/home; 4610 Carey Ave., Cheyenne

PRICING	Varies by seat and entertainment
BEST TIME TO VISIT	Open for 10 days, from mid- to late July
AGE RANGE	5 and older

Rodeos were conceived of as far back as the 19th century as a way for cowboys to show off their skills and compete for bragging rights, and the colorful displays of showmanship and athleticism continue to be immensely popular in the West. The Cheyenne Frontier Days Rodeo claims to put on the largest rodeo in the country, and also offers up a festival of western culture and art that is family-friendly and educational.

For 10 days in July, the Professional Rodeo Cowboys Association—sanctioned event features 1,500 contestants demonstrating skills like bareback bronco riding, bull riding, steer roping, barrel riding, and wild horse races, and the $1 million in prizes attracts the best rodeo athletes in the world. In addition, in the evening world-class entertainers perform in large-scale arenas; past years have featured country artists like Brad Paisley, Reba McEntire, and Blake Shelton. Activities during the festival include grand parades throughout town; an expansive carnival midway with rides, games, and food booths; a chuck wagon cook-off competition; behind-the-scenes tours; and free pancake breakfasts on select mornings. Native Americans host an Indian Village display, which includes American Indian dancing, storytelling, authentic food, and art exhibits. Nearby the

> The adjacent Cheyenne Frontier Days Old West Museum (on Carey Ave., in the northeast corner of Frontier Park) is open year-round and includes exhibits and educational programs that seek to preserve the legacy of the frontier days of this region.

Wild Horse Gulch exhibit includes costumed living historians demonstrating pioneer crafts, roping, open-range cooking, and blacksmithing, while actors portray western characters like Wild Bill Hickok and Wyatt Earp.

501 Fort Laramie National Historic Site

CONTACT 307-837-2221, www.nps.gov/fola; off WY 160, Fort Laramie

PRICING	$–$$
BEST TIME TO VISIT	Year-round
AGE RANGE	7 and older

Fort Laramie originated as Fort William in 1830, and served as an important trading post for the fur industry. The fort is in the upper Platte River Valley, at the confluence of the Laramie and North Platte Rivers, making it an ideal go-between location to facilitate trading among the Native American hunters who bartered animal pelts for goods like guns, ammunition, and tools. This location also landed the fort along the Oregon Trail, and thus its most important role in history was as a way station for pioneers migrating west. Federal troops garrisoned here during the era of westward migration were charged with protecting the wagon trains passing through from attacks by Native Americans. In addition, wagon trains restocked supplies at the fort before making their way to Oregon and California. In 1861, during the American Civil War, the troops at Fort Laramie were reassigned to fight the Confederate army in the East, and volunteer regiments moved into the fort to take their place for the next five years. The fort also played a role in several Indian conflicts through the years. Once the transcontinental railroad was completed in the late 19th century, the fort diminished in importance, as fewer and fewer wagon trains passed by. The fort was officially decommissioned in 1890, and the compound was opened to homesteaders for settlement.

Today the site attracts visitors, who can tour 11 restored buildings, including officers' quarters, cavalry barracks, a general store, a stone guardhouse, and a bakery. A museum on site offers displays of artifacts from the days of the Oregon Trail. The fort hosts seasonal living history demonstrations and offers periodic guided tours, including a popular moonlight tour available in summertime.

502 Grand Teton National Park

CONTACT www.nps.gov/grte; off U.S. 189/191, north of Jackson

PRICING	$
BEST TIME TO VISIT	Late spring through early fall
AGE RANGE	5 and older

There aren't enough superlatives to describe the spectacle of the Grand Tetons: The jutting peaks of the snowcapped mountain range, the sparkling lakes, and the sweeping valleys filled with wildlife combine for an unforgettable, inspiring sight—and surprisingly, this gorgeous park is often overlooked because of its proximity to the much more heavily trafficked nearby Yellowstone National Park. The park comprises more than 300,000 acres that include the 40-mile-long Teton Range and the adjacent valley of Jackson Hole. The mountain range includes the eponymous Grand Teton peak, which tops out at 13,770 feet; plus, there are a dozen additional mountains that stretch to more than 12,000 feet. There are seven beautiful morainal lakes at the base of the mountain range, and more than 100 lakes can be found in the backcountry.

The Grand Teton National Park is joined to Yellowstone (only 10 miles away) via the John D. Rockefeller Jr. Memorial Parkway, and together these three entities are managed as part of the Greater Yellowstone Ecosystem, one of the largest intact mid-latitude ecosystems in the world. This vast expanse of wilderness ensures an extended range for even large mammals, and this in turn guarantees enormous species diversity. The Grand Tetons are home to more than 1,000 species of plants, 300 species of birds (such as the fairy-tale-like trumpeter swans), and 60 species of mammals—including the spectacularly entertaining pronghorn antelope (herds of which bound and leap across the valleys), moose, black and grizzly bears, bison, and diminutive yellow-bellied marmots.

In addition to the showcase mountain range that is the jewel of the park, everywhere you look there is something startling and beautiful to see. Don't miss these attractions:

- **Jackson Hole Museum** (Glenwood St. and Deloney Ave., Jackson): This small local museum chronicles the history of the homesteaders and Native Americans who settled in this rugged terrain in the early days of the American West.

- **Jackson Lake:** Jackson Lake is the biggest body of water in the park carved by glaciers. Trails circumnavigate the lake, which is the site of water sports like sailing, windsurfing, and fishing. There are three marinas that provide boat access, and a handful of prime picnic grounds that overlook the water.

- **Jenny Lake:** Jenny Lake is a smaller, picturesque alpine lake, south of Jackson Lake, that is a longtime favorite with paddlers and hikers. Another way to view the scenery is via the Jenny Lake Scenic Drive, a 4-mile loop road that circles the Grand Teton Range.

- **Jenny Lake Visitor Center** (open June through September): This visitor center includes a relief model of the Teton Range and an exhibit that explains the geology behind the massive peaks.

Grand Teton National Park Courtesy Wyoming Tourism

In addition to jaw-dropping scenery, the park is a mecca for outdoor lovers. Grand Teton is famous as one of the few places in the world to catch fine-spotted cutthroat trout, and in general is a favorite with fly fishermen. Other outdoor activities popular in the park include backcountry camping, boating, cross-country skiing in-season, horseback riding, hiking, and mountaineering (the mountains in this range are recommended only for experienced climbers). The park is a great place for birding, and in the spring the meadows burst with wildflowers. If your kids need a little push to get out into the wilderness, check out the Nature Explorer's Backpack Program, designed for children 6 through 12. Rangers from the Laurance S. Rockefeller Preserve Interpretive Center (3 miles north of the Granite Canyon entrance) will lend pint-sized explorers a nature journal and a backpack full of activities that will keep them engaged along the trails of the Rockefeller Preserve.

A word of warning about the weather: The short spring and summer seasons in Grand Teton are glorious, with mostly mild temperatures, predominantly clear skies, and an explosion of greenery and blooms. But the long, bitter winters here are beyond extreme. The coldest temperature in the park was recorded at -63 degrees Fahrenheit. In addition, ice and snow close access roads and make hiking treacherous. Families traveling with children should limit visits to the late spring (when snow is still not uncommon) through very early fall.

nosaur skeletons—*and* they can get out into the field and actually help excavate fossils. The site is a relatively recent scientific discovery: The first bones were found in 1993, weathering out of the mountains surrounding the nearby Big Horn Basin. Since then, more than 10,000 bones have been removed from the site. The museum is located right where dino remnants from the Jurassic period have been recently unearthed. The center displays close to 30 complete skeletons, as well as dinosaur eggs, a large collection of Devonian fish, and fossils from the pre-Mesozoic. Look for one of the most recent additions, a 106-foot-long supersaur. In warmer months, guests can take a guided tour into the excavation quarry (only a few miles away), once an allosaur feeding site that still holds the remains of sauropod bones and footprints from various dinosaurs. Afterward, guests can observe as professionals clean and catalog the bones in the adjacent laboratory.

The center provides a unique opportunity to actually participate in an excavation as well. The Dig for a Day program invites kids to an all-day program, which starts with an orientation at the museum; participants are then transported to dig sites and given tools and digging instructions. The costs are a bit steep—$150 for adults and $80 for children—and any child under 18 must be accompanied by an adult; in addition, advance reservations are a must—but this is an incredible opportunity to literally dig through the past. The center also offers kids-only summer day programs for 8- to 10-year-olds, who will have the chance to excavate at an active dinosaur quarry.

503 Wyoming Dinosaur Center

CONTACT 307-864-2997, www.wyodino.org; 110 Carter Ranch Rd., Thermopolis

PRICING	$$ (dino digs and excavation tours are extra)
BEST TIME TO VISIT	Year-round
AGE RANGE	3 and older

If your child is a budding paleontologist, the Wyoming Dinosaur Center is not to be missed: Guests can view a wonderful, compact museum full of di-

504 Yellowstone National Park

CONTACT Yellowstone Visitor Services Office, 307-344-7381, www.nps.gov/yell; Yellowstone National Park (predominantly in northwest Wyoming, but park borders cross into Montana and Idaho)

PRICING	$
BEST TIME TO VISIT	Spring and fall
AGE RANGE	5 and older

Yellowstone attracts visitors from around the globe, but despite the international appeal, this is a quintessentially American experience, steeped in the history of the Wild West and epitomizing the open range and the great outdoors. This *is* the place where the deer and the antelope roam. The park (which spills over into Montana and Idaho) is an astonishing expanse of wilderness comprising 2.2 million acres, but despite the enormous size it's accessible by car, thanks to a double loop road that leads to most of the well-known sites. And what a lot of sights there are to see here: gushing geysers, colorful hot springs, bubbling mud pots, smoking fumaroles (a fancy word for steam vents), massive herds of bison roaming the seemingly endless grasslands, crystalline rivers and lakes, waterfalls, mountains, grasslands, and canyons. This national park belongs on everyone's bucket list, but it's especially grand for children. Families can spend weeks exploring this huge area and not run short on outdoor adventures, geology lessons, or wildlife-spotting opportunities.

Geyser in Yellowstone National Park © Debbie K. Hardin

Geysers, Hot Springs, and Mud Pots

Yellowstone sits on top of the largest geological hot spot in the world, and although the volcanoes are dormant, there is evidence all around that there is something very different going on just beneath the surface of the earth. The park is famous for its geysers, erupting fountains of boiling water and steam that range from the up-to-200-foot displays of Giantess, which erupts a handful of times every year, to the more modest showings of tiny, unnamed fountains that bubble up a few inches.

The most famous of these is Old Faithful, located in the Upper Geyser Basin, near the beloved Old Faithful Inn—and just off an always-crowded parking lot that brings in geyser-gazers by the thousands to watch the regular eruptions every 85 or so minutes. Old Faithful is not the largest geyser in the park, or even the prettiest—but for some reason it is the most popular. Do yourself a favor and take a hike along the raised wooden walkways that wind through this basin past dozens of other geysers and hot springs to get an even better show. First a word of warning: Watch your children carefully around all thermal features: The

water and steam can be boiling, and the crusts surrounding geysers and near hot springs are thin. Stay on designated pathways—and make sure the kiddos do, too—and *never* be tempted to touch the superheated water: It could be a deadly experience. With that said, the pathways are eminently safe for walking and are sited at distances appropriate to allow for eruptions. For the best viewing of the other thermal features in the Old Faithful area, take the path around Geyser Hill, which is just across the Firehole River. Some of the most beautiful thermal features in the park are the colorful hot springs, which range in hue from aquamarine to deep sapphire to emerald, often with streaks of vibrant yellow and orange bacterial rings around the edges.

North of this region is Midway Geyser Basin, which offers another easily walkable loop path winding around one of the largest features in the park: the 370-foot-across Grand Prismatic Spring. Children might not enjoy the sulpfurish scents here, and the 170-degree water sometimes raises the summer temperatures to unpleasant heights—but even so, this is not to be missed: It looks, feels, and *smells* like another world, and kids cannot help but wonder about the geological forces at work that have created such a place.

Nearby is the Fountain Paint Pot region, accessible from the Firehole Lake Drive that loops off the main park road. A short trail from the parking area leads to a collection of small bubbling mud pots that blurp and gurgle in ways that are sure to make children giggle. What is most astonishing is the range of colors of mud—from white and gray to yellow and orange to reddish brown.

Near the northern border of the park, Mammoth Hot Springs is an ever-changing collection of hot springs in the form of stepped terraces created when the calcium-carbonate-rich hot water trickles through sedimentary limestone, resulting in delicate pools that change colors as the water flow shifts, from chalky gray terraces that no longer hold water to pearly white structures that are filled with light blue pools.

Animal Sightings

A favorite activity in Yellowstone is looking for animals, which are delightfully abundant in this park. To maximize your chance of seeing wildlife, get up early in the morning (at dawn). Come equipped with binoculars or cameras with telephoto lenses. If your family doesn't do mornings, you are still very likely to see a good share of wildlife along trails and even driving along the loop roads: Just watch for cars stopped inexplicably in the middle of the road. This usually means there is a wild mammal nearby.

What can you expect to see? Wild bison (what are commonly, but incorrectly, referred to as buffalo), elk, mule deer, and pronghorn antelope are plentiful and not particularly shy of people. Also abundant but harder to spot are grizzly and black bears, wolves, moose, and bighorn sheep. The park is home to mountain lions, but it is extremely unlikely you'll see one. Favorites with children are the diminutive and entertaining yellow-bellied marmots, whose underground dens can be found throughout the region. A trip to

Hayden Valley almost guarantees wildlife sightings: This grassland area is a special favorite with huge herds of bison (which often cause massive traffic jams when they cross the park roads) and elk. Lamar Valley is equally as scenic, and although it takes patience to spot them, this is a prime spot to look for grizzly and black bears. Madison River in the east is home to a large population of snow-white trumpeter swans.

Other Extraordinary Viewpoints

A surprise to many visitors, the Grand Canyon of the Yellowstone is one of the most picturesque sites in the park. The 20-mile canyon has been carved through the millennia out of brightly colored cliffs of yellow, orange, white, and pink. The thunderous Lower Falls that cuts through the canyon and plummet more than 300 feet is one of the loveliest waterfalls in the United States and is best viewed from the aptly named Inspiration Point.

Yellowstone Lake is often overlooked in this park full of other superlative sites: Don't miss it. With more than 100 miles of shoreline, dotted in spots by thermal features that make the otherwise frigid waters steam, this is a lovely place for a picnic. In warmer months the water is dangerous for swimming (because of potential microbes that live in the waters and cold temperatures year-round) and boating (because of potentially tumultuous conditions that can turn for the worse very quickly). Most of the year it is covered over in ice.

The Yellowstone River, which threads through the Yellowstone Lake in the south and into the Grand Canyon of Yellowstone in the north, is also worthy of note. Check out the pretty Fishing Bridge just north of the lake (although, oddly, fishing is not allowed here) and lovely Tower Fall, north of the canyon. There are dozens of idyllic picnic spots along the river, and trails along the way offer premium vistas of the tallest peaks in the southeastern corner of the park.

Sunrise over Tidal Basin © Debbie K. Hardin

WASHINGTON, DC

505 Cherry Blossom Festival

CONTACT www.nationalcherryblossomfestival.org; held throughout Washington, DC

PRICING	$
BEST TIME TO VISIT	End of March, beginning of April
AGE RANGE	7 and older

The District of Columbia is known as the City of Trees, and every spring the city goes particularly wild over one flowering variety: the ethereal cherry blossom. In 1912 Mayor Yukio Ozaki of Tokyo donated more than 3,000 cherry blossom trees to the city of Washington, to celebrate a growing friendship between Japan and the United States. First Lady Helen Taft and Viscountess Chinda, the wife of the Japanese ambassador stationed in Washington, planted the first of these trees along the Tidal Basin in West Potomac Park, now site of the Jefferson Memorial and the Franklin D. Roosevelt Memorial. The much-beloved trees blossom into clouds of pale pink in very early spring, and to celebrate the city puts on a two-week party every year in late March/early April to coincide with the peak blossom period. Highlights of the National Cherry Blossom Festival include a colorful, eclectic parade down Constitution Avenue that features lively taiko drumming by corps from Japan and the United States; delicately decorated floats adorned with Cherry Blossom princesses; and oversized balloon characters. Visitors can purchase grandstand seats and watch the parade from bleachers along the route or just show up early and watch from the sidewalk. Another standout of the festival is the Sakura Matsuri, a one-day exhibition of Japanese culture that includes multiple live performance venues, karate demonstrations, a Japanese beer garden, traditional Japanese arts like ikebana (flower arrangement), and *kamishibai* (Japanese folktales) for children.

Cherry blossoms along the Tidal Basin   © Debbie K. Hardin

506 Chesapeake and Ohio Canal

CONTACT 202-653-5190, www.nps.gov/choh, 1057 Thomas Jefferson St., Washington, DC, NW; and 301-767-3714, 11710 MacArthur Blvd., Potomac, MD

PRICING	$–$$
BEST TIME TO VISIT	Late spring through early fall
AGE RANGE	3 and older

The Chesapeake and Ohio Canal, a nearly 185-mile waterway that runs parallel to the Potomac River from Cumberland, Maryland, to Washington, DC, operated from 1831 to 1924, and it was once essential to moving products and raw materials through the DC area. The canal pathway changes elevation by about 600 feet, and to accommodate the geography the builders engineered 70-some canal locks that raise and lower the water level.

Today the C&O Canal is a National Historic Park, and it runs through some of the most beautiful scenery in the DC area, including an extremely picturesque portion of Georgetown, a historic residential neighborhood in the west end of the city. Visitors to the park enjoy hiking, biking, and jogging along the towpath that runs beside the canal; it's even possible

Chesapeake and Ohio Canal, Georgetown   © Debbie K. Hardin

National Archives   © Debbie K. Hardin

to ride horses here through most portions of the park.

Kids will not want to miss the chance to get out on the canal and really experience life as it might have been in the 19th century. The National Park Service operates hour-long mule-drawn canal boat rides and interpretive ranger programs, starting in both Georgetown and Potomac, Maryland. The reproduction vessels are hosted by period-dressed park rangers, who are well versed in the history of the canal. As you pass through several of the historic lift locks, the lively guides explain what life was like back in the 1800s. If you're lucky, you'll be treated to period tunes performed by a musically inclined ranger. Don't forget to bring along some fruit or veggies to feed the mules! Additional special historical walks can also be arranged out of the C&O Visitor Center during the summer, delving into the neighborhood's architecture and Civil War history.

507 Constitution and Declaration of Independence in the National Archives

CONTACT 866-272-6272, www.archives.gov; 700 Pennsylvania Ave., NW

PRICING	$
BEST TIME TO VISIT	Year-round (but avoid spring break crowds)
AGE RANGE	10 and older

The National Archives is a repository of documents that includes the most important papers in the history of the United States: Inside the Rotunda, guests can view the Constitution, the Bill of Rights, and the Declaration of Independence. Although the three documents are heavily guarded and kept within immense glass cases, it is still possible to get a good look at these historic papers—especially if the Rotunda isn't too busy and you can take your time. The ornate handwriting is faded and hard to read, but kids will get a kick out of picking out the oversized signature of John Hancock.

Other exhibits include the "Public Vaults" exhibit, which displays original Indian treaties, formerly classified audio recordings of presidents, and rare film footage from the earliest days of movies. Most of these exhibits are multimedia presentations, and many are interactive. In addition to the artifacts on display, the Archives catalogs and stores the country's most extensive collection of census figures, federal documents, birth and death records, and military service records, which are available to any adult wishing to do genealogical research.

Spring crowds are oppressive, especially in March and April when thousands of school groups descend

To avoid a long line to get inside the National Archives (most of which is outside and exposed to the elements), secure tickets by emailing visitorservices@nara.gov at least six weeks in advance to reserve space in a self-guided tour group, or call 202-357-5450 for a spot on a guided tour.

PRICE KEY
$ free–$5
$$ $6–10
$$$ $11–20
$$$$ $21+

on the city—and almost all of them make a stop at the National Archives. If you can, come instead in what Archives officials claim are the best months to visit: between June and February (not counting the days immediately surrounding the Fourth of July). Whenever you visit, it's best to leave purses and bags at home to make the thorough security check quicker; no backpacks are allowed.

508 Ford's Theatre and Lincoln Museum

CONTACT 202-347-4833, www.fordstheatre.org; 511 10th St., NW

PRICING	$
BEST TIME TO VISIT	Year-round (although the theater is sometimes closed for rehearsals)
AGE RANGE	12 and older

The U.S. Civil War was a bloody, destructive campaign that exacted an enormous toll. In some 10,000 battles approximately a million Americans were killed,

Ford's Theatre © Debbie K. Hardin

nearly two-thirds of whom died from disease or infection. The lengthy war ended on April 9, 1865, when General Robert E. Lee surrendered to General Ulysses S. Grant in Appomattox, Virginia, and thereafter the Confederacy collapsed. Less than a week after Lee's surrender, on April 14, 1865, President Abraham Lincoln was shot and killed by John Wilkes Booth at Ford's Theatre, just a few blocks from the White House, while the president was attending a play with his wife. Booth, a famous actor of the time, believed himself to be aiding the Confederacy, and after shooting Lincoln he jumped on the stage and cried out before the horrified witnesses, "*Sic simper tyrannis*" (meaning "thus always to tyrants").

After being fatally wounded, the dying president was carried across the street to the Petersen House, where he perished the next morning. After Lincoln's death, Ford's Theatre was closed for more than 100 years. As a tribute to Lincoln's love of the theater, however, the site was reopened in the late 1960s. (Today the theater is still the site of contemporary performances, and tours are thus sometimes closed temporarily to the public because of rehearsals.) Today visitors can view the theater, now designated a National Historic Site, including Lincoln's presidential box, and head across the street to visit the bedroom where he died, which is furnished with period pieces and the bloodstained pillow that Lincoln used. This experience is macabre and too intense for young children and older kids who are particularly sensitive, but it is a memorable outing that will help older children understand the passion behind those who fought and died in the Civil War.

509 Fourth of July on the National Mall

CONTACT 202-789-7000; held on the National Mall, NW; for the Folk Life Festival, www.festival.si.edu/explore_festival/year.aspx

PRICING	$
BEST TIME TO VISIT	July 4
AGE RANGE	7 and older

Fireworks over the National Mall

Carol M. Highsmith's America, courtesy Library of Congress, Prints and Photographs Division

There is probably no better place in the country for a spectacular Independence Day celebration than the National Mall in Washington, DC. The day's festivities include the National Independence Day parade down Constitution Avenue; a reading of the Declaration of Independence at the National Archives; and a truly fabulous free evening concert on the west steps of the Capitol Building featuring the National Symphony Orchestra and internationally recognized guest performers. Throughout the day there are concerts on the open-air stage just east of the base of the Washington Monument as well. The festivities overlap with the outdoor Smithsonian Folk Life Festival held annually from late June through mid-July; the expansive festival is located on the Mall between the Smithsonian Museums, and every year celebrates the culture and food of one country and one U.S. state. The cherry on top, of course, is that the city puts on one of the biggest July 4 fireworks displays in the nation, which is best viewed from the 2-mile stretch of the Mall from the Lincoln Memorial to the Capitol Building. The light show begins when the sun sets (usually around 9), and the colorful explosions are timed to coincide with patriotic music provided by the NSO. The Mall is *really*

For security reasons, the National Mall is cordoned off during big events such as the July 4 celebrations, and guests must pass through security checkpoints. Be sure to arrive early, as these checks can take hours when it is truly crowded.

crowded, so this isn't an adventure to be enjoyed by anyone with claustrophobia or aversion to huge numbers of people—and it is absolutely imperative to take public transportation to the Mall, because there is no parking to be had—but celebrating the nation's Independence Day with the Washington Monument and the White House in the background is an experience your family won't soon forget.

510 Franklin D. Roosevelt Memorial

CONTACT 202-426-6841, www.nps.gov/frde/index.htm; off the Tidal Basin, Washington, DC

PRICING	$
BEST TIME TO VISIT	Year-round
AGE RANGE	All ages

Franklin D. Roosevelt (1882–1945) was the 32nd president of the United States, and the only president to have been elected to more than two terms. He presided over the country during the Great Depression, and worked with Winston Churchill to lead the Allied Forces against Germany and Japan during World War II. He is best remembered for his New Deal—a panoply of government programs committed to creating economic reform and a social safety net. A surviving program is Social Security for aged citizens. What many Americans didn't know about Roosevelt

Franklin D. Roosevelt Memorial   © Debbie K. Hardin

at the time of his administration is that he was disabled by a bout with polio; he was generally photographed sitting down, so most Americans were unaware the president could not walk freely.

Just off the Tidal Basin, the Franklin Delano Roosevelt Memorial dedicated to the president's memory is an outdoor garden that stretches across 7.5 acres, with cherry blossom trees, extensive water features (including a roaring waterfall made from granite blocks), and statuary displayed in four outdoor "rooms." Each room represents one of FDR's terms in office and is demarcated by granite walls, many of which are engraved with quotations from the eloquent president. In addition to a large statue of a seated FDR with his dog, Fala (his nose worn shiny by kids who like to rub it), guests will also encounter a sculpture grouping depicting a bread line from the Great Depression; a man hunkered close to an old-fashioned radio, presumably listening to a "fireside chat"; and a statue of the president's wife, Eleanor Roosevelt (the first such memorial to a First Lady). Shortly after the memorial was complete, outcry by citizen groups who were unhappy that Roosevelt's disability was not represented anywhere in the memorial prompted then president Bill Clinton and the Congress to secure funding to add an additional sculpture that shows the former president in a wheelchair. Visitors can find this small addition at the front of the memorial.

Frederick Douglass House
Carol M. Highsmith's America, courtesy Library of Congress, Prints and Photographs Division

race, ethnicity, or gender. He was a noted orator and writer; he also served as U.S. marshal for the District of Columbia, the U.S. minister to Haiti, and the chargé d'affaires to the Dominican Republic.

At the end of the Civil War, Douglass moved to Washington, DC, buying his home at Cedar Hill, where he lived until his death. This National Historic Site located at the former home of the "Sage of Anacostia," as he was known, preserves the 1893–95 appearance of his home. Guests can tour the cozy parlor, guest bedrooms, a small kitchen, and the private bedrooms of the Douglass family. Check out the large collection of books in Douglass's library. Reservations are recommended.

511 Frederick Douglass National Historic Site

CONTACT 202-426-5961, www.nps.gov/frdo; 1411 W St., SE

PRICING	$
BEST TIME TO VISIT	Year-round
AGE RANGE	7 and older

Abolitionist and statesman Frederick Douglass (c. 1818–95) was arguably the most influential African American in the 19th century. He was born into slavery but escaped to the North and to freedom as a young man. Thereafter he worked to free others and further equality among all people, regardless of

512 International Spy Museum

CONTACT 202-393-7798, www.spymuseum.org; 800 F St., NW

PRICING	$$$; OperationSpy requires a separate ticket
BEST TIME TO VISIT	Year-round
AGE RANGE	5 and older

Visitors to the DC area might know that nearby Langley, Virginia, is home to the Central Intelligence Agency (CIA)—but don't expect to be issued an invitation to the headquarters. The CIA grounds, not surprisingly, are strictly off limits. But kids wanting to

International Spy Museum   © Debbie K. Hardin

which combined give guests the chance to think and act like an agent in the field. Younger children can participate in overnight adventures in which they have similar (but less intense) hands-on fun with the exhibits.

513 Jefferson Memorial

CONTACT	202-426-6841, www.nps.gov/thje; East Basin Dr., SW
PRICING	$
BEST TIME TO VISIT	Cherry blossom season (late March through early April)
AGE RANGE	All ages

learn more about espionage have only to look to the International Spy Museum in downtown DC. Permanent exhibits at the museum include the largest collection of international spy-related artifacts on public display—and it's just good fun to visit. Start by participating in an interactive exhibit that begins when you assume an identity: Memorize your new name and background, and then check in at video screens along the way to make sure you've kept your cover. At each stop you'll receive additional details of your mission, which gets increasingly complicated. Throughout you'll watch archival films that include OSS and C-130 training films from World War II; interviews with former intelligence agents who explain their often-complex motivations; cartoon shorts from WWII that encourage citizens to pay their "taxes to beat the Axis"; and a training video on how to pick a lock. Check out gadgets that would make Maxwell Smart drool, like a compass hidden in a button; a Bulgarian umbrella that can fire a poison-filled pellet; a KGB-issue shoe with a heel transmitter; a cigarette pistol; and eyeglasses that conceal a cyanide pill. Kids will not want to miss the chance to crawl through overhead ductwork to eavesdrop on conversations.

For kids 12 and older, check out Operation Spy, an interactive hour-long adventure in which participants search for a hypothetical missing nuclear device. The activity features live action, video, and special effects,

Located directly on the cherry-tree-studded Tidal Basin, the Jefferson Memorial is a colonnaded white-marble rotunda that was built to honor the nation's third president, Thomas Jefferson. The memorial was modeled after the Pantheon in Rome, and the neoclassical structure also mimics the architecture of Monticello (Jefferson's home in Charlottesville, Virginia) as well as the University of Virginia—both of which Jefferson designed himself. Original memorial architect John Russell Pope began the exterior of the memorial, but died before he was able to complete it; Daniel P. Higgins and Otto R. Eggers took over in 1937. Franklin Roosevelt laid the cornerstone in 1939 and ordered that all the trees between the memorial and

Jefferson Memorial   © Debbie K. Hardin

☞ Although parking is always tight anywhere near the National Mall, one of the lesser-known lots lies behind the Jefferson Memorial on Ohio Drive. If you come early or late in the day, you're more likely to find a spot here than anywhere else within easy walking distance of a DC memorial.

Kennedy bust, inside John F. Kennedy Center for the Performing Arts   © Debbie K. Hardin

the White House be cut down so that the view between the two was unobstructed—FDR was a great admirer of Jefferson, and he wanted to be able to look out his window and see the memorial every day. (If you're ever lucky enough to visit the White House, you'll see that this view is preserved to this day.) In 1941 artist Rudolph Evans was commissioned to create the 19-foot bronze statue of Jefferson that now resides inside the rotunda; the statue gazes directly toward the White House. Five quotations taken from Jefferson's writings are engraved on the walls of the memorial. Rangers present 30-minute programs throughout the day, but, if possible, visit at night when the exterior is flooded with light and the interior glows. Or better still, visit in early spring to see the incredible snowy show from the cherry blossom trees that ring the adjacent Tidal Basin. For a real treat, reserve a paddle boat (202-479-2426, www.tidalbasinpaddleboats.com) and take a spin around the small basin that fronts the memorial.

514 John F. Kennedy Center for the Performing Arts

🎸

CONTACT 202-467-4600, www.kennedy-center.org; 2700 F St., NW

PRICING	$ for tours; prices for performances vary
BEST TIME TO VISIT	Year-round
AGE RANGE	7 and older

The expansive John F. Kennedy Center on the banks of the Potomac River is the site of world-class performances by renowned artists, and it is a monument to

America's commitment to the performing arts. Although Dwight Eisenhower was the president to sign bipartisan legislation to fund and create this national cultural center back in 1958, the stunning theater complex—opened in 1971—was ultimately named after President John F. Kennedy to honor his lifelong commitment both to the arts and, during his presidency, to funding the center. The Kennedy Center is the premier performance venue in Washington, DC, and comprises several theaters under one roof, including the magnificent Concert Hall where the National Symphony Orchestra performs; the Opera House, home of the very popular Washington National Opera company as well as host to international ballet companies; the Eisenhower Theater, where dramatic productions are staged; the charming Terrace Theater, home of chamber music and smaller productions; and the Theater Lab, which offers new plays and experimental works. Look for special matinee performances of original plays aimed at youngsters, which are generally significantly discounted.

Prepurchase tickets for plays, ballets, or musical theater, or line up in late afternoon for the chance to enjoy a performance at no cost: As part of an encompassing community outreach program, the Kennedy Center presents free one-hour concerts at 6 every evening on the Millennium Stage, ranging from live jazz to string quartets to full-blown orchestral concerts. (Note: This is an extremely popular series, so it is imperative you arrive at least an hour before the performance to wait on line. Bring books or travel

Underground parking at the Kennedy Center is extensive, but it'll cost you more than $20 (although there is free one-hour parking on Level B to allow guests to purchase tickets at the box office or to visit the gift shop—be sure to get your ticket validated at the time of purchase). Instead consider taking the Metro subway system; the center runs a free shuttle bus every 15 minutes between 9:30 AM and midnight from the Foggy Bottom Metro station to the Kennedy Center.

games for the kids and wear comfy shoes: This is likely to be the best free concert you will ever experience, so it will be well worth the wait.) Free tours of the facility are offered every day of the week.

515 Korean War Veterans Memorial

CONTACT 202-426-6841, www.nps.gov/kwvm; Independence Ave., SW

PRICING	$
BEST TIME TO VISIT	Year-round
AGE RANGE	All ages

One of the most accessible memorials on the Mall, the Korean War Veterans Memorial commemorates the sacrifice and service of more than 1.5 million Americans who participated in the three-year Korean War, a civil war between North Korea and South Korea that was aided by international forces (nearly 90 percent

Korean War Veterans Memorial   © Debbie K. Hardin

of which were American soldiers). The memorial includes the serene "Pool of Remembrance" surrounded by a thick grove of trees and the "Field of Service," which depicts eerily life-like statues patrolling with heavy packs and foul-weather gear. Nearby is a 164-foot granite wall with etched depictions of individuals who served in the war. There is also a listing of the 22 nations that contributed to the United Nations's campaign in Korea.

516 Library of Congress

CONTACT 202-707-8000, www.loc.gov; 10 1st St., SE

PRICING	$
BEST TIME TO VISIT	Year-round
AGE RANGE	10 and older

If your children love to read, this is the place for your family! Founded in 1800, the Library of Congress was conceived as a repository of books and papers for use by members of Congress. The library was housed within the Capitol itself until 1814, when the collection of 3,000 volumes was destroyed when British soldiers tried to burn down the city during the War of 1812. A few months after the fire, Thomas Jefferson offered his extensive personal library for sale to replenish the collection. The U.S. government bought 6,487 volumes from Jefferson for $23,950. Sadly, another fire destroyed nearly two-thirds of these books in the mid-19th century. It didn't take long, however, for the library to build back its collection—and then some.

Today the Library of Congress is the largest library in the world, with more than 130 million items in its permanent collection, including such priceless treasures as one of three surviving Gutenberg Bibles and what is said to be the smallest book in the world—*Old King Cole*, which measures one twenty-fifth of an inch square (you'll need a needle to turn its pages). There are more than 530 miles of bookshelves here; in addition the library collects maps, recordings, photographs, letters, and manuscripts, including presidential papers dating back to George Washington; the earliest daguerreotype of the U.S. Capitol;

Interior of Jefferson Building, Library of Congress
© Debbie K. Hardin

and the first surviving film registered for copyright (*Fred Ott's Sneeze*, 1894). Each day the library adds another 10,000 or so new items to its collection; these vast resources remain available to members of Congress as well as to the American public.

The library occupies three buildings on Capitol Hill: The magnificent Thomas Jefferson Building, which dates to 1897; the John Adams Building (1939); and the James Madison Memorial Building (1981). The Jefferson Building—with a must-see interior—is an extraordinary example of Italian Renaissance—style architecture; inside, guests will find miles of intricate marble floor mosaics, allegorical paintings on the ceilings that are worthy of a Roman cathedral, more than 100 murals, a soaring staircase that seems too fine to be housed in a public building, and ornate plasterwork and embellishments reminiscent of a European castle. Visitors will also find numerous exhibits open to the public, including *American Treasures of the Library of Congress*, which offers a rotating display of some of the rarest items in the library's collection, including the Bible on which Abraham Lincoln took the oath of office and one of Thomas Jefferson's rough drafts of the Declaration of Independence.

Beneath the massive dome in the Jefferson Building is the stunning Reading Room, which is accessible to visitors on 45-minute docent-led tours, offered regularly throughout the day. (Pick up a ticket at the information desk at the front entrance for same-day tours.) In addition, individuals 16 and older wishing to do research in the Reading Room may do so after first securing a reader identification card; cards are free and can be obtained in Room LM 140 on the first floor

of the Madison Building, near the Independence Avenue entrance. Present a valid driver's license, passport, or state-issued ID and complete a computerized self-registration process in person; the library will verify the information, take an ID photo, and issue a photo card on the spot.

The library's Coolidge Auditorium is the site of numerous arts performances throughout the year, including live music and dance. Tickets to these performances are free, but seats must be secured in advance through Ticketmaster (1-800-551-SEAT). The tiny Mary Pickford Theater, housed in the Madison Building, has frequent free screenings of early films and TV programs as well.

517 Lincoln Memorial

CONTACT 202-426-6841, www.nps.gov/linc; westernmost end of the Mall, between Constitution and Independence Aves.

PRICING	$
BEST TIME TO VISIT	Spring through fall
AGE RANGE	All ages

One of the most beloved monuments in DC is the Lincoln Memorial, which honors America's 16th president, Abraham Lincoln. Architect Henry Bacon designed the memorial to the "Great Emancipator" to

Lincoln Memorial
© Debbie K. Hardin

resemble a Greek temple, with 36 columns to reflect the 36 states of the Union at the time of Lincoln's death. Dominating the interior space is a commanding 19-foot white marble statue of a seated Lincoln designed by Daniel Chester French. The memorial, which was completed in 1922, also features murals by artist Jules Guerin, and the interior walls are engraved with moving passages from the Gettysburg Address and Lincoln's second Inaugural Address. To the east of the monument is the 2,000-foot-long Reflecting Pool that points to the World War II Memorial and the Washington Monument (and Capitol) beyond. In August 1963, the Lincoln Memorial was the site of Martin Luther King Jr.'s "I Have a Dream" speech and the largest protest demonstration in U.S. history (250,000 Americans gathered to lobby for passage of sweeping civil rights measures by Congress); an inscription on the 18th step down from the top of the memorial was added later to mark the exact spot where King delivered this historic address. If you have the chance, save the Lincoln Memorial for a nighttime tour; the view from the top of the steps looking over the reflecting pool is one of the most iconic in the city, and the huge sculpture of Lincoln is even more majestic when it is lighted up in the evening.

Martin Luther King Jr. Memorial   Courtesy National Park Service

Have a Dream," which was delivered in the summer of 1963 on the steps of the Lincoln Memorial during the largest political demonstration in American history. Dr. King was assassinated in Memphis, Tennessee. He has since been awarded posthumously the Congressional Gold Medal and the Presidential Medal of Freedom. The Martin Luther King Jr. Memorial is the newest large-scale memorial along the National Mall, and it is the first to honor not a president or a military leader but a citizen activist.

518 Martin Luther King Jr. Memorial

CONTACT www.nps.gov/mlkm/index.htm; 1964 Independence Ave., SW

PRICING	$
BEST TIME TO VISIT	Spring through fall
AGE RANGE	All ages

The Reverend Dr. Martin Luther King Jr. (1929–68) was the voice of the American civil rights movement in the 1960s, advocating for nonviolent protests as a way to pressure policy makers to further the rights of African Americans, and King remains an icon in American history. Although his safety was often in danger during his many appearances and speeches rallying the cause of civil rights, he persevered. He is possibly best remembered for his moving speech "I

519 Mary McLeod Bethune Council House

CONTACT 202-673-2402, www.nps.gov/mamc; 1318 Vermont Ave., NW

PRICING	$
BEST TIME TO VISIT	Year-round
AGE RANGE	7 and older

Mary McLeod Bethune (1875–1955) was an African American civil rights leader, teacher, and founder of the Bethune-Cookman University. Bethune had intended to become a missionary in Africa, but instead worked tirelessly to further education for African Americans in the United States. She was active in politics and worked in President Franklin D. Roosevelt's reelection campaign in 1932. Bethune became a member of Roosevelt's "Black Cabinet," as an adviser

Mary McLeod Bethune Council House
Carol M. Highsmith's America, courtesy Library of Congress, Prints and Photographs Division

on African American concerns and as an ambassador to African American communities, whom Roosevelt hoped would vote for the Democratic party. Bethune founded the National Council of Negro Women to advance the opportunities available to black women in the United States. The Mary McLeod Bethune Council Home preserves the lovely three-story Victorian townhouse where Bethune lived and worked. Visitors can tour the home, which remains largely unchanged, and view an orientation film.

520 National Air and Space Museum

CONTACT 202-633-1000, www.nasm.si.edu; Independence Ave. and 7th St., SW

PRICING	$
BEST TIME TO VISIT	Year-round (although less crowded when school is in session)
AGE RANGE	5 and older

Since opening in 1976, the National Air and Space Museum has been among the most visited museums in the world—and the ubiquitous crowds show no signs of shrinking. The museum boasts the world's largest collection of historic air- and spacecraft, with more than 50,000 artifacts that encompass the earliest attempts at flight through the current space age. Favorites include the *Spirit of St. Louis*, the plane in which Charles Lindbergh made the first nonstop solo transatlantic flight; the *Apollo 11* command module *Columbia*, which brought home the astronauts from the first moon landing; and *SpaceShipOne*, the first privately piloted ship to enter outer space. Don't miss the touchable moon rock displayed just beyond the security checkpoint near the front door. To orient yourself when exploring this huge space, remember that airplanes and aviation are on the west end of the building, and rockets and spacecraft are on the east. Near the entrance is an IMAX theater, which features a rotating collection of movies about flight and space. Tickets are required for IMAX movies, as well as for the Albert Einstein Planetarium upstairs, which also shows films about space on a 70-foot dome and offers lectures on the night sky as well as multimedia presentations on astronomy. To ensure you secure tickets to the movie and time you want, head to the box office as soon as you arrive in the museum. By midmorning on busy days, shows sell out.

Space wing, National Air and Space Museum
© Debbie K. Hardin

521 National Gallery of Art

🎸

CONTACT 202-730-4215, www.nga.gov; 4th St. and Constitution Ave., NW

PRICING	$
BEST TIME TO VISIT	Year-round
AGE RANGE	7 and older

The National Gallery of Art is one of the finest art museums in the world and houses more than 100,000 paintings, sculptures, and mixed-media pieces dating from the Middle Ages to the present. The museum is divided into two distinct wings: the original West Wing and the newer East Wing. The East Wing, designed by I. M. Pei, is dedicated to modern and contemporary art, and is accessed via a separate entrance east of the original building or through an underground passageway between the buildings, which passes beneath Pei's signature glass pyramids.

Note that many visitors to DC mistake the National Gallery as part of the Smithsonian Institution: It is not, but it is readily accessible to Smithsonian visitors because it is located along the National Mall. It can be challenging to bring children to any art museum—especially young children—but there are treasures to behold here for all ages. Try making the experience as interactive as possible to keep kids engaged: Let them bring along their own sketchbooks, and encourage them to copy the pieces they like most or ask them to find artwork depicting children (they will find a lot here, especially in the impressionist galleries in the West Wing). Pick out a few favorites to enjoy, and don't overdo the time you spend in the museum. And if the kids get squirrelly before you're ready to call it a day, make a quick trip to the fabulous underground cafeteria for a pick-me-up cookie or ice cream.

Better yet, take the children outside to enjoy more of the collection and run off some energy in the process: The National Gallery of Art Sculpture Garden is located across from the West Wing on 7th Street, and encompasses two city blocks displaying close to 20 large-scale sculptures set amid a mature garden.

Rodin group, National Gallery Outdoor Sculpture Garden   © Debbie K. Hardin

Kid-friendly pieces include a lyrical, oversized typewriter eraser by Claes Oldenburg and Coosje van Bruggen; a leaning tower of blue chairs by Lucas Samaras; and a cartoonesque playhouse by Roy Lichtenstein that seems to defy perspective. A beautiful central fountain is transformed into an ice-skating rink from mid-November through mid-March.

522 National Holocaust Memorial Museum

🔔

CONTACT 202-488-0400, www.ushmm.org; 100 Raoul Wallenberg Place, SW

PRICING	$; timed tickets are required March through August
BEST TIME TO VISIT	Year-round
AGE RANGE	13 and older

This is arguably the most important museum in Washington, DC, and undeniably the most difficult to visit. The National Holocaust Memorial Museum was founded to document, interpret, and study Holocaust history, and serves as a testament to the millions of people who were killed during the most far-reaching genocide of the modern era. The exhibits encourage visitors to reflect on this unfathomable atrocity as well as on the legacy of both Holocaust victims and survivors.

In addition to scores of photographs depicting

National Holocaust Memorial Museum   © Debbie K. Hardin

victims, TV screens scattered throughout the exhibit space show newsreels of the day, and there are moving collections of everyday items that were lost to those shipped to the concentration camps—photographs, personal letters, and mementos, including a particularly disturbing pit full of tens of thousands of shoes that were left behind. Visitors will walk through a freight car that was actually used to transport thousands of victims to the concentration camps; pass by bunks taken from Auschwitz II—Birkenau; and view a horrifying diorama of a gas chamber.

Downstairs is the "Hall of Remembrance" where an eternal flame burns in memory of the more than six million people who were murdered during the Holocaust. Guests may also light candles. In addition, the "Wall of Remembrance" is a tribute to the 1.5 million children killed during the Holocaust. American schoolchildren designed and painted the more than 3,000 ceramic tiles that make up the heartbreaking memorial.

When most people think of Washington, DC, they imagine the National Mall: The nearly 2 miles of acreage running from the Lincoln Monument east to the U.S. Capitol Building, near the White House and the Jefferson Memorial—are home to a wealth of historical and cultural treasures, and Americans grow up seeing the iconic landmarks on TV and in films.

A note of caution: Newcomers are often fooled by the deceptive scale of the National Mall. The towering monuments, federal buildings, and enormous Smithsonian museums make the distances between them seem closer than they actually are. It is certainly possible to walk from one end of the Mall to the other in one visit, with stops at major points along the way, but it makes for a long, tiring day—and can make for a rushed experience, especially if you try to hit the museums, too. A more practical way to navigate is to divide the Mall into manageable chunks. Explore, say, the west end of the Mall one day: Take in the Tidal Basin and the Roosevelt, MLK, Lincoln, Jefferson, Korean War, and Vietnam Memorials. Then, on a second day, tackle the World War II Memorial, the Washington Monument, and one or two of the Smithsonian museums. On yet another day, focus on the east end, exploring the U.S. Capitol, the Library of Congress, the U.S. Supreme Court Building, and a few more museums. Of course, if your time is limited, by all means see as much as you can: Get an early start, wear comfortable shoes, and plan a meal break. The benches lining the green space between the museums are good spots for an impromptu picnic, and food carts along the mall and food trucks parked on adjacent streets offer refreshments. (Look for carts selling yummy hot chestnuts in winter!)

523 National Mall

CONTACT www.nps.gov/nacc/index.htm; between the Lincoln Memorial in the west and the U.S. Capitol Building in the east, between Madison and Jefferson Drs.

PRICING	$
BEST TIME TO VISIT	Spring through fall
AGE RANGE	All ages

National Mall   Courtesy National Park Service

524 National Museum of African Art

CONTACT 202-633-1000, http://africa.si.edu; 950 Independence Ave., SW

PRICING	$
BEST TIME TO VISIT	Year-round
AGE RANGE	7 and older

Accessed from the serene Enid A. Haupt Garden, just behind the Smithsonian Castle, the subterranean National Museum of African Art celebrates the rich cultural and artistic heritage of Africans and African Americans. The permanent collection includes beautiful examples of intricately carved wood, ivory, and stone; fine historic masks from nations throughout the African continent; and astonishing textiles and pottery. The extraordinarily well-designed display space is bright and cheerful, and artifacts are often displayed in freestanding glass cases, which makes it possible to wander among the art pieces in a way that traditional against-the-wall displays don't allow. This is not a heavily trafficked museum, and thus it is a nice place to escape the crowds during busy seasons. The museum sponsors regular family activities such as storytelling, musical performances, and hands-on art workshops.

National Museum of African Art   Courtesy Smithsonian Institution

525 National Museum of American History

CONTACT 202-633-1000, www.americanhistory.si.edu; 14th St. and Constitution Ave., NW

PRICING	$
BEST TIME TO VISIT	Year-round
AGE RANGE	7 and older

If you can see only one Smithsonian museum while visiting DC with your children, make this the one: The exhibitions of the National Museum of American History focus on the history and culture of the United States, from the Revolutionary War to the present day. Visitors will find otherwise mundane items that hold special significance because of their historical, political, or cultural importance—objects like Thomas Edison's lightbulb, Abraham Lincoln's top hat, Jacqueline Kennedy's inaugural gown, and Dorothy's slippers from *The Wizard of Oz*. On entering the new grand atrium space (added in a recent, extensive renovation), you'll immediately notice the Star-Spangled Banner, the enormous flag that inspired Francis Scott Key to write the national anthem. The three-million-plus-artifact collection is mind boggling, and visitors of all ages and interests are sure to find something appealing. The on-site Historic Theater offers living history interpretations and performances throughout the year. And don't miss the Flag Folding demonstration, where guests learn to fold a full-sized replica of the 30-by-42-foot Star-Spangled Banner (held throughout the summer months).

National Museum of American History   Courtesy Smithsonian Institution

526 National Museum of the American Indian

CONTACT 202-633-1000, www.nmai.si.edu; 4th St. and Independence Ave., SW

PRICING	$
BEST TIME TO VISIT	Year-round
AGE RANGE	7 and older

The architecture of the National Museum of the American Indian, the newest museum on the National Mall (opened in 2004), stands apart from that of its older siblings. The rough limestone exterior the color of sand curves organically, seemingly wind-carved, and derives from ancient places like Chaco Canyon and Mesa Verde. The main entrance faces the rising sun (and the Capitol) in the east. The structure was designed by Douglas Cardinal, a Blackfoot who worked with a team of Native American architects and artists to make sure the building respected its natural surroundings. The permanent collection offers more than 800,000 works of aesthetic, cultural, historical, and spiritual significance to Native Americans, including a dizzying array of gold coins, tomahawks and other weaponry, fine examples of basketry and beading, elaborate feather bonnets, wood and stone carvings, and spiritual artifacts. The collections span more than 12,000 years of history and more than 1,200 Native cultures throughout the Americas. In the summertime, look for an outdoor garden that contains traditional Native crops like maize, beans, and medicinal herbs. Pick up a *Family Guide* at the front desk to help you find your way through the museum's offerings. Every Wednesday and Saturday afternoon, the museum hosts family events like cultural demonstrations and hands-on craft workshops.

527 National Portrait Gallery

CONTACT 202-633-1000, www.npg.si.edu; 8th and F Sts., NW

PRICING	$
BEST TIME TO VISIT	Year-round
AGE RANGE	7 and older

National Museum of the American Indian   © Debbie K. Hardin

The National Museum of the American Indian has a second site, in downtown Manhattan (215-514-3700, 1 Bowling Green, New York City). The New York site offers permanent and temporary exhibitions and numerous events that include music and dance performances, storytelling, and films.

National Portrait Gallery   Courtesy Smithsonian Institution

A gallery offers the only complete collection of presidential portraits outside the White House.

The building that houses the National Portrait Gallery started out as the U.S. Patent Office and was the site of President Abraham Lincoln's inaugural ball: The grand space makes quite an impression to this day. The gallery features portraits of important Americans from pre-colonial days through the Revolutionary and Civil Wars, and also showcases 20th-century Americans, including pop icons like Marilyn Monroe, Babe Ruth, and Tallulah Bankhead. A second-floor gallery offers the only complete collection of presidential portraits outside the White House, including Gilbert Stuart's famous painting of George Washington.

528 The Newseum

CONTACT 888-639-7386, www.newseum.org; 555 Pennsylvania Ave., N.W

PRICING	$$$–$$$$
BEST TIME TO VISIT	Year-round
AGE RANGE	12 and older

Since the early days of the Republic, journalists have shaped the impressions American citizens have about our leaders and the events of the day. As early as the 1770s, there were nearly 90 newspapers published in the American colonies, and the people who wrote these publications had an immense impact on the American Revolution. Today there are tens of thousands of publications across the country, in addition to 24-hour news broadcasts on television, radio, and the Internet, and the influence of the journalists who provide this information continues to be formidable.

The Newseum is devoted to the art and science of journalism: It is a unique attraction that offers visitors a mix of journalism history, up-to-the-minute news, and myriad hands-on exhibits, all of which serve to educate the public on how news is disseminated and to memorialize the people who have made journalism their life's work. The impressive Newseum building is dominated by a massive wall of glass that fronts some of the most elite real estate in the country: It sits between the White House and the U.S. Capitol, just off the National Mall, and the views from inside are nothing short of breathtaking. (Don't miss the chance to step outside on the Hank Greenspan Terrace for an unparalleled photo opportunity.)

The museum comprises seven levels of galleries, theaters, shops, and restaurants, and there are a lot of hands-on opportunities for the whole family. Head straightaway to the NBC News Interactive Newsroom, where children (and adults) can try their hands at preparing news stories and then delivering them on camera. Also worth visiting is the Pulitzer Prize Photography Gallery, which offers a revolving collection of famous historic photos and more recent pictures, displayed in a thoughtful way that is educational and aesthetically pleasing. The Berlin Wall Gallery includes the largest display of the original wall outside of Germany, with eight 12-foot sections of concrete alongside Checkpoint Charlie, a three-story East German guard tower that served as a crossing point between East and West Germany before the wall fell. And to keep in touch with what is happening at the moment, the Front Pages Gallery includes the current front pages of 80 newspapers from around the world.

The complex also includes 15 theaters showing a wide variety of news coverage, from historical reels to current sports. Guests also have the opportunity to hear prominent speakers in journalism that have included the most famous names in the business.

NBC Interactive Newsroom, The Newseum

Photo by Maria Bryk, courtesy Newseum

529 Renwick Gallery

CONTACT 202-633-1000, www.americanart.si.edu; 1661 Pennsylvania Ave., NW

PRICING	$
BEST TIME TO VISIT	Year-round
AGE RANGE	7 and older

Located across the street from the White House, the Renwick Gallery is dedicated to American crafts from the 19th century onward, including pieces in glass, ceramic, wood, metal, textiles, and mixed media. The museum's claim to fame is George Catlin's "Indian Gallery," a collection of more than 250 paintings—including many portraits, landscapes, and animal studies—the early-19th-century artist created to document the lives of Native Americans. The structure itself is breathtaking: The Second Empire–style brick structure was designed by architect James Renwick Jr., and it was completed in 1874. It was meant to house the private art collection of philanthropist William Wilson Corcoran, but this quickly outgrew the space and moved across the street. The building was used for a time by the U.S. Court of Claims, but in 1972 the Smithsonian restored the building to its current splendor.

Renwick Gallery   © Debbie K. Hardin

530 Smithsonian Institution

CONTACT www.si.edu; addresses and phone numbers for individual museums given below

PRICING	$
BEST TIME TO VISIT	Year-round
AGE RANGE	7 and older

Many people think of the Smithsonian as the famous fanciful red-brick structure adorned with romantic spires, leaded-glass windows, and soaring towers. But that extravagant building, nicknamed "the Castle," is actually only the figurehead of the museum complex, which now comprises 19 museums (some outside of Washington) and the National Zoo. A family could spend weeks exploring the offerings of each collection, but most children will not have the patience to visit every one.

Several museums of the Smithsonian are listed as separate adventures throughout this section. Below are a few other kid-pleasing favorites. Choose those options that will appeal to *your* children the most, and be sure to drop by the information desks at each site for free activity books and special tour information designed for children.

- **Freer Gallery of Art and Arthur M. Sackler Gallery** (202-633-1000, www.asia.si.edu; 1050 Independence Ave., SW). The Freer Gallery and the Sackler Gallery collectively represent the finest collection of Asian art in the nation. The Freer Gallery collection spans 6,000 years and myriad cultures. Besides Asian art, the Freer also has a collection of 19th- and 20th-century American art, including the largest collection of work by James McNeill Whistler in the world. The adjacent Sackler Gallery was founded to extend the coverage of Asian art to include contemporary art and works in various media.

- **Hirshhorn Museum and Sculpture Garden** (202-633-1000, www.hirshhorn.si.edu; Independence Ave. and 7th St., NW). Dedicated to modern and contemporary art, this dramatic museum opened in 1974 thanks to philanthropist Joseph Hirshhorn, who donated his massive collection of artwork to the Smithsonian Institution. Today the permanent collection of more than 11,000 pieces includes paintings, sculpture, and mixed media representing the most important modern and contemporary artists from around the world. The striking building is a modern art statement itself, designed by architect Gordon Bunshaft in the form of a hollow cylinder 82 feet high and 231 feet wide, with a large, round fountain slightly off center inside.

- **National Museum of Natural History** (202-633-1000, www.mnh.si.edu; 10th St. and Constitution Ave., NW). Opened in 1910, the lovely Beaux-Arts National Museum of Natural History houses extensive specimens of gems and minerals, fossils, and insects. The enormous exhibition hall encompasses more than 325,000 square feet of public space—it is large enough to fit 18 football fields inside!—and houses 126 million natural science specimens and artifacts. The museum's unofficial mascot, an African bush elephant that stands 13 feet 2 inches at the shoulder and weighs nearly 12 tons, greets visitors in the massive rotunda at the entrance, and from there exhibits radiate outward and upward. This museum is extremely popular with children, likely because of the extensive first-floor collection of dinosaur bones that include woolly mammoths and a 65-million-year old *Tyrannosaurus rex*, among the thousands of other ancient species represented. Another favorite is the Geology, Gems, and Minerals Hall on the second floor, which boasts the famous Hope Diamond.

- **National Zoo** (202-633-4800, www.nationalzoo.si.edu; 3001 Connecticut Ave., NW). An outpost of the Smithsonian in the upper Northwest quadrant of DC, the zoo successfully draws legions of visitors—and with good reason. Orangutans swing overhead on an open cable system; lions and tigers and bears prowl in their simulated environments; and indoor exhibits like the Reptile and Amphibian House, the Invertebrate House, and the Bat Center offer shelter from any impending storm. The multistory Amazonia building reflects the diverse climate of that South American ecological treasure, complete with a walk-through rain forest and profiles of its resident animals. But arguably the zoo's biggest draws are the lovable pandas.

The Castle, Smithsonian Institution   © Debbie K. Hardin

- **Smithsonian Institution Building** (aka the Castle) (202-633-1000; 1000 Jefferson Dr., SW). The Smithsonian Institution was named after James Smithson, a wealthy English scientist who never set foot in the United States. He died during the 19th century and bequeathed a large portion of his considerable estate to the United States for the purposes of establishing a museum. He also donated a vast collection of minerals and a significant scientific library. The Castle currently houses Smithson's crypt, as well as the Smithsonian membership desk—a good place to pick up maps and brochures; guests can also catch an informative orientation video here. In the east wing of the building you'll find an exhibit hall offering a preview of the Smithsonian museums in DC, with a handful of items on display from each one.

531 Supreme Court Building

CONTACT 202-479-3211, www.supremecourt.gov; 1 1st St., NE

PRICING	$
BEST TIME TO VISIT	October through April, when court is in session
AGE RANGE	12 and older

The Supreme Court Building is home to the highest judicial authority in the United States. Construction

Supreme Court Building

© Debbie K. Hardin

of this exceptionally beautiful classical building, which resembles a Greek temple, began in 1932. Designed by Cass Gilbert, the building boasts an outcropping of splendidly ornate and perfectly symmetrical Corinthian columns over which is inscribed EQUAL JUSTICE UNDER LAW. There are also fine sculptural works in bas-relief on the pediments and massive bronze doors. Court is in session here October through April; during this period, the Court usually sits for two weeks each month and hears arguments 10–noon and 1–3 on weekdays. Members of the public can view cases Monday through Wednesday, but be prepared to wait for hours; seats are limited (about 100 spots) and provided on a first-come, first-served basis. Call for specifics in advance, or check the argument calendar at www.supremecourt.gov. When Court is not in session, visitors can tour the building and catch a live lecture on the inner workings of the Court. These lectures, generally available on the hour, are subject to change and cancellation.

532 U.S. Capitol Building

CONTACT 202-225-6828, www.aoc.gov; 1st St., between Constitution and Independence Aves.

PRICING	$
BEST TIME TO VISIT	Year-round: closed to tours on Sunday
AGE RANGE	7 and older

No visit to Washington, DC, is complete without a peek at the U.S. Capitol Building. This regal structure at the eastern end of the National Mall has housed Congress since 1800. The west-facing steps of this recognizable building are the site of modern presidential inaugurations, and inside is the location of the annual State of the Union address. President Abraham Lincoln's funeral was held within the halls of the ceremonial Rotunda (the room that lies beneath the enormous dome), and most presidents who have died in the modern era have lain in state here as well. Construction on this neoclassical beauty began in 1793, and George Washington laid the cornerstone. The Capitol was built on top of a hill so that it would tower over the rest of the city—and in fact, in 1901 Congress passed a law that ensured the Capitol dome would remain the tallest building in the city: It is 287 feet, 5.5 inches tall, and by law no building in DC may exceed this height. The emblematic statue *Freedom*, rendered by artist Thomas Crawford, was added to the top of the dome in 1863.

Since 9/11, there have been numerous security updates to the building, and a new visitor center was built underground in the past several years. The tragedy of 9/11 has also drastically changed the accessibility of this building (and every other federal building in the country): Guests are no longer allowed to visit without a prearranged tour. If you want to get a look inside, secure tickets the same day in person at the visitor center or make advance reservations through your congressional representative. Tours begin at 9 AM and lines queue up as early as 7 to secure timed tickets. Be sure to arrive no later than 10, because tickets are limited and are generally gone by late morning. In the busy summer and spring vacation seasons, expect a very long line to get tickets. Note that each member of your party must be present to obtain a timed ticket. Once you secure tickets, line up 10 minutes before the appointed time, and expect the total tour (including the security check) to take a little more than an hour. Visitors may not bring food or liquids into the Capitol, and no bags larger than 14 inches by 13 inches by 4 inches are allowed. Other prohibited items include aerosol and nonaerosol bottles and cans; any sort of sharp object, including knitting needles; and, of course, all weapons (even toys) and ammunition.

Your group will share the floor with at least a

U.S. Capitol Building   © Debbie K. Hardin

dozen others, and the sounds inside this big old stone structure are cacophonous. Add to this the frustrating requirement that you stay in one spot with your designated tour guide, which means you'll see most of the room from a distance. If you can stomach the crowds and noise, however, the place is magnificent. The Rotunda is tall enough to accommodate an upright Statue of Liberty (if she were standing in her bare feet). Most impressive, however, is the enormous painting on the inside of the dome, 180 feet above the Rotunda floor. Painted by Constantino Brumidi and titled *The Apotheosis of Washington*, the classical scene shows George Washington surrounded by symbols of democratic progress. Brumidi also painted many of the corridors and other rooms throughout the Capitol, as well as a good portion of the frieze depicting scenes from American history that encircles the Rotunda.

Next on the tour is the Old Hall of the House of Representatives, which is now called National Statuary Hall, so named because of the dozens of state-owned statues that have been placed here. Children will wonder at the variety of people memorialized here, from Confederate general Robert E. Lee to King Kamehameha I of Hawaii; states may place (at their own expense) whatever statues they wish in the hall, as long as the subject is deceased and the statue is made from marble or bronze. The ornate moldings throughout the hall, its off-center dome, and the plethora of statuary are interesting, but kids are likely to most enjoy the irregular acoustics in the space. Because of the architecture of the dome, it is

possible to hear a whisper from across the room. Encourage your kids to give this a try.

If you would like to get a little closer to the folks who decide how your tax dollars are spent, be sure to visit your representative or senator. To find your House representative, head to the Cannon, Longworth, and Rayburn Buildings on the south side of the Capitol. Offices of senators are on located in the Dirksen, Hart, and Russell Buildings on the north side of the Capitol, on Constitution Avenue. When Congress is in session, you may also obtain tickets to visit the galleries that overlook the government in action. (Note: You can tell when Congress is in session by looking for the flags that fly over the House and Senate on those days. At night, look for the light that shines from the torch of *Freedom*.) Secure these passes in advance from your House representative; most will be able to accommodate your request the day of your visit, but it's a good idea to call ahead to verify availability. Non-U.S. citizens may obtain gallery tickets at the security office once inside the building.

533 Vietnam Veterans Memorial

CONTACT 202-426-6841, www.nps.gov/vive; northeast of Lincoln Memorial

PRICING	$
BEST TIME TO VISIT	Spring through fall
AGE RANGE	All ages

The Vietnam Veterans Memorial is a moving, simple statement of loss that honors the American men and women who sacrificed and served during the Vietnam War. The centerpiece of the memorial (known as "the Wall") was completed in 1982, after then college student Maya Lin's elegant design won a national contest. Because of the controversial nature of the war, Lin envisioned a memorial that makes no political statement. The stark, reflective black granite of the Wall is inscribed with nearly 60,000 names of fallen soldiers, as well as those still considered missing in action, listed in chronological order of loss (starting on the west end of the Wall). The National Park Serv-

Vietnam Veterans Memorial   © Debbie K. Hardin

ice occasionally adds names as individuals continue to die from injuries sustained during the war. Information books located at the western end of the Wall chronicle every name inscribed, along with the number of the panel on which it can be found; thin slips of paper and pencils are provided so that visitors can make rubbings of names. In 1984 a life-sized statue of three soldiers who seem to be staring at the Wall was created by Frederick Hart and installed nearby. And in 1993 the Vietnam Women's Memorial, designed by Glenna Goodacre, was erected on the grounds. This memorial shows three uniformed women nurses caring for a wounded soldier. Guests should exercise decorum when visiting the grounds of this memorial; it is an overwhelmingly emotional place for many who come to pay tribute to their loved ones, most of whom died much too young.

534 Washington Monument

CONTACT 202-426-6841, www.nps.gov/wamo; on the National Mall, midway between the Capitol and the Lincoln Memorial

PRICING	$
BEST TIME TO VISIT	Year-round
AGE RANGE	All ages

Arguably the most recognizable architectural feature in Washington, DC, the Washington Monument is an elegant, commanding memorial to the nation's first president, George Washington. Despite its seeming simplicity—it is rendered in the style of a classic Egyptian obelisk—the monument is on a grand scale, topping out at a little more than 555 feet tall and weighing in at more than 90,000 tons. The structure is made with 36,491 blocks of white marble and is surrounded by 50 flags at the base, each symbolizing a state of the Union. The monument was designed by architect Robert Mills, who originally conceived of a much more elaborate memorial: The current obelisk was to be surrounded by statues of Revolutionary War heroes along with a large statue of a toga-clad Washington driving a chariot. Money—and enthusiasm for the grand theme—ran short, however, and eventually the plans were scaled back. In 1848, the cornerstone of the obelisk was laid on the Fourth of July. But building progressed slowly because of financial constraints, and by 1854 funds dried up completely. The country entered into the bitter Civil War at this time, and the monument thus stood unfinished for more than 20 years. When the war was finally over and construction began again, the stones dug from the same quarries were a slightly different shade of white. If you look about a third of the way up

Washington Monument   Courtesy Jon Preimesberger

the monument, you'll see the demarcation between the old construction and the newer.

Today the tiny observation floor at the top of the Washington Monument, accessed via an elevator that can complete the trip in 70 seconds, offers one of the best views in the city. Although the tour of the monument is free, all visitors must have tickets (even small children). The ticket kiosk at the base of the monument on 15th Street opens at 8:30 AM (although lines often form as much as an hour and a half earlier). Free tickets are available by advance reservation online (www.recreation.gov). There is a small fee per order to reserve tickets. Pick up these passes at the will-call window of the monument ticket kiosk the day of your tour or get tickets on a first-come, first-served basis at the Washington Monument Lodge on 15th Street.

535 White House

CONTACT 202-456-1414, www.nps.gov/whho; 1600 Pennsylvania Ave., NW

PRICING	$
BEST TIME TO VISIT	Year-round (winter holidays to see special decorations, Tuesday through Saturday)
AGE RANGE	7 and older

The White House is where the president of the United States and First Family live, but it is and has always been the "People's House," and as such remains as accessible to the public as is possible given the enormous security challenges this presents. Don't miss the chance to view the north entrance exterior of the building from Pennsylvania Avenue, which is easily visible by peering through the iron fence; the building is especially lovely at night. But for a real treat, arrange for a tour inside the home, which is not as imposing as you might suppose.

City architect Pierre L'Enfant's original plan for the District of Columbia called for the White House to be nearly 10 times its current size to keep it in proportion to the much larger Capitol Building. But later planners scaled back the size of the president's house

White House © Debbie K. Hardin

considerably, and today many visitors are surprised by how small the White House really is—especially considering the West Wing houses many employees of the Executive Office of the President and the East Wing houses largely ceremonial rooms. Although the building has been renovated many times over the years, the original concept came from James Hoban, who won a government-sponsored competition with his Georgian design. John and Abigail Adams were the first occupants; George Washington was the only president who never lived here.

As a result of increased security post-9/11, White House tours can only be arranged through your congressional representative. Note that these must be requested at least 21 days in advance, but it is recommended that they be arranged as much as six months ahead of time. You will be notified of your specified day and time a month in advance; note, however, that the White House can and does cancel these tours at a moment's notice. Call the visitor information desk, 202-456-7041, the day before your scheduled tour to confirm it. Guests with confirmed tickets will enter the complex from the corner of 15th Avenue and Hamilton Place. Also note that the White House has a long list of prohibited items: Visitors may not bring purses or bags of any type; cameras, video recorders, or audio recorders; strollers; tobacco; and personal grooming products like lotions, lipsticks, brushes, and combs. Not surprisingly, sharp objects that can be used as weapons and any actual weapons or explosive devices are also not allowed.

There are 132 rooms on six floors in the White

House, but if you are lucky enough to get a White House tour you will see only a limited section that includes ceremonial public rooms like the Red Room, the Blue Room, the Green Room, the East Room, the State Dining Room, and the China Room. Public tours do not get anywhere near the Oval Office, nor will visitors be allowed to see the presidential residence.

There are also seasonal tours, the tickets for which are distributed on a first-come, first-served basis. The annual White House Garden Tour is held over one weekend in April; you can obtain tickets the day of the tour from the Ellipse Visitor Pavilion at 15th and E Streets, but line up as early as possible because these tickets are hot commodities. The tour passes through Jacqueline Kennedy's Rose Garden, the Children's Garden, and the South Lawn. The Monday after Easter the White House hosts the Annual Easter Egg Roll, a tradition dating back to 1878 when President Rutherford B. Hayes opened the White House for egg hunting to local children. Today children and their families attending the Easter festivities (held on the South Lawn) will enjoy traditional egg rolling, arts and crafts, and live musical performances. The president generally makes an appearance at this event, as do the children and grandchildren of other high-level government officials—and tickets for civilians are distributed via lottery system.

If you cannot arrange a White House tour, don't

Next door to the White House, on 17th Avenue, NW, is the Eisenhower Executive Office Building, or EEOB (formerly the Old Executive Office Building, or OEOB). This building's extravagant French Empire—style structure houses much of the White House staff. Nicknamed the "Wedding Cake," the building has been derided by many architectural critics over the years for its over-the-top exterior; wit Mark Twain called the EEOB the "ugliest building in America," and in the early 20th century there were plans to cover the building with a Greek Revival facade. Thankfully for those of us who are fans of this fanciful structure, funding ran short and the remake never happened. Although you cannot tour the EEOB, it is worth taking a look at its exterior. Suggest that kids try to count the exterior columns on this exuberant facade: There are 900!

Interior of Woodrow Wilson House   © Debbie K. Hardin

despair: Visit the White House Visitor Center (at the southeast corner of 15th and E Sts., NW) to see an exhibit on the architecture of the White House, as well as displays on artifacts and furnishings. There is also a 30-minute video about the history of the structure and its famous occupants through the years.

536 Woodrow Wilson House

CONTACT 202-387-4062, www.woodrowwilsonhouse.org; 2340 S St., NW

PRICING	$–$$
BEST TIME TO VISIT	Year-round; closed Monday
AGE RANGE	7 and older

Woodrow Wilson (1856–1924) was the 28th president of the United States. He was a onetime president of Princeton University as well. During his administration Wilson passed an incredible number of progressive reform acts, including the Federal Reserve Act, the Federal Farm Loan Act, and the Federal Trade Commission Act. He presided over the White House during World War I, and was a vocal advocate for women's rights (especially the right to vote).

This surprisingly large 1915 brick structure was home to Woodrow Wilson and his second wife in the years immediately following his presidency. It is a delight to find the home much as the Wilsons left it: It still seems residential (you have to ring the doorbell to be admitted), and 95 percent of the contents are those that the Wilsons owned themselves, still in their original settings. Begin the tour with a somewhat dry 15-minute orientation film about the former president, and then you will be led among the 1920s-style furnished rooms, including Wilson's personal office (nicknamed "the Dugout" because of his love of baseball), a well-stocked library that also features a movie screen, and a fascinating kitchen and pantry stocked with foods typical of the era. While visiting you can sneak a peek into Mrs. Wilson's closet, and you might even have the chance to plunk out a tune on the Wilsons' grand piano.

537 World War II Memorial

CONTACT 202-426-6841, www.nps.gov/nwwm; on the National Mall, east of the Lincoln Memorial

PRICING	$
BEST TIME TO VISIT	Year-round
AGE RANGE	All ages

The World War II Memorial is an oval, 7-acre park built in 2004 to honor the 16 million Americans who served during World War II, including the more than 400,000 people who gave their lives doing so. The memorial sits at the eastern base of the Lincoln Reflecting Pool. The neoclassical park features 56 granite pillars arranged in a semicircle; each 17-foot pillar is adorned with two bronze wreaths and marked with the name of a state or U.S. territory. On either side of the pillars are massive archway pavilions symbolizing the wars in the Atlantic and the Pacific, and in the center of the central plaza is a large pool with explosive fountains. The "Freedom Wall" to the west contains more than 4,000 stars—one for every 100 soldiers who died during the war. Visitors will find a registry kiosk to look up the names of veterans. (Note that this is also available at www.wwiimemorial.com.)

World War II Memorial   Courtesy Jon Preimesberger

APPENDIX A

Choosing the Adventures Right for Your Family

To help you decide which adventures will appeal most to your kids, use this handy reference chart. The numbers before each site correspond to the order in which these sites are presented in this book.

Animals

#7 Denali National Park and Preserve
#8 Glacier Bay National Park and Preserve
#10 Katmai National Park and Preserve
#59 San Diego Zoo
#88 Biscayne National Park
#92 Everglades National Park
#95 Pelican Island National Wildlife Refuge
#119 Hanauma Bay Nature Preserve
#178 National Mississippi River Museum
and Aquarium
#376 Theodore Roosevelt National Park
#396 Crater Lake National Park
#416 Block Island National Wildlife Refuge
#442 Great Smoky Mountains National Park
#457 Zion National Park
#469 Chincoteague and Assateague Islands
#482 Shenandoah National Park
#487 Olympic National Park
#502 Grand Teton National Park
#504 Yellowstone National Park
#530 Smithsonian Institution

Archaeology

#2 Moundville Archaeological Park
#15 Canyon de Chelly National Monument
#16 Casa Grande Ruins National Monument
#20 Montezuma Castle National Monument
#22 Pueblo Grande Museum and Archaeological
Park
#25 Tuzigoot National Monument
#34 Parkin Archeological State Park
#36 Toltec Mounds Archaeological State Park
#68 Hovenweep National Monument

#69 Mesa Verde National Park
#102 Etawoh Mounds
#108 Ocmulgee National Monument
#128 Puako Petroglyph Archaeological Preserve
#131 Pu'ukohola Heiau
#147 Cahokia Mounds State Historic Site
#177 Mines of Spain Archaeological Site
#179 Toolesboro Indian Mounds
#184 El Cuartelejo
#206 Poverty Point State Historic Site
#217 Whaleback Shell Midden
#321 Aztec Ruins National Monument
#322 Bandelier National Monument
#325 Chaco Culture National Historical Park
#328 Pecos National Historical Park
#329 Petroglyph National Monument
#330 Puye Cliff Dwellings
#331 Salinas Pueblo Missions National Monument
#490 Grave Creek Mound Archaeological Complex
#495 Aztalan State Park

Architecture and engineering marvels

#23 San Xavier del Bac
#42 El Presidio de Santa Barbara State Historic Park
#43 El Pueblo de Los Angeles State Historic Park
#45 Golden Gate Bridge
#47 Hearst San Simeon State Historical Monument
#52 Mission Basilica San Diego de Alcala
#85 Nemours Mansion and Gardens
#111 Swan House
#114 Byodo-In
#122 Iolani Palace
#136 Cataldo Mission

#149 Chicago Architecture Foundation
#152 Frank Lloyd Wright Home and Studio
#159 Willis Tower
#205 Oak Alley Plantation
#213 Museums of Old York
#215 Portland Head Light
#216 West Quoddy Head Lighthouse
#235 Harvard University
#275 Gateway Arch
#299 Hoover Dam
#301 Las Vegas Strip
#327 Palace of the Governors
#328 Pecos National Historical Park
#330 Puye Cliff Dwellings
#331 Salinas Pueblo Missions National Monument
#332 Taos Pueblo
#337 Central Park
#340 Empire State Building
#341 Erie Canalway National Heritage Corridor
#354 Statue of Liberty
#356 Vanderbilt Mansion National Historic Site
#359 Biltmore Estate
#361 Cape Hatteras Lighthouse
#367 Tryon Palace
#385 Serpent Mound Archaeological Site
#408 Independence Hall
#409 Liberty Bell
#420 Newport Rhode Island Mansions
#422 Touro Synagogue National Historic Site
#423 Boone Hall Plantation
#424 Burt-Starke Mansion
#427 Drayton Hall
#432 Crazy Horse Memorial
#436 Mount Rushmore
#447 El Paso Mission Trail
#455 Temple Square
#470 Colonial Williamsburg
#480 Pentagon
#488 Seattle Space Needle
#497 Pabst Mansion
#498 Taliesin
#506 Chesapeake and Ohio Canal
#516 Library of Congress
#523 National Mall
#531 Supreme Court Building
#532 U.S. Capitol Building
#534 Washington Monument
#535 White House

Art, music, and theater

#33 Ozark Folk Center State Park
#44 Getty Villa Malibu
#47 Hearst San Simeon State Historical Monument
#80 Wadsworth Atheneum
#87 Winterthur Museum
#113 Bernice Pauahi Bishop Museum
#146 Art Institute of Chicago
#163 Eiteljorg Museum of American Indians and Western Art
#173 Grant Wood Studio
#228 Boston Museum of Fine Arts
#241 Norman Rockwell Museum
#246 Peabody Essex Museum
#282 Scott Joplin House State Historic Site
#322 Bandelier National Monument
#326 Georgia O'Keeffe Museum
#329 Petroglyph National Monument
#334 Apollo Theater
#336 Broadway Theaters
#349 Metropolitan Museum of Art
#351 Pollock-Krasner House and Studio
#388 Centennial Land Run Monument
#391 National Cowboy and Western Heritage Museum
#420 Newport Rhode Island Mansions
#462 Shelburne Museum
#463 Simon Pearce Glass Factory
#498 Taliesin
#514 John F. Kennedy Center for the Performing Arts
#521 National Gallery of Art
#524 National Museum of African Art
#527 National Portrait Gallery
#529 Renwick Gallery
#530 Smithsonian Institution

Battles and military history

#35 Prairie Grove Battlefield State Park
#97 Andersonville National Historic Site
#100 Chickamauga and Chattanooga National Military Park
#101 Civil War Exhibit at the Atlanta History Center
#126 Pearl Harbor: USS *Arizona* Memorial
#171 Tippecanoe Battlefield
#192 Camp Nelson Civil War Heritage Park
#207 World War II Museum

Beaches

Books

Cowboys, Native Americans, and western culture

#141 Nez Perce National Historical Park
#163 Eiteljorg Museum of American Indians and Western Art
#171 Tippecanoe Battlefield
#182 Dodge City
#187 Old Cowtown Museum
#272 Natchez Trace Parkway
#286 Crow Fair and Rodeo
#288 First People's Buffalo Jump
#290 Little Bighorn Battlefield
#293 Fort Kearny
#294 Fort Robinson
#371 Fort Abraham Lincoln
#372 Fort Mandan
#374 Knife River Indian Villages National Historic Site
#389 Chisholm Trail Heritage Center
#391 National Cowboy and Western Heritage Museum
#394 Red Earth Festival
#395 Washita Battlefield
#432 Crazy Horse Memorial
#437 Wounded Knee Memorial
#484 Fort Vancouver
#499 Buffalo Bill Historical Center
#500 Cheyenne Frontier Days Rodeo
#526 National Museum of the American Indian
#529 Renwick Gallery

Cultural diversity

#6 Alaska Native Heritage Center
#12 Sitka National Historical Park
#13 Totem Bight State Historical Park
#18 Heard Museum
#33 Ozark Folk Center State Park
#39 Chinatown San Francisco
#43 El Pueblo de Los Angeles
#51 Manzanar
#77 Mashantucket Pequot Museum and Research Center
#113 Bernice Pauahi Bishop Museum
#114 Byodo-In
#120 Hawaii's Plantation Village
#122 Iolani Palace
#124 Kona History Center Museum
#125 Mookini Heiau State Monument
#127 Polynesian Cultural Center
#132 Queen Emma Summer Palace
#135 Basque Museum and Cultural Center

#140 Minidoka National Historic Site
#172 Danish Immigrant Museum
#198 Shaker Village of Pleasant Hill
#199 Acadian Village
#202 Magnolia Mound Plantation
#234 Hancock Shaker Village
#268 Voyageurs National Park
#276 The Griot Museum of Black History
#286 Crow Fair and Rodeo
#305 Canterbury Shaker Village
#325 Chaco Culture National Historical Park
#332 Taos Pueblo
#339 Ellis Island
#347 Lower East Side Tenement Museum
#394 Red Earth Festival
#399 Kam Wah Chung Company Building
#522 National Holocaust Memorial Museum
#524 National Museum of African Art

Dinosaurs and fossils

#50 La Brea Tar Pits
#64 Comanche National Grassland
#65 Dinosaur National Monument
#67 Florissant Fossil Beds National Monument
#240 New Bedford Whaling Museum
#287 Dinosaur Trail
#292 Ashfall Fossil Beds State Historical Park
#398 John Day Fossil Beds National Monument
#431 Badlands National Park
#434 Mammoth Site
#446 Dinosaur Valley State Park
#503 Wyoming Dinosaur Center

Exploring

#32 Louisiana Purchase State Park
#38 Cabrillo National Monument
#115 Captain Cook Monument
#139 Massacre Rocks State Park
#142 Sacajawea Interpretive, Cultural, and Educational Center
#144 Three Island Crossing State Park
#154 Lewis and Clark State Historic Site
#180 Western Historic Trails Center
#189 Santa Fe Trail
#279 Museum of Westward Expansion
#295 Homestead National Monument
#296 Pioneer Village
#366 Roanoke Island

#372 Fort Mandan
#397 Fort Clatsop National Memorial
#400 National Historic Oregon Trail Interpretive Center
#473 Jamestown
#496 Madeline Island Historic Museum

Festivals and parties

#58 Rose Parade
#167 Johnny Appleseed Festival
#176 Iowa State Fair
#200 French Quarter, New Orleans
#203 Mardi Gras in New Orleans
#204 New Orleans Jazz and Heritage Festival
#212 Maine Annual Lobster Festival
#267 St. Paul Winter Carnival
#320 Albuquerque International Balloon Fiesta
#348 Macy's Thanksgiving Day Parade
#505 Cherry Blossom Festival
#509 Fourth of July on the National Mall

Forts

#29 Fort Smith National Historic Site
#82 Fort Delaware State Park
#89 Castillo de San Marcos National Monument
#90 Dry Tortugas National Park
#103 Fort Pulaski National Monument
#151 Fort de Chartres State Historic Site
#185 Fort Scott National Historic Site
#194 Fort Boonesborough
#209 Colonial Pemaquid
#210 Fort Knox
#223 Fort McHenry
#255 Colonial Michilimackinac
#256 Fort Mackinac
#263 Fort Snelling
#293 Fort Kearny
#294 Fort Robinson
#307 Fort at Number 4
#313 Fort Lee Historic Park
#343 Fort Ticonderoga
#371 Fort Abraham Lincoln
#372 Fort Mandan
#373 Fort Union Trading Post
#379 Fort Meigs
#390 Fort Gibson
#397 Fort Clatsop National Memorial
#429 Fort Sumter

#473 Jamestown
#484 Fort Vancouver
#493 Prickett's Fort State Park
#501 Fort Laramie National Historic Site

Heroes and trailblazers

#1 Ivy Green
#3 Selma to Montgomery Historic Site
#31 Little Rock Central High
#48 John Muir National Historic Site
#74 Amistad Memorial
#75 Eli Whitney Museum and Workshop
#79 Noah Webster House
#84 John Dickinson Plantation
#106 Martin Luther King Jr. National Historic Site
#123 King Kamehameha Statue
#142 Sacajawea Interpretive, Cultural, and Educational Center
#168 Levi Coffin Home
#175 Hitchcock House
#181 Carrie Nation Home
#186 Nicodemus Historic District
#191 Ashland
#214 Portland Freedom Trail
#221 Benjamin Banneker Historical Park and Museum
#222 Clara Barton House
#245 Paul Revere's House
#248 Pilgrim Hall Museum
#252 Sojourner Truth Memorial
#262 Charles Lindbergh Boyhood House
#281 Pony Express Museum
#296 Pioneer Village
#304 American Independence Museum
#306 Daniel Webster Birthplace Site
#312 Boxwood Hall
#317 Thomas Edison National Historical Park
#319 Washington Crossing State Park
#333 9/11 Memorial
#342 Federal Hall Memorial
#344 Harriet Tubman Home
#355 Susan B. Anthony House
#357 Women's Rights National Historical Park
#369 Wright Brothers National Memorial
#381 National Underground Railroad Freedom Center
#382 Rankin House Abolitionist Site
#392 Oklahoma City National Memorial
#401 Benjamin Franklin National Memorial
#402 Betsy Ross House

#404 Declaration House
#405 Franklin Court
#411 National Constitution Center
#417 First Baptist Meeting House
#418 General Nathanael Greene Homestead
#428 Fort Hill
#439 Davy Crockett Birthplace
#460 Ethan Allen Homestead Museum
#466 Arlington House
#467 Arlington National Cemetery
#480 Pentagon
#481 Red Hill
#507 Constitution and Declaration of Independence
#511 Frederick Douglass National Historic Site
#518 Martin Luther King Jr. Memorial
#519 Mary McLeod Bethune Council House

Learning how things work

#81 Windham Textile and History Museum
#112 World of Coca-Cola
#117 Dole Pineapple Plantation
#155 Museum of Science and Industry
#196 Louisville Slugger Museum and Factory
#201 Frogmore Cotton Plantation
#258 The Henry Ford
#323 Bradbury Science Museum
#363 Duke Homestead and Tobacco Factory
#407 Hersheypark
#419 Museum of Work and Culture
#421 Slater Mill Historic Site
#458 Ben and Jerry's Factory
#461 Maple Sugaring in Vermont
#463 Simon Pearce Glass Factory
#489 Beckley Exhibition Coal Mine
#512 International Spy Museum

Natural wonders

#7 Denali National Park and Preserve
#8 Glacier National Park and Preserve
#17 Grand Canyon National Park
#19 Meteor Crater
#21 Petrified Forest
#26 Buffalo National River
#40 Death Valley National Park
#49 Kings Canyon and Sequoia National Parks
#56 Redwood National Park
#61 Yosemite National Park
#62 Cave of the Winds

#63 Colorado Trail
#70 Pike's Peak
#71 Rocky Mountain National Park
#88 Biscayne National Park
#92 Everglades National Park
#116 Diamond Head Volcano
#118 Haleakala National Park
#119 Hanauma Bay Nature Preserve
#121 Hawaii Volcanoes National Park
#129 Punalu'u Black Sand Beach
#134 Wailua Falls
#137 Craters of the Moon National Monument and Preserve
#143 Shoshone Falls
#150 Field Museum of Natural History
#170 Marengo Cave
#178 National Mississippi River Museum and Aquarium
#208 Acadia National Park
#264 Grand Portage National Monument
#265 Mille Lacs Kathio State Park
#268 Voyageurs National Park
#289 Glacier National Park
#300 Lake Tahoe
#324 Carlsbad Caverns
#346 Lake George
#350 Niagara Falls
#360 Blue Ridge Parkway
#376 Theodore Roosevelt National Park
#431 Badlands National Park
#442 Great Smoky Mountains National Park
#453 Bryce Canyon National Park
#457 Zion National Park
#482 Shenandoah National Park
#485 Mount St. Helens National Volcanic Monument
#487 Olympic National Park
#491 Harpers Ferry National Historical Park
#492 New River Gorge National River
#502 Grand Teton National Park
#504 Yellowstone National Park

Pop culture

#37 Alcatraz
#41 Disneyland
#46 Grauman's Chinese Theatre
#91 Epcot
#112 World of Coca-Cola
#196 Louisville Slugger Museum and Factory

#260 Motown Historical Museum
#383 Rock and Roll Hall of Fame
#393 Oklahoma Route 66 Museum
#440 Graceland Mansion
#441 Grand Ole Opry
#458 Ben and Jerry's Factory
#525 National Museum of American History
#527 National Portrait Gallery
#528 The Newseum

Presidents

#27 Clinton Presidential Library and Museum
#57 Ronald W. Reagan Presidential Library
and Museum
#104 Jimmy Carter Library and Museum
#110 Roosevelt's "Little White House"
#145 Abraham Lincoln Presidential Library
and Museum
#157 New Salem Historic Site
#158 Ulysses S. Grant Home
#161 Benjamin Harrison Home
#164 Grouseland
#169 Lincoln Boyhood Home National Monument
#174 Herbert Hoover National Historic Site
#183 Dwight D. Eisenhower Presidential Library
and Museum
#190 Abraham Lincoln Birthplace National
Historical Park
#197 Mary Todd Lincoln House
#237 John F. Kennedy Presidential Library and
Museum
#247 Peacefields
#257 Gerald Ford Museum
#269 Beauvoir
#277 Harry Truman Library and Museum
#283 Ulysses S. Grant National Historic Site
#308 Franklin Pierce Homestead
#345 Home of Franklin D. Roosevelt National
Historic Site
#352 Sagamore Hill
#376 Theodore Roosevelt National Park
#378 First Ladies National Historic Center
#380 Lawnfield
#384 Rutherford B. Hayes Presidential Center
#386 Warren G. Harding Home
#387 William McKinley Library
#403 Carpenters' Hall
#415 Wheatland

#436 Mount Rushmore
#438 Andrew Johnson National Historic Site
#443 Hermitage
#448 George H. W. Bush Library and Museum
#449 Lyndon B. Johnson Presidential Library
#451 Sixth Floor Museum at Dealey Plaza
#459 Calvin Coolidge Homestead District
#468 Ash Lawn
#476 Monticello
#477 Montpelier
#478 Mount Vernon
#494 Washington Heritage Trail Byway
#508 Ford's Theatre and Lincoln Museum
#510 Franklin D. Roosevelt Memorial
#513 Jefferson Memorial
#517 Lincoln Memorial
#527 National Portrait Gallery
#534 Washington Monument
#535 White House
#536 Woodrow Wilson House

Space travel

#5 U.S. Space and Rocket Center
#94 Kennedy Space Center
#452 Space Center Houston
#520 National Air and Space Museum

Sports

#9 Iditarod Trail Sled Dog Headquarters
#26 Buffalo National River
#72 Ski Colorado
#99 Centennial Olympic Park
#133 Surfing at Waikiki Beach
#160 Wrigley Field
#166 Indianapolis Motor Speedway
#195 Kentucky Derby
#196 Louisville Slugger Museum and Factory
#219 Babe Ruth Museum
#232 Fenway Park
#300 Lake Tahoe
#335 Baseball Hall of Fame
#492 New River Gorge National River
#500 Cheyenne Frontier Days Rodeo

Time travel and living history

#24 Tombstone
#29 Fort Smith
#30 Historic Washington State Park

#78 Mystic Seaport
#82 Fort Delaware State Park
#83 Hagley Museum and Library
#85 Nemours Mansion and Gardens
#98 Archibald Smith Plantation Home
#109 Pebble Hill Plantation
#111 Swan House
#130 Pu'uhonua o Honaunau National Historic Park
#148 Chaplin Creek Historic Village
#156 Naper Settlement
#162 Conner Prairie Interactive History Park
#188 Old Prairie Town Ward-Meade Historic Site
#193 Cumberland Gap National Historical Park
#194 Fort Boonesborough
#198 Shaker Village of Pleasant Hill
#199 Acadian Village
#201 Frogmore Cotton Plantation
#202 Magnolia Mound Plantation
#209 Colonial Pemaquid
#213 Museums of Old York
#224 Historic St. Mary's City
#225 The Star Spangled Banner Flag House
#229 Boston Tea Party Cruise
#233 Freedom Trail
#234 Hancock Shaker Village
#238 *Mayflower II*
#244 Old Sturbridge Village
#249 Plimouth Plantation
#255 Colonial Michilimackinac
#264 Grand Portage National Monument
#305 Canterbury Shaker Village
#310 Strawbery Banke Museum
#315 Morristown National Historical Park
#316 Old Barracks
#347 Lower East Side Tenement Museum
#370 Bonanzaville USA
#423 Boone Hall Plantation
#424 Burt-Starke Mansion
#425 Charles Town Landing
#430 Old Slave Mart Museum
#456 This Is the Place Heritage Park
#470 Colonial Williamsburg

#472 Gadsby's Tavern
#473 Jamestown
#491 Harpers Ferry National Historical Park

Trains, planes, automobiles, and ships

#4 Tuskegee Airmen National Historic Site
#14 White Pass and Yukon Railway
#55 *Queen Mary*
#66 Durango & Silverton Narrow Gauge Railroad
#78 Mystic Seaport
#153 Illinois Railway Museum
#165 Hoosier Valley Railroad Museum
#220 Baltimore and Ohio Museum
#226 U.S. Naval Academy Museum and Gallery of Ships
#227 USS *Constellation*
#229 Boston Tea Party Cruise
#253 USS *Constitution*
#258 The Henry Ford
#259 Model T Automotive Heritage Complex
#261 Walter P. Chrysler Museum
#303 Virginia and Truckee Railroad
#368 USS *North Carolina*
#369 Wright Brothers National Memorial
#377 Dayton Aviation Heritage National Historic Park
#412 Steamtown National Historic Site
#454 Golden Spike National Historic Site
#486 Museum of Flight

Treasure hunting

#11 Klondike Gold Rush Park
#24 Tombstone
#28 Crater of Diamonds State Park
#60 Sutter's Mill
#73 U.S. Mint
#138 Land of Yankee Fork State Park
#285 Bannack State Park
#291 Virginia City
#298 Chollar Mine Tour
#302 Rhyolite

APPENDIX B

Suggested Lodging

Price categories given at the end of each lodging entry reflect the rates for one night, not including occupancy or sales taxes (which in some cities can tack on as much as 25 percent to the final bill), for the least expensive standard room that will accommodate two adults and two children. Note that many properties also charge additional resort fees, and hotels in big cities almost always charge a hefty fee for parking. Unless otherwise specified, rates refer to high season.

A word about recommended lodging: I have included only a very few options in each locale, and have focused information primarily on big cities and towns that are near major attractions. Each property highlighted offers something special for families—a premier location, kid-pleasing amenities, a historical setting, or an extraordinary experience (tepee camping near Glacier National Park in Montana, a balcony overlooking a faux African savanna in Orlando, swimming with dolphins on the Big Island of Hawaii, milking a goat on an organic farm in Albuquerque, wrangling longhorns at a dude ranch near Tulsa . . .). I've included options that reflect a range of rates, from splurges to penny-pinching choices to everything in between. When choosing among lodging options, focus on how much time *your* family plans to spend in the accommodations—and what amenities are important to you. There's no point in paying extra for a fabulous pool if no one in your party likes to swim; likewise, sometimes the convenience of a property near a beloved attraction or the luxury of a four-star resort is well worth the extra investment. Do your research, make reservations in advance for popular destinations, and look for online specials if budget is a factor. And don't be afraid to be picky: At check-in, specify your need for a quiet room (if this an issue for you), and if there is space available you will be sited away from elevators and ice makers. If you want a particular view (and this isn't considered a premium at your location), let the agent know before she or he assigns your room. And if you aren't satisfied with the accommodations you are assigned, ask to see other options on the property. Even rooms within chain properties can vary considerably in size and decor (especially if the property is in the middle of ongoing renovations).

Alabama

Gulf Shores

The Beach Club (877-331-9576, www.beachclubal.net; 925 Beach Club Trail). Spacious condominiums on the shore. Extensive kid-friendly amenities like playgrounds and sports courts, with a robust children's program and an on-site grocery store. $$$.

Montgomery

Staybridge Suites EastChase (866-599-6674; 7800 EastChase Parkway). Huge suites, free breakfast and afternoon snacks, nice pool. $.

Selma

St. James Hotel (www.historichotels.org/hotels-resorts/st-james-hotel-al; 1200 Water Ave.). Historic riverfront motel downtown, with classic southern charm. Beautiful views. $$.

Alaska

Anchorage

Hotel Captain Cook (800-843-1950, http://captain hook.com; 939 W. 5th Ave.). Luxury accommodations downtown, with spectacular views and world-class service. Suites offer lots of space for families. $$$$.

Puffin Inn (907-243-4044, www.puffininn.net; 4400 Spenard Rd.). Pet-friendly hotel with a range of choices, from deluxe boutique spaces to modest motel lodging. Some rooms with kitchenettes. Special welcome gifts for children (must be prearranged). $$.

Denali National Park and Preserve

McKinley Chalet Resort (800-276-7234, www.denali
parkresorts.com/accommodations/mckinley-cha
let-resort.aspx; Mile 238.5 George Parks Hwy.). Just
outside the Denali park entrance, with beautiful
views of a glacier-fed river. Spacious two-room suites
are ideal for families. $.

Glacier Bay

Glacier Bay's Bear Track Inn (907-697-3017,
www.beartrackinn.com; Gustavus). Remote location near Glacier Bay. Timber construction, large
rooms. Package rates include transportation from
Juneau, lodging, and meals. $$$.

Katmai

Brooks Lodge (907-243-5448,
www.katmailand.com/lodging/brooks.html;
Katmai National Park). Secluded, rustic accommo-
dations in the park. Within walking distance of
Brooks Falls, the best place in the park to view
bears. $$$.

Arizona

Grand Canyon

Bright Angel Lodge (928-638-2631, www.grand
canyonlodges.com; South Rim, Grand Canyon
National Park). Lovely rustic stone-and-timber
lodge near Bright Angel Trail. Reserve *very* early
(a year in advance) to secure a rim cabin, with the
best views of any park lodging. $.

El Tovar (928-638-2631, www.grandcanyon
lodges.com; South Rim, Grand Canyon National
Park). Historic, luxurious lodge directly on the
canyon rim, in the heart of Grand Canyon Village.
Standard rooms include air-conditioning—a must
in the Arizona summer. $$$.

Phoenix Area

The Buttes (www.marriott.com/hotels/travel/
phxtm-the-buttes-a-marriott-resort; 2000 West-
court Way, Tempe). Unique architecture, centrally
located in Tempe near Phoenix and Scottsdale.
Volleyball courts and a spectacular pool. $$.

Wigwam Golf Resort and Spa (623-935-3811,
www.wigwamresort.com; 300 E. Wigwam Blvd.,
Litchfield Park). Contemporary western architecture and decor. On-site golfing and four pools,
which include a 25-foot tower and twisting water-
slides. $$$.

Wigwam   Courtesy Greater Phoenix Convention and Visitors Bureau

Tombstone Area

Shady Dell Trailer Park (520-432-3567, www.the
shadydell.com; 1 Douglas Rd., Bisbee). Mid-
century vintage trailers in a park setting offer a
blast from the past. Vintage diner onsite adds to
the ambience. $$$.

Tucson

Westward Look Resort (800-722-2500, www.west
wardlook.com; 245 E. Ina Rd.). Large guest rooms,
three pools, and 80 acres of desert grounds. $$$.

Arkansas

Eureka Springs

1886 Crescent Hotel and Spa (877-342-9766,
www.crescent-hotel.com; 75 Prospect Ave.).
Historic spa with daily activity programming for
kids. Traditional hotel rooms plus cozy two-
bedroom cottages. Activities include ghost tours,
history talks, and art classes. $$.

Hot Springs

The Springs Hotel and Spa (501-624-5521, www.the
springshotelandspa.com; 135 Central Ave.).
Recently renovated historic property with com-
modious rooms. Thermal mineral baths, live
entertainment on weekends. $.

Little Rock

Markham House (501-666-0161, www.markham
housesuites.com; 5120 W. Markham). Allergy-
sensitive apartment lodging with daily and weekly
rates. Includes continental breakfast; cribs and
rollaway beds available. $.

Peabody Hotel Little Rock (501-906-4000,
www.peabodylittlerock.com; 3 Statehouse Plaza).

PRICE KEY
$ $150 or less
$$ $151–200
$$$ $$201–275
$$$$ $276+

Luxury accommodations at a prime location downtown. Features the famous Peabody ducks, which waddle down a red carpet to a lobby fountain twice daily. $$.

California

Anaheim/Disneyland

The Anabella (714-905-1050, www.anabella hotel.com; 1030 W. Katella Ave.). Ecofriendly property with space and smart layout designed for families. Walking distance to Disney theme parks and the Anaheim Convention Center. $.

Disney's Grand Californian (714-956-6425, www.disneyland.com; 1600 S. Disneyland Dr.). Pricey and elegant, just a short walk from the entrance of Disneyland and Disney's California Adventure. Some rooms offer bunk beds. $$$$.

Disneyland Hotel (714-778-6600, www.disneyland.com; 1150 Magic Way). Spacious rooms with superior kid-friendly service and a grand themed pool. Recently renovated. $$$.

Kings Canyon and Sequoia

Wuksachi Village and Lodge (559-253-2199, www.visitsequoia.com; Sequoia National Park). Authentic timber-and-stone lodge; offers campfire programs, nighttime hikes, and a near guarantee of seeing deer grazing at dusk. $$.

Los Angeles

Andaz WeHo (323-656-1234, http://westhollywood.hyatt.com/hyatt/hotels/index.jsp; 8401 Sunset Blvd., West Hollywood). Sleek, youthful property on the famous Sunset Strip, with free soft drinks and candy. Teenagers will appreciate the ample rock-and-roll history. $$$.

Beverly Hills Hotel and Bungalows (800-283-8885, www.beverlyhillshotel.com; 9641 Sunset Blvd., Beverly Hills). Glamorous, iconic property: "If these walls could talk . . . ," the pink grande dame would speak of onetime residents like Marilyn Monroe, Elizabeth Taylor, and Warren Beatty. $$$$.

Fairmont Miramar Hotel and Bungalows (310-576-7777, www.fairmont.com/santamonica; 101 Wilshire Blvd., Santa Monica). Classic beach hotel in the heart of Santa Monica, with easy access to the shore and the Santa Monica Pier. $$.

Westin Bonaventure (213-624-1000, www.thebona

Hard Rock Hotel San Diego   Courtesy Hard Rock Hotel

venture.com; 404 S. Figueroa St.). Surprisingly affordable accommodations in the center of downtown. Extensive on-site restaurants and shops and a large outdoor deck and rooftop pool. $$.

San Diego

Hard Rock Hotel (619-702-3000, www.hardrock hotelsd.com; 207 5th Ave.). In the hip Gaslamp Quarter downtown. Extremely high cool quotient that teenagers will adore; the public spaces double as a museum of rock and roll. $$$.

Hotel del Coronado (619-435-6611, www.hoteldel.com; 1500 Orange Ave., Coronado). Grand historic resort on the sands of Coronado island, just across the bay from downtown. Tiny rooms, extensive kids' activities in the summer. $$$.

Omni San Diego (619-231-6664, www.omnihotels.com/FindAHotel/SanDiego.aspx; 675 L St.). Near the Convention Center and connected by skyway to the Padres' Petco Park downtown. This sleek high-rise is a mecca for baseball lovers, who will find an impressive collection of memorabilia on display. $$.

San Francisco

Fairmont San Francisco (866-540-4491, www.fairmont.com/san-francisco; 950 Mason St.). Centrally located grand historic property in Nob Hill neighborhood. On request guest rooms can be stocked with child-sized robes and a special toiletries package that includes baby shampoo, bubble bath, kid-flavored toothpaste, and a stuffed animal. $$$$.

Good Hotel (415-621-0701, www.thegoodhotel.com; 112 7th St.). Billed as a hotel with a conscience, because of numerous green initiatives. Comfortable, trendy, in the South of Market District. Tremendous value. $.

Hotel Drisco (415-346-2880, www.hoteldrisco.com; 2901 Pacific Heights). Small, luxurious hotel with elegant breakfast included. Slightly off the beaten path, but restful and indulgent. $$$.

Hotel Triton (415-394-0500, www.hoteltriton.com; 342 Grant Ave.). Trendy boutique property downtown, adjacent to Chinatown. Rooms are small; staff is exceedingly friendly and welcoming to children. $$.

Santa Barbara

Fess Parker Double Tree Resort (805-564-4333, www.fessparkersantabarbarahotel.com; 633 E. Cabrillo Blvd.). Family-friendly resort across the street from the beach, south of Stearns Wharf, with shuffleboard, a heated pool, tennis courts, and spacious rooms. $$.

Harbor View Inn (800-755-0222, www.harborviewinnsb.com; 28 W. Cabrillo Blvd.). Charming, moderately sized property with casually elegant accommodations, all with spacious balconies or patios, and many with ocean views and fireplaces. $$.

Yosemite National Park

The Ahwahnee (801-559-4884; Yosemite Valley, Yosemite National Park). Luxurious, historic lodge near Yosemite Falls. The epitome of "parkitecture." Kids will love the complimentary cookies served by a roaring fire in winter. $$$$.

Wawona Hotel (801-559-4884; off Hwy. 41, north of the South Entrance, Yosemite National Park). Far-flung Victorian beauty near the Mariposa Grove. Kids will enjoy the icy pool and the herd of deer that roam the sequoia-studded grounds. $$.

Colorado

Aspen

Molly Gibson Lodge (888-271-2304, www.mollygibson.com; 101 W. Main St.). Comfortable one- and two-bedroom condos offer plenty of space for families, in contemporary surrounds. Includes free airport shuttle, continental breakfast, evening reception. $$.

Colorado Springs

The Broadmoor (800-755-5088, www.broadmoor.com; 1 Lake Ave.). Spectacular views of the Rocky Mountains in an upscale resort atmosphere. The pet-friendly property offers a children's concierge, summer camp programs, and babysitting services. $$$$.

Mesa Verde

Far View Lodge (800-449-2288, www.visitmesaverde.com/accommodations; Mesa Verde National Park). Southwestern decor within the park boundaries. Convenient to Mesa Verde visitor center. $.

Rocky Mountain National Park

The Stanley Hotel (800-976-1377, www.stanleyhotel.com; 333 Wonderview Ave., Estes Park). Elegant 1909 resort 6 miles from the Rocky Mountain National Park. Fans of Stephen King will appreciate that this was the setting for *The Shining*. $$$.

Steamboat Springs

The Steamboat Grand (877-269-2628, www.steamboatgrand.com; 2300 Mount Werner Circle). Easy walking to the resort gondola; large property with kid-friendly amenities like an arcade. Offers hotel rooms, multiroom condominiums, and penthouses. $$.

Telluride

Mountain Lodge Telluride (866-368-6867, www.mountainlodgetelluride.com; 457 Mountain Village Blvd.). At nearly 10,000 feet, pretty log-cabin-style accommodation offers lodge rooms, private cabins, and multi-bedroom condominiums. $$.

Vail

Montaneros (800-444-8245, www.montaneros.com; 641 W. Lionshead Circle). Condominium lodge with one- to four-bedroom accommodations with full kitchen, sauna, year-round heated pool. $$.

Connecticut

Greenwich

Delamar Greenwich Harbor Hotel (203-661-9800, www.delamargreenwich.com; 500 Steamboat Rd.). Gracious, airy guest rooms with seaside decor; at the marina, with private pier and boat docking privileges. $$$–$$$$.

Hartford Area

Avon Old Farms Hotel (860-677-1651, www.avon oldfarmshotel.com; 279 Avon Mountain Rd., Avon). Ten minutes from downtown. Luxury property with down beds, cheerful traditional decor. Pet-friendly. $$.

The Farmington Inn and Suites (860-677-2821, www.farmingtoninn.com; 827 Farmington Ave., Farmington). A small, elegant country inn with well-appointed rooms. Complimentary coffee and cookies; breakfast included. $.

Litchfield Hills Area

Winvian Cottages (860-567-9600, www.winvian.com/cottages; 155 Alain White Rd., Morris). Eighteen unique, private, beautifully decorated cottages, nestled amid 113 acres, among them an adorable log cabin, a garage space that includes a helicopter, and a tree house. All-inclusive packages are available. $$$$.

New Haven

Omni New Haven at Yale (203-772-6664, www.omnihotels.com/FindAHotel/NewHaven Yale; 155 Temple St.). Downtown, steps from Yale campus and the New Haven Town Green. Welcome gift for kids, milk and cookies at bedtime. Large, comfortable rooms. $$.

Delaware

Rehoboth Beach

Admiral Hotel (302-227-2103; 2 Baltimore Ave.). A block from the ocean and boardwalk with good views from the shared balcony. Extremely inexpensive during off-season, and moderately so in peak months. $.

Boardwalk Plaza (302-227-7169, www.boardwalk plaza.com; 2 Olive Ave.). Luxurious pink Victorian beauty directly on the boardwalk, with spectacular views and extreme attention to period detail. Offers a unique indoor-outdoor pool, afternoon high tea, and a summertime kids' program. $$$.

Wilmington

Hotel du Pont (302-594-3100, www.hoteldupont.com; 11th and Market). Palatial historic property in downtown financial district. Offers packages that include admission to Fort Delaware, Eleutherian Mills, and the Hagley Museum. $$$.

Florida

Destin

Hilton Sandestin Beach Golf Resort and Spa (850-267-9500; 4000 Sandestin Blvd.). Looking over a long stretch of snow-white beach. Large pool, some rooms with bunk beds. $$.

Key West

Parrot Key Hotel and Resort (888-665-6368; 2801 Roosevelt Blvd.). Tropical feel with charming decor, inside and out. Four pools, 100 percent nonsmoking. $$.

Southernmost Point Guest House (305-294-0715; 1327 Duval St.). Centrally located, classic Old Key West home with airy rooms—each one unique. Kitchenettes available. $$.

Miami

Acqualina (305-936-9088; 17875 Collins Ave., Miami Beach). European design, with a kids' center and a science-based day camp. $$$.

Newport Beachside Resort (800-327-5476; 16701 Collins Ave., Miami Beach). On a lovely beach, with stellar views. Lots of kids' amenities, like a beach-front playground, arcade, and regular children's activities. $$$.

Surfcomber (305-532-7715; 1717 Collins Ave., Miami Beach). Great location on South Beach. High-style yet playful, with kids' welcome gift and child-sized robes. $$$$.

Orlando

Animal Kingdom Lodge (407-934-7639; 2901 Osceola Pkwy.). On the Disney World property. Designed to resemble an African lodge, many rooms overlook a 30-acre savanna populated by captive exotic animals. $$$$.

Hard Rock Hotel (407-502-7625; 5800 Universal Blvd.). On the Universal Studios Orlando property. Offers a huge heated pool and plenty of rock-and-roll cachet. $$$.

Nickelodeon Suites Resort (877-642-5111, www.nickhotel.com; 14500 Continental Gateway). Nickelodeon-themed suites, with on-site water park and roaming characters like SpongeBob SquarePants and Dora the Explorer. Near Disney World. $.

Port Orleans Resort—Riverside (407-934-6000; 1000 W. Buena Vista Dr.). On the Disney World property. New Orleans—themed resort, with an entertaining waterslide and convenient food court. Take a water taxi on adjacent river to Downtown Disney. $$.

Georgia
Atlanta

The Ellis Hotel (888-471-8161; 176 Peachtree St. NW). Downtown luxury property, gorgeous bathrooms, premier service. $$$.

Omni Hotel at CNN Center (404-659-0000; 100 CNN Center). Near Centennial Olympic Park downtown. Welcome gift for kids, plus nighttime cookies and milk and toys and games to borrow. $$.

The Inn at Serenbe (770-463-2610; 10950 Hutcheson Ferry Rd., Chattahoochee Hills). Southwest of Atlanta. Collection of cottages and guesthouses, located on a beautiful farm chock-full of kid-friendly animals like rabbits and goats. Hayrides and evening marshmallow roasts. $$.

Savannah

Hamilton-Turner Inn (912-233-1833, www.hamilton-turnerinn.com; 330 Abercorn St.). Stunning mansion on Lafayette Square. Exquisitely furnished guest home. Gourmet breakfast. Children 10 and older are welcome. $$.

Inn at Ellis Square (912-236-4440; 201 Bay St.). A 150-year-old property smack in the middle of the historic district, with courtyard pool. $.

Marshall House (800-589-6304, www.marshallhouse.com; 123 E. Broughton St.). A cozy, historic bed & breakfast that welcomes children with southern hospitality. Courtyard suites offer separate parlor space to accommodate family lodging. Excellent hot breakfast. $$.

The President's Quarters Inn (800-233-1776, www.presidentsquarters.com/savannah-bed-breakfast.html; 225 E. President St.). Beautiful guest rooms, charming courtyard. Inn claims Robert E. Lee as one of its most famous guests. $$.

Hawaii
Honolulu, Oahu

Halekulani (808-923-2311, www.halekulani.com; 2199 Kalia Rd.). Enormous, elegant accommodations on Waikiki Beach. Welcoming, relaxing environment with impeccable service. $$$$.

Royal Hawaiian   Courtesy Hawaiian Tourism Authority

Outrigger Reef on the Beach (808-923-3111, www.outrigger.com/hotels-resorts/hawaiian-islands; 2169 Kalia Rd.). Prime location on Waikiki Beach, with beautiful views of Diamond Head. Lots of shopping and dining options within walking distance. $$$.

Queen Kapiolani Hotel (866-970-4164, www.queenkapiolani.com; 150 Kapuhulu Ave.). Near Waikiki, and at the foot of Diamond Head; affordable beachfront property with third-floor pool deck, self-serve laundry, some rooms with fridge and microwave. $.

Royal Hawaiian (808-923-7311, www.royal-hawaiian.com; 2259 Kalakaua Ave.). Infamous "Pink Palace" on Waikiki offers luxury and indulgence with plenty of island style. Kids will enjoy the pool waterslides and beach activities, like stand-up paddle classes and outrigger canoe rides. $$$$.

Kona Area, Hawaii

Hilton Waikoloa Village (808-866-1234, www.hiltonwaikoloavillage.com; 69-425 Waikoloa Dr., north of Kona). Astonishing, meandering resort, beautifully landscaped and interconnected with canals, ancient petroglyphs and native artwork, enormous pools with waterfalls, grotto Jacuzzis, and a protected snorkeling lagoon. $$$$.

Royal Kona Resort (805-480-0052, www.royalkona.com; 75-5852 Ali Dr., Kailua-Kona). Sculptural midrise directly on the coastline with private lagoon, tennis courts, beautiful oceanfront swimming pool. Site of popular luau. $$.

Idaho
Boise

The Grove Hotel (208-333-8000, www.grovehotelboise.com; 245 S. Capitol Blvd.). Luxe accommodations in downtown with indoor Olympic-sized pool. Offers packages with museum and attraction passes. $$.

Harrison Hotel (800-376-3608, www.harrison hotelboise.com; 409 S. Cole Rd.). Comfortable, centrally located downtown, with free breakfast and a nice pool. $.

Twin Falls

Shilo Inn Suites (800-222-2244, www.shiloinns.com; 1586 Blue Lakes Blvd.). Well-priced motor inn with family suites, in-room refrigerator and microwave, indoor pool. $.

Illinois

Chicago

The Drake (312-787-2200, www.thedrakehotel.com; 140 E. Walton). A grand property on the Miracle Mile. Packages include the American Girl Experience, which offers an in-room doll bed, milk and cookies in the evening, and voucher for pink lemonade at the fabulous Palm Court. $$–$$$.

Hotel Burnham (866-690-1986, www.burnham hotel.com; 1 W. Washington St.). Embrace the architectural glory of Chicago at the Hotel Burnham, in the famous Reliance Building, one of the first glass-walled skyscrapers. $$$.

Peninsula Chicago (312-337-2888, www.peninsula. com/Chicago; 108 E. Superior St.). Comfortable elegance with jaw-dropping views. Family specials May through December that include treats, welcome gifts, and special children's programs. $$$$.

Indiana

Indianapolis

Canterbury Hotel (317-634-3000, www.canter buryhotel.com; 123 S. Illinois St.). European-style historic property in downtown. Packages include sporting event and theater tickets. $$.

Gatehouse Suites Indianapolis (877-851-6763; 3553 Founders Rd.). Modest accommodations with plenty of room for families to spread out. Full kitchens, plus complimentary breakfast buffet. $.

Omni Severin Hotel (317-634-6664, www.omni hotels.com/FindAHotel/IndianapolisSeverin.aspx; 40 W. Jackson Place). Nonsmoking property with indoor pool. Welcome gift for kids at check-in,

Hotel Julien Dubuque   Courtesy Hotel Julien Dubuque

plus cookies and milk in the evening. Toy and books available for lending. $.

Iowa

Des Moines

Hotel Fort Des Moines (515-243-1161, www.hotel fortdesmoines.com; 1000 Walnut St.). Smoke-free property with storied Hollywood past. $.

Hotel Pattee (515-465-3511, www.hotelpattee.com; 1112 Wills Ave., Perry). Individually decorated guest rooms, with public spaces adorned with art by local artists. Kids will love the on-site two-lane bowling alley. $$.

Dubuque

Hotel Julien Dubuque (563-556-4200, www.hoteljuli endubuque.com; 200 Main St.). Elegant boutique hotel with beautiful indoor pool. Remarkable value. $.

Kansas

Topeka

Capitol Plaza Topeka (785-431-7200, www.capitol plazahoteltopeka.com; 1717 SW Topeka Blvd.). Comfortable downtown accommodations, with indoor pool. Nonsmoking, pet-friendly. $.

Hyatt Place Topeka (785-273-0066, http://topeka. place.hyatt.com/hyatt/hotels-topeka-place; 6021 SW 6th Ave.). All-suites property with spacious accommodations, free WiFi, heated pool, complimentary breakfast. Near shopping mall. $.

Wichita

Hotel at Old Town (316-267-4840, www.hotelat oldtown.com; 830 E. 1st). Spacious suite accommodations with fully equipped mini kitchens.

Old Town location within walking distance of restaurants and shopping. $$.

Kentucky
Lexington
Crown Plaza Lexington (877-270-1395; 1375 S. Broadway). Pretty swimming pool, plentiful suites, accommodations with enough space for even large families. $.

Inn at Shaker Village (800-734-5611, www.shakervillageky.org; 3501 Lexington Rd., Harrodsburg). Southwest of Lexington, part of Shaker Village of Pleasant Hill living history museum. Charming period-decorated guest rooms and private cottages scattered among 13 19th-century structures. $.

Louisville
Brown Hotel (502-587-7006, www.brownhotel.com; 335 W. Broadway). Grand hotel in Louisville theater district, home of the famous Lobby Bar. Gracious service, including babysitting services. $$$.

Louisiana
Lafayette
Juliet Hotel (337-261-2225, www.ascendcollection.com; 800 Jefferson St.). Boutique property downtown. Smoke-free, free WiFi, pretty outdoor pool. $.

New Orleans
Hotel Modern (504-962-0900, www.thehotelmodern.com; 936 St. Charles Ave.). High-style, whimsical decor, located near several museums. iPod stations and candy in every room. Limo service available, along with babysitting. $$.

Hotel Monteleone (504-523-3341, http://hotelmonteleone.com; 214 Royal St.). In the heart of French Quarter with plenty of Old World charm. Onetime favorite of American luminaries like William Faulkner, Ernest Hemingway, and Tennessee Williams. Heated rooftop pool, pet-friendly. $$$.

International House (504-553-9560, www.ihhotel.com; 221 Camp St.). Located in the quiet central business district. Elegant, stylish decor; upscale electronics. $$.

Loews Hotel New Orleans (800-235-6397, www.loewshotels.com/New-Orleans-Hotel; 300 Poydras St.). Check-in gift for kids under 10. Parents can borrow strollers, cribs, potty seats, baby bathtubs, toys, and more. Teenagers get two music download cards, plus borrowing privileges for Xbox 360, DVD players, and board games. $$$.

Maine
Acadia National Park and Bar Harbor
Acadia Inn (207-288-3500, www.acadiainn.com; 98 Eden St., Bar Harbor). Large rooms, near the park. With free breakfast and laundry facilities. $.

Bar Harbor Grand Hotel (207-288-5226, www.barharborgrand.com; 269 Main St., Bar Harbor). Castle-like structure located downtown. Suites and two-bedroom units available. $–$$$.

Portland
Eastland Park Hotel (207-347-6521, www.eastlandparkhotel.com; 157 High St.). Downtown, with sweeping views of Casco Bay. Renovated interiors. $$$.

Portland Harbor Hotel (888-798-9090, www.portlandharborhotel.com; 468 Fore St.). Luxury, high-style accommodations in the Old Port District. Charming courtyard and impeccable service. $$–$$$.

Maryland
Annapolis
Historic Inns of Annapolis (410-263-2641, www.historicinnsofannapolis.com; 58 State Circle). Collection of three historic, charming hotels in downtown (The Maryland Inn, Governor Calvert House, Robert Johnson House), each dating back to the 17th or 18th century. $$.

Baltimore
Admiral Fell Inn (410-522-7380, www.harbormagic.com; 888 S. Broadway). European-style hotel with Old World charm, 18th-century furnishings, and according to legend a few resident ghosts. Nice views. $$.

Pier 5 Hotel (410-539-2000, www.harbormagic.com; 711 Eastern Ave.). Chic boutique property right on the water. High-style rooms, centrally located, with larger options for families. $$$.

Massachusetts
Boston and Cambridge
Best Western Tria (866-333-TRIA, www.hoteltria.com; 220 Alewife Brook Pkwy., Cambridge).

Modest chain hotel offering true value in an expensive city. Free shuttle to the subway and Harvard Yard. $.

Liberty Hotel (617-224-4000, www.libertyhotel.com; 215 Charles St., Boston). Once the Charles Street Jail, this quirky luxury hotel offers hip design. Centrally located, with commanding views from top floors. Nonsmoking, pet-friendly. $$$$.

Omni Parker House (617-227-8600, www.omnihotels.com; 60 School St., Boston). Oldest operating hotel in the United States, located on the Freedom Trail. Offers a nice welcome gift to kids; deluxe rooms are spacious (baths are not). Home of Parker House rolls and Boston cream pie. $$$.

Royal Sonesta (617-806-4200, www.sonesta.com/boston; 40 Edwin Land Blvd., Cambridge). Near the science museum, just over the bridge from Boston, with commanding views of the Charles River. Exceptional service. $$.

Plymouth Area

John Carver Inn & Spa (508-746-7100, www.johncarverinn.com; 25 Summer St., Plymouth). Near historic attractions. Lavish Pilgrim-themed indoor pool with a replica of the *Mayflower* and 80-foot waterslide. $.

Omni Parker House   Courtesy Omni Parker House

Plymouth Bay Inn and Suites (781-585-3831, www.plymouthbay.com; 149 Main St., Kingston). Modest motel accommodations, with indoor and outdoor pools. Rooms include refrigerator and microwave. $.

Michigan

Detroit Area

The Henry, Autograph Collection (313-441-2000, www.marriott.com/hotels/hotel-information/travel/dtwak-the-henry-autograph-collection; 300 Town Center Dr., Dearborn). Boutique Marriott property that includes indoor pool, video games, modern art collection. $$$.

Roberts Riverwalk Hotel Detroit (313-259-9500, www.detroitriverwalkhotel.com; 1000 River Place). Elegant design and spacious rooms. In Central Detroit, on the river boardwalk. $.

Mackinac Island

The Grand Hotel (906-847-3331, www.grandhotel.com; 286 Grand Ave.). Gorgeous historic resort property, popular with well-heeled vacationers since 1887. Each guest room is unique. Frothy, sorbet-hued guest room decor, fabulous views. Complimentary children's programs. $$$$.

Traverse City Area

Sugar Beach Resort Hotel (231-938-0100, www.tcbeaches.com/reservations/sugar-beach.html; 1773 US 31 N., Traverse City). Pretty beach resort on the lake. Private balconies, refrigerator and microwave in the room. $$.

White Birch Lodge (231-264-8271, www.whitebirchlodge.org; 571 Meguzee Point Rd., Elk Rapids). All-inclusive family lake resort with extensive kids' programming and plenty of water sports. Includes three meals a day. $$.

Minnesota

St. Paul/Minneapolis Area

Best Western Plus Bloomington at Mall of America (952-854-8200, www.bestwesternbloomington.com; 1901 Killebrew Dr., Bloomington). Comfortable, spacious rooms and extensive suites five minutes from Mall of America. Small indoor water park. $.

Graves 601 Hotel Wyndam Grand (612-677-1100, www.graves601hotel.com; 601 N. 1st Ave.,

Minneapolis). Sophisticated downtown location with hip design and impeccable service. Connected by skyway to shopping and dining. $$$.

Sofitel Minneapolis (952-835-1900, www.sofitel.com/gb/hotel-0539-sofitel-minneapolis; 5601 W. 78th St., Bloomington). Stylish accommodations near Mall of America. Walk-in rain showers, well-equipped gym facilities. $$.

St. Paul Hotel (800-292-9292, www.saintpaulhotel.com; 350 Market St., St. Paul). Classic design in downtown, near Rice Park. Complimentary local transportation; offers package deals with Science Museum passes. $$$.

Mississippi

Biloxi

South Beach Biloxi Hotel and Suites (228-388-2627, www.sbbiloxihotel.com; 1735 Beach Blvd.). Beachfront, nonsmoking midrise with good views of the Gulf. Fresh, bright family suites include full kitchens and washer/dryer units. $–$$.

Greenwood

The Alluvian (662-453-2114, www.thealluvian.com; 318 Howard St.). Boutique property downtown, offering complimentary southern breakfast buffet, library of southern literature and films to borrow, children's games. Adjacent Viking Cooking School offers lessons for families and children. $$$.

Jackson

Old Capitol Inn (601-359-9001, www.oldcapitolinn.com; 226 N. State St.). Traditional, gracious accommodations in downtown Jackson. Full southern breakfast and wine and cheese in the evenings. $.

Missouri

St. Louis

Chase Park Plaza (314-633-3000, www.chaseparkplaza.com; N. Kingshighway Blvd.). Stunning luxury accommodations in downtown. Piazza with fabulous heated outdoor pool; adjacent to a beautiful cineplex. $$$.

Drury Plaza Hotel at the Arch (800-378-7946, wwwc.druryhotels.com; 2 S. 4th St.). Classic accommodations near the St. Louis Arch. Complimentary breakfast, free sodas and popcorn in the afternoon, free appetizers and beverages in the evening. Microwaves and refrigerators in each room. $.

Moonrise Hotel (314-721-1111, www.moonrisehotel.com; 6177 Delmar in the Loop). Luxury boutique high-style property at bargain-basement prices. Quirky design elements like an ever-changing iridescent lobby wall and moonscape art. $.

Montana

Glacier National Park Area

Glacier Park Lodge (406-892-2525, www.glacierparkinc.com/glacier_park_lodge; at the junction of Hwys. 2 and 49). Historic property in East Glacier; the giant log-cabin lobby is cacophonous but beautiful. $$.

Lake McDonald Lodge (406-892-2525, www.glacierparkinc.com/lake_mcdonald_lodge; Glacier National Park). Centrally located hotel rooms and cozy cottages on Lake McDonald. Horse stables on site. $.

Many Glacier Hotel (406-892-2525, www.glacierparkinc.com/many_glacier_hotel; Glacier National Park). Stunning 1915 Swiss-style chalet on the shores of Swiftcurrent Lake, with fine views of Mount Grinnell. Family rooms are available. $$$.

Tipi Village (www.blackfeetculturecamp.com; off Durham Rd., Browning). Experience an unforgettable overnight in an authentic tepee on the scenic Blackfeet Reservation. Bring your own sleeping bag and mattress pad, or rent them (with advance notice). The Blackfeet Nation offers a traditional meal of bison, elk, or seafood at additional cost. $.

Browning tepees   Courtesy Montana Office of Tourism

Nebraska

Lincoln

Settle Inn (402-435-8100, www.settleinn.com/hotels/lincoln; 7333 Husker Circle). Smoke-free property with free continental breakfast and indoor pool. Kids will like the castle decor throughout, including suits of armor in the lobby and murals in the guest rooms. $.

Omaha

Ramada Plaza Omaha Hotel (402-393-3950, www.ramada.com/hotels/nebraska/omaha; 3321 S. 72nd St.). Modest chain hotel accommodations with four-star kids' amenities: an indoor water park with three 40-foot waterslides, a lazy river, large heated pools, and plentiful water-play zones. $.

Hotel Deco XV (402-991-4981, http://hoteldeco omaha.com; 1504 Harney St.). Contemporary, stylish property with impeccable service. Plasma TVs, iPad rentals, spa-like showers. $$$.

Magnolia Hotel Omaha (402-341-2500, www.magno liahotels.com/omaha/magnolia-hotel-omaha.php; 1615 Howard St.). Elegant downtown property that has the look of an Italian villa. Lofts and extended-stay suites available. $$.

Nevada

Las Vegas*

The cost of a hotel room in Las Vegas on a weekend can be up to three times higher than it would be on a weeknight. Prices given here are based on weeknight rates.

Mandalay Bay Hotel and Casino (702-632-7777, www.mandalaybay.com; 3950 Las Vegas Blvd. S.). Luxurious, spacious accommodations on the Strip. Fabulous outdoor water park, including a lazy river, wave pool, and beachfront area. Also boasts a shark tank. Parents will appreciate that reaching the check-in desk doesn't require walking through the casino. $$$$.

New York New York Hotel and Casino (866-815-4365, www.newyorknewyork.com; 3790 Las Vegas Blvd. S.). Another mega-resort on the Strip, with clean-line rooms and great views. Includes an amazing on-site roller coaster and Coney Island–style midway (but there's no avoiding walking past smoke-shrouded slot machines). $.

The Venetian Casino, Hotel, and Resort (866-834-2320, www.venetian.com; 3355 Las Vegas Blvd. S.). Luxe resort modeled after an Italian palazzo and filled with priceless artwork. Kids will flip for the indoor canal and gondola rides (which are almost as pricey here as in the real Venice). $$–$$$.

New Hampshire

Concord

The Centennial (603-227-9000, www.thecentennial hotel.com; 96 Pleasant St.). Refined service, modern design in a classic Victorian structure. Complimentary cookies every evening. Exceptional on-site restaurant. $$.

Hampton

Lamies Inn (603-926-0330, www.oldsaltnh.com; 490 Lafayette Rd.). Homey, colonial property that dates to 1740. Adjacent to famous restaurant The Old Salt. $.

Lake Winnipesaukee

The Inns and Spa at Mill Falls (800-622-6455, http://millfalls.com/inns/mill_falls.htm; 312 Daniel Webster Hwy., Meredith). Traditionally styled guest rooms on picturesque grounds. Connected to the pretty Marketplace by covered bridge overlooking a waterfall. $$–$$$.

White Mountain National Forest Area

The Lodge at Bretton Woods (800-680-6600, http://brettonwoods.com; 2653 Rt. 302 E., Bretton Woods). Pretty country property; part of the Mount Washington Resort, including golf, tennis, skating, and trail riding. Easy access to ski resorts. $.

New Jersey

Atlantic City**

**The cost of a hotel room in Atlantic City on a weekend—particularly in the summer—can be up to three times more expensive than it would be on a weeknight. Prices given here are based on weeknight rates.*

The Chelsea (800-548-3030, www.thechelsea-ac.com; 111 S. Chelsea Ave.). Youthful, elegant property overlooking the ocean and famous Boardwalk. One of the few hotels in this area that doesn't offer gambling; outdoor saltwater pool. Nonsmoking property. $–$$.

Tropicana Casino and Resort Atlantic City (800-345-8767, www.tropicana.net; 2831 Boardwalk). In the heart of the action, with shopping, fine dining, and gambling for parents steps away and the beach and Boardwalk attractions outside the front door. Stylish, exotic decor. $.

Cape May

Ocean Club Hotel (609-884-7000, www.capemay oceanclubhotel.com; 1035 Beach Ave.). New property with stunning pool overlooking the ocean. Private balconies, beach lounge service. $$.

Princeton

The Peacock Inn (609-924-1707, http://peacock inn.com; 20 Bayard Lane). Small boutique property in downtown Princeton sited in an 18th-century colonial mansion. Spa showers and upscale toiletries. $$$$.

New Mexico

Albuquerque

Andaluz (877-987-9090, www.hotelandaluz.com; 125 2nd St. NW). Downtown historic property, dripping with luxurious southwestern flair. Beautiful local artwork throughout. Restful guest rooms. On-site library. $$$.

Los Poblanos Historic Inn and Organic Farm (505-344-9297, www.lospoblanos.com; 4803 Rio Grande Blvd., Los Ranchos de Albuquerque). Set amid a lavender field and organic farm. Lovely historic property, with tranquil gardens and exquisite dining. Kids can help gather eggs or milk a goat. Welcome gift for children by special arrangement. $$.

Santa Fe

Hotel St. Francis (505-983-5700, www.hotelstfran cis.com; 210 Don Gaspar Ave.). Historic small inn just off the Santa Fe Plaza. Spanish missionary style, with clean-line guest rooms. Extraordinary concierge. Free historic walking tours of the city. $–$$.

Inn of the Governors (505-982-4333, www.innofthe governors.com; 101 W. Alameda St.). Near the Plaza. Delicious and hearty New Mexican–style breakfast buffet; complimentary tea and sherry in the afternoon. Charming courtyard pool, heated year-round. $.

La Fonda (505-982-5511, www.lafondasantafe.com; 100 E. San Francisco St.). Popular landmark property located smack in the middle of the historic Santa Fe Plaza. Spacious rooms, many with kiva fireplace. $$$$.

New York

Adirondacks

Sagamore (866-385-6221, www.thesagamore.com; 110 Sagamore Rd., Bolton Landing). Lovely upscale resort on an especially pretty stretch of Lake George in Bolton Landing. Beautiful pool, extensive kids' programming. Families will enjoy the complimentary lake cruises aboard the *Morgan*, a replica of a 19th-century touring boat. $$$$.

New York City

70 Park Avenue Hotel (877-707-2752, www.70park ave.com; 70 Park Ave., Manhattan). Boutique property in Midtown. Eco-friendly, pet-friendly, nonsmoking, high-style. $$$$.

Hotel Le Bleu (866-427-6073, www.hotellebleu.com; 370 4th Ave., Brooklyn). High-style property in Brooklyn, near Coney Island. Lots of extras included—free WiFi, movies, snacks, breakfast, and more. $$.

The Michelangelo (800-237-0990, www.michelangelo hotel.com). Beautiful luxury property with Italian style, near Times Square. Deep whirlpool bathtubs, deluxe bedding. Complimentary Italian pastries and cappuccino in the lobby. $$$$.

Library Hotel (212-983-4500, www.libraryhotel.com; 299 Madison Ave., Manhattan). Designed around the Dewey Decimal system: Each floor is themed to match one of the 10 categories. All guest rooms include a collection of books, and the property boasts more than 6,000 on display. Reading room,

Hotel Sagamore   © Debbie K. Hardin

free cappuccino, cookies, fruit, extensive DVD library. Complimentary breakfast. $$–$$$.

The Plaza (866-940-9361, www.theplaza.com; 5th Ave. at Central Park, Manhattan). Indulgent opulence that offers plenty for kids, including a children's concierge; extensive child's room service menu; and the fabulous (super-pricey) "Eloise Suite," a dreamy pink space designed by Betsey Johnson and based on the children's book *Eloise* by Kay Thompson. $$$$.

Niagara Falls

Giacomo (716-299-0200, www.thegiacomo.com; 222 1st St.). Small trendy boutique hotel in a historic art deco office structure. Walking distance of the falls. With free hot breakfast. $$.

North Carolina

Asheville

Grove Park Inn (800-438-5800, www.grovepark inn.com; 290 Macon Ave.). Distinctively decorated accommodations in the Blue Ridge Mountains, including a '50s-themed suite, an art deco suite, and a groovy '60s pad. Extensive kids' programming. $$.

Inn on Biltmore Estate (866-336-1245, www.bilt more.com; 1 Lodge St.). Grand guest accommodations on Biltmore property, with service fit for American royalty. $$$$.

Outer Banks***

***Rates in the Outer Banks are determined by season. Low season (winter and spring) is generally half or less the price of high season (summer and fall). Rates given here are for low season.

First Colony Inn (252-441-2343, www.firstcolony inn.com; 6715 S. Croatan Hwy., Nags Head). Charming rooms at a small property off the main highway into the Outer Banks. Hot breakfast, afternoon tea. Croquet, pool, boardwalk to the dunes. $.

Oasis Suites Hotel (252-441-5211, www.oasissuites.com; 7721 S. Virginia Dare Trail, Nags Head). Elegant accommodations that include family suites, views of the lovely Albemarle Sound, private balconies, and spa tubs. Dockside fishing and crabbing, with on-site grills. $$$.

Raleigh–Durham–Chapel Hill

Carolina Inn (800-962-8519, www.carolinainn.com; 211 Pittsboro St., Chapel Hill). Elegant country decor, near the University of North Carolina–Chapel Hill. $$.

Millennium Hotel Durham (919-383-8575, www.mil lenniumhotels.com/millenniumdurham; 2800 Campus Walk Ave., Durham). Comfortable, modest rooms near Duke University. Free shuttle service to campus sporting events. $.

The Umstead Hotel and Spa (866-877-4141, www.the umstead.com; 100 Woodland Park Dr., Cary). Spacious, relaxing, elegant accommodations near Raleigh. Beautiful pool and lake on site. $$$$.

North Dakota

Bismarck

Fairfield Inn and Suites Bismarck (701-223-9077, www.marriott.com/hotels/travel/bisfi-fair field-inn-and-suites-bismarck-north; 1120 E. Century Ave.). Newly renovated, bright, pretty rooms. Indoor pool, laundry facilities. $.

Fargo

Hotel Donaldson (701-478-1000, www.hoteldonald son.com; 101 Broadway). Urban loft-style accommodations in a tiny boutique hotel, housed in historic downtown property. Spa bathrooms, individual decor. $$.

Grand Forks

Lakeview Hotel and Resort (www.lakeviewhotels. com&inn; 3350 32nd Ave.). Modest rooms with warm, western decor. Indoor pool, free WiFi, DVD library. Near outlet malls. $.

Grove Park Inn   Courtesy Grove Park Inn

Ohio

Cincinnati

21c Museum Hotel Cincinnati (www.21cmuseum hotels.com/cincinnati; 609 Walnut St.). New luxury property in historic structure; in the arts district downtown. State-of-the-art electronics in guest rooms and public spaces. Pet-friendly, smoke-free. $$$.

The Cincinnatian Hotel (513-381-3000, www.cincin natianhotel.com; 601 Vine St.). Opulent landmark hotel. Deluxe accommodations, unforgettable spa bathrooms, superior service. $$$.

Garfield Suites (513-421-3355, http://garfieldsuites hotel.com; 2 Garfield Place). All-suites property downtown, with plenty of space for a large family. Accommodations include full kitchens. $.

Dayton

Dayton Grand (937-461-4700, www.daytongrand hotel.com; 11 S. Ludlow). Comfortable, stylish lodging with spacious rooms. Rooftop indoor pool, free WiFi. $.

Studio Plus Dayton (800-804-3724, www.studioplus. com/hotels/dayton-hotels.html; 3131 Presidential Dr.). Lived-in, modest accommodations at a discount. Spacious suites, kitchenettes, laundry facilities, outdoor pool. $.

Sandusky

Cedar Point's Castaway Bay (419-627-2106, www.castawaybay.com; 2001 Cleveland Rd.). Extremely family-friendly, tropic-themed waterpark resort, near Cedar Point, with a wave pool, water coaster, large arcade, and planned kids' activities. $$.

Oklahoma

Oklahoma City

Colcord (405-601-4300, www.colcordhotel.com; 15 N. Robinson). Modern style in historic building downtown. Newly renovated, with large showers, extra-comfy beds. Located in OKC's first skyscraper. $$–$$$.

Skirvin (405-272-3040, www.skirvinhilton.com; 1 Park Ave.). Revitalized property downtown, near hip Bricktown area. Unusual artist-in-residence program allows guests to experience a working art studio and view art in progress. $$.

Tulsa Area

Ambassador Hotel (918-587-8200, http://tulsa. ambassadorhotelcollection.com; 1324 S. Main St.). Classic accommodations downtown. Fresh flowers in guest rooms, pet-friendly. $$$.

The Mayo Hotel (918-582-6296, www.themayohotel. com; 115 W. 5th St.). Hip style in historic structure downtown. Grand lobby with whimsical furnishings. Guest rooms include huge flat-screen TV, iPod docking station. Local shuttle service. $$.

Meadowlake Inn and Dude Ranch (www.bbonline.com/united-states/oklahoma/ sand-springs/meadowlake.html; 3450 S. 137th West Ave., Sand Springs). Rambling dude ranch west of Tulsa. Western-themed decor, plenty of opportunities to wrangle, rope, play horseshoes, fish, and enjoy an evening campfire. Chose your experience: log cabin or tepee. $.

Oregon

Crater Lake Area

The Cabins at Mazama Village (888-774-2728, www.craterlakelodges.com/mazama-village-mo tor-inn; Crater Lake National Park). Basic yet cozy cabins tucked in a beautiful forest located 10 miles from the crater. Especially peaceful: Lodging does not include TVs. $.

Crater Lake Lodge (888-774-2728, www.craterlake lodges.com/crater-lake-lodge-1842.html; Crater Lake National Park). Perched on the edge of the caldera, overlooking Crater Lake. Beautiful, welcoming lobby; pleasant rooms, most with outstanding views. $$.

Portland

The Heathman Hotel (503-241-4100, http://portland. heathmanhotel.com; 1001 SW Broadway at Salmon). Grand downtown property near Pearl District. "Bed menu" allows guests to choose among a feather bed, pillow-top, or Tempur-Pedic mattress. $$.

Hotel Monaco Portland (506-222-0001, www.mona co-portland.com; 506 SW Washington St.). Stunning downtown boutique hotel with trendy, elegant decor. Pet-friendly, with loaner bicycles. Wine reception every evening for parents. $$$.

McMenemins Kennedy School Hotel (503-249-3983, www.mcmenamins.com/427-kennedy-school-home; 5736 NE 33rd Ave.). Eclectic, fun accommodations in a historic schoolhouse, with guest rooms complete with blackboards and themed around beloved books, including Beverly Cleary's *Beezus and Ramona*, Sue Monk Kidd's *The Secret Life of Bees*, and Ursula Le Guin's *Earthsea Cycle*. $.

Pennsylvania

Hershey

Hershey Lodge (800-437-7439, www.hersheylodge.com; 325 University Dr.). At Hersheypark. Kids' check-in desk, with sweet gift on arrival; discount on Hersheypark tickets. Activities like chocolate bingo, s'mores roasts, crafts, and Wii room. $$.

Hotel Hershey (800-437-7439, www.thehotelhershey.com; 100 Hotel Rd.). Elegant historic resort property at Hersheypark. Home of the Chocolate Spa, which offers a whipped cocoa bath and chocolate bean polish. Seasonal kids' club. Chocolate Kisses at turndown. $$$$.

Philadelphia

Alexander Inn (215-923-3535, www.alexanderinn.com; 12th and Spruce Sts.). Historic nonsmoking property in Center City. Complimentary breakfast buffet plus 24-hour snack and fruit table. $.

aloft (267-298-1700, www.starwoodhotels.com/aloft hotels/property/overview/index.html?property ID=3181; 4301 Island Ave.). Half a mile from the airport, with free shuttle service. Small, chic rooms with oversized showers, free WiFi, in-room games. Goodie bag for kids on arrival, plus pint-sized air mattresses and bedding. $.

Rittenhouse 1715 (www.rittenhouse1715.com; 1715 Rittenhouse Square St.). Tiny boutique property housed in a classic row house downtown. Fabulous complimentary breakfast, gourmet snacks throughout the day. $$.

Pittsburgh

Omni William Penn (412-281-7100, www.omnihotels.com/FindAHotel/PittsburghWilliamPenn; 530 William Penn Place). Elegant, historic property downtown. Kids' welcome gift, milk and cookies in the evening, rolling backpack of toys and books to borrow. $$$.

Rhode Island

Newport

Hotel Viking (401-847-3300, www.hotelviking.com; 1 Bellevue Ave.). Classic Newport luxury at value rates, with comfy bedding, luxurious furnishings, and rich artwork. $$.

The Newport Harbor Hotel and Marina (800-955-2558, www.thenewport-hotel.com; 49 America's Cup Ave.). Swanky accommodations on the water with a 60-slip marina. Nice indoor pool. $$$.

Providence

Hotel Providence (800-861-8990, www.hotelprovidence.com; 139 Mathewson St.). Clubby, luxe downtown property filled with books, local artwork. Guest rooms include sitting area, deep soaking tub. $$.

Providence Biltmore (800-294-7709, www.providencebiltmore.com; 11 Dorrance St.). Beautiful downtown property, near Brown University and Rhode Island Convention Center. Large rooms, California king beds available, suites with kitchenettes. $.

South Carolina

Charleston Area

Shem Creek Inn (843-881-1000, www.shemcreekinn.com; 1401 Shrimpboat Lane, Mount Pleasant). Across the Cooper River Bridge from Charleston, waterfront property. Charming views of shrimp boat fleet, elegant rooms. Lovely pool overlooking Shem Creek. $.

Vendue Inn (843-577-2913, www.vendueinn.com; 19 Vendue Range, Charleston). Classic southern style with fresh, whimsical details. In downtown French Quarter, steps from the waterfront. Several rooms boast fireplace. $$–$$$.

Wentworth Mansion (888-466-1886, www.wentworthmansion.com; 149 Wentworth St., Charleston). Opulent, gracious accommodations dripping with crystal chandeliers, marble fireplaces, and fine polished furniture. Complimentary breakfast, house-made chocolates. $$$$.

South Dakota

Custer

Rock Crest Lodge and Cabins (877-41-CABIN, http://rockcrestlodge.com; 15 W. Rushmore Rd.).

Cozy log cabins with kitchens, some accommodating large families, and lodge guest rooms. Free breakfast, outdoor pool and playground. Pet-friendly. $–$$.

Hill City

High Country Guest Ranch (www.highcountry guestranch.com); 12138 Ray Smith Dr.). Experience the West in spacious log cabins scattered amid scenic Black Hills. Trail riding, horse rentals, volleyball, free outdoor movie theater, pony rides for kids. $.

Keystone/Mount Rushmore

Presidents' View Resort (800-504-3210, www.presi dentsviewresort.com; 1800 Boardwalk, Keystone). Extremely affordable accommodations in downtown Keystone. Suites with kitchens, offering balconies with views of Mount Rushmore. Indoor pool. $.

Roosevelt Inn (605-666-4599, www.rosyinn.com; 206 Old Cemetery Rd., Keystone). No-frills rooms in a small, family-run property at the base of Mount Rushmore. $.

White House Resort (866-996-6835, www.white houseresort.com; 1880 Boardwalk, Keystone). Pet-friendly, kid-friendly hotel with basic accommodations. In downtown Keystone, near Mount Rushmore. $.

Tennessee

Memphis

Elvis Presley's Heartbreak Hotel–Graceland (www.elvis.com/graceland/heartbreak_hotel. aspx; 3677 Elvis Presley Blvd.). Across the street from Graceland. Heart-shaped outdoor pool, kitschy decor the King himself would approve of. Affordable year-round, but also includes some *very* pricey themed suites. $.

River Inn of Harbor Town (901-260-3300, www.river innmemphis.com; 50 Harbor Town Square). Overlooking the Mississippi River, near downtown. Beautiful, traditional southern decor. Every floor features a library sitting area. Free breakfast. $$$–$$$$.

Nashville

Hermitage Hotel (615-244-3121, www.thehermitage hotel.com; 231 6th Ave.). Traditional opulence downtown. Historic property, lavish bathrooms.

With advance notice, room can be stocked with baby food, cribs, and bed guards. $$$.

Hutton Hotel (615-340-9333, www.huttonhotel.com; 1808 West End Ave.). Chic, ecofriendly lodging that boasts reclaimed wood and bamboo furnishings, uses biodegradable cleaning products and energy-saving lighting and plumbing. Courtesy vehicles are hybrid SUVs. $$$$.

Texas

Austin

Austin Motel (512-441-1157, www.austinmotel.com; 1220 S. Congress Ave.). Hip, retro motor inn with pretty grounds and kidney-shaped pool located in trendy "SoCo" neighborhood. $.

Barton Creek Resort and Spa (866-572-7369, www.bartoncreek.com; 8212 Barton Club Dr.). Swanky Texas Hill Country resort with premier golf club on site. Beautiful pools, in-room Nintendo, touches of cowboy chic. $$$.

Hotel Saint Cecelia (512-852-2400, www.hotelsaint cecilia.com; 112 Academy Dr.). Named after the patron saint of music; aesthetic evokes Beat Generation writers and musicians. Poolside bungalows and suites available. $$$.

Dallas/Fort Worth

The Joule (214-261-4575, www.thejouledallas.com; 1530 Main St., Dallas). Downtown boutique property filled with modern art, bold design, dramatic public spaces. Stunning rooftop pool. $$$$.

Hotel Zaza (214-468-8399, www.hotelzaza.com; 2332 Leonard St., Dallas). Youthful, colorful uptown Dallas accommodations. Themed suites available with extra space. Very trendy. $$$.

Stockyards Hotel (817-625-6427, www.stockyards hotel.com; 109 E. Exchange Ave., Fort Worth). Quintessential Texas, with hunting trophies on the walls, leather on myriad surfaces, and ubiquitous western art. $$.

Houston

Alden-Houston Hotel (855-212-6780, www.alden hotels.com; 1117 Prairie St.). Centrally located downtown hotel with fresh, hip design. DVD library, courtesy car, same-day laundry service. $$.

The Magnolia Hotel (888-915-1110, www.magnolia hotels.com/houston/magnolia-hotel-houston; 1100 Texas Ave.). Large guest rooms with luxurious furnishings in bright hues. Pretty rooftop pool deck. $$.

San Antonio

Hotel Valencia Riverwalk (210-227-9700, www.hotel valencia-riverwalk.com; 150 E. Houston St.). Sophisticated accommodations within the popular arts and dining Riverwalk district. Pretty courtyard overlooking the river. Free WiFi. $$$.

Menger Hotel (210-223-4361, http://mengerhotel.com; 204 Alamo Plaza). Historic property dating to 1859; near the Alamo. Quiet Spanish garden, large heated outdoor pool, lots of western touches. $.

Utah

Bryce Canyon National Park

Bryce Canyon Lodge (435-834-8700, www.bryce canyonforever.com; Bryce Canyon National Park). Within steps of the Bryce Amphitheater. Book well in advance to secure charming, rustic Western Cabin. $$.

Ruby's Inn (435-834-5301, www.rubysinn.com; 300 S. Main Hwy. 63). Touristy but convenient motel near the park, with restaurants and shopping. Children will enjoy camping in authentic tepees in adjacent campground. $.

Salt Lake City

Inn on the Hill (801-328-1466, www.inn-on-the-hill. com; 225 N. State St.). Elegant B&B in the historic Capital Hill neighborhood. Individually decorated nonsmoking guest rooms and one mini suite. Great views of downtown in the distance. $.

Metropolitan Inn (801-531-7100, www.metropolitan inn.com; 524 SW Temple). Small, modest art deco property featuring prints of *Wizard of Oz* charac-

Cable Mountain Resort   © Debbie K. Hardin

ters above the beds. Complimentary breakfast, baby furniture on request. $.

Zion National Park

Cable Mountain Lodge (435-772-3366, www.cable mountainlodge.com; 147 Zion Park Blvd., Springdale). Luxurious suites accommodations with kitchenettes and separate bedrooms. Gorgeous setting, within steps of the entrance to Zion National Park. $$$.

Zion Lodge (435-772-7700, www.zionlodge.com; Zion National Park). Historic, well-worn lodge inside the park, with stunning views of the mountains. Book a cozy cabin with a fireplace or a more commodious motel room. $$.

Vermont

Lake Champlain Area

Basin Harbor Club (800-622-4000, www.basin harbor.com; 4800 Basin Harbor Rd., Vergennes). Sprawling seasonal resort on the shores of Lake Champlain. No TV, but plenty of outdoor recreation like bicycling, canoeing, golfing, tennis, and kayaking. Art classes. Daily kids' club throughout the summer. $$$$.

Montpelier

Comfort Inn and Suites (802-262-6117, www.comfort inn.com; 213 Paine Turnpike N.). Cheerful, updated accommodations within minutes of state capitol; expansive suites with kitchenettes. Complimentary beverages, cookies, and breakfast. $.

Stowe

Stowe Mountain Lodge (888-478-6938, www.stowe mountainlodge.com; 7412 Mountain Rd.). Beautiful chalet-style ski lodge with spectacular mountain views. Offers ski valet, fly-fishing service, golf concierge, children's programming. Dog-friendly. $$$.

Virginia

Alexandria/Mount Vernon

Morrison House (703-838-8000, www.morris onhouse.com; 116 S. Alfred St., Alexandria). Re-created historic feel in Old Town Alexandria, with impeccable service. $$$.

Arlington

Hotel Palomar Arlington at Waterview (703-351-

Morrison House   © Debbie K. Hardin

9170, www.hotelpalomar-arlington.com; 1121 N. 19th St.). High-style accommodations just across the Potomac River from Georgetown, with stunning views of the city and waterfront. $$$.

Colonial Williamsburg

Williamsburg Colonial Houses (757-229-1000; 306B E. Francis St.). Perfectly restored historic homes within Colonial Williamsburg. An unforgettable chance to *experience* history. $$$$.

Woodlands Hotel and Suites (757-229-1000; 105 Visitor Center Dr.). Within half a mile of Colonial Williamsburg; spacious enough for large families. Comfortable and well appointed. $.

Richmond

The Berkeley Hotel (888-780-4422, www.berkeley hotel.com; 1200 E. Cary St.). Adjacent to the historic Shockoe Slip. Gracious, spacious accommodations. $$$.

Linden Row Inn (800-348-7424, http://lindenrow inn.com; 100 E. Franklin St.). Accommodations in a row of seven mid-19th-century Greek Revival townhouses, plus their garden dependencies

Colonial House, Williamsburg   © Debbie K. Hardin

(small, separate buildings). Each guest room is meticulously restored and decorated with antiques. $$.

Washington

Mount Rainier Area

Alta Crystal Resort (800-277-6475, www.altacrystal resort.com; 68317 State Rt. 410 E., Greenwater). Chalet-style architecture, with evening bonfires and barbecues. Outdoor pool. Just outside the national park entrance. $$.

Paradise Inn (360-569-2275, www.mtrainierguest services.com; Ashford, Mount Rainier National Park). Historic Paradise Inn dates to 1916, with awe-inspiring views of adjacent Mount Rainier. Hiking trails starting on the property, offering views of glaciers and waterfalls. $$.

Olympic National Park Area

Kalaloch Lodge (866-875-8456, www.nationalpark reservations.com/olympic_kalaloch; Olympic National Park). Picturesque inn in the national park, on a cliff overlooking the ocean. Rustic lodge rooms, plus a variety of private cabins. $–$$$.

Lake Quinault Lodge (866-875-8456, www.national parkreservations.com/olympic_lakequinault; Olympic National Park). Cozy, no-frills lodging on the shores of Lake Quinault; vintage feel with heated indoor pool and sauna, arcade. Some guest rooms with fireplace. $–$$.

San Juan Island

Earthbox Motel and Spa (800-793-4756, www.earth boxmotel.com; 410 Spring St., Friday Harbor). Vintage motel meets hip boutique hotel. Near ferry terminal. Free use of beach cruiser bikes; indoor heated pool. $$.

Seattle

Arctic Club Seattle (206-340-0340, http://thearctic clubseattle.com; 700 3rd Ave.). Downtown lodging, within walking distance of Pike Place Market. Country club feel, masculine design. $$$$.

The Edgewater (206-728-7000, www.edgewater hotel.com; 2411 Alaskan Way, Pier 67). Fun location on a pier on the Seattle waterfront. Tranquil ambience. Amazing views over Elliott Bay and beyond to Olympic Mountains. $$$.

Maxwell Hotel (206-286-0629, www.themaxwell hotel.com; 300 Roy St.). Bright, modern accommodations near the Space Needle. Indoor pool, loaner bikes, smoke-free, ecofriendly cleaning products. Free popcorn. $.

West Virginia

Charleston

Charleston Plaza Hotel (304-345-9779, www.charlestonplazahotel.com; 1010 Washington St. E.). Comfortable, modest accommodations near the Civic Center. Complimentary breakfast. Pet-friendly. $.

Harpers Ferry

The Town's Inn (877-489-2447, www.thetowns inn.com; 179 High St.). Lodging in two picturesque, pre–Civil War stone homes, sited within the national historic park. Substantial midweek discounts. $.

White Sulphur Springs

The Greenbrier (855-453-4858, www.greenbrier.com; 300 W. Main St.). Splurge-worthy grand resort with championship golf, world-class spa, stunning indoor pool. Extensive kids' programs, plus magical Christmas events. Tour the underground bunker designed as an emergency shelter for the U.S. Congress during the Cold War. $$$$.

Wisconsin

Madison

The Dahlmann Campus Inn (608-257-4391, www.the campusinn.com; 601 Langdon St.). At the University of Wisconsin. Includes complimentary breakfast, appetizers, and desserts. Nonsmoking property. $.

HotelRED (608-819-8228, www.hotelred.com; 1501 Monroe St.). Trendy, spacious accommodations with well-stocked kitchenettes, whimsical art, ultramodern bathroom fixtures. Near Camp Randall Stadium. $$.

Milwaukee

Iron Horse Hotel (888-543-4766, www.theironhorse hotel.com; 500 W. Florida St.). Across from the Harley-Davidson Museum. Amenities include in-room boot storage, indoor motorcycle parking, and a bike wash. $$.

The Pfister (414-273-8222, www.thepfisterhotel.com; 424 E. Wisconsin Ave.). Historic downtown properties, blocks from Lake Michigan. Palatial public spaces, lavish classical guest rooms. Book a room in a top floor for premier views. $$–$$$.

Wyoming

Cody

The Chamberlin Inn (307-587-0202, www.chamberlin inn.com; 1032 12th St.). Small property near historic main street. Accommodations include traditional guest rooms, cottages, and garden studio apartments. $.

Jackson Hole/Grand Tetons

Hotel Terra (307-631-6281, http://hotelterrajackson hole.com; 3335 W. Village Dr.). Ecofriendly rambling resort with contemporary western design. Includes studios with kitchens and multi-bedroom suites to accommodate large families. $$.

Jenny Lake Lodge (307-543-2811, www.gtlc.com/lodging/jenny-lake-lodge; Grand Teton National Park). Beloved property within the boundaries of the national park, featuring private, tranquil cabins. Breathtaking views of the Tetons, glacial lakes. Rates include hearty breakfast, gourmet dinner, guided horseback riding, loaner bicycles. Book well in advance. $$$$.

Yellowstone National Park

Lake Yellowstone Hotel and Cabins (866-439-7355, www.yellowstonenationalparklodges.com;

Old Faithful Inn   © Debbie K. Hardin

Yellowstone National Park). Charming lakeside cottage-style lodging, with comfortable hotel rooms and Spartan cabins. $$.

Old Faithful Inn (866-439-7355, www.yellowstone nationalparklodges.com; Yellowstone National Park). Historic lodging next to Old Faithful geyser; no telephone or air-conditioning. Kids will love the log cabin within a log cabin in the lobby. Book far in advance. $$$.

Roosevelt Cabins (866-439-7355, www.yellowstone nationalparklodges.com; Yellowstone National Park). Secluded, nonsmoking cabins for a real wilderness experience. "Roughrider" cabins have shared bathroom facilities. $.

Washington, DC

Hay-Adams (202-628-6600, www.hayadams.com; 800 16th St., NW). Posh historic property across the street from the White House. Freshly baked cookies at the front desk. $$$$.

Hotel Monaco (202-628-7177, www.monaco-dc.com; 700 F St., NW). Stylish, playful accommodations in central location, near International Spy Museum. Guest rooms come with pet goldfish. $$.

The River Inn (202-337-7600, www.theriverinn.com; 924 25th St., NW). All-suites hotel in centrally

Hay-Adams   © Debbie K. Hardin

located, quiet residential Foggy Bottom neighborhood near the Kennedy Center. Contemporary design, spacious accommodations with kitchenettes. $$.

Willard Intercontinental Washington (202-628-9100, www.washington.intercontinetal.com; 1401 Pennsylvania Ave., NW). Spectacular Beaux-Arts grande dame that has been playing host to presidents and heads of state since 1850. Luxe decor, superior service, and some of the best restaurants in the city on site. $$$$.

index

Heading toward adventure   Courtesy Jo Legg